P9-DHJ-470

A HARD ROAD TO GLORY

A HISTORY OF THE AFRICAN-AMERICAN ATHLETE 1919-1945

ARTHUR R. ASHE, JR.

A HARD ROAD TO GLORY

A HISTORY OF THE AFRICAN-AMERICAN ATHLETE 1919-1945

WITH THE ASSISTANCE OF
KIP BRANCH, OCANIA CHALK, AND FRANCIS HARRIS

WARNER BOOKS

A Warner Communications Company

An Amistad Book

Copyright © 1988 by Arthur R. Ashe
All rights reserved
Warner Books, Inc., 666 Fifth Avenue, New York, NY 10103

 A Warner Communications Company

Printed in the United States of America
First Printing November 1988
10 9 8 7 6 5 4 3 2

Library of Congress Cataloging-in-Publication Data

Ashe, Arthur.
   A hard road to glory : a history of the African-American athlete,
1919-1945 / Arthur R. Ashe, Jr.
   p. cm.
   ISBN 0-446-71007-5
   1. Afro-Americans—Sports—History—20th century. 2. Afro
-American athletes.   I. Title.
GV583.A754 1988   88-20680
796'.08996073—dc19   CIP

Packaged by Rapid Transcript, a division
of March Tenth, Inc.

To my wife, Jeanne, and my daughter, Camera

Contents

Foreword

This book began in a classroom at Florida Memorial College in Miami, Florida, in 1983. I was asked to teach a course, The Black Athlete in Contemporary Society, by Jefferson Rogers of the school's Center for Community Change. When I tried to find a book detailing what has surely been the African-American's most startling saga of successes, I found that the last attempt had been made exactly twenty years before.

I then felt compelled to write this story, for I literally grew up on a sports field. My father was the caretaker of the largest public park for blacks in Richmond, Virginia. Set out in a fanlike pattern at Brookfield Playground was an Olympic-size pool, a basketball court, four tennis courts, three baseball diamonds, and two football fields. Our five-room home was actually on these premises. Little wonder I later became a professional athlete.

My boyhood idol was Jackie Robinson, as was the case with every black kid in America in the late 1940s and early 1950s. But I had no appreciation of what he went through or, more importantly, what others like him had endured. I had never heard of Jack Johnson, Marshall Taylor, Isaac Murphy, or Howard P. Drew—icons in athletics

but seldom heralded in the post-World War II period.

These and others have been the most accomplished figures in the African-American subculture. They were vastly better known in their times than people such as Booker T. Washington, William E.B. Du Bois, or Marcus Garvey. They inspired idolatry bordering on deification, and thousands more wanted to follow. Indeed, in the pretelevision days of radio, Joe Louis's bouts occasioned impromptu celebration because, between 1934 and 1949, Louis lost only once.

But if contemporary black athletes' exploits are more well known, few fully appreciate their true Hard Road to Glory. Discrimination, vilification, incarceration, dissipation, ruination, and ultimate despair have dogged the steps of the mightiest of these heroes. And, only a handful in the last 179 years have been able to live out their post-athletic lives in peace and prosperity.

This book traces the development of African-American athletes from their ancestral African homelands in the seventeenth century through the present era. Their exploits are explored in a historical context, as all African-American successes were constrained by discriminatory laws, customs, and traditions.

As I began to complete my research, I realized that the subject was more extensive than I had thought. All of the material would not fit into one volume. Therefore, I have divided the work as follows:

Volume I covers the emergence of sports as adjuncts to daily life from the time of ancient civilizations like Egypt through World War I. Wars tend to compartmentalize eras and this story is no different. Major successes of African-Americans occurred in the ninteenth century, for example, which are simply glossed over in most examinations of the period.

Volume II examines black athletics during that vital twenty-year period between the World Wars. No greater contrast exists than that between the 1920s—the Golden Decade of Sports—and the Depression-plagued 1930s. The infrastructure of American athletics as we know it today was set during these crucial years, and the civil rights apparatus that would lead to integration in the post–World War II era was formalized. Popular African-American literature and its press augmented the already cosmic fame of athletes such as Jesse Owens and Joe Louis, who were the first black athletes to be admired by all Americans.

Volume III is set between World War II and the present. It begins with an unprecedented five-year period—1946 through 1950—in which football, baseball, basketball, tennis, golf, and bowling became integrated. These breakthroughs, coupled with the already heady showings in track and

boxing, provided enough incentive for African-Americans to embark on nothing less than an all-out effort for athletic fame and fortune.

The reference sections in each volume document the major successes of these gladiators. These records are proof positive of effort and dedication on the playing field. More importantly, they are proof of what the African-American can do when allowed to compete equally in a framework governed by a set of rules.

Each volume is divided into individual sport histories. Primary source materials were not to be found in the local public library and not even in New York City's Fifth Avenue Public Library. Chroniclers of America's early sports heroes simply left out most of their darker brothers and sisters except when they participated in white-controlled events. Much had to be gleaned, therefore, from the basements, attics, and closets of African-Americans themselves.

Interviews were invaluable in cross-referencing dubious written records. Where discrepancies occurred, I have stated so; but I have tried to reach the most logical conclusion. Some unintentional errors are inevitable. The author welcomes confirmed corrections and additions. If validated, they will be included in the next edition of this work.

Today, thousands of young African-Americans continue to seek their places in the sun through athletics. For some African-Americans the dream has bordered on a pathological obsession. But unless matters change, the majority may end up like their predecessors. Perhaps this history will ease the journey with sober reflections of how difficult and improbable the Hard Road really is. In no way, however, do I care to dissuade any young athlete from dreaming of athletic glory. Surely every American at some time has done so.

A word about nomenclature. Sociologists have referred to nearly all immigrant groups in hyphenated form: Irish-Americans, Italian-Americans, and Jewish-Americans. African-Americans are no different, and this term is correct. Throughout this book, I shall, however, use the modern designation *"black"* to refer to African-Americans. The appellations *Negro* and *colored* may also appear, but usually in quotes and only when I thought such usage may be more appropriate in a particular context.

Acknowledgments

A Hard Road to Glory would have been impossible without the help, assistance, contributions, and encouragement of many people. Initial moral support came from Reverend Jefferson Rogers, formerly of Florida Memorial College; Professor Louis "Skip" Gates of Cornell University; Howard Cosell; Marie Brown; my editor, Charles F. Harris; and my literary agent, Fifi Oscard. All made me believe it could be done. An inspiring letter urging me to press on also came from Professor John Hope Franklin of Duke University, who advised that this body of work was needed to fill a gap in African-American history.

My staff has been loyal and faithful to the end these past four years. I have been more than ably assisted by Kip Branch, who has stood by me from the first day; and by Ocania Chalk, whose two previous books on black collegiate athletes and other black athletic pioneers provided so much of the core material for *A Hard Road to Glory*. To my personal assistant, Derilene McCloud, go special thanks for coordinating, typing, filing, phoning, and organizing the information and interviews, as well as keeping my day-to-day affairs in order. Sandra Jamison's skills in library science were invaluable in the beginning. Her successor, Rod Howard, is now a virtual walking encyclopedia of information about black athletes, especially those in college. To Francis Harris, who almost single-handedly constructed the reference sections, I am truly grateful. And to Deborah McRae, who sat through hundreds of hours of typing—her assistance is not forgotten.

Institutions have been very helpful and forthcoming. The people at the New York Public Library Annex went out of their way to search for books. *The New York Times* provided access to back issues. The Norfolk, Virginia, Public Library was kind and considerate. This book could not have been done without the kind help of the Schomburg Library for Research in Black Culture in Harlem, New York. Its photography curator, Deborah Willis Thomas, found many photographs for me, and Ernest Kaiser followed my work with interest.

The Enoch Pratt Free Library in Baltimore, Maryland; the Moorland-Spingarn Library at Howard University in Washington, D.C.; and the Library of Congress not only assisted but were encouraging and courteous. The offices of the Central Intercollegiate Athletic Association, the Southern Intercollegiate Athletic Conference, the Mideastern Athletic Conference, and the Southwest Athletic Conference dug deep to find information on past black college sports. The National Collegiate Athletic Association and the National Association for Intercollegiate Athletics were quick with information about past and present athletes. The home offices of major league baseball, the National Basketball Association, the National Football League, and their archivists and Halls of Fame were eager to provide assistance. Joe Corrigan went out of his way to lend a hand.

The staffs at Tuskegee University and Tennessee State University were particularly kind. Wallace Jackson at Alabama A&M was helpful with information on the Southern Intercollegiate Athletic Conference. Alvin Hollins at Florida A&M University was eager to assist. Lynn Abraham of New York City found a rare set of boxing books for me. Lou Robinson of Claremont, California, came through in a pinch with information on black Olympians, and Margaret Gordon of the American Tennis Association offered her assistance.

Many people offered to be interviewed for this project. Two of them, Eyre Saitch, Nell Jackson, Dr. Reginald Weir and Ric Roberts, have since passed on, and I am truly grateful for their recollections. Others who agreed to sit and talk with Kip Branch, Ocania Chalk, or me include William "Pop" Gates, Elgin Baylor, Oscar Robertson, Anita DeFranz, Nikki Franke, Peter Westbrook, Paul Robeson, Jr., Afro-American sportswriter Sam Lacy, A.S. "Doc" young, Frederick "Fritz" Pollard, Jr., Mel Glover, Calvin Peete, Oscar Johnson, Althea Gibson, Mrs. Ted Paige, Charles Sifford, Howard Gentry, Milt Campbell, Otis Troupe, Beau Jack, Coach and Mrs. Jake Gaither, Lynn Swann, Franco Harris, Dr. Richard Long of Atlanta University, Dr. Leonard Jeffries of the City College of New York, Dr. Elliot Skinner of Columbia University, and Dr. Ben Jochannon.

Dr. Maulana Karenga of Los Angeles and Dr. William J. Baker of the Unversity of Maine offered material and guidance on African sports. Dr. Ofuatey Kodjo of Queens College in New York City helped edit this same information. Norris Horton of the United Golfers Association provided records, and Margaret Lee of the National Bowling Association answered every inquiry with interest. To Nick Seitz of *Golf Digest* and *Tennis*, I offer thanks for his efforts. Professors Barbara Cooke, Patsy B. Perry, Kenneth Chambers, Floyd Ferebee, and Tom Scheft of North Carolina Central University were kind enough to read parts of the manuscript, as did Mr. and Mrs. Donald Baker. Professor Eugene Beecher of Wilson College, an unabashed sports fan, shuttled many clippings our way.

To the dozens of people who heard about my book on Bob Law's *Night Talk* radio show and sent unsolicited but extremely valuable information, I cannot thank you enough. And to the hundreds of unsung African-American athletes who played under conditions of segregation and whose skills and talents were never known to the general public, I salute you and hope this body of work in some measure vindicates and redresses that gross miscarriage of our American ideals.

Finally, to my wife Jeanne Moutoussamy-Ashe, I owe gratitude and tremendous appreciation for her understanding, patience, tolerance, and sacrifice of time so I could complete this book.

                                   Arthur R. Ashe, Jr.
                                   1988

A HARD ROAD TO GLORY

A HISTORY OF THE AFRICAN-AMERICAN ATHLETE 1919-1945

Introduction

"America's Young Black Joe"

I'm America's YOUNG BLACK JOE.
Most times good natured, smiling and gay
My sky is sometimes cloudy
But it won't stay that way.
I'm comin,' I'm comin'—
But my head *ain't* bending low!
I'm walking proud! I'm speaking out
    loud!—
I'm America's YOUNG BLACK JOE!

The years between the ends of the two World Wars offered about as much contrast as our nation could handle. The 1920s was known as the "Golden Decade of Sports" because of the prevalence and fame of such stars as Babe Ruth, Harold "Red" Grange, Bill Tilden, Jack Dempsey, and Bobby Jones. Of course, it should have been more appropriately called the "Golden Decade of [white] Sports," for black athletes were shut out of major league baseball, eased out of professional football, not allowed to join a fledgling professional basketball league, barred from Forest Hills in tennis, and unlawfully kept out of contention for the heavyweight boxing crown. Most sobering of all was the complete disappearance of the black turf jockey from a sport he dominated a mere twenty years before.

In the period just prior to the Second World War, America had its confidence

badly shaken by a depression so deep that college professors were selling apples on the street. It is a wonder that some sports survived at all. Government programs kept many people on "make work" jobs that ordinarily would have been in low demand. Some of these projects involved building sports facilities.

Despite the large migration of blacks to the North during the First World War, the majority of them still lived in the South at the end of the 1920s. If a black youngster in the North were lucky, he or she could go to a fairly decent public school where sports were a standard part of the extracurricular activities program. In the South, a black youngster would be lucky to finish the seventh grade before being forced by economic necessity to work. Even if he or she had the time, the imbalance in facilities was blatant.

In a 1928 study of recreation in the South, it was found that "In the case of public parks . . . 4 out of 17 southern cities

*From Arnold Rampersad, *The Life of Langston Hughes: Volume 1: 1902-1941: I, Too, Sing America* (New York: Oxford University Press, 1986), pp. 391-392.

have facilities for whites only; one half of those cities which have recreation centers have none for Negroes; 3 have public bathing beaches for whites only, and 10 out of 17 have swimming pools for whites only."[1] The South just did not spend much on recreation per capita; partly because the weather was warm.

The migration northward during the First World War had swamped the public recreational facilities. Factories, churches, Urban League chapters, Travelers Aid Societies, fraternal organizations, YMCAs, and YWCAs struggled to make life more pleasant for the new arrivals. School buildings were commandeered. In Detroit just after the war, the use of public school buildings at night and public high school buildings for evening sports was a method to alleviate the demand for athletics. It did not get appreciably better in the 1920s.

Northern high schools built new sports grounds to handle the increased demand. Gyms and football/track fields were constructed as newspapers increased their coverage of sports. In 1920, the *New York Herald*, for instance, allotted 60 percent of its local news coverage to sports. The *New York World* gave 40 percent. The black-owned paper, the *Chicago Defender*, had a circulation of over 280,000, two-thirds of which was outside Chicago. The nation was going sports crazy but facilities were frequently off-limits to blacks or nonexistent, as in the South.

There were, however, some solid gains in the 1920s. The Negro National League was formed in baseball by the charismatic Andrew "Rube" Foster. William DeHart Hubbard won a gold medal at the 1924 Olympics in the long jump. Blacks participated in the fledgling National Football League, though they were ultimately barred for thirteen years between 1934 and 1946. The United Golfers Association was formed to enhance opportunities for blacks on the links. Two of the most famous basketball teams ever formed—the New York Renaissance and the Harlem Globetrotters—began their tours; and Chicago replaced New York City as the black sports capital of America.

Chicago's importance cannot be understated. The city's black newspaper, the *Chicago Defender*, had heavy sports coverage and was carried by black railroad porters to points south and west. The Chicago Romas, the Savoy Big Five, and the Harlem Globetrotters basketball teams were all Chicago based. Mrs. C. O. "Mother" Seames also had her famous one-court tennis instruction program in Chicago. Rube Foster and three Negro League baseball teams also made Chicago their home. The East-West All-Star Negro League baseball game was played at Chicago's Comiskey Park.

The Golden Gloves Boxing Tournament was begun there by Arch Ward, sports editor of the *Chicago Tribune*. Jack Johnson, the former heavyweight champion, lived in Chicago; as did Joe Louis at the height of his career. In football, Amos Alonzo Stagg was the coach of the University of Chicago football team and had won more games than any other college coach. Richard Hudlin, a black player from St. Louis, was captain of the University of Chicago tennis team. Soldier Field stadium was the largest in the country and black professional football players were on the Chicago Cardinals NFL team. Wendell Phillips High School had a predominantly black student body and was nationally known for its sports teams. In short, no other city, not even New York City, could match Chicago in black sports participation and accomplishment between 1920 and 1940.

Two events, however, occurred in 1929 that profoundly affected sports for blacks and everyone else. One was the stock market crash that plunged the nation into the Great Depression. The other was the commissioned Carnegie Report that highlighted widespread abuses of rules in college sports programs. The report recommended a deemphasis of sports on campuses which meant that for the already underfunded black land grant colleges, hard choices had to be made. For a time, only football mattered. As the February 2, 1935, *Norfolk Journal and Guide* newspaper, a black publication, wrote, "There hardly seems to be any other dish on the table for local fans except football. Efforts have been made to interest the public in sport for every season, but that seems to have gone for naught." In some places, the Depression made talk of sports perfunctory.

Certain black colleges were granted funds to refurbish their sports facilities. Virginia State (Petersburg, Virginia) received $70,000 in 1935 to erect an indoor pool, locker rooms, and to resod its football field. But blacks had little voting control over these decisions. As late as 1940, only three of the seventeen black land grant colleges had black board members with voting power. Thousands of black students in the 1930s and 1940s could not go to college because there was simply no room for them at black schools and there were quotas at northern white schools. In the 1930s when black groups placed more pressure on white southern schools to open up, the southern state supreme courts upheld the right of white colleges to deny black enrollment. At Ohio State in 1933, the Ohio Supreme Court upheld that school's right to deny dormitory space to black coeds because it might have forced a "family-like" atmosphere between black and white girls.

At the end of the 1930s, most black sports observers were only cautiously optimistic about the future in spite of the fame of performers like Jesse Owens and Joe Louis. In the first definitive historical review of black sports, Edwin B. Henderson noted in his book, *The Negro in Sports* (1939), that "...the records show no outstanding Negro champions in archery, auto racing, badminton, billiards, bob-sledding, bowling, canoeing, casting, chess, court tennis, cricket, curling, fencing, gymnastics, handball, hockey, horseshoe pitching, ice-skating, lacrosse, lawn bowling, motor boating, polo, rackets, rowing, rugby, skeet shooting, trap-shooting, skiing, squash, swimming, table tennis, wrestling, and yachting."[2] What had emerged for blacks was a Big Five: baseball, basketball, football, boxing, and track.

Blacks had begun to concentrate on those sports stressed in the public school systems because they were free of charge. The school systems in turn stressed team sports that occupied as many students as possible. Hence, with the exception of boxing, the other four of the Big Five formed the nucleus of future black participation. Historical and traditional links to the past, like jockeys and wrestling, were forgotten. Only the Big Five really mattered.

Few civil rights groups, like the National Association for the Advancement of Colored People (NAACP), got involved in sports disputes. Games were thought to be quasi-frivolous anyway. All that changed, however, in the early 1940s when the labor movement assumed the leadership role for black advancement. Leaders such as A. Philip Randolph of the Brotherhood of Sleeping Car Porters, made a cause of the entry of blacks in major league baseball. Such an event was, in his mind, a test of President Franklin D. Roosevelt's true intentions concerning fairness in employment. The slogan, "If he's good enough for the Navy, he's good enough for the majors [leagues]" became a favored expression during the Second World War. This positive role of black civil rights leaders, particularly labor leaders, in effecting progress in sports has been historically underestimated.

The war itself provided many American males—black and white—with their first sustained exposure to one another on the athletic field. For most southern whites, it was a difficult adjustment to make since blacks dominated sports contests in all branches of the armed forces. It put to rest notions of the natural superiority of whites over blacks—there was now proof in the flesh.

The nation as a whole was more receptive to the participation of blacks in professional sports leagues after the war, though there probably would not have been too many problems beforehand. This increased receptiveness notwithstanding, blacks took matters into their own hands and pressed for redress in practically every sport around. The result was an unprecedented five-year period between 1946 and 1950, when the American sports establishment was literally forced to open their doors to blacks. The South remained a problem but it, too, in time gave way.

This twenty-five-year period is best remembered for the exploits of Jesse, Joe, and Jackie: Jessie Owens, Joe Louis, and Jackie Robinson. These three black athletes left indelible impressions on America and the world. Owens was the fastest, Louis was the strongest, and Robinson was the bravest. Each in his own way forced the country to see the folly of erecting barriers between the races in the athletic arena. Each represented the best at his sport and was an example of what an individual could do if only given the chance. That is all anyone can ask and the black athlete was no different.

Notes

1. Edwin B. Henderson, *The Negro in Sports* (Washington, D.C.: Associated Publishers Inc., 1939 and 1949), p. 766.
2. Ibid., p. 220.

Boxing

Jack Johnson's Legacy

America's boxing authorities after the First World War believed they had rid themselves of blacks as contenders for the heavyweight title. Jack Johnson had lost his world heavyweight title to Jess Willard while in exile in 1915. Noted black heavyweights like Joe Jeanette, Sam Langford, Sam McVey, et al., were getting old or, at best, not worthy of title contention—so authorities thought. There was no longer a need for a "white hope."

William Henry "Jack" Dempsey stepped up in the racially torn summer of 1919 and won the world heavyweight crown from Willard on July 4. He followed his victory with only two defenses in 1920. He also let it be known that he would draw the color line and refuse to fight blacks. Such was the bitter taste that Jack Johnson's flamboyance and flouting of social convention left in the mouths of white America. In his wake, other black heavyweights paid a heavy price for his iconoclasm.

The first to suffer was Harry Wills, born on May 15, 1892, in New Orleans. Like Jack Johnson before him, Wills was a stevedore and stood a massive six feet two inches and weighed 220 pounds. Because he had refused to fight the same blacks over and over, he spent much of his time before the war in Panama, where race was not so large a factor. He returned to the United States and on July 26, 1920, he became the legal number one contender for Dempsey when he scored a third-round knockout over Fred Fulton at New York City's First Regiment Armory. Dempsey himself was present to see Wills' victory.

Knowing of Dempsey's prior decision to decline fights with blacks, Paddy Mullins, Wills' manager, decided to stick to his long-range plans for a title shot. He would have Wills fight Dempsey or no one else. Mullins knew the law was on his side. Boxing had been legalized once again in New York State in 1920, because of lobbying by such influential groups as the American Legion. It was difficult to say "no" to such a publicly patriotic group. But when Dempsey refused to fight, Mullins was forced to book fights wherever he could find them—including Cuba. Wills even became the Colored heavyweight champion in 1922 when he defeated Bill Tate.

Finally, so the story goes, Wills was signed by George Lewis "Tex" Rickard, the major domo of boxing promoters, to fight Dempsey in 1923, but Rickard reneged. A year later, James Farley, the chairman of the New York State Athletic Commission, ordered Dempsey to select Wills as his next opponent but Rickard refused to promote it, claiming that "higher ups" in Albany (the state capital) instructed him to leave it alone.

Some believed Rickard, who controlled the sport at Madison Square Garden, was afraid Dempsey might lose. But Nat Fleischer wrote that Rickard had no choice. "There was nothing personal in the denial to Wills of a chance to battle for the heavyweight championship."[1] Rickard was doing what his political superiors told him to do, according to Fleischer. However, the October 5, 1918, *New York Age*, a black newspaper that followed Wills's fortunes closely, had quoted Dempsey's manager, Jack Kearns, as saying, "I never was in favor of mixed bouts...Willard squelched the Colored heavyweight division when he squelched Jack Johnson in Cuba. Why resurrect it again?" That certainly sounded like Kearns too meant to keep blacks out of title contention. Still Rickard announced on May 1, 1924, that Wills and Dempsey would fight on September 6 of that year, but it never came to pass.

Wills and Mullins sat through two years of frustration and were finally offered a bout with a white contender, Gene Tunney, to "clear up" the matter. Mullins, according to Fleischer, screamed, "NO!" It would be "Dempsey or nobody."[2] Wills was then told by Rickard that if he refused to fight Tunney he would forfeit his title chances. Mullins' demands to Farley went unheeded. Rickard then staged the first million-dollar fight in history between Dempsey and Tunney—in Philadelphia. This bout went to the City of Brotherly Love because Dempsey was legally bound in New York State to fight Wills. Wills' demise was one of the most blatantly discriminatory maneuvers in sports history.

Wills was reportedly paid $50,000 for his forfeit, but the Dempsey–Tunney bout grossed $1,895,733; the richest ever. Wills ended 1926 with a loss to Jack Sharkey at Ebbetts Field in Brooklyn and later fought a twelve-round no-decision bout against Louis Firpo at Boyle's Thirty Acres in Jersey City, New Jersey. Nicknamed "the Brown panther," Wills fought Sam Langford fourteen times, Sam McVey four times, and Joe Jeanette twice. He did, however, retire financially secure with major holdings in several Harlem apartment buildings.

In the lower weight classes after the war, opposition to advancement was not nearly as severe. Louis "Battling Siki" Phal of Senegal became the first black holder of the world light-heavyweight title in 1922, but three years later, on December 15, 1925, he died of gunshot wounds in the back. On August 19, 1926, Theodore "Tiger" Flowers, better known as "the Georgia Deacon" because he was constantly seen reading Bible verses, won the world middleweight title over Harry Greb at Madison Square Garden. This first-ever middleweight crown for a native-born black American drew a gate of $101,134.70, and a crowd of 16,311. But in a freakish accident, Flowers died following a routine eye operation on November 11, 1927.

It was during this era of the festive 1920s, and the literary flowering of the Harlem Renaissance, that some blacks began attending the fights at Madison Square Garden in their finest sartorial splendor.

Madison Square Garden was relatively new and after the bouts, hordes of fans—black and white—headed "uptown" to Harlem seeking fun and cabaret entertainment. New York was *the* sports capital of America and the modern Madison Square Garden was the most famous indoor arena extant. Yankee Stadium was the most well-known outdoor sports palace.

There was still a dark side to the boxing business and that remained the ever-present influence of organized crime and their betting schemes and parlors. George Godfrey (a.k.a. Feabe Smith Williams), the black heavyweight, was forced to "throw" a fight against the Italian, Primo Carnera, on June 23, 1930. While everyone knew that Carnera's life was controlled by underworld figures, timely hints to other fighters worked just as well. As Nat Fleischer noted, "Carnera's fight with Godfrey was fixed for the former to win."[3]

Other blacks who sought glory in the ring in this era include, among others, Joe Johnson and Bruce Flowers in the lightweight division, Jack McVey and Lee Anderson in the middleweight class, Buddy Sanders among the welterweights, and Ace Clark and Black Bill in the heavyweight division. Some who fought in several weight classes were Jack Thompson, Larry Johnson, John Lester Johnson, Kid Norfolk, "Baby" Joe Gans, Chick Suggs, Harry Sellers, Larry Gaines, Billy Jones, and Frankie Ansel. All of them laced up their gloves hoping for a way out of their ghetto existence. The best way to start was to first try their luck in the amateur Golden Gloves competitions.

The Golden Gloves, which began in 1923, were staged in the beginning by *Chicago Tribune* sports editor Arch Ward to test Illinois' anti-boxing law. Scheduled for a three-night run, it was so popular that it had to be held over because 424 boxers showed up to register. Groups such as the National Reform Association tried to stop the tournament but a court injunction kept them at bay. In 1926, boxing was legalized in Illinois. Not to be outdone in New York City, the *Daily News* began a New York version in 1927. A year later, the *Tribune* invited boxers from a wider area of the Midwest than just Chicago and thus was born The Golden Gloves Tournament of Champions, which debuted on March 24, 1928.

With successful events in both Chicago and New York, it was only natural that the respective winners meet in a National Tournament of Champions. This format thrived and afforded many young fighters their opportunities for supervision and instruction. Blacks were welcomed from the very beginning and the Golden Gloves became their most important steppingstone to professional success. It also helped to partially remove the sport from the cloistered and unprotected clubs to the public arenas where the light of thoughtful scrutiny prevailed. Its rise occurred just in time, for Tex Rickard died in 1929 during an appendicitis attack, and left the sport floundering as the Great Depression began.

For some black fighters, these hard times were only slightly more discernible than their pre-Depression existence. Two blacks won world titles. Cecil Lewis "Young Jack" Thompson, who was born in San Francisco in 1904, defeated Jackie Fields on May 9, 1930, at The Olympia in Detroit in fifteen rounds to capture the welterweight crown. Thompson weighed in at 142¾ pounds to Fields' 145¾ pounds. He lost his crown four months later to Tommie Freeman at the Public Hall in Cleveland, Ohio, and then regained it in twelve rounds from Freeman at the same place on April 14, 1931. Thompson died prematurely of a heart attack in 1946 at age forty-two.

The other black world titleholder was William "Gorilla" Jones, who was born on May 12, 1906, in Memphis, Tennessee. A prolific boxer, he once had sixty-two bouts in a three-year period. Jones won one of two competing elimination tournaments to choose a successor to Mickey Walker, who resigned the middleweight title in early 1931. Jones defeated Tiger Thomas in Milwaukee on August 25, 1931, in ten rounds, to win the National Boxing Association (NBA) version of the crown. He lost the title when he was beaten by the Frenchman Marcel Thil on a foul in the eleventh round in Paris on June 11, 1932. Jones finished with a record of ninety-seven wins, twenty-three losses, thirteen draws, three no-contests (exhibitions), and five no-decisions (no verdicts).

However successful the lighter classes may have been, the heavyweight division was a mess after Rickard's death. There were few quality boxers around in that class and, beginning in 1930, there were five different winners in as many years. A new hero was needed; someone who captured the public's imagination like Babe Ruth in baseball and Red Grange in football. The elements were in place, the time was propitious, and the Depression provided an added incentive. Out of the feeder system of the recently organized Golden Gloves and Amateur Athletic Union

(AAU) came the savior of the entire sport. And he was black. His name was Joseph Louis Barrow.

The Brown Bomber

No era of sporting excellence for blacks had such an inauspicious beginning as the one defined by the rise and fall of Joseph Louis Barrow. Boxing was more affected by the Depression than most other sports because its very existence depended upon the thousands of employed, single men who lived in northern urban areas like New York City, Chicago, Philadelphia, Detroit, and Baltimore. With fewer dollars in their pockets, they were more choosy about entertainment.

While great numbers of whites found themselves in similar predicaments, they could afford to be more optimistic about the future; they would be first in line if the economy improved. No such optimism floated about the black communities of America. They could only aspire to so much before hitting an artificial ceiling placed there by racism. Consequently, many young blacks sought a quick way out of their predicaments. The fastest route seemed to pass through the boxing ring where, in spite of the Depression, boxers made more money in less time than in any legitimate enterprise known to the average black American. Joe Louis did just that and became the most famous black man on earth since Jack Johnson.

Johnson had many detractors; Louis had no more than a handful. Johnson was born in the South and migrated northward;

Louis was born on May 13, 1914, in Lafayette, Alabama, and eventually settled in a northern ghetto in Detroit. Johnson had to chase his quarry all over the world to get a chance for the world heavyweight title; Louis could try right here at home. But most important, Johnson took a not-so-secret delight in piquing white America with his white wives; Louis heeded his counsel to avoid even being photographed alone with a white woman.

Joe Louis started out as Joe Barrow to a father, Munro, who was committed to a state hospital for the mentally ill. His mother Lily, hearing that her husband had died, married Patrick Brooks who had eight children of his own. The Barrow-Brooks clan soon moved to Detroit to work in the automobile industry. The poorly educated young Louis was brought face to face with harsh racial and urban realities like ethnic street gangs, flushing toilets, brick school-houses, and trolley cars. Of his prior life, he said, "There didn't seem to be anything bad between whites and blacks in Alabama but you have to remember I was a little boy...I never heard about lynchings; nobody ever called me a nigger until I got to Detroit."[4]

In the matter of education, Louis had more in common with another future champion, Floyd Patterson, who ducked school because he did not want anyone to see him in dirty clothes. At Detroit's Duffield Elementary School, though he was twelve years old, he was placed in the fifth grade, but he never cultivated any special interest in books. Because of his insecurities, he developed a stutter. Patterson avoided school by hiding in subway tunnels all day. At the Bronson Trade School, Louis became a fairly good catcher on the baseball team and a teacher prophetically noted he was "Good in manual training. This boy some day should be able to do something with his hands."[5] Quite an understatement.

In 1931 when he was seventeen, Louis was out of school and working in the Briggs Automobile Factory for a dollar a day. He also hauled ice blocks—as did Jack Johnson—and began taking violin lessons. After being badgered by a friend, Thurston McKinney, to take boxing lessons, he finally gave it a try at the Brewster East Side Gymnasium. With the fifty cents his mother gave him for his violin lessons he rented a locker and borrowed a pair of trunks and some ill-fitting shoes. He never took another violin lesson.

Louis entered a world already traipsed by hundreds of blacks before him. Radio broadcasts of the big fights were in their infancy and the sports sheets catered to fans everywhere. "Jack Dempsey was the one hero that I had when I was a kid," said Louis. "We listened to his fights on the radio. It was always Dempsey does this, Dempsey does that."[6] Louis did not realize that he idolized a man who refused to fight blacks after winning the title.

Atler Ellis arranged for Louis' training and placed him on the Brewster team. He promptly lost his first sanctioned bout to Johnny Miler at the Detroit Athletic Club in the fall of 1932. He remembered that he "...was a badly beaten and bruised boy when I slipped into the house that night. I didn't want anyone to see me, so I ducked upstairs."[7] He had been knocked down seven times and was given a merchandise check for seven dollars.

Though he was by then working for Ford Motor Company and training at the same time, he steadily improved and managed to reach the finals of the 1933 AAU National Light-heavyweight Tournament in Boston. He lost to Max Marek. A year later on May 13, he won this crown in St. Louis. After an amateur career of fifty-four bouts, which included AAU and Golden Gloves titles, he was ready to turn professional.

No matter how good he was, he needed connections with managers and promoters to advance his career. Boxing's reputation in the early 1930s was not the best around and blacks were particularly vulnerable because they placed a higher personal psychic value upon sports than did whites. Consequently, they could be persuaded more easily with less temptation. Louis wanted a black manager but was not sophisticated enough at the beginning to know that that was not enough for a heavyweight. No black boxer had fought for the heavyweight title since Jack Johnson in 1915—almost twenty years before.

In 1933, Louis happened to meet John Roxborough, a black Detroit businessman and a friend of local sports clubs for blacks. He was also the king of the illegal numbers rackets in the city's black neighborhoods. But to Louis, Roxborough became "...the best friend I ever had."[8] Roxborough agreed to manage Louis and enlisted the help of a black Chicago-based mortician, Julian Black, who was in the numbers rackets as well. Black also owned an eatery, Elite Number Two, which was a much frequented watering hole for Chicago's sports set.

Black knew the best trainers in the Midwest and called upon one of them, an ex-fighter named Jack Blackburn, to help

the young AAU champion become a professional. The resulting bond between Louis and Blackburn became one of the strongest, warmest, and most trusting in all of sports history. Since Louis weighed only 175 pounds in 1934, he faced an uphill struggle and needed all the help he could get. But he soaked up the advice from the former boxer which began with lessons on balance. "If you're off balance after you throw a punch, then it wasn't thrown right," noted Blackburn.[9] They also worked on adding more poundage. Most important, Louis was taught how to become a model black American heavyweight because of the residue of white disdain from the Jack Johnson era. If Louis were to get his shot at the title, he could not take any unnecessary chances.

Louis was literally groomed to be a champion. He was told he had to knock out opponents rather than risk the judges' decisions, for judges were routinely "bought off" by organized crime. Roxborough gave him lessons on personal hygiene and proper table manners. Russ Cowans, a sports reporter for the *Michigan Chronicle*, provided English lessons to improve his diction, and all concerned advised him "...for God's sake, after you beat a white opponent, don't smile."[10] With these cues and a powerful punch, he turned professional on July 4, 1934, after an amateur record of fifty-four wins and four losses.

In his first professional bout he scored a first-round knockout of Jack Kracken and earned $59—almost three week's wages at Ford Motor Company. By May 5, 1935, his record was twenty-two wins, no losses, and no bout went past ten rounds. But he had not fought in New York City, the nation's boxing capital. Ordinarily a black fighter had to "throw" a few fights—like Joe Gans, Joe Walcott, and George Godfrey—if he wanted to get ahead, but so far Roxborough and Black had been able to resist these demands. As one promoter said to Roxborough, "I can help your boy, but you understand he's a nigger and can't win every time he goes into the ring."[11]

Roxborough and Black needed a New York connection and they found one in Michael "Uncle Mike" Strauss Jacobs, a promoter and ticket agent. They agreed that Jacobs would promote Louis' fights and his managers would take 50 percent of Louis' share for ten years. (It was not atypical for managers then to take half a fighter's purses. They figured they were taking a big chance and they had to pay off the organized crime mobsters from their share. But 50 percent of a national champion's earnings seemed excessive.) Jacobs then assured Roxborough and Black that Louis would not have to throw any bouts; that he "...can win every fight he has, knock'em out in the first round if possible. I promise if Joe ever gets to the top, he'll get the shot at the title."[12] Jacobs kept his promise and twenty years after Jacobs had died, Louis said he was "...one of the finest men I ever knew."[13]

Primo Carnera was chosen for Louis' New York debut. The hulking six-feet-seven-inch, 275-pound Italian was, of course, completely controlled by the Mafia and had hit an opponent so hard on February 10, 1933, that he died five days later. Carnera would simply do whatever his handlers wanted if he could. However, in their bout on June 25, 1935, Louis knocked him to the floor in the sixth round. But there was more to this bout than the win. It almost did not happen.

Front-page stories blared the news that Italy, under fascist dictator Benito Mussolini, was preparing to invade Ethiopia, ruled by its monarch Haile Selassie I. Newspaper publisher William Randolph Hearst wanted to have the bout cancelled because his wife's Milk Fund charity was a recipient of some of the fight proceeds. Louis was obviously seen by some as a symbol of the oppressed Ethiopians in his bout against the Italian giant. The distinguished black historian Rayford W. Logan of Atlanta University commented that "I am afraid that the defeat of Carnera by Louis will be interpreted as an additional insult to the Italian flag, which will promote Mussolini to start again the recent attempt by Italy to annihilate Abyssinia [Ethiopia]."[14] A compromise was reached by having a pre-fight announcement made at ringside that urged all concerned to view the bout as a contest between two fighters and nothing more. But to many observers it was an example of American democracy versus Italian fascism.

After Louis' victory over Carnera, his stock in the black community soared. He was as popular as Satchel Paige at a time when, as one black newspaper noted, "It takes twice as much effort to turn ordinary colored citizens into fight fans...when they hear of hard striving boys of their race being robbed of decisions by crooked referees, or forced to lay down to inferior white opponents...."[15] The primary obstacle was the powerful black church which was generally not in favor of boxing as a profession. Intellectuals like W.E.B. Du Bois were strongly against boxing.

Louis seemed befuddled by all this attention at first. After church services with his mother following the Carnera win, he said, "When I walked in the church, you'd have thought I was the second coming of Christ...Rev. J.H. Maston...talked about how God gave certain people gifts...and through my fighting I was to uplift the spirit of my race. I must make the whole world know that Negro people were strong, fair, and decent....He said I was one of the chosen. I thought to myself, 'Jesus Christ, am I all that?'"[16]

Next, Louis defeated another ex-champion, Maximillian Adalbert "Max" Baer who stood six feet two and a half inches and weighed 220 pounds. Baer fell in four rounds at Yankee Stadium. But just four hours before this bout, Louis had impulsively married nineteen-year-old Marva Trotter, his girlfriend for some time. He was now nearly twenty-five pounds heavier than his professional debut weight and already one of the wealthiest black men in America. For his last two fights alone, he had grossed $300,000.

Louis finally received his comeuppance on June 19, 1936. In a bout for which he used a future heavyweight champion, "Jersey" Joe Walcott, as a sparring partner, he lost in another controversial bout to the German Max Schmeling in a twelfth-round knockout. Some say he had not trained according to Blackburn's instructions, he had played too much golf, and was not in proper shape. In addition, his trainer Blackburn, who was an alcoholic, was involved in a shootout in late 1935 in which an elderly man had died. Though he was acquitted, Blackburn had to be watched.

The Nazis in Adolf Hitler's Germany were jubilant over Schmeling's victory. One of their writers, George Spandau, called it a cultural achievement for the white race.

The October 1936 issue of the National Association for the Advancement of Colored People's magazine, *Crisis*, reprinted a complete transcription of an article from the German magazine, *Der Weltkampf*. In part, it read: "The Negro is of a slave nature, but woe unto us if this slave nature is unbridled, for then arrogance and cruelty show themselves in the most bestial way...these three countries—France, England, and white North America—cannot thank Schmeling enough for his victory, for he checked the arrogance of the Negro and clearly demonstrated to them the superiority of white intelligence." Earlier that year in August, Jesse Owens had burst Hitler's racist balloon by winning four gold medals at the Olympic Games in Berlin.

Like a rider thrown from a horse, Louis was back in the ring in less than two months with a third-round knockout of Jack Sharkey, another ex-champion. The world now knew that Louis deserved a shot at the title. No more excuses. No more alibis. No more flimsy subterfuge as was the case with Harry Wills. As promised by Jacobs, he got it on June 22, 1937, at Chicago's Comiskey Park against the current champion, James J. Braddock.

This bout against Braddock almost failed to come about because Braddock had signed to fight Schmeling. But Joe Gould, Braddock's manager, figured that Louis would be easier since he had lost to Schmeling and that Braddock would not have to run the gauntlet of anti-Nazi Jewish demonstrators. In reality, the issue was over who would promote the bout, Jacobs or Madison Square Garden. Jacobs won when Judge Guy T. Fake ruled that the only valid agreement was Louis-Braddock. (It is interesting that Madison Square Garden allowed semi-naked black boxers to fight there yet denied black college basketball teams berths in their much heralded doubleheaders on Saturday afternoons.)

The twenty-three-year-old Louis never trained harder for a bout in his life. He had six tune-up bouts since his Sharkey win, and at his Kenosha, Wisconsin, camp, he scheduled nineteen sessions of boxing with workouts on Saturdays, Sundays, Tuesdays, and Thursdays. Braddock, thirty-two, came into the ring not having fought in two years, so Louis was a 2-to-1 betting favorite. On fight night, 20,000 of the 45,000 in attendance were black—the largest number of blacks ever to see a live bout.

In the first round Louis was dropped by a right hand, but bounced up quickly and waited for time to take its toll. The champion had obviously counted on a quick knockout for he knew he could not go the distance. By the eighth round it was clear to all that, barring an act of God, Louis would win. Blacks in the crowd were delirious with joy. Some of them began crying, hugging one another, holding hands, laughing, mimicking Louis' every blow, wincing with every blow he took. They were witnessing a historic occasion, as no black person present had traveled to Sydney, Australia, in 1908 to see Jack Johnson win his title. These 20,000 were the chosen few.

At one minute, ten seconds into the eighth round, referee Tommy Thomas counted out James Braddock and Joseph Louis was the new world heavyweight champion.

But Louis would not feel complete until he conquered Max Schmeling. As Ja-cobs ironed out the details of a Louis-Schmeling rematch, he was aware of the increasing tensions between Germany and Austria and the atrocities against the Jews there. As a Jew himself, Jacobs knew there would be trouble, which was partially dampened by a friendly meeting Louis had with President Franklin D. Roosevelt. The President told the new champion, "Joe, we need muscles like yours to beat Germany."[17] It was also at this time he found out his father, Munro, was not dead as presupposed, and the champion subsequently arranged for his care until his passing in 1938.

The date for Schmeling was set for June 22, 1938, at Yankee Stadium, just as word of Nazi concentration camps for Jews was spreading. Many now worried about a Louis loss to Schmeling. In short, Louis had to win or all of America would suffer the psychological consequences of more Nazi drivel about racial supremacy over blacks and Jews. If Louis lost, Jacobs, himself, would be considered a traitor to *his* own people. But Louis reportedly told Jacobs that he had no plans to return to Ford Motor Company and that he, Jacobs, would not have to go back to selling lemon drops on the Staten Island Ferry.

In mid-May, Louis' camp in Pompton Lakes, New Jersey, was picketed by pro-Nazi sympathizers. When Louis was asked if he was scared, he replied, "Yeah, I'm scared. I'm scared I might kill Schmeling."[18] The source of Louis' anger was a late hit by Schmeling in their first bout and he meant to get even.

Never before, save possibly the Jack Johnson fight with Jim Jeffries, had black America been so consumed by a single event. No political happening, no other sports occasion, no war, no imminent passing of any law could compare with the possibility of a Louis victory. Ask any black person who was alive and over ten years of age when Joe Louis fought Max Schmeling, and he or she would remember it clearly. Neither Jesse Owens' four Olympic gold medals nor Jackie Robinson's signing with the Brooklyn Dodgers equaled the elation of this night. The emotional immediacy of a Louis victory over the "Nazi" Schmeling was wildly compelling.

Two other factors made this bout special: direct radio broadcasts and the accreditation of black journalists. Jacobs initially believed that live radio would hurt the live gate and had not allowed it. The inability of black sports reporters getting credentials was another matter. Joe Bostic of the *New York Age* explained, "They [major stadium and arena managers] would turn us off by saying that working press tickets were only for people from the daily press.... We would get what they called tax tickets; you still had to pay a tax but there was no admission price. The seats were far from ringside. After Louis fought [Jorge] Brescia [October 9, 1936], we got our first boxing press credentials."[19]

On the day of the fight, an unusually calm Louis weighed 198 to 193 pounds for Schmeling. "This is it Chappie. It's your chance to prove you're a real champ," explained Blackburn, who had Louis trained to his outer limits as they entered the ring. Referee Arthur Donovan brought the two boxers together and afterwards, Louis stood in his corner rather than rest on his stool a few extra minutes. He was critically aware of the burden he was shouldering. Never before had as many Americans—all Americans—pulled for a reigning champion as they were for Louis. It was a rerun of the Louis–Carnera bout but with far graver circumstances. Before he sat down again, he would erase all doubts that he was the best in the world.

At the sound of the opening bell, Louis charged across the ring and began assaulting Schmeling with stinging left jabs that found their marks. Schmeling got in one right hand that did little damage. Four more Louis left jabs and then he saw an opening for a right to the jaw. Hit flush on the left side of his face just below his ear, Schmeling caromed off the ropes to be met with a right to the body which, Louis said later, made the German squeal "..like a stuck pig."[20] Donovan scored it a knockdown.

After a count of one, the challenger was back in the center of the ring and another right to the jaw put him on the floor for a three-count. Up again, he took a left and a right to the head and fell to his knees for a count of two—solely because his mind could not follow the referee's count. His fighter's training forced him up a third time, and Louis let fly with a left hook and a right to the jaw. It was over. In two minutes, four seconds of the first round, the Brown Bomber had convinced all doubters that, racial theories to the contrary, he was the undisputed world champion.

The entire nation celebrated but blacks were euphoric. No need to hide their joy this time. There were no murders or retributive acts of racial revenge, as was the case when Jack Johnson defeated "the white hope" Jim Jeffries in 1910. Louis was, at that moment, more idolized than any black athlete had ever been before, until the prime of Muhammad Ali. He took seven months off to enjoy himself before granting the black world light-heavyweight champion, John Henry Lewis, a title shot. In this second heavyweight title bout between two blacks—the first was Jack Johnson versus Jim Johnson—Louis mercifully knocked out Lewis after two minutes, twenty-nine seconds into the first round.

Though no one any longer questioned his fistic talents, he did pile up some personal problems. His marriage began to fail, he lost thousands of dollars on the golf course, and he gave money away to friends and relatives. As late as 1942 when he enlisted in the army, his bouts since 1934 had grossed nearly $2 million and certified Treasury records showed a federal and state tax bite of $227,746. Yet his net income totaled only $84,500 for the period, as his managers were taking 50 percent and training expenses came out of his own share. Louis did not comprehend the tax consequences of his actions.

After the second Schmeling bout, Louis fought four times in 1939 and four times in 1940. He then began what was called a "bum-of-the-month" tour from January through November in 1941. Only one opponent lasted the fifteen-round limit and that was Arturo Godoy who afterwards rushed over to Louis and kissed him on the mouth. The bum-of-the-month tour barely covered expenses but Louis kept spending. In 1942, he donated the entire proceeds of his fight with Buddy Baer—$89,092—Max's brother, to the navy Relief Fund, though the navy, which includes the marines, was clearly the most discriminatory of the armed forces branches. The marines were also the last of the armed forces to integrate.

Two months later, on March 27, he donated another $36,146 to the Army Relief Fund from his fight with Abe Simon. He did not fully understand that these sums were still considered income by the government. Actually, Louis was left to his own devices by Roxborough and Black after they tried to get him to temper his spending. But Roxborough was sent to prison, in 1941, for two and a half years for operating a numbers business. By the end of 1942, Louis' beloved Blackburn had died of heart disease. He was by then in the army and owed the government $117,000 in back taxes, Roxborough $41,000, and the Twentieth Century Sporting Club $60,000. Given a chance to clear up some of this debt with a $300,000 payday in September 1942, Sergeant Joe Louis was denied the opportunity to fight by Secretary of War Henry Stimson.

When Louis received his honorable discharge from the army in October 1945, he was broke though he had fought ninety-six exhibitions, traveled 70,000 miles, and had done all he was asked. His wife Marva was divorcing him and when she agreed to accept a $25,000 cash settlement, he did not have it to pay. But he was still the world heavyweight champion and everybody loved him.

It was a wonderfully expectant time to be a talented black athlete. Jackie Robinson had signed with the Brooklyn Dodgers to break the color line in team sports, and basketball and football were ready to admit blacks as well. Much of the goodwill for black athletes generated in the dozen years leading to the end of the war was due to the positive image that Louis had created. He could build on that reputation to see his way out.

Those Other Black Champions

Joe Louis so dominated the 1930s and 1940s that his fellow black boxers in lower weight classes sometimes failed to attract their just due. But they all shared the same condition as members of the black underclass making their way during the Depression, since few middle-class young men, black or white, aspired to be professional boxers.

The aforementioned John Henry Lewis became the world light-heavyweight champion on October 31, 1935, when he defeated Bob Olin in St. Louis in fifteen rounds. He started out in Los Angeles where he was born on May 1, 1914, just thirteen days before Joe Louis. It is claimed that he was a great-great nephew of Tom Molineaux, the early nineteenth-century boxing contender, but, true or not, his boxing skills were certainly respected.

Lewis' father was a boxer who taught his son in Phoenix, Arizona, where the family had moved so the elder Lewis could work as a trainer at a local college. John Henry turned professional at sixteen, and thirteen of his first fourteen fights were won by knockouts before the seventh round. One of these opponents, Sam Terrain, died as a result. Lewis, at five feet eleven inches and 174 pounds, was a powerful puncher. But the big purses were in the heavyweight division. So he fought constantly. In June 1936 and April 1937, he fought four times in each thirty-day period.

At one time Lewis was managed by Gus Greenlee who was responsible for the resurrection of baseball's Negro National Leagues in 1933. His prior manager, Ernie Lira, arranged both light-heavyweight and heavyweight opponents. His first loss came on November 16, 1932, to "Slapsie" Maxie Rosenbloom in ten rounds, but he avenged that loss with two wins over Rosenbloom in three weeks, in July 1933.

After defeating Olin for the title, Lewis successfully defended his crown five times before abdicating in 1938. It was just too difficult to maintain the weight limit as a light-heavyweight. He was thus the first native-born black American world light-heavyweight champion and the first to retire from his division undefeated. His bout with Joe Louis on January 25, 1939, was in fact arranged to provide Lewis with a big pay-day—$17,000. Days later, the truth surfaced that Lewis was half-blind in his right eye before the bout. He never fought again and died in Berkeley, California, on April 18, 1974.

Another who competed with Joe Louis for publicity was Henry "Hammering Hank" Armstrong who was born in Columbus, Mississippi, on December 12, 1912. With the possible exception of George Dixon, Armstrong was the first to be thought of as, pound-for-pound, the best ever. Armstrong began his life as Henry Jackson, to a father who had fifteen children. He saw his mother die of tuberculosis when he was six and an older brother died from a beating he took from attracting the wrong girl. After moving to St. Louis, he worked on a construction gang and read about Kid Chocolate making $75,000 for fighting a half hour in the ring. On the spot, so the story goes, he quit his construction duties and told his grandmother he wanted to be a fighter.

Henry Armstrong's wise grandmother told him, "...son, you can't fight. You ain't no Jack Johnson."[21] But he proceeded anyway and met Harry Armstrong, who became his manager, at the Colored YMCA. With his quick fists and nonstop style, he was soon the featherweight king of St. Louis with no one to fight. So he turned professional in 1931, under the name "Mellody Jackson" and lost his first fight because all he could afford to eat was bread and water. Harry Armstrong had not been told about his diet.

After traveling to California in a box car, Mellody Jackson and Harry Armstrong arranged to sell their management contract to Tom Cox for three dollars. Jackson then decided he wanted to fight as an amateur again so he adopted the name Henry Armstrong. He had by then fought under three different names: Henry Jackson, Henry Armstrong as an amateur, and Mellody Jackson as a professional. But it was probably not the first time it had occurred.

Armstrong tried to make the 1932 Olympic team as a bantamweight but losing the required weight made him so weak that he lost miserably. His contract was then sold by Cox to Wirt "One Shot" Ross for three hundred dollars (a multiple of one-hundred over the three dollar price), as he turned professional for good under the name Henry Armstrong. Immediately, he ran into trouble. Freddie Miller, the feather-weight champion, would not meet him because of Armstrong's outstanding record. In Mexico for a "fixed" match against a local favorite, Baby Arizmendi, he intentionally lost as agreed and later had his share stolen away, so he fought for nothing.

He fought Arizmendi a second time with an agreement to lose and complied. During a third "fix," Armstrong doublecrossed Arizmendi and crushed him unmercifully. This third bout was watched by the famed entertainer, Al Jolson (who performed in black-face makeup), who, with the actor George Raft, put up $5,000 to buy Armstrong's contract from Ross for Eddie Mead, a local manager. With these connections, he was ready for Madison Square Garden.

When he got his chance, Armstrong overwhelmed the featherweight king, Petey Sarron, in six rounds to capture the title on October 29, 1937. He was awarded *Ring* magazine's Merit Award even though Joe Louis won the heavyweight title that same year. But, as he noted, "...everyone was saving their money to see Joe Louis fight because he's knocking out everybody."[22] Armstrong figured the only way he could get any attention was to win world titles in three weight classes—featherweight, lightweight, and welterweight.

Lou Ambers, the lightweight champion, declined an offer to fight Armstrong but Barney Ross, the Jewish welterweight holder, agreed. After gorging himself with water and high-calorie foods, Armstrong barely made the lower limit for the welterweight class of 147 pounds. Luckily the bout was postponed after the weigh-ins were finished, and when they met on May

31, 1938, Armstrong weighed 133 ½ pounds to Ross' 142. Armstrong won a unanimous fifteen-round decision. Two titles down; one to go.

The lightweight title affair with Ambers was, said Armstrong, "...the bloodiest fight I ever had in my life."[23] The referee, Arthur Donovan, almost stopped it. To solve the problem for himself, Armstrong simply swallowed his own blood from the thirteenth round on. In the fifteenth and final round, he fought in a state of delirium and had to be pulled off of Ambers and carried to his dressing room where he blacked out. When he was revived, he thought he had lost but could remember nothing. He had become the first man in history to hold three world titles at once, and he did not even recall the third one.

Armstrong then abdicated his featherweight crown and lost his lightweight title to Ambers. A try for the middleweight title on March 1, 1940, against Ceferino Garcia failed and on October 4 of that year, he then lost his welterweight crown to Fritzie Zivic. Comebacks failed and two of these included losses to Beau Jack and Sugar Ray Robinson. Though Armstrong's purses totaled over a million dollars, he lost almost all of it to bad advice and bad investments. He now works with the Boy's Clubs in St. Louis and is an ordained minister. That was the way it was for a poor, uneducated child of the Depression.

Between the end of 1940 and the end of 1942, Joe Louis was the only black American world boxing champion. But on December 18, 1942, he was joined by a Georgia-born bootblack, Sidney "Beau Jack" Walker, who won the New York State version of the world lightweight title. As a teenager, Beau Jack worked at the Augusta National Golf Club and was later assisted by Bobby Jones, a club member and winner of golf's Grand Slam titles. Like Henry Armstrong, Beau Jack was raised by his grandmother, who once spanked him for letting another boy take his shoe polish. The next time the adversary tried to nip his polish, Beau Jack fought back and won. "That's the way I want you to be," his grandmother replied approvingly.

Little did his grandmother know what she had started. Beau Jack made his way to Springfield, Massachusetts, to train and eventually wound up in an elimination tournament for Sammy Angott's vacated lightweight title. On December 18, 1942, the five-foot-six-inch boxer's nonstop style won for him the New York State version of the title. Five months later, he lost the title to Bob Montgomery; then regained it on November 19, 1943; then lost it for good to Montgomery on March 3, 1944. He now works at the Konover Hotel in Miami Beach, Florida, and helps to train aspiring fighters.

Bob Montgomery, who twice won the lightweight crown from Beau Jack, was also southern-born in Sumter, South Carolina, on February 10, 1919. After his second title victory he enlisted in the army, and later lost the crown to Ike Williams on August 4, 1947. Montgomery now lives in Philadelphia.

The third and final lightweight champion of the 1940s was Ike Williams of Brunswick, Georgia. After his birth on August 2, 1923, he moved to Trenton, New Jersey, and turned professional at age seventeen. (Black boxers from the South just could not remain at home and hope to succeed in the ring. All the big money fights were up North, especially New York, Chicago, Detroit, Philadelphia, and so on.) He won the National Boxing Association version of the lightweight crown from Juan Zurita in Mexico City on April 18, 1945, on a second-round knockout. Immediately afterwards, bricks, bottles, and cans started flying all over the place and Williams was held up at gunpoint. His championship belt was stolen and he has not seen it since.

In a measure of revenge from Montgomery, Williams won the undisputed world title from him on August 4, 1947, and then lost it to James Carter in 1951. His more long-lasting losses, however, came on the golf course where he came up short in high-stakes games with hustlers. Ike Williams retired in 1955 in modest circumstances.

By the end of the Second World War, it seemed black America could not produce a world champion who could exit the ring gracefully with his earnings safely invested. Still, the professional ranks, at the beginning of the war, had many quality fighters. Some heavyweights, notwithstanding Joe Louis included Roscoe Toles, Turkey Thompson, Harry Bobo, and Lou Brooks. Light-heavyweights around were Jimmy Reeves, Booker Beckwith, Mose Brown, and Lloyd Marshall. Middleweights saw enough of Charley Burley who refused to go to the 1936 Olympics because he disagreed with Adolf Hitler's policies.

Archie Moore, the future world light-heavyweight titleholder, fought for a time as a middleweight in the 1940s, and was joined by Holman Williams. Other welterweights were Jimmy Edgar, Kid Cocoa, and Earl Turner. Willie White and Cleo Shane were lightweights and Davey Crawford fought in the featherweight ranks.

In 1938, one of our black Olympic medalists became involved in a three-way drama stretching over five years. On October 29, 1937, Henry Armstrong defeated Petey Sarron to win the world featherweight crown. Armstrong then resigned in early 1938, because he could no longer make the weight. In an elimination event to find Armstrong's successor, Joey Archibald won the National Boxing Association (NBA) and New York State version of the title. Archibald later lost his NBA title because he refused to defend it, but New York State let it stand. This set up the possibility of dual champions.

The NBA's new designated champion, Petey Scalzo, lost his title to Richie Lemos on July 1, 1941. Lemos then lost it to the black Olympic silver medalist, Jackie Wilson, on November 18 of that same year. Two months earlier, Albert "Chalky" Wright, another black fighter, won the New York State title over Archibald in eleven rounds. Thus two black champions held the same title at the same time, though Wright's crown was considered more important. Such things happened in boxing's strange world sometimes and it persists to this day. Wilson, who was born in Arkansas in 1909, was five feet five inches, fought seventeen years as a professional, and compiled a 74–41–5 record, including one no-contest and one no-decision.

The Sugar Man

In *The Black Athlete: Emergence and Arrival*, the authors rightfully stated that "If there is any major connecting link through those war years in boxing, it is personified by 'Sugar Ray' Robinson, whom many consider, pound for pound, the best fighter ever."[24] This author agrees. Seldom have such superlatives fit a fighter so well. In terms of finesse, body control, flair, hand speed, endurance, athletic ability, and showmanship, no boxer in history matched Robinson. He redefined the very image of the consummate pugilist.

Robinson was born with the name Walker Smith, Jr. to a very poor family in Detroit on May 3, 1920. He hung out at the Brewster Center Gymnasium where Joe Louis trained in the early 1930s. He even became a Louis tag-a-long for a time. After a separation from her husband, his mother brought him and his two sisters to New York City in 1932, first to a lower West Side area known as Hell's Kitchen and then to Harlem. In Harlem, he became infatuated with Bill "Bojangles" Robinson, the black dancer, and performed his routines for money on downtown streets such as Fifth Avenue.

He eventually found his way to the Salem-Crescent Club and its boxing coach, George Gainford. Initially interested, the young Smith sold his first donated boxing outfit and Gainford had second thoughts about training him. However, "...the dance-happy kid who loved to play also got a bang out of the routine of training...he learned fast."[25]

Smith was taken to various boxing shows by Gainford and during one such extravaganza, the promoter needed a last-minute substitute and Gainford offered Smith. But there was a problem: Smith needed an AAU registration card and did not have one. So Gainford did what thousands of his counterparts would have done; he faked it. He arranged to use the card of a recently retired fighter, Ray Robinson, from Richmond, Virginia. Smith-Robinson fought as a substitute and won.

He picked up the sobriquet "Sugar" in Watertown, New York, when a local reporter witnessed Smith-Robinson in action and told Gainford, "You got a mighty sweet boy there."[26] Hence the name Sugar Ray Robinson. Sugar Walker Smith just did not sound appealing; it did not roll off the tongue. Sugar Ray Robinson had almost 125 amateur fights—eighty-nine recorded—and registered sixty-nine knockouts, forty-four of which were in the first round.

As an amateur Robinson won the 1939 Golden Gloves featherweight title and the 1940 lightweight crown, as well as the New York City-Chicago Intercity title. Then he turned professional in 1940 under the management of Kurt Horrman, a wealthy heir to a brewing fortune. Horrman retained Gainford as trainer and arranged for Robinson's Madison Square Garden debut on October 4, against Joe Echeverria. Robinson won in a second-round knockout and then proceeded to win another thirty-nine in a row, twenty-eight by knockout.

Robinson could not hope to match the lure of Joe Louis but he had his own personal following during the war. He kept his reputation clean and his fighting style was inimitable. He had the endurance of Beau Jack, the relentlessness of Henry Armstrong, the finesse was all his own. Few critics had seen anyone glide across the canvas like Robinson. All that dancing on Fifth Avenue had paid off. Finally, as had happened to just about everyone, he lost. Jake LaMotta decisioned him in ten rounds on February 5, 1943, in their second meeting. Undaunted, the Sugar Man began another winning streak of ninety-six bouts without a loss that stretched over eight years. Included in that second string of victories was a win over the aging Henry Armstrong, three of his six world titles, and an army tour that ended in 1946. Save Jack Johnson and Joe Louis, Sugar Ray Robinson influenced his craft more than any other black fighter until the coming of Muhammad Ali.

The Olympians

Though the professionals received most of the ring publicity, there was a group of amateur Olympians who made names for themselves. Ben Pointeau was part of the 1920 Olympic squad but did not win a medal. The 1936 Games in Berlin offered opportunities for five black Americans in four weight classes. They were Arthur Oliver, heavyweight; Willis Johnson, heavyweight alternate; James C. Atkinson, middleweight; Howell King, welterweight alternate; and Jackie Wilson, bantamweight. The highly touted Charley Burley earned a place on the squad but declined.

Jackie Wilson's silver medal was the only prize won by the group. His loss in the finals to Italy's Ulderico Sergo was Wilson's sole defeat as an amateur. By every account, Wilson's demise was a political move because of Italy's partnership with Adolf Hitler. When Wilson met Sergo one year later, he won and left the amateur ranks with a record of fifty wins and one loss. He was also the AAU flyweight winner that same year.

The amateurs as a group had made tremendous advances by the beginning of World War II, and most of them were trained east of the Mississippi River. By 1943, six of the eight national AAU champions were black as were five of the eight national Golden Gloves winners. New York City's Salem-Crescent Club in particular fielded many talented fighters. Boxing was used in the armed forces to toughen the men, and the quality of the instruction and intra-service competition was quite high. The respectability of the sport had never been better. Even the middle-class-oriented NAACP got involved.

In Washington, D.C., in 1945, for instance, the NAACP sued the local AAU affiliate to integrate its boxing tournament. Eugene Meyer, whose paper, the *Washington Post*, sponsored the event, threatened to withdraw his patronage if the AAU did not open up. By a vote of 12 to 4, the AAU Washington, D.C., affiliate changed its previously all-white tournament. The future looked promising for those who wanted to pursue "the sweet science" as a profession.

But a look back could not have provided much encouragement. Yes, the money to be made was more than the average person could earn in several lifetimes. But as Edwin B. Henderson noted in the August 21, 1948, *Afro-American* newspaper, "...professional boxers...theirs is a sad story. For every one who plummets upward to fame and money the road is strewn with punch drunk wrecks."[27] He was right. However, after the war, new generations of young black athletes decided to follow their predecessors into the ring; motivated by the same personal experiences of poverty, a lack of respect for segregated education, and a strong belief that there was just no other way to untold riches. They, too, traveled a "Hard Road to Glory."

Notes

1. Nat Fleischer, *Black Dynamite: The Story of the Negro in the Prize Ring from 1782 to 1938* (New York: *Ring* magazine, 1947) Vol. 5, p. 49.
2. Ibid., p. 50.
3. Ibid., Vol. 5, p. 106.
4. Doug Smith, Monograph, 1985, p. 4.
5. Margery Miller, *Joe Louis: American* (New York: Hill & Wang, 1945), p. 20.
6. Gerald Astor, *And a Credit to His Race: The Hard Life and Times of Joseph Louis Barrow* (New York: Saturday Review Press, 1974), p. 27.
7. Joe Louis, *My Life Story* (New York: Duell, Sloan & Pearce, 1947), p. 27.
8. Ibid., p. 29.
9. Ibid.
10. Gerald Astor, *And a Credit to His Race: The Hard Life and Times of Joseph Louis Barrow*, p. 42.
11. Ibid., p. 60.
12. Ibid., p. 80.
13. Ibid., p. 67.
14. Ibid., p. 97.
15. *California Eagle*, 31 August 1934.
16. Doug Smith, Monograph, 1985, p. 11.
17. Gerald Astor, *And a Credit to His Race: The Hard Life and Times of Joseph Louis Barrow*, p. 169.
18. Doug Smith, Monograph, 1985, p. 15.
19. Gerald Astor, *And a Credit to His Race: The Hard Life and Times of Joseph Louis Barrow*, p. 176.
20. Joe Louis, *My Life Story*, p. 101.
21. Peter Heller, *In This Corner: Forty World Champions Tell Their Stories* (New York: Simon & Schuster, 1973), p. 196.
22. Ibid., p. 211.
23. Ibid., p. 24.
24. Edwin B. Henderson and *Sports* magazine, *The Black Athlete: Emergence and Arrival* (Cornwell Heights: Pennsylvania Publishers Co. Inc., 1968), p. 157.
25. Ibid., p. 179.
26. Ibid., p. 182.
27. *Baltimore Afro-American*, 21 August 1948.

Baseball

Black College Baseball's
Last Hurrah

Baseball was the nation's number one sport after World War I, as returning black veterans flocked to black colleges to make up for lost time. In that period between the end of the war and the onset of the Depression, baseball at these institutions had their finest results but it was short-lived. With a few exceptions, the sport never figured very prominently again after 1940, as track superseded it in importance.

But what a decade black college sports had in the 1920s! The centerpiece of the season remained the Easter Monday game featuring long-established rivalries. In Charlotte, North Carolina, in 1922, 7,000 fans showed up to watch Livingstone defeat Biddle 9–3. Few Negro league professional games could boast that many attendees. There were four major black college rivalries at the time—Howard-Lincoln, Fisk-Tuskegee, Wiley-Prairie View, and Livingstone-Biddle—each pair drew thousands of their faithful.

Their popularity also brought the problem of professionalism to the fore. The black athletic conferences had clear rules against professionals playing on college teams. Article VI, Section 5 of the Colored (now Central) Intercollegiate Athletic Association (CIAA) constitution, for instance, said the only exceptions for off-season play-for-pay was if a student worked at a resort hotel or on a steamboat. Violations were rampant.

Throughout the twenties the issue never waned in the black press. If anything, it worsened. As late as 1927, a March 27 *Pittsburgh Courier* article stated: "It is an open secret that a large number of college men play summer baseball...in the Negro National and the Eastern Colored leagues....The work is more dignified than dish washing, hotel work, dining car and Pullman car services."[1] It came down to practicalities; for many schools, the results of their athletic teams were the primary means of disseminating favorable publicity about themselves, and they were not about to abandon it.

In the CIAA, member schools were playing baseball schedules of a dozen games per season and some played against white schools. On May 6, 1921, Wilberforce defeated Antioch College 6–5. On April 16, 1925, Durham State College defeated Harvard University 9–8 in eleven innings. These interracial match-ups never occurred in football or track. In addition, the relatively lengthy schedules gave several players a chance to star. Hubert Lockhart of Talladega College was easily among the best known pitchers of the early 1920s. In 1922, he tossed a no-hit, no-run game against Morris Brown College.

Harry "Wu Fang" Ward was a standout at Wilberforce from 1923 to 1927. Another star pitcher was Lamon Yokeley of Livingstone. In 1925, Yokeley's last year, he played in a losing Easter Monday effort against Johnson C. Smith (formerly known as Biddle), 7–3. These two teams set an all-time black college attendance record, in 1928, of 10,000. Yokeley later played for the Baltimore Black Sox in the Negro leagues. Other college players who tried the Negro leagues included Charles Taylor of Benedict College; John "Steel Arm" Taylor of Biddle; Dave Malarcher and Bobby Williams of Xavier; and Dick Lundy of Edward Waters College.

History of a different sort was made on June 2, 1925, when the Howard University nine played a touring squad from Japan's Meiji University. Howard won 4–3 in ten innings. Meiji had previously defeated Harvard, Yale, and Princeton during its trip. But by the end of the "Golden Decade of Sports"—as the 1920s are called—even games against foreign teams could not save black college baseball.

Football was the number one attraction and track competed for attention in the spring semester. The Depression effectively ended baseball as a major sport on black college campuses, though shortened varsity schedules remained. Gone were the crowds in the thousands, and with them the Easter Monday games. The favorites of black America by the early 1930s were the resurging Negro league teams and local

nines that played in regional associations. In fact, at their zenith the Negro leagues constituted the largest black-owned business in the country. But at one time these transient professionals nearly "failed to reach first base."

A League At Last

An outstanding war record did not help blacks break into the major leagues in 1919. Andrew "Rube" Foster, owner of the Chicago American Giants, the most dominant force in black baseball, had challenged the organizers of the white Federal league in 1915 to integrate, but he was turned down. Race riots during the "Red Summer of 1919" had further reinforced the "gentlemen's agreement" among major league owners that integrated ball was not a good idea.

White players feared for their jobs; white owners feared their white fans would desert them; white managers feared for the harmony on their teams; and a new white commissioner in 1920, Kennesaw Mountain Landis, wanted an all-white major league lineup. There had occurred in the World Series of 1919 the worst scandal in major league history and Landis' mandate was to clean it up. The last thing he wanted to deal with was the delicate subject of integrated baseball. The black teams just had to form their own league.

Black teams had had their own problems and the owners were fed up with the irresponsibility of the players. Rube Foster declared: "Ball players have had no respect for their word, contracts or moral obligations, yet they are not nearly as much to blame as the different owners of clubs."[2] By Foster's reasoning, the players could not jump from club to club if the owners refused to pay them. So he decided to start with the owners he knew best.

At Foster's urging, a select group of club owners met at the Colored YMCA in Kansas City on February 13–14, 1920, and the Negro National League (NNL) was born. Those present were Foster of the Chicago American Giants; C.I. Taylor of the Indianapolis ABC's; Joe Green of the Chicago Giants; J.L. Wilkerson (white) of the Kansas City Monarchs; Lorenzo S. Cobb of the St. Louis Giants; J.T. Blount of the Detroit Stars. John Marcos of the Cuban Stars was ill and not physically present, but he agreed to the group's formation. The Columbus (Ohio) Buckeyes were initially considered but did not attend this meeting. The NNL became the first black long-term league in any professional sport.

The NNL slogan was "We are the ship; all else the sea." In attendance to witness this historic occasion was Dave Wyatt of the *Indianapolis Ledger,* Elwood C. Knox of the *Indianapolis Freeman,* Cary B. Lewis of the *Chicago Defender,* and attorney Elisha Scott of Topeka, Kansas, who wrote the NNL constitution. The fact that the group had a decidedly midwestern makeup did not deter the attendees. Each franchisee paid $500 as good faith money and began formulating rules.

Much to everyone's surprise and consternation, Foster, who was elected chairman, had already written his own set of rules which he passed out for review. In the back of his mind was the possibility that black teams might one day join the major leagues. So in his words, "We have to be ready when the time comes."[3] He left nothing to chance and he certainly would not wait until there was total unanimity on

everything. As an indiction of the magnitude of the potential for major league participation, George Herman "Babe" Ruth's contract was sold by the Boston Red Sox to the New York Yankees in 1920 for $125,000.

The new NNL planned to begin in April 1921, but changed its mind and reset May 1920 as the debut. The biggest hurdles were the lack of trusted umpires, the lack of enough parity among the teams, and most important, the lack of NNL-owned parks in which to play their games. Acquiring these facilities was priority number one. Otherwise, they would always be dependent upon white booking agents like Nat Strong to schedule games. Problems or not, the first game was played on May 2, 1920, when the Indianapolis ABC's defeated the Chicago Giants 4 to 2 at home before a crowd of 8,000.

Perhaps encouraged by the success of the NNL, another group of black teams formed the Southern Negro League (SNL) in March of 1920. The SNL included the Chattanooga Black Lookouts, the New Orleans Black Pelicans, the Birmingham Black Barons, the Atlanta Black Crackers, the Jacksonville (Florida) Red Caps, and the Nashville Elite (pronounced EE-lite) Giants. Though they agreed to play against non-SNL squads, they kept a separate record for games among themselves.

At the time, eastern teams just played ad hoc schedules and depended upon the black press to publicize their important games. A breakthrough of sorts was effected on July 17 of that year, when the Atlantic City Bacharach Giants played the Lincoln Giants at Ebbetts Field before 16,000 fans. This represented the first time black teams had played in a major league park—the home of the Brooklyn Dodgers. The response was overwhelmingly positive for the teams but offered a win-win situation for the white park owners; they could now continue to keep blacks out of the major leagues and rent their large parks to them on idle days. The Cuban Stars became the regular tenant in a big-league park— Redland Field in Cincinnati—and paid about $4,000 per year for the privilege.

Interwoven with the optimism were serious problems. Umpiring, for instance, remained poor. "There was no umpiring, only guesses,"[4] proclaimed Pepper Bassett. Thirty-one years after the last black player was kicked out of organized ball, this was still the number one gripe. Schedules were uneven because of the problems of park ownership. At the end of the 1921 season, for example, the Chicago American Giants had played sixty-two games, the Kansas City Monarchs played eighty-one games, but the Chicago Giants played only forty-two games. Comparisons were impossible.

Foster's motives were constantly being questioned not only by his fellow owners but by the black press. F.A. "Fay" Young of the *Chicago Defender* saw Foster's purpose "...in forming the league as an effort to keep Nat Strong from controlling all Negro baseball...."[5] Writer Al Monroe thought Foster "...was determined to extend his booking agency as far west as Kansas City and as far south as Birmingham, and the only way to perform this miracle was to form a race [black] baseball league."[6]

The much respected former Xavier star Dave Malarcher disagreed, saying, "...Foster was too great and too big a man to stoop to petty and selfish ambition such as perpetuating a booking agency."[7]

Though the true answers may never be known, it is no secret the owners were very jealous of one another, which flew in the face of model changes in the major leagues. In 1921, the old three-man commission was replaced by a single commissioner, Kennesaw Landis, who now ruled alone. Radio broadcasts of major league games had also begun and these innovations were not lost on the farsighted Foster, who sought to do the same thing in black baseball. Foster was handed further proof in 1922, when the United States Supreme Court decreed major league baseball *not* to be commerce or trade in the ordinary sense and was therefore not subject to the laws governing corporations. Black and white owners were now strengthened in their dealings with recalcitrant players.

Three years after the NNL's formation, it was joined by a new league of teams from the East. In 1923 the Mutual Association of Eastern Colored Baseball Clubs, better known as the Eastern Colored League (ECL), agreed to form an alliance with the NNL. Meeting on December 16, the following teams came aboard at Philadelphia: Brooklyn Royal Giants, New York Lincoln Giants, Atlantic City Bacharach Giants, Baltimore Black Sox, Hilldale of Philadelphia, and the Cuban Stars. The ECL was nominally run by a six-man commission, but in truth it was controlled by Nat Strong, who booked all the games.

Wrote *Pittsburgh Courier* reporter W. Rollo Wilson, "Nat Strong is more than a name in the Eastern League, and will get out only when it suits Nat Strong to do so."[8] It is safe to say that Wilson's comment was tinged with frustration and dismay, for blacks wanted to do their own booking but simply did not have the necessary connections.

Nineteen twenty-three was a good year nevertheless. The NNL's total attendance was 402,436, or about 1,650 per game. Total receipts were $197,218, and player salaries were a combined $101,000. Train fares amounted to $25,212, and $7,965 was spent on baseballs at $23 per dozen. In addition, a new livelier ball was introduced in 1921 that quickened the pace of games. Such good luck could not last forever.

A war broke out in 1924 over players because the ECL paid higher salaries, but a truce was effected just before the first World Series for black baseball. The Kansas City Monarchs won five games to four over Hilldale in a series played from October 3 to 20. But this was not a typical World Series and the bickering was intense. It was played in four different cities and the total attendance was 45,857, with receipts totaling $52,113.40. Each Kansas City player received $307.96, and the losers received $193.23. The Monarchs' superior pitchers, "Bullet" Rogan and Jose Mendez, each won twice and William Bell once. Nip Winters pitched three winning games for Hilldale.

After Hilldale won the 1925 World Series, league officials realized something was missing. Fans wanted to see more stars from more teams, not just the two best from the NNL and ECL, both of which lacked parity among themselves. From 1920 through 1925, the Monarchs averaged $41,000 per year from NNL games; the Chicago American Giants averaged $85,000; but most others managed only $10,000 to $15,000 per year. Moreover, noted sports reporters like Fay Young labeled the World Series a joke. As Ocania Chalk put it,

"The World Series had not caught on in fan appeal."[9]

Reporters like Fay Young of the *Chicago Defender* and all of those from the *Pittsburgh Courier* were the sport's severest critics. They came from cities with strong sports histories. In Pittsburgh, for example, there were nearly a dozen black quality teams that had strong local backing in their communities. The same was true of Chicago. Pittsburgh's teams were somewhat integrated and there was a highly publicized recreational league that featured some of the best players in the city. The teams in several sports that centered around the Crawford Bath House took exceptional pride in their results. From the best to be found in the early 1930s, the Pittsburgh Crawfords emerged as one of the NNL's premier teams and their local reporters minced few words in support.

Rube Foster had forced a showdown in 1925 with his fellow NNL owners to settle arguments. He forced them to pay him 5 percent of all league games receipts to run the NNL. He began by firing six umpires. Unfortunately, Foster suffered a nervous breakdown in 1926, and with it came the slow demise of the NNL. He could not even comprehend his Chicago American Giants' World Series victory in 1926. A black judge, W.C. Hueston, became chairman of the NNL in 1927, and the ECL disbanded one year later on April 30.

The NNL continued operations while other leagues surfaced to maintain some semblance of order. The Negro Southern League (NSL) organized on May 1, 1926, from remnants of the old SNL. The new NSL lineup included the Birmingham Black Barons, Atlanta Black Crackers, Nashville Elite

Giants, Albany (Georgia) Giants, Memphis Red Sox, Chattanooga White Sox, and the Montgomery Grey Sox. Out in the Southwest, a Texas-Oklahoma-Louisiana League (TOL) formed in 1927 though it, too, died out shortly thereafter. Three of its premier teams were the San Antonio Giants, the Austin Black Senators, and the Galveston Crabs.

This predicament in 1927 was similar to that attending black baseball in 1890, when all of white organized ball had managed to rid itself of every black player. Then, as in 1927, some of the dispossessed turned to clowning for a living. The Texas Giants and the New York All-Stars toured Canada and put on humorous displays interspersed with legitimate baseball. To players who had no other skills, clowning was better than no jobs at all.

With two years of off-the-cuff scheduling in the East, another attempt was made to form a league to replace the defunct ECL. On January 17, 1929, the American Negro League (ANL) began with Hilldale, the Baltimore Black Sox, the Lincoln Giants, the Cuban Stars, the Bacharach Giants, and the Homestead Grays (Pittsburgh) in the lineup. But alas, the ANL folded after one season. Meanwhile, that same season, the NNL had what Chicago American Giants' manager "Candy" Jim Taylor called "...the poorest [season] from the standpoint of playing and attendance...mainly because no club in the league was able to put a club on the field in condition to play."[10]

As if the NNL and the ANL did not have enough troubles, the stock market crash of 1929 at season's end stopped everything. Black college baseball all but disappeared in importance for a time. Black professional players tried augmenting their salaries with winter league baseball in Puerto Rico, the Dominican Republic, Mexico, and Cuba. But nothing demonstrated the critical need for new leadership more than the death of the father of black baseball, Rube Foster.

Foster died on December 9, 1930, never fully understanding what had happened since his breakdown in 1926. His remains lay in state for three days and his funeral was one of the largest ever seen for a black man in Chicago. The *Chicago Defender* stated that Foster was the most commanding figure in the history of the game— black or white.

To complete the circle, the incomparable John Henry Lloyd retired in 1931, just as the NNL itself disbanded. (Since 1905, Lloyd had played shortstop, first base, and managed for twenty-five years.) Throughout the eleven-year history of the NNL, only three teams ever won the pennant: the Chicago American Giants, the Kansas City Monarchs, and the St. Louis Stars—too few for long-term stability even in good times. If recovery were possible, the owners had to stop bickering, financial backing had to be firmer, player contracts had to be honored, and the black press needed more stars to write about. Some of those who remained, however, were among the best ever.

Stars of the Twenties

Organizational squabbles notwithstanding, some of the players in the NNL, ECL, SNL, and the ANL were without peer and could have performed with any team anywhere. Oscar Charleston was the most powerful hitter of the decade and it is a shame he never locked horns with Babe Ruth. He came from Indianapolis where he was a bat boy for the Indianapolis ABC's. He later ran away from home to join the army. After playing for the all-black 24th Infantry, he returned to play for the ABC's.

The left-handed Charleston was born in 1896 and stood a sturdy five feet eleven inches and weighed 190. He played the outfield so well that Satchel Paige said "He would outrun the ball."[11] Dave Malarcher added that Charleston "...could play the whole outfield by himself."[12] An exaggeration perhaps, but no one complained about his salary of $325 per month in his prime in the thirties. *Pittsburgh Courier* writer Chester Washington noted that he "... was to Philadelphia [while playing there] what Smokey Joe Williams was to New Yorkers...their hero....Scores of school children turned out to see Oscar perform. He was to them what Babe Ruth was to kids of a lighter hue."[13]

Washington's comment about Babe Ruth left the impression that Ruth was not particularly appealing to black youngsters. This view is buttressed by a strange quote from Ruth on the attraction blacks might have had in the major leagues: "...the colorfulness of Negroes and their sparkling brilliancy on the field would have a tendency to increase attendance at games."[14] Everyone knew Ruth did not speak in such terms so they were probably written for him by his agent Christy Walsh.

Leroy "Satchel" Paige was in a class by himself. He was simply the best known of all the players in black baseball before Jackie Robinson. He earned the moniker "Satchel" from carrying bags or satchels at the train station in his native Mobile, Ala-

bama. After time spent in the St. Meigs Reform School for troubled youngsters, he began his pitching career with the Mobile Tigers, in 1924, at age eighteen. At six feet three inches and 180 pounds, he had exceptionally long arms and wore a size twelve shoe.

In 1926, he was throwing out the opposition for the Chattanooga Black Lookouts and the New Orleans Black Pelicans for $50–200 per month. Newt Allen, a premier second baseman, recalls that "Paige struck out eighteen of us at three o'clock in the afternoon. His arms were so long, he'd raise up that big foot and the next thing you'd know the ball was by ya."[15] But Paige never did play in the NNL or ECL while Foster was in control. His name guaranteed many a sold-out ballpark on Sunday afternoons around the country.

Clinton Thomas of Hilldale was a .300 plus hitter. Floyd "Jelly" Gardner of the Chicago American Giants had blazing speed on the base paths. Oliver "Ghost" Marcelle of New Orleans was a standout at third base when he kept his fiery temper in check. Marcelle once hit Oscar Charleston over the head with a bat. Historian Robert Peterson says the switch-hitting Dick Lundy was the best shortfielder in the 1920s.[16] Lundy had to go to court once in the early 1920s for signing contracts with three separate clubs for the same period.

William "Judy" Johnson was the standard by which other third basemen were measured. At five feet eleven inches and 150 pounds, he had sure hands and a quick mind. He later became a scout in the major leagues. William "Bill" Yancey did double duty as a classy shortstop and as a starter for the famed New York Renaissance basketball team. Newt Allen of Texas had one of the longest careers in black baseball—from 1922 to 1943. A switch-hitter, this five-feet eight-inch 170-pound second baseman's best years were with the Kansas City Monarchs.

Willie Wells was five feet seven inches and weighed only 160 pounds but, as Buck Leonard reminds us, "...he could always get that man at first—he would toss you out, the boys used to say."[17] Had he been born a decade later, he may have been the first black player in the major leagues since the 1880s instead of Jackie Robinson.

Elwood "Bingo" DeMoss played second base for the ABC's and the Chicago American Giants. A motion picture was made in the 1970s that featured a character based on DeMoss. This Topeka, Kansas-born performer was outstanding and he ended his career managing Joe Louis' team, the Chicago Brown Bombers.

George "Mules" Suttles was a powerful hitter from Louisiana who enjoyed a long career. Beginning in 1918, he sojourned with many teams until he finished with the New York Black Yankees in 1943. Louis "Top" Santop Loftin drew one of the highest salaries from Hilldale at $500 per month. "Top" liked to show the fans beforehand where he might hit a home run and sometimes he did just that.

Raleigh "Biz" Mackey was, with no reservation, the best catcher before the Depression. Born in San Antonio, Texas, in 1897, this switch-hitter's life on the diamonds spanned thirty-two years. Beginning with the San Antonio Giants in 1918, he finished with the Newark Eagles in 1950 as their manager. Black Hall of Famer Roy Campanella credits Mackey with teaching him the basics of catching.

Jesse "Nip" Winters was the best pitcher in the ECL. He was a left-hander who began with the Norfolk (Virginia) Stars in 1919 and, after starring at Hilldale, finished with the Bacharach Giants in 1933. William "Dizzy" Dismukes pitched for the Philadelphia Giants in 1913 and then pitched, coached, and managed until the early 1950s. He was a mainstay with the Kansas City Monarchs in the early 1940s.

The pitcher Willie Foster was Rube Foster's half-brother. Noted Bill Yancey, "That guy would give you ten hits and shut you out. He could really pitch."[18] He played for his brother's Chicago American Giants after starting for the Memphis Red Sox. He later became a coach at Alcorn A & M in Mississippi.

The foregoing and more were common names in the black press in the 1920s and 1930s. They were as familiar to black Americans as the major leaguers were to all Americans. Yet they never had the chance to play among all their peers. They had their faults; they broke contracts and sometimes made side deals with owners. But they were also forced to look out for themselves at a time when the future seemed dim. Fortunately, some of them were around to play in the reborn NNL that began in 1932.

The New Negro National League

The death of Rube Foster necessitated a complete revision of the way the NNL had been run. The ANL folded after only one season in 1929, but the struggling NNL and the star players kept hopes alive for a continuation of black professional league baseball. With the Depression in full swing in 1932, recovery would be slow. What was needed were teams with financial backing to weather not only the effects of the poor economic climate, but the fickleness of the players as well. The new benefactors came from an unusual source: the black "numbers" or "policy" kings. Some of their beneficiaries would later play in the major leagues.

In 1931 the NNL actually disbanded, but the separate teams continued to play some games in 1931. The few games played by these teams in 1932 were almost a complete washout. Cumberland Posey of Pittsburgh proposed an East-West game in January, but that idea never materialized. Then, knowing an opportunity when he saw it, Gus Greenlee, the policy king of Pittsburgh's Hill district, decided to give this legitimate business a try. From his own pocket he spent $100,000 to build the first completely black-owned stadium on Bedford Avenue. Simultaneously, he persuaded his fellow black racket operatives in other cities to join him.

Among those who said "yes" were Abe Manley in Newark, New Jersey; Ed Bolden in Philadelphia; Tom Wilson in Nashville; Ed "Soldier Boy" Semler in New York City; and Sonny "Man" Jackson in nearby Homestead, Pennsylvania. Noted Don Rogosin in his book *Invisible Men*, "...all were numbers bankers, personal friends of Gus Greenlee..."[19] The new NNL began in 1933, and Cole's American Giants (Chicago) won the first half of the season and claimed the second half.

From 1933 until 1937, the NNL had no major competition in the East and Midwest, though the Kansas City Monarchs were not members and other local leagues continued operating. The following clubs made up the NNL at various times in this period: Cole's American Giants, Baltimore Black Sox, Detroit Stars, Philadelphia Stars, Cleveland Red Sox, Columbus Elite Giants, Brooklyn Eagles, Washington Elite Giants, New York Black Yankees, Pittsburgh Crawfords, Nashville Elite Giants, Columbus (Ohio) Blue Birds, Newark (NJ) Dodgers, Bacharach Giants, Homestead Grays, New York Cubans, and the Newark (NJ) Eagles.

Concurrent with the revival of the NNL came Posey's idea of an East-West or All-Star Game. Supposedly the plan of Greenlee's assistant, Ray Sparrow, the game was played between teams of players who received the most votes in polls conducted by the *Chicago Defender* and the *Pittsburgh Courier* newspapers. In the inaugural game in 1933, the West defeated the East 11 to 7 behind the pitching of Willie Foster. Sam Streeter was the losing pitcher. Attendance was an astounding 20,000. Black professional baseball was on its way again.

Six factors seems to make a difference in the following decade: one, the East-West game was a huge success and was played in a major league stadium—Comiskey Park in Chicago; two, barnstorming tours in California, the Caribbean, and the Midwest by white major leaguers against black all-star aggregations; three, the *Denver Post* Baseball Tournament; four, the National Baseball Congress Tournament in Witchita, Kansas; five, more black teams were playing more often in major league parks for regular season games; and six, the players were exciting.

Two of those players were Josh Gibson and James "Cool Papa" Bell. Gibson may have been, with Oscar Charleston, the best long ball hitter in the game—bar none. He started with the Homestead Grays on July

25, 1929, as a substitute catcher when the regular catcher, Charles Williams, split his finger on a fastball. Still in high school, Gibson was called out of the stands where he was watching the game against the Kansas City Monarchs. Judy Johnson said Gibson "...would walk up there...turn his left sleeve up...he'd lift that left foot up..."[20] swing the bat, and the ball was gone out of the park.

Gibson's rise and discovery illustrates how some black players wound up in the Negro leagues. His father was from Buena Vista, Georgia, where young Josh was born. He brought his family to Pittsburgh after he found work at the Carnegie-Illinois Steel Company. Josh left school at fourteen and worked for Westinghouse and in Gimbels department store. Gimbels had a baseball team and a local black sports enthusiast, Harold Tinker, spotted him and persuaded him to think about playing for the Crawfords at Ammond Field. Once in the lineup, he stayed.

Gibson hit seventy-five homers in 1931 and sixty-nine homers in 1934 for the Pittsburgh Crawfords. That same year, 1934, he hit a ball to left field over the bull pen and out of Yankee Stadium. Another time in the same stadium, he cracked the longest homer ever seen, which landed two feet from the top of the centerfield wall—580 feet from home plate. Unfortunately, Gibson was an alcoholic; this eventually caused his death in 1947 of a stroke. His prowess with a bat was legendary.

Bell had no peer as a base runner. In centerfield he was a perennial all-star, playing in the East-West classic from 1933 to 1936. Before his death, sports reporter Ric Roberts told the author a little anecdote about Bell. It seems the players used to say that "Cool Papa bunts, bounce twice, put it in your pocket."[21] No man was faster and the NNL teams emphasized speed.

To set themselves apart from the major leagues, Negro league baseball stressed bunts, squeeze plays, hit-and-run tactics, and daring steals. But there was a bit of clowning as well. Touring teams like the Cincinnati/Indianapolis Clowns, the Tennessee Rats, the Zulu Cannibals, and the Miami Clowns were famous for their slapstick routines during play. These teams were definitely looked down upon by most serious players.

Life for players like Gibson and Bell was never easy. The travel was incessant in cramped buses or cars that frequently broke down. Restaurants seldom served blacks and sleeping accommodations were always a problem. Players were responsible for their own uniforms, and medical insurance for injuries was nonexistent for most of them. Still, as Judy Johnson admitted, "We would get tired from the riding, we would fuss like a bunch of chickens, but when you put the suit on it was different. We just knew that was your job...and you'd just do it...there were some sad days too, but there was always sun shining someplace."[22]

The sun shone brightest when they played the white major leaguers. Being shut out of organized ball made them play their hardest in these encounters. Most of these dates continued to be booked by whites such as Nat Strong, Ed Gottlieb, and Eddie Loesch. The black team owners would rather have had a black booking agent but, as in boxing, black agents were short on influence. There was really nothing to be done about it. Solace was taken in playing one's best and defeating the major leaguers.

Another place to show their skills was the *Denver Post* Tournament. The Kansas City Monarchs were the first black team invited in 1934, and they lost to the all-Jewish House of David squad in the finals. This House of David team was an interesting group of devoutly religious men who wore long beards that sometimes reached to the knees. Chet Brewer struck out nineteen batters during this series. The sterling play of Brewer and others was putting to rest the theories that the quality in the NNL was substandard. This fact would play a major role later when integration of the major leagues was imminent.

Other than the Pittsburg Crawfords, the Kansas City Monarchs were the favored team for black and white opponents. Their white owner, J.L. Wilkinson, kept them in good condition and they were not members of the NNL. Wilkinson believed he could make more money and feel freer to schedule if he were independent. Wilkinson's team was even credited with racial breakthroughs in their area. The black newspaper, the *Kansas City Call*, wrote that "...from a sociological point of view the Monarchs have done more than any other single agent in Kansas City to break the damnable outrage of prejudice that exists in this city...."[23]

The Crawfords, on the other hand, were decimated in 1937, when three of their top stars—Satchel Paige, Cool Papa Bell, and Josh Gibson—accepted an invitation from Dominican Republic President Rafael Trujillo to play on his team. The Crawfords dropped from first place in 1936, to next to last place in 1937. That was life in the NNL.

At one time, however, the Crawfords had five future Hall of Fame players on their roster: Gibson, Paige, Charleston, Johnson, and Bell.

A year after the *Denver Post* event, the National Baseball Congress Tournament was held in Witchita, Kansas. The $10,000 first prize was won by a team from Bismarck, North Dakota, which included Ted "Double Duty" Radcliffe, Chet Brewer, Hilton Smith, Quincy Troupe, and Paige. Again, major league scouts were in attendance and black players made good impressions.

Of all the touring match-ups from the *Denver Post* event or the Baseball Congress or from All-stars, the most anticipated duels were between Satchel Paige and the then current major league fastball artists. In the 1930s it was Paige versus Dizzy Dean. A Paige-Dean game drew 20,000 spectators and always gave Paige the notion that he was a law unto himself. Even Dean paid homage to Paige's artistry: "I know who's the best pitcher I ever see and it's old Satchel Paige, that big lanky colored boy."[24] Dean, of course, was just another big league white pitcher in a lengthening line of twirlers—Rube Waddell, Walter Johnson Grover C. Alexander, Lefty Grove—who lost games to Negro league pitchers.

In the same year that Paige defected to the Dominican Republic, the NNL finally received some serious competition. A new Negro American League (NAL) was formed in 1937, and it offered some southern teams a chance to show their talents. The anchor team was the Kansas City Monarchs and the supporting cast included the St. Louis Stars, the Indianapolis Athletics, the Cincinnati Tigers, the Memphis Red Sox, the

Detroit Stars, the Birmingham Black Barons, and the Chicago American Giants. This NAL roster was characterized by an almost total lack of racket influence and heavy promotion. Their opening day game featured two bands and a parade.

A feeling gained credence among blacks that the integration of the major leagues was not a dream anymore. General interest in baseball was never greater. Both the NNL and the NAL drew well. The black track star Jesse Owens and the heavyweight champion Joe Louis were idolized by all Americans. The famed black dancer, Bill "Bojangles" Robinson of Richmond, Virginia, even owned a part of the New York Black Yankees. But most important, the black civil rights organizations began offering assistance in seeking admittance to the major leagues. It was simply a matter of finding the right time and the right person.

The Major Leagues Give In

The East-West game played at Chicago's Comiskey Park was, by 1938, the most well known black sports event on earth and was attended by more blacks than any other single occurrence. No Thanksgiving Day college game, no basketball game featuring the Harlem Globetrotters or the New York Renaissance, not even a Joe Louis title fight brought as many blacks together as this All-Star Game.

These games featured Willie Wells, "Mules" Suttles, Walter "Buck" Leonard, Ray Dandridge, Newt Allen, "Turkey" Stearns, and others. They were living proof that the talent was there. The black press that picked the teams lobbied hard to tell the world how good these players were. Hall of Famer Monte Irvin said, "They gave the players tremendous local publicity. They would pick out the stars, like Josh [Gibson], Buck [Leonard], and Satch [Paige]. Jocko Maxwell of the New Jersey *Afro-American* became efficient at producing good human interest stories..."[25]

The most read of the sports scribes were Fay Young of the *Chicago Defender,* Wendell Smith and Ric Roberts of the *Pittsburgh Courier,* Sam Lacy of the *Afro-American,* Joe Bostic of the *New York Age* and the *People's Voice,* and Romeo Dougherty. Two other influential papers were the *Kansas City Call* and the *California Eagle* in Los Angeles. Southern papers like the *Richmond* (Virginia) *Planet* and the *Montgomery* (Alabama) *Advertiser* were sympathetic but always faced the possibility of reprisals if their editorials were too strong. In some parts of the rural South, the *Chicago Defender* and the *Pittsburgh Courier* were not even read in public for fear of offending some whites. All of these papers campaigned for the integration of the major leagues.

One of the major league team owners, Clark Griffith of the Washington Senators, gave a lengthy interview to Sam Lacy in 1938, and hinted at the possibility of integrated ball. He told Lacy that "Both the commissioner [Judge Landis] and I know that colored baseball is deserving of some recognition in the organized game.... However, I am not so sure that the time has arrived yet....A lone Negro in the game will face rotten, caustic comments. He will be made the target of cruel, filthy epithets....I would not want to be the one to have to take it."[26] Out in Los Angeles that same season, Kenny Washington of UCLA was the

Pacific Coast League collegiate batting champion.

There was some nastiness that year as well. Jake Powell, a New York Yankee outfielder, told a reporter that in the off-season he worked as a policeman in Dayton, Ohio, where he kept in shape by cracking "niggers" over the head. He was suspended for ten days and literally begged forgiveness from the *Chicago Defender.*

But the pressure was mounting. In 1939 in Connecticut, the New Haven Youth Conference forced the State Baseball League to admit blacks. In St. Louis the major league Cardinals' manager, Ray Blades, told another reporter that "The owners will admit Negroes if the [white] fans demand them."[27] Even white reporters began to campaign for black players. Westbrook Pegler, Heywood Broun, Dan Parker, and the *Washington Post's* Shirley Povich went public with their pleas.

On April 7, 1939, Povich wrote, "There's a couple of million dollars worth of baseball talent on the loose, ready for the big leagues, yet unsigned by any major league clubs....Only one thing is keeping them out of the big leagues—the pigmentation of their skin....That's the crime in the eyes of the big league club owners....It's a tight little boycott that the majors have set up against colored players."[28]

Conversely, other white writers were just plain stupid in their comments. In the July 27, 1940, edition of the *Saturday Evening Post,* writer Ted Shane snidely commented that "...their [Negro League] baseball is to white baseball as the Harlem Stomp is to the sedate ballroom waltz...they play faster...clown a lot, go into dance steps, argue noisily and fun-

nily...they undoubtedly are better baserunners than their white confreres...some are positive magicians at bunting...."[29] Then Shane caricatured Oscar Charleston in stereotyped black English: "We plays for bunts." Articles like this made it difficult to gain acceptance.

In the black community at least, part of the negative image left by writers like Ted Shane was thwarted by the burgeoning civil rights movement. At the beginning of the Depression, a DON'T-BUY-WHERE-YOU-CAN'T-WORK compaign was initiated and effective in some northern cities. In the early 1940s the phrase "If he's good enough for the navy, he's good enough for the majors" became a nationwide slogan among blacks.

A. Phillip Randolph, president of the Brotherhood of Sleeping Car Porters, threatened a massive march on the nation's capital unless the federal government moved to end discrimination in employment. Twenty thousand blacks appeared at a rally in New York City's Madison Square Garden on June 16, 1941, in support of Randolph's foreboding. Nine days later on June 25, President Franklin D. Roosevelt issued Executive Order Number 8802, which established the Federal Fair Employment Practices Commission. All of professional baseball wondered if this new order applied to them as well.

Major league officials responded in several ways. Clark Griffith invited Josh Gibson and Buck Leonard to his office for a chat but nothing came of it. Roy Campanella, the catcher for the Baltimore Elite Giants, actually left his team to seek a tryout with the major league Philadelphia Phillies and was embarrassed at being turned down. Leo "The Lip" Durocher said he would use blacks if he thought they could help win ball games. Commissioner Landis reiterated the known fact that no rule existed to prevent blacks from playing in the major leagues.

On the field, sterling play continued and parks were full as blacks had money to spend but fewer material items to purchase because of war shortages. The East-West game attracted 50,256 in 1941. It also featured the first players who eventually played in the major leagues: Monte Irvin, Roy Campanella, Dan Bankhead, and Satchel Paige.

In 1942, the East-West game attracted 48,400 fans to Comiskey Park. A month later on September 26, Randolph specifically mentioned sports when delivering the keynote address to the policy conference of the March on Washington Movement: "...our nearer goals include the abolition of discrimination, segregation, and Jim Crow in the government, the army, navy, air corps, U.S. marines, coast guard...in hotels, restaurants, on public transportation conveyances, in educational, *recreational*, cultural, and amusement and entertainment places...."

A Citizens Committee to Get Negroes Into the Big Leagues was formed late in that summer with the assistance of the black press. It was motivated by a comment from American League president Larry McPhail who had said that the Negro leagues would fold if blacks were brought into the major leagues. Mrs. Effa Manley, owner of the Newark Eagles since her husband, Abe, had died, replied, "The majors draft dozens of players from the minors every season, but do those leagues fold up?...I have absolute confidence that our players will be successful in the big time."[30] A true statement of fact considering the splendid seasons the NNL was having.

Nineteen forty-three was momentous. An embarrassing incident occurred in California in the spring when Clarence "Pants" Rowland, manager of the Los Angeles Angels of the Pacific Coast League, reneged on a promise to grant a tryout to Howard Easterling, Chet Brewer, and Nate Moreland. In February, Charles D. Perry, a New York State senator, sponsored a resolution condemming major league baseball that cited President Roosevelt's antidiscrimination Executive Order. Wendell Smith reported that "...every team...with the possible exception of one, realized a profit of at least five thousand dollars...three teams went over the fifteen-thousand-dollar mark."[31] The East-West game drew its largest crowd ever, 51,723, and total receipts for the combined NNL and NAL were approximately two million dollars—the largest black business in the nation. It was a strange season of ups and downs that all seemed to point toward a real breakthrough.

Getting blacks into the majors was now a test of the intentions of the white establishment and a much publicized goal of the civil rights movement. The publishers of the major black papers sought and obtained an audience with major league officials in early December 1943—just a month after Brooklyn City Councilman Peter Cacchinore, a communist, offered a resolution to force the majors to integrate. This meeting between the Negro Newspapers Publishers Association and a joint session of the two major leagues was a first. In the past, the major league owners would not even have bothered with it; nor would the publishers have banded together like this to risk their influence on sport and games. For some reason, all concerned thought this was different. Baseball was now more that just a game to black America.

On hand at this New York City confab were John Sengstacke of the *Chicago Defender,* Howard Murphy of the *Afro-American,* Dr. C.B. Powell of the *New York Amsterdam News*, Ira Lewis of the *Pittsburgh Courier,* Louis Martin of the *Michigan Chronicle,* William Walker of the *Cleveland Call* and *Post,* and Dan Burley and Wendell Smith as advisors. Also invited was the athlete-author-singer Paul Robeson. Robeson opened the meeting with a stirring plea for justice and fair play. Sengstacke, Lewis, and Murphy, the group's spokesmen, laid out a plan whereby black players would be graded and graduated through the minors just like white players, and he also mentioned that track and boxing were virtually free of racial incidents from fans. No promises were made about future actions.

Nineteen forty-four was marked by two benchmarks: the East-West game outdrew the major leagues' All-Star Game by 46,247 to 29,589. Commissioner Landis died on November 25. (Landis was disliked almost as much as Avery Brundage, the American Olympic Committee president who, blacks felt, was grossly insensitive and bigoted.) Landis' death had removed a major obstacle to the participation of blacks. It was clear for some time that the despised Landis did not want blacks in the majors during his administration.

Finally in 1945 through the convergence of the war's end, changed public attitudes, the civil rights movement, the black press, the undeniable talents of some

NNL and NAL players, and government pressure, the long awaited breakthrough arrived. First, a new Negro Southern League (NSL) formed with the Atlanta Black Crackers, the Knoxville Grays, the Mobile Black Bears, the Nashville Black Vols, the Little Rock Travellers, the Chattanooga Choo-Choos, the Asheville Blues, and the New Orleans Black Pelicans.

Within weeks of the NSL announcement came news of another league of black teams by Branch Rickey, president of the major leagues' Brooklyn Dodgers. This United States League would begin soon and Rickey indicated he would begin immediately to recruit for his team, the Brooklyn Brown Dodgers. A thoroughly skeptical Fay Young thought Rickey was trying to be another Abraham Lincoln. Rickey was further embarrassed when Joe Bostic, of New York City's *People's Voice* newspaper, showed up unannounced with Terris McDuffie and David "Showboat" Thomas for a tryout at Bear Mountain Park, New York, in front of news cameras. What neither Young nor Bostic realized was that Rickey had a plan to integrate his all-white Brooklyn Dodgers but dared not tell a soul. The United States League was a decoy for his true intentions.

Most reports relate Rickey's rage at the stunt pulled by Bostic but in his 1948 book, *Jackie Robinson: My Own Story,* Robinson wrote that McDuffie and Thomas were cordially treated and that, as a result of seeing them perform, Rickey "...decided then that the Negro leagues were worth watching and he sent qualified scouts out to round up Negro players."[32] The major leagues certainly could have used some talent that season. Rather than sign quality black players to fill gaps left by war call-ups, some teams actually used one-armed (Pete Gray of the St. Louis Browns in 1945) and one-legged (Bert Shepard of the Washington Senators) white players. The New York Yankees were picketed on opening day.

On April 16, Jackie Robinson, Sam Jethroe, and Marvin Williams were given tryouts by the Boston Red Sox in a move Cumberland Posey thought was "...the most humiliating experience Negro baseball has yet suffered from white organized baseball."[33] On May 1, the black communist Manhattan City Councilman Benjamin Davis called for a formal investigation of discrimination in professional baseball. (The American Communist Party had tried mightily since the early 1930s to enlist blacks in its cause to no avail.) On July 1, the Ives-Quinn Law went into effect in New York State barring discrimination in employment. Both major league home offices were in New York.

On August 11, New York City Mayor Fiorello LaGuardia invited ten prominent citizens to study the color issue in baseball. They were Dr. John H. Johnson, the black rector of St. Martin's Church, chairman; Dr. Daniel Dodson, New York University professor; Charles Golden, New York Supreme Court justice; Jeremiah Mahoney, former New York Supreme Court justice; Daniel Higgins, of the New York City Board of Education; Edward Lazansky, Appellate Court judge; Arthur Daley, *New York Times* sports columnist; Bill "Bojangles" Robinson, the black actor/dancer; Lawrence McPhail, New York Yankees president; Robert Haig, Columbia University professor; and Branch Rickey; a blue-ribbon panel if there ever was one.

On August 27, this committee held its first meeting. Two days later, Branch Rickey had *his* first meeting with his choice to become the first black player in white organized ball since 1889: Jackie Robinson. Robinson did not come about in this selection through the most predictable course. He had not endured years of barnstorming in the Negro leagues. He was a college-educated (UCLA), former army officer who was born in Cairo, Georgia, but grew up in Pasadena, California.

Robinson knew racism in Pasadena when he was called "nigger," and his family was made to feel unwelcome. He was spared the grind of the Negro leagues. Even the incomparable Satchel Paige spoke of the frequent lethargy and aimlessness of the tour: "I used to feel so bad before I got to the clubhouse I didn't know what to do. But when I put that ballsuit on I don't know where I got the spark to save my life."[34] Robinson , however, experienced very little of that.

Rickey was blunt in that initial session with Robinson. He came right to the point: "You are not here as a candidate for the Brooklyn Brown Dodgers. I've sent for you because I'm interested in having you as a candidate for the Brooklyn National league club....How do you feel about it?"

"Me?" replied Robinson incredulously, "Play for the Dodgers?"

"We're tackling something big here, Jackie; if we fail, no one will try it again for 20 years."[35] "I know you're a good ball-player. What I don't know is whether you have the guts."[36] With the Charles Thomas affair of 1904 still fresh in his mind, Rickey explained to Robinson what a difficult time he would have at first.

Robinson then asked, "Mr. Rickey, are you looking for a Negro who is afraid to fight back?"[37]

Rickey shot back, "Robinson, I'm looking for a ballplayer with guts enough not to fight back!"[38]

Robinson had plenty of experience in delicate racial situations, though not so public. In Pasadena, he fumed at the rule that allowed blacks to swim in the municipal pool only on Tuesdays. With the help of his mother, Mallie, and brothers—Frank and Mack in particular—and a friend, Reverend Karl Downs, he had channeled his energies into a spectacular athletic career at John Muir High School, Pasadena Junior College, and UCLA. At UCLA, he became the school's first four-letter athlete, starring in football, baseball, track, and baseketball. While there, he met his future wife, Rachel Isum.

After leaving UCLA before graduation, he became an assistant athletic director at the National Youth Administration Camp at Atascadero, California. He then went to Hawaii for semiprofessional football with the Honolulu Bears on weekends, while building houses on the weekdays. Luckily, he left Hawaii just forty-eight hours before the Japanese bombed Pearl Harbor on December 7, 1941. The spring of 1942 found him in the army at Fort Hood, Texas, where he refused to play on the post football team because he was once threatened with a court martial for not going to the back of an army bus. Branch Rickey knew all of this and liked what he found out.

Robinson landed with the Kansas City Monarchs just five months before the meeting with Rickey. He was given a tryout with the Monarchs on the recommendation of a friend and was accepted at a salary of $400 per month. Though the money was satisfactory, he hated the life of a Negro leaguer. At the East-West game that summer, Robinson was approached by Rickey's chief scout, Clyde Sukeforth, about playing for the Brooklyn Brown Dodgers and agreed to go to New York City to talk it over.

After talking it over with his wife, Rachel, Robinson agreed in August to join the Dodger organization, but he would keep the pact a secret until later. Though only Rickey's family ostensibly knew of his plans to hire a black player, Red Barber, in his book, *When All Hell Broke Loose in Baseball,* said he was informed of the impending move in March at Joe's Restaurant, in Brooklyn, following a Red Cross meeting. Barber was the most influential baseball announcer in New York, but Rickey obviously thought he could be trusted with this bombshell. As far as the black press was concerned, Wendell Smith put it best in the September 8 *Pittsbhurgh Courier*: "It does not seem logical he [Rickey] should call in a rookie player to discuss the future organization of Negro baseball."[39]

On October 17, Roy Campanella also had a meeting with Rickey. Rickey did not want Robinson to be the lone black player in his organization but when Campanella was asked about playing for him, Campanella turned down the chance. Mistakenly, Campanella thought Rickey was asking about the Brown Dodgers. Later, the dejected catcher was sick at losing the opportunity. Three days later, Mayor LaGuardia's committee published its findings, the most important of which was that blacks were kept out of major league baseball because of sheer prejudice and tradition. Now was the time for Rickey to act.

The official announcement finally came on October 23, 1945, in Montreal, Canada. The assembled reporters had no idea why Rickey had called them in. Robinson, they were told, was being assigned to the Dodgers' minor league affiliate Montreal Royals for a bonus of $3,500 and a salary of $600 per month. He had *not* been signed to play for the Dodgers themselves. Predictably, the reactions ranged from outrage to euphoria.

Alvin Gardner of the Texas League said blacks would never play in the South with its Jim Crow laws. The renowned Rogers Hornsby said, "It won't work."[40] Dixie Walker, a Dodger player, said, "As long as he isn't with the Dodgers, I'm not worried."[41] The New York *Daily News'* Jimmy Powers said Robinson was a thousand-to-one shot to make it. But Robinson supporters included Red Smith of the *New York Herald,* Dan Parker of the *New York Daily Mirror,* and Shirley Povich of the *Washington Post.*

The black press was jubilant. Sam Lacy, Joe Bostic, Fay Young, Wendell Smith, Ric Roberts, et al., along with civil rights groups, felt a large measure of vindication. One sour note came from the Kansas City Monarchs' new owner Tom Baird. Declaring that "We won't take this lying down,"[42] Baird acted on the premise that he still had a valid contract with Robinson. Robinson thought he "...merely had a verbal agreement to play as long as $400 was laid on the line each month.[43]

So it had come to pass that a sixty-four-year-old major league owner had enough courage to do the morally correct thing: grant a human being his rightful chance to succeed or fail. Nothing more; nothing less. Team sports in America have not been the same since that day. Robinson's signing was another demerit for the ideals embodied in the United States Constitution, in that for the second time—the first being Jack Johnson's world heavyweight title victory in Sydney, Australia, in 1908—a black American athlete had to travel outside his country to gain his athletic freedom.

Jackie Robinson's sojourn was just beginning in the spring of 1946. He was a twenty-seven-year-old black rookie in the most tradition-bound sport in the nation. He and his wife would become the most publicized black couple in the country for a time. He had a "Hard Road to Glory" still ahead.

Notes

1. *Pittsburgh Courier,* 27 March 1927.
2. Robert Peterson, *Only the Ball was White* (Englewood Cliffs, N.J.: Prentice-Hall Inc., 1970), p. 83.
3. Don Rogosin, *Invisible Men: Life in Baseball's Negro Leagues* (New York: Antheneum Press, 1983), p. 180.
4. Ibid., p. 73.
5. Robert Peterson, *Only the Ball Was White,* p. 113.
6. Ibid.
7. Ibid.
8. Peterson, *Only the Ball Was White,* p. 88.
9. Ocania Chalk, *Pioneers in Black Sports* (New York: Dodd, Mead & Co., 1975), p. 54.
10. Peterson, *Only the Ball Was White,* p. 91.
11. Rogosin, *Invisible Men: Life In Baseball's Negro Leagues,* p. 13.
12. Ibid., p. 12.
13. Peterson, *Only the Ball Was White,* p. 243.

14. Rogosin, *Invisible Men: Life in Baseball's Negro Leagues,* p. 182.
15. Ibid., p. 16.
16. Peterson, *Only the Ball Was White,* p. 233.
17. Ibid., p. 234.
18. Ibid., p. 210.
19. Rogosin, *Invisible Men: Life in Baseball's Negro Leagues,* p. 17.
20. Peterson, *Only the Ball Was White,* p. 160.
21. Ric Roberts telephone interview with author, 9 July 1983, Washington, D.C.
22. Rogosin, *Invisible Men: Life in Baseball's Negro Leagues,* p. 91.
23. Ibid., p. 35.
24. Peterson, *Only the Ball Was White,* p. 129.
25. Union College Seminar, 23 September 1984.
26. *Baltimore Afro-American,* 25 June 1938.
27. *New York Daily Worker,* 18 August 1939.
28. *Washington Post,* 7 April 1939.
29. *Saturday Evening Post,* 27 July 1940.
30. *New York Daily Worker,* 13 August 1942.
31. *Pittsburgh Courier,* 18 December 1943.
32. Jackie Robinson, *Jackie Robinson: My Own Story* (New York: Greenburg Publishers, 1948), p. 64.
33. Peterson, *Only the Ball Was White,* p. 185.
34. Rogosin, *Invisible Men: Life in Baseball's Negro Leagues,* p. 91.
35. A.S. "Doc" Young, *Great Negro Baseball Stars* (New York: Barnes & Co., 1953), p. 41.
36. Jackie Robinson, *I Never Had It Made* (Greenwich, Conn.: Fawcett Publications, 1972). p. 40.
37. Ibid., p. 41.
38. Ibid.
39. Rogosin, *Invisible Men: Life in Baseball's Negro Leagues,* p. 211.
40. Red Barber, *1947: When All Hell Broke Loose in Baseball* (Garden City, N.Y.: Doubleday & Co., 1982), p. 52.
41. Ibid.
42. Young, *Great Negro Baseball Stars,* p. 24.
43. Peterson, *Only the Ball Was White,* p. 192.

Chapter

3

Basketball

Though basketball grew rapidly after its invention in 1891, it was hampered for the first forty years by poor facilities. This winter game was played in makeshift halls with poor indoor lighting. The gymnasiums in the first quarter of this century were just not built with spectator basketball in mind. Court sizes were standardized, but most teams took what they could get, or settled for what was most convenient. So small were the playing arenas that floor-to-ceiling nets had to be strung up to keep the fans from the players—hence the term "cagers" used to describe basketball performers.

Basketball was also limited by the normal six-day work week. Saturday and Sunday night games were the most popular but they ran counter to many states' "blue laws" which forced some Sunday night games to begin at midnight. Then there were, of course, the vast distances between the good teams. With only five players to a squad, it was so easy to form a team that good ones were rare. By far, most of the talent emerged from the northern ghettos—of Chicago and New York City in particular.

Down South the game was still subject to the tourist season. The winters were warm and when wealthy northerners headed for the local resorts in Arkansas, Florida, Louisiana, Mississippi, and the Car-

olinas, many would-be basketball players were carrying luggage and waiting on tables. It is no wonder then that energetic and resourceful clubs fielded the strongest teams. Since these aggregations grew out of organizations that featured more than just basketball—like Brooklyn's Smart Set Club—their teams proved more cohesive and entertaining than those from schools.

Between the two World Wars, the white club teams tried to form leagues similar to those in major league baseball but without success. It was only after the Second World War, when black players were finally accepted into these professional league ranks, that the leagues themselves matured. Within a few short years of this breakthrough in 1946, the sport featured, by common consensus, the very best athletes in the entire world.

The Great Club Teams

World War I forced many women to work in the northern urban factories and the very image of the American woman underwent subtle changes. Victorian attitudes toward female manners, dress, behavior, and sports changed from strict adherence to established norms to one of modified permissiveness. Females were

44

even allowed the opportunity to vote in 1920. Two black female basketball teams emerged in the first fifteen years following the war that featured two of our nation's best-ever athletes.

The first of the two teams was the Chicago Romas, organized by Edward "Sol" Butler, formerly of Dubuque College and Seminary. Their starting lineup included Isadore Channels, Corinne Robinson, Mignon Burns, Lillian Ross, Virginia Willis, and Lula Porter. Channels was the star and, in addition, was a four-time winner of the American Tennis Association (ATA) Women's Singles title. (The ATA was the black counterpart to the white United States Lawn Tennis Association.) The Romas dominated ladies' basketball in the Chicago and Midwest regions.

The second dominant team was the *Philadelphia Tribune* squad, that was sponsored by the black newspaper of the same name. Black and white papers frequently sponsored sports events and/or teams to enhance their image and increase sales. The *Tribune* must have done a bit of both because the team, which was begun in 1931, seldom lost. Coincidentally, the *Tribune's* leading player was another tennis star, Ora Washington, who won an unprecedented eight ATA Singles titles during her career. Washington, a center, also later played for the Germantown Hornets of Philadelphia.

The *Tribune* squad, as well as the YWCA and other club teams, played the typical six-players-per-team style which had separate threesomes for offense and defense at opposite ends of the court. This was done so as to minimize the "strain" on the players. It was still fervently, but er-roneously, believed that women had innately delicate natures and too much exercise would damage their equilibrium. Hence, women never played full-court basketball until well into the 1960s. Frequently though, the *Tribune* team did use men's rules and the results were usually the same. Miss Washington's teammates included Gladys Walker, Virginia Woods, Lavinia Moore, Myrtle Wilson, Rose Wilson, Marie Leach, Florence Campbell, and Sarah Latimere. They were named by most black papers as national champions during most of the 1930s.

In 1938 the Tribunes toured the South in February and March, giving clinics, offering advice and encouragement, and demonstrating for crowds the high quality basketball of which women were potentially capable. The Philadelphia Tribune was black America's first premier female sports team. When it disbanded in 1940, its fame was superseded only by the women's track team at Tuskegee, which was the AAU national champion.

The two stellar men's squads—the New York Renaissance Big Five and the Harlem Globetrotters—came from New York City and Chicago, respectively. This came as no surprise since these cities' public school, club, YMCA, church, American Legion, and college teams were nationally recognized. It so happened that the rise and subsequent demise of these squads as basketball powerhouses fell almost neatly between the two World Wars.

The New York Renaissance, better known as the Rens, began as the Spartan Braves of Brooklyn. The Spartan Braves became the Spartan Five that later still became the Rens in 1923. The Braves had joined New York City's Metropolitan Basketball Association (MBA) but the MBA in 1922 ordered the Braves to suspend Frank Forbes and Leon Monde for a violation. The Spartans refused and were fined. The following year—the same year the YMCA held its first national event—the Braves' owner, Robert J. Douglas, took Forbes and added four others to form the Rens. It was the first full-salaried, black professional basketball team.

Full credit must go to Douglas who is now referred to as the father of black basketball. His keen eye for talent and sound business acumen enabled his squad to survive until the late 1940s. He was born on the Caribbean island of St. Kitts in 1885, and had brought with him to America those traits of perserverance and hard work that so typified the black West Indian immigrants. A. S. "Doc" Young went so far as to say that "Never before, or since, in American sports history has an all-Negro team operated by Negroes earned the national acclaim that accrued to the Rens."[1]

The Rens first starting five were captain Hilton Slocum, Frank Forbes, Hy Monte, Zack Anderson, and Harold Mayers. The team got its name from Harlem's Renaissance Ballroom on 135th Street and 7th Avenue. To show they were to be taken seriously, the Rens won their debut game, 28 to 22, against the Collegiate Big Five on November 3, 1923. They finished the season with a 15–8 record.

The Rens soon had little difficulty finding opponents. Their main black rivals were the Harlem Globetrotters, the Chicago Hottentots with Joe Lillard, the Chicago Collegians, the Chicago Studebakers, and the Savoy Big Five. Other opponents included the Celtics, the Philadelphia Sphas, the Detroit Eagles, and the Akron Firestones. The most intense games were those against the Globetrotters and the Celtics. In the past such rivalries often led to violence on the court between teams. Before the rules changes of the 1930s and 1940s, play was often plodding. There was a jump ball after every basket, and everyone clogged the middle.

There was also heavy betting, poor officiating, and selfishness. Douglas saw this shortcoming early and insisted his players perform more like a team, with strict adherence to discipline and the good of the team over that of the individual. Things had gotten so out of hand earlier that the *Chicago Defender* editorialized for a change. "The first thing to be done to help make this game one of the cleanest and best played and liked of games," it said, "is to cut out some of the rough stuff....Another big fault is gallery playing and what might be termed as clique playing. Players...sent into the game have been refused the opportunity to handle the ball....The biggest and most important of all things is choice of referees."[2]

The *New York Age* was just as adamant. "...some teams began to fight among themselves. By the end of the 1921 season, basketball in this city was in an unhealthy condition, although from outward appearances, the game was never more popular, or the clubs more prosperous."[3] The Rens tried to compensate with teamwork. Noted the late Rens player Eyre "Bruiser" Saitch, "We didn't even have a coach! We didn't have positions; we played the man."[4] He further claimed that after playing together so often, it was just easier for the same five players to adjust to one another. A man's position on the team in those days mattered less than now. A center—now the tallest player on a team—was so named in the 1920s only because he was used to jump-center at the beginning of a play. After that, positions made little difference.

Saitch did, however, deplore the necessity to combine the social with the athletic. A highly skilled athlete, he wanted to see the game stand on its own but that never came to pass in the 1920s. "We had to have a dance afterwards or nobody would come to the damn thing...the Renaissance [Ballroom] was right across the street from The Red Rooster [nightclub]....If you didn't get there by seven o'clock, you didn't get in the damn door. The big game didn't start until 10 o'clock."[5] Such was the case in the socio-athletic milieu of the nation's black cultural capital during the Harlem Renaissance period of the 1920s.

How much did players make back then? Saitch mentions salaries of between $800 to $1,000 per month and noted that "a loaf of bread was only a nickel and the best apartment was $60 a month."[6] But they more than earned their pay since they were on the road 75 percent of the time. Of particular importance was their annual swing through the South in the early spring to play against some black college teams.

William "Pops" Gates recalled that "We'd tour the South and play the Negro colleges, sometimes playing three teams in the same day. In Atlanta, we'd play Morehouse, Morris Brown, and Clark twenty-minute periods each."[7] Saitch added that "We played in some areas where they didn't have backboards; just a net attached to an iron pipe."[8]

Unfortunately, this was often seen as out-of-bounds for a professional team and much worse for the colleges. Fay Young of the *Chicago Defender* was against college-versus-professional games. However, the colleges needed all the help they could get. But it was 1930 before any school had a twenty-game schedule per season, and facilities were poor. Otis Troupe, the Morgan State star, said he and his teammates "...had to go into town to practice at the New Albert Casino one or two nights a week."[9] Imagine trying to field a quality team with twice-a-week practices! The farther South a school was located, the more likely its schedule and practice time was to be interrupted by the tourist season. But these college-versus-professional games were scheduled anyway, despite conference rules against it. The demand for such matchups was high, the experience was invaluable for the collegians, and the schools needed the revenue. The professionals simply used this time to work on new plays, get into condition, and integrate new players into the lineup. Indeed, new players did come in and out of the team.

In addition to the original five, some other players of the late 1920s, the 1930s, and early 1940s included William "Wee Willie" Smith, Charles "Tarzan" Cooper, Eyre "Bruiser" Saitch, Clarence "Fats" Jenkins, George Fiall, James "Pappy" Ricks, Clix Garcia, Walter Saunders, and Bill Yancey. Later Rens included Johnny Isaacs, William "Pops" Gates, Clarence "Puggy" Bell, Zack Clayton, Johnny "Casey" Holt, Al Johnson, and for a very short time, Wilmeth Sidat-Singh. Nearly all came from New York City schools, clubs, and public parks before 1930.

Ricks had been a star for Loendi before joining the Rens in 1924, After that year, Loendi lost much of its initial strength. This was confirmed somewhat in the February 23, 1924, edition of the *Pittsburgh Courier*: "Loendi has lost more games this season than any other season...one or more players...neglect their defense entirely in efforts to score more field goals continuously."[10] In Ricks' second year, the Rens tied a heated six-game series, 3–3, against the all-white Original Celtics (then so-called because other teams also used the name "Celtics"), the acknowledged world professional champions, with its star Joe Lapchick. These games secured the reputation of the Harlem-based team and earned it a tremendous following.

In 1925, the American Basketball League (ABL) was organized without inviting any black teams to join. The Original Celtics themselves refused to join partly because ABA rules may have disallowed games against black fives. This snub of blacks came in the same year the National Football League began to ease its black players from its member teams. But, like the best white major league baseball squads, the best white professional teams actually sought out confrontations against the premier black aggregations. These interracial games virtually guaranteed a jammed box office.

In 1927, the Rens were joined by another black team, the Harlem Globetrotters, that would in time rival it in fame though not in the record books. Some players like Zachary Clayton wore the uniforms of both teams. Though the Rens now had company, the addition of the Globetrotters enhanced all of black basketball; fans took it more seriously and a sort of intra-racial rivalry began.

In the latter part of the 1920s the Rens were playing 150 games per year against club, YMCA, and college fives. They would appear for a guarantee plus expenses. Robert Douglas' Rens team was booked as much as an entire season in advance for certain games. In one of these highly publicized contests against Morgan State on March 18, 1927, the Rens won 26–22 at their home base, the Renaissance Casino. As usual, the post-game dance began right after the game in the same hall. On March 20, 1929, Morgan State finally defeated the Rens 41–40.

The Celtics rivalry, too, continued to blaze. In 1928, the Rens won even though Lapchick and Nat Holman were in uniform for the Celtics. But the following year the Celtics won 38–31, in front of 10,000 fans. Tarzan Cooper had ten points for the Rens. Lest these scores seem low by today's standards, there was a jump ball after every basket, players continued clogging the middle, and there was no rule requiring teams or players to advance the ball beyond the mid-court stripe in any length of time. A "fast break" was unheard of and was not even considered a part of the language of the sport.

Partly because of the low scores and the spectator demand for a faster pace, the rules were revolutionized during a twelve-year period beginning in 1932. The ABL had disbanded the year before and the need for adjustments was obvious and clear. The first rule to be changed struck at the very heart of the pace of play. Teams had to advance the ball past the aforementioned mid-court stripe within ten seconds toward their own end of the court. In addition, no player with the ball could stand in the foul lane more than three consecutive seconds. These changes forced teams with large leads to play more aggressively and to emphasize teamwork more than brute strength. Scores immediately increased almost 50 percent in some instances.

In 1936, the three-second rule was further amended to disallow *any* players on offense to stand in the foul lane more than three consecutive seconds. Blacks particularly liked this innovation because the fancy passing that ensued was entertaining as well as productive. Now, all ten players were constantly in motion, juggling for position and looking for fakes and picks. The fans loved it and an added premium was placed on compatibility.

A year later in 1937, the center jump after each basket was eliminated, and players on defense could no longer interfere with the ball while it was above the rim of the basket. The immediate result was the introduction of what was then termed the "race horse" maneuver, which is known today as the "fast break." Teams henceforth had to have backcourt players who were not only adept ball handlers but they had to be quick to exploit a weak defense. Black players turned out to be among the quickest ever seen. (Coincident with that year's rule change came the new National Basketball League [NBL], which also declined to invite black squads to join. Black teams like the Globetrotters and the Rens had now been snubbed twice.)

Saitch had this to say about the elimination of the center jump. "In those days...we played by halves and then changed to fifteen-minute quarters...the referees only called flagrant fouls...with no jump ball, we just outran everybody...."[11]

In 1944, "goal tending," which forbade players on defense from interfering with the ball once it was on its way in its *downward* path after a shot, was made illegal. Defenders had to then block shots in the ball's upward path only. All these changes over a dozen seasons resulted in increased demand for the sport among public schools, clubs, churches, fraternal leagues, YMCAs, YWCAs, industrial leagues, colleges, and the professionals.

Just before the first series of rules changes in 1932, the Rens won their first world professional championship from the Celtics 37–34 on March 30. On April 3 they beat them again 30–23—with a team that included Lapchick and Henry "Dutch" Dehnert. The reigning world champions then made a six-state sweep that included stops in Pennsylvania, Maryland, Washington, D.C., North Carolina, Georgia, Alabama, and Tennessee. Douglas believed such a tour could not only enhance the image of his team but help to improve the quality of the game itself among blacks. He knew about the "iron pipe" baskets and the lack of coaching, but he also thought that firsthand experience with the world champions would be a tremendous morale boost to any fledgling team. He was correct, of course.

For the record, that world championship squad incuded Saitch, Cooper, Jenkins, Slocum, Yancey, Holt, Smith, and Ricks—one of the best teams before World War II.

The following season, 1932–33, was marked by an eighty-eight game winning streak that was finally broken by, of all teams, the Celtics, on April 3, 1933. Two years after that, another memorable encounter involved a win over the New York Celtics by one point when the Rens, featuring Johnny Isaacs, controlled the ball for the last six minutes of play. Crowds in this mid-Depression era sometimes reached 15,000 a true testament to the popularity of this famous five from New York City. Douglas' team was in its prime.

But there was a price to pay for this fame that attended anyone who was black, even someone like Bill "Bojangles" Robinson, the black actor/dancer. As in the Negro leagues for baseball, Saitch said he and his teammates sometimes "...slept in jails because they wouldn't put us up in hotels...standard equipment for us was a flint gun; we'd spray all the bedbugs before we went out to play and they'd be dead when we got back....We sometimes had over a thousand damn dollars in our pockets and we couldn't get a good goddamn meal. Our per diem was $2.50 a day. 'Fats' Jenkins was so tight that he'd save the tea balls and later ask for a cup of hot water. Man, he was tight [laughter]!"[12]

Nineteen thirty-nine was the Rens' last good year. They were then coached by Eric Illidge and they won the world professional title again at Chicago Stadium. The Globetrotters went down 27–23 in the semifinals and the Oshkosh All-Stars succumbed 34–25 in the finals. Each Rens player received $1,000 for his efforts. In 1943—during the war—the Rens changed their name to the Washington Bears and won the world professional title in 1943, before 12,000 of their faithful in Chicago Stadium. Zack Clayton, a Bears player, had then played on three world championship teams; for the Rens, the Globetrotters, and the Bears.

At war's end, the Bears changed their name back again to the Rens but took the name Dayton Rens in 1948, and joined the National Basketball League as a replacement for the Detroit Vagabonds, an all-white team. Still owned by Douglas, the Dayton Rens had a 16–43 season and played their last game against the Denver Nuggets on March 21, 1949, at Rockford, Illinois. The Rens' lifetime record was an astounding 2,318 wins and 381 losses. They were the first black team to win a world professional title in any sport and led the way for the post-World War II surge of blacks who eventually dominated the sport at every level.

The Rens' alter ego, the Harlem Globetrotters, were also formed from earlier fives that needed an overhaul. The Savoy Big Five of Chicago—managed by Dick Hudson, and formerly named the Giles Post (Negro American Legion) team—featured the football star Joe Lillard. A Jewish businessman, Abe Saperstein, thought he detected more potential if the marketing of the team were improved. The Rens had provided enough evidence to convince him that in the face of continuing prejudice, another all-black team had appeal. Saperstein, only five feet three and a half inches tall, decided to assume complete control of the Savoy squad and called his new team the Harlem Globetrotters, although they were based in Chicago. Though he did not know it, he had created what eventually became the most well-known team in sports history.

A.S. "Doc" Young said, "In all the history of American sports, no team has made a greater impact on the international scene than the Harlem Globetrotters professional basketball team...who are more personally familiar to fans in the remotest crannies of the world than the New York Yankees...or the Boston Celtics."[13] This was true in 1962 when Young wrote it, and even more true today in the mid-1980s.

Saperstein's starting five were Walter "Toots" Wright, Byron "Fat" Long, Willis "Kid" Oliver, Andy Washington, and Al "Runt" Pullins. In 1929, he replaced Washington with Inman Jackson, who became the first Globetrotter clown. Jackson played for fourteen years and made people laugh. But the Globbies could be and were a serious team as well. Even the name Globetrotters was just a dream at first. "...When the Globetrotters came into being, the possibility that the team would someday justify the 'Globetrotters' part of its title seemed as remote as some far distant planet."[14]

Saperstein's choice was based on hard business practices. No black teams belonged to the ABL, and they were not about to, for that would give them access to Madison Square Garden and other sports palaces on a regular basis. Black-versus-black games had little appeal unless the squads were truly superior; so the Globetrotters became a well-paid troupe of players who put on a good show and played well. They are also the oldest cur-rent black professional team in existence and still going strong. In the beginning, though, they were compared with the Rens and in fact its rivalry began in the early 1930s. By the late 1930s the Globbies were in the Chicago Herald American's world professional tournament, finishing third in 1939.

By 1940, the Globetrotters were better than the Rens; they won the professional title over their black rivals 37–36 in the semi-finals and over the Chicago Bruins in the final game. Not taking their success for granted, the Globbies organized their first fall training camp in 1940. The sport was by then more intense, more competitive, and required better conditioning and coordinated teamwork. This meticulous preparation paid off as they won the International Cup Tournament in Mexico City, in 1943, over stiffening competition.

Both the Globetrotters and the Rens suffered from the lack of a black league. Seating facilities remained small well into the war years, though by 1942 some black college fives had national followings. Distances between the quality teams remained vast and there were no super highways for cars. The turnpikes were not yet built, let alone the modern interstates. A trip that averaged forty miles per hour in a car was considered swift.

As the Globetrotters came into their own relatively late and during the war, they played many colleges as morale boosting experiences with diminished resistance from the press, but with problems from the college conferences. (Virginia Union University had their CIAA title taken away in the

1940–41 season because they played the Globetrotters.) A game against the University of Washington in 1943 for the Servicemen's Fund drew over 10,000 fans, though the author wonders how much of that went to black servicemen. These displays of patriotism were not enough to elicit an invitation to join the Basketball Association of America (BAA) that was formed in 1946.

Another theory much believed by the black press was that, being white, Saperstein made an arrangement with the owners of the white teams to keep blacks out so that his Globetrotters could always have the pick of the best blacks. This would accomplish two ends: ensure that the Globetrotters always had quality black players; and, with no black players in the white leagues, the white players would never complain. This was never proven one way or the other. Nevertheless it was believed by many black players and fans.

With the integration of the professional leagues, the Globetrotters in 1949 switched entirely to entertaining rather than trying to find a place as a serious team. This again was a sound business decision if albeit, a sad athletic one. Major league baseball did not allow any Negro league teams to enter their domain and the basketball leagues thought along the same lines. Black players? yes; black teams? no. Black America had to look toward its college squads to find all-black teams to follow. But they, too, had a rocky transition after the First World War.

Black College Basketball

Basketball at black colleges after World War I was little more than a diversion at best and, in most places, an afterthought. Howard University stopped the sport for a while in 1919. Except for the CIAA, other conferences either did not exist or did not play for a title. The facilities were just not there at the majority of schools and spectator seating was usually standing-room-only. Coaches were more attuned to football and baseball and they were not hired full-time; they had to teach academic subjects as well. The segregated and poorly outfitted black public schools in the South—where all but a handful of the colleges were located—had either no facilities or makeshift dirt courts.

Competition was usually of the intramural variety or against other colleges or YMCAs. Even less attention was paid to competition for women; if at all. Then there was the need of players to leave college to work during planting and harvesting seasons and to fill the choice jobs (for blacks) in the resort hotels in the winter. Most schools just closed during these times. It was no surprise then that the decade of the 1920s was spent building both interest and courts.

Hampton probably had the best team around in 1920 since it had an indoor gymnasium. It could draw upon local Virginia high school players that were reasonably competent in athletic ability. The state also had St. Paul's, Virginia Normal and Industrial, Virginia Union, and Howard University located virtually within a three-hour train ride. In the West, the SWAC conference had formed in 1920, but did not host a title competition until 1928. The sport could only improve in importance.

In 1925, Morehouse won the first tournament played (outdoors) among black colleges in the South. They defeated Atlanta

University 37–13 and followed this victory with a 9–0 undefeated season in 1926. But nine games were hardly enough to build a quality team and test its compatibility, and frankly, nothing of grand importance except pride was hanging in the balance. There were no athletic scholarships, no professional leagues save local groups up North, and no high expectations. The primary benefit was merely the chance to garner some favorable publicity for the college.

Some thought the schools took this approach too far when games were scheduled against professional teams. There were definite conference rules forbidding these contests, but administrators just winked and proceeded as if they had not noticed. Conference cohesion was sorely tested in the mid-1920s as a result, when schools such as Howard railed against losing their perceived independence. After all, Howard was black America's most famous college.

In any event, some standards were set. Horace "Itty" Dalton, of Clark College, scored 336 points in 1927; quite a feat, but it included games against all opponents—collegiate and otherwise. In 1928, the Southern Intercollegiate Athletic Conference (SIAC) was formed and immediately embraced basketball. Schoolboy teams looked up to these squads. There was even an attempt to establish a high school league in Virginia in 1928. The Deep South was catching up.

The westernmost colleges joined the ranks of basketball fives in 1928, when Sam Houston in Texas won the first Southwest Athletic Conference (SWAC) title. Two years later, every section of the country that had black colleges had at least two or three schools that played varsity basketball. But they all took a back seat to the teams from Morgan State College in Baltimore. Morgan State teams in the late 1920s and early 1930s could, on any given day, defeat any squad, amateur or professional.

From 1927 until 1934, Morgan never lost a home-court game until Howard stopped the streak. Its 41-40 victory over the professional Rens squad in 1929 was the greatest college victory of the decade. For a time, only Virginia Seminary could give coach Eddie Hurt's team any competition. With Morgan State in the CIAA, it assured a conference of premier standing among the others. Morgan State's conference mate, Howard University, played and won a game, 32–26, against Lincoln University (Penn.) in New York City, in 1930. Both teams had tremendous followings at the game due to their football rivalry.

As the decade of the 1930s began, facilities remained a problem. Few schools could justify the expense of building special gymnasiums just for basketball. Scores were low because of rules that did not penalize stalling; conferences were imbalanced; and the sport lacked a tradition akin to that for baseball or football. Baseball had a traditional Easter Monday game; football a Thanksgiving Day game; but basketball was bereft of national social importance. Where would a school's alumni sit even if they came to see a big game?

General purpose gymnasiums could be found at Talladega, Tennessee A&I, Morehouse, Hampton, and Howard; exceptions all. Even mighty Morgan State lacked its own on-campus site. The farther south a school's location, the more likely that school played its games outdoors. Black high schools in the South had no gymnasiums at all; sports facilities were outdoors. The best of these secondary school teams were found in the Midwest and on the East Coast; in Indiana, Kentucky, and the Carolinas; in Chicago, Philadelphia, New York City, Wilmington (Delaware), Baltimore, and Washington, D.C. School teams with regional reputations were DeWitt Clinton in New York; Dunbar and Armstrong in Washington, D.C.; Wendell Phillips in Chicago; and Roosevelt in Gary, Indiana. There were attempts to organize national tournaments for high school teams but the cost was prohibitive and a venue could never be agreed upon. No thought whatever was given to such competition for girls.

Into these circumstances appeared a few college teams that competed for column space in the black press. (There were no radio or television broadcasts.) Morgan State fielded outstanding teams until the mid-1930s. They were CIAA champions from 1931 to 1934 then tied for the title with Virginia State in 1937–38. Morgan's lineup included big names from the gridiron, plus others: Edward "Lanky" Jones, Pinky Clark, Cutie Brown, Babe Jones, Skippy Gibson, Otis Troupe, Tom "Big Tank" Conrad, and Howard "Brutus" Wilson. Troupe, Conrad, and Wilson also played football. Jones was later instrumental in assisting former Lincoln University (Pa.) football star, Dr. Robert W. Johnson, with his junior tennis program that produced Arthur Ashe.

Wiley College enjoyed the first serious winning streak in the SIAC, a thirty-three-game record that ended in 1936. Under coach F.T. Long, it featured such players as Stretch Byrd, Crab Neely, John Aikens, Bill Spiller, Chuck Johnson, and Fess Widemon. The SIAC and the South Central Athletic

Conference (SCAC) began title awards in 1934.

Xavier University in New Orleans had some of the best teams before the Second World War during the 1935-38 period. Their stars were Cleveland Bray, Leroy Rhodes, Tilford Cole, Charlie Gant, and William McQuitter. At one time this fivesome had a record of sixty-seven wins and two losses. One loss was to LeMoyne, 33–32, in 1935, and the other to Clark, 27–26, in 1937. The unique feature of this team was that the five stars all came from Chicago's Wendell Phillips High School. On two occasions it played the Rens, losing 38–37 and 24–20, before the largest crowd to see black college basketball in the South. Though not a part of this illustrious team, Frank "Blotto" Crozier, in 1939, set a new single–season scoring record of 343 points.

Virginia Union fielded its famous "dream team" in the 1939–40 season. It had won the CIAA title in 1939, and the press believed the squad of Mel Glover, Gerald "Pickles" Frazier, Obie Knight, Kavanzo Hyde, and Wylie "Soupy" Campbell were the pick of the year. Other members were Howard Jones, Wendell Williams, Alvin Storres, Floyd Atkins, Lewis White, Vincent Tinsley, and Norman Hines. Mel Glover claims that Virginia Union actually won the CIAA title in both the 1940 and 1941 seasons, but the conference officials would not acknowledge it because the school played against the Globetrotters. "We are still mad about that," noted Glover, "because other schools did it too but we were pretty good and they wanted to make an example out of us."[15] It seemed as if the college game had sprouted new talent all at once but, in reality, it was only maturing. On the cusp of its growth during the Depression, basketball had a deepening constituency.

Part of this effort resulted in the first games against white schools. Under the direction of its athletic director, Charles H. Williams of Hampton, that school played Brooklyn College in 1938, losing 46–31, at Brooklyn. Virginia Union and Kentucky State followed in 1939 with games against Long Island University. (Back in 1934, Ned Irish had begun his soon-to-be-famous college doubleheaders at Madison Square Garden but black teams were never invited.) In 1940, Glover and Campbell starred for Virginia Union, as it defeated Brooklyn College 54–38 before 3,500 fans. The black press campaigned for this game to be played in Madison Square Garden, but it did not materialize.

Clark College also had a notable team in 1939. A decade earlier it had been behind its other Atlanta University sister schools, Morris Brown and Morehouse, but with the stellar play of Abbey Henderson, Sonny Younger, Hank DeZowie, Joe Johnson, Dale Pemberton, and the incomparable William "Pops" Gates, Clark was the best in the Southeast.

North Carolina College (now North Carolina Central) won the CIAA title in 1940–1941 and was 14–0. It also played Brooklyn College that same year, winning 37–34. Langston University in Oklahoma had a fifty-game winning streak that began in 1942. South Carolina State had Henry "Mice" Holden who scored fifty points against Delaware State and 458 points for the season in 1942. Under coach Ollie

Dawson, Holden's teammates included Ezra Moore, Charles Penn, William "Ducky" Copeland, Luther "Pepsi-Cola" Bligen, Curtis Torrey, Walter "Dynamite" Palmer, Curtis Moreland, and Morris Esmond.

With all this talent, a national tournament was suggested and planned to be held in Cincinnati, but it was a financial disaster. At least it was tried. By the end of World War II, the college game in the South was much less susceptible to the resort season and plantings and harvestings. Farm machinery had improved the productivity of the average farmer and he was less dependent on black labor to work the fields and pick the crops. Thus, basketball benefitted black colleges and high schools.

The most compelling and positive force for change, though, was the imminent integration of the professional leagues. Along with baseball and football, basketball—by 1950—brought three blacks into its professional ranks and two of them were products of black colleges. This was proof enough that these institutions had arrived as sports powers.

Blacks at White Colleges

The basketball policy of the various white athletic conferences was mixed toward blacks between the two World Wars. The Ivy League and other schools that competed in the Intercollegiate Amateur Athletic Association of America (ICAAAA) competitions were generally receptive. There was a history of black participation dating back to William T.S. Jackson and John B. Taylor in track; and baseball and football had already bestowed national honors on their token darker brethren. Jim Crow laws and white racist customs in the South, however, kept all blacks out of white colleges there. Princeton University, in New Jersey, had a "whites only" policy until 1944. Black cagers simply had to weave their way through a maze of obstacles if they wanted to play.

John Howard Johnson was Columbia University's first black player and as the following report shows, he was not afraid to defend himself. "Johnson, Columbia's Negro center, and Peck, a Quaker [University of Pennsylvania] guard, lost their heads and exchanged blows under the Columbia basket."[16] Peck seemed to have taken on more than he could handle since Johnson was a much larger center. Johnson graduated in 1921.

Ralph Bunche, the future Nobel Peace Prize recipient, was a standout at UCLA in the mid–1920s, though he stood only five feet ten inches. The tallest players in this era were around six feet five inches as in the case of famed Celtic star, Joe Lapchick. Charles Drew, who later received acclaim for his work on blood plasma, played at Amherst in 1923. He won his school's Ashley Trophy as the best all-around athlete.

George Gregory, a graduate of New York City's DeWitt Clinton High School, was elected Columbia's captain in 1930. He was also named to the Helms Foundation All-America team in 1931, alongside the soon-to-be legendary UCLA coach, John Wooden. In his three-year career, Gregory scored 509 points in sixty-two games. James D. and Samuel E. Barnes were the first black siblings to play at Oberlin in Ohio, where there was a long tradition of

black participation. As at black colleges, competition for women was strictly intramural and informal almost everywhere.

Most black sports enthusiasts had hoped the records of George Gregory and others would help counter the wave of re-segregation taking place in American athletics in the latter half of the 1920s. However, the controversial legacy of the black former heavyweight champion Jack Johnson had caused Harry Wills, another black heavyweight, to be denied his rightful title opportunity. The National Football League had begun to freeze out its black players; in 1933 they banned all of them for thirteen years. Major league baseball gave no hint of integrating, and black jockeys had been systematically driven off the tracks by the eve of World War I. Northern white college basketball's odd-league-out was the Big Ten. While it showcased black football talent, it refused to allow black basketball players until after World War II.

In January 1934, the University of Michigan—a Big Ten school—caused an uproar when it dismissed Franklin Lett from its freshman squad. Lett had been informed by coach F.C. Cappon that "There has never been a colored boy to play basketball in the Big Ten. It has been a mutual agreement between the coaches not to use a colored boy in basketball."[17] In a letter to Cappon, Roy Wilkins, the young assistant secretary of the National Association for the Advancement of Colored People, angrily replied that Cappon's remarks were an insult to young Lett personally and to blacks in general.

Two weeks later, the January 27 *Afro-American* newspaper reported that "…an alleged agreement between the Big Ten coaches to keep colored players off basketball teams...was broken this week when...Michigan was forced to place Franklin Lett, star athlete, back on the freshman squad."[18] Lett, however, never played varsity basketball for Michigan. Two years before, Michigan track star Eddie Tolan won two gold medals at the Los Angeles Olympic Games. Michigan's and the Big Ten's treatment of black basketball players was patently unfair and discriminatory. As if to verify the University of Michigan's racist policies, all-white college basketball doubleheaders at New York City's Madison Square Garden were begun the same year.

Some white schools *did* continue to use black players and a partial listing includes Horace Johnson at Dakota College from 1936 to 1938; Bobby Yancey and Ben Franklin at Boston University in 1937; and Lawrence Bleach at Detroit University in 1937. Of particular interest was William "Dolly" King at Long Island University. King was a graduate of Brooklyn's Alexander Hamilton High, where he lettered in three sports (basketball, baseball, and football), for three years. King was the first black player in the National AAU tournament, in 1937. On November 29, 1939, he performed a unique double by playing in a football and a basketball game on the same day. After his college years, King played professionally for the Scranton Miners, the Rens, the Washington Bears, and in 1946 for the Rochester Royals, a National Basketball League squad.

Frank "Doc" Kelker played at Western Reserve from 1936 to 1938. Kelker gradu-ated Phi Beta Kappa after three varsity seasons. Wilmeth Sidat-Singh, the adopted son of Dr. Samuel Sidat-Singh, starred at Syracuse University after attending DeWitt Clinton High in New York City. As had happened on his school's football team, Sidat-Singh was left off the team in a game against Navy. His 1939 squad was 14–0. He joined the Syracuse Reds after graduation and played for the Rochester Seagrams in 1940, in the World Professional Tournament. After attending Tuskegee's (Alabama) Army Air Corps Flying School, he became a member of the all-black 332nd Fighter Group stationed at Selfridge Field, Michigan. He was unfortunately killed on June 9, 1943, when his military plane caught fire and crashed in Lake Huron.

Another in the news was Jackie Robinson at UCLA in 1939–40. He won the Pacific Coast Conference-Southern Division scoring title in his first year with 148 points in twelve games. The following season he won the title again with 133 points in twelve games. Back East, Jim Coward was at Brooklyn College; Ed Younger at Long Island University; Tom Wood and Norman Skinner at Columbia; Jay Swift at Yale; Sonny Jameson at City College of New York; Dick Culberson at Iowa; Dick Wilkins scored 345 points in 1944 at the University of Oregon; and Art White became Princeton's first black player in 1944.

These players seldom had the impact of their black football brothers. No basketball player garnered the publicity accorded Cornell's All-America football star Jerome Holland, for example. Seldom did a white school play more than one black player at the same time, and there were few black substitutes. All of them were tokens since there were always more blacks qualified to play than were allowed on varsity fives.

The racial logjam was finally broken during the five years from 1946 to 1950. Joe Louis, Jackie Robinson, Althea Gibson, and Jesse Owens left such positive impressions upon their respective sports that the entire American sports establishment felt freer to experiment. Old groundless fears were proven to be just that—groundless. But most important, the world found out just how good black athletes were and how eager they were to compete. As for basketball, the best was yet to come.

Notes

1. A.S. "Doc" Young, *Negro Firsts in Sports* (Chicago: Johnson Publications, 1963), p. 81.
2. *Chicago Defender*, 18 January 1921.
3. *New York Age*, 8 April 1922.
4. Eyre Saitch interview with author, 7 April 1984, New York City.
5. Ibid.
6. Ibid.
7. William "Pops" Gates telephone interview with author, 24 April 1985.
8. Eyre Saitch interview with author, 7 May 1984, New York City.
9. Ocania Chalk, *Black College Sports* (New York: Dodd, Mead & Co., 1976), p. 28.
10. *Pittsburgh Courier*, 23 February 1924.
11. Eyre Saitch interview with author, 7 May 1984, New York City.
12. Ibid.
13. Young, *Negro Firsts in Sports*, p. 230.
14. Ibid., p. 78.
15. Mel Glover interview with author, 17 March 1987, New York City.
16. *New York Times*, 26 January 1919.
17. *Pittsburgh Courier*, 13 January 1934.
18. *Baltimore Afro-American*, 27 January 1934.

Tennis

The Sport of Kings

Before horse racing assumed the title of "the sport of kings" in the mid-1700s, tennis lay claim to that category. The French called it *tenez* and played their version indoors. The English followed in turn and, depending on which sets of rules were followed, it was referred to more properly as *real tennis* or *court tennis*. In 1415, Charles, Duke of Orleans, played tennis while imprisoned by the English after the Battle of Agincourt. King Henry VIII was an avid player.

The English brought it outdoors, changed the court dimensions, and eventually Mary Outerbridge brought the sport to America in 1874. The first national tournament was held in 1881 at Newport, Rhode Island, and the entries were predominantly the members of elite private clubs of the Northeast. No blacks or socially outcast players were permitted but, by 1890, several professional black families had built courts on their properties.

There were no public courts in the 1890s and it had little appeal to working class folk. Players traditionally dressed in all-white with the men in flannel pants, long-sleeved shirts, and ties. The women wore long ankle-length full skirts and blouses up to the neck. Their shoes were leather-soled and high-topped. Most courts were of closely cut grass that required steady maintenance. Tennis, along with crew and golf, was identified with the upper classes and strictly for amateurs. The United States National Lawn Tennis Association (USNLTA), its governing body, meant to keep it just the way it began.

Tennis among blacks took root at the Ivy League colleges where the well-to-do sent their children—if they could get in. Eventually the campuses of Howard University, Lincoln University, Tuskegee Institute (now Tuskegee University), and others had courts for their faculty. Records at Tuskegee show tournaments were held there as early as 1895. The organizers were E.T. Atwell, Emmett J. Scott, Warren Logan, and S.E. Courtney.

Not to be outdone, enterprising blacks in Philadelphia held a tournament in 1898 which was won by Thomas Jefferson of Lincoln University. The Philadelphia contingent, headed by Reverend W.W. Walker, had also invited fellow blacks from Washington, D.C., to compete in team play in 1898 and 1899. The Washington, D.C., group, led by Dr. Henry Freeman, went down to defeat. One of Freeman's members was Charles C. Cook, Howard University's first football coach who had attended Cornell University.

By the first decade of this century, professional blacks along the East Coast had formed clubs and were playing regular intercity matches. Socially prominent blacks found tennis an ideal sport and encouraged their children to learn. Teachers, preachers, professors, doctors, lawyers, dentists, and merchants sought refuge in fraternal and sororal associations at their local courts. Out in Chicago, Mrs. C.O. "Mother" Seames, a legendary figure in tennis circles there, began teaching on a single court at the turn of the century.

The equipment then was quite crude and expensive by today's standards. The rackets were wooden and unwieldy with large bare handles (no leather grips), the strings were thicker and they loosened considerably as time passed. The balls were slightly smaller and lost their fuzzy nap much sooner, even though most courts were grass. Courts used by blacks, however, were nearly always made of clay. On a typical tennis outing, players had to even bring a net to the site as few were permanently provided.

By 1910, the black press reported on the doings of the Monumental Club of Washington, D.C.; the Chautauqua Tennis Club in Philadelphia; the Flushing Tennis Club of New York City; and others in Wilmington, Delaware; New Rochelle, New York; New Haven, Connecticut; Annapolis, Maryland; Atlanta; Durham, North Carolina; Charleston, South Carolina; and New Orleans. That same year, the members of the Washington, D.C., YMCA team conducted a traveling tour of several cities to show the rudiments of the game to interested groups. Play in the Far West and Midwest seemed limited as Edwin B. Henderson noted that there was "...only one court available to colored citizens..."[1] in St. Louis, Missouri.

Among the Washington, D.C., troupe was John F.N. Wilkinson, who was the best player between 1910 and World War I. Other names that appear as having exceptional records were Rev. Walker, Edgar Brown, Henry Freeman, E.J. Ridgely, Ralph Cook (Charles' brother), H. Stanton McCard, Gerald F. Norman, Daisy Reed, Dora Cole Norman, and Lucy Diggs Slowe. Dora Cole Norman was also the best basketball player in her day and Miss Slowe eventually became dean of women at Howard University.

On the eve of World War I, Edwin B. Henderson and Roscoe C. Bruce, the new assistant superintendent of Colored Schools of Washington, D.C., had introduced the sport to some public school youngsters and black colleges were playing informal matches. Virginia Union, Hampton Institute (now Hampton University), Howard, and Atlanta University had the best teams. Enough sustained interest seemed present to form a national body to cultivate even more interest in the black community. The result was the formation of the American Tennis Association (ATA). It became the oldest, continuously operated black sports group in the country, outside of collegiate circles.

The American Tennis Association

In 1916, the Association Tennis Club of Washington, D.C., invited local players and those from Baltimore to form a national body. The initial attendees at the ATA's formation were Henry Freeman, John F.N. Wilkinson, and Talley Holmes from Washington, D.C., and H. Stanton McCard, William H. Wright, B.M. Rhetta, and Ralph Cook from Baltimore. McCard was elected president and Gerald Norman of the Ideal Tennis Club in New York was executive secretary.

The ATA had four goals: to develop tennis among black people in the United States; to encourage the formation of clubs and the building of courts; to encourage the formation of local associations; and to encourage and develop junior players. To that end and to inaugurate its efforts, the first ATA Nationals were held at Baltimore's Druid Hill Park courts, in August 1917. Twenty-three clubs sent players and from the thirty-nine entries, Talley Holmes emerged the winner of the Men's Singles. The first Women's winner was Lucy Diggs Slowe. Miss Diggs thus became the first black female national champion in any sport. Junior Singles and Women's Doubles did not begin until 1924.

In spite of the success of the ATA, tennis remained confined to the black professional classes and collegians. A survey was made in 1926 which showed little or no interest from fifty-six of seventy colleges queried, only thirty-six schools with courts, and only four of them with coaches. Dr. Elwood Downing of Roanoke, Virginia; Charles Williams of Hampton's faculty; and Cleveland Abbott at Tuskegee helped remedy this shortcoming.

The best opportunities came at white colleges with their superior facilities, tough competition, and quality coaching. Four blacks played on these varsity squads before the Depression: Richard Hudlin at the University of Chicago; Douglas Turner at the University of Illinois; Henry Graham at Michigan; and Reginald Weir at the City College of New York (CCNY). Hudlin was captain of his team in 1927, Turner was runner-up in the Big Ten Championships in 1929; and Weir was captain three years running at CCNY.

In 1929, the ATA and the USNLTA had its first confrontation over the entries of Weir and Gerald Norman, Jr. in the USNLTA's Junior Indoor event at New York City's seventh Regiment Armory. Relations between the two groups had been cordial until then. In 1921, Dwight F. Davis, the donor of the Davis Cup and the secretary of war, had umpired a semi-final match at the ATA Nationals. But the USNLTA had an unwritten rule barring blacks from participation. Now, however, some blacks were good enough to compete with the best around.

Weir and Norman had paid their one dollar entry fee and showed up to play. When informed that his son could not participate, Norman's father, Gerald Sr., complained to the National Association for the Advancement of Colored People (NAACP). The NAACP assistant secretary, Robert Bagnoll, complained but received the following reply: "...the policy of the USLTA [they had deleted the word "National" from their title] has been to decline the entry of colored players in our championships....In pursuing this policy we make no reflection upon the colored race but we believe that as a practical matter, the present method of separate associations...should be continued."[2] Neither Weir nor Norman played.

It is interesting that the NAACP was brought into the predicament when very little input from them was forthcoming in other sports like baseball. But tennis was a middle class sport and the NAACP—at the time—had a middle-class following, with virtually all of its officers drawn from the black professional class. The NAACP did not, for instance, try to intercede on behalf of the boxer Harry Wills, who was summarily cut out of his rightful heavyweight title opportunity by Tex Rickard and other boxing authorities.

The denials of Weir and Norman did not disguise the talent in ATA events. Eyre Saitch was one of the best and most athletic of ATA Nationals winners. He was more famous as a member of the famed New York Renaissance basketball team. Among the women, Isadore Channels and Ora Washington were clearly the best yet. Channels won four ATA Nationals crowns between 1922 and 1926. Washington won a record eight crowns between 1929 and 1937. Both Channels and Washington were, like Saitch, star performers on the basketball courts as well.

Washington was so good that Chicago's black paper, the *Chicago Defender*, noted on March 14, 1931, that "Ora Washington, now of Chicago, again holds her position as national champion, having gone through the season without a defeat. We don't even recall her losing a set....Her superiority is so evident that her competitors are frequently beaten before the first ball crosses the net."[3] So complete was the dominance of a few women players that

in the first twenty years of the ATA's history, there were only five different winners.

Washington was also quite unorthodox in her approach. She held the racket half way up the handle and seldom took a full swing. But no woman had her foot speed, which she honed while playing basketball for the *Philadelphia Tribune* team. She was clearly the first black female to dominate a sport. Lulu Ballard finally stopped her winning streak in 1936. Completing the list of outstanding female players were Flora Lomax of Detroit and the Peters sisters, Roumania and Margaret. The latter twosome won the ATA Women's Doubles crown a whopping fourteen times, unmatched by any doubles team—male or female.

Ora Washington's reign came during the Depression years of the 1930s, which turned out to be a blessing and a curse for black tennis. The blessing came in the form of more facilities built during President Franklin D. Roosevelt's Works Progress Administration programs. Hundreds of public courts were erected in parks where blacks played. The curse, of course, was that few people had enough resources to do much of anything, let alone play games.

The Depression Years and World War II

With more balanced interest and facilities in more places, the ATA moved its Nationals event to different venues during the 1930s. But soon the courts at Wilberforce College in Ohio became the most centrally located because of the increased entries from Texas, Arkansas, and even California. The Nationals remained east of the Mississippi River, however, until 1975, when they were played in San Diego.

College play greatly enhanced the appeal of ATA events, which fitted in neatly with the group's middle-class orientation. Interest had expanded since the end of World War I, and the Colored (Now Central) Intercollegiate Athletic Association (CIAA) was by far the strongest conference. Smith, Morgan State, Howard, and St. Augustine all won titles during the 1930s and 1940s. The Midwestern Athletic Association (MWAA), the Southwest Athletic Conference (SWAC), the South Central Athletic Conference (SCAC), and the Eastern Intercollegiate Athletic Conference (EIAC) fielded mediocre teams at best. The talent in the clubs and in the collegiate ranks remained in the Northeast though Tuskegee was an exception.

Tuskegee compiled the best record of any black school in any sport on the tennis courts but, in truth, their competition was woefully inadequate. They had a club team beginning in 1909 and their coach, Cleveland Abbott, became an ATA president. They also had two courts built exclusively for women staff and students. When the ATA Nationals were held there in 1931, fourteen courts were in place with a covered grandstand for 1,000 people. Quite an achievement in the Depression. The other solid southern team was at Xavier University in New Orleans, thereby taking advantage of that city's long history of blacks in sports. The SWAC did not even have a conference championship until 1942.

To capitalize on the growing interest, the ATA, at its 1937 annual meeting, arranged an exhibition tour for some of its best players at schools and colleges. Starting on February 4, 1938, Lulu Ballard, Ernest McCampbell and others visited twenty-one colleges and eight high schools in a journey that must rank as a noble effort to upgrade black tennis across the eastern half of the country. That there were possible rewards in the offing (for those who heeded their advice) came in the form of a continuing black presence on some white college varsities. Dan Kean had played at Michigan in 1933 and Maceo Hill was at Ohio State that same year.

The styles of play of players like Kean and Hill had changed considerably since the era of Rev. Walker and Henry Freeman. Early participants used lots of chops and spins and the next wave of players made better use of the power derived from better equipment. By 1930, the best black players were copying the best white players in strokes and swings. Although white players could not be seen at events held at private clubs, they could be viewed at places like the seventh Regiment Armory in New York City.

The Jackson brothers, Nathaniel and Franklin, were baseline experts like the legendary Don Budge, the white champion, and well-coached by Cleveland Abbott. They dominated the ATA Doubles events in the 1930s. Jimmy McDaniel was the first good player from California. Beginning in 1939 he won four ATA crowns. His style, as opposed to that of Kean, Hill, and the Jackson brothers, was the serve-and-volley variety developed on the fast cement courts in Los Angeles. California had few if any slow clay courts, so their players played very aggressive tennis. McDaniel was so impressive that he was involved in an historic interracial exhibition in July 1940 with Budge, winner of the four major world titles in 1938.

This exhibition took place at the Cosmopolitan Tennis Club on Convent Avenue in Harlem, New York. Budge won 6–1, 6–2 on the club's best clay court in front of the largest crowd ever to watch a match there. Sandwiched as it was among tall apartment buildings, the club could not hold all who wanted to witness this historic happening, but it was the best that Harlem had to offer at the time. After the singles, Budge and Reginald Weir played a doubles match against McDaniel and Richard Cohen, the reigning ATA champions.

While Budge's appearance was certainly inspirational and appreciated, blacks were still *persona non grata* at the USLTA Nationals at the West Side Tennis Club at Forest Hills, New York. Of the ATA Nationals winners, only Lloyd Scott and the 1950 champion, Oscar Johnson of Los Angeles, had practiced regularly against whites. Said Johnson of that period: "At the time, blacks were literally not allowed to play in tourna-ments against whites. Players before me could not enter...Jimmy McDaniel was very good in his day. The only encounter...he had playing against a white was in a tournament in New York, an all-black tournament."[4] However, McDaniel and Johnson were not the only eminently qualified players to face discrimination.

Pressures were mounting nonetheless for the USLTA to admit blacks to its sanctioned events. After World War II, the most important breakthrough came from an unlikely source—a street-smart, lower-middle-class female named Althea Gibson. She and Johnson would force the USLTA to amend its tournament entry policies and lead a new wave of black players who went to the very top of the rankings.

Notes

1. Henderson, *The Negro in Sports*, p. 312.
2. *Montgomery Advertiser*, 28 December 1929.
3. *Chicago Defender*, 14 March 1931.
4. *Tennis West Magazine*, March 1984, p. 140.

Chapter
5

Golf

The sport of golf developed along paths similar to that of tennis. It originated in the Scottish Highlands and by the 1700s, the Scottish Parliament was issuing decrees to regulate it. It quickly spread to the rest of the British Isles and Holland as well. When the country club movement began in the 1800s here in America, golf was its centerpiece. Since these clubs had very selective memberships and the number of public courses was small, golf acquired an initial aura of exclusivity. Black participation, therefore, remained relatively minor compared to that for other, more accessible sports.

The rugged, athletic President, Theodore Roosevelt, even tried to hide his fondness for the game. Fearing the average American thought golf too unmanly, he expressed his reservations in a letter to William Howard Taft. In part, he wrote: "It would seem incredible that anyone would care one way or the other about your playing golf, but I have literally received hundreds of letters from the West protesting it. I myself play tennis, but that game is a little more familiar; besides you never saw a photograph of me playing tennis, I am careful about that; photographs on horseback, yes; tennis, no. And golf is fatal."[1]

Golf was certainly not fatal to Dr. George F. Grant, a black Harvard University graduate and prominent dentist. To him goes the distinction of patenting the first golf tee, in 1899. Tees are small, cone-shaped, solid pieces of wood with slightly concave tops on which the ball rests for the first shot on a hole. Before Dr. Grant's invention in Boston, players had to construct small mounds of dirt on which to place their balls. His patented tee, United States patent number 638,920, changed all that.

Dr. Grant's tees did not make him rich. Though born before the Emancipation Proclamation, he made no attempt to capitalize on his invention's popularity. Noted his daughter, Frances Grant, "My father had burlap bags of golf tees, but he gave them away instead of selling them. He was an avid golf fan."[2] The tees in wide use today were adapted from Dr. Grant's and are properly known as Reddy tees.

John and Cyrus Shippen

Inventions aside, the first notable black players are the subject of continuing controversy and dispute. John Shippen was, it is believed, part Indian and part

65

black and played in the 1913 United States Open—he finished fourth. He, along with his brother Cyrus, was a teaching professional at such clubs as Merion in Philadelphia, and in East Hampton, Long Island. If in fact he thought of himself as black, he managed to keep it hidden long enough to play in places where blacks would definitely have been excluded as members.

Then again, professional play before World War I was so reprehensible to country club members that there were few protests when Shippen played in tournaments. The author could find no authoritative sources to verify Shippen's race, though numerous articles and books, including Edwin B. Henderson's *The Negro in Sports*, claim him as such. What *is* known is that Dewey Brown was the first black member of the Professional Golfers Association (PGA) in the 1920s. The early playing professionals, according to one golf historian, "...never seemed to consider golf as a field of social differences."[3]

The PGA itself was organized in 1916, when the scion of a wealthy Philadelphia family, Rodman Wanamaker, put up $2,500 to sponsor a professional event. The PGA had no formal restrictions on membership then, and Brown though too old to play competitively in PGA tournaments, was a teacher in clubs in southern New Jersey. His most well-known position was at the Buckwood Inn at Shawnee-on-Delaware.

The United Golfers Association

Though the majority of black golfers after World War I were educated, professional people, they did not have as much success as their tennis counterparts. The resources needed to build and maintain courses were simply beyond their means. The overwhelming majority of blacks played on public courses and they were usually—though not always—restricted to certain days or hours or both. Yet there were enough players from different places by the mid-1920s to form a national body. Thus the United Golfers Association (UGA) was born.

The UGA was organized, in 1926 at Stowe, Massachusetts, by a group of golf-playing doctors from Washington, D.C. George Adams and Albert Harris had tired of the Jim Crow rules in their home city which forced them to travel to New England each summer to play. The courses in the nation's capital would not allow blacks to play every day and conditions were similar elsewhere. Robert Hawkins of the Mapledale Club in Boston was the group's first president.

The winners of their inaugural event were Harry Jackson of Washington, D.C., and Marie Thompson of Chicago. Though Thompson was just a club player, Jackson earned his living partly from playing and teaching the game. It immediately became clear to the early UGA officials that their member clubs had to upgrade the quality of play if they hoped to be taken seriously. The Shady Rest Country Club became a good example.

Shady Rest was founded in 1921 in Westfield, New Jersey, and numbered among its members some of the most prominent blacks in the New York City–New Jersey area. Shady Rest had about two hundred members who paid approximately twenty dollars per year in dues but "...if they [prospective members] couldn't make the grade socially all the money in the world wouldn't get them in...."[4] To the extent that UGA club tournaments pretended to represent the best black players, it fell short due to some exclusionary membership rules. Still, interest remained strong and an all-women's club, Wake Robin Golf Club, was formed in Washington D.C., in 1927.

The best players were not difficult to identify. By far the most outstanding early performers were Robert "Pat" Ball and Walter Speedy of Chicago among the men. Laura Osgood of Chicago, Lucy Williams of Indianapolis, Marie Thompson, Ella Able, Melanie Moye, and Cleo Ball (Robert's wife) were prominent women players. Robert Ball won the professional UGA title in 1927, 1929, 1934, and 1941.

Following Ball in prominence was Howard Wheeler of Atlanta, a five-time UGA winner between 1933 and 1958. Wheeler was famous for his cross-handed grip. Though right-handed, he unconventionally held his clubs with his right hand on top of his left, near the butt of the handle. But it worked. Wheeler's frequent playing partner was John Dendy of Asheville, North Carolina, and A.D.V. Crosby, who played varsity golf at the University of Michigan. Crosby won his school's All-Campus event in 1930; the runner-up was another black player, R.G. Robinson.

The UGA never managed to enroll the majority of black golfers, just as the American Tennis Association—its tennis counterpart—failed to enroll the bulk of black tennis players. But its member clubs still sponsored the most events and began to lure such luminaries as heavyweight boxing champion Joe Louis as supporters. This suited the black professionals because in the mid-1930s, they were dependent to a large degree on "hustling" or winning bets to make a living. Golf was indeed a betting man's game.

Louis' loss to Max Schmeling in 1936 was blamed by some observers in part because he played too much golf. He sponsored a $2,500 UGA tournament and hired some black professionals as teachers. He also admits that he lost considerable sums betting in high-stakes games. The biggest loser, though, may have been the boxer Ike Williams. Williams said, "I did a first class job of managing my money real bad. Gambling on golf, playing golf....I had bet a thousand dollar Nassau on one game, which means you can lose three thousand. I lost some playing golf...."[5] Sounds like he lost more than a few bucks.

There were two other places where blacks found opportunities to play: in the army and at black colleges. Though neither had formal connections with the UGA, this national body benefitted blacks nonetheless. For some blacks the army courses were the only places they were able to play a full eighteen holes. (At many municipal courses that were segregated, a nine-hole course was all there was for blacks.) Private Jerry Reid of Atlanta—and a former caddie for Grand Slam winner Bobby Jones—once placed fourth in the Central Pacific championships.

Private Calvin Searles of Montgomery, Alabama, even played in the 1944 All-American event at Chicago's Tam O'Shanter course and acquitted himself well in the company of professionals like Byron Nelson. Wrote F.A. "Fay" Young of Searles' efforts then: "...Searles holds a position higher than any other colored golfer has ever enjoyed in golf in the United States."[6] Unfortunately, Searles died in action in World War II. Through the war years, the event at the Tam O'Shanter course was the only white-run professional tournament that allowed blacks to play.

Though not in the armed services, other players of note during the early 1940s included Ed Jackson and Bennie Davis of Detroit; Calvin Ingram and Frank Radcliffe of Chicago; Peter Fortunes of Suffolk, Virginia; and Hoxey Hazzard of Montgomery, Alabama. Nearly all were caddies as youngsters and were largely self-taught. Certainly few of them bothered to read manuals or could afford lessons. Most were simply shown the grips by a mentor, and after settling on what felt most comfortable, they just played when they could. The result was an amalgam of unorthodox styles epitomized by the cross-handed play of Howard Wheeler.

Some colleges also offered chances not found at public facilities. The UGA never sent a touring troupe of teachers to black colleges as had the American Tennis Association. Golf was at best a side-bar in even the most dedicated collegiate sports program. When Edwin B. Henderson completed his second edition of *The Negro in Sports* in 1949, golf was not even listed among conference titles awarded. Yet golf was pursued because a large percentage of the black college graduates would become professional people—doctors, lawyers, etc.—and golf would later come in handy in certain social situations.

The only black school with its own course was Tuskegee. A three-hole course was constructed in the 1920s and soon replaced by a five-hole layout. When the legendary Cleveland Abbott became director of athletics there, he finished four more holes for half a course of nine holes. In 1938, Tuskegee sponsored the first intercollegiate tournament with the following schools: Tuskegee, Alabama State, Florida A & M, Morehouse, and Morris Brown. The winners were Alfred Holmes and Maxwell Vails, both of Tuskegee. The women's event was won by Cora Lee McClinick. Fort Valley State College also sent a women's squad.

The reception was so positive at this 1938 inaugural event that a National Interscholastics tournament was added in 1940. Black high schools from Tuskegee, Atlanta, and Montgomery participated. Both of these events were dropped in 1944 because of the war, but the collegiate tournament was revived in 1950. Among blacks at white colleges, Hayden Golden was a varsity member at the University of Oregon in the mid-1930s, and he played in the Negro Northwest Open that had its debut in 1938 at Seattle's Earlington Golf Club. There was, by 1940, a substantial black golf community that needed only the opportunities to demonstrate its potential. The PGA, unfortunately, was not very accommodating.

Roadblocks

To white golfers on the fledgling PGA circuit in the 1930s, the most well-known black performer was a caddie, not a player. He was known as "Stovepipe" and he was a famous caddie at the Augusta National Club in Augusta, Georgia. In 1935, he was credited with assisting Gene Sarazen in winning that year's Masters tournament.

Sarazen was trailing Craig Wood after the fourteenth hole on the last day of play. He asked Stovepipe what it would take to win from his position. Stovepipe reportedly replied, "Four threes, Mr. Gene. Three, three, three, three."[7] Sarazen won the tournament. Another black employee at Augusta in that era was Beau Jack, the boxing champion, who was a bootblack there. Thirty-eight years after Stovepipe's story, the Augusta club became the source of bitter complaints from black professionals since none had been invited to play in the Masters tournament.

If black caddies were acceptable on the PGA tour, black players were not so welcomed in the 1940s. The group had an unwritten policy of not admitting blacks to its tour stops. The PGA ban against blacks approximated the unwritten policies of the major leagues and the National Football League. In 1943, a woman applied for membership and while her application was being reviewed, the issue of blacks arose. In a statement that Graffis writes as expressing the general sentiment at their annual meeting, someone said, "Show us some good golf clubs Negroes have established, and we can talk this over again."[8]

The Michigan delegation then proposed the following amendment to the PGA constitution: "Professional golfers of the Caucasian race, over the age of eighteen years, residing in North or South America, and who have served at least five years in the profession...shall be eligible for membership."[9] It passed. The clause left open the possibility of white women as members, but closed the door altogether to black golfers.

The challenge facing black golfers was formidable as the war ended. The UGA continued to offer opportunities for recreational players to test their skills against other blacks on public courses. Except for a layout in Los Angeles owned by Neil and Oscar Clisby at Fifty-first Street and Central Avenue in the early 1930s, no eighteen-hole course was black-owned—public or private. If blacks were going to show the world they could tee up with the best, another breakthrough was needed. That logjam was broken in 1948 by Bill Spiller, Ted Rhodes, and Madison Gunter. They forced the PGA to rethink its exclusionary membership rules and black golfers eventually became among the best ever.

Notes

1. Benjamin G. Rader, *American Sports* (Englewood Cliffs, N.J.: Prentice-Hall, Inc. 1983), p. 224.
2. Guil Jones, "Historically Speaking," United States Golf Association, p. 13.
3. Herb Graffis, *The PGA: Official History of the PGA of America* (New York: Thomas Y. Crowell Co., 1975), p. 199.
4. *New York Sun*, 11 July 1922.
5. Heller, *In This Corner: Forty World Champions Tell Their Stories*, p. 272.
6. *Baltimore Afro-American*, 2 September 1944.
7. *Sports Illustrated*, 8 April 1985, p. 60.
8. Graffis, *The PGA*, p. 236.
9. Ibid.

Wrestling

Almost every society, tribe, clan, grouping, and nation has lauded its wrestlers. There are probably more references to wrestling than to any other form of sport going back as far as recorded history. In some instances, it served as a substitute for war. In most cases it was just a much favored form of entertainment with the highest of accolades to the winners. From ancient Ethiopia and Egypt to seventeenth century West Africa to enslaved African-Americans to black freedmen in the twentieth century, wrestling in some form has not only endured; it has prospered.

The first famous European wrestler was Plato, the Greek philosopher, whose original name was Aristocles. His wrestling coach named him "Plato" which has remained since then. Olympic wrestlers in the ancient Games performed in the nude and later the Romans introduced bloody no-holds-barred "battle royals," which were wrestling matches with weapons. In the European Dark Ages and the Middle Ages, the sport was mainly local until it became associated with the lower classes during the Renaissance. In the handbooks for courtiers and royalty, wrestling was much too dirty an affair for the learned and refined.

They tended more toward tennis and horse racing.

In West Africa, the sport had been exalted above all others. Some matches held between wrestlers from neighboring tribes or villages had the appeal of today's Super Bowl. Great expectations awaited the contests and they occasioned more betting than anything else. Tribal champions were memorialized by village and societal historians known as *griots* and by latter day African novelists who used wrestlers to relate stories of success and failure.

In his book, *Things Fall Apart,* African writer Chinua Achebe's main character is a young man of eighteen named Okonkwo who defeated "Amalinze the Cat." Amalinze had brought honor to his village because he had not lost a wrestling match in seven years. He was given the nickname Cat because his back never touched the ground when competing. When Okonkwo defeated him, it was as if his entire village had won, for success depended on those qualities cherished by Africans: strength, agility, suppleness, mental alertness, quickness, and determination.

The late French anthropologist Charles Beart spent many hours documenting African village life and noted the careful preparation that preceded official matches. There were ceremonies beforehand that reinforced the importance and solemnity of the match. The match itself followed very precise rules rooted in history, for the object was not to maim but to simply throw one's opponent to the ground on his back. The most popular time for these games was after the sowing season and the harvest. The winners were adorned with cowrie shells and bells. In some instances, the outcome of wrestling matches determined either which males could marry or who they could marry. It is imagined that many a champion won the tribal chief's daughter's hand in marriage.

In colonial America, wrestling was so popular that it had to be regulated. Public notices were posted to advise all concerned of "wrastlling" matches and prizes such as tobacco, guns, and sugar were awarded to the winners. The Native Americans in particular loved to wrestle and they spent an inordinate amount of time at it. The straight-laced, puritan white settler could not understand such attention to a frivolity. But for the Native American adult male, it was a serious endeavor and a prominent way to demonstrate his manhood.

Black slaves also wrestled when they had the time and they, too, considered the sport vital to their status. One such slave who later became the most outspoken and well-known political figure of his time was Frederick Douglass. In his autobiography, Douglass wrote of the favored days between Christmas and New Year's Day when "The

sober, thinking, industrious ones [slaves] would employ themselves in manufacturing...but the majority spent the holidays in sports, ball-playing, wrestling, boxing, foot races...."[1]

Concurrent with the celebrations of whites, slaves held their own wrestling matches on Easter Monday, Shrove Tuesday, County Court Day, at county fairs, and on military training days. They could not participate in the activities of whites so they created their own and wrestling was a favorite sport. After the Emancipation Proclamation, wrestling continued as a pastime of fraternal and sports clubs that formed in the late 1800s.

The first historical mention of black wrestlers by name was Viro "Black Sam" Small who was born a slave in Beaufort, South Carolina, in 1854. He was abandoned as a nine-year-old during the Civil War, and eventually found employment in a foundry in Richmond, Virginia. Later he went to New York City to work in a slaughterhouse. According to Charles Morrow Wilson in his book, *The Magnificent Scufflers,* this five-foot nine-inch, 185-pound professional wrestler made his debut at Owney's Bastile in the Bowery section of New York City in 1870.

The first mention of black collegiate performers by name occurred during World War I. Walter Gordon, of the University of California at Berkeley from 1916 to 1918, was a Pacific Coast Conference heavyweight champion. Eugene Gordon of Washington, D.C., was a 125-pound winner while at Harvard University in 1917. Benner C. Turner was a 125-pound champion in New

England in 1926, and Russell Minton was a member of Penn State's squad.

In spite of the notices of black varsity wrestlers at white colleges, the sport lost favor after the First World War because there were so many competing leisure possibilities. At black colleges, where it might be expected to see a continuation of this tradition, there was almost no interest at all. The Colored (now Central) Intercollegiate Athletic Association (CIAA) was the only conference to offer wrestling and that did not begin until 1934. Lincoln University and Hampton Institute (now Hampton University) dominated the standings. Between 1934 and 1949, only Virginia State College (now Virginia State University)—in 1940–41—intruded. There were few coaches, little competition, and insufficient funds to provide the necessary leadership for quality teams. But the primary problem was the loss of the tradition from West Africa. It was almost forgotten, as wrestling thrived best in small, intimate surroundings.

However, that changed after the Second World War when white midwestern colleges began recruiting blacks with high school experience. The first breakthrough came in 1957, when Simon Roberts of the University of Iowa won the National Collegiate Athletic Association (NCAA) title for 147-pounders. There has been steady improvement since then.

Since 1950, wrestling has been sharply divided into professional or entertainment grappling and the more traditional forms that include loose, catch-hold, and belt-and-jacket styles. Professional wrestling, which is not considered a serious sport, remains popular among black television viewers and fans, while the latter categories are found in official competitions like the Olympics and the NCAA. For an update on professional black wrestlers, see Volume III, Chapter 8.

Notes

1. Frederick Douglass, *The Life and Times of Frederick Douglass* (New York: Bonanza Books, 1962), 145-146.

Track

Herculean strides were made between the two World Wars by black track and field athletes. Most of the gains came in the 1930s and early 1940s, as contrasted with the slow pace of progress in the 1920s. The talent was overwhelmingly concentrated in white college varsity teams and in clubs that were formed for this very purpose. Black colleges were woefully unable to offer anything resembling a track program until well into the 1930s. They had squads but their results were not very substantial.

Black schools struggled just to meet their academic demands, which increased considerably after the First World War. In addition, track suffered the same fate as basketball since it fell within the tourist season down South, where all but five black colleges were located. Baseball was the primary spring sport and it was buttressed by a traditional Easter Monday game, which usually attracted several hundred former alumni to campus for reunions and other festivities.

Track and field facilities were lacking, coaching was rudimentary, conference competition did not begin until 1924, with the Colored Intercollegiate Athletic Association (CIAA) meet, and there were no role models to follow. Football and baseball were the most important activities and every other sport was secondary. The track

programs at the segregated public high schools in the South were present in name only—if present at all. Typically, blacks were not expected to go to school after the seventh grade. Nearly everyone was engaged in farming or its subsidiary businesses. In short, track was just not very important.

Black clubs in the northern cities with access to quality competition fared well. Some had a long history of performers dating back to the early 1900s and many of their members wound up in prestigious white schools. None of these clubs belonged to the Amateur Athletic Union (AAU) until the mid-1920s, but informal arrangements with meet organizers were usually enough to gain admission for a select number of competitors. Few blacks had the time or the inclination to train for a sport that offered no professional outlet. The usual work week was six days and time off meant money lost.

At some white colleges, black athletes were able to gain worldwide attention. Competition began in dual meets with other schools and was augmented—for the very best—by conference meets, Intercollegiate Amateur Athletic Association of America (ICAAAA) meets, National Collegiate Athletic Association (NCAA) meets, AAU meets, special invitational meets, and the Olympic Games, which never saw a product from a black college until after the Second World War.

Facilities at white schools were state-of-the-art and supplemented by government funds in some instances, as when the Reserve Officers Training Corps (ROTC) was established and monies were provided for drill fields. Black colleges never saw a dime of these appropriated stipends. Another prime source of support came from wealthy alumni who donated, bequeathed, or just built athletic facilities for their alma mater. What with all these advantages and a willingness born of long-standing tradition, it is no wonder that black America's most illustrious track and field athletes matriculated at these institutions.

It would have been foolhardy to go on record in 1919 and predict that, within a quarter of a century, blacks would hold nearly all the world sprinting and jumping records. But that is exactly what happened in spite of their having to suffer the most vicious form of institutionalized racism which went undirected at their less athletically gifted brethren.

Black College Track

Within three years of the end of the First World War, the sport of track took giant organizational strides to meet the growing demand for quality competition. Of all the major sports played in America, track was the most universally known and the easiest to arrange. It was the centerpiece of the Olympics and a victorious America was eager to maintain her preeminence.

The YMCA staged its first national meet in 1920; the Olympics resumed in 1920 after an eight-year hiatus because of World War I (though Germany, Austria, Hungary, Turkey, and Russia were not invited); the NCAA began its meets in 1921; and the CIAA finally held its inaugural meet in 1924. But black college track programs were, in most instances, nonexistent. Only Hampton Institute (now Hampton University) could claim more than elementary expertise. Their dominance was such that only Lincoln University (Pennsylvania) and Morgan State won CIAA titles between 1924 and 1931. The Southern Intercollegiate Athletic Conference (SIAC) began track in 1916 and then discontinued it until 1938. Southern, segregated white colleges were not that interested in track either. Less than a half a dozen of them placed their stars on the Olympic teams before 1932. As at black colleges, only football and baseball mattered.

Howard University won that first CIAA meet and a sample of the winning times and distances makes interesting reading today. The results were: 100-yard dash = 10.2 seconds; 440-yard dash = 53 seconds; long jump = 20' 10"; pole vault = 9' 3"; high jump = 5' 6". It is important to avoid drawing the wrong inferences from these results. In the 1920s, black colleges were bastions of privilege for a small number of students in three separate departments: grade school, preparatory department, and the college-level department. In 1924, there was simply no history of track superiority to emulate.

It was 1927 before any black land grant schools—the state-supported institutions—received their accreditation and that was bestowed by the *northern* branch of the Association of Colleges and Secondary

Schools. The southern branch would not dare accredit black schools for fear their graduates would press for jobs reserved for whites. The one major, prestigious competition that would accept blacks was the Penn Relays at Franklin Field in Philadelphia. In 1923, Lincoln University won the one-mile relay there.

As if to reinforce the egalitarian code of this competition, Dr. George Overton, the Penn Relays director in the 1920s, mentioned to the *Chicago Defender* reporter William White that he would see to it that racial discrimination would not be a factor. Furthermore, he added that black colleges were backward in athletics but that, in track at least, they could develop performers like John B. Taylor and Howard Porter Drew. One particularly bright result was George D. Williams of Hampton Institute, who in 1930 placed second in the javelin and a year later set a meet record of 197' 1½".

Tuskegee copied the format of the Penn Relays and began its own Relay Carnival on May 7, 1927; the first by a black college. The May 14 *New York Age* printed this account of Tuskegee athletic director Cleveland Abbott's success: "...Tuskegee's entire student body with a large number of visitors from Columbus [Georgia], Montgomery, Atlanta and other points were on hand to witness a thorough and comprehensive demonstration of the possibilities of the youth of our race."[1] It is worth noting that a northern black newspaper like the *New York Age* thought enough of the Carnival's potential to provide wide coverage for the event.

When Abbott began his school's Relay Carnival, there were no events for women at the Penn Relays, but he did not forget them.

He inserted two events that first year: the 100-yard dash and a 440-yard relay. In 1930, he added the 50-yard dash and the discus. None of the CIAA schools had varsity competition for women at the time, so he broke new ground against establishment opposition.

In 1917 in France, a Women's Sports Federation was formed, and four years later the Women's International Sports Federation was organized to minister to women's athletics and to formulate policy. In 1922 the first Olympics for women were held in Paris, that led to their inclusion at regularly scheduled Olympiads beginning in 1928. In 1924, the AAU staged its first national championships for women. In 1926, Gertrude Ederle, white, swam the English Channel in fourteen hours and twenty-three minutes and broke the men's record by two hours. That same year at Lincoln Park in Chicago, Viola Edwards set a new AAU record in the high jump at 5' ⅛", surpassing the old mark of 4' 9". All of these developments led Abbott to believe that women should not be ignored.

But Abbott's foresight was not shared by everyone. Most black women spent very little time engaged in competitive, organized sport. They worked in the home with few appliances of convenience. There were no washers and dryers, no dishwashers, no disposable diapers, and the average work day was twelve hours long. In the South, two-thirds of all black women who worked outside their own homes did so as domestics in the homes of whites. The only times for recreation were Saturday and Sunday afternoons. The percentage of black college women heavily involved in sport was probably less than 5 percent.

As late as 1930, one black paper, the *California Eagle,* reported on March 14 that "Colored girls are showing a smaller percentage engaged in regular athletic sports than any other race in the Los Angeles area....In this wonderful climate, where outdoor sports may be played year-round, and there's no color bar set up at the gym door or the playgrounds, is there any reason why our girls have fallen so far behind our boys?"[2] The answer was yes, they had work to do and society considered track to be a masculine endeavor. Inez Patterson of Temple University was the outstanding exception to this trend.

In the 1930s, two more black college conferences began track competition—the Midwestern Athletic Association (MWAA), in 1933, and the Southwestern Athletic Conference (SWAC), in 1939. Wilberforce University won all save one of the MWAA titles through the decade, but in 1937 there was no conference meet at all. The SWAC's focus was football until well into the 1940s—football was the *only* conference title awarded until 1939, when basketball and track were added. Normal black occupational routines were to go to school through the sixth or seventh grade if possible, and then get a job wherever someone could pull some strings. Willie Mays, perhaps the most versatile baseball player ever, almost went to work in a saw mill because his father was there.

Consequently, by the end of the decade, southern black track aspirants had only three major meets in which to perform: the Penn Relays, the CIAA meet, and a new Tuskegee Carnival. Anything of significance was likely to come out of one of these events and that is exactly what hap-

pened. Abbott paid increasing attention to his female students and the results were positive. He felt encouraged enough to enter a team in the 1936 AAU Nationals, and their second place finish was the highest yet attained by a black school in any AAU National meet.

When Abbott came to Tuskegee in the mid-1920s he did so in the aftermath of a devastating resolution passed by the Council on Women's Sports in 1923. Through ignorance, custom, and chauvinism, the council resolved to urge women's sports organizations to deemphasize keen competition. Abbott thought the advice was too strong and proceeded to build a powerhouse track team—the best by any black college until World War II. He even hired a female, Amelia C. Roberts, as the team's coach. In 1937, the team won the AAU Nationals and began the black female domination of some events that exists in America today.

In that first championship season, the team amassed thirty-three points at Trenton, New Jersey, and the star was Lula Mae Hymes who competed and scored in the 100 meters, the long jump, and the 400-meter relay. Tuskegee even had a second team entered. The members of that winning squad were Hymes, Cora Gaines in the hurdles, Florence Wright in the shotput, Lelia Perry in the long jump, Mable Smith and Esther Brown in the sprints, Margaret Barnes in the javelin, Melissa Fitzpatrick in the baseball throw, and the relay team of Hymes, Brown, Jessie Abbott (Cleveland Abbott's daughter), and Celestine Birge. The coach was Christine Evans Petty who had replaced Miss Roberts. Here are their times and distances.

- 80-meter hurdles . . . . 1st place
  Cora Gaines . . . . 12.8 seconds
- long jump . . . . 1st place
  Lula Hymes . . . . 17′ 8½″
- 50-meter dash . . . . 2nd place
  Lula Hymes . . . . 6.8 seconds
- high jump . . . . 2nd place
  Cora Gaines . . . . 4′ 10½″
- 400-meter relay . . . . 2nd place
  Birge, Abbott, Smith, Hymes   51 seconds
- shotput . . . . 2nd place
  F. Wright . . . . 37′ 5″
- discus . . . . 2nd place
  F. Wright . . . . 105′ 1″
- baseball throw . . . . 2nd place
  M. Fitzpatrick . . . . 229′ 5″
- 100 meters . . . . 4th place
  Jessie Abbott . . . . 12.8 seconds
- 200-meter dash . . . . 4th place
  Mable Smith . . . . 27 seconds

In the previous AAU meet in 1936, Mable Smith set a new American citizenship record in the long jump at eighteen feet. Smith and her teammates would have never received this kind of attention in a white college track program. Most of the female AAU participants came not from universities but from clubs. White college varsity sports for women in the 1930s followed the 1923 Women's Sports Council resolutions to the letter. Their roughest activity was probably field hockey.

It might be expected that Tuskegee's main competition would come from another black school but it in fact came from northern clubs, especially the Mercury Athletic Club in New York City and the Illinois Women's Athletic Club. Two Mercury stalwarts were Gertrude Johnson and Ivy Wilson. Johnson was the AAU 200 meters winner in 1937 and the 50 meters winner in 1939. At another AAU sanctioned meet, Johnson became the first contestant to enter and score in five events: the 50-yard dash, the 100-yard dash, the 220-yard dash, the baseball throw, and the long jump. Wilson won the 50 meters title in 1936. Other members of that Mercury team included Ida Byrne, Pearl Edwards, Romona Harris, Etta Tate, and Esther Dennis. Mercury won the 1937 AAU 400-meter relay event and a year later they annexed the Canadian National Outdoor title under coach Leroy Alston.

Tuskegee's women speedsters continued their winning ways through the eve of the 1948 Olympics in London. They repeated as team victors in 1938 through 1942 and won the inaugural AAU Indoor title in 1941. In 1943, the Cleveland Polish team, led by Stella Walsh, captured the honors but Tuskegee returned to form in 1944 through 1948. Alice Coachman assumed the leadership role from Hymes in 1942 by contending for the sprints and the high jump. She won the AAU Outdoor 50-meter title four times, the 100 meters three times, and the high jump title an incredible nine times. Indoors, she won the 50-meter title twice, and the high jump three times. At five feet eight inches, this Albany, Georgia, native had first attracted attention as a seventh-grader when she vaulted 5′ 4½″, less than an inch from the world mark. Keep in mind that in this era the jumpers took off with both feet flying rather than taking off with one foot as today. Coachman literally *owned* the high jump for a decade.

Rounding out the Tuskegee teams of the war years, the featured student-athletes were Lillie Purifoy, a three-time AAU 80-meter hurdles winner and long jump victor;

Lucy Newell, a 50-meter dash winner; Juanita Watson, a 50-meter and 100-meter winner; and the incomparable Hattie Turner, black America's first superlative performer in the discus and the baseball throw.

Tuskegee's one major black college competitor was Wilberforce, which was in the MWAA conference. That institution's Betty Jean Lane won the AAU Outdoor 50-meter title in 1940, the 100-meter title in 1940-41, and the 200-meter title in 1941. Indoors, she captured the 50-meter and 100-meter crowns in 1941. The only other groups to show consistently good results in this period were the West Philadelphia Athletic Club and the Harrisburg (Pennsylvania) Athletic Association. If it had not been for the black college, track for black women in the South would have been non-existent.

The mantle began to pass to another black school in 1944, when Jessie Abbott left her father's school to become track coach at Tennessee A&I (now Tennessee State). Walter Davis of Tennessee A&I was convinced that Cleveland Abbott's program could be cloned and he meant to try. "Good physical training...and good discipline would be good for the girls rather than harmful....We knew that there was nothing to prove that competitive sports was harmful. And we decided to go into it....We had seen Abbott win the AAU with Negro girls, and being a geneticist I know that individuals are born equal...and it's the environment that makes the difference."[3] Tennessee State dominated women's track in the 1950s.

While black women garnered most of the publicity at black schools, there were a few men who made the headlines. After

George Williams' high jump performances in 1932, Lloyd Thompson of Xavier University (New Orleans) followed him with an AAU victory in 1937 at 6' 6". Two years later, John Borican of Virginia State College (now Virginia State University) smashed several distance marks. He was American record holder at 600 yards (1 minute 10.2 seconds in 1941), 880 yards (1 minute 50.5 seconds in 1940), 800 meters (1 minute 50 seconds in 1942), and the AAU pentathlon winner in 1938, 1939, and 1941. He was the most talented all-around black performer between 1936 and 1942.

Lilburn Williams of Xavier was the AAU shotput winner in 1939. Mozelle Ellerbee of Tuskegee was the collegiate 100-yard dash champion in 1938 at 9.7 seconds and in 1939 at 9.8 seconds. Mel Walker of Tennessee State was high jump winner in 1941 at 6' 6½". Adam Berry of Southern University (Baton Rouge, Louisiana) leaped the same height—6' 6½"—in 1942. And Lewis Smith of Prairie View A&M was the AAU 600-yard indoor champion in 1943. He later attended Virginia Union. The only pole vault notable was Virginia Union's Howard Jones, who managed 13' 3" in 1936 with a wooden pole; fiberglass was not yet standard equipment.

By 1940, the South Central Athletic Conference (SCAC) began its competitions and joined the CIAA, SWAC, SIAC, and MWAA in trying to upgrade performances. Problems remained much as before: lack of adequate facilities, coaches like Morgan State's Eddie Hurt were overworked, fewer competitions, and the inability to secure certification for meet records in AAU standings. No American or world record set in a black college meet would have been accepted by the AAU or the ICAAAA. This fact alone was often reason enough for a promising black speedster to seek his education at a white school. It was little wonder then that white college results were looked upon as the times and distances to emulate.

Stars on White College Tracks

A berth on a major white college track team was nearly all any runner could want. The facilities were the best to be found, the competition was always keen, the coaching was at least adequate, and any records set were instantly certified. But as with other black students on white campuses, such problems as housing, jobs, and the limited use of university amenities were insulting but tolerated. After all, the alternative was either a black school or a club with AAU recognition. In most cases, if it were not for their athletic prowess, blacks would not be attending at all. However insulted, by the end of the Second World War, these token black athletes had rewritten the record books.

The big names just after the First World War were Fred "Duke" Slater, who starred in weight events at Iowa, and Edward Solomon Butler of Dubuque Seminary, who was a long jumper. Butler made the Olympic team in 1920, only to injure himself in his first leap in Antwerp, Belgium. But the most fuss was caused by two all-purpose athletes from the University of Michigan and Harvard: William DeHart Hubbard and Ned Gourdin.

Hubbard had attended Walnut Hills High School in Cincinnati, Ohio, and entered Michigan in 1921. He was an immediate sensation as a freshman in tying the

school record in the 50-yard dash, setting a freshman record in the long jump at 24' 6¾", winning the AAU long jump title at 24' 5½", winning the hop, step, and jump at 48' 1½", and being named an All-America. Michigan even lengthened the jumping pit just for him.

In his sophomore year, Hubbard set Big Ten marks in the 50-yard dash and the long jump at 25' 1½", and captured the hop, step, and jump again. In 1924, the Olympic year, he was Big Ten winner in the 100-yard dash at 9.8 seconds and the long jump. He might have been a threat on Michigan's football team but its coach, Fielding "Hurry Up" Yost, did not allow blacks on the team. At the Olympic Games in Paris, Hubbard captured a gold medal in the long jump— 24' 5⅛"—after qualifying on his second leap.

Still improving as a senior, he tied the 100-yard dash world record in a dual meet against Ohio State at 9.6 seconds, and later won the national title. His most illustrious feat, however, was a 25' 10⅞" long jump world mark on June 13, 1925, at Stagg Field in the NCAA championships. Hubbard's record was inspirational, noted the *California Eagle* in its June 26 edition, "...your blood tingled with pride and you shared with Michigan's greatest athlete his big triumph....We bow to King Hubbard, the persistent one."[4] A physical education major at school, he later took a position with the Cincinnati Recreation Department. When he graduated, Hubbard was one of only eight blacks in a class of 1,456.

One of Hubbard's Olympic teammates was Edward Orval "Ned" Gourdin of Jacksonville, Florida. Gourdin managed to graduate from Cambridge Latin Preparatory

School in Boston before entering Harvard. He was not planning to try out for track; he fancied himself a baseball player. But he certainly fooled everyone in 1921. In the Harvard–Yale meet he won the long jump at 24′ 4″; the 100-yard dash in 10.4 seconds on a muddy track; and finished second in the 220-yard dash. Against Princeton—which did not admit blacks then—Gourdin won all three of the above events. His long jump performance set a new collegiate record at 24′ 6″. Said Princeton's coach, Keene Fitzpatrick, "There goes a whole track team and a man who ranks with [Alvin] Kraenzlein, who was the greatest all-around I ever saw in action."[5]

On July 23 at a Harvard–Yale and Oxford–Cambridge meet, Gourdin became the first to break the 25-foot barrier in a leap of 25′ 3″, which the August 21 *New York Telegram* said was a jump that "...was considered almost impossible....We may begin to think of a day when the 26-footer will arrive...the achievement of Gourdin stands out, however, as the greatest feat in track and field in a generation."[6] Just to tease his opposition, on October 12, he captured the AAU Pentathlon at Travers Island, New York, by amassing twelve combined points in the long jump, javelin, 100-meter dash, discus, and 1500 meters. He repeated this pentathlon win in 1922 and won a silver medal in the 1924 Olympic long jump event.

Gus Moore hailed from Brooklyn's Boys High School and later the University of Pittsburgh. He was the fastest schoolboy miler ever—at 4 minutes 28.2 seconds—in 1925, only three-fifths of a second slower than the collegiate mark that year. In college, he broke R. Earl Johnson's six-mile

cross country record in 27 minutes 32.6 seconds, while winning the title in 1928-29. He was AAU 10-mile champion in 1930.

The AAU National meet in 1927 set a precedent by relocating from New Orleans to Lincoln, Nebraska, because of possible racial discrimination. New Orleans meet officials just refused to accept black entrants so the venue was changed. Had this been football with more money at stake, the black performers would have merely been left at home. But some schools had little chance of winning without their black student-athletes. As the 1920s closed, blacks had distinguished themselves in the long jump and were about to serve notice in the sprints.

The black domination in the short races began with two Olympians in 1932, and put into overdrive with the most acclaimed athlete of the first half of this century. Thomas "Eddie" Tolan, Jr. and Ralph Metcalfe both came from the Midwest and were promising athletes as far back as high school. Tolan attended Detroit's Cass Technical High School and Metcalfe went to Chicago's Tilden Technical High. Tolan entered the University of Michigan and Metcalfe went to Marquette. Both wound up side-by-side at the 1932 Olympics in Los Angeles.

Tolan, at five feet six inches and 130 pounds, was the American schoolboy champion in the 100-yard and 220-yard dashes. He set a new world record in the 100-yard mark on May 25, 1929, at 9.5 seconds. Two weeks later, George Simpson, white, lowered the mark to 9.4 seconds using starting blocks which were disdained at first. (For a time, two separate sets of records were kept for dashes using blocks and for those set without them.) In 1930, Tolan was Big Ten champion Indoors for 60 yards in 6.2 seconds, the outdoor 100-yard winner at 9.6 seconds, and the 220-yard winner at 20.9 seconds. His black teammate, Booker Brooks, was Big Ten discus champion in 1930, with a heave of 142′ 6″ and second in the shotput at 46′ 6⅜″.

On July 1, 1930, Tolan set a new world record in the 100-meter dash at 10.2 seconds that included a win over Simpson and Percy Williams, the Olympic champion at that distance. That summer also proved to be a trying time for him. In September, Tolan, Gus Moore, and John Lewis were denied lodging at the Illinois Athletic Club and the Chicago Athletic Club where their teammates were staying for an AAU event against Great Britain. Threatening to leave, Tolan was told by an AAU official that he would "…be through in athletics forever…" if he quit the team.[7]

Tolan wired his mother for advice and was urged to run his heart out, though others advised him to leave. The three athletes eventually stayed at the Grand Hotel, a black inn on Chicago's South Side. Phil Edwards, the black British runner, stayed with his team members at the Medinah Athletic Club. Metcalfe, from Chicago originally, stayed at home. It was a classic case of suffering the indignity of racial rejection if he stayed, or of missing out on a solid accomplishment if he left. It would not be the last time it happened to them.

Metcalfe was born in Atlanta, Georgia, on May 29, 1910, and moved to Chicago with his family. At five feet eleven inches and 180 pounds, he had burst upon the scene in 1930 when, as a member of the Chase Athletic Club, he won the AAU Junior 100-yard dash title in 9.7 seconds. His big day came on June 11, 1932, when he shattered the world record in the 220-yard dash and tied Tolan's 100-yard dash mark at 9.5 seconds. But for both Metcalfe and Tolan, the supreme test was the 1932 Olympic Games in Los Angeles, where the city had raised $1.5 million in bonds to be added to state funds of another million to showcase America's first Olympics since 1904. The most awaited event was the 100-yard dash final with Tolan, Metcalfe, and Simpson at the starting line.

Metcalfe was favored but he false-started and was away last with the second shot of the starter's pistol. Tolan led at fifty meters and Metcalfe caught him at ninety meters but "The timer's clock, however, caught the Michigan marvel's chest a hair's breadth ahead of Metcalfe at the end."[8] Tolan's time was 10.3 seconds, a new Olympic and world record. He returned to capture the 200 meters as well in 21.2 seconds for another Olympic record. It was the first gold medal performance for a black American athlete in a sprint event. Michigan's Willis Ward said that "Tolan slackened near the finish enabling Metcalfe, the favorite, to win…" in the trials.[9] If Ward is correct, Tolan must have wanted Metcalfe to shoulder the pressure of being the favorite in the Games; in any case it worked.

Ed Gordon of the University of Iowa won the long jump gold medal at 25′ ¾″. He had collected the collegiate title earlier at 25′ 3⅜″. Other blacks who just missed making the United States team were discus thrower Booker Brooks of Michigan; high jumper Willis Ward of Michigan; Eugene Beatty, a hurdler from Michigan Normal (State); John Brooks, a long jumper; Ben

Eastman, a quarter-miler; and the javelin expert George Williams of Hampton Institute.

James Johnson of Illinois State Normal was a victim of an unfortunate turn of events. He was left off the 400-meter relay team after finishing fifth in the 100-meter dash trials. Past tradition had put the fifth and sixth place finishers in the 100-meter and the 200-meter finals on the 400-meter relay team, but at the last minute Johnson was replaced by Bob Kiesel and Hec Dyer with no explanation. Maybe the authorities meant to start a new tradition or just continue an old one of dispensing with blacks at will.

The two black women team members, Louise Stokes and Tydie Pickett, were members of the 400-meter relay but did not win a medal. Stokes ran for the Onteona Athletic Club in Malden, Massachusetts. She finished in a tie for fourth in the 100-meter dash trials while Pickett finished sixth in the 400-meter trials.

Those memorable 1932 Olympic Games were elementary compared to the 1936 Games in Berlin, Germany. More has been written about this Olympiad than about any other because of three facts: the German leader, Adolf Hitler, planned to demonstrate his theories of Aryan racial superiority through athletics; the undeniable talents of Jesse Owens, a black American sprinter and jumper; and reports of atrocities against Jews in Germany at the time. But the center of attention was Jesse Owens, who came upon his fame due to an unlikely set of circumstances.

Jesse Owens was named James Cleveland Owens after his birth on September 12, 1913, in Oakville, Alabama. One

of twelve children of Henry and Emma Owens, Jesse was one of nine that survived. He did not grow up in good health, having suffered from bronchitis brought on from drafty winter winds and growths on his legs and chest that doctors could not decipher. Owens was not an especially good student, but he later acquired an ability to express himself quite well.

His family members were very religious, which may have helped him withstand the racial discrimination meted out to blacks in Alabama. Though Owens never had many unkind words to say about his early life there, another black Alabama sprinter contemporary, Eulace Peacock, lamented that "When I look back over my lifetime I can get so bitter about things that happened to me. And actually I should hate white people, but fortunately my family didn't bring me up that way."[10] Young Jesse must have had similar sentiments.

Owens' family moved to Cleveland, Ohio, in the early 1920s, and he again faced a new set of segregated movies and other recreational amenities. At the Bolton Elementary School, his teacher misunderstood Owens to say "Jesse" when asked his name rather than "J.C." in his slow, southern drawl. "Jesse" stuck. At Fairmont Junior High School, he met his future wife, Minnie Ruth Solomon, and discovered the joys of organized sports, mainly basketball and track. He also met his primary mentor and friend, Charles Riley, the school's coach and physical education teacher.

Riley, who was white and of average build—five feet eight inches—may have seen something of William DeHart Hubbard in Owens' speed, because he literally made his young protégé his life's work.

Henry Armstrong, shown shortly after winning the welterweight title from Barney Ross on May 31, 1938. Armstrong is the only man to hold three world boxing titles at the same time—featherweight, lightweight, and welterweight. *(Courtesy of Ocania Chalk)*

In 1943 Sergeant Joe Louis embarked upon a hundred-day War Department–sponsored tour of army bases and hospitals. The "morale building" tour included refereeing and exhibition bouts by Louis and his entourage. With the champion is also P.F.C. "Sugar" Ray Robinson, who was being called the "uncrowned" welterweight champion, and Sergeant George Nicholas, one of Louis' sparring partners. *(Life Magazine, December 1944)*

Joe Louis towers over a fallen Max Schmeling in the first round of their rematch on June 22, 1938. Schmeling did not get up after 2 minutes and 4 seconds. *(AP/Wide World Photos)*

Harry Wills, prizefighter, circa 1926. Wills was unjustly denied a
heavyweight title fight against Jack Dempsey.
(Courtesy of the Van Der Zee Collection)

Joe Louis wins the World Heavyweight title over James Braddock (slumping to the canvas) at Comiskey Park in Chicago on June 23, 1937. *(AP/Wide World Photos)*

Francis Alfred "Jazz" Byrd of Lincoln University, during a 77-yard touchdown run against Howard University, November 30, 1922. *(Courtesy of Lincoln University)*

All-America selection Julius Franks, guard, of the Uiversity of Michigan, 1942. *(AP/Wide World Photos)*

Archie Harris, the brilliant end for Indiana University, 1939. *(AP/Wide World Photos)*

Jerome Heartwell Holland, of Cornell. Holland, from Auburn, New York, was one of the two juniors to make All-America, 1937.
(AP/Wide World Photos)

John "Big Train" Moody, Morris Brown star. *(Courtesy of Morris Brown College)*

Wilmeth Sidat-Singh, Syracuse University triple-threat star. Shown about 1937. *(Courtesy of Syracuse University)*

Joe Lillard of the Chicago Cardinals, number 19, being chased by Red Grange, number 77, in a 1933 NFL game. *(Courtesy of the Saint Louis Cardinals)*

The incomparable Ben Stevenson of Tuskegee Institute, the most heralded black college football player before World War II. *(Courtesy of Tuskegee University)*

Jerome Heartwell "Brud" Holland, Cornell University All-America in 1937. *(Courtesy of Cornell University)*

The Renaissance Basketball Team, 1925. *(Courtesy of the Van Der Zee Collection)*

First Colored World Series. *(Source unknown)*

Ralph Johnson Bunche, future Nobel Peace Prize winner, shown as guard on the UCLA basketball team in 1925.

New York Black Giants, 1930. *(Courtesy of the Van Der Zee Collection)*

The New York Black Yankees, circa 1930. *(Courtesy of the Van Der Zee Collection)*

Paul Robeson, second row, third from left, of the Rutgers University varsity baseball team, 1919. *(Courtesy of Rutgers University)*

The new Negro League administrators gather for a commemorative photo at New York City's Polo Grounds in 1934.
(Courtesy of the Van Der Zee Collection)

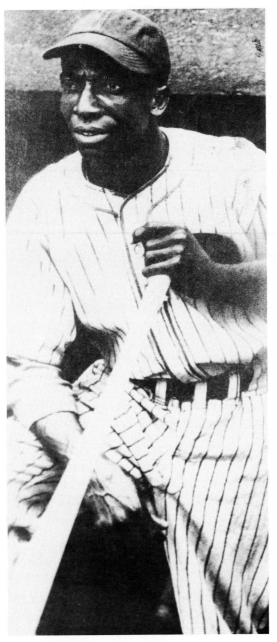

Josh Gibson, of the Homestead Grays, the most powerful hitter in the Negro Leagues in the late 1930s and 1940s.
(Photograph by Bill Yancy)

James "Cool Papa" Bell, all-time great Negro League star and Hall of Famer. His career in the Negro League spanned the years 1922–1946.
(Courtesy of John Holway)

Owens even lunched at Riley's home, where Riley spared no efforts in making him faster. Within a year, Owens had clocked 11 seconds in the 100-yard dash and at age fifteen he set world marks for a junior high school student of 6' in the high jump and 22' 11¾" in the long jump. Riley even arranged for Owens to meet Hubbard, who had set the world record in the long jump in 1925.

In 1930 Owens was in East Technical High School, in a group of blacks that made up less than 5 percent of the students. In two years, he was the hottest track property in the country, bar none. He competed in the 1932 Midwest Olympic Preliminaries but lost in the long jump, the 100 meters, and the 200 meters. He became a father on August 8 when his daughter, Gloria, was born to Minnie Ruth. He then finished high school after setting a schoolboy record in the long jump of 24' 3¾". Later, at the National Interscholastic meet at Stagg Field in Chicago, Owens soared 24' 9⅝" in the long jump, tied the world mark in the 100-yard dash in 9.4 seconds, and set a new world record in the 220-yard dash in 20.7 seconds. Of East Tech's fifty-four total points, Owens accounted for thirty of them. He was even feted with a parade back in Cleveland. Strangely, not a single black college made an attempt to recruit him, so he wound up at Ohio State after seriously considering a few others.

But Ohio State had a sordid reputation among black Ohioans in the early 1930s. In 1931, William Bell, a black Ohio State football player, was benched in a game against Vanderbilt (Tennessee) that was played at *home*. In 1933, the Ohio State Supreme Court upheld the university's right to deny housing to a black co-ed, Doris Weaver, because, as school president Dr. George Rightmire said, "Knowing the feelings in Ohio, can the administration take the burden of establishing this relationship—colored and white girls living in this more or less family way?"[11] Rightmire must have been talking about the feelings of white Ohioans.

The black press urged Owens to think twice before entering his choice of schools. "Why help advertise an institution that majors in prejudice?"[12] cried the *Chicago Defender*. Nevertheless, with his 73.5 high school grade-point-average, Owens enrolled in Ohio State in the fall of 1933. He had to share a boarding house apartment with some other black students because on-campus housing was barred to blacks. For him and his black friends, only one movie theater was accessible—upstairs, no university restaurants would admit them, and Owens himself was given the least visible job as a freight elevator operator in the State Office Building. The passenger elevator job was reserved for white athletes. Owens did not complain for he was paying his own way through college; he did not have a free ride as is the possibility today. (In those days, a scholarship was in fact a ready-made job for a student.) But 1933 was not all bad. John Brooks was Big Ten long jump champion at the University of Chicago; James Luvalle was ICAAAA winner in the 440-yard dash; and Eulace Peacock was the national pentathlon victor.

Problems aside, Owens' track potential seemed harnessed until the end of his sophomore season when he exploded with stellar performances on one Saturday afternoon. At the National Intercollegiates in Ann Arbor, Michigan, on May 25, 1935,

Owens put on a mind-boggling display that resulted in three world records and a tie in another. The new marks were a 20.3-second clocking in the 220-yard dash, a 22.6-second time in the 220-yard low hurdles, a leap of 26′ 8¼″ in the long jump, and a tied world mark in the 100-yard dash in 9.4 seconds. It was simply the most superlative feat ever accomplished in the history of the sport.

The black press was understandably effusive in praise. Said the June 8, 1935, *Norfolk* (Virginia) *Journal and Guide:* "Owens...is without doubt the greatest individual performer the world has ever known."[13] It also noted that coverage in the white daily papers in Birmingham and Atlanta was relegated to page three. Up North, the June 2, 1935, *New York Times* carried a banner headline, "Owens' Record-Breaking Feats Presage Brilliant Olympic Mark" and then reopened a discussion of why blacks make better runners. The *Times* added that "A theory has been advanced that through some physical characteristic of the race involving the bone and muscle construction of the foot and leg the Negro is ideally adapted to the sprints and jumping events."[14] Need more be said about this ridiculous notion that was thought to be just the reverse before Eddie Tolan and Ralph Metcalfe won the sprints at the 1932 Olympics? No matter what blacks did, white experts had to concoct a "theory" to explain it.

Owens' accomplishments overshadowed other outstanding performances by black stars. Willis Ward had defeated Owens in a 60-yard Indoor event on March 2 of that year, and again in the hurdles. In July, at the AAU Championships, Eulace

Peacock also beat Owens twice—in the 100-meter dash in 10.2 seconds and in the long jump at 26′ 3″. Owens and Peacock were envisioned as another one-two sprint punch for the upcoming Olympics like Tolan-Metcalfe in 1932. With this kind of talent, it is not surprising that Adolf Hitler was worried about America's "Black Auxiliaries," as he called our black runners.

As controversial as the 1936 Olympics themselves were, problems started for the American team and for Owens even before they left for Berlin. Owens suffered a few personal problems in July 1935 in California, and performed poorly at the AAU Championships in Lincoln, Nebraska. Then he got married and was later told that he may have endangered his amateur standing by accepting a job as a "page" in the Ohio House of Representatives. That taken care of, he fared badly in his studies and found himself academically ineligible for the 1935–36 indoor track season.

Compounding all these problems was a mounting campaign to boycott the 1936 Olympics. On September 15, 1935, Adolf Hitler issued the Nuremberg Laws which stripped German Jews of their citizenship rights and equal treatment under German law. The AAU then voted in the fall of 1935 to boycott unless Germany changed its treatment of their Jewish athletes. The American Olympic Committee sent several leaders—including Avery Brundage, its president—to Germany to see for themselves. They came back with high marks for the Germans. What, pray tell, raged the black press, did Brundage and his cohorts see? Brundage remained a despised figure to the majority of black athletes the rest of his days.

Black stars like Owens were also reminded by the black press that, here at home, neither the major leagues nor the National Football League admitted blacks. The New York *Amsterdam News* urged our black athletes to stay put, as did Owens' two hometown black papers, the *Cleveland Call and Post* and the *Cleveland Gazette*. To make matters worse for him, because of his troubles as a "page," the AAU ordered Owens' name removed from consideration for the Sullivan Award, given annually to the nation's most outstanding amateur athlete. Thus Owens' May 25 performance—the most acclaimed athletic feat of the century—went unrewarded by the sport's highest authorities.

Owens had to be slightly unsure since Peacock had beaten him five straight times since July 1935. But then Peacock tore a hamstring muscle at the Penn Relays on April 24, 1936, while Owens regained his form. Owens, by now at five feet ten inches and 165 pounds, broke the world mark in the 100-yard dash in 9.3 seconds on May 16, won all of his events at the Big Ten Championships, and easily qualified for the American Olympic squad at New York City's Randall's Island. His other black teammates were Ralph Metcalfe and Mack Robinson (Jackie Robinson's brother) in the sprints, David Albritton and Cornelius Johnson in the high jump, Archie Williams and James Luvalle in the 400 meters, "Long" John Woodruff in the 800 meters, Fritz Pollard, Jr. in the 110-meter hurdles, and John Brooks in the long jump. The sprinter Louise Stokes and hurdler Tydie Pickett made the women's team. Willis Ward of Michigan, Mel Walker (Owens' Ohio State teammate), and Peacock missed their berths. One favorable note was the designation of Tuskegee as the site for semi-final trials for women—a first for a black school.

The team sailed on the S.S. *Manhattan* on July 15, and arrived in Bremerhaven, Germany, nine days later. Owens was mobbed by German autograph seekers as he and his teammates tried to adjust to the time change. When the Games began a week later, everything seemed in order except for the banning of Howell King, a black boxer, for supposedly pilfering a camera from a store. Then on the very first day, what began as a perceived slight in time mushroomed into legend.

After Hitler watched two German athletes win gold medals, he ordered them to his box for personal congratulations. He did the same for a Finnish athlete. Then Cornelius Johnson won the high jump over David Albritton but Hitler left just before the playing of the American national anthem. No one will ever know for sure if Hitler was purposely avoiding a face-to-face confrontation in full public view with a black athlete, but the American press played the "snub" for all it was worth. According to William J. Baker, "Not until the next day did Owens win his first gold medal. By then the president of the International Olympic Committee, Henri de Baillet-Latour of Belgium, had gotten word to Hitler that as the head of the host government he must be impartial in his accolades.... Hitler stopped inviting winners to his stadium box."[15]

The snub to Johnson was eventually transposed to a snub to Owens that Owens himself initially denied but later erroneously admitted was true. Owens won his first gold medal on the second day,

August 3. In the semi-final heats on the first day, he broke the world record in the 100 meters at 10.2 seconds, but it was wind-aided. In the final on that Monday, he lined up against Metcalfe and Frank Wykoff of the United States, and the runners from Germany, Sweden, and the Netherlands. He drew the inside lane but officials had moved everyone one lane out because the distance runners had chewed up the lane nearest the curb. But it did not matter as Owens won by three yards in 10.3 seconds with Metcalfe second. One down, three to go.

On Tuesday morning, August 4, Owens qualified for the 200-meter finals with Mack Robinson. In both of his heats he clocked 21.1 seconds for new world marks around a turn, but trouble loomed in the afternoon long jump trials. American jumpers had won every long jump event since 1896. After Owens took a practice run through the long jump pit, an official raised his red flag to signify an attempt. Practice runs were not allowed in Germany. On his second try, his take-off foot stepped over the front edge of the board and he fouled again. He had one last try to qualify and here more legend surfaced.

Many accounts had Owens' chief rival, the German Lutz Long, as coming over to him to offer words of encouragement. In the book, *Jesse: The Man Who Outran Hitler,* Long supposedly said, "I Luz Long. I think I know what is wrong with you."[16] In actuality, Long did no such thing and Owens later admitted as much to close friends. But the first version was more dramatic and many sportswriters let him get away with this little slip. In any event, Owens qualified and set up a real confrontation with Long. Owens held a small lead at 25' 9¾" after the first round of jumps but Long matched it. Then Owens sailed beyond 26' and Long failed to keep up. But Owens still had more in reserve though his second gold medal was already in his pocket. On his last solo try, he sprung himself out to a new Olympic record of 26' 5¼". Two down, two to go.

Both Owens and Mack Robinson qualified in the morning rain on August 5 for the 200-meter finals. In the finals in the afternoon, Owens and Robinson crouched next to two Dutchmen, a Swede, and a Canadian. With the starter's pistol Owens catapulted his lithe figure to victory in an Olympic record time of 20.7 seconds. Robinson was second in a borrowed pair of shoes in 21.1 seconds. But the attention once again centered on Owens who had just won his third gold medal, the first since 1900. Three down, one to go. He rested and watched Fritz Pollard, Jr. win a bronze medal in the 110-meter hurdles on August 6.

Ordinarily, Owens would have been finished competing, but he surprisingly found himself having to lead off the 400-meter relay team. The team was told at the Randall's Island trials that the fourth, fifth, sixth, and seventh finishers in the 100-meter trials would make up the 400-meter relay squad. That was Foy Draper, Marty Glickman, Sam Stoller, and Mack Robinson. But at the last minute the coaches changed their minds in a ploy that looked as though the two Jewish runners, Glickman and Stoller, were intentionally overlooked and that favoritism for the University of Southern California (USC) was involved.

Though Robinson had qualified for the 200 meters, he was replaced by Frank Wykoff who was a USC student. The coach of the relay squad was Dean Cromwell, also of

USC. Glickman and Stoller had resisted protests back home for going to Nazi Germany in the first place and this was another blow. In addition, Cromwell had Glickman, Stoller, and Draper run in a special 100-meter race next to the Olympic Village to see who would run in what order in the relay. Both Glickman and Stoller finished ahead of Draper in this dry run. But Lawson Robertson, the head coach, decided to drop both Glickman and Stoller in favor of Draper and Wykoff.

According to William J. Baker, Metcalfe and Wykoff thought Owens had selfishly wanted to win a fourth gold medal and had not protested the exclusion of the Jewish runners. Glickman said he vividly remembers Owens saying in a meeting: "Coach, let Marty and Sam run. I've had enough. I've won three gold medals. Let them run, they deserve it. They ought to run." To which one of the coaches snidely replied, "You'll do as you're told."[17] Back home the press concerning the benching of Glickman and Stoller was lost in the euphoria of the team's victories.

Metcalfe, who lost twice to Eddie Tolan at Los Angeles in 1932, finally got his gold medal in the relay; Archie Williams won the 400 meter dash in 46.5 seconds; John Woodruff captured the 800-meter run in 1:52.9 minutes; and James Luvalle, the only Phi Beta Kappa in the field, won a bronze medal in the 400 meters. John Brooks placed sixth in the long jump. All returned home as conquering heroes in an election year that saw black Americans courted as never before.

After a series of economic and occupational mishaps, Owens finally settled down as a representative for the Atlantic Richfield Company, while Woodruff, Pollard, Williams, Albritton, and Metcalfe finished college and went on to respectable lives. Luvalle earned his doctorate in chemistry and became a college professor at Stanford University. Neither Stokes nor Pickett won medals at Berlin in the women's events.

In 1950, the Associated Press named Owens as the "Athlete of the Half-Century," an especially welcomed honor since he failed to win the Sullivan Award in 1936, given to the nation's most outstanding amateur athlete. In late 1936, Owens publicly backed the losing presidential candidate, Alf Landon. He also lost his amateur standing because of oral agreements made to cash in on his Olympic fame. Not only did these offers fail to materialize, but he became involved in a series of business disasters that sullied his name for a time. His stature was resurrected by presidential appointments for world tours to promote sports and international understanding. Through it all, his wife Ruth stood by his side.

In 1972 his alma mater awarded Owens an honorary doctorate, and in 1974 the NCAA presented the Theodore Roosevelt Award to him in honor of his college contributions. He was made a charter member of the Track and Field Hall of Fame. In 1976, President Gerald Ford awarded him the highest accolade a civilian could receive—the Presidential Medal of Freedom.

The victories of black Americans at Berlin served as a beacon for all Americans of African descent. The Depression was beginning to ebb and another migration from South to North had started. More runners were competing in more events as the Second World War decimated the college campuses. But the black dominance in sprinting and jumping had begun in earnest despite the plaudits of Woodruff and Williams at Berlin. The increasingly learned coaches of young black speedsters funneled them into the shorter races so they could perform like Jesse Owens. They found inspiration in his exploits.

A host of long jumpers emulated Owens including Mel Walker of Ohio State; Edward Burke of Marquette; Albert Threadgill of Temple; Gilbert Crutcher of Colorado; Paul Robeson, Jr. of Cornell; Don Barksdale of UCLA; Joshua Williamson of Camp Plauche, Louisiana; Lloyd Thompson of Xavier; Adam Berry of Southern University; Kermit King of Pittsburgh (Kansas); William Lacefield of UCLA; and on through Herb Douglas, the AAU champion in 1945.

Said Douglas, "When I was thirteen, Jesse Owens influenced me...I had the opportunity to meet him....During the 30s...the Big Ten did not allow any Blacks to play basketball....I knew if I could go and excel in track and field, I could get an education."[18] Only in track and field at a white college before 1950 could a black athlete reach his full potential. Basketball in some conferences was closed to him, professional football banned him from 1934 until 1946, and major league baseball had him barred since 1889. He could not do any better than the cinder paths.

Nowadays, experts think back to Owens and Metcalfe and wonder which of the two was better on closer inspection. Owens won the AAU 100-meter title only once; Metcalfe won it three times. Owens failed to win the AAU 200-meter title; Metcalfe won it five times in a row. Owens won the Intercollegiate 100-yard dash twice; Metcalfe three times. And again in the Intercollegiate 220-yard dash, Owens won it twice to three times for Metcalfe. What does all this prove? Maybe nothing but the results are surprising when compared with the relative publicity they received.

Our black distance runners were not difficult to identify at all. After Archie Williams and John Woodruff came James Herbert of New York University (NYU) with a world record at 600 yards in 1:11 minutes. Woodruff was the AAU, Intercollegiate, and ICAAAA champion in the half-mile. Others who chased his trail were George Carr at Marquette, Dave Bolen at Colorado, Robert Kelly at Illinois, Reginald Pearman and Stan and Maurice Callender at NYU, among others. But on the eve of the 1948 Olympics, no black runner held a world record beyond 880 yards. Conversely, no white person had high jumped beyond 6' 9" as of 1939. Three blacks—Cornelius Johnson, David Albritton, Mel Walker—had all crossed this bar.

In the mile, only James T. Smith of Indiana University and Frank Dixon of NYU stirred passions. Smith had clocked 4:11 minutes, and Dixon had begun as a cross country star at New York City's James Monroe High School in 1938. By 1942, Dixon had captured the AAU and ICAAAA cross country titles and the AAU mile crown. As a freshman at NYU, he had a 4:9.6 minutes time under his belt in the mile. In the weight events, Bill Watson of Michigan was a Big Ten champion in the discus, long jump, and the high jump. He won the AAU decathlon in 1940 and in 1943.

It had been a glorious run for these stars on campuses where all but a select few of the black students were athletes, or sons and daughters of professionals. For most of them, athletic talents were their entry to a prestigious education and a chance for honors on the track. After World War II, there would be new hurdles—racial and athletic—to overcome. White southern schools waited until forced by legal procedures to admit blacks in the early 1970s. At other institutions where blacks had already established a presence, new and subtler barriers to free expression surfaced to make campus life horrid in the 1960s. Some of those at white schools wound up organizing the most memorable protests ever mounted by black athletes, while continuing to burn up the track. For this new generation of runners, life would be, as it was for James Cleveland Owens, "A Hard Road to Glory."

Our Club Stars

Lest we forget, there were a few runners who did not go to any college at all, or who earned their honors while representing their home clubs. These organizations filled the gaps left by the limits of black colleges and the tokenism of white schools. Many of the clubs had been formed in the first decade of this century by middle-class blacks to field track squads and basketball fives. A surprising number of them were filled with upwardly mobile West Indians who were first-generation immigrants. All of them stressed education and "social" members—those joining for status, and so on—also made up a sizable portion of the total. The overwhelming majority of these groups whose members appear in national track listings were based in New York City, Philadelphia, Boston, Washington, D.C., Chicago, western Pennsylvania, and northern New Jersey.

R. Earl Johnson, for instance, who won the AAU 10,000-meter run from 1921 to 1923, represented Thompson Steel. He made the 1920 Olympic team, but was forced to quit in the fifteenth lap due to stomach cramps. Johnson may have been the first black Olympian to write a guest column for a black newspaper—the *Afro-American*—while at the Olympics. Tom Anderson represented New York City's St. Christopher Club in the weight events in the early 1920s. Louis Watson, a high jumper from the Alpha Physical Cultural Club, just missed qualifying for the Olympic team. Black America's first pair of top-flight marathoners were also club-affiliated. Many thought Clifton Mitchell of St. Christopher should have been selected to the 1920 team. Aaron Morris of the New York Runners club finished in sixth place in the Boston Marathon on April 19, 1919.

Cecil Cook, who won the 1925 AAU 400-meter run, represented Salem-Crescent, one of the oldest black clubs from Brooklyn. Louise Stokes, who was on the 1932 Olympic team, was a member of the Onteona Athletic Club in Malden, Massachusetts. The prowess of the Mercury Athletic Club members has been previously mentioned. As early as the 1920s, some athletes ran for their schools from September through the following June and then for a club. Ned Gourdin of Harvard ran for the racially integrated Dorchester Athletic Club of Boston in the summers.

A thorny problem for black clubs was their inability to receive AAU accreditation. Authorities simply refused to grant the credibility which ensued to sanctioned clubs. William DeHart Hubbard finally secured the first such sanction in 1926. This official recognition meant that clubs could then enter teams in AAU meets; they could hold meets themselves provided certain minimum standards were met; and they could certainly use their status to attract the best runners as members. When club memberships were impractical, some ran unattached. Archie Harris, for example, won the AAU discus title in 1941 though he belonged to no club. But that was rare and usually occurred in weight events.

The inability of blacks to form AAU-affiliated clubs in the South seriously hampered their track progress until well into the 1950s. Most efforts centered around the black colleges, but unless there were dynamic organizers like Cleveland Abbott to run them, a void resulted. In fact, not a single black AAU-affiliated club representative won a national title prior to World War II. However, the list of black national winners from northern clubs is lengthy, as is the list of southern-based black baseball teams. The irony is that while major league berths were barred to blacks until 1946, they nevertheless formed dozens of teams in the South. Track imposed no limits but southern blacks failed to show enough interest to take advantage of the opportunities. Against this background, the success of the Tuskegee women's squad in the late 1930s and early 1940s is even more extraordinary, coming as it did with exclusively home-grown talent.

After the war, club membership assumed more importance since the available college scholarships were limited at a time of increasing demand. But the commercialization of the sport at every level and the developing rivalry with the Soviets provided a niche for clubs with quality programs, quality coaches, and state-of-the-art facilities. Colleges just could not turn out enough record-breaking perfor-

mers. Later, as track participation became a vocation like any other with stipends and appearance fees, clubs dominated the list of national winners. For the black athlete, it all began in the early 1900s with far-sighted groups like Smart Set, St. Christopher, Alpha Physical Culture, Wissahickon Boys Club, and Salem-Crescent. A tremendous debt is owed them for leading the way.

The sustained success of black track and field performers between the two World Wars is well documented. Unlike baseball, football, and basketball, track—along with boxing to a large degree—allowed blacks to demonstrate their talents and be judged accordingly. Perhaps because the judging of track races is so objective, it was relatively difficult for white authorities to deny any talented runner his or her rightful place on the starting line. International competition such as the Olympics also served to force American officials to field the best team, regardless of ethnic or religious backgrounds. But, as just mentioned, two Jewish athletes at the 1936 Olympics—Sam Stoller and Marty Glickman—were denied opportunities in the 400-meter relay because a coach favored his own college pupil. This had happened to blacks for generations.

The post-World War II era is characterized by an all-out assault on the record books. More scientific methods of training, the sub-discipline of exercise physiology—unheard of in 1945—and computer analysis would result in new training procedures and techniques. Super performances from super athletes ensued as the Olympic Games were joined by other competitions like the Pan-American Games, the Asian Games, the Pan-African Games, the World

University Games, and the Commonwealth Games, among others, to show the world just how far, how fast, and how high men and women can truly move.

Notes

1. *New York Age,* 14 May 1927.
2. *California Eagle,* 14 March 1930.
3. Nolan Thaxton, *Documentary Analysis of Women's Track at Tuskegee and Tennessee State* (Tuskegee University, formerly Tuskegee Institute, Tuskegee, Alabama), p. 66.
4. *California Eagle,* 13 June 1925.
5. *Boston Telegram,* 25 May 1921.
6. *New York Telegram,* 21 August 1921.
7. *Chicago Defender,* 6 September 1930.
8. Henderson, *The Negro in Sports,* p. 54.
9. John Behee, *Hail to the Victors!* (Ann Arbor, Michigan: Ulrich's Books, 1974), p. 17.
10. William J. Baker, *Jesse Owens: An American Life* (New York: The Free Press, 1986), p. 12.
11. Ibid., p. 35.
12. Ibid.
13. *Norfolk Journal and Guide,* 8 June 1935.
14. *New York Times,* 2 June 1935.
15. Baker, *Jesse Owens: An American Life,* pp. 90-91.
16. Jesse Owens, *The Man Who Outran Hitler* (New York: Fawcett Gold Medal Books, 1978), p. 71.
17. Baker, *Jesse Owens: An American Life,* p. 104.
18. *Dollars and Sense* magazine (June-July 1983), p. 28.

Football

Football had a dramatic impact on the nation between the two World Wars. Next to baseball it was the most exciting sport and white college games, in particular, riveted the country's attention on fall Saturday afternoons. Black Americans also cheered for their heroes, although a quota existed which kept the number of black players to "agreeable" limits. The bravery of black soldiers in the First World War had not earned enough good will to allow their athletically gifted brethren to be chosen on merit alone.

Beginning in 1919, the saga of football until the end of the Second World War is, for blacks, three separate stories: their participation at white colleges, at black colleges, and a shameful and splintered twenty-seven years in the professional game. Through this period, blacks performed at a level much in excess of what their percentage of the total population would predict. If sports indeed related something of the character of the country between 1919 and 1945, then football was a less than satisfactory commentary on American life.

White College Experiences

Frederick Douglass "Fritz" Pollard and Paul Robeson were stellar names in 1918,

the last year of World War I. Pollard was the first black All-America running back and Walter Camp, the acknowledged "father of football," said Robeson was the finest ever to play the end position. But Pollard and Robeson were the legators of future generations of black players at white schools. The first so noted was the last Camp selection as Third Team All-America, Fred "Duke" Slater, a tackle at Iowa in 1919.

Slater played in thirty games and was an Iowa All-State pick four consecutive years. In 1920, Iowa was undefeated at 7–0. Slater moved up to Second Team All-America in 1921 in most selections and in his senior year, he was a First Team member in the International News Service, the Newspaper Enterprise Association, the Walter Eckersall All-America list, and the Walter Trumbull list for the *New York Herald*. In a famous game against Illinois in 1920, Slater even played without a helmet. He later played in the National Football League (NFL) before it banned all black players.

Joseph Collins of Coe College was another standout in the state of Iowa. His coach, Moray Eby, praised his running back in saying, "Collins is one of the best football players ever developed in the state of Iowa and I consider him on my all-time college eleven."[1] The third black Iowa-based player of the time was Edward Solomon "Sol" Butler of Dubuque, who had performed exceptionally well at the Inter-Allied Track and Field Games in Paris, in 1919.

Iowa sports buffs were impressed enough in 1918 that the December 15 *Des Moines Register* said this about these three performers: "The outstanding feature of this year's All-State selections is the fact that two Negroes, Slater of Iowa and Collins of Coe, are named on the first selection and that Butler of Dubuque College and Seminary, another Negro, is placed on the second eleven."[2] In one game for Dubuque (which also had a black trainer, B. Butler), Butler had a 100-yard punt return against Buena Vista.

These exceptional performances aside, some coaches were shunning the idea of playing blacks because of the problems attendant to their presence. Alumni groups, jealousies among the white players, and southern teams on their schedules were often more than the staffs were willing to handle. There were plenty of examples. Charles "Prunes" West of Washington and Jefferson was a star half back for four years, and was the second black to play in the Rose Bowl. But Washington and Lee (Virginia) demanded West be benched if they played in 1923. Washington and Jefferson's president S.S. Baker refused, saying, "I respect the tradition which Washington and Lee followed in refusing to play the game, but Washington and Jefferson is a northern school with traditions, too. It has never made any distinctions against color or creed in enrolling its students."[3]

The black press was quick to acknowledge Baker's stand. The October 23, 1923, *New York Age* noted that "...in acting to refuse catering to southern prejudice by taking Charles West from its lineup, [Baker] is heartening to colored people generally and colored athletes in particular."[4] In another example, Jack Trice, who played at Iowa State, died on October 5, 1923, of internal bleeding and a broken collar bone suffered in a game against Minnesota. Trice was deliberately injured in that encounter and his death occurred in a train taking him back to campus for treatment.

More slights began in the mid-1920s when the famed sportswriter Grantland Rice took over the All-America selections from Walter Camp. In twenty-eight years of picks, Rice selected only five black players: Jerome Holland of Cornell in 1937, Julius Franks of Michigan in 1942, Don Coleman of Michigan State in 1951, Ollie Matson of the University of San Francisco in 1951, and J.C. Caroline of the University of Illinois in 1953. How he could have left out William "Dolly" King of Long Island University (LIU), Kenny Washington of the University of California at Los Angeles (UCLA), and Wilmeth Sidat-Singh of Syracuse University, among others is strange indeed.

Another player who was supposed to be left out was Brice Taylor of the University of California at Berkeley (UCB). In the 1929 Rose Bowl, UCB lost to Georgia Tech who asked for Taylor to be benched. UCB refused. That same year, David Myers of New York University *was* left off his team not once, but twice—against West Virginia Wesleyan and Georgia. NYU's coach, John T. "Chick" Meehan, was brutally frank about Myers' choices. His black player could "...sit on the bench, or in the stands, or not come to the game at all if he did not want to."[5] Myers' black teammate, William

O'Shields, elected to sit on the bench. While at Ohio State, William Bell was left off his squad against—of all teams—Navy.

Matters got so bad that, from 1924 until 1937, not a single black player made All-America First Team selections. Ray Kemp of Duquesne University (Pittsburgh, Pennsylvania), the last black player in the NFL in 1933, was an Honorable Mention pick in 1929. But snubs aside, black stars on white college elevens were the best known in the nation and were apparently too visible on Saturday afternoons when America turned its radios to college gridiron contests. After Walter Camp died in 1925, his successors did not show the same objectivity.

In the 1930s, many schools had new stadiums to fill and more blacks were recruited to play. But sensitivities to racial wrongs were heightened. All black players suffered social discrimination, and housing was never convenient and mostly substandard. Student unions and co-operatives were frequently off-limits. Invitations to dances were not forthcoming and interracial dating was at the top of the list of no-no's and entirely clandestine if dared to be tried at all. Of course, the alternative was an almost complete absence of black co-eds enrolled. But on-field discrimination continued as well.

In 1934, Willis Ward of Michigan was benched in a game against Georgia Tech, but the entire campus came to Ward's defense. This support would not have happened a mere decade ago. The school's newspaper, the *Michigan Daily*, complained that Michigan's "...principles are incompatible with the South's position on racial differences. Let Michigan of the future play with those who are of her own eminently worthwhile type.'"[6] Athletic administrators did not interpret these slights so seriously.

Coaching staffs and administrators had treated benchings as so commonplace that the furor over Ward showed the callousness of their positions. Michigan's president, Alexander Ruthven, exclaimed that "My life is being made miserable by arguments with the colored brethren...."[7] To which the National Association for the Advancement of Colored People (NAACP) Assistant Secretary Roy Wilkins replied: "What about the feelings of Negro athletes who have carried the name and fame of the University of Michigan to the ends of the earth with Olympic victories?"[8] Well said, with Eddie Tolan, Michigan's double gold medal winner in the sprints in the 1932 Olympics in mind.

Michigan's coach, Fielding "Hurry Up" Yost, was believed by black America to harbor an aversion to using blacks when possible. Edwin B. Henderson clearly had Yost in mind when he noted in his 1939 edition of *The Negro In Sports* that "It is known that one of the coaches [Yost], although of national stature in his capacity, had been little inclined to use or be tolerantly fair to colored football candidates."[9] For his part, Yost said, "I never dreamed there would be so much agitation about the matter."[10] Ozzie Simmons at Iowa encountered problems as well.

Jerome "Brud" Holland of Cornell University was different. He was an exception and a brilliant one at that. He was the most acclaimed black player of the 1930s save possibly Kenny Washington of (UCLA). Born on January 6, 1916, in Auburn, New York, Holland had a deformity to his legs as a child which his grandmother helped massage away. After a superior showing at Auburn Academic High School, he was interested in attending Cornell by a local white YMCA official, H. Ralston Ross. He was the college's first black player when he entered in 1935, and two years later he was an All-America selection at the end position.

Holland's 1937 honors pointed out the difficulties facing black players when southern college elevens were beginning to catch up in publicity and talent. By the mid-1930s, every white sportswriter worth his salt felt confident enough to issue his own All-America list, but the most prestigious at the time—a decade after Camp's death—were the New York *Daily News* poll conducted by its sports editor Jimmy Powers, the Hearst Newspaper selections, and the *New York Times* picks. Neither the *Times* nor the Hearst polls selected Holland but the *Daily News* did.

The *Daily News* poll was the most complete. It was conducted among the leading sportswriters and Holland received fifty-two votes, of which twenty were from southern papers. Said the Associated Negro Press' (ANP) Al White of the *Daily News'* courage: "All credit to Jimmy Powers of the *Daily News* and the 113 sportswriters who helped pick the 1937 All-America football team, for in spite of fears that Southern newspapers wouldn't print the pictures of the team they selected, Brud Holland, the greatest end in the East...was named to that mythical eleven...."[11] As implied in White's comment, southern white daily papers refused to print the photos of blacks who excelled in anything except crime. (Similarly, music albums recorded by black

artists never had their faces on the cover for fear of offending southern customers.) In the final *Daily News* balloting, only Chuck Sweeney of Notre Dame, with seventy-seven votes, outpolled Holland.

The black community was beside itself after over a decade of relative neglect and kowtowing to southern writers who gained in influence. Holland, however, was so good that he was not denied his place in the sun. Edwin B. Henderson positively gushed in saying "...what a player Brud Holland was! A volume could scarcely contain the commentary complimentary to the skill, strength, endurance and sportsmanship of Holland...."[12] In company with Holland that year in All-America honors were Marshall Goldberg and a future United States Supreme Court Justice, Byron "Whizzer" White.

Sadly, Holland's career had to stop with his Cornell kudos, for even though the NFL began the college draft in 1935, Holland received nary an inquiry from the NFL because of its gentlemen's agreement against signing blacks. A few black players, like Joe Lillard of the University of Oregon, had continued with semi-professional squads here and there.

Ozzie Simmons was another star in the 1930s, at Iowa, whom the white press publicized and the black press made larger than life. Simmons hailed from Gainsville, Texas, and, like Holland, was enticed into attending Iowa by a former white alumnus of that school. In the midst of the Depression, the athletic exploits of blacks were touted as a viable way out of a dreary future. Said the February 15, 1936, *Pittsburgh Courier*, a black paper, of Simmons: "...if he stayed in Gainsville in faraway Texas? He might still have been a mechanic's flunkie in a pair of greasy overalls. He would have been thrown for heavy losses before he got started down the glamorous highway which leads toward greatness in football's glittering Hall of Fame."[13]

The implication here is that a poor southern black boy could not aspire to much else and that football glory at a white school like Iowa was better than menial labor, even though there was no professional future. It did not end that well for Simmons. He was roughed up so badly that he could not finish the full schedule of games. Two years later in 1938, Homer Harris was elected captain of the Iowa eleven.

Other names in the era of Holland and Simmons were sprinkled about by the press. Frank "Doc" Kelker had a spectacular two-year career at Western Reserve from 1936 to 1937 at the end position, and was an All-America on some lists. Following his bronze medal performance in the 110-meter hurdles at the 1936 Berlin Olympics, Frederick Douglass "Fritz" Pollard, Jr. starred at North Dakota for three years as running back. His father, Fritz Sr., was the first black running back named an All-America by Walter Camp back in 1916. Horace Bell played guard at Minnesota from 1936 to 1938, while his brother, William, was at Ohio State.

Bernard Jefferson was a standout running back at Northwestern University in 1937-38. Archie Harris was a premier end at Indiana in 1938. William "Dolly" King was a powerful fullback at Long Island University in 1937, where he lettered in three sports and reckoned to be one of the best athletes

ever seen in the East. In 1946, King became one of the first two blacks to break into the previously all-white professional basketball league.

The success of so many blacks prompted the black press to campaign for games between white and black colleges. Morgan State College, a black school near Baltimore, had a record so good that many believed a game between them and a white school could generate tremendous interest and goodwill. The October 17, 1936, *Chicago Defender,* another black paper, suggested "Why not a game between Race [Black] and White college teams? The sports fans would take to it with the same relish as they take a Black man and a White man in the ring,...or high school gridirons."[14] It never came to pass. But what did come to pass was a charity game at Chicago's Soldier Field on September 23, 1938, between the NFL's Chicago Bears and a representative aggregation of black stars from black and white schools. It did not, however, become an annual event.

After Jerome Holland, there were four very special players on the eve of World War II who captured the imagination of the entire country: Kenny Washington and Jackie Robinson of UCLA, Wilmeth Sidat-Singh of Syracuse University, and Julius Franks of Michigan. Of the four, Washington was the most acclaimed. He was born Kenneth Stanley Washington on August 8, 1918, in Los Angeles, and was a varsity player at Lincoln High School. Enrolling at UCLA in 1936, he was a three-time All-Pacific Coast quarterback, while lettering in baseball, track, football, and boxing. In 1939, this six-feet-one-and-a-half-inch, 210-

pound athlete led the nation in total offense and played in 580 of 600 possible minutes of play.

In 1937, his first varsity year, UCLA's record was 2–6–1, but in Washington's junior year it was 7–4–1, and the following year 6–0–4. He was joined on the team in 1939 by Jackie Robinson and other black teammates, Woodrow Wilson "Woody" Strode and Ray Bartlett. But the magnitude of Washington's respect by his fellow opponents was borne out in the 1939 *Liberty Magazine* poll for All-America selections. This periodical sent "all-players" forms to every letterman on the 110 major school teams. Varsity players were asked to select their toughest opposing player with two provisions: they could not pick a teammate and they had to select someone they actually played against.

In the January 6, 1940, issue of the magazine, the article read, "Only one player of the 664 named received the vote of every player who opposed him. He was Kenny Washington, UCLA's great halfback. One hundred and three players who competed against the Negro star agreed in the returns that he was the outstanding backfield man they met."[15] But, like Jerome Holland, he received no immediate professional offers. Nor was he selected an All-America by the Associated Press, United Press International, or Grantland Rice. Those honors went to Tom Harmon of Michigan and Nile Kinnick of Iowa, both white and deserving. Washington later played semi-professional football with the Hollywood Bears (California) in the early 1940s and with the San Francisco Clippers in 1944, before joining the newly integrated NFL in 1946. Of his

non-selection to the All-America teams or the College All-Star Game for 1939, Washington said, "It's unfair. It's because I'm a Negro that they don't want me to play."[16]

Wilmeth Sidat-Singh of Syracuse also had his troubles. He was born in Washington, D.C., and became the adopted son of a Hindu; hence the non-English sounding name. Singh was a phenomenal passer and had an arm that Grantland Rice described as a "howitzer."[17]

In 1937, Sidat-Singh was benched in a game against the University of Maryland, which refused to play against blacks. He could have headed for a brilliant professional career in basketball or football, but was killed in a plane crash while in the military. Two years after Singh's benching, Lou Montgomery of Boston College was benched three times—against the University of Florida, Auburn University, and Clemson University in the Cotton Bowl—in one season. But this time, Montgomery admitted the benchings were voluntary. He had talked things over with his coach, Frank Leahy, and told the *Chicago Defender* that "If I could play in the game [Cotton Bowl] and go about socially down there as I have all through high school and college days; in other words be free to be myself, I would love to go."[18] So he did not go. Montgomery's statement neatly summarized the dilemma facing all black players at white schools.

Less than ten months after Lou Montgomery's admission, another cause celebre surfaced over Leonard Bates' exclusion from a New York University game against Missouri. Bates, however, was told beforehand that he would not get to play in games against some opponents, the University of Missouri in particular. He admitted as much in a signed letter before accepting a scholarship to NYU. When knowledge of Bates' compromised position came to light, campus and other groups rallied to his defense. The most encouraging support came from Jewish student organizations; very few blacks were allowed to attend NYU at the time.

Speaking for the campus Jewish contingent, Zinko Funcich said, "This is not a question of Bates alone. This is a part of the discrimination against Negro and Jewish students. We have to remind Missouri that we fought the Civil War and this is a question of fighting it all over again—perhaps."[19] Even the former black All-America Paul Robeson pleaded for justice. In a telegram to the Negro Cultural Association, he wrote, "All American football stars deplore the reports of the gentlemen's agreement between NYU and Missouri University to discriminate against Bates."[20] To which NYU athletic director Philip O. Badger coldly replied. "...the petitions have nothing to do with it. I'll do what I want."[21] He did. Bates did not play.

Fortunately, Julius Franks, a six-foot, 187-pound guard did not have to be benched while he played at Michigan and was a *Colliers Magazine* Third Team All-America selectee in 1942—the twenty-fourth Michigan player so honored. He came along just as white college elevens were being decimated by the draft for World War II. Teams were skeletons of their former strength and attention turned to squads at the major training stations. There were six of these teams that caught the public's favor during the war: Camp Lee in Virginia; Great Lakes Naval Training Center on Lake Michi-

gan; McDill Field in Florida; Army Air Force in Hawaii; Camp Beale in California; and Fort Warren in Wyoming. While units of the army, navy, and marines remained segregated until 1948, the commanders at these posts allowed integrated teams in selected sports with few problems.

Paul Brown, who later coached the incomparable Jim Brown while with the NFL's Cleveland Browns, was also the coach at the Great Lakes Naval facility in 1944–45. The first black varsity player at this station was Graham Edward Martin, in 1943. Two years later, another showed up who would one day be classed among the best that ever wore a pair of cleats: Marion Motley of South Carolina State and the University of Nevada. The other five post teams were similarly constituted; that is, there were black teams and white teams, but for special occasions an integrated squad might be formulated.

Special mention must be made of a benefit game on Thanksgiving Day of 1945—November 22—when Bert Piggott, who had played at the University of Illinois, led the all-black Tuskegee Army Air Force team to a 14–7 win over the all-white Navy Submarine Base squad from New London, Connecticut. The contest was played on New York City's old Polo Grounds before 19,862 fans. It was well played and a grand time was had by all. Contests like this one provided clues to the coming re-integration of the NFL. President Franklin D. Roosevelt had issued an Executive Order to outlaw discrimination in employment and segregated sports had become test cases of his intentions.

There were a few others who graced the gridiron before the end of the war in 1945. William "Bill" Willis of Ohio State was

Tidye Pickett and Louise Stokes made the 1932 women's Olympic track and field team of sixteen—but were mysteriously replaced. Ms. Pickett (shown in Berlin in 1936) made the 1936 team, but was disqualified when in the heat her trailing leg hit a hurdle, breaking her foot. She was entered in the 80-meter hurdles. *(Courtesy of AP/Wide World)*

Jesse Owens on the victory stand after winning the long jump at the 1936 Olympic Games at Berlin. Note the official and Luz Long (silver medalist) giving "Heil Hitler" salute. *(Courtesy of AP/Wide World)*

Willis Ward, class of 1935 at the University of Michigan, was a football end and a sprinter in track. Shown here in 1934.
(Courtesy of the University of Michigan)

On Saturday, May 23, 1935, Jesse Owens put on the greatest one-man performance in the history of track athletics. He broke three world records and tied a fourth. At 3:15 P.M. he tied the 100-yard dash world's record in 9.4 seconds. At 3:25 he leaped 26 feet and 8¼ inches to break the broad jump record. At 3:34 he broke the world's record in the 220-yard dash in 20.3 seconds. At 4:00 Owens won the 220-yard low hurdles (shown here) in 22.6 seconds, establishing a new world's record in this event. *(Courtesy of AP/Wide World)*

Jesse Owens and Luz Long, after Owens' long-jump victory at the 1936 Olympic Games in Berlin, Germany. *(AP/Wide World Photos)*

Eddie Tolan, center, and Ralph Metcalfe, left, after finishing first and second in the 1932 Olympic Games 100-meter dash. *(AP/Wide World)*

William Dehart Hubbard in action at the 1924 Olympic Games, where he won the long jump. *(Courtesy of United States Olympic Committee)*

Frederick D. Pollard, Jr., after being selected to the 1936 Olympic team. He placed second in the 110-meter hurdles trials at Randall's Island, New York. *(AP/Wide World Photos)*

Archie Williams, right, wins 400-meter dash at the Berlin Olympic Games in 1936. Second was Arthur Brown of Great Britain. *(AP/Wide World Photos)*

"Long" John Woodruff, number 745, races to victory in the 1936 Olympic Games 800-meter run. Mario Lanzi, of Italy, was second; Phil Edwards, number 74, of Canada, was third. *(AP/Wide World Photos)*

James Luvalle, of UCLA, wins NCAA 440-yard dash at Berkley, California, in 1935. John McCarthy of USC was second, and Glenn Hardin, the favorite of Louisiana State, was third. *(AP/Wide World Photos)*

John Borican, former Virginia State University star, leads Glenn Cunningham across the tape in a special 1,000-yard race at Newark, New Jersey, in 1939. *(AP/Wide World Photos)*

Eulace Peacock, of Temple University, wins the 100-yard dash at the 1937 Penn Relays. His time of 9.7 seconds placed him first, ahead of Columbia University's Marty Glickman. *(AP/Wide World Photos)*

George Williams, of Hampton Institute, won the Penn Relays javelin throw by one inch—197 feet 1½ inches—in 1931. *(AP/Wide World Photos)*

Ralph Metcalfe, of Marquette University, second from right, equalled the AAU meet record in the 100-meter dash in 1934, in a time of 10.4 seconds. Jesse Owens, of Ohio State, was second. *(AP/Wide World Photos)*

What a pair! Jesse Owens and Ralph Metcalfe relax during the 1936 Central Intercollegiate track meet in June at Milwaukee. *(AP/Wide World Photos)*

Ralph Metcalfe, of the Marquette Club, Milwaukee, shown as he won the first heat in the 100-meter dash. Ben Johnson, of the New York Curb Exchange A.A., was second. The year is 1936. *(AP/Wide World Photos)*

High jumpers Cornelius Johnson, of Compton, California, and David Albritton, of Ohio State, aboard the *S.S. Manhattan,* en route to the 1936 Olympic Games. *(AP/Wide World Photos)*

"Flying" Ed Gourdin in mid-air during the 1932 Olympic Games at Los Angeles. His jump of 25 feet ¾ inch won first place. *(AP/Wide World Photos)*

Jesse Owens, the one-man track team from Ohio State University, is caught here by the camera, flying through the air to an "Olympic Triple" in the broad jump event at the Olympic Games in Berlin, 1936. *(AP/Wide World Photos)*

Jesse Owens cruising to victory in the 1936 Olympic trials. At far left is Mack Robinson of Pasadena, California, who finished second. Robert Packard, of Georgia, was third. *(AP/Wide World Photos)*

CLEVE L. ABBOTT

Cleveland Abbott, Tuskegee Institute's famed coach and athletic director. *(Courtesy of Tuskegee University)*

a tackle from 1942 to 1944. At six feet two inches and 215 pounds, he helped lead his school to a 9–0–0 record in 1944. He was also the first black player in the starting lineup for the College All-Star Game—in 1944. He later became the head coach at Kentucky State after a career in the NFL.

The aforementioned Marion Motley began at a black college, South Carolina State in 1939, but wound up at the University of Nevada. This Hall of Fame fullback from Leesburg, Georgia, lettered at Nevada from 1940 to 1942. Bert Piggott played at the University of Illinois. Paul Robeson, Jr., the son of the legendary Paul Robeson Sr., played at Cornell University. The brightest light toward the end of the war was shone by Claude "Buddy" Young of Chicago.

Young only played at Illinois two seasons—1944 and 1946—but he was nothing short of splendid. He had first attracted attention at Wendell Phillips High School where he won the city scoring title in 1943. In a highly publicized game against St. George, 80,000 fans appeared at Soldier Field to see him—in a high school game. At Illinois in 1944, he tied Harold "Red" Grange's single-season scoring record as a freshman with thirteen touchdowns. After a year in the army in 1945, he returned in 1946 and led Illinois to a 45–14 rout of UCLA in the 1947 Rose Bowl. He could do no wrong.

Black players had come quite a distance since the days of Fritz Pollard and Paul Robeson. There was still tokenism on white college teams in 1945, and certain positions were off-limits though teams still used one set of eleven men to play both offense and defense. Housing was still a problem on most campuses. On-campus dormitory or apartment units were prac-

tically impossible for black students to secure. In addition, their social life was difficult at best. Equipment had improved for everyone, the coaching was better, and most important, the prospect loomed that the NFL and the new All-America Football Conference (AAFC) would sign black players. But it was too late for Jerome Holland, Bernard Jefferson, and Ozzie Simmons, and others who deserved their chance for professional fame.

What they did leave behind was proof that the talent was there all along, and that discrimination alone kept them from reaching for the brass ring. They must have been partially consoled later when their black legacees took up the new challenges and excelled far beyond what anyone could have expected. Some, however, looked back in anger at all the wasted talent that could have thrilled us on Saturday and Sunday afternoons between 1919 and 1945.

Black College Play

The second era of black college sports began in 1912 with the formation of the Colored (now Central) Intercollegiate Athletic Association (CIAA), that represented some of the oldest institutions. But while this organizational structure was maturing, the physical infrastructure necessary for implementing its new plans was not in place. The legal provisions had been made in the second Morrill Act of 1890, to provide for what is termed "land grant" schools with state assistance. The black land grant schools (BLG's), however, never received their rightful share of monies.

By 1900, white southern congressmen were already siphoning off some of the funds meant for BLG's, and the feelings of many of them were summarized by the following comment from George T. Winston, president of North Carolina A&M (now North Carolina State), in 1900. Winston complained that "The wasteful expenditure of money for negro literacy education in the public schools of the South should be changed into profitable and useful training in industrial schools, shops, and farms...."[22] In Winston's mind, if black public schools were to be nothing more than institutions that taught the trades, then BLG's should not aspire to much more.

Thus all black colleges—and nearly all are located in the South—faced a growing demand for sports facilities with less than their rightful share of congressionally appropriated funds to help provide them. While the white land grant institutions (WLG's) were building stadiums, the BLG's were just "making do" with what was offered. In truth, part of the cost of the athletic facilities for the WLG's was financed by monies meant for the seventeen BLG's. The other privately funded black colleges were even worse off in athletic facilities.

Against this backdrop, the black schools began their athletic programs after the First World War, and football was the linchpin of the entire effort. Crowds were anxious to see rivalries renewed and Howard and Lincoln obliged in 1919, settling for a 0–0 tie as the famed Fritz Pollard coached the Lincoln eleven in front of 18,000 fans. Other Thanksgiving Day game rival matchups included Livingstone-Johnson C. Smith; Fisk-Tuskegee; Wiley-Prairie View; Virginia Union-Virginia State; and Hampton-Morgan.

These games were, without a doubt, the most "must see" events in black America at the time. The major black papers went all out to provide coverage. The *Pittsburgh Courier,* for example, sent five reporters to cover the Howard-Lincoln game alone; who was there, what they were wearing, and any gossip of interest. The trains that brought the fans were known as "flapper specials" and some were festooned with banners and ribbons. There was simply nothing like it until the Negro Leagues East-West All-Star baseball games began in 1933 at Chicago's Comiskey Park. Though a school like Howard had its own stadium, by 1922 it had to use Griffith Stadium—the major leagues' Washington Senators' home park—when it played against Lincoln.

The undisputed king of the first five years of this era was Franz Alfred "Jazz" Bird of Lincoln. He was built like Fritz Pollard, only five feet seven inches, and weighed 145 pounds, but he was nicknamed "the Black Red Grange." Lincoln did not lose to Howard while Bird was on the team. Bird's teammate, Robert W. Johnson, another running back known as "Whirlwind," later began junior tennis programs that helped produce champions Althea Gibson and Arthur Ashe. In 1926, Bird himself became the athletic director at Florida A&M in Tallahassee.

The decade of the 1920s was still plagued by rule infractions and a lack of parity among teams. Many games were forfeited and eligibility requirements were sometimes simply ignored. Equipment standards were frequently compromised. In 1924, Haywood "Speed" Johnson of Howard died at Freedman's Hospital in Washington,

D.C., of injuries in a game. That same year, Howard University withdrew from the CIAA because of a censure over the illegal use of Robert Miller on their team. Lincoln was censured in 1925.

Frankly, both schools cared more about winning and the money to be made playing each other than strictly adhering to the eligibility rules. Making note of this growing problem, Gideon Smith of the *Chicago Defender* wrote on January 24, 1925, "A student is in school to finish courses leading to some definite goal.... The tramp athlete cannot do this.... The CIAA has to rid itself of this type of tramp athlete.... If schools get in the habit of drawing out of an association and forming new ones, when rules pinch them a little, it will be impossible to form strong, lasting organizations."[23]

Rules or no rules, the acknowledged premier player in the history of black college football performed for Tuskegee, a Southern Intercollegiate Athletic Conference (SIAC) school, and played eight seasons. Yes, eight seasons. His name was Benjamin Franklin Stevenson and he was a six-feet three-inch, 215-pound running back from 1924 through 1931. In his career, he had forty-two runs of fifty or more yards and, in a 1926 game against Lincoln, he scored all of his team's twenty points for a 20–16 victory. Partly in response to Stevenson's longevity, the CIAA passed a rule in 1928 limiting a player's eligibility to four years; but some rules were broken anyway.

The black press was always tougher on CIAA schools. Its member institutions were the most well-known and it was supposed to set the standards for the rest. The individual schools, however, did not want to give up any of their autonomy. A plea borne of exasperation appeared in the November 22, 1929, New York *Amsterdam News* that chastised Howard for its transgressions: "The public expects the best of everything from Howard; the best scholarship, the best sportsmanship, and the best athletic competition.... President [Mordecai] Johnson alone is to be blamed for the miserable football team...this year. He cut out the training table a couple of years ago because he feared the survey being made by the Carnegie Foundation."[24] This *Amsterdam News* article was partly correct and partly incorrect.

As some semblance of parity crept into the college game in the latter part of the decade, Howard found it difficult to balance the use of declining receipts from football games with the demands of the players. In 1927, Howard's team went on strike because President Johnson suspended their special training table meals and room payments. (There were no real scholarships in those days for athletes.) The Board of Athletic Control then threatened to cancel the entire season if players did not report to practice by October 11. The players did return after meeting with Johnson.

Though this "Golden Decade of Sports" closed with the stock market crash of 1929, some of the players deserve mention. Milton Roberts, who has extensively studied these players and the records of the schools, had this to say about the following selected performers. Napoleon Rivers, end, of Talladega, had great hands, was smart, and was a good receiver. John T. Williams, end, of Langston, was quite tall—six feet four inches—and an exceptional receiver. Ted Gallion, tackle, of Bluefield Institute, was a superb tackler and played without a helmet. A. Louis Irving, tackle, of Morehouse, was a smart, natural leader; the silent type. And Harry "Wu Fang" Ward, halfback, of Wilberforce, was a powerful runner.

The powerhouse teams of the 1930s could look back on some correctable problems left over from the 1920s. Bluefield Institute was undefeated in 1928 and 1929; they defeated Morristown College (Tennessee) 129–0 in 1928. Wiley was also undefeated in 1928 and 1930. Fisk and Johnson C. Smith were unbeaten in 1929. In 1930, South Carolina State and Morehouse were similarly unbeaten or tied. If these scores sound like those of blockbuster schools, they are not. Conference opponents were still woefully inadequate and some schools were much richer in resources than others. The pressure to field football teams caused some to do so without a prayer of success; hence some one-sided victory margins.

Coaching was only marginally better at the end of the 1920s than just after the First World War. No players had to check in before the fall semester began as is the case today. Practice sessions did not start until the school year began, and the offensive plays were still relatively simple, since most students' positions were precarious anyway. The average game was still attended by fans, who more than likely stood rather than sat, and there were no public address systems. Concession stands served homemade ham and chicken sandwiches and lemonade out of paper cups. Most people brought their own food, though the tradi-

tion of tailgating had not caught on as yet. Like the basketball games of the New York Renaissance and the Globetrotters, football games were also social occasions where alumni and friends got together and partied for a long weekend.

The last two items of significance in 1929 were the first post-season bowl game sponsored by Prairie View A&M, and the appointment of Edward Paulette Hurt as coach at Morgan State. The former signaled the optimism felt by black college football in spite of the stock market crash. The latter proved to be the start of the most winning dynasty in the history of black collegiate games.

The Depression-dominated decade of the 1930s was marked by the play of Morgan State College under the guidance of Edward Hurt and his assistant, Talmadge L. Hill, and the general rise in the quality of play at all colleges. Morgan State, though, was in a class by itself. From 1930 until the eve of World War II, it won seven CIAA titles. From 1930 through 1935 its record was 41–3–4 and beginning in 1932, it amassed an unbeaten streak of fifty-four games—forty-seven wins and seven ties. It finally came to an end on Thanksgiving Day 1938, when Virginia State humbled them 15–0 at Petersburg, Virginia. This tied them for third place with the University of California for consecutive games without a loss. The record was fifty-six games held by Michigan. It was fitting that Virginia State broke the streak since they were one of only two other schools to win the CIAA title in the 1930s.

Hurt was part of that first generation of black college coaches to learn the scientific game in the 1920s. Like his fellow coaches at other black schools, he was a teacher first and foremost. He noted that "When I went to Morgan in 1929, I had no assistants, no help. And yet I taught and coached the football, baseball, and track teams, and then taught math. I don't know how, but I did it."[25]

As with his fellow black coaches, Hurt recruited everywhere he believed he could find good student-athletes. One of his stars, Otis Troupe, was plucked from a pool room. Said Troupe admiringly, "Coach Hurt went out and got the best athletes from both white and black high schools."[26] Two other big names who played under Hurt were Thomas "Tank" Conrad and quarterback Howard "Brutus" Wilson. Other CIAA standouts were halfback Ivory "Ike" Richmond and tackle Samuel "Thunderbolt" Gaines of Hampton; fullback Eugene Bailey, halfback Henry Briscoe; center Roscoe "Turk" Lewis of Virginia State, and Fred "Cannonball" Cooper, a running back at Virginia Union.

Partially as a result of Hurt's success, the Howard-Lincoln scrapes lost some of their fizz in the 1930s. In 1933, fewer than 5,000 fans attended, and no flapper specials were organized. They did not even play in 1936. The game was now Hampton-Morgan. Down South, Tuskegee continued its winning ways, dominating the SIAC. It won five conference titles under Cleveland Abbott, but this conference was decidedly weaker than the CIAA. Tuskegee and Morehouse were the most powerful in their area by a large margin. From 1916 to 1933, one of these two schools won its conference title all but three years. In Benjamin Stevenson's last year in 1931, Tuskegee was 9–0–1.

In the latter half of the 1930s, Florida A&M (FAMU), Alabama A&M, Alabama State, and Morris Brown improved their football fortunes in the SIAC. FAMU stars included fullback James Alonzo Adams, guard Roy Gant, quarterback Henry Butler, and halfback Stanley Strachan. Morris Brown boasted halfback William "Shag" Jones, tackle Major Powell, and, beginning in 1938, a five-foot seven-inch, 216-pound halfback named John Clifford "Big Train" Moody. During his time at Morris Brown, Moody averaged eleven yards per carry, scored thirty-nine touchdowns, and thirty-two extra points for a total of 266 career points.

Also in his own category was Alabama State guard William Coger. Coger was still in school while in his mid-twenties and, as a former miner, his strength was legendary. By all accounts, he could have played professional football with little or no adjustments. Down in New Orleans, Xavier University lineman Hiram Workman was described by Cleveland Abbott as "...the greatest tackle I've ever seen play in the South."[27] Workman's teammate, Madison Doram, could punt forty yards with either foot. It would have been inspiring to see some of these players in the NFL, but college varsity play was the height of their careers.

Out West, the SWAC schools had nothing to look forward to but football all year. From its beginning in 1921, only football awarded conference titles, until basketball and track were added in 1939. The most exciting event during this entire period was the 1936 game between Wiley and Prairie View in the Cotton Bowl in Dallas, Texas. That contest drew 20,090 fans, a record for a black college game west of the Mississippi River. The distances between schools in the SWAC conference made it difficult to play games on a regular basis, and there were no super highways in the mid-1930s. Conversely, the distance between Howard and Morgan State was about forty-five minutes in a car.

Wiley stars were fullback Elza "Tip" Odell and halfback Andrew Patterson. Southern University in Baton Rouge, Louisiana, claimed guard Reedy Spignor and halfback Raymond "Pelican" Hill. Bishop College in Dallas boasted guard Eulos Von Rettig. Langston (Oklahoma), which won four SWAC titles in the 1930s, had halfback Tim Crisp. Prairie View listed running backs Jeru Marks and Shelton Mason as standouts.

The South Central Athletic Conference (SCAC) was better known for its baseball teams. They did not award any football titles until 1930, and that initial distinction went to Tougaloo College. The SCAC was hampered by lack of funds and it had only one land grant school, Alcorn A&M, among its members. Their most illustrious player was from tiny Leland College, Eddie Robinson, who later became the most winning college football coach in history—black or white.

The Midwestern Athletic Conference (MWAC) began in 1932, and quickly assembled a powerful group of schools in a very short period. They had three BLG's— Kentucky State, West Virginia State, and Tennessee State—and two old and prestigious institutions—Wilberforce (Ohio) and Lincoln, which switched from the CIAA. None of these schools tried to field quality baseball squads but all were formidable in football, track, and basketball. Wilberforce won the first two MWAC titles and their heroes were Art Wilson and center Pat McPherson.

West Virginia, the 1936 conference winner, had guard James Ware and halfback Floyd Meadows in starring roles. Lincoln, seeking to regain lost glory, showed tackle Richard "Dynamite" Kane in their starting lineup. Tennessee State quarterback John Cox was noted for his accurate passing. Kentucky State won four titles and was acclaimed "National Champions" by the Chicago Defender in 1934 with a record of 7–0. It was not unusual for the leading black papers to name a national champion in this period, as was done for white colleges.

Some of Kentucky State's players were among the best ever. Ends William Reed and Robert Hardin were compared with Paul Robeson. Tackle William "Wild Man" Coleman was nationally known. Running back George "Big Bertha" Edwards terrorized opposing linemen. But the star of stars was quarterback Joseph "Tarzan" Kendall. Experts rate Kendall as the best Black quarterback before World War II and his prowess was further aided by a reduction in the size of the football in 1934. Milton Roberts said Kendall "...was the first great collegian, black or white, to feature the forward pass, anywhere, anytime, on the field."[28]

Kendall and his fellow players helped make the names of their colleges well known. Football was the primary means for favorable publicity for these schools since a black school's name would not ordinarily be printed in papers outside their local area. In particular, black papers like the Chicago Defender, the Pittsburgh Courier, the Kansas City Call, and even the California Eagle out in Los Angeles kept up with football results from these schools. How else could they hope to favorably reach as many people who may have known nothing of their programs. If it had not been for sports, many black schools would have been much less visible than they were.

Few of their playing fields held more than a few thousand people, but in the rural South a few thousand was noteworthy. Locker room facilities were distinctly no-frills. Officiating was still a problem as it was before the war, but it had improved since many ex-players served as referees. The most trying but discussed problem that defied solution was the naming of the aforementioned national champion.

Three difficulties arose: one, there were simply not enough inter-conference games to make a valid comparison; two, schools did not all play the same number of games per season; and three, there was no radio or television and the raters could not possibly see every game or team. Therefore, an impersonal method had to be devised. The schools decided to use the Dickinson Rating System which seemed to satisfy most critics.

Dr. Frank Dickinson's plan ignored such intangibles as weather, size of scores, the number of first downs, or the length of the visitors' trip. All that mattered was whether a team lost or tied a game. He divided conferences into first and second divisions; first division teams won more games than they lost during a season. Points were then awarded according to losses or ties against these first or second division teams, and percentages were computed accordingly. Teams were ranked by

their percentages provided at least six games were played. Dickinson's system was copyrighted and used by most black papers for national rankings.

As the Second World War began, the Dickinson Ratings were one item of constancy in a muddled five-year period. Equipment was difficult to acquire and teams were uneven because of the draft. The Howard-Lincoln rivalry resumed and Morgan State's stranglehold was now over. In 1940, Lincoln defeated Howard 63–0 and even used a white center, Ralph Oves, on its team. On December 6, 1941—just one day before the Japanese bombed Pearl Harbor, Hawaii—the Peach Blossom Classic was inaugurated in Columbus, Georgia. North Carolina College narrowly won from Morris Brown 7–6. That was an unusual score. In 1943, Morgan State defeated FAMU 50–0 in Washington, D.C.'s Griffith Stadium.

Selecting the All-America teams for black schools then was, as Fay Young of the *Chicago Defender* noted, "...like putting together a puzzle."[29] There was little disagreement, however, over the choice of superstars of the war years. That honor went to John "Big Train" Moody of Morris Brown and guard Herbert "Lord Herbie" Trawick of Kentucky State. As explained, Moody was one of the best ever witnessed. Milton Roberts called Trawick a "...devastating blocker...a mountain man on defense."[30]

Rounding out the roster of newsmakers before the war's end were Howard Gentry, a tackle from FAMU; Warren Cyrus, an end, and William Bass, a halfback, from Kentucky State; Jack Brayboy, an end, at Johnson C. Smith; tackles Heywood Settles and William Wysinger at Morris Brown; quarterback Clarence Pollard at Texas College; and center Ulysses Jones from Southern University.

After the war, black veterans returned to campuses but black colleges would start to lose more and more of their talent to white northern institutions. Though southern white schools did not admit blacks until the early 1970s, they offered less resistance to playing against them. Black colleges had to rethink their role in the totality of sports offered their students. Some took the necessary but regrettable step of abolishing football altogether. Others upgraded their entire system, changed conferences, and recruited more fiercely. The very process of recruiting was done informally and through personal contacts. Mel Glover, of Virginia Union University's "dream team" basketball squad in 1940, said that "No one had any money set aside to recruit in those days. A coach depended entirely on an informal network of friends who may have been former alumni or someone who wanted to give a poor kid from high school a chance for a college education. Most of us who went to public school in the North had never heard of half these Black colleges in the South. And when we got to these schools, we found out that a 'scholarship' really meant a job at the school and we were lucky to get it."[31] Glover had captained the basketball team at New York City's DeWitt Clinton High School.

By 1946, the success and positive images of Joe Louis, Jesse Owens, Claude "Buddy" Young, and the NFL's decision to readmit blacks to the professional ranks combined to offer the next generation of players more choices than ever before. But with these new opportunities came a new set of problems as racism became more subtle. There was still "A Hard Road to Glory" ahead.

The Black Professionals

The professional game had begun before the turn of the century, but it never threatened the college game. The play-for-pay performers struggled through haphazard scheduling and a relatively sparsely populated Midwest locale that made it difficult to attract crowds. At the end of World War I, however, some teams hoped to capitalize on the game's popularity by forming the American Professional Football Association (APFA). The APFA formally organized in 1919 with the 1912 Olympics star, Jim Thorpe, as president.

The first black professional was Charles Follis back near the turn of the century, but the first APFA member was none other than Frederick "Fritz" Pollard, the former Brown University running back, who signed to play for the Akron Indians in 1920. Pollard was one of thirteen blacks who played from 1920 through 1933 in the APFA and its successor, the National Football League (NFL). The NFL was organized from remnants of the APFA on September 9, 1921. But the year before, Pollard helped lead his Akron Pros (a name change from the Akron Indians) to a share of the APFA title with a 0–0 tie game against the Decatur Staleys in Cubs Park in Chicago. George Halas played right end for the Staleys which are known today as the Chicago Bears.

Players were not very trustworthy in that two-year period of the APFA. They jumped from team to team and this instability prompted the formation of the NFL. As the NFL gained in credence and financial backing, it, too, began thinking like major league baseball in regard to blacks. A glance at the full rosters of black players from 1920 through 1933 clearly illustrates the point. Only five teams in any one season ever employed blacks, and only in two years did any team have three of them—Milwaukee in 1922 and Hammond in 1925; yet black talent abounded.

Increasingly ingrained in the American consciousness in the 1920s was the idea that blacks and whites *should* have separate athletic agendas. In baseball, the Negro leagues began in 1920 and the major leagues encouraged the racially divided circuits through its new commissioner, Kennesaw Mountain Landis. In boxing, the former heavyweight champion Jack Johnson had so incensed white America by flouting its traditions that Harry Wills, the black number one contender in 1920, was never given his rightful shot at the title. On the track, a black speedster was not even considered for the Olympic team if he did not attend a white college. In basketball, ethnically homogeneous squads made more at the box office than mixed teams, however good they were. The so-called "Golden Decade of Sports"—as the 1920s were called—could more appropriately be termed the White Decade of Sports.

Of the names associated with this decade—Jack Dempsey, Gene Tunney, Bill Tilden, Bobby Jones, Red Grange, Babe Ruth—all were white.

Despite the discrimination, black players were stalwarts on their teams. As in the college game, one-platoon teams were the norm. Everybody played offense and de-fense. Pollard was a player/coach during his entire career in the APFA/NFL, sharing these duties with Elgie Tobin at Akron in 1920. He played long enough to see plenty of good and bad. Once, when he was denied accommodation at a Dayton, Ohio, motel, his teammates, "…which included a number of Southern boys, walked out."[32] After a winning effort against a team in the hills of western Pennsylvania one afternoon, the windows of the Akron team bus were shot out.

In 1922, Pollard helped organize, played for, and coached the new Milwaukee Badgers squad. He also coached at Lincoln University and returned to coach for the Hammond (Indiana) Pros. As the highest paid black player in the first half of the 1920s, Pollard was earning about $1,500 per game. After his playing days were finished, he became a theatrical agent and later owned an investment firm that was wiped out by the stock market crash of 1929. When his good friend Paul Robeson made the movie *Emperor Jones*, Pollard supplied most of the black talent for it. In 1935, he formed an all-black football team—the New York Brown Bombers, named for Joe Louis—and got involved in black professional baseball. In 1954, he earned some measure of vindication by being inducted into the National Football Hall of Fame.

Robeson played only three years in the NFL because he was earning enough money to pay for his law school tuition at Columbia University. Robert Marshall had played semi-professional football after starring at the University of Minnesota. Jaye "Inky" Williams played six years with four different teams; sometimes with two teams in the same season, which was not unusual then. The most important player in the NFL that decade, though, was Harold "Red" Grange, who was white and was the most acclaimed college player ever, while at Illinois.

He came to the Chicago Bears in 1925 after scoring thirty-one touchdowns in college, and immediately drew 35,000 fans on Thanksgiving Day. A week later, 70,000 came to watch him battle the New York Giants at the Polo Grounds. Grange was severely criticized in many quarters for turning professional as there still existed a stigma against it. So powerful was he and his manager, C.C. "Cash and Carry" Pyle, that they formed their own football association, the American Football League, in 1926, which lasted one year. He did, however, add needed legitimacy to the fledgling NFL.

Two years after Grange's debut, a shakeout of black players began under the guise of weeding out weaker teams and less experienced performers. Players were making about $1,500 to $1,800 per season and white players felt this much money should go to them. After all, was this not the way it worked in the major leagues? By 1928, Fred "Duke" Slater was the only black player for the second consecutive year when there were only ten teams. He was so good that no one could say he lacked experience or seniority. Slater became a Chicago judge after his playing days were over.

Joe Lillard's name is listed for only two years, 1932 and 1933, but he left his imprint on the NFL. He was all alone as the only black NFL player in 1932, and had brought a reputation of being a disciplinary problem. He graduated from Mason City (Iowa) High School and played at the University of Oregon. Nicknamed "the Midnight Ex-

press," Lillard had been suspended for two games when it was discovered he played semi-professional baseball for the Gilkerson Union Giants in the summer of 1931. He claimed he only drove the team bus, which does not sound very plausible.

His 1933 season with the Chicago Cardinals was tumultuous. In the first game, he faced the only other black player, Ray Kemp, of the Pittsburgh Steelers. Against Cincinnati on October 8, the six-foot one-inch, 185-pound Lillard was punched by Lester Caywood. He retaliated with an uppercut and both players were ejected, but the incident did not seem to affect his play. On October 15, he returned a punt fifty-one yards against the Bears. In taking advantage of a new rule legalizing all forward passes behind the line of scrimmage, Lillard was lionized by the critics: "One of the longest passes completed at Ebbetts Field this season was produced by the Cardinals' Lillard" in a 7-0 losing effort against the Brooklyn Dodgers.[33] In an earlier victory against Boston, 9–0, he had runs of twenty and ten yards, a drop-kick extra point, a forty-four-yard punt return, a twenty-yard kickoff return, and a ten-yard completed pass.

As Ray Kemp noted, "Joe could do it all—punt, pass, and run. He did it all with great abandonment."[34]

Kemp himself was the last black NFL player before the owners' gentlemen's agreement to follow major league baseball and ban all blacks. His brief time with the Steelers as a tackle was on-again, off-again. The six-foot one-inch, 215-pounder was released after the third game of the season by Art Rooney, and then recalled for the last three games. Rooney was quoted as saying he had to cut his squad and "Experienced men will be given preference."[35] In actuality, Rooney and other NFL owners were catering to demands from white players that blacks be dropped. The official reason given for the ban was that owners feared mass attacks on black players like that on Lillard.

Pollard, Lillard, and Kemp were swift with replies. Pollard angrily noted that "I played twenty years with white teams and against them, and was never hurt so I had to quit the game....I weighed only 160 pounds or so, and they never made me or Inky Williams quit either. So they can't say that's the reason they're keeping us out of the game..."[36]

Lillard was even more forthright in his criticism. "...The pro league and the way they are supposed to hand out the lumps is a joke. Why, I never got hurt among the pros like I did when I was in college."[37]

Kemp was equally dismayed. "...It wasn't long before I became aware of the fact that professional football too had its version of racism on both local and national levels...even though I received thunderous applause when I took the field in the Pirates' [the Pittsburgh Steelers were first known as the Pittsburgh Pirates] first game, and gave, evidently a rather outstanding account of myself, I soon was assigned to an off-again, on-again status...."[38] Kemp later became a professor of sociology at Tennessee A&I (now Tennessee State University).

The excuses given for the exclusion of blacks were all lies of course, but the ban applied just the same. Only the black press complained bitterly about it and life went on in the NFL. From 1934 through the 1945 season, no blacks played on nor were invited to try out for NFL teams. This twelve-year period has to be one of the blackest spots on the record of American professional sports. It was also the second time in thirty years that blacks were completely shut out of a professional sport; jockeys were banned by 1912. Boxing and track were the only avenues open for blacks at the time to reach their true potential; and those could only be realized with white managers. All NFL records should properly show asterisks besides any records made during this era.

At the end of the Second World War, blacks were again made a part of the professional game, though there still existed some racially stereotyped notions that they could only play certain positions. According to Joe Horrigan, the curator of the Pro Football Hall of Fame, the thirteen blacks who played from 1920 through 1933 were squeezed into just four positions: seven running backs, three ends, two tackles, and one guard. None came from a black college. Thus the impression was left (for over twelve years) that blacks were only good at certain positions and those from black schools were not very good at all.

These impressions were less troublesome on the West Coast where, by 1945, blacks were already playing on teams in the Pacific Coast Professional Football League (PCPFL). The PCPFL ranked second only to the NFL in importance and thirteen blacks played on six of its teams—the Los Angeles Bulldogs, the Hollywood Bears, the Oakland Giants, the San Francisco Clippers, the San Jose Mustangs, and the San Diego Bombers. Thus the PCPFL had technically reintegrated the professional game before the NFL rehired blacks. Two facts had made the hiring of blacks worthwhile: one, there was more demand for professional teams than the NFL could supply; and two, black players were not only drawing fans in the PCPFL, they were usually the crowd favorites.

Americans had money to spend during the war but few material things to spend it on. They enjoyed football but there was no NFL franchise west of Green Bay, Wisconsin. Arch Ward, the sports editor of the *Chicago Tribune*, helped to organize the All-America Football Conference (AAFC) and convinced over one hundred NFL players to switch leagues. With the stroke of a pen, AAFC teams began operating in Miami, Chicago, Buffalo, Brooklyn, New York City, Cleveland, San Francisco, and Los Angeles. To compete, the NFL moved its Cleveland Rams team to Los Angeles and, following the publicly stated intentions of the AAFC to do so, signed its first black players since 1933. What would the NFL have done if the AAFC had not planned to sign black players? Probably nothing.

The sport had grown in sophistication and public acclaim since the end of World War I. Now another world conflict forced Americans to focus on discrimination at home. Had not the Second World War been partially fought over ethnic prejudice and genocide? In time, football, especially the professional variety, would supplant baseball as the primary outlet for the sports fans' emotions. Believe it or not, America, black players became the object of most of that attention.

Notes

1. Henderson, *The Negro in Sports*, p. 119.
2. *Des Moines Register*, 15 December 1918.
3. Chalk, *Black College Sports*, p. 186.
4. *New York Age*, 23 October 1923.
5. Chalk, *Black College Sports*, p. 327.
6. Behee, *Hail to the Victors!*, p. 26.
7. Ibid.
8. Ibid.
9. Henderson, *The Negro in Sports*, p. 116.
10. Behee, *Hail to the Victors!*, p. 26.
11. Al White, *Associated Negro Press*, 1 December 1937.
12. Henderson, *The Negro in Sports*, p. 127.
13. *Pittsburgh Courier*, 15 February 1936.
14. *Chicago Defender*, 17 October 1936.
15. *Liberty* magazine, 6 January 1940.
16. *Daily Worker*, 18 October 1939.
17. Henderson, *The Negro in Sports*, p. 124.
18. *Chicago Defender*, 30 December 1939.
19. *New York Age*, 26 October 1940.
20. *Daily Worker*, 22 October 1940, p. 8.
21. Ibid.
22. William E. Truehart, *The Consequences of Federal and State Resource Allocation and Development Policies for Traditionally Black Land Grant Institutions: 1862-1954.* (A Thesis) Cambridge, Ma. Doctoral for Graduate School of Education, Harvard University, 1979, p. 86.
23. *Chicago Defender*, 24 January 1925.
24. *Amsterdam News*, 22 November 1929.
25. *Dollars and Sense* magazine (June-July 1983), p. 83.
26. Chalk, *Black College Sports*, p. 283.
27. *Associated Negro Press*, 23 September 1938.
28. Milton Roberts, *50 Years of the Best in Black College Football*, Monograph, *Black Sports*, June 1976.
29. *Chicago Defender*, 16 January 1943.
30. Roberts, *50 Years of the Best in Black College Football*.

31. Mel Glover telephone interview with author, 17 March 1987.

32. Ebony magazine, January 1972, p. 106.

33. New York Times, 29 October 1933.

34. Chalk, *Pioneers in Black Sports,* p. 226.

35. *Pittsburgh Courier,* 14 October 1933.

36. Chalk, *Pioneers in Black Sports,* p. 252.

37. Ibid.

38. Ibid.

Reference Section

AUTHOR'S NOTE: *Most of the reference data regarding collegiate athletic conferences from their formation to the present appears in* A Hard Road to Glory: The History of the African-American Athlete, 1919-1945, *this volume, which is the middle volume of this three-volume work. I decided to place this material here even though, chronologically, parts of it belong elsewhere, in order to allow the reader to find this comprehensive and critical information all in one place.*

KEY TO ABBREVIATIONS

C	Center		LB	Linebacker
D	Decision		LD	Loss by Decision
D	Draws		LF	Loss by Foul
DB	Defensive Back		LJ	Long Jump
DE	Defensive End		M	Meters
DMR	Distance Mile Relay		MC	Meter Champion
DMRT	Distance Mile Relay Team		MD	Meter Dash
DT	Defensive Tackle		MH	Meter Hurdles
E	End		MR	Meter Run
Exh.	Exhibition Match		MR	Meter Relay
F	Flanker		NC	No Contest
F	Forward		ND	No Decision
FB	Fullback		NDC	North Division Champion
G	Guard		NT	Nose Tackle
HB	Halfback		OD	Outdoor
HH	High Hurdles		OMR	One Mile Run
HJ	High Jump		P	Punt
HJC	High Jump Champion		PCC	Pacific Coast Champion
ID	Indoor		PV	Pole Vault
IH	Intermediate Hurdles		Q	Quarterback
KO	Knockout		QB	Quarterback
KOBO	Knockout by Opponent		QM	Quarter Mile
KO BY	Knockout by Opponent		R	Relay
L	Lineman		RB	Running Back
L	Loss		S	Safety

S	Sprint		WF	Win on Foul
SC	Steeplechase		WR	Wide Receiver
SP	Shotput		WT	Weight
SPC	Shotput Champion		YD	Yards
T	Tackle		YDHH	Yard High Hurdles
TB	Total Bouts		YDR	Yard Run
TE	Tight End		YH	Yard Hurdles
TKO	Technical Knockout		YHC	Yard Hurdle Champion
TJ	Triple Jump		YHH	Yard High Hurdles
W	Win		YR	Yard Relay
WD	Win by Decision		YRT	Yard Relay Team

OUTSTANDING AFRICAN-AMERICANS IN COLLEGE SPORTS
(1919-1945)

Bishop College
Dallas, Texas 75241

Coaches of Varsity Teams

Football

Collins, George 1923–25
Purdy, 1926–27
Mumford, A.W. 1927–30
Collins, George 1931–32
Taylor, Brice 1933–36
Weatherford, Fish Head 1936–37
Stevens, Jimmy 1937–41

Boston College
Chestnut Hill, Massachusetts 02167

Other Outstanding Athletes

Football

Montgomery, Louis[1]

[1] Montgomery, Louis-he was not allowed to make the trip with the Boston College football team to the 1940 Cotton Bowl in Dallas because of segregation. In 1941 he made the trip to the Sugar Bowl in New Orleans and was still denied the privilege to play

Boston University
Boston, Massachusetts 02215

Other Outstanding Athletes

Football

Chase, Jesse[1]
Forte, Moreland[2]
Smith, Chester[3]
Bernard, Roland[4]
Thomas, Charles[5]

Baseball

Crosson, George "Deedy"[6]

Track

Wharton, Clifton[7]
Franklin, Benjamin[8]

[1]Chase, Jesse—played on the 1934 Boston University team
[2]Forte, Moreland—played on the 1934 Boston University team
[3]Smith, Chester—played on the 1935 and 1936 Boston University teams
[4]Bernard, Roland—played on the 1938 Boston University team
[5]Thomas, Charles—earned nine varsity letters in three sports from 1939 to 1942
[6]Crosson, George "Deedy"—played on the 1922–24 Boston University teams
[7]Wharton, Clifton—captain on the 1921 Boston University team
[8]Franklin, Benjamin—captain on the 1938 Boston University team

Case Western Reserve University
Cleveland, Ohio 44106

All-American

Football

Keller, Frank "Doc" 1936

Other Outstanding Athletes

Baseball

Spencer, Booker T.[1]
Brooks, Robert A.[2]

[1]Spencer, Booker T.—played on the 1926 Case Western Reserve University team
[2]Brooks, Robert A.—played on the 1936 and 1937 Case Western Reserve University teams

Columbia University
New York, New York 10027

All-American

Men's Basketball

Gregory, George[1] 1931

Outstanding Athletes

Men's Basketball

Wood, Tom[2]
Skinner, Norman[3]

Baseball

Rivero, Manuel[4]

Football

Calloway, George[5]

[1]Gregory, George—first black American voted College All-American in basketball
[2]Wood, Tom—played for Columbia University in the mid-1940s
[3]Skinner, Norman—played for Columbia University in the mid-1940s
[4]Rivero, Manuel—played on the 1932 and 1933 Columbia University teams
[5]Calloway, George—played on the 1920 and 1921 Columbia University teams

Cornell University
Ithaca, New York 14851

All-American

Football

Holland, Jerome "Brud" 1937–38

Track

Robeson, Jr., Paul[1] 1944

[1]Robeson, Jr., Paul—Honorable Mention; 1946 IC4A Indoor High Jump Champion; also played left end and place kicker in football

Dartmouth College
Hanover, New Hampshire 03755

Outstanding Athletes

Football

Bullock, Matthew[1]
Shelbourne, John[2]

Baseball

Thompson, Harry[3]

[1]Bullock, Matthew—played on the 1901–03 Dartmouth College teams
[2]Shelbourne, John—played on the 1919–21 Dartmouth College teams
[3]Thompson, Harry—played on the 1919 Dartmouth College team

Dusquesne University
Pittsburgh, Pennsylvania 15282

Outstanding Athletes

Football

Kemp, Ray[1]
Shelton, Buzz[2]
Velar, Simeon[3]

Other Outstanding Athletes

Jackson, Bruce[4]

[1]Kemp, Ray—first black American to play football at Duquesne University, 1929–31
[2]Shelton, Buzz—competed in football in 1926
[3]Velar, Simeon—competed in football in 1926
[4]Jackson, Bruce—athletic trainer

Florida A&M University
Tallahassee, Florida 32207

Athletic Directors

Bragg, J.B.
Bell, William

Coaches of Varsity Teams

Football

Sampson, George 1920–22
Bragg, J.B. 1922–25
Byrd, Franz 1925–30
Bragg, J.B. 1930–32
Wright, Theodore 1932–33
Bragg, Eugene 1934–36
Bell, William 1936–44
Gaither, Alonzo "Jake" 1944–45

Baseball

Sampson, George 1920–23
Griffin, Peter 1940–45

All-American (Black College)

Football

Bragg, Eugene 1926
Calhoun, Soloman 1934
Everett, James 1934–35
McKeekins, Alphonso 1937

Butler, Henry 1938
Neely, Murray 1938
Griffin, Robert "Pete" 1938
Jones, Tom 1938
Mays, Jesse 1939
Strachan, Stanley 1939
Horton, William 1940
Gentry, Howard 1941
Gant, R.R. 1941
Williams, Macon 1942
Howard, John A. 1944
Ingraham, Bernard 1945
Cromartie, Leroy 1945

Fort Valley State College
Fort Valley, Georgia 31030

Athletic Directors

O'Shields, William D. 1941

Coaches of Varsity Teams

Football

Brwaters, Sr., Leroy 1920
Richardson, Richard 1920
Beasley, Robert 1930
Horne, Frank 1930
Alexander, Ernest 1939–40
O'Shields, William D. 1942–45

Grambling State University
Grambling, Louisiana 71245

Coaches of Varsity Teams

Football

Jones, Ralph Waldo Emerson 1926–32
Smith, Ira 1932–33
Williams, Joe 1933–34
Johnson, Osiah 1934–35
Hines, Emory 1935–40
Robinson, Ed 1941–46

Baseball

Jones, Ralph Waldo Emerson 1926–46

Hampton University
Hampton, Virginia 23668

Coaches of Varsity Teams

Football

Smith, Gideon 1921–40
Griffin, Sr., James 1941–42
Moore, Sylvius 1943–44
Neilson, Herman 1945–46

All Central Intercollegiate Athletic Association

Football

Butler, Adee 1923
Coleman, Theodore 1923
Lee, William 1923–27
Pindle, O.A. 1925
Alexander, James 1925
Davis, George 1925–26
Williams, William 1926
Munday, Reuben 1926
Robinson, Theodore 1927
Gates, Harold 1928
Hill, Carl 1928
Jones, Oscar 1928
Perkins, Sylvester 1928
Gaines, Samuel 1928–31
McGowan, Charles 1929
Thomas, Maxwell 1930
Edwards, 1931
Rivers, George 1931–32
Unthank, James 1931–33
Richmond, Ivory 1933
Owens, Larney 1936
Hopson, Raymond 1936
Griffin, James 1939
Stuart, James 1939–40
Grice, William 1941
Ware, David 1942
King, Robert 1942
Mann, Robert 1943

Harvard University
Cambridge, Massachusetts 02138

Outstanding Athletes

Baseball

Brown, Earl[1]

[1]Brown, Earl—played on the 1923 Harvard University team

Howard University
Washington, D.C. 20059

Coaches of Varsity Teams

Football

Morrison, Edward 1920–23
Watson, Louis 1923–24
Morrison, Edward 1924–25
Watson, Louis 1925–28
Morrison, Edward 1928–29
Verdell, Tom 1929–34
West, Charles 1934–36
Payne, Harry 1936–41
Rowland, James 1941–43
Chambers, James "Ted" 1944–45

Men's Basketball

Morrison, Dr. Ed 1920–23
Burr, Jr., John H. 1923–30
Waller, Aubrey O. 1930–31
Burr, Jr., John H. 1931–46

Tennis

Davis, 1941–45
Tyrance, Herman J. 1945–46

Track

Morrison, Edward 1920–23
Watson, Louis 1924–25
West, Charles 1926–27
Verdell, Tom 1930
Burr, John C. 1936–38
Payne, Harry 1938
Chase, 1942

Swimming

Pendelton, Sr., Clarence M. 1928

All Central Intercollegiate Athletic Association

Football

Doweby, Charles 1923
Marshall, John 1930
Ware, Joseph 1933
Cole, Joseph 1933
Gaither, Booker 1934
White, Robert 1937

Indiana University
Bloomington, Indiana 47405

Outstanding Athletes

Football

Lyons, Fitzhugh[1]
Babb, Jesse[2]

[1]Lyons, Fitzhugh—played on the 1931–33 Indiana University football teams
[2]Babb, Jesse—played on the 1932–33 Indiana University football teams

Iowa University
Iowa City, Iowa 52242

All-American

Football

Simmons, Ozzie 1935

Other Outstanding Athletes

Football

Galloway, LeDrue[1]

[1]Galloway, LeDrue—played on the 1927 Iowa University football team

Jackson State University
Jackson, Mississippi 39217

Athletic Directors

Pinkett, John R. 1920–25
Lawson, B.V. 1925–39
Ellis, T.B. 1939–46

Coaches of Varsity Teams

Football

Bragg, 1911–20
Richards, Earnest 1920–25
Lawson, B.V. 1925–38
Ellis, T.B. 1939–46

Johnson C. Smith University
Charlotte, North Carolina 28216

Coaches of Varsity Teams

Football

Williams, "Silent Wop" 1926
Thomas, John F. 1930
Byarm, Lonnie P. 1931–32
Griffin, William 1933–35
Penn, Herbert 1936
Jackson, Edward 1937–44
Bynum, George O. 1945

All Central Intercollegiate Athletic Association

Football

Bogle, John 1930
Meadows, Milton 1937–39
Powell, Kenneth 1940
Brayboy, Jack 1940–42
Malone, Garland 1942
Fletcher, Elbie 1942
Fisher, James 1944
Taylor, Christopher 1944
Turner, Ed 1945

Kentucky State University
Frankfort, Kentucky 40601

Athletic Directors

Kean, Henry Arthur 1931–32
Willis, William 1945–46

Coaches of Varsity Teams

Football

Evans, Durall B. 1921–24
Harper, Jr., Louis J. 1924–25

Brown, Scott 1926
Vaught, Roscoe C. 1927
Williams, John T. 1928–30
Kean, Henry Arthur 1931–42
Passmore, Norman 1944
Willis, William 1945

All Mid-Western Conference

Football

Hackett, 1935
Davidson, 1935
Kendall, Joe 1935
Corbin, Richard "Nick" 1945

All-American (Black College)

Football

Coleman, William 1932–34
Bumphas, Alphonso 1934
Davidson, William "Bus" 1934
Hardin, Robert 1934
Edwards, George "Big Bertha" 1934–37
Kendall, Joe 1937–38
Toomer, Eugene 1938
Scaife, William 1938
Bailey, Melvin 1939
Rogers, Redford 1939
Thurman, Hoy 1941
Trawick, Herbert 1941
George, Warren 1941
Cyrus, Warren 1942

Women's Basketball

Serrell, Viola 1936–42

Lincoln University
Lincoln University, Pennsylvania 19352

Athletic Directors

Grim, Harold F. 1920–33
Rivero, Manuel 1934–46

Coaches of Varsity Teams

Football

Robeson, Paul 1920
Shelburne, J. 1921

Law, J.H. 1922
Young, U.S. 1923–26
Morrison, W.E. 1927–28
Taylor, William S. 1929–31
Smith, E.M. 1932
Martin, Julie F. 1933
Rivero, Manuel 1934–46

Basketball

Law, J.L. 1922–23
Walls, Ted 1927–28
Taylor, William S. 1929–32
Martin, Julius 1933–34
Ballard, C. 1934–38
Rivero, Manuel 1939–46

Wrestling

Bryant, "Panicky" 1934
Jones, Charles "Chuck" 1935
Turner, Jasper 1938–39
Holland, Jerome 1940–42
King, Benny 1943

Boxing

Bryant, "Panicky" 1933–34
Jones, Charles 1934–35
Turner, Jasper 1936–38
Holland, Jerome 1939–42
Pearcy, Milton 1942–43

Baseball

Grim, Harold 1920–26

All Central Intercollegiate Athletic Association

Football

Lee, Tom 1926
Goodman, George 1926
Kane, Richard (Sugar) 1931
Bergen, C.W. 1933
Brown, Wendell 1937

All-American (Black College)

Football

Bellinger, Charles 1921
Williams, Bruce 1921
Johnson, Dr., Robert "Whirlwind" 1924
Byrd, Franz "Jazz" 1925

Wood, Rev., William D. "Stye" 1925
Crudup, Byrd, D. 1925
Lancaster, Theo W. 1926
Martin, Julius 1928
Kane, Richard "Sugar" 1933

Livingstone College
Salisbury, North Carolina 28144

Athletic Directors

Willis, Arthur 1931–33
Gill, Robert L. 1933–34
Parker, Harry K. 1934–35
Barnes, Samuel 1936–41

Coaches of Varsity Teams

Football

Gill, Robert L. 1921–26, 1933–34
Parker, Harry K. 1934–35
Barnes, Samuel 1936–41
Hargreaves, Benjamin 1941
Peterson, Earl 1942–46

Long Island University
Brooklyn, New York 11201

Outstanding Athletes

King, William "Dolly"—played on the 1936, 1937 Long Island University basketball and baseball teams

Marquette University
Milwaukee, Wisconsin 53233

Outstanding Athletes

Track

Metcalfe, Ralph[1]

[1]Metcalfe, Ralph—member of the 1936 United States Olympic team

Morgan State University
Baltimore, Maryland 21239

Athletic Directors

Hurt, Eddie 1929–45

Coaches of Varsity Teams

Football

Laws, James 1923–25
Drew, Dr. Charles 1926–27
Taylor, William 1928
Hurt, Eddie 1929–45

Trainers

Hammond, Wally 1927–32

All-American (Black College)

Football

Williams, James 1933
Conrad, Thomas "Tank" 1934
Troupe, Otis 1936

Men's Basketball

Jones, Ed "Lanky" 1930
Wheatley, Thomas "Rap" 1930

All Central Intercollegiate Athletic Association

Football

Conrad, Thomas 1931
Wilson, Howard 1933
Williams, Jams 1933
Crawford, Hubert 1933–34
Drake, Carl 1934
Troupe, Otis 1934
Sowell, Richard 1936–37
Mosby, Walter 1936–37
Lampkin, William 1937
Ryans, Mason 1938
Gordon, Frank 1938
Holly, Waymond 1939
Mosby, Wallace 1939–41
Kee, Horace 1940
Cain, William 1940
Fauntleroy, Arthur 1941, 1946–47
Givens, Oscar 1941–42, 1946
Grimsley, Preston 1942
Couch, Flan 1943
Irvin, Calvin 1943
Gaines, Clarence 1943–44
Burgess, Fred 1943–44
Frazier, Charles 1944
Day, Terry 1944
Rahming, E. 1945

North Carolina
Agricultural and Technical State University
Greensboro, North Carolina 27411

Coaches of Varsity Teams

Football

Byarm, Lonnie 1925–29
Jefferson, Harry 1930–31
Breaux, Inman 1932–38
Harris, Homer 1939–40
Bernard, Roland 1941
Deberry, Morrow 1942
Bell, Horace 1945

All Central Intercollegiate Athletic Association

Football

Coleman, Herman 1925–27
Miller, Jesse 1926
Hester, Clarence 1926
Patterson, M.E. 1927
Miller, J. 1927
Streeter, J.A. 1927
Lane, J.F. 1927–28
Horsey, Julius 1934
Norman, McHenry 1934
Lynch, Allen 1938
Bruce, Sam 1939
Clarke, Earl 1941
Gearing, Roy 1943
Weaver, Charles 1944–46
Childs, Leroy 1945

All-American (Black College)

Football

Weaver, Charles 1945

North Carolina Central University
Durham, North Carolina 77707

Athletic Directors

McLendon, John 1942–45

Coaches of Varsity Teams

Football

Eagleson, Wilson V. 1923–26

Waters, Benny 1927–28
Crudup, B.D. 1929–31
Townsend, Leo 1931–35
Adams, E.H. 1936
Burghardt, William F. 1937–41
Turner, E.C. 1942

Basketball

Crudup, B.D. 1928–29
Waters, David, 1930–31
Townsend, Leo 1935–36
Adams, E.H. 1936–37
Burghardt, William F. 1937–40

All Central Intercollegiate Athletic Association

Football

Malone, William P. 1932
Holmes, Irwin 1933
Alston, Edward 1934
Peerman, William 1940
Hall, William 1941
Mack, George 1941
Gaines, William 1941–42

Northeastern University
Boston, Massachusetts 02115

Outstanding Athletes

Baseball

Chandler, G. Lewis[1]
Simms, Leslie[2]

Fencing

Henry, Richard[3]

[1]Chandler, G. Lewis—played for the 1925 and 1926 Northeastern University teams
[2]Simms, Leslie—played for the 1925 and 1926 Northeastern University teams
[3]Henry, Richard—competed on the 1926 Northeastern University team

Northern Illinois University
DeKalb, Illinois 60115

Other Outstanding Athletes
Cooper, Elzie[1]

[1]Cooper, Elzie—believed to be the first black athlete to play any sport or win a letter at Northern Illinois University, 1933–36

Northwestern University
Evanston, Illinois 60201

Outstanding Athletes

Football

Taylor, Samuel[1]
Vedeu, Tom[2]
Hinton, Clarence[3]
Jefferson, Bernard[4]
Cross, Irv

Baseball

Taylor, Samuel[5]

[1]Taylor, Samuel—played on the 1922 team
[2]Vendeu, Tom—played on the 1927 and 1928 teams
[3]Hinton, Clarence—played on the 1935–37 teams
[4]Jefferson, Bernard—played on the 1936–38 teams
[5]Taylor, Samuel—played on the 1927 team

Ohio State University
Columbus, Ohio 43210-1166

All Big-Ten Conference

Football

Bell, William 1931

All-American

Football

Willis, Bill 1944

Track

Owens, Jesse[1] 1936
Albritton, David[2] 1936–38
Walker, Melvin—HJ 1936

[1]Owens, Jesse—member of the 1936 United States Olympic track and field team
[2]Albritton, David—High Jump; winner of three NCAA titles; member of the 1936 United States Olympic track and field team

Ohio University
Athens, Ohio 45701

Other Outstanding Athletes
Central Intercollegiate Athletic Association

Football

Jefferson, Harry[1]

[1]Jefferson, Harry—first commissioner of the Central Intercollegiate Athletic Association; played football at Ohio University in 1922

Princeton University
Princeton, New Jersey 08544

Outstanding Athletes

Wilson, Arthur[1]

[1]Wilson, Arthur—first black basketball player in Princeton University history, 1942

San Diego State University
San Diego, California 92182

All-Southern California Intercollegiate Athletic Conference (SCIAC)

Men's Basketball

Moss, Clinton 1935

Savannah State College
Savannah, Georgia 31404

Coaches of Varsity Teams

Football

Richardson, Richard 1929–35
Dwight, Arthur 1935–39
King, W. McKinley 1940–41
Myles, John 1942–46

Men's Basketball

Richardson, Richard 1928–34
Dwight, Arthur 1934–40
King, W. McKinley 1940
Bruce, Clarence 1941
Myles, John 1942

Women's Basketball

Lester, Janie 1927–39

All-South Atlantic Athletic Conference

Football

Battle, David 1941

Shaw University
Raleigh, North Carolina 27611

All Central Intercollegiate Athletic Association

Football

Gill, H.H. 1924
Martin, J.T. 1925
Govan, Claude 1938
Worthy, Fred 1941

South Carolina State University
Orangeburg, South Carolina 29117

Coaches of Varsity Teams

Football

Brooks, Robert 1932
Dawson, Oliver C. 1940–42

Southern University
Baton Rouge, Louisiana 70813

Athletic Directors

Mumford, A.W. 1936–46

Coaches of Varsity Teams

Football

Mumford, A.W. 1936–46

Basketball

Mumford, A.W. 1937–46

Syracuse University
Syracuse, New York 13210

Outstanding Athletes

Football

Jackson, Chester[1]
Sidat-Singh, Wilmeth[2]

[1] Jackson, Chester—played on the 1928 Syracuse University Team
[2] Sidat-Singh, Wilmeth—starred in football and basketball 1936-39 at Syracuse University

Temple University
Philadelphia, Pennsylvania 19122

Outstanding Athletes

Track

Peacock, Eulace[1]
Threadgill, Albert[2]
[1]Peacock, Eulace—competed for Temple University 1935–38; broad jump
[2]Threadgill, Albert—competed for Temple University 1937–38; high jump

Tennessee State University
Nashville, Tennessee 37203

Athletic Directors
Kean, Henry Arthur, Sr. 1943–45

Coaches of Varsity Teams

Football

Scruggs, Joe E. 1920–24
Davenport, George 1925–26
Gales, Felton "Zip" 1927
Long, Harry 1928
Jackson, Alton 1929
Vaughn, Joe 1929
Upshaw, T.D. 1930–31
Benjamin, Harry 1932
Davis, Walter S. 1933–36
Mundy, Reuben 1937
Simmons, Lawrence 1938–39
Kean, Henry A. 1944–45

Basketball

Kean, Henry A. 1945–46

Boxing

Harris, Tom 1944

Men's Track

Harris, Tom 1945–46

All-Mid-Western Conference

Football

Drummond, Robert 1945
Bolden, John 1945
Bass, William 1945
Whitmon, Raymond 1945
Wynn, Earl 1945

All-American (Black College)

Football

Strange, Forrest—the first All-American at Tennessee State
University 1934
Cox, William 1935
Umphrey, Albert 1936–37
Braudnex, William 1937
Harris, Jimmie 1937
Bass, William 1944–45
Drummond, Robert 1945

University of California, Berkeley
Berkeley, California 94720

Coaches of Varsity Teams

Football

Gordon, Sr., Walter A. (Assistant) 1937–39, 1941–43

University of California, Los Angeles
Los Angeles, California 90024

All Coast

Football

Strode, Woody 1939
Washington, Ken 1939

All Pacific Coast Conference (Southern Division)

Basketball

Robinson, Jack 1940

University of Colorado
Boulder, Colorado 80309

Other Outstanding Athletes

Track

Croter, Gill[1]
Walton, Claude[2]

[1]Croter, Gil—competed in track, 1936
[2]Walton, Claude—compete in track, 1937

University of Illinois, at Urbana-Champaign
Champaign, Illinois 61820

All-American

Football

Young, Claude "Buddy" 1944

University of Maryland, Eastern Shore
Princess Anne, Maryland 21853

Athletic Director

Johnson, Dr. R. C. 1939–46

University of Michigan
Ann Arbor, Michigan 48109

All-American

Football

Franks, Julius 1942

Track

Hubbard, William Dehart[1] 1924
Tolan, Thomas "Eddie"[2] 1932

Other Outstanding Athletes

Track

Brooks, Booker
Ward, Willis

[1]Hubbard, William Dehart—member of the 1924 United States Olympic track and field team; the first black American to win a Gold Medal in the Olympics
[2]Tolan, Thomas "Eddie"—member of the 1932 United States Olympic track and field team

University of Minnesota
Minneapolis, Minnesota 55455

Outstanding Athletes

Football

Harpole, Ellsworth[1]
Bell, Horace[2]
Reed, Dwight[3]

[1]Harpole, Ellsworth—played on the 1932 team
[2]Bell, Horace—played on the 1936–38 teams
[3]Reed, Dwight—played on the 1935–37 teams

University of Oregon
Eugene, Oregon 97403

All Pacific Coast

Men's Track

Robinson, Robert—NDC, PV 1929
Robinson, Mack—BJ, PCC 1938
Browning, Allen—NDC, 100/200 YD 1943

All-American

Men's Track

Robinson, Mack[1] 1938

[1]Robinson, Mack—1938 NCAA champion, 200-meter dash; member of the 1936 United States Olympic track and field team

University of Pennsylvania
Philadelphia, Pennsylvania 19104

Outstanding Athletes

Track

Jones, Ed[1]
Rogers, C. Dewey[2]
Granger, Lloyd[3]
Alexander, Raymond P.[4]

Men's Basketball

Wideman, John E.[5]

[1]Jones, Ed—ran track from 1919 to 1921
[2]Rogers, C. Dewey—ran track from 1919 to 1921
[3]Granger, Lloyd—ran track from 1919 to 1921
[4]Alexander, Raymond P.—ran track from 1920
[5]Wideman, John E.—Rhodes Scholar; Big-Five Hall of Fame

University of Pennsylvania, at Cheyney
Cheyney, Pennsylvania 19319

Coaches of Varsity Teams

Men's All Sports

Rafer, 1920–23
Brown, Theodore R. 1925–27
Williamson, James C. 1928–46

University of Pittsburgh
Pittsburgh, Pennsylvania 15213

Outstanding Athletes

Men's Track

Woodruff, John Y.[1]

[1] Woodruff, John Y.—member of the 1936 United States Olympic track and field team.

University of Southern California
Los Angeles, California 90089-0602

All-American

Football

Taylor, Brice 1925

Virginia State University
Petersburg, Virginia 23803

Coaches of Varsity Teams

Football

Watson, Louis 1921–22
Graves, H. 1923
Lawrence, Jesse 1923
Johnson, W.R. 1924
Hurt, Ed 1925–28
Thompson, Ted 1929
Williams, Jesse 1930–31
Cook, Tindolph 1933
Jefferson, Harry 1934–45

All Central Intercollegiate Athletic Association

Football

Brown, Governor 1925
Slaughter, Tanner 1925–27
Dabney, Red 1928, 1930–31
Shelton, James 1928
Pegram, Richard 1928
Royall, Samuel 1929
Lee, Albert 1929
Oliver, Basil 1929–30

Bounds, Earl 1929–30, 1932
Johnson, L.M. 1929–31
Lewis, Roscoe 1930–32
Scott, Cabell 1931
Boyd, Theodore 1932
Dixon, Richard 1936
Craddock, Claiborne 1936–37
Briscoe, Henry 1936–38
Brewer, James 1937–39
Lamb, George 1938
Brewer, John 1938
Nelson, James 1938
Bartee, Lawrence 1939
Harris, Donald 1940
Carter, Oscar 1941
Hurley, Walter "Doc" 1942, 1946–47
Williams, Charles 1942
Battle, David 1943, 1945
Ferebee, Melvin 1943
Perry, General 1944
Porter, Leroy 1944
Taylor, Morris 1944
Whaley, Benjamin 1944–48
Price, Charles 1945
Jolly, Francis 1945

Virginia Union University
Richmond, Virginia 23220

Coach of Varsity Teams

Football

Hucles, Henry 1920–42

All Central Intercollegiate Athletic Association

Football

Miller, R.E. 1923
Sheilds, Jams 1924
Anderson, Roger 1926
Breaux, Inman 1926–27
Washington, Herman 1927
Burton, Thomas 1929
Thompson, B.H. 1929
Smith, Bernard S. 1929

Robinson, Theodore 1930
Robinson, Maxie 1930
Williams, John 1930–31
Williams, Lloyd 1932
Poole, Everett 1932, 1934
Jenkins, Samuel 1932, 1934
Campbell, Francis 1937
Cooper, Fred 1939–40

West Virginia State College
Institute, West Virginia 25112

Coaches of Varsity Teams

Baseball

Dunlap, Samuel 1920
Brock, George D. 1921
Hamblin, Adolph 1922–29

Basketball

Hamblin, Adolph P. 1921–33
Brown, Dallas 1933–34
Hawkins, Charles C. 1934–35
Ellis, Arthur W. 1936–37
Clement, Fred A. 1938–44
McCarthy, Horace 1944–45
Cardwell, Mark 1945–46

Men's Track

Barnette, Leonard 1924–25

Football

Dunlap, Samuel 1920–21
Brock, George D. 1921–22
Hamblin, Adolph P. 1922–44
Caldwell, Mark 1945–46

All Central Intercollegiate Athletic Association

Football

Lynch, Wesley 1942
Green, Linwood 1945

All-American (Black College NAIA)

Football

Jones, H. Smith 1923
Moore, William G. 1923
Anderson, John 1923
Barnes, John 1923
Whitted, Palmer 1923
Hodges, Marcell 1924–25
Greene, Oliver 1927–30
Saunders, Harry W. 1928–29
Gamble, Samuel A. 1928–29
Froe, Dreyfus W. 1928–29
Smoot, Thomas 1928–29
Lynch, John 1928–29
Leveridge, Charles 1930–33
Scott, James L. 1931–34
Wares, James T. 1932–33
Stevenson, Homer 1932–33
Thompson, Carroll 1932–35
Bates, Pervis 1932–35
Jackson, William S. 1932–35
Burroughs, Knute 1932–35
Robinson, William "Will" 1932–35
Stewart, Jr., Colston R. 1933
Price, Roderick 1933–36
Phillips, Sleepy 1936–40
Jennings, Thomas 1936–40
Johnson, Max 1936–40
Burris, Chester A. 1936–40
Webster, Amos 1936–40
Washington, Andrew 1936–40
Harvey, Harold 1936–40
Murphy, James 1941–43
Starling, Carol 1941–43
Wilson, James M. 1941–43
Taylor, Jack 1941–43

Baseball

Drewery, William 1921–23
Nash, James 1927
Johnson, Ernest M. 1933
Woodruff, George 1936

OUTSTANDING AFRICAN-AMERICANS IN COLLEGE SPORTS (1946–1986) BY CONFERENCE

MISSOURI VALLEY CONFERENCE

1. Wichita State University
2. University of Tulsa
3. Indiana State University
4. Creighton University

5. Drake University
6. Southern Illinois University
7. West Texas State University

Wichita State University
Wichita, Kansas 67208

Coaches of Varsity Teams

Football

Jeffries, Willie (Head), 1978–83
Hudson, Clarence (Assistant), 1976–78
Blacknall, Roy (Assistant), 1979–83
Goodwin, Sam (Assistant), 1979–83
Montgomery, John (Assistant), 1981–83
Hickson, Frank (Assistant), 1983
Tompkins, Mark (Assistant), 1983
Raye, James (Assistant), 1984–Present

Basketball

Guydon, Gus (Assistant), 1976–78
Jones, Jeff (Assistant), 1977

Track

Foote, Cyril (Assistant), 1985

All Missouri Valley Conference

Football

Lakes, Roland, 1960
Farr, Miller, 1962
Jones, Jimmie, 1966–67
Robertson, Pete, 1968
Jackson, Randy, 1971
Dobbs, Leon, 1976
Shuman, Ron, 1976
Brooks, Alvin, 1976–77
Smith, Willie, 1976–77
Vincent, Ted, 1977
Taylor, Sherman, 1977
Woods, Rodney, 1979
Collins, Mickey, 1980
Davis, David, 1980
Wilson, Billy, 1980

McCoy, Mark, 1980–81
Murphy, Kevin, 1981
Weston, Robert, 1981
Whitten, Curtis, 1981
McJunkins, Prince, 1981–82
Kennell, Lonnie, 1982
Stewart, Glen, 1982
Eckels, Reuben, 1982–83
Jones, Anthony, 1983
Blackman, Greg, 1983
Denson, Eric, 1983
Geathers, James, 1983

Basketball

Littleton, Cleo, 1952–55
Tate, Al, 1959
Wiley, Gene, 1961–62
Stallworth, David, 1963–65
Bowman, Nate, 1964
Pete, Kelly, 1965
Armstrong, Warren, 1966–68
Carney, Greg, 1970
Benton, Terry, 1971–72
Morsden, Rich, 1974–75
Wilson, Robert, 1974–75
Elmore, Robert, 1977–79
Johnson, Lynbert "Cheese," 1977–79
Levingston, Cliff, 1980–82
Carr, Antoine,[1] 1980–83
Sherrod, Aubrey, 1983
McDaniel, Xavier,[2] 1983–85

Baseball

Howard, Davis, 1979
Carter, Joe, 1979–81

Track and Field

Person, Roy, CC, 1967
Pratt, Nate, LJ, 1968–69
Carrington, Preston, LJ, 1971–72

All-American

Basketball

Littleton, Cleo, 1955
Stallworth, David, 1964
Carney, Greg, 1970
Johnson, Lynbert "Cheese," 1979
Carr, Antoine, 1983
Sherrod, Aubrey, 1984
McDaniel, Xavier, 1984–85

Baseball

Carter, Joe, 1978, 1980–81

Track and Field

Carrington, Preston, LJ, 1971–72

Athletic Trainers

Banks, Roland,[3] 1977–Present

Other Outstanding Athletes

Santos, Gus

[1] Carr, Antoine—1983 Missouri Valley Conference Player of the Year
[2] McDaniel, Xavier—1984 and 1985 Missouri Valley Conference Player of the Year
[3] Banks, Roland—Equipment Manager

University of Tulsa
Tulsa, Oklahoma 74104

Coaches of Varsity Teams

Basketball

Richardson, Nolan (Head), 1980–85

All Missouri Valley Conference

Football

Ashton, Josh, 1970
McGill, Ralph, 1971
Schrivener, Drane, 1972
Webster, Cornell, 1976
McGowen, Mel, 1976
Smith, Lovie, 1977–79
Watts, Rickey, 1978
Blackmon, Don, 1978–80
Lacy, Ken, 1982
Gunter, Michael, 1982

Basketball

Smith, Bobby,[1] 1968–69
Lewis, Dana,[2] 1970–71
Bracey, Steven, 1972
Biles, Willie, 1973–75
Brown, David, 1981
Pressey, Paul,[3] 1981–82
Stewart, Greg, 1981–82
Ross, Ricky, 1983–84
Harris, Steven,[4] 1983–85

All-American

Basketball

Smith, Bobby, 1969
Pressey, Paul, 1982
Harris, Stevens,[4] 1985

Other Outstanding Athletes

Football

Pearson, Drew
Johns, Paul

Basketball

Anderson, Michael

[1] Smith, Bobby—1969 Missouri Valley Conference Player of the Year; Honorable Mention
[2] Lewis, Dana—1970 Missouri Valley Conference Newcomer of the Year
[3] Pressey, Paul—1982 Missouri Valley Conference Player of the Year
[4] Harris, Steven—1982 Missouri Valley Conference Newcomer of the Year; Honorable Mention

Indiana State University
Terre Haute, Indiana 47809

Coaches of Varsity Teams

Cross Country

Draper, Dr., Fred (Head), 1970–79

Football

Cooks, Johnnie (Assistant), 1973–74
Turner, Robert (Assistant), 1975–82

Men's Basketball

Daniels, Mel (Assistant), 1978–82

All Missouri Valley Conference

Football

Allen, Vincent, 1977
Jackson, Don, 1977
Allen, Reginald, 1979
Ruffin, Ed, 1979–80
Wilson, Kirk, 1979–81
Moore, Hubert, 1980–81
Seaphus, Walter, 1982
Martin, Ed, 1982–83
Ramsey, Kevin, 1983
Mikell, Quintin, 1983
Clardy, Darrold, 1984
Davis, Wayne, 1984

Basketball

Morgan, Harry, 1978 ʼ
Nicks, Carl, 1979–80
Williams, John, 1983–84

Women's Basketball

Graves, Barbara, 1983

All-American

Football

Brumfield, Jim, 1968
Allen, Vincent, 1975
Hicks, Chris, 1977
Martin, Ed, 1983
Davis, Wayne, 1984

Basketball

Nicks, Carl, 1980

Baseball

Johnson, Wally, 1979

Indiana State University's Hall of Fame

Football

Walder, Verbie

Creighton University
Omaha, Nebraska 68178

Coaches of Varsity Teams

Basketball

Reed, Willis (Head), 1980–85

All Missouri Valley Conference

Basketball

Stovall, Daryl, 1982
Benjamin, Benoit, 1984–85
Moore, Vernon, 1984–85

All-American

Basketball

Silas, Paul, 1962–64
Baptiste, Cyril,[1] 1971
Benjamin, Benoit,[2] 1985

Other Outstanding Athletes

Gibson, Robert[3]

[1] Baptiste, Cyril—Honorable Mention
[2] Benjamin, Benoit—Honorable Mention
[3] Gibson, Robert—competed in basketball and baseball

Drake University
Des Moines, Iowa 50311

Coaches of Varsity Teams

Basketball

Anderson, Mark (Assistant)
Green, Mel (Assistant)
Guydon, James "Gus" (Assistant)
Proctor, Joe (Assistant)

All Missouri Valley Conference

Football

Bright, John, 1951
Holmes, Rudy, 1973
Lott, Glenn, 1973–74
Allen, Rodney, 1974
Herndon, Jim, 1975
Ferguson, Phil, 1977

Glover, David, 1978
Wright, Wardell, 1979
Benton, Greg, 1980
Ware, Amero, 1980–82

Basketball

Guydon, Gus, 1960–61
Foster, Jerry, 1962
Torrence, Marv, 1962
McLemore, McCoy, 1964
Foster, Billy, 1964
McCarter, Willie, 1968–69
Halliburton, Jeff,[1] 1970–71
Bell, Dennis, 1973
Harris, Ken, 1976–77
Lloyd, Lewis,[2] 1980–81
Mathis, Melvin, 1984
Lloyd, Daryl, 1985

All-American

Football

Bright, John, 1951

Basketball

McCarter, Willie, 1969
Lloyd, Lewis, 1980–81

Men's Track

Drew, Howard, 1912
Ford, Jim, 1951
Betton, Arnold, 1952
Durant, Charles, 1961
Martin, Sterling, 1985

Women's Track

Blackman, Carlon, 1983

Other Outstanding Athletes

Basketball

Watson, Herman

Men's Track

Nolan, George
Harris, James A.
Durant, Charles

Women's Track

Pulliam, Dolph

[1] Halliburton, Jeff—1971 Missouri Valley Conference Player of the Year
[2] Lloyd, Lewis—1980 and 1981 Missouri Valley Conference Player of the Year

Southern Illinois University
Carbondale, Illinois 62901

Athletic Directors

Sayers, Gale (Director of Men's Athletes), 1976–81

Coaches of Varsity Teams

Women's Volleyball

Locke, Sonya (Assistant), 1984–Present

All Missouri Valley Conference

Football

Honore, Bryon, 1978–79
Quinn, Burnell, 1978–79
Phillips, James, 1978–80
House, Kevin, 1979
Craddock, Oyd, 1979
Davis, Darrin, 1980–81
Poole, Walter, 1981
Harper, John, 1981
Shipp, Gregg, 1981
Butler, Granville, 1982–83
Haywood, Sterling, 1983
Foster, Ken, 1983
Taylor, Terry, 1984

Basketball

Abrams, Corky, 1976
Glenn, Michael,[1] 1976–77
Wilson, Gary, 1978–79
Abrams, Wayne, 1978–80

All-American

Football

Antwine, Houston,[2] 1950's
Brown, Jr., William,[3] 1950's
Shannon, Carver,[4] 1950's

Basketball

Vaughn, Charles "Chico,"[5] 1960
Glenn, Michael, 1976

Track

Dupree, Jim, 1960's
Moore, Oscar, 1960's
Crockett, Ivory, 1971

Southern Illinois University's Hall of Fame

Football

Antwine, Houston
Battle, Jim
Bullocks, Amos
Brown, Jr., Willie
Shannon, Carver
Silas, Sam

Basketball

Bryson, Seymour[6]
Vaughn, Charles "Chico"
Frazier, Walter[7]
Garrett, Dick
Glenn, Michael
Meriweather, Joe C.

Track

Payton, Eugene[8]
Dupree, Jim
Crockett, Ivory

Other Outstanding Athletes

Track

Benson, Charles
Brown, Lonnie
Lee, David
Rock, Rick
Duncan, Parry
Geary, Randy
Robins, Phil
Franks, Michael
Wray, Stephen

Gymnastics

Johnson, Julius[9]

Sims, William
Williamson, Lawrence

[1] Glenn, Michael—1976 Missouri Valley Conference Player of the Year; Honorable Mention
[2] Antwine, Houston—Little All-American
[3] Brown, Jr., William—Little All-American
[4] Shannon, Carver—Little All-American
[5] Vaughn, Charles "Chico"—Little All-American
[6] Bryson, Seymour—presently Dean of the College of Human Resources at Southern Illinois University
[7] Frazier, Walter—1967 National Invitational Tournament Most Valuable Player Award recipient
[8] Payton, Eugene—first black American to earn a letter at Southern Illinois University
[9] Johnson, Julius—captain of the 1957 team

West Texas State University
Canyon, Texas 79016

Coaches of Varsity Teams

Track

Willis, David (Head)

Basketball

Reaux, Tom (Assistant)

All Missouri Valley Conference

Football

Pritchett, William, 1971
Hibbler, Walter, 1972
Jones, Floyd, 1974
Kelson, Michael, 1975
Mayberry, Robert, 1976
Fifer, William, 1976–77
Robinson, Bo, 1976–78
Holt, John, 1979
Keller, Elvin, 1979–81
Nelson, Michael, 1980
McElroy, Reginald, 1981
Bennett, Curtis, 1982

Basketball

Smith, Dallas, 1976
Cheeks, Maurice, 1977–78
Adolph, Terry, 1980–81
Steppes, Robert, 1983

All-American

Football

Morris, Eugene, 1968
Thomas, Duane, 1969

Basketball

Hill, Simmie, 1969

Other Outstanding Athletes

Football

Anderson, Ralph
Washington, Hank
Brown, Raymond
Holt, John
Baker, Milt
Thompson, Rocky
McGee, Victor
Hemphill, Darryl

SUN BELT CONFERENCE

1. University of South Alabama
2. Old Dominion University
3. Jacksonville University
4. University of North Carolina, Charlotte

5. University of New Orleans
6. University of Alabama, Birmingham
7. Western Kentucky University

University of South Alabama
Mobile, Alabama 36688

All Sun Belt Conference

Basketball

White, Rory,[1] 1978, 1981–82
Rains, Ed,[2] 1979–81
Andrew, Herb, 1980–81
Gerren, Michael, 1983–84
Catledge, Terry,[3] 1983–85

Baseball

Coachman, Peter,[4] 1984
Johnson, Lance, 1984

Other Outstanding Athletes

Women's Basketball

Jenkins, Lasandra

Baseball

Lowe, Ledell
Saunders, Marvin
Lee, Ed

[1] White, Rory—1979 Sun Belt Conference Player of the Year
[2] Rains, Ed—1981 Sun Belt Conference Player of the Year
[3] Catledge, Terry—1984 Sun Belt Conference Player of the Year
[4] Coachman, Peter—1984 Sun Belt Conference Most Valuable Player

Old Dominion University
Norfolk, Virginia 23508

Coaches of Varsity Teams

Women's Basketball

Thaxton, Barbara, 1981–Present

All Sun Belt Conference

Men's Basketball

West, Mark, 1983
Gattison, Ken,[1] 1985–86

All-American

Men's Basketball

Copeland, Joel, 1975
Washington, Wilson, 1977
Valentine, Ron,[2] 1980
McAdoo, Ron,[3] 1981
West, Mark,[4] 1983
Gattison, Ken,[5] 1986

Women's Basketball

Claxton, Tracey, 1984–85
Dixon, Medina, 1984–85

[1] Gattison, Ken—1986 Sun Belt Conference Player of the Year
[2] Valentine, Ron—Honorable Mention
[3] McAdoo, Ron—Honorable Mention
[4] West, Mark—Honorable Mention
[5] Gattison, Ken—Honorable Mention

Jacksonville University
Jacksonville, Florida 32211

All Sun Belt Conference

Men's Basketball

Glover, Kent, 1977
Young, Felton, 1977
Ray, James,[1] 1978–80
Hackett, Michael, 1980–82
Rouhlac, Maurice, 1982
Smith, Otis, 1983–86
Murphy, Ron, 1984

All-American

Men's Basketball

Gilmore, Artis, 1971

Other Outstanding Athletes

Men's Basketball

Dublin, Chip[2]
Burrows, Pembrook
Fox, Harold
Fleming, Ernest
Steward, Abe
Benbow, Leon
Williams, Henry
Taylor, Butch
Williams, Anthony "Cricket"

[1] Ray, James—1980 Sun Belt Conference Player of the Year
[2] Dublin, Chip—the first black athlete to play at Jacksonville University, 1968

University of North Carolina
Charlotte, North Carolina 28223

Coaches of Varsity Teams

Rifle Team

Matthews, Willie (Head), 1984–Present

All Sun Belt Conference

Men's Basketball

Maxwell, Cedric, 1977
Massey, Lew, 1977–78
Kinch, Chad, 1978–79

Ward, Phil, 1981
Johnson, Melvin, 1983–84

All-American

Men's Basketball

Maxwell, Cedric, 1977

Women's Basketball

Bennett, Paula, 1981–82
Walker, Patricia, 1982

Other Outstanding Athletes

Baseball

Dickerson, James
Morgan, Kenneth

Men's Tennis

Berry, Dana
Caldwell, Ed

Women's Volleyball

Barrett, Rita

University of New Orleans
New Orleans, Louisiana 70122

All Sun Belt Conference

Basketball

Cooper, Wayne,[1] 1977–78
Mills, Nate, 1977–78

All-American

Basketball

Webster, Butch, 1970
Cooper, Wayne, 1978
Hodge, Sandra,[2] 1984

Other Outstanding Athletes

Basketball

Holland, Wilbur
Eckles, Ledell

[1] Cooper, Wayne—1978 Sun Belt Conference Player of the Year; Honorable Mention
[2] Hodge, Sandra—Honorable Mention

University of Alabama
Birmingham, Alabama 5294

Coaches of Varsity Teams

Men's Basketball

Catlin, Oscar (Assistant)
Prince, John (Assistant)

All Sun Belt Conference

Men's Basketball

McCord, Keith, 1980
Robinson, Oliver,[1] 1981–82
Gilkes, Caris, 1981–82
Pruitt, Cliff, 1983
Mitchell, Steven, 1984–86
Mincy, Jerome, 1985–86

[1] Robinson, Oliver—1982 Sun Belt Conference Player of the Year

Western Kentucky University
Bowling Green, Kentucky 42101

Coaches of Varsity Teams

Men's Basketball

Haskins, Clem, 1980–86

All Ohio Valley Conference

Men's Basketball

Haskins, Clem,[1] 1965–67
McDaniels, Jim,[2] 1969–71
Bryant, Aaron, 1977
Turner, Darryl, 1978
Johnson, James, 1978
Jackson, Greg, 1979
Bryant, William, 1980

All Sun Belt Conference

Men's Basketball

Wilson, Tony, 1983

All-American

Men's Basketball

Haskins, Clem, 1967
McDaniels, Jim, 1971

Women's Basketball

Haskins, Clemmette, 1986

[1] Haskins, Clem—1981 Ohio Valley Conference Coach of the Year, 1986 Sun Belt Conference Co-Coach of the Year; 1965–67 Ohio Valley Conference Player of the Year
[2] McDaniels, Jim—1970–71 Ohio Valley Conference Player of the Year

PACIFIC COAST ATHLETIC ASSOCIATION

1. University of Nevada, Las Vegas
2. University of California, Irvine
3. California State University, Long Beach
4. New Mexico State University
5. California State University, Fullerton
6. San Jose State University

University of Nevada
Las Vegas, Nevada 89154

Coaches of Varsity Teams

Football

Nunnely, Wayne (Head), 1986–Present

All West Coast Athletic Conference

Men's Basketball

Washington, Booker, 1971–73
Baker, Jimmie, 1973–74

Sobers, Ricky, 1975
Owens, Eddie, 1975

All Pacific Coast Athletic Association

Football

Cunningham, Randall, 1982–84

Men's Basketball

Green, Sidney,[1] 1983
Adams, Richie,[2] 1984–85
Jones, Anthony,[3] 1986
Banks, Fred, 1986–87
Gilliam, Armon, 1987

All-American

Men's Basketball

Gilliam, Armon, 1987

Other Outstanding Athletes

Men's Basketball

Theus, Reginald
Williams, Flintie Ray
Smith, Robert
James, Frank
Basknight, Jarvis
Paddio, Gerald
Graham, Gary

Football

LeFrance, Reginald

[1] Green, Sidney—1983 Pacific Coast Athletic Association Player of the Year
[2] Adams, Richie—1984 and 1985 Pacific Coast Athletic Association Player of the Year
[3] Jones, Anthony—1986 Pacific Coast Athletic Association Co-Player of the Year

University of California
Irvine, California 92717

Coaches of Varsity Teams

Men's Track and Field/Cross Country

Roberson, Bo (Head), 1971–72

Women's Track and Field

Williams, Dan (Head), 1982–Present

All Pacific Coast Athletic Association

Men's Basketball

Magee, Kevin, 1981–82
McDonald, Ben, 1983–84

Track

King, La Monte, 100M, 200M, LJ 1978–79
Chambers, Tim, 400MR, MR 1979
McGee, Darryl, 400MR, MR 1979
Frazier, Thomas, 800M, MR 1979–80
Kidd, Carlysle, 400M, MR 1979–81
Wells, Tony, 400M, MR 1979–81
Corrin, Michael, LJ 1980

Chapman, Phil, HJ 1981
Carey, Ed, 200M, 400M, MR 1981–82
Holliday, Rick, TJ 1983
Powell, Michael, 400MR, HJ 1984
Todd, Harold, 400MR 1984
Clarke, Selwyn, 400MR 1984

Other Outstanding Athletes

Women's Basketball

Hamilton, Katherine[1]
Lewis, Dorothy[2]

Women's Track

Westbrook, Brenda
Kelley, Michelle
Stanford, Carole

Baseball

Granger, Lee

[1] Hamilton, Katherine—played on the 1979–83 University of California, Irvine, team (All-Time Leading Scorer—1,768 Points)
[2] Lewis, Dorothy—played on the 1981–85 University of California, Irvine, team

California State University
Long Beach, California 90840

Coaches of Varsity Teams

Basketball

Palmer, Ron, 1984–Present

All Pacific Coast Athletic Association

Football

Dunn, Broddie, 1969
Burns, Leon, 1969–70
Metcalf, Terry, 1971
Berry, Reginald, 1971
Jones, Leanell, 1975
Lusk, Herb, 1975
Mathis, Julius, 1976
Smith, Jerrell, 1976
Henry, Vernon, 1978
Parker, Herman, 1978–79
Rudolph, Ben, 1979–80
Cobbs, Ervin, 1979–80
Moore, Art, 1980
Thomas, Kim, 1980

Land, Doug, 1981
Taylor, Lloyd, 1982
Howard, David, 1982–83
Golden, Tim, 1983
Johnson, Eric, 1983
Lockett, Charles, 1984
Hendy, John, 1984

Basketball

Trapp, George,[1] 1970–71
Ratleff, Ed,[2] 1971–73
Pondexter, Roscoe, 1973
Gray, Leonard,[3] 1974
Johnson, Richard, 1975
Ruffen, Clarence, 1976
McMillian, Lloyd,[4] 1977
Wise, Francois, 1978–80
Williams, Rickey, 1979
Wiley, Michael, 1980
Hodges, Craig, 1982

All-American

Football

Burns, Leon, 1969–70
Metcalf, Terry, 1971

Basketball

Trapp, George, 1971
Ratleff, Ed, 1972–73
Gray, Leonard, 1974
Pondexter, Clifton, 1974
McMillian, Lloyd, 1977

[1] Trapp, George—1970 and 1971 Pacific Coast Athletic Association Player of the Year
[2] Ratleff, Ed—1972 and 1973 Pacific Coast Athletic Association Player of the Year
[3] Gray, Leonard—1974 Pacific Coast Athletic Association Player of the Year
[4] McMillian, Lloyd—1977 Pacific Coast Athletic Association Player of the Year

New Mexico State University
Las Cruces, New Mexico 88003

Coaches of Varsity Teams

Basketball

Drew, Weldon (Head), 1979–Present

Football

Adams, Willie (Assistant), 1975–76

Gill, Ted (Assistant), 1977
Williams, Ivy (Assistant), 1978
Graves, Fred (Assistant), 1979–81
Cole, Lawrence (Assistant), 1983–Present

All Pacific Coast Athletic Association

Football

Gaithers, Bob, 1960
Young, Fred, 1982

Basketball

Grant, Roland, 1974
Jones, Albert "Slab," 1978–80
Patterson, Ernest, 1983
Colter, Steven, 1984

All-American

Football

Atkins, Pervis, 1960
Jackson, Ralph, 1974–75

Basketball

Criss, Charles, 1969
Collins, Jimmy, 1970
Lacey, Sam, 1970
Williamson, John, 1972

Other Outstanding Athletes

Football

Harris, Duriel

California State University
Fullerton, California 92634

Coaches of Varsity Teams

Men's Basketball

McQuarn, George (Head), 1981–83

Football

Brown, Jerry (Assistant), 1979–84

All Pacific Coast Athletic Association

Football

Graves, Obie, 1978

King, Leonard, 1978
Gilbert, Daren, 1984
Allen, Damon, 1984

Basketball

Bunch, Gregory, 1976–78
Roberts, Calvin, 1979–80
Wood, Leon, 1982–84
Neal, Tony, 1985
Henderson, Kevin, 1985

All-American

Basketball

Wood, Leon,[1] 1983–84

Other Outstanding Athletes

Baseball

Hudson, Tony[2]

[1] Wood, Leon—member of the 1984 United States Olympic Basketball Team
[2] Hudson, Tony—Most Valuable Player in the 1979 College Baseball World Series

San Jose State University
San Jose, California 95192–0062

Coaches of Varsity Teams

Track and Field

Livers, Larry (Assistant), 1972–80
Poynter, Robert (Assistant), 1980-present

Football

Sullivan, Richard (Assistant), 1973–76, 1979–82

Basketball

Berry, William (Assistant), 1979–Present

All Pacific Coast Athletic Association

Football

Jones, Cody, 1971
Wright, Louie, 1974
Small, Gerald, 1975–77
Nichols, Mark, 1979
Thomas, Ken, 1979–81
Willhite, Gerald, 1980–81
Bailey, Stacey, 1980–81

Byrd, Gill, 1980–82
Cockcroft, Sherman, 1983
Richardson, Eric, 1983

Basketball

Williams, Sid, 1981
McNealy, Chris, 1982–83

All-American

Football

Thomas, Lloyd, 1938
Small, Gerald, 1976–77
Nichols, Mark, 1979
Thomas, Ken, 1979–81
Bailey, Stacey, 1980
Willhite, Gerald, 1980–81
Byrd, Gill, 1980–82
Clarkson, Steven, 1981–82
Kearse, Tim, 1981–82
Richardson, Eric, 1983
Cockcroft, Sherman, 1983

Basketball

Williams, Sid, 1981
McNealy, Chris, 1983

Track and Field

Wyatt, Herman, 1952–53
Norton, Ray, 1958–59
Poynter, Robert, 1959
Williams, Errol, 1959–60
Compton, Maurice, 1966
Herman, Wayne, 1966
Smith, Tommie, 1966–68
Evans, Lee, 1968–69
Davis, Sam, 1968–69
Anderson, Marion, 1969
Clayton, Kirk, 1969
Smith, Ronnie Ray, 1969
Carty, George, 1969–71
Whitaker, Ron, 1975
Livers, Ron, 1975, 1977–78
Cooper, Dedy, 1976–77
Prince, Cleve, 1981
Thomas, Ken, 1981
Green, Dwayne, 1981
Torrence, Virgil, 1981
Holloway, Bernie, 1982

San Jose State University's Hall of Fame

Lewis, William
Minter, Aubrey
Allen, Johnny
Steele, Willig
Matthews, Larry
Donahue, Oscar

Roberts, Walter
Johnson, John
Jackson, Cass
Harraway, Charlie
Jones, Cody
Wright, Louie

WESTERN ATHLETIC CONFERENCE

1. University of Wyoming
2. University of Utah
3. University of Texas at El Paso

4. San Diego State University
5. Colorado State University
6. University of New Mexico

University of Wyoming
Laramie, Wyoming 82071

Coaches of Varsity Teams

Football

Daniel, James Edward (Assistant)
Whitt, Joseph (Assistant)

Basketball

Anderson, Tevester (Assistant)

All Western Athletic Conference

Football

Speights, Richard, 1966–67
Washington, Vic, 1966–67
Huey, Gene, 1967–68
Kyle, Aaron, 1975
Gaines, Lawrence, 1976–77
Howard, Walter, 1977–78
Hardeman, Myron, 1977–78
Dennis, Michael, 1978
Pittman, Dan, 1979
Bradford, Charles, 1978–80
Frazier, Guy, 1980
Williams, James, 1981
Goffigan, Walter, 1983

Basketball

Robinson, Flynn, 1963–65

Clark, Leon, 1964–66
Hall, Harry, 1967–69
Ashley, Carl, 1968–70
Roberson, Willie, 1971
Bradley, Charles, 1978, 1980–81
Martin, Tony, 1984
Denbo, Fennis, 1986–87

Track

Robinson, Herman, 1964
Washington, Vic, 1967
Johnson, Huey, 1969
Frazier, Michael, 1969
Jones, Arabia, 1971
Black, Robert, 1974
Benhom, Ben, 1974
Kyle, Aaron, 1975
Williams, Gladstone, 1978
White, Michael, 1980

Women's Track

Johnson, Tanya, 1976
Bradley, Jeannette, 1980
Miller, Pat, 1980

All-American

Basketball

Robinson, Flynn, 1965
Denbo, Fennis,[1] 1987

[1] Denbo, Fennis–Honorable Mention

University of Utah
Salt Lake City, Utah 84112

Coaches of Varsity Teams

Football

Gill, Ted (Assistant), 1974–76
Graves, Fred (Assistant), 1982

All Sky-Line Conference

Football

Fleming, Marv, 1961

Basketball

McGill, William, 1960–62

All Western Athletic Conference

Football

Jefferson, Roy, 1963–64
Coleman, Ron, 1964
McBride, Norman, 1967–68
Thomas, Louis, 1968
Thompson, Norman, 1969–70
Pritchett, Robert, 1972
Odom, Steven, 1973
Stepide, Jack, 1976
Walker, Lewis, 1979
Griffin, Jeff, 1980
Rodgers, Del, 1980
Reed, Tony, 1981
Monroe, Carl, 1982
Lawson, Lonnie, 1982
Walker, Carlton, 1984
Johnson, Ed, 1984

Basketball

Chambers, Jerry, 1966
Jackson, Merv, 1967–68
Sojourner, Michael, 1974
Burden, Luther, 1974–75
Matheney, Buster, 1978

All High Country Conference

Women's Basketball

Lee, Leshia, 1985

All-American

Football

Jefferson, Roy, 1964
Thompson, Norman, 1970
Odom, Steve, 1973
Griffin, Jeff, 1980
Walker, Carlton, 1984

Basketball

McGill, William, 1961–62
Chambers, Jerry, 1966
Jackson, Merv, 1968
Sojourner, Michael, 1974
Burden, Luther, 1975

University of Texas
El Paso, Texas 79968

Coaches of Varsity Teams

Women's Basketball

Thornton, Wayne (Head), 1978–83

Football

Ivory, Donald (Assistant), 1977–78
Atkins, David (Assistant), 1979–80
Simon, Matt (Assistant), 1979–80

Basketball

Shed, Nevil (Assistant), 1980–81
Forbes, James (Assistant), 1981–1983

Women's Basketball

Stoney, Be (Assistant), 1981–Present

All Border Conference

Basketball

Hill, Bobby Joe, 1962
Richardson, Nolan, 1962

All Western Athletic Conference

Football

Cavness, Grady, 1968
Coleman, LaFreddie, 1974
Elliott, Robaert, 1975–77
Garcia, Bubba, 1977–78

Forkerway, Ed, 1978
Besses, Melvin, 1979
Morris, Raymond, 1983

Basketball

Archibald, Nate, 1970
Bailey, Gus, 1974
Forbes, James, 1974
Burns, Anthony, 1979–80
Amie, Roshern, 1981
White, Terry, 1982
Reynolds, Fred, 1982–84
Walker, Byron, 1983
Goodwin, Luster, 1984

Track

Jackson, Harrington J.J.,[1] 1970–72
Deal, Jerome,[2] 1978–81
Scott, Carlos, 1980

All-American

Basketball

Barnes, Jim, 1964
Hill, Tyrone Bobby Joe, 1966

Men's Track

Beamon, Robert,[3] 1967–68
Turner, Kim,[4] 1983–84

Other Outstanding Athletes

Football

West, Charles[5]
Carr, Fred[6]
Randle, Thurman[7]

Basketball

Brown, Charles[8]
Artis, Orsten[9]
Worsley, Willie[10]
Florney, Harry[11]
Lattin, David[12]
Cager, Willie[13]

[1] Jackson, Harrington J.J.–1972 Western Athletic Conference 100-Meter Dash Champion
[2] Deal, Jerome–1981 Western Athletic Conference 100-Meter Dash Champion
[3] Beamon, Robert–1967 NCAA Indoor Long Jump Champion; member of the 1968 United States Olympic Track Team
[4] Turner, Kim–1984 NCAA 100-Meter Hurdle Champion; member of the 1984 United States Olympic Track Team

[5] West, Charles–played on the 1965–67 Texas Western University teams
[6] Carr, Fred–played on the 1965–67 Texas Western University teams
[7] Randle, Thurman–played on the 1965–67 Texas Western University teams
[8] Brown, Charles–first black athlete to receive a basketball scholarship at University of Texas, El Paso, 1956
[9] Artis, Orsten–started on the 1966 NCAA National Championship teams
[10] Worsley, Willie–started on the 1966 NCAA National Championship teams
[11] Florney, Harry–started on the 1966 NCAA National Championship teams
[12] Lattin, David–started on the 1966 NCAA National Championship teams
[13] Cager, Willie–member of the 1966 NCAA National Championship teams

San Diego State University
San Diego, California 92182

Coaches of Varsity Teams

Men's Basketball

Gaines, David "Smokey" (Head), 1980–87

Women's Basketball

Riggins, Earnest (Head), 1983–Present

Football

Atkins, David (Assistant), 1981–Present

Men's Basketball

Evans, Jesse (Assistant), 1982–Present

All California Collegiate Athletic Association CCAA

Football

Pinkins, Braxton, 1958
Carson, Kern, 1962
Petties, Neal, 1962
Howard, Robert 1966
Moses, Haven, 1967

Men's Basketball

Pinkins, Tony, 1955–57

All Pacific Coast Athletic Association

Football

Reynolds, Tom, 1969, 1971
Allison, Henry, 1970
Hayes, Tom, 1970
Youngs, Ty, 1971
Buchanon, Willie, 1971
Curtis, Issac, 1972
Lavender, Joe, 1972
Minor, Claude, 1973
Hayes, Billie, 1973

Weathers, Carl, 1973
Nogle, Darold, 1973
Denson, Keith, 1973
Henderson, Robert, 1973–74
Jackson, Monte, 1973–74
McDonald, Dwight, 1974
Fergerson, Duke, 1975
Jacobs, Mel, 1975

Men's Basketball

McMurray, Chris, 1972

All Western Athletic Conference

Football

Inge, Peter, 1978–79
Williams, Henry, 1978
Stapler, Steven, 1979
Allen, Tony, 1979
Ward, Terrell, 1979
Mitchell, Kevin, 1980
Dean, Vernon, 1981
Durham, Darius, 1982

Men's Basketball

Cage, Michael,[1] 1983–84

1983 Western Athletic Conference Co-Player of the Year

1983 United Press International West Coast Player of the Year

All-American

Football

Petties, Neal, 1963
Moses, Haven, 1967
Allison, Henry, 1970
Buchanon, Willie, 1971
Reynolds, Tom, 1971
Williams, Henry, 1978
Inge, Peter, 1978–79
Allen, Tony, 1979
Stapler, Steven, 1979
Ward, Terrell, 1979
Mitchell, Kevin, 1980
Dean, Vernon, 1981
Durham, Darius, 1982

Men's Basketball

Cage, Michael, 1983–84

Women's Basketball

Hutchinson, Tina,[2] 1985

Men's Track and Field

Steele, Willie,[3] LJ, 1947–48
Williams, Wes, 440 IH 1969–70
Robinson, Arnie,[4] LJ, 1970–71
Williams, Steve, 100M 1974
Wheeler, Quentin, 400M,[5] 1976

Other Outstanding Athletes

Baseball

Gwynn, Tony
Gwynn, Chris[6]
Meachem, Robert
Newman, Al
Wiggins, Kevin
Howard, Robert

Men's Track

Blaylock, Chris, 100M
McDonald, Brad, 200M
Almbruster, Michael, 800M
Robinson, Earl, 1500M
Martin, Otis, 5000M
Shy, Don, 110MH

Discus Throw

Ridge, Houston

Women's Track

Taylor, Anovia, 100M
Smith, Lori, 100MLJ
Sheffield, Lantanya, 100M
Chambers, Rene, 200M, 400M
Bryson, Yolanda, 110MH
Bullard, Yvette, 400M
Charles, Donna, 400M

Women's Basketball

Porter, Judy
Toler, Penny
Haynes, Jessica[7]

[1] Cage, Michael–1983 Western Athletic Conference Co-Player of the Year; 1983 United Press International West Coast Player of the Year
[2] Hutchinson, Tina—Honorable Mention
[3] Steele, William–member of the 1948 United States Olympic Track and Field team

[4] Robinson, Arnie–member of the 1972 United States Olympic Track and Field team
[5] Wheeler, Quentin–member of the 1976 United States Olympic Track and Field team
[6] Gwynn, Chris–member of the 1984 United States Olympic Track and Field team
[7] Haynes, Jessica–1986 Freshman All-American

Colorado State University
Fort Collins, Colorado 80523

All Skyline Conference

Football

Hanna, Eddie, 1948

All Western Athletic Conference

Football

McCutcheon, Lawrence, 1970–71
Kennedy, Jim, 1973
Stemrick, Greg, 1973
Baker, Al, 1977
Featherstone, Cliff, 1977
Jones, Larry, 1978
McDonald, Donzell, 1979
Lewis, Alvin, 1980
Goolsby, Tony, 1980
Hall, Richie, 1982

Basketball

Shegogg, Cliff, 1970
Fisher, Rick, 1971
Childress, Michael, 1971
Price, George, 1972
Cash, Lorenzo, 1976
Cunningham, Alan, 1977–78
Hughes, Eddie, 1979–80

All-American

Basketball

Green, William, 1963

Other Outstanding Athletes

Basketball

Rule, Bob
Wright, Lonnie

University of New Mexico
Albuquerque, New Mexico 87131

All Skyline Conference

Football

Perkins, Don, 1958–59

All Western Athletic Conference

Football

Dennard, Preston, 1974–76
Cole, Robin, 1975–76
Williams, Michael, 1976–78
Fields, Sharay, 1979
Baker, Charles, 1979
Carter, Jimmie, 1981–83
Carter, Michael, 1982
Jackson, John, 1982–83

Basketball

Harge, Ira, 1963–64
Daniels, Mel, 1965–67
Monroe, Ben, 1967
Howard, Greg, 1968–69
Long, Willie, 1970–71
Minniefield, Darryl, 1973
Hardin, Bernard, 1974
Cooper, Michael, 1977–78
Johnson, Marvin, 1977–78
Belin, Larry, 1979
Page, Ken, 1980–81
Smith, Phil, 1984

All-American

Basketball

Daniels, Mel, 1967

Men's Track

Howard, Richard, 440 MH 1959
Plummer, Adolph, 440 YD 1961
Kennedy, Larry, 660 YD 1964
Robinson, Clarence, LJ 1965
Rivers, Bernie, 440 YR 1966
Matison, Rene, 440 YR 1966

Robinson, Ira, LJ 1966
Baxter, Art, TJ 1966–67
Mitchell, Clark, 660 YD 1967

Solomon, Michael, 60 YD 1977
Moore, Roger, 2-Min. R 1983
Rudd, Dwayne, LJ 1983–84

MID-AMERICAN CONFERENCE

1. Ohio University
2. University of Toledo
3. Miami University
4. Eastern Michigan University

5. Kent State University
6. Northern Illinois University
7. Western Michigan University

Ohio University
Athens, Ohio 45701–2979

Coaches of Varsity Teams

Football

Bryant, Cleve (Head), 1984–Present

Basketball

Brown, Bill (Assistant)
Backus, Michael (Assistant), 1978–80

Football

Jackson, Sherrill (Assistant)

All Mid-American Conference

Football

Brooks, Bob, 1960
Harrison, Bob, 1960
Fowlkes, Ron, 1963–64
Turner, Chuck, 1964
Bryant, Cleve,[1] 1968
Allen, Bob, 1970–71
Benton, Al, 1970–71
Caldwell, Don, 1971–72
Dampier, Bert, 1972
Lyons, L.C., 1974
Madison, Ed, 1974–75
Lockett, Greg, 1976
Welcher, Arnold, 1976
Washington, Ed, 1983
Carter, Sherman, 1983

Basketball

Adams, Bunk, 1960–61
Jackson, Jerry, 1964
Hilt, Don, 1964–65
Fowlkes, Ken, 1966
McKee, Gerald, 1969
Corde, Tom, 1972
Green, George, 1973
Brown, Bill, 1974
Luckett, Walter,[2] 1974–75
Devereaux, John,[3] 1983–84

Wrestling

Johnson, Russ—177 lbs. 1970–72
Daniels, Andy—118 lbs.[4] 1976–78
Scott, Randolph—167 lbs. 1976

Track

Mitchell, Darnell, 1962–63, 1965

All-American

Basketball

Adams, Bunk,[5] 1960–61
Luckett, Walter, 1975

Track and Field

Mitchell, Darnell, 800M 1965
Taylor, Emmett, 200M 1968

Other Outstanding Athletes

Track

Perkis, Rupel A., 1950–51
Carney, Les,[6] 1960

[1] Bryant, Cleve–1968 Mid-American Conference Player of the Year
[2] Luckett, Walter–1974 Mid-American Conference Player of the Year
[3] Devereaux, John–1984 Mid-American Conference Player of the Year
[4] Daniels, Andy–chosen Outstanding Mid-Eastern Athletic Conference Meet Wrestler, 1977 and 1978
[5] Adams, Bunk–selected as an alternate member on the 1964 United States Olympic Basketball Team; Honorable Mention
[6] Carney, Les–first black athlete from Ohio University to compete in the Olympics; member of the 1960 United States Olympic Track and Field Team

University of Toledo
Toledo, Ohio 43606

Coaches of Varsity Teams

Men's Track and Field
Jones, Eugene (Head)

Women's Track and Field
Kearney, Beverly (Head)

Men's Basketball
Joplin, Stan (Assistant)

Football
Jackson, Sherill (Assistant)
Simmons, Robert (Assistant)
Jackson, Fred (Assistant)

All Mid-American Conference

Football

Triplet, Mel, 1954
Umbles, Clayton, 1956
Hodge, Roy, 1957
Burt, Occie, 1958
Smith, Robert, 1960
Baker, Frank, 1961
Gray, Jim, 1964
Burch, Henry, 1966
Sneed, Barry, 1966
Tucker, Mel, 1967–68
Moss, Roland, 1967–68
Johnson, Curtis, 1968–69
Tyler, Jim, 1969
Harris, Tony, 1969
Long, Mel,[1] 1969–71
Ealey, Chuck,[2] 1969–71
Cole, Charles, 1970
Saunders, John, 1971
Baker, Al, 1971

Duke, Willie, 1972
Young, Keith, 1973
Bivins, Aaron,[3] 1976–77
Menefee, David, 1981
Meadows, Darryl, 1982
Brandon, Mark, 1983

Basketball

Jones, Larry, 1962
Aston, Robert, 1966
Cole, Larry, 1975–76
Knuckles, Harvey, 1981

Track and Field

Harris, Byron, 1983–84

All-American

Football

Johnson, Curtis, 1969
Long, Mel, 1970–71
Ealey, Chuck, 1971

Track and Field
Hopkins, Aaron,[4] 1966–67

University of Toledo's Hall of Fame

Cole, Emerson
Pierce, James
Craig, Richard
Hutson, Dr. Richard
Nash, Robert
Clemons, Frankie

Other Outstanding Athletes

Hamlar, Davis
Rhodes, Lenny
Jackson, Jeff
Wright, Darrin
Palmer, Gerald
Tunnel, Emlen
Manuel, Jim
Crockett, Dan

[1] Long, Mel–1971 Mid-American Conference Defensive Player of the Year
[2] Ealey, Chuck–1969–70 Mid-American Conference Offensive Player of the Year
[3] Bivins, Aaron–1976 Mid-American Conference Defensive Player of the Year
[4] Hopkins, Aaron–NCAA Indoor Champion

Miami University
Oxford, Ohio 45056

Coaches of Varsity Teams

Women's Track

Williams, Joselyn, 1982–84

All Mid-American Conference

Football

Burton, Tirrel, 1955
Triplett, Bill, 1961
Tyler, Scott, 1962
Moore, Al, 1965–67
Thompson, Larry, 1968–69
Hitchens, Robert,[1] 1971–72
Jackson, Herman, 1973
Spicer, Joseph, 1974
Edwards, Mel, 1975
Smith, Sherman, 1975
Taylor, Rick, 1975
Hunter, Mark, 1978
Springs, Kirk, 1978–79
Crowder, David, 1979
Jones, Greg, 1980–81
Peterson, Jay, 1982
William, David, 1982
Swarn, George, 1986

Basketball

Barnette, Don, 1956–57
Embry, Wayne, 1958
Winguard, Ed, 1959
Benson, LeVern, 1962
Foster, Fred,[2] 1967–68
Dunlap, Darrell, 1972
Hampton, Rich, 1973
Lumpkin, Phil, 1973–74
Aldridge, Archie, 1978
Harper, Ron,[3] 1984–86

Track

Downing, Ted, 1967–68

Baseball

Byrd, Greg, 1980–81

All-American

Football

Hitchens, Robert, 1972

Track

Downing, Ted, 1968

Miami University's Hall of Fame

Embry, Wayne
Burton, Tirrel
Bronston, Robert
Hitchens, Robert
Smith, Sherman
Downing, Ted
Lumpkin, Phil

[1] Hitchens, Robert–1972 Mid-American Conference Offensive Player of the Year
[2] Foster, Fred–1968 Mid-American Conference Player of the Year
[3] Harper, Ron–1985 and 1986 Mid-American Conference Player of the Year

Eastern Michigan University
Ypsilanti, Michigan 48197

Athletic Directors

Smith, Dr. Albert E., 1975–76
Smith, Gene, 1985–Present

Coaches of Varsity Teams

Men's Basketball

Scott, Ray (Head), 1976–79
Boyce, James (Head), 1979–Present

All Mid-American Conference

Football

Johnson, Ron, 1976–77

Basketball

Cofield, Fred, 1984–85

All-American

Football

Pureifory, David, 1970–71

Basketball

Gervin, George,[1] 1972

Eastern Michigan University's Hall of Fame

Campbell, Garion H.
Beatty, Charles Eugene
Jones, Hayes
Pureifory, David
Sabbath, Clarence
Bibbs, James
Kirksey, Daniel Webster

[1] Gervin, George–Little All-American

Kent State University
Kent, Ohio 44242

Coaches of Varsity Teams

Men's Basketball

Boyd, Michael (Interim Head), 1/9/78–6/78

Men's and Women's Track and Field

Richburg, Orin (Head), 1978–Present

Tennis

Gatewood, Lucian (Head), 1973–74
Fuller, Brian (Head), 1975–78

All Mid-American Conference

Football

Owens, Luke, 1956
Collins, Booker, 1964
Asbury, William,[1] 1965
Brooks, Jon, 1965–66
Harris, Lou, 1967
Tinker, Gerald, 1973
Harmon, Bernard, 1973
Poole, Larry, 1973–74
Elliott, Marvin, 1974
Winnins, Larry, 1974
Brown, Cedric, 1974–75
Deadmond, Glenn, 1976

Basketball

Wallace, Oliver, 1958–60
Yance, Ruben, 1971–72
McGhee, Burrell, 1977–79

Grooms, Trent, 1980

Track

Curry, Norman, HJ 1964–66
Richburg, Orin, 100M/200M 1967–69
Harris, Ted, 800M 1971
Turner, Len, 100M/200M 1971–72
Tinker, Gerald, 100M 1973
Gregory, Calvin, 400IH/110MHH 1975
Carter, Terry, 100M 1979
Thrist, Harrison, LJ 1980
Jefferson, Thomas, 100M/200M 1982–84

All Mid-American Conference

Wrestling

McNair, Clarence, 1957–58

All-American

Football

Tate III, Penefield, 1952
Owens, Luke, 1956

Track

Hughes, Ron, IT 1965
Richburg, Orin, OT 1967
Tinker, Gerald, IT and OT 1973
Harris, Ted, IT 1973
Carter, Terry, IT 1979

Wrestling

McNair, Clarence, 1959
Whitaker, Tim, 1971

Kent State University's Hall of Fame

Asbury, William Wesley
Little, Wilbur
Owens, Luke
Poole, Larry
Tinker, Gerald Alexander
Turner, Len
Richburg, Orin

[1] Asbury, William–1965 Mid-American Conference Offensive Player of the Year

Northern Illinois University
Dekalb, Illinois 60115

Athletic Directors

Davis, McKinley "Deacon" (Executive Director for Intercollegiate Athletics), 1968–82

Coaches of Varsity Teams

Basketball

Luck, Emory (Head), 1973–77

Cross Country

Kimmons, Willie (Head)

All Mid-American Conference

Basketball

Hicks, Matt,[1] 1976–77
Dawkins, Paul,[2] 1978–79

All-American

Football

Hatter, Willie,[3] 1972–73

Basketball

Bradley, Jim, 1972–73
Hicks, Matt,[4] 1977
Dawkins, Paul,[5] 1979

Wrestling

Johnson, Johnny B.—190 lbs. 1972
Johnson, Larry—158 lbs. 1973

Other Outstanding Athletes

Football

Moore, Ken
Latin, Jerry

Basketball

Booker, Abe

Northern Illinois University's Hall of Fame

Football

Cooper, Elzie[6]

Basketball

Bradley, Jim

Wrestling

Johnson, John B.

[1] Hicks, Matt—1977 Mid-American Conference Player of the Year
[2] Dawkins, Paul—1979 Mid-American Conference Player of the Year
[3] Hatter, Willie–Honorable Mention
[4] Hicks, Matt–Honorable Mention
[5] Dawkins, Paul–Honorable Mention

Western Michigan University
Kalamazoo, Michigan 49008

Athletic Directors

Brinn, Chauncey (Interim AD), 1/79–6/79

Coaches of Varsity Teams

Football

Comer, Charles (Assistant), 1968–74
Lewis, Terry (Assistant), 1975–76
Hardy, William (Assistant), 1977
Harris, William (Assistant), 1978–81
Samuel, Tony (Assistant), 1982–Present

Basketball

Roberts, Joe (Assistant), 1970–71
Walker, Rich (Assistant), 1975–78
Quarles, Larry (Assistant), 1979
Byrdsong, Rick (Assistant), 1980
Wesley, Walter (Assistant), 1981–84

Track

Lewis, Fletcher (Assistant), 1969
Bowman, Boice (Assistant), 1970–74
Richburg, Orin (Assistant), 1975–77
Bates, Halbert (Assistant), 1978–Present

All Mid-American Conference

Football

Coleman, Lovell, 1958
Collins, Jerry, 1967–68
Lawson, Roger, 1970
Davis, Vern, 1970
Thomas, Bernard, 1971–72
Cates, Larry, 1971–72

Carter, Michael, 1973
Persell, Jerome,[1] 1976–78
Manns, Eric, 1978–79
Howard, Robert, 1979–80
Bullock, George, 1980
Hughes, Allen, 1980–81

Basketball

Newsome, Manny, 1962–64
Ford, Gene, 1968–69
Washington, Chuck, 1971
Jenkins, Earl, 1971
Pettis, Earnest, 1972
Cunningham, Ken, 1980
Russell, Walker D., 1981–82

Women's Basketball

Charity, Pat, 1981

Women's Tennis

Whitfield, Marla, 1984

Women's Gymnastics

Gill, Carmine, 1982

Men's Track

Taylor, Ed, 1948
Murchinson, Ira, 1954, 1957–58
Skinner, Byron, 1955
Littlejohn, Alonzo, 1961–62
Johnson, Joel, 1962
Randolph, Tom, 1968–69
Pruitt, Terry, 1970
Rencher, Don, 1970
Gaines, Homer, 1972
Baker, Alan, 1974

White, Craig, 1974
Miles, Dana, 1974
Williams, Darrell, 1978
Lockhart, Michael, 1980
Hamilton, Carol, 1981–82
Ellis, Ian, 1982
Washington, Alex, 1983–84
Williams, James, 1983–84

All-American

Football

Cheatham, Clarence, 1958
Coleman, Lovell, 1959
Persell, Jerome, 1976–77

Basketball

Newsome, Manny, 1964
Ford, Gene, 1969

Track

Murchinson, Ira, 1957–58
Littlejohn, Alonzo, 1961
Randolph, Tom, 1968
Washington, Alex, 1983

Western Michigan University's Hall of Fame

Coleman, Sr., Horace
Dunlap, Sam
Mallard, Louis "Bo"
Murchinson, Ira
Newsome, Manny
Salter, Ed

[1] Persell, Jerome–1976, 1977, and 1978 Mid-American Conference Offensive Player of the Year

SOUTHEASTERN CONFERENCE

1. University of Georgia
2. University of Kentucky
3. Mississippi State University
4. Vanderbilt University
5. University of Mississippi

6. Auburn University
7. University of Alabama
8. University of Tennessee
9. University of Florida
10. Louisiana State University

University of Georgia
Athens, Georgia 30613

All Southeastern Conference

Football

McClendon, Willie,[1] 1978
Hudson, Nat, 1980
Walker, Herschel,[2] 1980–82
Payne, Jimmy, 1980–82
Scott, Lindsay, 1981
Weaver, Eddie, 1981
Harper, Jimmy, 1982
Gilbert, Freddie, 1982–83
McIntyre, Guy, 1983
Flack, Tony, 1985–86

Basketball

Hogue, Ronnie, 1972
Bassett, Tim, 1973
Dorsey, Jackie, 1975–76
Daniels, Walter, 1976–79
Mercer, Lavon, 1979–80
Wilkins, Dominique,[3] 1981–82
Fleming, Vern,[4] 1983–84

Men's Track

Lattany, Mel,[5] 100M, 400MR, 60Y 1979–81
Christian, Clarence, 1980
Walker, Herschel, S, 400MR 1981–82
Simmons, Darryl, LJ 1982
Blalock, Stanley, 300MR 1984

Women's Track

Rankins, Kathy, LJ 1984

All-American

Football

Walker, Herschel, 1980–82

Payne, Jimmy, 1982
Gilbert, Freddie, 1983

Men's Basketball

Wilkins, Dominique, 1982
Fleming, Vern, 1984

Women's Basketball

Locke, Bernadette, 1980
Harris, Janet, 1983–85
Edwards, Teresa, 1984–85
McLain, Katrina

Men's Track

Lattany, Mel, 1980–81
Johnson, Paul, 1981
Richards, William, 110MHH 1981
Christian, Clarence, LJ 1982
Walker, Herschel, ID 60YH 1982

Women's Track

Walker, Veronica, 100MD, 400MR 1982
Rankin, Kenny, LJ 1984

---

[1] McClendon, Willie–1978 *Nashville Banner* Southeastern Conference Most Valuable Player Award recipient
[2] Walker, Hersche–1982 Southeastern Conference Back of the Year (given by the Atlanta Touchdown Club); 1980/81/82 *Nashville Banner* Southeastern Conference Most Valuable Player Award recipient; 1982 Walter Camp National Player of the Year; 1982 Heisman Memorial Trophy recipient
[3] Wilkins, Dominique–1981 United Press International Southeastern Conference Player of the Year; 1981 Associated Press Southeastern Conference Player of the Year; 1981 Most Valuable Player at the Southeastern Conference Tournament
[4] Fleming, Vern–1983 Most Valuable Player at the Southeastern Conference Tournament; member of the 1984 United States Olympic Basketball Team
[5] Lattany, Mel–member of the 1980 United States Olympic Track and Field Team; 400-Meter Relay; 1981 World University Games 100-Meter Champion; 1981 World Cup 200-Meter Champion

University of Kentucky
Lexington, Kentucky 40506–0019

Coaches of Varsity Teams

Wrestling

Carr, Fletcher (Head), 1973–82

Football

Carr, Fletcher (Assistant), 1973–75
Kirksey, Larry (Assistant), 1977–81
Sharpless, Rod (Assistant), 1982–Present

Basketball

Hamilton, Leonard (Assistant), 1974–86

All Southeastern Conference

Football

Bishop, Darryl, 1972–73
Collins, Sonny,[1] 1973–75
Bryant, Warren, 1974–76
Still, Art, 1976–77
Ramsey, Derrick, 1977
Adams, George, 1984

Basketball

Payne, Tom, 1971
Givens, Jack, 1976–78
Bowie, Sam, 1980
Minniefield, Dirk,[2] 1981–83
Hord, Derrick 1982
Turpin, Melvin, 1982–84
Walker, Ken,[3] 1984–86

Women's Basketball

Still, Valerie, 1982–83

Men's Track and Field

Green, Jim, 1968–71
Mayes, Marvin, 1970
Lightsey, William, 1970
Grimes, Hamil, 1980

Women's Track and Field

Lowe, Tanya, 1983–84

Wrestling

Carr, Joe, 1975–77

Carr, Jim, 1975–77
Smith, Harold, 1977–80
Rayford, Earl, 1980

Baseball

Bryant, Derek, 1971

All-American

Football

Stephens, Elmore, 1974
Bryant, Warren, 1976
Still, Art, 1977

Basketball

Givens, Jack, 1977–78
Bowie, Sam,[4] 1980–84

Women's Basketball

Still, Valerie, 1982–83

Men's Track and Field

Green, Jim, 1968
Mayes, Marvin, 1970
Grimes, Hamil, 1980

Wrestling

Carr, Joe, 1975–77
Carr, Jim, 1977
Smith, Harold, 1977

[1] Collins, Sonny–1973 *Nashville Banner* Southeastern Conference Most Valuable Player Award recipient
[2] Minniefield, Dirk–1982 Southeastern Conference Tournament Most Valuable Player Award recipient
[3] Walker, Ken–1986 Southeastern Conference Player of the Year
[4] Bowie, Sam–member of the 1980 United States Olympic Basketball Team

Mississippi State University
Mississippi State, Mississippi 39762

Coaches of Varsity Teams

Football

Ford, Robert (Assistant), 1982–Present

Basketball

Jeffries, Edgar (Assistant), 1977–79
Peck, Wiley (Assistant), 1980–81
Brown, Michael (Assistant), 1981–82

Track

White, Vernon (Assistant), 1976–78

Southeastern Conference

Football

Dowsing, Frank, 1971
Packer, Walter, 1974–75
Hull, Harvey, 1974–76
Costict, Ray, 1975–76
Gillard, Larry, 1977
McDole, Mardye, 1978–80
Cooks, Johnie, 1980–81
Collins, Glen, 1980–81
Haddix, Michael, 1981–82
Jackson, William, 1981–83
Knight, Danny, 1982

Basketball

Jenkins, Jerry, 1975
White, Ray, 1976, 1978–79
Brown, Ricky, 1977–78
Peck, Wiley, 1979
Malone, Jeff,[1] 1981–83

All-American

Football

Dowsing, Frank, 1971
Hull, Harvey, 1976
McDole, Mardye, 1980
Cooks, Johnie, 1981
Collins, Glen, 1981
Jackson, Billy, 1981

Basketball

Brown, Rickey, 1980
Malone, Jeff, 1983

Track

Jennings, Evis,[2] 1976
Washington, George,[3] 1982
Hadley, Michael[4]
Jones, Darryl[5]
Moore, Michael[6]

Other Outstanding Athletes

Track

Whitelead, Les, HJ
Gray, Samuel, MR
Darby, Jimmy, LJ
Milsap, Leroy, TJ
Spane, Charles, R

[1] Malone, Jeff–1983 United Press International Southeastern Conference Player of the Year
[2] Jennings, Evis–1976 NCAA 440-Yard Dash Champion
[3] Washington, George–member of the 440-Yard Relay Team
[4] Hadley, Michael–member of the 440-Yard Relay Team
[5] Jones, Darryl–member of the 440-Yard Relay Team
[6] Moore, Michael–member of the 440-Yard Relay Team

Vanderbilt University
Nashville, Tennessee 37240

Coaches of Varsity Teams

Football

Malone, Fred (Assistant), 1973–75
Alexander, Hubbard (Assistant), 1975–79

Basketball

Culley, David (Assistant), 1979–81
McClendon, Leroy (Assistant), 1984

Women's Basketball

Lawrence, Teresa (Assistant), 1981–Present

All Southeastern Conference

Football

Wilson, Bernard, 1976–77
Brown, Preston, 1979
Buggs, Waymon, 1981
Matthews, Allama, 1982
Coleman, Leonard, 1983

Basketball

Wallace, Perry,[1] 1970
Davis, Charles, 1978–79, 1981
Springer, Tom, 1979
Jones, Willie, 1982

Women's Basketball

Brumfield, Harriet, 1982–83

All-American

Football

Matthews, Allama, 1982

Other Outstanding Athletes

Football

Edwars, Charles
Heflin, Van
Gurley, Rodney
Jordon, Walter
Pointer, John
Myrick, Ron

Basketball

Sneed, John

[1] Wallace, Perry–first black American to compete in basketball in the Southeastern Conference and at Vanderbilt University, 1968; 1970 Southeastern Conference Sportsmanship Award recipient

University of Mississippi
University, Mississippi 38677

All Southeastern Conference

Football

Williams, Ben, 1973–75
Johnson, Lawrence, 1975
Weathers, Curtis, 1977–78
Cage, Charlie, 1978
Townsend, Andre, 1982–83
Nunn, Freddie Joe, 1983

Basketball

Ball, Coolidge, 1972–73
Turner, Elston, 1980–81
Clark, Carlos, 1982–83
Laird, Eric, 1984

Men's Track

Nelson, Nicky, 880, TMR, ID 1983–84
Tate, Cornelius, 880, TMR, ID 1984

Cartlidge, Perry, MR, ID, 1984
Dean, Melvin, MR, ID, 1984
Spry, Ralph, LJ, OD, 1982–83
Daniel, Clarence, 400M, OD, 1983
Dees, Tony, 110H, OD, 1983

All-American

Football

Williams, Ben, 1975

Men's Track

Spry, Ralph, LJ 1982–83
Dees, Tony, 60HH 1983–84
Daniel, Clarence 1983–84

University of Mississippi's Hall of Fame

Williams, Ben

Auburn University
Auburn University, Alabama 36849

Coaches of Varsity Teams

Football

Daniel, James Edward (Assistant)
Whitt, Joe (Assistant)

Basketball

Anderson, Tevester (Assistant)

All Southeastern Conference

Football

Cribbs, Joe,[1] 1978–79
Brooks, James, 1980
Humphrey, Donnie, 1981–83
James, Lionel, 1982–83
Jackson, Bo, 1982–83, 1985
Robinson, Gerald, 1983–85
Thomas, Ben, 1984
Fullwood, Brent, 1987

Basketball

Johnson, Eddie, 1974–76
Mitchell, Michael, 1977–78
Barkley, Charles,[2] 1983–84
Pearson, Charles,[3] 1984–86
Ford, Frank, 1987

Women's Basketball

Jackson, Becky, 1981–84
Monroe, Lori, 1983
Orr, Vickie, 1986–87

Baseball

Brown, J.B., 1978

Men's Track

Outlin, Cliff, 100YD 1974–75
Easley, Tony, 60YD, LJ 1976
Glance, Harvey, 100M, 60YD 1976–78
Walker, James, 60YHH, 110MHH, 400MH 1976–78
Smith, Willie, 440Y, 400M 1977–78
Strother, Steven, DMRT 1979
Floyd, Stanley, 100M, 60YD 1980
Miller, Eugene, 110MH 1980
Franklin, Byron, 1980

All-American

Football

Jackson, Bo,[4] 1983–85
Fullwood, Brent, 1986

Men's Track

Outlin, Cliff, 1974–75
Easley, Tony, 1976
Glance, Harvey, 1976–77
Miller, Eugene, 1980
Franklin, Byron, 1980
Brooks, Larry, 1980
Brooks, Calvin, 1983–84

[1] Cribbs, Joe–1979 *Nashville Banner* Southeastern Conference Most Valuable Player Award recipient
[2] Barkley, Charles–1984 Southeastern Conference Tournament Most Valuable Player Award recipient; 1984 United Press International Southeastern Conference Player of the Year Award recipient; 1984 Associated Press Southeastern Conference Player of the Year Award recipient
[3] Pearson, Charles–member of the 1984 United States Olympic Basketball Team
[4] Jackson, Bo–1985 Heisman Memorial Trophy recipient

University of Alabama
University, Alabama 35486

Coaches of Varsity Teams

Football

Croom, Sylvester (Assistant), 1976–Present

Basketball

Gray, Kevin (Assistant), 1984–Present

All Southeastern Conference

Football

Mitchell, John, 1972
Jackson, Wilbur, 1973
Lowe, Woodrow, 1973–75
Washington, Michael, 1974
Shelby, Willie, 1974
Croom, Sylvester, 1974
King, Tyrone, 1975
Newsome, Ozzie, 1976–77
Davis, John, 1977
Stephenson, Dwight, 1977–79
McNeal, Don, 1979
Junior, E.J., 1979–80
Boyd, Thomas, 1979–80
Castille, Jeremiah, 1981–82
Pitts, Michael, 1981–82
Lewis, Walter, 1983
Moore, Rick, 1983
Hand, Jon, 1984–85
Bennett, Cornelius, 1985–86

Basketball

Hudson, Wendell,[1] 1972–73
Cleveland, Charles, 1973–75
Douglas, Leon, 1974–76
Murray, Anthony, 1976–78
Dunn, T.R., 1977
King, Reginald,[2] 1977–79
Phillips, Eddie, 1980–82
Whatley, Ennis, 1982–83
Hurt, Bobby Lee, 1983–85
Richardson, Eric, 1984
Johnson, Buck, 1984–85
McKey, Derrick, 1986–87

All-American

Football

Mitchell, John, 1972
Lowe, Woodrow, 1973–75
Croom, Sylvester, 1974
Newsome, Ozzie, 1976–77
Davis, John, 1977
Stephenson, Dwight, 1979
McNeal, Don, 1979
Junior, E.J., 1980
Boyd, Thomas, 1980–81
Pitts, Michael, 1982
Castille, Jeremiah, 1982
Moore, Rick, 1983
Lewis, Walter, 1983
Hand, Jon, 1985–86
Bennett, Cornelius,[3] 1986–87

Basketball

Hudson, Wendell, 1973
Douglas, Leon, 1975–76
Dunn, T.R., 1977
King, Reginald, 1978–79
Whatley, Ennis,[4] 1984
Johnson, Buck,[5] 1985–86
McKey, Derrick,[6] 1987

[1] Hudson, Wendell–1973 United Press International Southeastern Conference Player of the Year; 1973 Associated Press Southeastern Conference Player of the Year
[2] King, Reginald–1978 and 1979 United Press International Southeastern Conference Player of the Year; 1978 and 1979 Associated Press Southeastern Conference Player of the Year
[3] Bennett, Cornelius–1987 Vince Lombardi Trophy recipient
[4] Whatley, Ennis–Honorable Mention
[5] Johnson, Buck–Honorable Mention
[6] McKey, Derrick–Honorable Mention

University of Tennessee
Knoxville, Tennessee 37901–9926

All Southeastern Conference

Football

Walker, Jackie, 1971
Stanback, Haskel, 1972–73
Holloway, Condredge, 1973
Morgan, Stanley, 1974–76

Harper, Reginald, 1978–79
James, Roland, 1978–79
Hancock, Anthony, 1980–81
Gault, Willie, 1982
White, Reginald,[1] 1983
Jones, Johnnie, 1983–84
Robinson, Tony, 1984
McGee, Tim, 1984

Basketball

Robinson, Larry, 1973
King, Bernard,[2] 1975–77
Jackson, Michael, 1976–77
Darden, John, 1977–78
Johnson, Reginald, 1978–80
Carter, Gary, 1981
Wood, Howard, 1981
Ellis, Dale,[3] 1981–83
White, Tony, 1986–87

Tennis

Harmon, Rodney, 1980

All-American

Walker, Jackie, 1970–71
James, Roland, 1979
Gault, Willie, 1982
White, Reginald, 1983
Robinson, Tony, 1984–85
McGee, Tim, 1984–85

Basketball

King, Bernard, 1975–77
Johnson, Reginald, 1979–80
Ellis, Dale, 1982–83
White, Tony, 1987

Track

James, Sam, SC 1979
Blair, Anthony, 400MD, 440YD 1979–80
Hancock, Anthony, LJ 1980
Miller, Michael, 60YD 1980
Gault, Willie, 100MHH, 60YH, 100MD, 110MH 1981–83
Towns, Reggie, 110MH 1983–84
Graddy, Sam, 100MD 1983–84
Wilson, Jerome, 110MH 400MH

Other Outstanding Athletes

Football

McClain, Lester[4]

[1] White, Reginald–1983 Southeastern Conference Lineman of the Year
[2] King, Bernard–1975 and 1976 United Press International Southeastern Conference Player of the Year; 1976 and 1977 (co-winner in 1977); Associated Press Southeastern Conference Player of the Year
[3] Ellis, Dale–1982 United Press International and Associated Press Southeastern Conference Player of the Year; 1983 Associated Press Southeastern Conference Player of the Year
[4] McClain, Lester–the first black American to play football at the University of Tennessee, 1968

University of Florida
Gainesville, Florida 32604

Athletic Directors

Tribble, Keith (Assistant Athletic Director), 1981–Present

Coaches of Varsity Teams

Football

Webster, James (Assistant), 1974
Reed, Lambert (Assistant), 1975–77
Parker, Jim (Assistant), 1978–82
Kendrick, Vince (Assistant), 1978–83
Morand, Elroy (Assistant), 1981–82
Kirksey, Larry (Assistant), 1984–Present

Basketball

Brown, James (Assistant), 1975–81
McCraney, Ken (Assistant), 1982–Present

Women's Basketball

Murphy, Donna (Assistant)

All Southeastern Conference

Football

Moore, Nat, 1972
Kendrick, Preston, 1974
Green, Sam, 1975
DuBose, Jimmy,[1] 1975
Williams, Michael, 1975
Chandler, Wes, 1976–77
Cowans, Alvin, 1976–77
Green, Tony, 1977
Little, David, 1980
Galloway, David, 1981

Marshall, Wilber, 1981–83
Jones, James, 1982
Dixon, Dwayne, 1983
Brown, Lomas, 1984
Johnson, Alonzo, 1984
Newton, Tim, 1984
Nattiel, Rick, 1985–86

Basketball

Glasper, Richard, 1978
Hannah, Reginald, 1980
Williams, Ron, 1981–84
McDowell, Eugene, 1983–85
Moten, Andrew, 1985–87
Maxwell, Vernon, 1986–87

Men's Track

Coleman, Ron, 1969–70, 1972
Jenkins, Nate, 1973
Brown, Beaufort, 1973–75
Bostic, Hesley, 1973–75
Rambo, Robert, 1974
Goings, Mitchell, 1974
Alexander, Winfred, 1974
Tuitt, Horace, 1976
Sharpe, Michael, 1976
Simmons, Palmer, 1976
Barriffe, Clive, 1976
Gray, Noel, 1976
Mayo, Wesley, 1977–78
Luckie, Dock, 1978–79
Pringle, Jim, 1979–80
Gray, Kenneth, 1980–81, 1983
Brown, Floyd, 1981
Miller, Hugo, 1981
Green, Rickey, 1981
Holmes, Stanley, 1981

Women's Basketball

Jackson, Tammy

Women's Track

Fowler, Oralee
Henry, Dee
Pitts, Alverretta
Bressant, Piper
Campbell, Donna
Lotmore, Sharon

All-American

Football

Green, Sammy, 1975
Chandler, Wes, 1976–77
Little, David, 1980
Marshall, Wilber, 1982–83
Brown, Lomas, 1984
Johnson, Alonzo, 1984
Nattiel, Rick, 1986

Men's Track

Brown, Beaufort, 1973–75
Goings, Mitchell, 1974
Rambo, Robert, 1974
Alexander, Winfred, 1974–75
Sharpe, Michael, 1975
Gray, Noel, 1975
Tuitt, Horace, 1975–76
Barriffe, Clive, 1978
Pringle, Jim, 1978–79
Green, Ricky, 1980
Mattox, Cullen, 1980

Women's Track

Allwood, Rose
Ray, Lorraine
Fergusan, Shonell
Dunlap, Patty
Lewis, Lori
Rodgers, Pam
Pitts, Alverretta
Bressant, Piper
Mercer, Lori

[1] DuBose, Jimmy–1975 *Nashville Banner* Southeastern Conference Most Valuable Player Award recipient

Louisiana State University
Baton Rouge, Louisiana 70893

Coaches of Varsity Teams

Football

Washington, Otis (Assistant), 1980
Harris, Bishop (Assistant), 1980–83
Lewis, Terry (Assistant), 1984

Basketball

Abernathy, Ron (Assistant), 1976–84

Gymnastics

Foster, Michael (Assistant), 1981–82

All Southeastern Conference

Football

Williams, Michael, 1974
Burrell, Clinton, 1976
Sibley, Lew, 1976
Robiskie, Terry, 1976
Carson, Carlos, 1977
Alexander, Charles,[1] 1977–78
Teal, Willie, 1978–79
White, Lyman, 1978–80
Williams, Chris, 1979–80
Richardson, Albert, 1980–82
McDaniel, Orlando, 1981
Scott, Malcolm, 1981–82
Smith, Lance, 1982
Britt, James, 1982
Dardar, Ramsey, 1982
Hilliard, Dalton, 1982–84
Hobley, Liffort, 1983
Martin, Eric, 1983–84

Basketball

Temple, Collis,[2] 1974
Higgs, Ken, 1976–78
Macklin, Durand, 1978, 1980–81
Green, Al, 1979
Scales, DeWayne,[3] 1979–80
Green, Lionel, 1979
Martin, Ethan, 1980–81
Carter, Howard, 1982–83
Mitchell, Leonard, 1982–83
Taylor, Derrick, 1984
Reynolds, Jerry, 1984–85
Williams, John, 1986
Wilson, Nikita, 1987

Women's Basketball

Walker, Joyce,[4] 1982–84
Doucet, Madaline, 1984

Women's Volleyball

Magers, Rose,[5] 1981
Rideau, Paula, 1983

All-American

Football

Williams, Michael, 1974
Alexander, Charles, 1977–78
Britt, James, 1982
Richardson, Al, 1982
Martin, Eric, 1983

Basketball

Macklin, Durand, 1981

Women's Basketball

Walker, Joyce, 1982–84

Wrestling

Evans, Michael, 1981
Jackson, Kevin, 1983

Other Outstanding Athletes

Basketball

Irvin, Fess
Wilson, Anthony
Woodside, Bernard

[1] Alexander, Charles–1977 *Nashville Banner* Southeastern Conference Most Valuable Player Award recipient
[2] Temple, Collis–first black American to compete in basketball at Louisiana State University
[3] Scales, DeWayne–1980 Southeastern Conference Tournament Most Valuable Player Award recipient
[4] Walker, Joyce–alternate member of the 1984 United States Olympic Basketball Team
[5] Magers, Rose–member of the 1984 United States Olympic Volleyball Team
83

TRANS-AMERICAN CONFERENCE

1. Northwestern State University
2. Houston Baptist University

3. Centenary College
4. North Texas State University

Northwestern State University of Louisiana Natchitoches, Louisiana 71497

Coaches of Varsity Teams

Football

Meadors, James (Assistant), 1983–Present

Basketball

Russell, Melvin (Assistant), 1984–Present

All Gulf South Conference

Football

Johnson, Donald 1972
Cage, Mario 1973
Kelly, John 1973
Dilworth, John 1974

All-American

Football

Walls, Larry 1972

Thornton, Sidney 1976
Delaney, Joe 1979–80
Richardson, Michael 1983

Men's Track

Brown, Michael, LJ, NAIA 1973–76
Hardwell, Robert, 100 and 200M, NAIA 1976
McIntosh, Robert, TJ, NAIA 1976
Handy, Jarrot, TJ, LJ 1980
Oatis, Victor, 400MR, NC 1981
Delaney, Joe, 400MR, NC 1981
Johnson, Mario, 400MR, NC 1981
Brown, Ray, 400MR 1982
Washington, Edgar, 400MR 1982
Johnson, Mario, 400MR 1982
McGloory, Percy, 400MR 1984
Johnsjon, Mario, 400MR 1984
Washington, Edgar, 400MR 1984
Evans, Cedric, 400MR 1984

Men's Basketball

Wilson, Vernon—NAIA 1973

Houston Baptist University
Houston, Texas 77074

All Trans-America Athletic Conference

Men's Basketball

England, Matt 1985

All-American

Men's Basketball

England, Matt[1] 1984

Men's Track

Thompson, Rick[2] 1983

Other Outstanding Athletes

Men's Basketball

Coleman, E.C.

[1] England, Matt—Honorable Mention
[2] Thompson, Rick—1983 NCAA Outdoor High Jump Champion

Centenary College
Shreveport, Louisiana 71134–0188

All Trans-America Athletic Conference

Basketball

Lett, George 1978–79
Rhone, Cherokee 1980–81
Jackson, Willie[1] 1981–84

All-American

Basketball

Parish, Robert 1974–76

[1] Jackson, Willie—leading scorer in Centenary College history

North Texas State University
Denton, Texas 76203

Administrators

Greene, Charles Edward "Joe"[1]

Coaches of Varsity Teams

Football

Barnes, Nelson (Assistant)
Shanklin, Ron (Assistant)
Jackson, Carl (Assistant)
Williams, Vic (Assistant)

Basketball

Gales, James (Assistant)

Track

Brown, Abe

All Missouri Valley Conference

Football

Haynes, Abner 1958–59
Perkins, Arthur 1960
Christle, William 1961
Love, John 1965
Harkless, Burkley 1965
Woods, William 1966
Greene, Joe 1966–68
Beatty, Charles 1967
Shanklin, Ron 1967–69
Taylor, Leo 1968
Holloway, Glen 1968–69
Hardman, Cedric 1969
Edwards, Dralves 1970
Dunlap, Leonard 1970
Scales, Hurles 1972

Basketball

Savage, John 1962–64
Russell, Rubin 1966–67
Hamilton, Joe 1969–70
Iverson, Robert 1974–75

All Southland Conference

Football

Hickman, Ron 1983
Cooks, Rayford 1983
Harper, Lester 1983

Men's Basketball

Lyons, Kenneth 1983

All-American

Football

Haynes, Abner 1959
Greene, Joe 1968
Holloway, Glen 1969

Other Outstanding Athletes

Football

Elliott, Tony
Haynes, Louis
Lewis, Reginald

Lockhart, Carl
Moseley, Andre
Phillips, Rudy
Pruett, Perry
Reece, Beasley
Smith, J.T.

Basketball

Jones, Albert
Winfield, Leroy

[1] Charles Edward "Joe" Greene—appointed a member of the North Texas State University Board of Regents in 1983. Term expires May, 1987.

EAST COAST CONFERENCE

1. American University
2. Hofstra University

3. University of Delaware

American University
Washington, D.C. 20016

Coaches of Varsity Teams

Men's Basketball

Tapscott, Ed (Head), 1982–Present

All East Coast Conference

Men's Basketball

Thomas, Wilbur[1] 1975
Brown, Calvin 1975–77
Bowers, Russell 1978–81
Nickens, Mark[2] 1981–83
Sloane, Ed 1983

All-American

Men's Basketball

Jones, Wil[3] 1960
Washington, Kermit[4] 1974

Other Outstanding Athletes

Men's Basketball

Lloyd, John
Hoey, Robin
Jones, Juan

Women's Basketball

Frazier, Jackie

[1] Thomas, Wilbur—1975 East Coast Conference Player of the Year
[2] Nickens, Mark—1982 East Coast Conference Co-Player of the Year
[3] Jones, Wil—College Division All-American
[4] Washington, Kermit—chosen to the 1970–80 Eastern College Athletic Conference All-Decade Team

Hofstra University
Hempstead, Long Island 11550

Coaches of Varsity Teams

Basketball

Tomlin, Bearnard (Assistant)

Football

Walker, Holly (Assistant)
McLeod, Chuck (Assistant)

Track

Jackson, John (Head)

All East Coast Conference

Basketball

Tomlin, Bernard 1975
Irving, John 1975–77

Laurel, Rich[1] 1976–77
Harvey, Lionel 1981

Other Outstanding Athletes

Williams, Wandy
White, Barry
Brower, Quinas
Mills, John
Singleton, Ken

Head Trainers

Shields, Gary
Hunter, Frank

[1] Laurel, Rich—1977 East Coast Conference Player of the Year

University of Delaware
Newark, Delaware 19716

Coaches of Varsity Teams

Football

Gregory, Ted (Assistant), 1972–77

All East Coast Conference

Men's Basketball

Luck, Ken 1981–82

Men's Lacrosse

Rogers, Ralph 1978–80

Women's Basketball

Price, Linny 1984

Women's Volleyball

Blair, Debra 1982

All-American

Football

Brown, Michael[1] 1963
Gregory, Ted[2] 1970
Hayman, Conway 1970
Johnson, Dennis[3] 1972

Beasley, Nate[4] 1974
Hyland, Vince[5] 1979

Men's Basketball

Luck, Ken[6] 1982

Other Outstanding Athletes

Football

Williams, Leonard[7]
Washington, Larry
Carroll, Craig
Roberts, Vernon
Gregory, Theo
Sully, Ivory
Randolph, Michael
Ramsey, Guy
Hammond, Paul

Women's Basketball

Phipps, Cynthia

Track

Brown, Michael, 50YD
Gordy, Frank, TJ, 600YD
Gregory, Ted, SPT
Ingram, Michael, LJ
Price, Calvin, 200MD
Ramsey, Guy, HJ
Luck, Ken, LJ
Thompkins, Nathaniel, WT
Madric, James, TJ, HH
Johnson, Anthony, HH
Miller, Dan, WT, SP
Weston, James, LJ

Wrestling

Lane, Brad

[1] Brown, Michael—College Division
[2] Gregory, Ted—Honorable Mention
[3] Johnson, Dennis—Honorable Mention; Division II
[4] Beasley, Nate—Division II
[5] Hyland, Vince—Honorable Mention
[6] Luck, Ken—Honorable Mention (*Sporting News*)
[7] Williams, Leonard—the first black American athlete at the University of Delaware, 1953–55

WEST COAST ATHLETIC CONFERENCE

1. University of San Francisco   2. Pepperdine University

University of San Francisco
San Francisco, California 94117

All West Coast Athletic Conference

Men's Basketball

Russell, William 1954–56
Jones, K.C. 1955–56
Brown, Gene 1958
Johnson, Ollie 1963–65
Ellis, Joseph 1964–65
Smith, Phil 1972–74
Redmond, Marion 1975–76
Boynes, Winford 1976–78
Hardy, James 1976–77
Cartwright, William 1976–79
Cox, Chubby 1977–78
Dailey, Quintin 1980–82
Bryant, Wallace 1981–82

All-American

Men's Basketball

Russell, William[1] 1955–56
Cartwright, William 1977–79
Dailey, Quintin 1982

Other Outstanding Athletes

Matson, Ollie[2]

[1] Russell, William—member of the 1956 United States Olympic Basketball team; 1956 United Press International College "Player of the Year" award recipient

[2] Matson, Ollie—played on the 1950–51 University of San Francisco team; member of the 1952 United States Olympic Track and Field team

Pepperdine University
Malibu, California 90265

All West Coast Athletic Conference

Basketball

Dugan, Larry 1954–55
Taylor, Mack 1957

Forbes, Sterling 1958–60
Blue, Robert 1959
Sims, Robert 1960
Warlick, Robert 1962–63
Betts, Roland 1964–65
Holmes, Tandy 1966
Grant, Hal 1967
Averitt, William 1972–73
Johnson, Dennis 1976
Matson, Ollie, Jr. 1976–79
Williams, Flintie Ray 1977
Brown, Ricardo 1979–80
Fuller, Tony 1980
Sadler, William 1981
Bond, Roylin 1981–82
Phillips, Orlando 1982–83
Suttle, Dane 1982–83
Anger, Victor 1984
Polee, Dwayne[1] 1985

Track

Johnson, Bill 1953–54
Walters, Jerome 1956

Baseball

Baptiste, Willie 1970

All-American

Football

Robinson, Wixie 1954–56

Basketball

Dugan, Larry 1955
Forbes, Sterling 1960
Warlick, Robert 1962
Averitt, William 1973
Bond, Roylin 1982

Track

Johnson, William 1953–54
Walters, Jerome 1956
Howard, Harold 1964–65
Coleman, Norman 1965
McNeil, Pablo 1967–68

Women's Track

Brown, Terrezene 1967
Charlton, Vilma 1967
White, Marilyn[2] 1967

Women's Basketball

Marcelin, Desi 1978

Tennis

Jones, Jerome[3] 1984

Pepperdine University's Hall of Fame

Dugan, Larry
Johnson, Bill

Robinson, Wixie
Walters, Jerome
Campbell, Dayle
Forbes, Sterling
Sims, Robert
Warlick, Robert
Averitt, William
Matson, Ollie, Jr.
Johnson, Dennis

[1] Polee, Dwayne—1985 West Coast Athletic Conference Player of the Year
[2] White, Marilyn—member of the 1964 U.S. Olympic Track and Field Team
[3] Jones, Jerome—won the 1984 NCAA Doubles Title with his partner

MID-WESTERN CITY CONFERENCE

1. University of Detroit
2. University of Evansville

3. Loyola University of Chicago
4. Oklahoma City University

University of Detroit
Detroit, Michigan 48221

Coaches of Varsity Teams

Fencing

Anderson, Elton (Head), 1973–77

Men's Basketball

Gaines, David "Smokey" (Head), 1977–79
McCarter, Willie (Head), 1979–82

Women's Basketball

Jones, DeWayne (Head), 1983–Present

Softball

Barnes, Milton 1983

Men's Basketball

Boyce, James (Assistant), 1973–75
Gaines, David (Assistant), 1973–77
McCarter, Willie (Assistant), 1978–79

Women's Basketball

Sims, Lydia (Assistant), 1978–81

All Missouri Valley Conference

Football

Russell, William 1955
Vaughn, Richard 1955

All Mid-Western City Conference

Men's Basketball

Davis, Jerry 1981–82
McNatt, Clarence 1983
Simms, Roy 1983
Doss, Bryan 1984
Gray, Keith 1984

Women's Basketball

Pack, Cassandra 1984
Pierce, Regina 1984

All-American

Football

Russell, William 1957

Men's Basketball

Murray, Dorle 1966
Haywood, Spencer 1969

Long, John 1978
Tyler, Terry 1978
Duerod, Terry 1979
Ross, Bryan[1] 1984
Gray, Keith[2] 1984

Women's Basketball

Johnson, Lydia 1980
Williams, Cheryl 1981
Pack, Cassandra 1984

Fencing

Blake, Ken 1971–73
Simmons, Tyrone 1971–73
Hooker, Fred 1972

University of Detroit's Hall of Fame

Bleach, Larry
Murray, Dorrie
Simmons, Tyrone

Other Outstanding Athletes

Women's Basketball

Daniels, Coretta
Blackburn, Lisa
Perry, Cynthia

[1] Ross, Bryan—Honorable Mention
[2] Gray, Keith—Honorable Mention

University of Evansville
Evansville, Indiana 47702–0329

All Indiana Collegiate Conference

Basketball

Smallwood, Ed[1] 1958–60
Humes, Larry[2] 1965–66

All Mid-Western City Conference

Basketball

Johnson, Richard 1982

All-American

Basketball

Smallwood, Ed 1958–60

Humes, Larry 1965–66
Johnson, Richard[3] 1982

Other Outstanding Athletes

Basketball

Scott, Tyrone

[1] Smallwood, Ed—1958 and 1960 Indiana Collegiate Conference Player of the Year
[2] Humes, Larry—1966 Indiana Collegiate Conference Player of the Year
[3] Johnson, Richard—Honorable Mention

Loyola University of Chicago
Chicago, Illinois 60626

Coaches of Varsity Teams

Men's Basketball

Wakefield, Andre (Assistant), 1981–Present

All Mid-Western Collegiate Conference

Men's Basketball

Clemons, Darius[1] 1980–82
Sappleton, Wayne[2] 1981–82
Hughes, Alfrederick[3] 1983–85
Battle, Andre 1983–85
Golston, Carl 1984–85
Moore, Andre 1985

All-American

Men's Basketball

Harkness, Gerald 1963
Sappleton, Wayne 1982
Hughes, Alfrederick 1985

Loyola University's Hall of Fame

Bluitt, Benjamin
Coleman, James
Harkness, Gerald
Hunter, Leslie
Martin, La Rue
McZier, Arthur
Miller, Ronald
Red, Clarence

Rouse, M. Victor
Tillman, Jim
White, Jr., Arthur M.
Billups, Ernest
White, Henry G.

Other Outstanding Athletes

Women's Volleyball

Anderson, Kathy

[1] Clemons, Darius—1981 Mid-Western Collegiate Conference Co-Player of the Year
[2] Sappleton, Wayne—1982 United Press International Mid-Western Collegiate Conference Player of the Year
[3] Hughes, Alfrederick—1983–85 Associated Press Mid-Western Collegiate Conference Player of the Year; 1983 United Press International Mid-Western Collegiate Conference Co-Player of the Year; 1985 United Press International Mid-Western Collegiate Conference Player of the Year

Oklahoma City University
Oklahoma City, Oklahoma 73106

All Mid-Western City Conference

Men's Basketball

Hill, Ernest 1980
Jackson, Rubin[1] 1980–82
Henry, Carl 1981
Campbell, James 1982
Johnson, Gary 1982

All-American

Men's Basketball

Wells, Jerry Lee 1966
Travis, Rich 1968–69
Edwards, Ozzie 1973

[1] Jackson, Rubin—1981 Mid-Western City Conference Co-Player of the Year

BIG EAST CONFERENCE

1. Georgetown University
2. Providence College
3. University of Pittsburgh
4. University of Connecticut
5. Seton Hall University

6. Boston College
7. St. John's University
8. Villanova University
9. Syracuse University

Georgetown University
Washington, D.C. 20057

Coaches of Varsity Teams

Men's Basketball

Thompson, John[1], (Head) 1972–Present
Riley, Michael, (Assistant) 1982–Present
Wilson, Gary, (Volunteer Assistant) 1981–Present

All Big East Conference

Men's Basketball

Duren, John[2] 1980
Shelton, Craig[3] 1980
Floyd, Eric[4] 1981–82
Ewing, Pat[5] 1982–85
Wingate, David 1985
Martin, Bill 1985

Jackson, Michael 1985
Williams, Reginald 1986–87

All-American

Men's Basketball

Floyd, Eric 1982
Ewing, Pat 1983–85
Williams, Reginald 1986–87

Other Outstanding Athletes

Men's Basketball

Holloway, Alonzo
Smith, Jonathan
Wilson, Merlin
Brooks, Gregory
Dutch, Al
Yeoman, Felix

Jackson, Derrick
Brown, Fred[6]
Smith, Gene
Graham, Michael
Riley, Michael
Spriggs, Ed
Hancock, Michael
Dalton, Ralph
Lynn, William
Long, Larry
Hopkins, Ed
Duren, Lonnie
Scates, Tom

[1] Thompson, John—first black American to coach a Division I NCAA basketball championship, 1984; 1980 Big East Coach of the Year; 1982 United States Basketball Writers Association Coach of the Year; 1985 National Association of Basketball Coaches' "Coach of the Year" Award recipient
[2] Duren, John—1980 Big East Conference Player of the Year
[3] Shelton, Craig—Most Valuable Player, 1980 Big East Tournament
[4] Floyd, Eric—Most Valuable Player, 1982 Big East Tournament
[5] Ewing, Pat—1984 and 1985 Big East Conference Co-Player of the Year; Most Valuable Player, 1984 Big East Tournament; 1982–85 Big East Conference Defensive Player of the Year; member of the 1984 United States Olympic Basketball Team; Most Valuable Player, 1984 NCAA Final Four Tournament
[6] Brown, Fred—1981 Big East Conference Rookie of the Year

Providence College
Providence, Rhode Island 02918

All Big East Conference

Basketball

Thorpe, Otis 1984

All-American

Basketball

Wilkins, Leonard R. 1959–60
Thompson, Jr., John R. 1963–64
Walker, James 1967
Barnes, Marvin[1] 1973–74
Thorpe, Otis 1984

Providence College's Hall of Fame

Brown, Malcolm H.[2]
Wilkens, Leonard R.
Thompson, Jr., John R.
Hadnot, James

Other Outstanding Athletes

Basketball

Westbrook, Dexter
Campbell, Bruce
King, Nehru
Tucker, Ricky
Knight, Raymond
Brooks, Delray
Wright, Steve

[1] Barnes, Marvin—a member of the 1970–80 Eastern Collegiate Athletic Conference All-Decade Team
[2] Brown, Malcolm H.—a member of the Providence College football team in the early 1930s. He later became the school's trainer until his death in 1938 from typhoid epidemic. A Mal Brown Award is given in his honor every year.

University of Pittsburgh
Pittsburgh, Pennsylvania 15213

Coaches of Varsity Teams

Football

Thompson, Don, (Assistant) 1982

Basketball

Warford, Reginald, (Assistant) 1979

All Eastern Athletic Association

Men's Basketball

Harris, Larry 1977–78
Knight, Terry 1979
Ellis, Sammie 1979–80
Clancy, Sam 1979–81
Everson, Carlton 1981
Vaughn, Clyde 1982

All Big East Conference

Men's Basketball

Vaughn, Clyde 1984
Smith, Charles[1] 1985–87
Lane, Jerome 1987

All-American

Football

Dorsett, Tony[2] 1973–74, 1976
Burley, Gary 1974

Holloway, Randy 1977
Green, Hugh[3] 1978–80
Jones, Gordan 1980
May, Mark[4] 1980
Dawkins, Julius 1981
Doleman, Chris 1985
Woods, Tony 1986

Men's Basketball

Knight, William 1974–75
Vaughn, Clyde 1984

Other Outstanding Athletes

Football

Weston, Lloyd
Wilson, J.C.
Chesley, Al
Logan, David
Parrish, Don
Johnson, Cecil
Williamson, Carlton
Pryor, Benjie
McMillan, Randy
Jackson, Ricky
Thomas, Pappy
Thomas, Lynn
Woods, Michael

Men's Basketball

Jinks, Ben
Bryant, Ernest
Sheffield, Cal
Edwards, Cleveland

Men's Track

Douglas, Herb[6]
Sowell, Arnold[7]
Utterback, Everett
Salter, Bryant
Barnwell, Mel
Farmer, Karl
King, Wes

[1] Smith, Charles—1985 Big East Conference Rookie of the Year
[2] Dorsett, Tony—1976 Heisman Memorial Trophy recipient
[3] Green, Hugh—1980 Vince Lombardi/Rotary Award recipient
[4] May, Mark—1980 Outland Trophy recipient
[6] Douglas, Herb—member of the 1948 United States Olympic Track and Field Team
[7] Sowell, Arnold—member of the 1956 United States Olympic Track and Field Team

University of Connecticut
Storrs, Connecticut 06268

All Big East Conference

Men's Basketball

Thompson, Corny 1981–82
Kelly, Earl[1] 1985–86

Other Outstanding Athletes

Men's Basketball

Hanson, Anthony C.[2]
Thomas, John[3]
McKay, Michael[4]
Hobbs, Karl[5]
Griscombe, Vernon[6]
Gamble, Phil

[1] Kelly, Earl—1983 Big East Conference Rookie of the Year; 1983 Widmer's Eastern College Freshman of the Year
[2] Hanson, Anthony C.—played on the 1974–77 teams; University of Connecticut Career Scoring Leader
[3] Thomas, John—played on the 1974–76 teams
[4] McKay, Michael—played on the 1979–82 teams
[5] Hobbs, Karl—played on the 1981–84 teams
[6] Griscombe, Vernon—played on the 1981–84 teams

Seton Hall University
South Orange, New Jersey 07079

Athletic Directors

Knight, Melvin (Associate Athletic Director), 1971–86

Coaches of Varsity Teams

Men's Basketball

Moon, John[1] (Head), 1970
Knight, Melvin (Assistant), 1976–82

Women's Track

Roman, Beverly (Assistant), 1983

Men's Basketball

Brown, Michael (Assistant), 1982

Men's Track

Presley, Ira (Assistant), 1977
Rogers, Earl (Assistant), 1982

All Eastern College Athletic Conference

Men's Basketball

Mosley, Glenn 1976–77
Tynes, Greg 1977–78

All Big East Conference

Men's Basketball

McCloud, Andre 1985
Major, James 1987

Men's Track

Shepherd, Kenneth[2] 1982
Denman, Brian, 400M ID 1982
Chambliss, Barron, 300M ID 1985

Women's Basketball

Bradley, Gloria 1984

All-American

Basketball

Dukes, Walter[3] 1953
Mosley, Glenn[4] 1977
McCloud, Andre[5] 1985

Men's Track

Fields, Benjamin F. 1976

Seton Hall University's Hall of Fame

Stanfield, Andrew[6]
Slade, Charles B.

Basketball

Thigpen, Phillip[7]
House, Kenneth
Dukes, Walter

Other Outstanding Athletes

Men's Basketball

Gaines, Richard W.[8]
Collins, Sir John
Bryant, Mark

Women's Basketball

Fairbanks, Leslie
Gorham, Ozelina

Baseball

Ben, Eli
Martin, Percy[9]

[1] Moon, John—1975 *Coach and Athlete* magazine's Man of the Year; 1981 Big East Conference Coach of the Year
[2] Shepherd, Kenneth—member of the 400-Meter Relay Team
[3] Dukes, Walter—1953 Haggerty Award recipient (given to the best player in the New York, New Jersey, Connecticut Tri-State area by the Metropolitan Basketball Writers Association)
[4] Mosley, Glenn—Honorable Mention
[5] McCloud, Andre—Honorable Mention
[6] Stanfield, Andrew—member of the 1952 United States Olympic Track and Field Team (200-Meter Gold Medalist), member of the 1956 United States Olympic Track and Field Team (200-Meter Silver Medalist)
[7] Thigpen, Phillip—1948 National AAU 1,000-Yard Champion; member of the 1951 National AAU 1,600-Meter Relay Team
[8] Gaines, Richard W.—competed in basketball 1954–57
[9] Martin, Percy—1974 National Collegiate Catholic Champion, 132 lbs.

Boston College
Chestnut Hill, Massachusetts 02167

Coaches of Varsity Teams

Football

Godbolt, Michael (Assistant), 1981

All Big East Conference

Basketball

Bagley, John[1] 1981–82
Garris, John 1983
Adams, Michael 1983–85

Other Outstanding Athletes

Basketball

Carrington, Robert
Cobb, Ernest[2]
McCready, Roger
Weldon, Melvin
Barros, Dana[3]

All-American

Football

Thurman, Anthony 1985

Basketball

Austin, John 1966

[1] Bagley, John—1981 Big East Conference Player of the Year
[2] Cobb, Ernest—recipient of the 1979 Eagle Award (given to school's best student athlete)
[3] Barros, Dana—1986 Big East Rookie of the Year

St. John's University
Jamaica, New York 11439

Coaches of Varsity Teams

Football

Bantum, Ken (Assistant)

Men's Basketball

Rutledge, Ron (Assistant)

Track and Field

Davis, Ken (Assistant)

All Big East Conference

Men's Basketball

Carter, Reginald 1980
Russell, David[1] 1982
Berry, Walter[2] 1985–86
Jackson, Mark[3] 1986–87

All-American

Football

Jamison, Todd 1982

Men's Basketball

Jackson, Tony 1960–61
Berry, Walter 1986
Jackson, Mark 1987

Other Outstanding Athletes

Men's Basketball

Dove, Lloyd "Sonny"
Ellis, Leroy
Johnson, George
Searcy, Ed
Smith, Bill "Beaver"
Goodwin, Bill
Abraham, Ralph
Williams, Kevin
Jones, Shelton
Moses, Michael
Stewart, Ron
McKoy, Wayne
Utley, Mel
Williams, Glen
Dupre, Joe

Men's Track

Fields, Carl[4]

[1] Russell, David—1980 Big East Rookie of the Year
[2] Berry, Walter—1986 Big East Conference Player of the Year; 1986 John Wooden Award recipient (given to the Player of the Year in college basketball); 1986 Associated Press Player of the Year; 1986 United Press International Player of the Year; 1986 United States Basketball Writers Association Player of the Year
[3] Jackson, Mark—1987 co-recipient of the Haggerty Award (given to the best player in New York, New Jersey, Connecticut Tri-State area by the Metropolitan Basketball Association)
[4] Fields, Carl—captain of the 1942 St. John's University team

Villanova University
Villanova, Pennsylvania 19085

Coaches of Varsity Teams

Men and Women's Track and Field and Cross Country

Jenkins, Dr., Charles (Head), 1981–Present

Women's Track and Field

Raveling, George (Assistant), 1967–68
Littlepage, Craig (Assistant), 1973–75
Thompson, James (Head), 1973–83

Football

Prescott, Spencer (Assistant), 1980–81
Jones, Brian, 1984–Present

All East

Football

Joe, Billy[1] 1962
Arthur, Eugene 1969
Miller, Joseph 1973
Thompson, Vince 1976
Martin, David 1978

Men's Basketball

White, Hubie[2] 1961–62
Jones, Wall[3] 1962–64
Washington, Jim[4] 1964–65
Jones, John 1968
Porter, Howard[5] 1969–71

All Eastern Athletic League

Men's Basketball

Herron, Keith 1977–78
Bradley Alexander 1979–80
Sparrow, Rory 1980

All Big East Conference

Men's Basketball

Granger, Stewart 1981–83
Pinckney, Ed[6] 1983–85
McClain, Dwayne 1984–85
Pressley, Harold 1984–86

All-American

Football

Thompson, Vince 1977–78

Basketball

Raveling, George 1960
White, Hubie 1962
Jones, Wali 1964
Porter, Howard[5] 1969–71
Pinckney, Ed[6] 1983

Big East Champions

Track

Wilson, Rodney—OD 110MHC, ID 55MHC 1981–83
Young, Carlton—OD 200MC, ID 400MC, OD 400MC 1982–83
Marshall, John—ID 800MC, ID 500MC 1983–84
Booker, Martin—OD 400MHC, OD 110MHC, ID 55MHC
   1983–85
Valentine, Tony—OD 400MHC 1984

IC4A Champions

Track

Jenkins, Charles—OD 440YC, ID 600YC 1955–57
Stead, Charles—ID HJC 1957–59
Reavis, Phil—ID HJC, OD HJC 1956–58
Collymore, Ed—ID 60YC, OD 220YC 1957–59
Joe, Billy—ID SPC, OD SPC 1961
Budd, Frank—ID 60YC, OD 100YC, OD 220YC 1960–62
Livers, Larry—OD 120YHC 1965
Hall, Erv—ID 60YC, OD 120YHC 1967–69

Other Outstanding Athletes

Track

Jenkins, Charles[7] 1955–57
Reavis, Phil[8] 1958

Stead, Charles[9] 1957–59
Collymore, Ed[10] 1958–59
Budd, Frank[11] 1961–62
Joe, Billy[12] 1961
Livers, Larry[13] 1965
Hall, Erv[14] 1969
James, Larry[15] 1968–70
Hymann, Lamonte[16] 1971
Dale, Tim[17] 1976–78
Cooper, Nate[18] 1977–79
Brown, Keith[19] 1979
Maree, Sydney[20] 1979–81
Wilson, Rodney[21] 1980–83
Young, Carlton[22] 1983

[1] Joe, Billy—All-Pennsylvania (Honorable Mention), 1961–62
[2] White, Hubie—1960–62 All Big-Five; 1962 Robert Geasey Memorial Trophy recipient (Big-Five Most Valuable Player)
[3] Jones, Wali—1962–64 All Big-Five 1963 and 1964 Robert Geasey Memorial Trophy recipient (Big-Five Most Valuable Player)
[4] Washington, Jim—1965 Robert Geasey Memorial Trophy recipient (Big-Five Most Valuable Player); 1963 and 1965 All Big-Five
[5] Porter, Howard—1969 and 1970 Robert Geasey Memorial Trophy recipient; co-winner each year (Big-Five Most Valuable Player); member of the 1970–80 Eastern College Athletic Conference All-Decade Team; 1971 Most Valuable Player in the NCAA Final Four Tournament
[6] Pinckney, Ed—1985 Most Valuable Player in the NCAA Final Four Tournament
[7] Jenkins, Charles—IC4A Outdoor 440-Yard Champion, IC4A Indoor 600-Yard Champion; member of the 1956 United States Olympic Track and Field Team (Gold Medalist)
[8] Reavis, Phil—NCAA High Jump Champion; IC4A Outdoor High Jump Champion; IC4A Indoor High Jump Champion; member of the 1956 United States Olympic Track and Field Team
[9] Stead, Charles—IC4A Indoor High Jump Champion
[10] Collymore, Ed—NCAA 222-Yard Champion; IC4A Outdoor 220-Yard Champion; 100-Yard Champion; IC4A Indoor 60-Yard Champion
[11] Budd, Frank—NCAA Outdoor 100-Yard Champion; NCAA Outdoor 220-Yard Champion; IC4A Outdoor 100-Yard Champion; IC4A 220-Yard Champion; IC4A Indoor 60-Yard Champion
[12] Joe, Billy—IC4A Indoor Shot Put Champion; IC4A Outdoor Shot Put Champion
[13] Livers, Larry—IC4A Outdoor 120-Yard Hurdles Champion
[14] Hall, Erv—NCAA Outdoor 120-Yard Hurdle Champion; IC4A Indoor 60-Yard Championship; IC4A Outdoor 120-Yard Hurdle Champion; 100-Yard Champion; NCAA Indoor 60-Yard Champion
[15] James, Larry—NCAA 440-Yard Champion; IC4A Indoor 600-Yard Champion; IC4A Outdoor 400-Yard Champion; member of the 1968 United States Olympic Track and Field Team
[16] Hymann, Lamonte—IC4A Indoor 440-Yard Champion
[17] Dale, Tim—IC4A Outdoor 400-Meter Champion; IC4A Indoor 440-Yard Champion
[18] Cooper, Nate—IC4A Indoor Triple Jump Champion; IC4A Outdoor Triple Jump Champion
[19] Brown, Keith—IC4A Indoor 440-Yard Champion

[20] Maree, Sydney—IC4A Three-Mile Champion; NCAA Outdoor 5000M Champion; IC4A Outdoor 5000M Champion; IC4A Indoor 5000M Champion; NCAA Outdoor 1500M Champion; IC4A Indoor 3000M Champion; member of the 1984 United States Olympic Track and Field Team

[21] Wilson, Rodney—NCAA Indoor 60-Yard Hurdles Champion; IC4A Outdoor 110-Meter Hurdles Champion; IC4A Indoor 55-Meter Hurdles Champion; Big East Conference Outdoor 110-Meter Hurdles Champion; Big East Conference Indoor 55-Meter Hurdles Champion

[22] Young, Carlton—NCAA Indoor 440-Yard Champion; IC4A Indoor 400-Meter Champion; Big East Conference, Outdoor 200-Meter Champion; Big East Conference, Outdoor 200-Meter Champion; Big East Conference, Indoor 400-Meter Champion; Big East Conference, Outdoor 400-Meter Champion

Syracuse University
Syracuse, New York 13210

All Big East Conference

Men's Basketball

Bouie, Roosevelt 1980
Orr, Louis 1980
Santifer, Eric 1983
Waldren, Eugene 1984
Addison, Rafael 1985
Washington, Dwayne "Pearl"[1] 1984–86
Douglas, Sherman 1987

All-American

Football

Brown, Jim 1956
Davis, Ernest[2] 1960–61
Little, Floyd D.[3] 1966
Preston, Ray 1976
Monk, Art 1980

Men's Basketball

Bing, David 1966
Duval, Dennis 1972

Hackett, Rudy 1975
Bouie, Roosevelt[4] 1980
Orr, Louis[5] 1980
Santifer, Eric[6] 1983
Washington, Dwayne 1985–86

Lacrosse

Brown, Jim 1956

Gymnastics

Oglesby, Sid

Wrestling

Nance, Jim
Baker, Art

Other Outstanding Athletes

Football

Morris, Joe[7]

Basketball

Moss, Ed
Bruin, Tony "Red"[8]
Hawkins, Andre[9]
Alexis, Wendell
Triche, Howard

[1] Washington, Dwayne "Pearl"—1984 Big East Conference Rookie of the Year
[2] Davis, Ernest—the first black American to win the Heisman Memorial Trophy, 1961
[3] Little, Floyd D.—1966 Eastern College Athletic Conference (University Division) Player of the Year
[4] Bouie, Roosevelt—Honorable Mention
[5] Orr, Louis—Honorable Mention
[6] Santifer, Eric—Honorable Mention
[7] Morris, Joe—1980 Eastern College Athletic Conference co-Offensive Player of the Year
[8] Bruin, Tony "Red"—1981 Big East Conference All-Tournament Team
[9] Hawkins, Andre—1984 Big East Conference All-Tournament Team

BIG EIGHT CONFERENCE

1. Oklahoma State University
2. University of Nebraska
3. University of Colorado
4. Iowa State University

5. University of Oklahoma
6. Kansas State University
7. University of Kansas
8. University of Missouri

Oklahoma State University
Stillwater, Oklahoma 74078

Coaches of Varsity Teams

Men's Basketball

Hamilton, Leonard[1] (Head), 1986–Present

Football

Cole, Robert (Assistant), 1973–78
Holton, Larry (Assistant), 1979–81
Falks, Frank (Assistant), 1981–82
Parker, Roberto (Assistant), 1981–82
Anderson, Willie (Assistant), 1982
Gardner, Steven (Assistant), 1984

Basketball

Smith, Steven (Assistant), 1973–77
Turner, Ken (Assistant), 1979–82
Stoglin, Andy (Assistant), 1984–85
Drew, Weldin (Assistant), 1985

All Big-Eight Conference

Football

Little, John, 1968–69
Steward, Darryl, 1972
Vann, Cleveland, 1972–73
Dokes, Philip, 1974–76
Miller, Terry, 1975–77
Butler, Daria, 1976–77
Corker, John, 1978
Richardson, Reginald, 1979
Taylor, Worley, 1979
Young, Ricky, 1979–81
Lewis, Gary, 1981–82
Anderson, Ernest, 1982
Green, Michael, 1982
Jones, Shawn, 1983
Rockins, Chris, 1983
O'Neal, Leslie, 1983–85

Brown, Rod, 1984
Harding, Rodney, 1984
Moore, Mark, 1984
Thomas, Thurman, 1986

Basketball

Moulder, Fred, 1965
King, James, 1965
Odom, Ed, 1980
Clark, Matt, 1981–83
Hudson, James, 1982
Combs, Leroy, 1983

Track

Hazley, Orlando,[2] 1959
Butler, James,[3] 1980

Women's Tennis

McNeil, Lori, 1982–83

All-American

Football

Vann, Cleveland,[4] 1973
Brown, Alvin,[5] 1973
White, James,[6] 1975
Dokes, Philip,[7] 1976
Miller, Terry, 1977
Corker, John,[8] 1978
Young, Ricky,[9] 1981
Anderson, Ernest, 1982
Brown, Rod, 1984
O'Neal, Leslie, 1985–86

Wrestling

James, Joe,[10] 1964
Ray, Ron,[11] 1975
Jackson, Jimmy,[12] 1976–78
Monday, Ken,[13] 1984

Track

Butler, James,[14] 1980–81

Other Outstanding Athletes

Track

Harris, Earl
Ingram, Ron
Blakely, Don

Women's Basketball

Nixon, Bridget

[1] Hamilton, Leonard–the first black head coach in basketball in Big-Eight Conference history
[2] Hazley, Orlando–220-Yard Dash Champion
[3] Butler, James–100-Yard and 200-Yard Dash Champion; 1980 Henry Schute Award recipient
[4] Vann, Cleveland–Honorable Mention
[5] Brown, Alvin–Honorable Mention
[6] White, James–Honorable Mention
[7] Dokes, Philip–Honorable Mention
[8] Corker, John–Honorable Mention
[9] Young, Rickey–Honorable Mention
[10] James, Joe–1964 NCAA Heavyweight Champion
[11] Ray, Ron–1975 NCAA 167 Lbs. Champion
[12] Jackson, Jimmy–1976–78 NCAA Heavyweight Champion
[13] Monday, Ken–1984 NCAA 150 Lbs. Champion
[14] Butler, James–100 and 200-Yard Dash

University of Nebraska
Lincoln, Nebraska 68588–0123

Coaches of Varsity Teams

Football

Thornton, William (Assistant)
Myles, William (Assistant)
Huey, Eugene (Assistant)

Basketball

Porter, Lonnie (Assistant)
Carter, Tim (Assistant)
Farley, Doug (Assistant)

Women's Basketball

Washington, Mavis (Assistant)

All Big-Eight Conference

Football

Bryant, Charles,[1] 1954
McWilliams, Jon,[2] 1955
Thorton, William, 1961
Robertson, Tyrone, 1962
Brown, Robert, 1962–63
Jeter, Tony, 1964–65

White, Freeman, 1964–65
Wilson, Harry, 1966
Davis, Richard, 1967
Geddes, Ken, 1968–69
Orduna, Joe, 1970
Rodgers, John, 1970–71
Harper, Willie, 1971–72
Glover, Rich, 1971–72
White, Daryl, 1973
Crenshaw, Marvin, 1974
Phillips, Ray, 1976
Fultz, Michael, 1975–76
Hipp, I.M., 1977
Miller, Junior, 1978–79
Redwine, Jarvis, 1979–80
Gary, Russell, 1980
Williams, Jamie, 1981–82
Williams, Jimmy, 1981
Rozier, Michael, 1981–83
Gill, Turner, 1982
Fryar, Irving, 1983
Dubose, Doug, 1984–85

Basketball

Turner, Hershell, 1960
Lantz, Stuart, 1967–68
Stewart, Marvin, 1971
Fort, Jerry, 1974–76
Banks, Brian, 1978

All Big-Eight Conference

Basketball

Smith, Andre, 1980–81

All-American

Football

Brown, Robert, 1963
Jeter, Tony, 1965
White, Freeman, 1965
Rodgers, John,[3] 1971–72
Harper, Willie, 1971–72
Glover, Rich,[4] 1972
Crenshaw, Marvin, 1974
Miller, Junior, 1979
Redwine, Jarvis, 1979
Rozier, Michael,[5] 1982–83
Fryar, Irving, 1983

Men's Track

Greene, Charles,[6] 1966–67
Lee, Jeff,[7] 1977

Women's Track

Murray, Normalee,[8] 1980–81
Ottey, Merlene,[9] 1980–82
McQueen, Alicia,[10] 1982
James, Debra,[11] 1982
Tate, Marcia,[12] 1982
Thacker, Angela,[13] 1982–83
Blanford, Rhonda,[14] 1982–83
Burke, Janet,[15] 1982–83
Powell, Debra, 1984
Ashmore, Holly, 1984
Smith, Heather, 1984

All Big-Eight Conference

Track

Case, Garth,[16] 1969–70, 1972
Greene, Charles,[17] 1965–67

---

[1] Bryant, Charles–All Big Seven
[2] McWilliams, Jon–All Big Seven
[3] Rodgers, John–1972 Heisman Memorial Trophy recipient
[4] Glover, Rich–1972 Outland Trophy recipient; 1972 Vince Lombardi/Rotary Award recipient
[5] Rozier, Michael–1983 Heisman Memorial Trophy recipient
[6] Greene, Charles–NCAA Champion 60-Yard Dash (Indoor)
[7] Lee, Jeff–NCAA Champion 60-Yard High Hurdles (Indoor)
[8] Murray, Normalee–300-Meter Dash; 800-Meter Sprint Medley; 1600-Meter Relay
[9] Ottey, Merlene–300-Meter Dash; 200-Meter Dash; 800-Meter Spring Medley; 60-Yard Dash
[10] McQueen, Alicia—60-Yard Dash; 300-Yard Dash
[11] James, Debra–400-Meter Relay; 60-Yard Dash; 880-Yard Relay
[12] Tate, Marcia–600-Yard Run; Mile Relay
[13] Thacker, Angela–60-Yard Dash; Long Jump; 200-Meter Dash
[14] Blanford, Rhonda–60-Yard Hurdles; 880-Yard Relay; 100-Meter Hurdles
[15] Burke, Janet–60-Yard Dash; 300-Yard Dash
[16] Case, Garth–Indoor, 600-Yard Run Champion
[17] Greene, Charles–Outdoor, 100-Yard and 200-Yard Dash

University of Colorado
Boulder, Colorado 80309

Coaches of Varsity Teams

Football

McGowan, Cottrell (Assistant)
Goldston, Ralph (Assistant)
Webster, Jim (Assistant)
Bassett, Harold (Assistant)

Dickerson, Ron (Assistant)
Caldwell, Jim (Assistant)

Basketball

Gentry, Alvin (Assistant)

All Big-Eight, Conference

Football

Wooten, John, 1957
Cooks, Wilmer, 1966
Bryant, Cullen, 1972
Cain, James V., 1972–73
Johnson, Charles, 1976
Reed, Tony, 1976
Spivey, Michael, 1976
McKinney, Odis, 1977
Haynes, Mark, 1978–79
Scott, Victor, 1982–83

Basketball

Gilmore, Wilky, 1962
Davis, Jim, 1963–64
Meely, Cliff, 1969–71
Lewis, Emmett, 1979
Hunter, Anthony "JoJo," 1981
Humphries, Jay, 1984

All-American

Football

Wooten, John, 1958
Bryant, Cullen ,1972
Haynes, Mark, 1979

Basketball

Meely, Cliff, 1971

Other Outstanding Athletes

Bolen, David–competed in track, 1948

Iowa State University
Ames, Iowa 50011

All Big-Eight Conference

Football

Webb, Don, 1959
Watkins, Tom, 1960

Vaughn, Tom, 1963–64
Barney, Eppie, 1965–66
Stowe, Otto, 1970
Murdock, Geary, 1972
Strachan, Michael, 1972–73
Hunt, Lawrence, 1973
Hill, Barry, 1974
Blue, Luther, 1976
Hawkins, Anthony, 1976
Green, Dexter, 1977–78
Crawford, Larry, 1980
Crutchfield, Dwayne, 1980–81
Osborne, Ron, 1982
Jacobs, Jason, 1983
Henderson, Tracey, 1983–84

Basketball

Crawford, John, 1958
Whitney, Henry, 1961
Smith, Don, 1966–68
Cain, William, 1969–70
Ivy, Hercle "Poison," 1975
Parker, Andrew, 1978–79
Stevens, Barry, 1984–85

Men's Track

Harris, Dan, 1984–85
Dixon, Leroy, 1985

Wrestling

Adams, Carl, 1970
Gadson, Willie, 1975–76
Carr, Nate, 1980–81
Cole, Wayne, 1983

Gymnastics

Galimore, Ron, 1980–81

All-American

Football

Watkins, Tom, 1960
Vaughn, Tom, 1963
Barney, Eppie, 1966
Murdock, Geary, 1972
Blair, Matt, 1973
Hill, Barry, 1974
Blue, Luther, 1976
Green, Dexter, 1978

Crutchfield, Dwayne, 1980
Henderson, Tracey, 1983–84

Basketball

Smith, Don, 1967

Wrestling

Watkins, Ellie, 1959
Carr, Virgil, 1961–63
Long, Veryl, 1963–65
Gillum, Ernest, 1965–66
Smith, Jason, 1968–70
Adams, Carl, 1969–70, 1972
Parker, Phil, 1970–72
Gadson, Willie, 1975–76
Gadson, Charles, 1978
Carr, Nate, 1981–83
Cole, Wayne, 1983
Crews, Murray, 1983

Men's Track

Carson, Steven, 1965–67
Harris, Dan, 1984

Women's Track

Wells, Sumetia, 1981–82
Hanna, Colleen, 1982
Bullocks, Denise, 1982

Gymnastics

Galimore, Ron, 1980–81

University of Oklahoma
Norman, Oklahoma 73019

All Big-Eight Conference

Football

Gautt, Prentice,[1] 1958–59
Hinton, Eddie, 1968
Pruitt, Greg, 1971–72
Hamilton, Raymond, 1971–72
Selmon, Lucious, 1972–73
Shoate, Rod, 1973–74
Washington, Joe, 1973–75
Selmon, Dewey, 1974–75
Selmon, Leroy, 1974–75
Henderson, Zack, 1975–77
Hunt, Darryl, 1976–78

Reference Section

Roberts, Greg, 1977–78
Lott, Thomas, 1977–78
Kinlaw, Reginald, 1977–78
Cumby, George, 1977–79
Mathis, Reginald, 1978
Sims, Billy, 1978–79
Ray, Darrol, 1979
Oubre, Louis, 1979–80
Wilson, Stanley, 1981
Dupree, Marcus, 1982
Bradley, Dan, 1984
Tillman, Spencer, 1985

Men's Basketball

Heard, Garfield, 1970
Barnett, Chuck, 1982
Tisdale, Waymon,[2] 1983–85
Kennedy, Darryl, 1986–87
McAllister, Tim, 1986–87

All-American

Football

Pruitt, Greg, 1971–72
Selmon, Lucius, 1973
Shoate, Rod, 1973–74
Jackson, Keith, 1986–87
Selmon, Dewey, 1974
Selmon, Leroy, 1974–75
Washington, Joe, 1974–75
Henderson, Zack, 1977
Kinlaw, Reginald, 1977
Hunt, Darryl, 1977
Roberts, Greg, 1977–78
Cumby, George, 1977–79
Sims, Billy,[3] 1977–79
Oubre, Louis, 1980

Men's Basketball

Tisdale, Waymon, 1983–85

Other Outstanding Athletes

Football

Holloway, Jamelle

Basketball

Grant, Harvey
Johnson, David

[1] Gautt, Prentice–the first black athlete to compete in any sport at the University of Oklahoma. Presently he is the Assistant Commissioner of the Big-Eight Conference
[2] Tisdale, Waymon–1983 and 1984 Big-Eight Conference Player of the Year; member of the 1984 United States Olympic Basketball Team
[3] Sims, Billy–1978 Heisman Memorial Trophy recipient

Kansas State University
Manhattan, Kansas 66506

Coaches of Varsity Teams

Baseball

Baker, David (Head), 1978–83

All Big-Eight Conference

Football

Robinson, Harold,[1] 1950
Switzer, Sr., Veryl,[2] 1951–53
Herron, Mack, 1969
Scott, Clarence, 1970
Lattimore, Marion, 1971
Jackson, Issac, 1973
Green, Charles, 1978
Walker, James, 1979–80
Singletary, Reginald, 1981–83
Wallace, Michael, 1982

Basketball

Boozer, Robert, 1957–1959
Murrell, Willie, 1963–64
Honeycutt, Steven, 1969
Venable, Jerry, 1970
Hall, David, 1972
Williams, Charles "Chuckie," 1975–76
Evans, Michael, 1976–78
Redding, Curtis, 1977
Blackmon, Rolando, 1979–81
Coleman, Norris, 1986–87

Women's Basketball

Gary, Priscilla, 1982–83
Boner, Angela, 1983–84
Dixon, Trina, 1984

Men's Track

Switzer, Sr., Veryl, 1952
McGill, Ray, 1970
Alexander, Dale 1974

Williams, Dean, 1974
Lee, Michael, 1974
Roland, Vance, 1974–75
Parrette, Vince, 1980
Switzer, Jr., Veryl, 1982

Women's Track

Hancock, Freda, 1978
Trent, Wanda, 1981
Graves, Rita, 1983
Suggs, Pinkie, 1984

All-American

Football

Switzer, Sr., Veryl, 1953
Scott, Clarence, 1970

Basketball

Boozer, Robert,[3] 1958–59
Blackman, Rolando,[4] 1981

Women's Basketball

Gary, Priscilla, 1983

Men's Track

Switzer, Jr., Veryl, 1982–83

Women's Track

Graves, Rita, 1983–84
Suggs, Pinkie, 1984

[1] Robinson, Harold–first black to play football in the Big-Seven Conference
[2] Switzer, Sr., Veryl–presently Dean of Minority Affairs at Kansas State University
[3] Boozer, Robert–member of the 1960 United States Olympic Basketball Team
[4] Blackman, Rolando–member of the 1980 United States Olympic Basketball Team; 1980 Big-Eight Conference Player of the Year

University of Kansas
Lawrence, Kansas 66045

Coaches of Varsity Teams

Women's Basketball

Washington, Marian (Head), 1972–Present
Woodard, Lynette (Assistant), 1984–85

Men's Basketball

White, Joseph (Assistant), 1981–83
Manning, Ed (Assistant), 1983–Present

Women's Track

Coffey, Carla (Assistant), 1980–Present

All Big-Eight Conference

Football

Floyd, Homer, 1958
McClinton, Curtis, 1959–61
Sayers, Gale, 1962–64
Pratt, Richard, 1965
Greene, John, 1967
Hicks, Emery, 1968–69
Lawson, Steven, 1970
Sheats, Ed, 1972
Edwards, Emmett, 1973–74
Smith, Laverne, 1974
Butler, Michael, 1975
Verser, David, 1979–80
Bell, Kerwin, 1980
Gardner, Stan, 1980
Capers, Wayne, 1981
Pless, Willie, 1983

Men's Basketball

King, Maurice,[1] 1956
Chamberlain, Wilt,[2] 1957–58
Bridges, William, 1959–61
Hightower, Wayne, 1960–61
Unseld, George, 1964
Wesley, Walter, 1965–66
White, Joseph "Jo Jo," 1967–69
Stallworth, Bud, 1971–72
Suttle, Rick, 1975
Cook, Norman, 1976
Douglas, John, 1977
Valentine, Darnell, 1978–81
Henry, Carl, 1984
Manning, Dan, 1985–87
Kellogg, Ron, 1986

Women's Basketball

Adams, Vickie, 1984–85

All-American

Football

Sayers, Gale, 1963–64

Men's Basketball

Chamberlain, Wilt, 1957–58
Bridges, William, 1961
Wesley, Walter, 1966
White, Joseph "Jo Jo,"[3] 1968–69
Stallworth, Bud, 1972
Valentine, Darnell,[4] 1980–81
Manning, Dan, 1986–87

Women's Basketball

Woodard, Lynette,[5] 1978–81

Men's Track

Shelby, Ernest—LJ, 220YH, 1958–59
Tidwell, Charles—100YD–200YH, 1958–59
Ard, Gary—LJ, 1967
Lewis, Ed—440YRT, 1974
Edwards, Emmett—440YRT, 1974
Wiley, Clifford[5]—100M–200M–MRT,[6] 1975–78
Newell, Kevin—400MRT, 1977–78
Blutcher, David—400MRT, 1978–80
Whitaker, Stan—MRT, 1978–79
Mickens, Lester—1,600MRT, 1980
Hogan, Deon—1,600MRT, 1980

NCAA Champions

Men's Track

Shelby, Ernest–OD, LJ, 1958–59
Tidwell, Charles–OD, 100MD, 220MD, 1958–60
Ard, Gary–OD, LJ, 1967
Jessie, Ron–ID, LJ, 1969
Ricks, Michael–ID, 600YD, 1980

University of Kansas Hall of Fame

Sayers, Gale
Hamilton, Theo
Newell, Kevin
Wiley, Clifford
Edwards, Emmett
Tidwell, Charles
Shelby, Ernest
Ard, Gary
Jessie, Ron
Ricks, Michael
Chamberlain, Wilt

Bridges, William
Westley, Walter
Stallworth, Bud
White, Joseph "Jo Jo"
Woodard, Lynette

[1] King, Maurice–All Big-Seven Conference
[2] Chamberlain, Wilt–All Big-Seven Conference
[3] White, Joseph "Jo Jo"–member of the 1968 United States Olympic Basketball Team
[4] Valentine, Darnell–member of the 1980 United States Olympic Basketball Team
[5] Woodard, Lynette–member of the 1984 United States Olympic Women's Basketball Team
[6] Wiley, Clifford–member of the 1980 United States Olympic Track and Field Team

University of Missouri
Columbia, Missouri 65205

Coaches of Varsity Teams

Football

Wynn, Michael (Assistant)

All Big Eight Conference

Football

Roland, John, 1962–63, 1965
Peay, Francis, 1965
Washington, Russ, 1967
Gray, Mel, 1969
Galbreath, Tony, 1974
Marshall, Henry, 1975
Towns, Morris, 1976
Winslow, Kellen, 1977–78
Bradley, Phil, 1978–80
Wright, Eric, 1979–80
Johnson, Demetrious, 1982
Bell, Bobby, 1983
Clay, William, 1986–87

Basketball

Smith, Willie, 1975–76
Drew, Larry, 1980
Berry, Curtis, 1980
Frazier, Ricky 1981–82
Chievious, Derrick, 1986–87

All-American

Football

Peay, Francis, 1965
Roland, John, 1965
Washington, Russ, 1967
Marshall, Henry, 1975
Towns, Morris, 1976
Winslow, Kellen, 1978
Clay, William, 1986–87

Basketball

Smith, Willie, 1976

Frazier, Ricky, 1982
Chievious, Derrick,[1] 1987

Baseball

Bradley, Phil, 1981

Other Outstanding Athletes

Football

Wilder, James

[1] Chievious, Derrick–Honorable Mention

SOUTHERN CONFERENCE

1. Furman University
2. Marshall University

3. Appalachian State University
4. Davidson College

Furman University
Greenville, South Carolina 29409

All Southern Conference

Football

Jennings, Stanford,[1] 1981–83
Gibson, Ernest, 1983

Basketball

Mayes, Clyde,[2] 1973–75
Leonard, Foster, 1973–75
Moore, Jonathan,[3] 1977–80
Daniel, Mel, 1980–81

All-American

Football

Jennings, Stanford, 1982–83
Gibson, Ernest, 1983

Men's Basketball
Moore, Jonathan,[4] 1980

[1] Jennings, Stanford–1981, 1982, 1983 Roy M. Hawley Award recipient (given to the Most Outstanding Player of the Southern Conference); 1984 Southern Conference Athlete of the Year
[2] Mayes, Clyde–1974, 1975 Malcolm U. Pitt Award recipient (given to the Most Valuable Player in the Southern Conference); 1975 Southern Conference Athlete of the Year
[3] Moore, Jonathan–1979 and 1980 Malcolm U. Pitt Award recipient (given to the Most Valuable Player in the Southern Conference)
[4] Moore, Jonathan–Honorable Mention

Marshall University
Huntington, West Virginia 25715–1360

Athletic Directors

Starling, Edward (Assistant), 1985–Present

All Mid-American Conference

Football
Lathan, Wilson, 1960

Basketball
Greer, Hal,[1] 1958

All Southern Conference

Basketball
Evans, Laverne,[2] 1984

All-American

Basketball

Lee, Russell,[3] 1972
Evans, Laverne,[4] 1984

Other Outstanding Athletes

Football

Fleming, Millard

Oliver, Reginald
Jackson, Mickey

Basketball

Carter, Phil
Stone, George
Gibson, Carlos

[1] Greer, Hal–First African-American athlete to compete in a Collegiate Sport at Marshall University
[2] Evans, Laverne–Most Valuable Player at the 1984 Southern Conference Tournament
[3] Lee, Russell–Honorable Mention
[4] Evans, Laverne–Honorable Mention

Wrestling

Anderson, Issac, 1979
Carmon, Lorenzo, 1979
Massey, Andre, 1979
Sumter, Todd, 1981
Hutchinson, Thomas, 1982
Jones, Chuck, 1983–84
Biggs, Thermus, 1984
Hampton, Johnathan, 1983–85
amar, Amalo, 1985

[1] Payton, Charles–1981 Malcolm U. Pitt Award recipient (given to the Player of the Year in the Southern Conference)

Appalachian State University
Boone, North Carolina 28608

Coaches of Varsity Teams

Football

Rucker, Ken (Assistant)
Leaks, Frank (Assistant)
Hixon, Stan (Assistant)
Cooper, Ron (Assistant)

Men's Basketball

Littles, Eugene (Assistant)
Searcy, Tony (Assistant)

Women's Basketball

Horton, Angelita (Assistant)
Moody, Gail (Assistant)

Wrestling

Anderson, Issac (Assistant)
Sumter, Glenn (Assistant)

All Southern Conference

Football

Hamilton, Emmitt, 1975
McKinney, Quinton, 1975
Parker, Alvin, 1982

Men's Basketball

Searcy, Tony, 1978
Hubbard, Mel, 1979
Robinson, Darryl, 1979
Payton, Charles,[1] 1981–82

Women's Basketball

Whiteside, Valorie, 1985

Davidson College
Davidson, North Carolina 28036

Coaches of Varsity Teams

Football

Williams, George (Assistant),
  1977–80
Wade, John (Assistant), 1973

Men's Basketball

Brown, James (Assistant), 1975–76
Wilson, Ray (Assistant), 1976–77

All Southern Conference

Maloy, Michael,[1] 1968–70
Wilson, Kenny, 1983–84

All-American

Football

Sinclair, Ray, 1981

Men's Basketball

Maloy, Michael, 1970

Other Outstanding Athletes

Football

Piercy, Gifford

Men's Basketball

Strong, Lester

[1] Maloy, Michael–1969 and 1970 Malcolm U. Pitt Award recipient (given to the Player of the Year in the Southern Conference)

EASTERN COLLEGE ATHLETIC CONFERENCE
(North Atlantic and Metro Divisions)

1. University of New Hampshire
2. Niagara University

3. Long Island University

Niagara University
Niagara University, New York 14109

Coaches of Varsity Teams

Men's Basketball

Walker, Andy (Assistant), 1984

All Eastern Collegiate Athletic Conference

Men's Basketball

Murphy, Calvin,[1] 1969–70
Phillips, Michael, 1982
Speaks, James, 1982

Women's Basketball

Williams, Cindy

All-American

Men's Basketball

Murphy, Calvin, 1969–70

Niagara University's Hall of Fame

Murphy, Calvin

Other Outstanding Athletes

Basketball
Fleming, Ed

[1] Murphy, Calvin–1969 Eastern Collegiate Athletic Conference Player of the Year

University of New Hampshire
Durham, New Hampshire 03824

All Yankee Conference

Football

Garron, Arnold, 1982–83
Garron, Andre, 1983–84

All Eastern College Athletic Conference (North Atlantic)

Basketball

Dixon, Robin, 1983
McClain, Al,[1] 1984

All-American

Basketball

Dixon, Robin,[2] 1983
Garron, Andre, 1984
McClain, Al[3], 1984

[1] McClain, Al–1981 Eastern College Athletic Conference North Atlantic Rookie of the Year
[2] Dixon, Robin–Honorable Mention
[3] McClain, Al–Honorable Mention

Long Island University
Brooklyn, New York 11201

All Eastern College Athletic Conference (Metro)

Men's Basketball

Clarida, Riley, 1981–82
Scurry, Carey,[1] 1985
Ervin, Andre, 1986

All-American

Men's Basketball

White, Sherman, 1950
Green, Luther, 1968
Scurry, Carey,[2] 1985

Outstanding Athletes

Men's Basketball

Cole, Robert
Fuller, Earl
Felix, Ray[3]

[1] Scurry, Carey–1985 Eastern College Athletic Conference (Metro) Player of the Year
[2] Scurry, Carey–Honorable Mention
[3] Felix, Ray–played on the 1951 and 1952 Long Island University teams

United States Naval Academy
Annapolis, Maryland 21402

All-American

Football

Cooper, Cleveland, 1972
Sapp, Jeff, 1976
Meyers, Ed, 1981
McCallum, Napoleon,[1] 1983

Basketball

Robinson, David,[2] 1986–87

Wrestling

Keaser, Lloyd, 1971–72
Fears, George, 1982

Fencing

Pace, George, 1980

Track and Field

Williams, Leo,[3] 1981–82

Other Outstanding Athletes

Track and Field

Owens, Ike

Anderson, Darryl
Colvin, Jeff

United States Naval Academy Hall of Fame

Football

Sapp, Jeff

Track and Field

Owens, Ike
Anderson, Darryl
Colvin, Jeff
Williams, Leo

Fencing

Pace, Greg
Mines, Gwendolyn

LaCrosse

Abernathy, Syd

Baseball

Liscomb, Jerry

[1] McCallum, Napoleon–1983 Eastern Collegiate Athletic Conference Co-Player of the Year
[2] Robinson, David–1987 John Wooden Award recipient; 1987 United Press International College Player of the Year
[3] Williams, Leo–1981 and 1982 NCAA High Jump Champion

YANKEE CONFERENCE

1. University of Vermont

University of Vermont
Burlington, Vermont 05405

All Yankee Conference

Men's Basketball

Lord, Clyde O., 1957–59
Isles, Jr. Charles H., 1960
Becton, Benjamin, 1961

Track

Howard, William C.,[1] 1951

Other Outstanding Athletes

Williams, Leroy[2]

[1] Howard, William C.–1950 New England Indoor 50 Yard Dash Champion
[2] Williams, Leroy–played on the 1956 and 1957 University of Vermont Football Teams (All-Vermont both years)

Division II Colleges

1. California State University, Los Angeles
2. California Polytechnic State University
3. Chicago State University
4. Texas A&I University
5. University of Puget Sound
6. Philadelphia College of Textiles and Sciences
7. University of Tennessee, Martin
8. City College of New York

California State University, Los Angeles
Los Angeles, California 90032

Coaches of Varsity Teams

Football

Thurmond, Walter (Head), 1969

Track

Coleman, Leon (Head Acting), 1983

Basketball

Maxey, Ken (Head), 1981–83
Newman, James (Head), 1984–85

Cross Country

Bryant, Rosalyn (Head), 1981

All California Collegiate Athletic Association

Football

Davis, Cliff, 1952
Sherrill, Ed, 1954
Evans, Irvin, 1959
Hankerson, Sam, 1960
Womack, Joe, 1959–61
cCauley, Ron, 1962–63
Johnson, Walter, 1963–64
Robinson, Art, 1964
Youngblood, George, 1964
Thurmond, Walter, 1964
Jones, Ray, 1964–65
Willard, Jess, 1964–65
Parks, Perry, 1965

Men's Basketball

Barber, John, 1953–54
Jackson, Frank, 1958
Hill, Leo, 1959–61
Wilson, C.D., 1964–65
Davis, Joe, 1966–67

Thomas, Charles, 1967–68
Smith, Cary, 1967–68
Knight, Ron, 1968–69
Pate, Edgar, 1978–79
Hester, Michael, 1979–80
Jordan, Mark, 1980
Bellamy, Nate, 1981
Catchings, Ed, 1982
Brown, Anthony, 1984–85
Yeal, Sam, 1985

Baseball

Carroll, William, 1967–68
Owens, Ted, 1968

Women's Basketball

Rhodes, Johanna, 1982
Finley, Veronda, 1985

All Pacific Coast Athletic Association

Football

Fontenot, Tyrone, 1969–70

Basketball

Knight, Ron, 1970
Thomas, Morris, 1970
Adolph, Mose, 1970–72
Murray, Rodney, 1971
Jackson, Michael, 1972
Lewis, Raymond, 1973
Lipsey, Tom, 1974
Mallory, William, 1974

All Southern California Baseball Association

Baseball

Brown, Darrell, 1977
Gwynn, Charles, 1979–81

All-American

Football

Womack, Joe[1]–Honorable Mention, 1959–61
McCauley, Ron, 1963
Johnson, Walter,[2] 1963–64
Jones, Ray,[3] 1965
Davis, Don[4]–Honorable Mention, 1965
Parks, Perrry,[5] 1965
Youngblood, George[6]–Honorable Mention, 1965
Fontenot, Tyrone[7]–Honorable Mention, 1970

Basketball

Hill, Leo[8]–Honorable Mention, 1959–60
Smith, Cary[9]–College Division, 1968
Lewis, Raymond[10]–Division I Honorable Mention, 1973
Lipsey, Tommie,[11] 1976
Brown, Darrell,[12] 1977
Veal, Sam,[13] 1985

All-American Division II

Track

Lewis, Tony–Long Jump, 1976
Adams, Keith–Pole Vault, 1977
Hart, Chester-High Hurles, 1977–78
Turner, Sam–400 Meter Hurdles, 1977–78, 1980
Peete, Gerald–400 Meters, 1978
Robinson, Craig–Pole Vault, 1978
Greene, Anthony–High Hurdles, Intermediate Hurdles, 1979
Hopper, Clarence–Intermediate Hurdles, 1980–81
Booker, Angelo–High Hurdles, 1981
Gray, Byron–Triple Jump, 1982
Lister, Tom–Shot Put, 1982
Holmes, Gregg–100 Meters, 200 Meters, 1982–83
illiams, Eric–200 Meters, 1983

Women's Track

Scott, Jarvis–AIAW, 1973
Bryant, Rosalyn–AIAW 100, 200, 400 Meters, 1976–78
Rich, Yolanda–AIAW 400 Meters, 1979–80
Williams, Diane–NCAAI, 100, 200 Meters, 1982–83
Howard, Denean–NCAAI, 400 Meters, 1983
Howard, Sherri–NCAAI, 100, 200 Meters, 1984
Dabney, Sharon–NCAAI, 400 Meters, 1985

California State University's Hall of Fame

Hill, Leo
Johnson, Walter
Bryant, Rosalyn
Scott, Jarvis

Head Trainers

McVey, Larry

[1] Womack, Joe–Little All-American
[2] Johnson, Walter–Little All-American
[3] Jones, Ray–Little All-American
[4] Davis, Don–Little All-American
[5] Parks, Perry–Little All-American
[6] Youngblood, George–Little All-American
[7] Fontenot, Tyrone–Little All-American
[8] Hill, Leo–Little All-American
[9] Smith, Cary–Little All-American
[10] Lewis, Raymond–Little All-American
[11] Lipsey, Tommie–*Basketball Weekly*
[12] Brown, Darrell–Division II All-American
[13] Veal, Sam–National Association of Basketball Coaches All-American

California Polytechnic State University
San Luis Obispo, California 93407

All-American

Football

Hill, Curtis,[1] 1960
Davis, Gary,[2] 1975
Childs, Jimmy,[3] 1977
Jackson, Louis,[4] 1980

Track and Field

Turner, Cecil[5]–100M, LJ, 1967–68
Brown, Reynaldo[6]–HJ, 1971–73
Edwards, Clancy[7]–100M, 200M, 1974–75
Williams, Bart[8]–400MH, 1978–79

Wrestling

Hall, Terry,[9] 1969–70

Other Outstanding Athletes

Football

McDaniel, Le Charles
Kaufman, Mel

Baseball

Smith, Ozzie

Basketball

Keys, Andre
Lucas, Kevin

[1] Hill, Curtis–Small College All-American
[2] Davis, Gary–Division II All-American
[3] Childs, Jimmy–Division II All-American
[4] Jackson, Louis–Division II All-American
[5] Turner, Cecil–Division II All-American
[6] Brown Reynaldo–Division II All-American
[7] Edwards, Clancy–Division II All-American
[8] Williams, Bart–Division II All-American
[9] Hall, Terry–NCAA Division II 115 lb. Champion, 1969 and 1970

Chicago State University
Chicago, Illinois 60628

Athletic Directors

Richey, Dorothy–First Female Black American Athletic
   Director in the Nation, 1975–76
Butler, Dr., Gerald, 1977–78
Herron, Bruce, 1984

Coaches of Varsity Teams

Men's Basketball

Buckhalter, Joe, 1975–77
Woods, Ed, 1977–78
McCray, Kevin, 1981–Present

Men's Swimming

Adams, William, 1976–81

Wrestling

Mackey, Chandler, 1981–82
Hardy, Derrick, 1981–Present

Track and Cross Country

Davis, Sudie–Men's/Women's, 1977–Present
Harris, Veronica–Men's/Women's, 1981–Present

Women's Basketball

Sailes, Gary, 1979–80

Men's Tennis

Sailes, Gary, 1977–84

All Chicagoland Collegiate Athletic Conference

Tillman, Curtis,[1] 1981
Leonard, Percy,[2] 1981

All Chicagoland Athletic Conference

Baseball

Hopkins, Willie, 1979
Johnson, John, 1983–84

Women's Basketball

Gilkey, Anita, 1984

Women's Volleyball

Cephas, Phyllis, 1984

All-American

Men's Basketball

Cyrus, Ken–NAIA, 1978
Eversley, Michael–NAIA, 1979
Dancey, Ken–NAIA, 1980
Arnold, Sherron–NAIA, 1982–83
Perry, Charles–NAIA, 1984

Men's Track

Curtis, Josephy–NAIA, 1978–79
Horton, Delwyn–NAIA, 1978–79

Wrestling

Mackey, Chandler–NAIA, 1979–80
Hardy, Derrick[3]–NCAA Div. II, 1980
Keys, Lionel–NAIA, 1984
Shepard, Frank[4]–NCAA Div. II, 1984

Swimming

Flemmister, Michael[5]–NCAA Div. II, 1978
Evans, Fred[6]–NCAA Div. II, 1978

[1] Tillman, Curtis–1981 Chicagoland Collegiate Athletic Conference Most
   Valuable Player
[2] Leonard, Percy–1981 Chicagoland Collegiate Athletic Conference Most
   Valuable Player
[3] Hardy, Derrick–Division II
[4] Shepard Frank–Division II
[5] Flemmister, Michael–Division II
[6] Evans, Fred–Division II

Texas A & I University
Kingsville, Texas 78363

Coaches of Varsity Teams

Football

Crawford, Andrew (Assistant), 1977–78
Starks, Glenn (Assistant), 1979
Pittman, Don (Assistant), 1979–83
Kelly, Robert (Assistant), 1983

Basketball

Thomas, Roy, 1980–83

All Lone Star Conference

Football

Blanks, Sid, 1960–61, 1963
Brown, James, 1963
Hill, James, 1964, 1966–67
Upshaw, Eugene, 1966
Harrison, Dwight, 1967–70
Scott, Ed, 1968
Douglas, Karl, 1968–70
Scott, Ed, 1969
Matthews, Alvin, 1969
Glenn, Henry, 1969
Small, Eldridge, 1969–71
Neal, Curtis, 1970
Price, Ernest, 1970–71
Johnson, Levi, 1971
Hill, David, 1973–75
Huff, Ruford, 1973
Hardeman, Don, 1973–74
Henderson, Howard, 1974–75
Evans, Ray, 1974–75
Avery, Leonard, 1974–76
Collins, Larry, 1974–77
Grady, Larry, 1975
McFarland, Larry, 1975–76
Starks, Glenn, 1975–77
Barefield, Johnny, 1975–77
Hawkins, Michael, 1976–77
Greene, Doug, 1976–77
Franks, Clem, 1976–77
Brooks, Randy, 1978
Wright, Ken, 1978
Waddy, Raymond, 1978

Sweeney, Bryan, 1978
White, Jafus, 1979
Poole, Robert, 1979
Hawkins, Andy, 1979
Washington, Don, 1979–80
Thompson, Emmuel, 1979–80
Bonner, Marcus, 1979–80
Barefield, Joe, 1980
Roquemore, Durwood, 1980–81
Green, Darrel, 1981–82
Lewis, Loyd, 1982–83

Basketball

Neal, Algie, 1972
Simmons, Hoegie, 1973
Johnson, James, 1976–78
Staten, Eric, 1978–Present
Kinzer, Robert, 1978–Present
Turner, Ed, 1979–81
Daniel, Michael, 1981–82
Farmer, Joe, 1982
Bailey, James, 1982
McCain, Michael, 1983

NAIA All-American

Football

Matthews, Alvin, 1969
Douglas, Karl, 1970
Johnson, Levi, 1971
Hardeman, Don, 1974
Hill, David, 1974–75
Collins, Larry, 1977
Starks, Glenn, 1977
Hawkins, Andy, 1979
Roquemore, Durwood, 1980–81

Basketball

Turner, Ed, 1979–81

Little All-American

Football

Blanks, Sid, 1963
Small, Eldridge, 1971
Johnson, Levi, 1971
Hill, David, 1975
Collins, Larry, 1977

Hawkins, Andy, 1979
Green, Darrell, 1982
Lewis, Loyd, 1983

All Lone Star Conference

Women's Basketball

Goodwin, Kay, 1982
Campbell, Sheryl,[1] 1982

Other Outstanding Athletes

Men's Track

Green, Darrell–100, 200, 400 MD
Gay, Stefan–800 MR
Sweeney, Bryan–100 MH
Martin, Demetrius–member 400 MRT
Green, Darrel–member 400 MRT

Women's Basketball

Denley, Altanette
Bonner, Rhonda
Glass, Gwen

Men's Basketball

Smith, Charles

Texas A & I University's Hall of Fame

Football

Upshaw, Eugene
Douglas, Karl
Blanks, Sid
Hickl, Ray
Starks, Glenn

Track

Haynes, Earnest

[1]Campbell, Sheryl–American Women's Sports Federation All-American, 1987

University of Puget Sound
Tacoma, Washington 98416

Coaches of Varsity Teams

Track

Peyton, Joe, 1968–Present

Softball

Medley, Al, 1983–Present

All Evergreen Conference

Football

Peyton, Joe, 1963–66

All-American NAIA

Football

Peyton, Joe, 1966

Men's Basketball

Lowery, Charles, 1971

Track

Peyton, Joe–LJ, 1964

Philadelphia College of Textiles and Sciences
Philadelphia, Pennsylvania 19144

All-American

Men's Basketball

Poole, Carlton, 1970
Sammons, Emery, 1976–77
Owens, Randy, 1979

Women's Basketball

Morris, Vincene, 1984

Soccer

Durham, Robert, 1969–70
Russell, Dale, 1973–76
Seale, Elson, 1974–76
Nusam, John, 1975–76
Alkins, Peter, 1979

University of Tennessee at Martin
Martin, Tennessee, 38238-5028

All Gulf South Conference

Football

Holmes, Nate, 1971
Williams, David, 1975–77
Washington, Larry, 1976
Watkins, Dan, 1976
Smalls, Alvin, 1977

Meredith, Terry, 1979–81
Williams, Ken, 1980–81
McKinney, Dwayne, 1981
Magee, Greg, 1983

Basketball

Carter, Larry, 1976–77
Boddie, Joe, 1978
Brooks, Larry, 1982
Smith, Darrell, 1982
Rudolph, Gus, 1983
Cherry, Sam, 1984

University of Tennessee at Martin's Hall of Fame

Hamilton, Leonard–the first black athlete recruited to the University of Tennessee at Martin.

City College of New York
New York, New York 10031

Coaches of Varsity Teams

Men's Basketball

Layne, Floyd (Head), 1974–Present

All-American

Men's Basketball

Jameson, Spenser–Honorable Mention, 1949
Warner, Ed,[1] 1950

City College of New York's Hall of Fame

Warner, Ed–played on the 1949 and 1950 City College of New York team that won the National Invitational Tournament and National Collegiate Athletic Association titles in 1950
Layne, Floyd–played on the 1949 and 1950 City College of New York team
Jameson, Spencer–played on the 1949 City College of New York team
Loyd, Otis, Jr.–City College of New York's All-Time leading scorer, 1970–1973.

[1] Warner, Ed–the first African-American to be named the Most Valuable Player at the National Invitational Tournament, 1950

GULF STAR CONFERENCE

1. Stephen F. Austin State University

Stephen F. Austin State University
Nacogdoches, Texas 75962

Coaches of Varsity Teams

Football

Allen, George (Assistant), 1979–Present

All Gulf-Star Conference

Football

Lane, Frank, 1966
Thompson, Dwight, 1972
Eaglin, Lawrence, 1972
Paterson, Ron, 1972
Simmons, Carl, 1972
Borner, Jesse, 1972

Tyler, William, 1973
Booker, Gordon, 1974
Norris, Odis, 1974
Mitchell, Robert, 1978
Haynes, Ron, 1978–79
Godfrey, Orlando, 1980
White, Melvin, 1982–83
Noble, James, 1982–84
Harris, R.L., 1983
Harkless, Darrell, 1984

Basketball

Oliver, Surry, 1967
Johnson, George, 1968–69
Silas, James, 1970–71
Harris, Pete, 1972–73
Evans, Vernon, 1976

Harrison, Hiram, 1982
Harrison, Winston, 1982
Hagan, Chris, 1983

Men's Tennis

Waters, Herb, 1984

All-American

Football

Booker, Gordon, 1974

Haynes, Ron, 1979

Basketball

Oliver, Surry, 1967
Johnson, George, 1968
Silas, James, 1970–71
Harris, Pete, 1972–73
Walker, Rosie,[1] 1979–80

[1] Walker, Rosie–member of the 1980 United States Olympic Women's Basketball Team

Division II Colleges

1. Wesleyan University

2. Seattle University

Wesleyan University
Middletown, Connecticut 06457

Coaches of Varsity Teams

Football

Clark, Norris, (Assistant), 1968–75

Outstanding Athletes

Football

Thomas, James
Greene, Jim

Men's Track

Logan, John
Johnson, James
Linder, Michael
Harris, Darrick
Cornwall, Milton
Robinson, Kevin
Smith, Al

Women's Track

Dillon, Neyga

Soccer

Harris, Darrick
Hamilton, Stan

Wrestling

Ferguson, James,[1] 1962–63
Logan, John,[2] 1966–67

[1] Ferguson, James–the first African-American captain at Wesleyan University
[2] Logan, John–New England Champion at 167 lbs. in 1966 and at 177 lbs. in 1967

Seattle University
Seattle, Washington 98122

All West Coast Athletic Conference

Men's Basketball

Richardson, Clint, 1976–79

All-American

Baylor, Elgin–1958 NCAA University Division Tournament Most Valuable Player

CENTRAL INTERCOLLEGIATE ATHLETIC ASSOCIATION

1. Virginia State University
2. Norfolk State University
3. Virginia Union University
4. Fayetteville State University
5. Hampton University
6. Livingstone College
7. Johnson C. Smith University
8. Elizabeth City State University
9. Winston-Salem State University
10. Shaw University
11. St. Augustine's College
12. St. Paul's College

Virginia State University
Petersburg, Virginia 23803

Football

Jefferson, Harry, 1946–48
Hall, Sal, 1949–52
Lawson, William W., 1953–69
Lovett, Walter L., 1970–72
Bennett, William, 1973
Marshall, John D., 1974–76
Morris, Thomas, 1977–79
Tabor, Al, 1980
Moody, George, 1981–Present

Basketball

Jefferson, Harry, 1946–48
Matthews, Shelton, 1949–54, 1957–63
Deane, Harold A., 1971–77, 1979
Laisure, Floyd, 1981–Present

Women's Basketball

Bey, Leon, 1980–Present

All-Central Intercollegiate Athletic Association

Football

Jones, John, 1947
Keene, Floyd, 1951–52
Miles, Leo,[1] 1951–52
Thompson, Charles, 1952
Callahan, Robert, 1952
Ellerbe, Steve, 1952
Wilson, Wilbur, 1952
Carter, Sidney, 1952
Day, Norman, 1953–54
Freeman, Clinton, 1954
Nash, John, 1954–55
Moody, George, 1958
Jeter, Dewayne, 1960

McNeil, Robert, 1961
Watkins, Joseph, 1963
Golder, Edward, 1964
Sharper, Harry, 1966
Mitchell, James, 1967–69
Helms, Dewey, 1967
Brooks, Larry, 1970–71
Mayes, Myron, 1971
Winslow, Joe, 1971
Bullock, Ronald, 1971
Jackson, Roddrick, 1971
Harper, William, 1971
Allen, John, 1971
Overton, Thomas, 1971
Davis, Ronald, 1971
Chambers, William, 1971–72
Chavis, Robert, 1972
Caul, Robert, 1972
Harris, Ronald, 1972
Hathaway, Harold, 1972
Hayes, Michael, 1972
Dunn, Walter, 1973

All-Central Intercollegiate Athletic Association

Football

Pearson, Joseph, 1973–74
Robinson, Linwood, 1975
Pleasants, Curtis, 1976
Hines, Herbert, 1976–77
Moore, Chris, 1976–77
Crawford, Rufus, 1977
Miles, Charles, 1978
Banks, Layard, 1979
Burnette, Carter, 1979
Johnson, Brad, 1981
Robinson, Mark, 1983
Ward, James, 1983

Basketball

Simmons, Samuel, 1960
Stephens, Frank, 1963
Brock, Ernest, 1968
Looney, Rodney, 1972–74
Johnson, Linwood, 1975–77
Tisdol, Doward, 1976
Bell, Jerome, 1976
Ware, Daniel, 1979
Stith, Darryl, 1981
Norman, Julius, 1981–82

All Tournament Team

Basketball

Bennett, Cleveland, 1947
Hurley, Walter, 1947
Banks, Leroy,[2] 1947
Oliver, Percy, 1957
Deane, Harold, 1961
Stephens, Frank, 1963
Johnson, Linwood,[3] 1974
Bell, Jerome, 1976
Tisdol, Doward, 1976–77
Stith, Darrell, 1981
Norman, Julius,[4] 1981

[1] Miles, Leo–Defensive Back, New York Giants
[2] Banks, Leroy–1947 CIAA Tournament Most Valuable Player
[3] Johnson, Linwood–1974 CIAA Tournament Most Valuable Player
[4] Norman, Julius–1981 CIAA Tournament Most Valuable Player

Norfolk State University
Norfolk, Virginia 23504

Coaches of Varsity Teams

Football

Archie, William, 1962–66
Smith, Willie S., 1967
Maddox, Curtis, 1968–71
Ledbetter, Robert, 1972–73
Price, William "Dick," 1974–83
Bailey, Willard, 1983–Present

Men's Basketball

Porter, Leroy
Turpin, John, 1953–62
Fears, Ernest, 1962–69

Smith, Robert, 1969–73
Christian, Charles, 1974–78
Mitchell, Lucias, 1979–81
Christian Charles, 1982–Present

All Central Intercollegiate Athletic Association

Football

Baker, John, 1963
Smith, Raymond, 1966
Ferguson, Eugene, 1968
Jarvis, Raymond, 1968–70
Jones, Leroy, 1971–72
Santiful, Adolph, 1973
Graeff, Steve, 1974
Trotter, Moses, 1974
Nance, Roger, 1975
Curry, Dexter, 1975–76
Powell, Robert, 1976
Flowers, Jim, 1976
Harrington, Larue, 1977–79
Ellis, Michael, 1977–79
Sweatt, Dwight, 1978
Belle, Joe, 1978
Robinson, James, 1979
Sturdifen, Melvin, 1979
High, John, 1980
Ricks, Alonzo, 1980
Smallwood, Reginald, 1980
Gunn, Jeffrey, 1980–81
Scott, Joseph, 1982
Evans, Brian, 1982
Goodhope, Orlando, 1983
Smith, Leon, 1983
Smith, Alphonso, 1985
Gillus, Willie, 1985
Bates, Theodore, 1986

Basketball

Morris, John, 1965
Pitts, Richard, 1966
Grant, James, 1966–67
Kirkland, Richard, 1968
Dandridge, Robert, 1968–69
Bonaparte, Charles, 1969
McKinney, John, 1970
Peele, Rudolph, 1971–72
Jones, Leroy, 1971–73
Wilson, Ronald, 1972–73

Mitchell, Roosevelt, 1974
Cunningham, Eugene, 1974–76
Burns, Melvin, 1975
Epps, Raymond, 1976–77
Wilkerson, Jesse, 1977
Isabelle, Robert, 1978
Evans, Ken, 1978
Tibbs, Terry, 1981
Pope, David, 1981–84
Tally, Ralph, 1984–87

All Tournament Team

Basketball

Pitts, Richard, 1964–66
Grant, James,[1] 1965–68
Thompson, Essesx, 1966
Kirkland, Richard,[2] 1968
Bonaparte, Charles, 1968–69
Dandridge, Robert,[3] 1968–69
Smith, Gerald, 1971
Peele, Rudolph, 1971–72
James, Morrall,[4] 1971
Jones, Leroy, 1971–73
Lassiter, Randolph, 1972
Wilson, Ronald, 1973
Mitchell, Roosevelt, 1973–74
Parks, James, 1974
Cunningham, Eugene,[5] 1974–76
Epps, Raymond, 1975–76
Burns, Melvin, 1975–76
Isabelle, Robert,[6] 1978–79
Evans, Kenneth, 1978–79
Simon, Lewis, 1979
Tibbs, Terry, 1980
Haynes, Ken, 1983
Allen, Tim, 1983
Pope, David, 1983–84
Talley, Ralph,[7] 1984–87

Norfolk State Alumni in the National Football League

Jarvis, Atlanta Falcons, (WR), 1971–72;
    Detroit Lions, (WR), 1974–78;
    New England Patriots, (WR), 1979
Jones, Earl, Atlanta Falcons, (DB), 1980–83

Reaves, Ken, Atlanta Falcons, (DB), 1966–73;
    New Orleans Saints, (DB), 1974;
    St. Louis Cardinals, (DB), 1974–77
Bolton, Ron, New England Patriots, (DB), 1972–75;
    Cleveland Browns, (DB), 1976–82
Moore, Alex, Denver Broncos, (RB), 1968
Ray, Ricky, New Orleans Saints, (DB), 1979–80;
    Miami Dolphins, (DB), 1981
Ferguson, Eugene, San Diego Chargers, (T), 1969–70;
    Houston Oilers, (T), 1971–72
Bell, Joe, Oakland Raiders, (DE), 1979
Harrington, La Rue, San Diego Chargers, (RB), 1980

Norfolk State Alumni in the National Basketball Association

Dandridge, Robert, Milwaukee Bucks, (F), 1969–77;
    Washington Bullets, (F), 1977–81
Epps, Ray, Golden State Warriors, (G), 1978–79
Pope, David, Utah Jazz, (F), 1984;
    Kansas City Kings, (F), 1985

[1] Grant, James–1965 CIAA Tournament Most Valuable Player
[2] Kirkland, Richard–1968 CIAA Tournament Most Valuable Player
[3] Dandridge, Robert–1969 CIAA Tournament Most Valuable Player
[4] James, Morrall–1971 CIAA Tournament Most Valuable Player
[5] Cunningham, Eugene–1975 and 1976 CIAA Tournament Most Valuable Player
[6] Isabelle, Robert–1978 CIAA Tournament Most Valuable Player
[7] Talley, Ralph–1984 CIAA Tournament Most Valuable Player, 1986 NCAA Division II Player of the Year

Virginia Union University
Richmond, Virginia 23220

Athletic Directors

Harris, Thomas
Marshall, J.D.
Bailey, Willard
Talley, Wilbeart
Battle, James F.

Coaches of Varsity Teams

Football

Taylor, Samuel, 1946–48
Harris, Thomas, 1950–70
Bailey, Willard, 1971–83
Taylor, Joseph, 1984–Present

Basketball

Hucles, Henry
Harris, Thomas, 1950–73
Moore, Robert, 1974–79
Robbins, David, 1980–Present

Women's Basketball

Harris, Thomas
Cannady, Nathan, 1974–82
Hearn, Louis, 1983–Present

All-Central Intercollegiate Athletic Association

Football

Roder, Andrew, 1951
Vaughn, Leroy, 1952
Pinkston, Frank, 1957
Braxton, Hezekiah, 1960
Davis, Jones, 1963
Anderson, Roger, 1963
Beard, Monroe, 1964
Patterson, Donald, 1967
Jenkins, Oscar, 1971
Dreher, Damon, 1971
Williams, Lofell, 1972
Evans, Clarence, 1972
Strickland, Irving, 1972
Jones, Bob, 1972
Shephered, Larry, 1973
Scott, Herbert, 1973
McCray, Frank, 1973
Macon, Richard, 1973
Eley, Vincent, 1973
Reed, Larry, 1973
Roberts, Larry, 1973–74
Leonard, Anthony, 1973–75
White, Clarence, 1974
Tate, Donald, 1974
Jones, Michael, 1974
McCray, Frank, 1975
Seward, Larry, 1975
Williford, Larry, 1975
Hill, Daryl, 1976
McNeil, Dale, 1976
Johnson, Bernard, 1976
Crawley, Michael, 1976–78
Thomas, Judge, 1976–78
Dark, Frank, 1977

Lyman, Curtis, 1977–79
Youngs, Ernesto, 1977–78
Adams, Leroy, 1978
Bullock, Plummer, 1978–79
Barnwell, Malcolm, 1979
Whaff, Wilbert, 1979
Adams, Leroy, 1979
Barnett, Oswald, 1979–80
Cunningham, Phillipe, 1980
Patterson, Kevin, 1980
Mayo, Gary, 1981
Wall, William, 1981
Collier, Robert, 1981
Barringer, Larry, 1981–83
Drew, Dwayne, 1981–83
Dillon, William, 1981–82
Cathion, Keith, 1982
Jordan, Roy, 1982
Curtis, Larry, 1983
Grooms, Samuel, 1983
Brown, Rick, 1985
Wright, Adrian, 1985
Chase, Thomas, 1985

Basketball

Gwin, Stephen, 1955
Spraggins, Warren, 1960–61
Jackson, Jackie, 1961
Davis, Michael, 1968–69
Hunter, Ralph, 1973
Hazley, Andrew, 1973
Carrington, Gregory, 1975
Valentine, Keith, 1979
Holmes, Larry, 1980
Lily, Derwin, 1980
Oakley, Charles, 1982–85
Waller, Jamie, 1985–87

All Tournament Team

Basketball

Bressant, Howard, 1946
Dilworth, James,[1] 1946
Ross, Donald,[2] 1947–49
Clements, Ozelius, 1951
Johnson, William, 1951
King, William, 1952
Wilson, William, 1952

Jones, Howard, 1954–55
Spraggins, Warren, 1959
Simmons, Edward,[3] 1959
Davis, Michael, 1967–69
Niles, Arthur, 1968
Cannady, Nathan, 1972
Hazley, Andrew, 1972
Hunter, Ralph, 1972–74
Benson, Charles, 1977
Lewis, Curvan, 1977
Holmes, Larry,[4] 1979
Echols, Lamont, 1979
Lilly, Derwin, 1979–80
Valentine, Keith,[5] 1979–80
Oakley, Charles,[6] 1985
Waller, Jamie, 1986–87

All-American (Black Colleges or NCAA Division II)

Football

Braxton, Hezekiah, 1960
Chavis, Jesse, 1967
Scott, Herbert, 1973
Leonard, Anthony, 1973
Thomas, Judge, 1976
Bullock, Plummer, 1978
Dillon, William, 1982
Curtis, Larry, 1983
Grooms, Samuel, 1983

All-American (Black College)

Men's Basketball

Oakley, Charles, 1985
Waller, Jamie, 1986–87

Virginia State Alumni in the National Football League

Jones, Robert, Atlanta Falcons, (DB), 1975–76
Braxton, Hezekiah, San Diego Chargers, (RB), 1962;
  Buffalo Bills, (RB), 1963
Scott, Herbert, Dallas Cowboys, (G), 1975–83
Lewis, Herman, Denver Broncos, (DE), 1968
Leonard, Anthony, San Francisco 49ers, (DB), 1976;
  Detroit Lions, (DB), 1978–79
Mallory, Irvin, New England Patriots, (DB), 1971
Anderson, Roger, New York Giants, (DT), 1965–68

Barnwell, Malcolm, Oakland/Los Angeles Raiders, (WR),
  1981–84;
  Washington Redskins, (WR), 1985
Oakley, Charles, Chicago Bulls, (F), 1985–87

[1] Dilworth, James–1946 CIAA Tournament Most Valuable Player
[2] Ross, Donald–1949 CIAA Tournament Most Valuable Player
[3] Simmons, Edward–1959 CIAA Tournament Most Valuable Player
[4] Holmes, Larry–1979 CIAA Tournament Most Valuable Player
[5] Valentine, Keith–1980 CIAA Tournament Most Valuable Player
[6] Oakley, Charles–1985 NCAA Division II Player of the Year

Fayetteville State University
Fayetteville, North Carolina 28301

Athletic Directors

Gaines, William A. "Gus," 1946–57
Scott, Harold, 1960–70
Bell, William, 1970–75
Robinson, Joe, 1975–79
Doubbs, Hubert (Interim), 1979–80
Marshall, John D., 1980–Present

Coaches of Varsity Teams

Football

Gaines, William A. "Gus," 1946–57
Bryant, William, 1957–59
Doubbs, Hubert, 1959–63
Robinson, Frank, 1963–66
Doubbs, Hubert, 1966–70
McDougal, Raymond, 1970–80
Morris, Thomas, 1980–81
Head, William, 1981–85
Pulliam, Robert, 1986–Present

Men's Basketball

Gaines, William A. "Gus," 1946–57
Bryant, William, 1957–62
Robinson, Frank, 1962–69
Reeves, Thomas, 1969–75
Hawkins, Otis, 1975–76
Robinson, Joe, 1976–79
Ford, Jake, 1979–86
Jones, Jeff, 1986–Present

Women's Basketball

Taylor, Leoretta, 1944–77
Hatcher, Cleophus, 1977–78
Smith, Maceo, 1978–79

Henderson, Robert, 1979–80
Edwards, Yvonne, 1980–82
Lamb, Mary, 1982–Present

All Central Intercollegiate Athletic Association

Football

Cox, Ronald, 1970
Walker, Larry, 1972
Pointer, Clarence, 1973
Wright, Michael, 1973
Young, John, 1974
Godwin, James, 1974–75
Simmons, Jackie, 1975
Franks, Maurice, 1975–76
Travis, Burnis, 1976–78
Gray, Willie, 1979
Guions, Ronald, 1979
Wadford, Bertie, 1979
Hall, Ike, 1979–80
Martin, Kevin, 1982
Kelly, Tyrone, 1983
Simms, Kendrick, 1983
Harris, Charles, 1985

Basketball

Evans, Ronald, 1957
Bibby, Fred, 1964
Monroe, William, 1969
Sneed, Michael, 1971–72
Barrows, John, 1977
Jefferson, Edward, 1979
Mims, Steve, 1981
McNeil, Bonny, 1982
Person, William, 1984

All Tournament Team

Evans, Ronald, 1957
Morgan, John, 1957
Sneed, Michael, 1972
McNeil, Earl, 1972
Cogdell, Alton, 1973
Tyus, James, 1973
McNeil, Bonny, 1982

Hampton University
Hampton, Virginia 23668

Coaches of Varsity Teams

Football

Griffin, Sr., James, 1947–48
Jefferson, Harry, 1949–56
Whaley, Ben, 1957–64
Labat, Mel, 1965–68
Van Cleve, Whitney, 1969–73
Lovett, Walter, 1974–80
Wyche, Ed, 1981–84
Freeman, Fred, 1985–Present

Basketball

McClendon, John, 1952–54
Whaley, Ben, 1954–57
Enty, Frank, 1957–61
Smith, Willie, 1961–62
Enty, Frank, 1962–63
Royster, Lee, 1963–64
Moorehead, Ike, 1964–71
Shackleford, Louis, 1971–73
Frazier, Solomon, 1973–75
Ford, Hank, 1975–Present

Women's Basketball

Gatling, Alberta, 1975–80
Sinclair, Marilyn, 1980–81
Sweat, James, 1981–Present

Men's Tennis

Neilson, Dr., Herman
Screen, Dr., Robert, 1970–Present

Women's Track

Sweat, Laverne, 1978–Present

Wrestling

Crocker, David 1980

All-Central Intercollegiate Athletic Association

Football

Casey, Tom, 1946–47
Lewis, W.C., 1948
Goodall, Luther, 1948
Ayers, Robert, 1951

Eason, Harry, 1953
Brown, George, 1956
Bey, Charles, 1966
Bowers, Sandy, 1966
Robinson, Betram, 1967–69
Johnson, Robert, 1971
Bascomb, Carl, 1975
Bey, Ronald Allen, 1975
Doss, Reginald, 1976–77
Midgett, Reginald, 1977
Jones, Leroy, 1978
Rose, Don, 1978
South, Victor, 1979
White, Ernest, 1979
Mahan, Dennis, 1980
Johnson, Michael, 1980
Smith, Anthony, 1980
Jackson, Reginald, 1982
Readon, Issacs, 1983
Skinner, Dark, 1985
Readon, Ike, 1985
Denby, William, 1985
Bailey, Clarence, 1985

Basketball

Amos, Edwin, 1956–57
Trader, Nathaniel, 1959
Ward, Walter, 1961
Youngblood, Willie, 1973
Britt, Wayne, 1974
Best, Tyrone, 1977
Payne, Marvin, 1977–79
Threatt, Tony, 1978
Tolliver, Keith, 1978
Mahorn, Rick,[1] 1978–80
Warwick, Darryl, 1981
Washington, Anthony, 1982–83
Hines, Gregory, 1983
Miller, Cedric, 1984

All-Tournament Team

Basketball

Trader, Nathaniel, 1960
Threatt, Tony, 1978
Tolliver, Keith, 1978

Mahorn, Rick, 1978–80
Warwick, Darryl, 1979
Hines, Gregory,[2] 1980–83
Moore, Gerald, 1982
Miller, Cedric, 1982
Washington, Tony,[3] 1982–83

All-American (Black College)

Football

Bey, Ron, 1975
Gamble, John, 1975
Midgett, Reginald, 1975
Seaton, Russ, 1975–76
Wickham, Nick, 1976
Graham, Leroy, 1976
Doss, Reginald, 1976
White, Ernie, 1977–78
Rose, Donovan, 1978
Thomas, Jon, 1979
Johnson, Michael, 1980–82
Mahan, Dennis, 1980–82
Ross, Kevin, 1981
Harrison, Phil, 1981–83
Lawson, John, 1982
Young, Wallace, 1982
Readon, Ike, 1983
Speller, Nepton, 1983

Men's Basketball

Best, Tyrome, 1977
Tolliver, Keith, NAIA 1978
Mahorn, Ricky, NAIA 1978–80
Warrick, Darryl, NAIA 1981–82
Washington, Tony, NAIA 1982–82
Hines, Gregory, NAIA 1982–83

Men's Track

Richardson, Paul, NAIA (HH) 1976
Watts, William, NAIA (TJ) 1976
Powell, Whitney, NAIA (MR) 1979
Ruffin, Michael, NAIA (MR) 1979
Williams, Willie, NAIA (MR) 1979
West, Richard, NAIA (MR) 1979
Dixon, David, NCAA (HH) (ID) 1981
Brown, Robert, NAIA 440 (ID) 400M (OD)

Symonette, Ed, NAIA (MR) (ID) 1982
Brown, Robert, NAIA (MR) (ID) 1982
Johnson, Freddie, NAIA (MR) (ID) 1982
Turner, Doug, NAIA (MR) (ID) 1982
Johnson, Freddie, NAIA 60 YD (ID) 1982
Marshall, Livingstone, 800M (OD) NAIA 1983
Skinner, Darryl, 100M, NAIA 1983
Delk, Lee Roy, 4x100R, NAIA 1983
Brown, Robert, 4x100R, NAIA 1983
Dannelly, Charles, 4x100R, NAIA 1983
Skinner, Darryl, 4x100R, NAIA 1983
Delk, Lee Roy, 200M, NAIA 1983
Fisher, Kenneth, 800M, NAIA 1983
Mason, Mark, Discus, NAIA 1983

Hampton Institute's Hall of Fame

Moore, Dr., Sylvius S.
Hill, Dr., Carl
Griffin, Dr., James
Williams, C.H.
Casey, Dr., Tom
Smith, Gideon

Hampton University Alumni in the National Football League

Reeberg, Lucien, Detroit Lions, (T), 1963
Rose, Donovan, Kansas City Chiefs, (DB), 1980
Doss, Reginald, Los Angeles Rams, (DE), 1978–86

Hampton University Alumni in the National Basketball Association

Mahorn, Rick, Washington Bullets, (F), 1980–85;
    Detroit Pistons, (F), 1985–87

[1] Mahorn, Rick–1979 Central Intercollegiate Athletic Association Player Of The Year
[2] Hines, Gregory–1982 Central Intercollegiate Athletic Association Most Valuable Player
[3] Washington, Tony–1983 Central Intercollegiate Athletic Associate Tournament Most Valuable Player

Livingstone College
Salisbury, North Carolina 28144

Athletic Directors

Mitchell, Edward, 1952–58
Brown, A.R., 1959–60
Cox, Charles R., 1960–64
Johnson, Elijah, 1964–65
Brown, Jr., Walter, 1965–70
Marshall, Jr., John D., 1970–73
Ponder, Fred, 1973–79
Robinson, Joe, 1979–83
Ponder, Fred, 1983–85
Clemmons, Edward, 1986–Present

Coaches of Varsity Teams

Football

Goodrum, William, 1946–48
Sneed, Maurice, 1948–49
Mitchell, Edward L., 1949–51
Greene, Luther, 1951–52
Mitchell, Edward L., 1952–58
Brown, Arthur T., 1959–60
Cox, Charles R., 1960–64
Johnson, Elijah, 1964–65
Marshall, J.D., 1965–73
Holman, Baxter D., 1973–78
Littlejohn, Andrew, 1978–80
Rose, Mel, 1980–85
Corley, David, 1986–Present

Basketball

Mitchell, Edward L., 1949–58
Warner, L.A., 1959–64
Brown, Walter L., 1965–70
Wiggins, Morris, 1970–74
Porter, Willie, 1974–76
Thomas, Fred, 1976–79
Robinson, Joe E., 1979–83
Fitch, Jerry, 1983–84
Corley, David, 1984–85

Track and Field

Mitchell, Edward L., 1957–58
Brown, Arthur T., 1959–60

Cox, Charles R., 1960–64
Marshall, J.D., 1964–65, 1967–68
Seales, Roger, 1968–70
Ponder, Fred, 1970–73
Holman, Baxter D., 1973–78
Littlejohn, Andrew, 1978–79
Rose, Mel, 1980

Tennis

Warner, L.A., 1960–61
Valencourt, Roy, 1961–62
Little, Harlee, 1962–63
Nelson, Grady, 1963–68
Marshall, J.D., 1968–70
Poe, Alfred, 1970–72
Marshall, J.D., 1972–73
Ponder, Fred, 1973–85

Golf

Warner, L.A., 1961–64
Jones, Fletcher, 1964–65
Nelson, Grady, 1965–66
Jones, Fletcher, 1970–71
Marshall, John D., 1971–72
Nelson, Grady, 1972–75
Jones, Fletcher, 1975–77
Rippy, Julius, 1977–79
Springs, Andre, 1979–81
Rose, Mel, 1981–83
Fitch, Jerry, 1983–84

Wrestling

Bartlett, William, 1971–72
Johnson, Richard, 1973–78
Vaughn, Samuel, 1978–80
Gorney, Blaine, 1980

Women's Basketball

Davis, Jeanne, 1947–48
Mitchell, Florence N., 1949–64
Martin, Rose, 1964–65
Williams, Anne L., 1965–69
Wrightsell, Emma M., 1969–74
Lawson, Patricia, 1974–79
Corley, David, 1979–83
Green, Peggy, 1983

All Central Intercollegiate Athletic Association

Football

Tyler, Alfred, 1966
Sutton, Sylvester, 1966
Smith, Gregory, 1968
Klutz, Paul, 1968–69
Brandon, Robert, 1970
Price, Perry, 1971
Brooks, David, 1971
Sawyer, Frank, 1971–73
Farrar, John, 1972
Thomas, Robert, 1973
Ballard, Horace, 1973
Ritter, Sylvester, 1974
Miller, John, 1974–75
Cooney, Andrew, 1974–76
Lee, Larry, 1975
Cuthrell, Herman, 76–77
Stoutamire, John, 1977
Long, Jesse, 1979
White, Joseph, 1981–82
Ford, Paul, 1983
Cunningham, Kevin, 1985
Asbury, Jerry, 1985

Basketball

Hamilton, Jerry, 1974–75
Davis, Antonio, 1982

Johnson C. Smith University
Charlotte, North Carolina 28216

Coaches of Varsity Teams

Football

Crudup, Byrd, 1946–49
Jackson, Robert H., 1953–57
McGirt, Edward, 1958–77
Harris, Wylie, 1978–83
Small, Horace, 1983–Present

Men's Basketball

Bynum, George, 1946
McKenney, T.E., 1948
Irvin, Calvin, 1950–52
Brayboy, Jack, 1953–54

McGirt, Edward C., 1960–62
McCullough, William, 1963–68
Fitch, Jerome, 1975–78
Moore, Robert, 1979–86

All-Central Intercollegiate Athletic Association

Football

Petty, Howard, 1952
Norman, Pettis, 1961
Farmer, Edward, 1967–68
Dusenberry, William, 1969
Reid, Paul, 1969
Duncan, Elroy, 1970
Fairley, John, 1970
Jones, Larry, 1970
Duke, Bruce, 1971
Corbett, Billy, 1971
Gunn, William, 1971
Lide, William, 1972
Carter, Luther, 1972–73
Hill, George, 1974
Bailey, Willie, 1974
Spindle, Linwood, 1975
Corley, Ronald, 1975–76
Grimsley, Chet, 1976
Stroman, Charles, 1978
Wring, Alfred, 1979
Abernathy, Alvarez, 1980
Beauford, Daniel, 1980–82
McDowell, Nate, 1981–82
Thomas, John, 1982
Wicker, Anthony, 1983
Warren, Craig, 1985
Swain, Michael, 1985

Basketball

Sanders, Claude, 1955
Crenshaw, Joseph, 1959
Hester, James, 1962
Neal, Fred, 1963
Turner, Charles, 1965
Randolph, Reginald, 1967
Butts, Robert, 1970–71
Cooper, George, 1974–75
Lewis, Robert, 1976
Entzminger, Herbaert, 1977–78

Proctor, Francis, 1978–80
Tibbs, William, 1979–82
Oliver, Larcell, 1980–82
Flores, Phil, 1981
McGrudder Roosevelt, 1984

All Tournament Team

Basketball

Saunders, Claude, 1952
Hargett, James, 1952
Hester, James, 1961
Neal, Fred, 1961–63
McMorris, Stoney, 1964
Schley, Stephen, 1964
Wilson, Jackie, 1965–67
Sanders, James, 1973–74
Cooper, George, 1973–75
Joplin, Willie, 1974
Wallace, Derek, 1975
Lewis, Robert, 1976
Entzminger, Herbaert, 1978
Flores, Phil, 1982
Oliver, Larcell, 1982
Smith, Phil, 1982

Elizabeth City State University
Elizabeth City, North Carolina 27909

All Central Intercollegiate Athletic Association

Football

Pugh, Jethro, 1963–64
Little, Thurlis, 1964
Walton, John, 1968
Bell, Ernest, 1969
Russell, Anthony, 1969
Moore, Donnell, 1969
Lewis, Alvin, 1969
Williams, Torain, 1970
Leigh, Ronald, 1970
Belton, Andy, 1971
Reynolds, Oliver, 1971
Johnson, Larry, 1972
Carmichael, Bruce, 1973
Stukes, David, 1973
Brooks, John, 1973–74

Newsome, Jerome, 1974–75
Holmes, Alfred, 1975
Hargrove, Fred, 1977
Farrington, Lester, 1977
Moses, Waddell, 1978
Thompson, Tony, 1978
Pugh, James, 1978
Hill, Michael, 1979
Wilson, Fred, 1979
Whitehurst, Stanley, 1980
Bright, Maryland, 1980
Evans, John, 1980
James, Elvin, 1981
Whitefield, Dwayne, 1981
Futrell, Robert, 1981–83
Langhorne, Reggie, 1983
Moore, William, 1985
Cofield, Tim, 1985

Basketball

Trotman, Marvin, 1962
Todd, Richard, 1965–66
Stubbins, Gary, 1966–67
Lewis, Frederick, 1967–68
Smith, Oscar, 1968
Oliver, Israel, 1969–70
Gale, Michael, 1970–71
Carmichael, Len, 1972
Windley, Glen, 1973–74
Carr, Charles, 1975
Blue, Thomas, 1975–77
Gaskins, Arthur, 1979–80
Bland, Pierre, 1982

All Tournament Team

Basketball

Smith, Oscar, 1968
Oliver, Israel, 1969
Moorer, Hubert, 1969–70
Gale, Michael, 1969–71
Carmichael, Len, 1972
Carr, Charles, 1975
Blue, Thomas, 1975
Gaskins, Arthur, 1981
Bland, Pierre, 1981
Gale, Michael, San Antonio Spurs, (G), 1976–80;
   Portland Trailblazers, (G), 1980–81

Winston-Salem State University
Winston-Salem, North Carolina 27110

Coaches of Varsity Teams

Football

Gaines, Clarence,[1] 1946–50
Conrad, Thomas, 1950–69
Wallace, C., 1970–75
Hayes, William, 1976–Present

Basketball

Gaines, Clarence, 1947–Present

All Central Intercollegiate Athletic Association

Football

Wallace, Cleo, 1951
Dupree, Benjamin, 1957
Rowe, Robert, 1957
Guthrie, Nelson, 1960–61
Souels, Richard, 1964
Grady, Daniel, 1968
McManus, Allen, 1969
Nelson, Frederick, 1972
Phiffer, Curtis, 1972
Garner, Robert, 1972
Gregg, Edward, 1972
Barbour, Bennie, 1972–74
Davis, James, 1973
Richardson, Curtis, 1974
Rodgers, Johnny, 1975–76
Winbush, James, 1977
Blount, Kermit, 1977–78
Newsome, Tim, 1977–79
Washington, Cornelius, 1977–79
Diggs, William, 1978
Harrington, Baxter, 1978
Jordan, Willie, 1978
Tyson, James, 1979
Jacobs, Daniel, 1979
Mack, Winfred, 1979
Jones, Arrington, 1980
Parson, Keith, 1980
Watson, Carlton, 1980
Lewis, John, 1981
Bryson, Dan, 1981
Stokes, Harrison, 1981–82

Nimmons, Jonathan, 1981–83
Moore, Danny, 1982–83
Powell, Alvin, 1983
Cameron, Jack, 1983
Sauls, Eddie, 1983
Holland, Keith, 1985
Turner, Barry, 1985

Basketball

Defares, Jack, 1955–56
John, Wilfred, 1958
Hill, Cleo, 1959–61
Foree, George, 1962
Glover, Richard, 1963
Blount, Theodore, 1963–65
Curry, Willie, 1964
Monroe, Earl, 1965–67
Cunningham, Tom, 1966
Ridgill, Howard, 1966
Reid, James, 1967
Smiley, Eugene, 1968
English, William, 1968–69
Williams, Donald, 1970
Smith, Sandy, 1971–72
Williams, Earl, 1972–74
Chavious, Arthur, 1973
Kitt, Harold, 1974
Paulin, Thomas, 1975
Helton, Donald, 1976
Terry, Carlos, 1976–78
Gaines, Reginald, 1978–80
Robinson, Michael, 1978–80
Harold, David, 1979
Greene, Therman, 1982
Russell, Troy, 1984

All Tournament Team

Basketball

Defares, Jack, 1955–57
John, Wilfred,[2] 1955–57
Hill, Cleo,[3] 1959–61
Foree, George,[4] 1960–62
Riley, Charles, 1961
Glover, Richard, 1963
Blount, Theodore,[5] 1962–63
Monroe, Earl,[6] 1965–67
Reid, James, 1967

English, William, 1967–69
Kimbrough, Vaughn, 1969
McManus, Allen,[7] 1970
Garner, Robert, 1973
Williams, Earl, 1973–74
Paulin, Thomas, 1975
Helton, Donald, 1975–76
Terry, Carlos,[8] 1975–78
Brown, Michael, 1976
Gibson, George, 1977
Dillard, Marco, 1977
Robinson, Michael, 1978
Gaines, Reginald, 1978–79
Whitfield, Cliff, 1983
Womack, Dan, 1983

Winston Salem State Alumni in the National Basketball Association

Monroe, Earl, Baltimore Bullets, (G), 1967–72;
   New York Knickerbockers, (G), 1972–80
Reid, Jim, Philadelphia 76ers, (F), 1967–68
Williams, Earl, Phoenix Suns, (F), 1974–75;
   New Jersey Nets, (F), 1976–77
Terry, Carlos, Washington Bullets, (F), 1980–83

[1] Gaines, Clarence–career coaching record 750 wins, 345 losses, .685 percentage, has more career wins than any other active collegiate coach.
[2] John, Wilfred–1957 CIAA Tournament Most Valuable Player
[3] Hill, Cleo–CIAA Tournament Most Valuable Player, 1960, 1961
[4] Foree, George–1962 CIAA Tournament Most Valuable Player
[5] Blount, Theodore–1963 CIAA Tournament Most Valuable Player
[6] Monroe, Earl–1966 CIAA Tournament Most Valuable Player
[7] McManus, Allen–1970 CIAA Tournament Most Valuable Player
[8] Terry, Carlos–1977 CIAA Tournament Most Valuable Player

Shaw University
Raleigh, North Carolina 27611

All-Central Intercollegiate Athletic Association

Football

Bellamy, Twille, 1947–49
Roper, Edward, 1949
Way, Leroy, 1949
Hammonds Eugene, 1957
McClain, Albert, 1958
Knight, Glenfield, 1958–60
Clark, Otis, 1961
Crenshaw, Chauncey, 1966
Wynecoff, Roderick, 1970

Green, Van, 1972
Artis, William, 1974
Williams, Curtis, 1976

Basketball

Mitchell, Ira, 1966
Utley, Kelly, 1970–71
Haskins, Raymond, 1971–72
Agee, Daniel, 1973
Richardson, Andrew, 1974
Moye, Joseph, 1975
Stuckey, Sammy, 1982
Lacy, David, 1984

All Central Intercollegiate Athletic Association's
All Tournament
Keitt, Frank, 1958
Utley, Kelly, 1971
Haskins, Raymond, 1971–72
Murchinson, Terrance, 1973
Richardson, Andrew, 1976
Hicks, Larry, 1977

St. Augustine's College
Raleigh, North Carolina 27611

All Central Intercollegiate Athletic Association

Football

Miles, Roland, 1950
Clements, Jesse, 1950
McAllister, William, 1952
Nicholson, Joseph, 1956
Richards, Earl, 1956

Basketball

Pritchett, Curtis, 1971–72
Powell, Sean, 1977
Cooper, William, 1980
Boggan, Anthony, 1981
Carroll, Donald, 1982
Franks, Randy, 1984
Rogers, Anthony, 1984

All Tournament Team

Basketball

Burks, Clarence, 1953
Stirrup, Al, 1960
Rand, Calvin, 1976
Powell, Sean, 1977
Rhodes, Larry, 1977
Preston, Calvin, 1980
Taylor, Gary, 1980
Cooper, William, 1980
Bogan, Anthony, 1980–81
Cook, Marvin, 1982
Carroll, Donald, 1982–83
Rogers, Anthony, 1982–83
Davis, Mark, 1983
Bannister, Ken, 1984
Franks, Randy, 1984

St. Augustine's Alumni in the
National Basketball Association

Bannister, Ken, New York Knickerbockers, (F), 1984–86

St. Paul's College
Lawrenceville, Virginia 23868

All Central Intercollegiate Athletic Association

Football

Woodson, James, 1974–77
Cosby, Samuel, 1975–76
Grimes, Willie, 1978
Bell, Willie, 1980
LeSane, Lydell, 1980
Freeman, Waldo, 1980

Basketball

Bacote, Ralph, 1954
Green, Michael, 1970
Roberts, Donnie, 1975–76
Cozart, William, 1976–77
Jackson, Gregory, 1980–81
Lewis, Bernard, 1981
Bell, Charles, 1984

MID-EASTERN ATHLETIC CONFERENCE

1. Morgan State University
2. North Carolina Central University
3. Delaware State College
4. South Carolina State College
5. University of Maryland, Eastern Shore
6. Florida A&M University
7. North Carolina Agricultural and Technical State University
8. Howard University
9. Coppin State University

Morgan State University
Baltimore, Maryland 21239

Athletic Directors

Hurt, Eddie, 1946–70
Bowie, Embra C., 1970–72
Banks, Earl, 1971–82
Dean, Tom, 1983–Present

Coaches of Varsity Teams

Football

Hurt, Edward, 1946–59
Banks, Earl, 1959–73
Taylor, Nathaniel, 1974–75
Lattimore, Henry, 1976–77
Thomas, Clarence, 1978–79
Phillips, James, 1984
Thomas, Jesse, 1985–Present

Men's Basketball

Wilson, Howard A. "Brutus," 1957–66
Frazier, Nathaniel, 1967–76
Johnson, Aaron, 1976–78
Goydon, Gus, 1978–80
Dean, Tom, 1984–85
McMillian, Ray, 1984–85
Frazier, Nathaniel, 1985–86

Women's Basketball

Fields, LaRue, 1978–85
Powell, Andy, 1985–Present

Trainer

Brown, Dr., Herman, 1943–47

All-American (Black College)

Football

Brown, Roosevelt "Rosie," 1953
Kelly, Leroy, 1964

Lanier, Willie, 1965
Queen, Jeff, 1967
Germany, Willie, 1970
Cherry, Stan, 1972
Simms, Eugene "Superman," 1973
Fowlkes, Joe, 1978
Holston, Michael, 1980

Men's Basketball

Webster, Marvin, 1973–74
O'Neal, Alvin, 1974

Men's Track

Rhoden, George, 1952
Bragg, Arthur "Art," 1953
Culbreath, Joshua "Josh," 1955
Lee, Nichols "Nick," 1966

All Central Intercollegiate Athletic Association

Football

Cragway, Roy, 1948
Rooks, George, 1948–50
Nelson, Athelstan, 1949
Hunter, Timothy, 1949
Whaley, Marvin, 1949
Robinson, Charles, 1950
Brown, Roosevelt, 1951–52
Buford, William, 1953
Gaines, Al, 1953
Porter, Charles, 1955
Prather, Gilbert, 1955
McArthur, Jerome, 1956
Rozier, Jack, 1956
Tinkler, William, 1961
Young, Robert, 1961
Dobbins, Oliver, 1963
Sheppard, Leroy, 1963
Phillips, James, 1964–66
Mayo, Earl, 1966

Nock, George, 1966–67
Palmore, Harvey, 1966
Johnson, Wade, 1966
Lanier, Willie, 1966
Dabney, Carlton, 1966–67
Queen, Jeffrey, 1966–67
Johnson, Daryl, 1967
Dean, Thomas, 1967
Boyd, Gerald, 1967
Hayes, Edward, 1967–68
Chester, Raymond, 1968
Smith, Robert, 1968–69
Washington, Mark, 1969
Bell, Harold, 1970
Caraway, Bruce, 1970
Germany, Willie, 1970

Basketball

Garrett, Ernest, 1954–55
Garner, Ronald, 1958
Brightful, Charles, 1958
Johnson, Harold, 1960–62
Turk, James, 1965

All Mid-Eastern Athletic Conference

Football

Hairston, Ray, 1971
Sykes, John, 1971
Freeland, Jeff, 1971
Ogle, Gregory, 1971
Andrews, John, 1971
Cherry, Stan, 1972
Simms, Eugene, 1972–73
Hammond, Robert, 1972–74
Davis, Curtis, 1973
Latta, Gregory, 1973
Tyuz, Richard, 1973
McQueen, Frank, 1973–74
Thompson, William, 1974
Baylor, Tim, 1973–75
Nicholson, Van, 1975
Lighty, William, 1975–76
Durden, Mark, 1975–76
Fowlkes, Joseph, 1976–78
Slade, Kevin, 1977
Ross, Allen, 1977
Munford, Nathan, 1977–78

Huggins, Gerald, 1977–78
Henderson, Curtis, 1979
Coulter, Darrell, 1979
King, Henry, 1979
Cook, Arthur, 1979
Dennis, Vaughn, 1979
Burton, Maurice, 1979
Franks, Elvis, 1979

Basketball

Davis, Chester, 1972–73
Webster, Marvin,[1] 1972–75
Newton, William, 1975–76
Evans, Eric,[2] 1976–78
Jennings, Maurice, 1977
Young, Anthony, 1977–79
Hopkins, Garcia, 1979
Witherspoon, Byron, 1979
Roberts, Yarborough, 1980

Morgan State Alumni in the National Football League

Chester, Raymond, Oakland Raiders, (TE), 1970–72;
    1978–81
    Baltimore Colts, (TE), 1973–77
Mayo, Ron, Baltimore Colts, (TE), 1974
Robinson, Charles, Baltimore Colts, (G), 1954
Dabney, Carlton, Atlanta Falcons, (DT), 1968
Germany, Willie, Atlanta Falcons, (S), 1972;
    Detroit Lions, (S), 1973;
    Houston Oilers, (S), 1975;
    New England Patriots, (S), 1976
Collier, Michael, Pittsburgh Steelers, (RB), 1975;
    Buffalo Bills, (RB), 1977–79
Dobbins, Oliver, Buffalo Bills, (DB), 1964
Tyler, Maurice, Buffalo Bills, (DB), 1972;
    Denver Broncos, (DB), 1973–74;
    Detroit Lions, (DB), 1976;
    New York Jets, (DB), 1977;
    New York Giants, (DB), 1978
Latta, Greg, Chicago Bears, (TE), 1975–80
Franks, Elvis, Cleveland Browns, (DE), 1980–85
Kelly, Leroy, Cleveland Browns, (RB), 1964–73
Mitchell, Alvin, Cleveland Browns, (DB), 1968–69;
    Denver Broncos, (DB), 1970
Washington, Mark, Dallas Cowboys, (DB), 1970–78;
    New England Patriots, (DB), 1979

Wade, Robert, Pittsburgh Steelers, (DB), 1968;
Washington Redskins, (DB), 1969;
Denver Broncos, (DB), 1970
Holston, Michael, Houston Oilers, (WR), 1981
Queen, Jeff, San Diego Chargers, (RB), 1969–71;
Houston Oilers, (RB), 1974
Anderson, John, Los Angeles Rams, (DE), 1975–76
Baylor, Tim, Minnesota Vikings, (S), 1979–80
Johnson, Darryl, Boston Patriots, (DB), 1968–70;
New England Patriots, (DB), 1971
Scott, Clarence, Boston Patriots, (DB), 1969–70;
New England Patriots, (DB), 1971–72
Carr, Thomas, New Orleans Saints, (DE), 1968
Brown, Roosevelt, New York Giants, (T), 1953–65
Fuqua, John, New York Giants, (RB), 1969;
Pittsburgh Steelers, (RB), 1970–76
Nock, George, New York Jets, (RB), 1969–71;
Washington Redskins, (RB), 1972
Hayes, Ed, Philadelphia Eagles, (DB), 1970
Person, Ara, St. Louis Cardinals, (TE), 1972
Sykes, John, San Diego Chargers, (RB), 1972
Lanier, Willie, Kansas City Chiefs, (L), 1967–77

Morgan State University's Athletic Hall of Fame

Football

Frazier, John "Stoop"
Hicks Raymond "Tim"
Lawless, Preston E.
Moore, William Coleridge
Morris, Arnold "Clip"
Turpin, Waters "Biffo"
Williams, Robert "Bob"
Holley, Waymon
Smith, Rubin "Whirlwind"
Fauntleroy, Arthur "Honeyboy"
Hill, Herbert "Chink"
Brown, Roosevelt
Locust, Irvin "Monk"
Gilbert, Albert C.
Robert, Richard "Reds"
Rooks, George "Choo Choo"
Turpin, James "Jim"
Byrd, Earl Wesley "Early"
Cragway, Roy "Craig"
Dennis, Jack "The Menace"

McIntyre, Theodore "Ted"
Pompey, Carmie, "Pete"
Young, Robert "Bobby"
Brightful, Charles "Bo"
Buford, William "Bill"
Burkett, Robert M.
Hawkins, Wilbur
Nelson, Athelson Thel
Dobbins, Oliver W.
Hurtt, Clarence "Mel"
Kelly, Leroy
Patterson, Donald "Pat"
Lyght, William "Bill"
Philips, James "Phil"
Thomas, Lorenzo "Joints"
Wade, Robert "Flakie"
Butler, J. Hiram "Steepy"
Henderson, Tillman "Tex"
Marcus, Jr., Matthew "Mack"
Nickens, J. Laws
Oliver, Isiah "Ted"
Chase, Anthony Driver
Rosedom, George "Rosie"
Lanier, Willie
Dean, Thomas "Tex"
Smith, Henry "Goose"
Thomas, Luther "Shag"

Football–Basketball

Clark, Daniel "Pinky"
Hill, Talmadge "Marse"
Turpin, Samuel "Sam"
Wheatley, Thomas "Rap"
Cain, William "Sugar"
Conrad, Thomas "Tank"
Crawford, Herbert "Hub"
Drake, Carl
Gibson, Charles "Skippy"
Lampkin, William "Bill"
Ryan, Maceo P.
Smith, Robert "Spooks"
Troupe, Otis "Whata Man"
Williams, James "Jim"
Wilson, Howard "Brutus"
Bowie, Embra C.
Brown, Alvin "Boo"
Brown, Thomas "Tom"

Byron, Cyril "Buns"
Day, Terry "Tippy"
Gaines, Clarence "Big House"
Gibson, Joseph "Deuce"
Grimsley, Preston "Grimmie"
Givens, Oscar
Howard, Ely "Tim"
Sowell, Richard "OJay"
Jones, Willie "Toe"

Men's Basketball

Jones, Ed "Lanky"
Sheffey, Powell B.
Hackett, Rufus "Legs"
Jones, William "Babe"
Murdock, Ezra "Ez"
Payne, William "Mack"
Spencer, Howard "Jack"
Garrett, Ernest
Cornish, Howard Lee
Covert, Bettilee "Jenks"
Whitted, Carl "Jet"
James, Albert "Sonny"
Clarke, Wilbur "Ace"

Football–Track

Bell, Alfred "Gator"
Spaulding, George "Hoss"
Stugis, John "Johnnie"
Burdnell, John "Baby"
Campbell, Jonathan "Unk"
Gibbs, James "Jim"
Gordon, Frank "Pickle"
Hurtt, Jesse "Flash"
Black, Joseph "Chico"
Harris, Elmo "Pepper"
Robinson, Charles "Bull"
Triplett, John "Trip"

Track

Ross, Wellington "Duckie"
Couch, Flan "Butte"
Barksdale, A. Robert "Barky Roll"
Bragg, Arthur "Art"
Brown, William "Bill"
Ellis, Nichols "Nick"
Labeach, Samuel "Speedy"
Rhoden, George V.

Tyler, Robert "Bo"
Culbreath, Joshua "Josh"
Thompson, Lancelot "L.C."
Lee, Nichols "Nick"
Martin, Lee
Dennis, George Robert
Rogers, James "Jimmy"
Bethea, John David
Brown, Kelsey Thurlow
Wade, Herman "Bitsey"
Waters, Edward "Dickey"
Gross, Harry Rudolph
Kake, Kenneth
Morgan, Howard Phipps
Winder, Paul Lewis
Labeach, Byron
Stanbury, Wardell

Coaches

Clark, Daniel
Hill, Talmadge
Taylor, William
Wilson, Brutus
Brown, Alvin

[1] Webster, Marvin–1973–74 Mid-Eastern Athletic Conference Player of the Year
[2] Evans, Eric–1977 Mid-Eastern Conference Player of the Year

North Carolina Central University
Durham, North Carolina 27707

Athletic Directors

McLendon, John, 1946–52
Newton, I.G., 1952–61
Younge, James W., 1961–67
Stevens, James, A., 1968–69
Younge, James W., 1969–75
Alston, Joseph L., 1975–76
Stevens, James, 1976–77
Silva, C. Francis A., 1977–80
Lattimore, Henry C., 1980–Present

Coaches of Varsity Teams

Football

Riddick, Herman H., 1945–64
Stevens, James A., 1965–67

Quiett, George L., 1968–72
Smith, Willie S., 1973–77
Clements, Jesse, 1977
Jackson, Robert, 1977
Greene, Ray, 1978
Lattimore, Henry C., 1979–86

Basketball

McLendon, John B., 1940–52
Brown, Floyd H., 1952–70
Edmonds, Harry J., 1970–73
Jones, Samuel, 1973–74
Holt, Sterlin M., 1974–78
Silva, Francis A., 1978–79
Clements, Jesse, 1979–84
Edmonds, Harry J., 1984–Present

Track

Walker, Dr. Leroy T., 1946–73
Jermundson, Aaron, 1973–75
Harvey, Robert, 1975–77
Lipscomb, George, 1977–81
Falcuma, McDougald-Mark Adams, 1981–82
McDonald, Larry, 1982

Coaches of Varsity Teams

Tennis

Brown, Floyd H., 1946–49
Younge, James W., 1950–74
Edmonds, Harry J., 1975

Women's Basketball

McCormick, Mickie, 1975–78
Wade, Calvin, 1978–79
Silva, Francis A., 1979–80
Gatling, Alberta W., 1980–82
Edwards, Yvonne M., 1982

Volleyball

Shuler, Sandra T., 1975–Present

All Central Intercollegiate Athletic Association

Football

Brown, John, 1946
Galbreath, Carl, 1946–48
Taylor, Butler, 1950

Warlick, Ernest, 1950–51
Crawley, William, 1951
Spener, Melvin, 1951
Floyd, Charles, 1952
Person, Joseph, 1953
Thornton, Amos, 1953–54
Harvey, Otto, 1954
Evans, Jerome, 1954
Montgomery, Al, 1956
Baker, John, 1956–57
Wallace, George, 1958
Brewington, James, 1958
Gatling, Issac, 1958
Jackson, Clifton, 1958
Hinton, Charles, 1961
Wilkins, Richard, 1961
Hayes, William, 1963
Currington, Robert, 1963
Jones, Edwin, 1966
Bell, Louis, 1966
Martin, Julian, 1967–69
Wilkerson, Doug, 1967–69
Paige, Lonnie, 1968
Gantt, Jerome, 1969
Matthews, Herman, 1969
Carson, Ollis, 1969
Singletary, Samuel, 1969
Quinn, Peter, 1969–70
Clayton, Larry, 1970
Holloway, Robert, 1970

All Mid-Eastern Athletic Conference

Football

Bonham, Bracey, 1971
Bellinger, Charles, 1971
Harrell, Joseph, 1971
Williams, Mahlon, 1971–72
Inmon, Jefferson, 1971–72
Caldwell, Jason, 1972
Armstrong, Gordon, 1972
Stone, Garvin, 1972
Williams, George, 1972
Williams, Owen, 1972
McNeil, Ronald, 1972
Barbee, John, 1972
Saxton, Thomas, 1972–73

Pettiford, Dwight, 1972–74
Gravett, Herman, 1972
Jones, Alexander, 1972–73*
Spencer, Maurice, 1972–73
Smith, James, 1974
Smith, Charles, 1974
Jones, Samuel, 1974
Breeden, Louis, 1975–76
Helton, Darius, 1976
Hines, Eric, 1976
Mack, Joseph, 1976–77
Smith, Reginald, 1977
Odom, Walter, 1978
Sanders, Carl, 1979
Birth, Rodney, 1979

All Central Intercollegiate Athletic Association

Football

Smith, Gary, 1980
Fraylon, Gerald, 1981
McKinstry, Chris, 1981
Bishop, John, 1981
Riddick, Andrew, 1981
Ingram, Lorenzo, 1981–82
Hunter, Victor, 1982
Washington, Sam, 1982
Tate, Benjamin, 1982
Pierce, Allen, 1982
Kersey, Clifton, 1983
Frizzell, William, 1983
Fraylon, Gerald, 1983–84
Clark, Robert, 1983–85
Patton, Gerald, 1984
Brown, Arnold, 1984
Harvey, Earl,[1] 1985–86

Basketball

Harrison, Charles, 1954
Jones, Samuel, 1954–57
Sligh, James, 1958
Bell, Carlton, 1959
Parker, Joseph, 1964
Manning, Theodore, 1965–66
Davis, Lee, 1967–68
Pridgen, Joseph, 1969
McCrimmon, Ronald, 1970
Leggett, Redden, 1971

All Mid-Eastern Athletic Conference

Basketball

Reddish, Allen, 1972
Little, Robert, 1975
Harrell, John, 1976
Monroe, Floyd, 1977
McClellan, Robert, 1977

North Carolina Central Alumni in the National Football League

Smith, Reginald, Atlanta Falcons, (WR), 1980–81
Gantt, Jerome, Buffalo Bills, (T), 1970
Romes, Charles, Buffalo Bills, (DB), 1977
Breeden, Louis, Cincinnati Bengals, (DB), 1978–85
Barnes, Ernest, New York Jets, (T), 1960;
    San Diego Chargers, (T), 1960–62;
    Denver Broncos, (T), 1963–64
Wilkerson, Doug, Houston Oilers, (T), 1970;
    San Diego Chargers, (T), 1971–81
Helton, Darius, Kansas City Chiefs, (G), 1977
Parker, John, Los Angeles Rams, (DT), 1958–61;
    Pittsburgh Steelers, (DT), 1963–67
Martin, Aaron, Los Angeles Rams, (DB), 1964–65;
    Philadelphia Eagles, (DB), 1966–67;
    Washington Redskins, (DB), 1968
Hinton, Charles, Pittsburgh Steelers, (DT), 1964–71;
    New York Jets, (DT), 1971
McAdams, Robert, New York Jets, (DT), (L), 1963–64
Brewington, Jim, New York Jets, (T), 1961
Sligh, Richard, Oakland Raiders, (T), 1967
Spencer, Maurice, St. Louis Cardinals, (DB), 1974
Tate, Franklin, San Diego Chargers, (L), 1975
Jones, Sam, Boston Celtics, 1957–69

[1] Harvey, Earl—1985 Central Intercollegiate Athletic Association Offensive Player of the Year

South Carolina State College
Orangeburg, South Carolina 29117

Athletic Directors

Football

Dawson, Oliver C., 1946
Simmons, Lawrence, 1951
Martin, John, 1953
Moore, Roy D., 1955–56
Parks, Jesse L., 1957–59
Dawson, Oliver C., 1966–67

Basketball

Dawson, Oliver C., 1955–63
Brown, William, 1964–66
Dawson, Oliver, 1967
Holmes, Roosevelt L., 1968–69
Hunter, Dr. Milton D., 1971–79
Ham, Dr. Willis C., 1980–86

Football

Simmons, Lawrence, 1946–51
Martin, John H., 1953–54
Moore, Roy D., 1955–59
Harris, William B., 1960–61
Bell, George, 1962–64
Banks, Oree, 1965–72
Jeffries, Willie, 1973–79
Davis, Bill, 1980–85
Thomas, Dennis, 1980–Present

Basketball

Martin, Edward A., 1955–67
Jobe, Ben, 1968–71
Autry, Tim, 1972–79
Jones, John, 1980–82
Caldwell, Percy Chico, 1983–Present

Women's Basketball

Simon, Willie J., 1974–85

All Southern Intercollegiate Athletic Conference

Football

Felton, Ed, 1952–54
Parker, Leon, 1953–54
Clinton, Taylor, 1953–55
Stanley, Charles, 1954
Weymer, David, 1954
Gardner, Alexander, 1956–58
Adams, Thomas, 1959
King, Ralph, 1961
Tucker, Wendell, 1961–62
Hoskins, Harry, 1963
Brown, James, 1963
Goodwin, Sam, 1963–64
Gilliam, John, 1964

Basketball

Wright, Ted, 1956, 1958–59

Morgan, William, 1961
Jackson, Ernest, 1961–62, 1964
Moody, Lindberg, 1961–62
Myles, Ron, 1962–64
Williams, Robert, 1964
Shields, Tyrone, 1965
Hillary, William, 1966
Lewis, Robert, 1966
Keye, Julius, 1966
Lewis, Robert, 1968

All Mid-Eastern Athletic Conference

Football

Wade, John, 1971
Bailey, Dennis, 1971
Evans, James, 1971
Taylor, Carlton, 1971–72
Chavious, Barney, 1972
Shell, Donnie, 1973
McCarthy, Darius, 1974
Smith, Razzae, 1974
Mason, Leroy, 1974
Carson, Harry,[1] 1974–75
Sims, Robert,[2] 1974–76
Dixon, Luther, 1975–76
Evans, Anthony, 1975–76
Edmonds, Erone, 1975–76
Burgess, Charles, 1976
Montgomery, Malcolm, 1976–77, 1979
Duncan, Leonard, 1976
Bryant, Rudolph, 1976
Moore, Bobby,[3] 1976–78
Anderson, Ricky,[4] 1977
Lester, Albert, 1977
Washington, M., 1977
Brown, Tommy, 1977
Sullivan, Walter, 1977–78
Prescott, Arthur, 1977–78
Rivers, Nate,[5] 1978
Reed, Jackie, 1978
Bess, Rufus, 1978
Robinson, Leroy, 1978–80
Bailey, Edwin, 1978–79
Parker, Erwin, 1978–79
Ragland, Chris, 1979
Turner, Terry, 1979
Murphy, Phillip,[6] 1979

Warren, Larry, 1979–80
King, Angelo, 1979–80
Odom, Henry, 1980
Brown, William, 1980
Judson, William, 1980
Burton, Ron, 1980
Alford, John,[7] 1980
Tutson, Tommy, 1980–81
Samuels, Edward, 1981
Colbert, Jeff, 1981
Reed, Anthony, 1981–82
Gardner, Alexander, 1981–82
Gatson, Desmond, 1981–82
Bussey, Barney,[8] 1981–83
Fulton, Sidney, 1981–82
Green, Ralph, 1982
Thomas, Zack, 1982
McCray, Harley, 1982
Anderson, Terrance, 1982
Courtney, John,[9] 1982
Jackson, Dwayne, 1982
Green, Ralph, 1983
Darling, Myles, 1983
Mattison, Dwayne, 1983
Roberts, Lonnie, 1983
Neal, Alan, 1983
Crutchfield, Johnson, 1983–84
Norman, David Lee, 1984
Nesmith, Larry, 1984
Braddy, Alonzo, 1984
Sykes, Bruce, 1984

Basketball

Thornton, John, 1972
Boswell, Thomas, 1972–73
Williams, Michael, 1974
Barron, Alex, 1974–75
Nickens, Harry, 1975–78
Green, Carl, 1976
Brown, Willie, 1977
Snipes, Arthur, 1978–79
Lane, Marty, 1980
Wilson, Gregory, 1980–81
Robinson, Joe, 1981–82
Haynes, Marvin, 1983
Giles, Franklin, 1983–84
Miller, Ralph, 1984
Parson, Sylvester, 1985
Williams, Dennis, 1985

All-American

Football

Caldwell, Tyrone, 1967
Evans, James, 1971
Chavous, Barney, 1972
Shell, Donnie, 1973
Carson, Harry, 1975
Sims, Robert, 1976
Anderson, Ricky, 1977
Murphy, Philip, 1979
Bailey, Edwin, 1980
Reed, Anthony, 1981–82
Jackson, Dwayne, 1981–82
Courtney, John, 1982
Green, Ralph, 1982–83

South Carolina State Alumni in the National Football League

Gilliam, John, St. Louis Cardinals, (WR), 1969–71;
    Minnesota Vikings, (WR), 1972–75;
    Atlanta Falcons, (WR), 1976;
    Chicago Bears, (WR), 1977
Bess, Rufus, Oakland Raiders, (DB), 1979;
    Buffalo Bills, (DB), 1980–81
Grate, Willie, Buffalo Bills, (TE), 1969–70
Parker, Ervin, Buffalo Bills, (L), 1980–83
Ross, Louis, Buffalo Bills, (DE), 1971–72;
    Kansas City Chiefs, (DE), 1975
Johnson, Jim, Cincinnati Bengals, (DB), 1968–69
Sims, Mickey, Cleveland Browns, (DT), 1977–79
Clinscale, Dexter, Dallas Cowboys, (S), 1980–85
King, Angelo, Dallas Cowboys, (L), 1981–85
Jones, David, Los Angeles Rams, (DE), 1961–71
    San Diego Chargers, (DE), 1972–73;
    Washington Redskins, (DE), 1974
Murphy, Phil, Los Angeles Rams, (DT), 1980–86
Gamble, R.C., New England Patriots, (RB), 1968–69
Carson, Harry, New York Giants, (L), 1976–85
Rivers, Nate, New York Giants, (RB), 1980
McClain, Clifford, New York Jets, (RB), 1970–73
Shell, Donnie, Pittsburgh Steelers, (S), 1974–85
Young, Al, Pittsburgh Steelers, (WR), 1971–72
Anderson, Rickey, San Diego Chargers, (RB), 1978
Jones, Ray, San Diego Chargers, (DB), 1972
Bailey, Edwin, Seattle Seahawks, (G), 1981–84

Thomas, Zach, Tampa Bay Buccaneers, (WR), 1984

Brown, Charles, Washington Redskins, (WR), 1982–84;
  Atlanta Falcons, (WR), 1985

Holman, Willie, Washington Redskins, (DE), 1971

[1] Carson, Harry–1974–75 Mid-Eastern Athletic Conference Defensive Player of the Year

[2] Sims, Robert–1976 Mid-Eastern Athletic Conference Defensive Player of the Year

[3] Moore, Bobby–1978 Mid-Eastern Athletic Conference Defensive Player of the Year

[4] Anderson, Ricky–1977 Mid-Eastern Athletic Conference Offensive Player of the Year

[5] Rivers, Nate–1978 Mid-Eastern Athletic Conference Offensive Player of the Year

[6] Murphy, Phillip–1979 Mid-Eastern Athletic Conference Defensive Player of the Year

[7] Alford, John—1980 Mid-Eastern Athletic Conference Defensive Player of the Year

[8] Bussey, Barney—1983 Mid-Eastern Athletic Conference Defensive Player of the Year

[9] Courtney, John—1982 Mid-Eastern Athletic Conference Defensive Player of the Year

Delaware State College
Dover, Delaware 19901

Athletic Directors

Jackson, Dr. Edward R., 1953–55

Mitchell, Preston, 1959–62

Williams, James, 1962–77

Wyner, Dr. W.R., 1977–79

Townsend, Nelson, 1979–Present

Coaches of Varsity Teams

Football

Conrad, Thomas, 1947–49

Johnson, Nathaniel, 1949

White, Robert, 1950

Jones, Willard S., 1951–52

Jackson, Edward R., 1953–55

George, Bennie J., 1956–58

Moore, Roy D., 1960–64

Washington, U.S., 1965

Moore, Roy, D., 1966

Jeter, Arnold, 1967–74

Wyche, Edmond,[1] 1975–78

Henderson, Charles, 1979–80

Collick, William, 1985–Present

Basketball

George, Bennie J., 1949–71

Mitchell, Ira, 1971–75

Emery, Marshall, 1976–79

Triplett, Ajac, 1979–83

Davidson, Joe Dean, 1983–85

Emery, Marshall, 1985–Present

Women's Basketball

George, Bennie, J., 1953–56

Franklin, Lucille, 1956–68

Wyche, Mary, 1968–69

McQuire, June, 1969–71

Johnson, Sal, 1971–76

Russell, Carrie, 1976–80

Jones, Byarie, 1980–81

Freeman, Marriana, 1981–83

McDowell, Stanley, 1983–85

Lamb, Mary, 1985–Present

Men's Track

Franklin, Frederick, 1953–67

Watson, Harrison B., 1967–70

Burden, Joseph, 1970–Present

Women's Track

Hackett, Marvin, 1973–80

Elliott, Scott, 1980–81

Tullis, Walter, 1981–82

Sowerby, Fred, 1983–Present

Baseball

George, Bennie, 1948–60

Blakely, Donald, 1960–68

Williams, James, 1969–84

Wrestling

Robinson, Jackie, 1978–81

Collick, William, 1981–84

Johnson, Randy, 1984–Present

Swimming

Moses, Harry, 1973–74

Cross Country

Burden, Joseph, 1980–81

Burke, Raymond, 1982–83

Sowerby, Fred, 1983–84

Athletic Trainers

Lang, Lawrence, 1974–78
Hunt, Roger, 1979–83
Knaar, John, 1983–Present

All Mid-Eastern Athletic Conference

Football

Howard, Luther, 1972
Dancy, Nate, 1974
Tullis, Walter, 1974–75
Crocker, David, 1975–77
Dixon, Andre, 1977
Brown, DeCosta, 1978
Wright, Gregory, 1978
Weathers, Clarence, 1980
Staples, Terry, 1982
Heflin, Victor, 1982
Dunn, Nigel, 1983
Lake, Eugene, 1983
Lane, Joseph, 1983
Taylor, John, 1984
Morgan, Everett, 1984
Burton, Joe, 1984

Basketball

Sheppard, Sam, 1972, 1974–75
Roundtree, James, 1973–75
Simmons, Fred, 1975
Rogers, James, 1976
Shealy, Charles, 1979–80
Maybin, Charles, 1979
Hill, William, 1979, 1980–82
Hunter, Robert, 1980
Gumbs, Jeff, 1981
Wallace, Edward, 1983
Sapp, Danny, 1983
Campbell, Bernard, 1984–85
Snowden, Dominic, 1984–85
Ball, Terrence, 1986

Women's Basketball

Leonard, Sabrina, 1984
Albury, Carlene, 1985–86

All-American (Black College)

Football

Lake, Eugene, 1983–84
Taylor, John, 1984
Lane, Joe, 1984

Men's Basketball

Campbell, Bernard, 1985

Women's Basketball

McCormick, Eve, 1978

Men's Track

Morris, Brad,[2] 1975
Tullis, Walter,[3] 1977
White, Gregory,[4] 1977
Howell, Emory,[5] 1977–79

Women's Track

Collins, Michelle, 1984
Dortch, Lorraine, 1984
Hunter, Sophia, 1984–85

[1] Wyche, Edmond–1977 Mid-Eastern Athletic Conference Coach of the Year
[2] Morris, Brad–NCAA All-American
[3] Tullis, Walter–NAIA All-American
[4] White, Gregory–NAIA All-American
[5] Howell, Emory–NAIA All-American

University of Maryland, Eastern Shore
Princess Anne, Maryland 21853

Athletic Directors

Thomas, Richard "Fess," 1946–48
McCain, Vernon "Skip," 1948–62
Gilliam, Roosevelt "Sandy," 1962–65
McCain, Vernon "Skip," 1965–68
Davis, Howard, 1968–71
Coursey, Dr. Leon, 1971–75
Townsend, Nelson, 1975–79
Lewis, Dr. Tyrone, 1980–81
Mack, Joel C., 1981–82
Coursey, Dr. Leon, 1982–84
Hall, Kirkland, 1984–Present

Coaches of Varsity Teams

Football

Coffey, J.C., 1946–48
McCain, Vernon "Skip," 1948–62
Gilliam Roosevelt "Sandy," 1962–66
Taylor, Robert, 1966–69
Smith, Willie, 1969–72
Gray, Harold "House," 1972–77
Redmon, Joe, 1977–78
Caldwell, Tyrone, 1978–79

Basketball

Kiah, Waldo, 1945
Waters, Slim, 1946–48
McCain, Vernon "Skip," 1948–54
Taylor, Robert, 1955–65
Davis, Howard, 1965–66
Robinson, Joe, 1966–71
Bates, John, 1971–74
Jones, Dan, 1974–77
Hall, Kirkland, 1977–84
Evans, Howie, 1984–86
Williams, Steve, 1986–Present

Track

McCain, Vernon "Skip," 1949–56
Watson, Pop, 1956–58
Ross, Wilbur, 1958–60
Anderson, Clifton "Cappy," 1960–79
Brown, Robert, 1979–80
Sowerby, Fred, 1980–83
Daley, Ian, 1983–Present

Baseball

Banks, Earl, 1955–59
Barnett, Thomas "Pete," 1960–64
Ballard, Arnold, 1964–66
Gilliam, Roosevelt "Sandy," 1966–70
Gray, Harold "House," 1970–75
Jackson, William "Red," 1975–77
Hall, Kirkland, 1977–80
Tate, Odell, 1980–82
Cassell, Allen, 1982–Present

Golf

Taylor, Robert, 1961–63

All Central Intercollegiate Athletic Association

Football

Plunckett, Sherman, 1954–56
Sample, John, 1954–57
Evans, Raleigh, 1956–57
Vaughn, Vernon, 1956–57
Brown, Roger, 1958
Gray, Harold, 1960
Hobbs, John, 1960
Taylor, Robert, 1960–61
Boozer, Emerson, 1962–64
Williams, Joseph, 1964
Shell, Art, 1966–67
Duncan, James, 1966–67
Belk, William, 1967
Kirksey, Roy, 1967
Thompson, William, 1967–68
Williams, Earvin, 1968
Denson, Moses, 1968
Cropper, Marshall, 1968
Baylor, Robert, 1969

Basketball

Williams, Sonny, 1956
Lloyd, Sonny, 1962
Santio, Al, 1962
Williams, Edward, 1963–65
Ford, Jake, 1968–70
Fontaine, Levi, 1969–70
Morgan, James, 1970–72
Bryant, Jackie, 1971–72

Track

Rogers, Russ,[1] 1961–63
Mays, Charles, 1961–63
Santio, Al, 1962
Cayenne, Benedict
Skinner, Ed, 1962
Gilbert, Elius, 1963
Jackson, Raymond, 1963
Jones, Cliff, 1963
Bush, Edward, 1963
Carmen, Jon, 1963
Rogers, Earl, 1963–65

All Mid-Eastern Athletic Conference

Football

Wilkins, Richard, 1971
Anderson, Greg, 1971
Boston, Charles, 1973
Woods, Harold, 1973
Shell, Kenneth, 1973
Hairston, Carl, 1973–74
Royale, Michael, 1974
Ennis, Reginald, 1979

Basketball

Bryant, Jackie, 1972
Collins, Rubin, 1973–74
Skinner, Talvin, 1973–74
Pace, Joe, 1974
Gordon, William, 1974
Simmons, Kenneth "Chick," 1977–79
Hay, Steve, 1980
Bonney, Donnell, 1984–85

Women's Basketball

Dallas, Cherryl, 1983
Felder, Monica,[2] 1984–85

Track

Daly, Ian, 1982
Thomas, Greg, 1982
Meekins, Rickey,[3] 1982–83
Bell, Robert,[4] 1982–83
Addison, David,[5] 1982–84
Harrigan, Annette, 1983–84
Anderson, Natalie,[6] 1983–85
Pierce, Kimberly, 1983–85
Tyer, Angela, 1983–85

All-American (Black College)

Football

Polk, Sylvester "Swifty," 1947–49

Basketball

Williams, Ed, 1965
Ford, Jake, 1970
Pace, Joe, 1974
Collins, Rubin,[7] 1974
Simmons, Ken, 1979

Other Outstanding Athletes

Football

Goodwin, Doug
Whye, Wayne
Gentry, Curtis

University of Maryland, Eastern Shore Alumni in the National Football League

Alston, Mack, Green Bay Packers, (TE), 1973–76;
    Baltimore Colts, (TE), 1977–80
Duncan, James, Baltimore Colts, (DB), 1969–71
Plunkett, Sherman, Baltimore Colts, (T), 1958–60;
    San Diego Chargers, (T), 1961–63;
    New York Jets, (T), 1964–67
Sample, John, Baltimore Colts, (DB), 1958–60;
    Washington Redskins, (DB), 1963–65;
    New York Jets, (DB), 1966–68
Stukes, Charles, Baltimore Colts, (DB), 1967–72;
    Los Angeles Rams, (DB), 1973–74
Belton, Willie, Atlanta Falcons, (RB), 1971–72
Goodwin, Doug, Buffalo Bills, (RB), 1966;
    Atlanta Falcons, (RB), 1968
Laster, Art, Buffalo Bills, (T), 1970
Gentry, Curtis, Chicago Bears, (DB), 1966–68
Thompson, William, Denver Broncos, (S), 1969–83
Brown, Roger, Detroit Lions, (DT), 1960–66;
    Los Angeles Rams, (DT), 1967–69
Taylor, Robert, New York Giants, (DE), 1963–64
Boozer, Emerson, New York Jets, (RB), 1966–75
Christy, Earl, New York Jets, (DB),(KR), 1966–68
Kirksey, Roy, New York Jets, (G), 1971–72;
    Philadelphia Eagles, (G), 1973–74
Irons, Gerald, Oakland Raiders, (L), 1970–75
Shell, Art, Oakland Raiders, (T), 1968–81;
    Los Angeles Rams, (T), 1982–86
Williams, Erwin, Pittsburgh Steelers, (WR), 1969
Bell, William, San Francisco 49ers, (DE), 1968–74
Deacon, Moses, Washington Redskins, (RB), 1974–75

[1] Rogers, Russ–member of the 1964 Olympic Track and Field Team
[2] Felder, Monica–Black College Female Freshman of the Year
[3] Meekins, Ricky–Cross Country Champion; 1500 Outdoor Champion
[4] Bell, Robert–Cross Country
[5] Addison, David–Cross Country
[6] Anderson, Natalie–Cross Country; Most Outstanding Female Performer at MEAC Outdoor Track Championship
[7] Collins, Rubin–NCAA Division II All-American; NAIA All-American; All NIT Team

Florida A&M University
Tallahassee, Florida 32207

Athletic Directors

Gaither, Alonzo "Jake"
Tookes, Hansel E.
Wilson, Roosevelt

Women's Athletic Directors

Bartley, Dr. Lua S.
Hill, Sarah

Coaches of Varsity Teams

Football

Gaither, Alonzo "Jake," 1946–69
Griffin, Robert "Pete," 1969–70
Montgomery, Theodore, 1970–71
Williams, Jim, 1971–74
Hubbard, Rudy, 1974–Present

Basketball

King, W. McKinley, 1930–33
Wright, Ted, 1933–37
Gaither, Alonzo "Jake," 1937–42
Nelson, Buck, 1942–50
Oglesby, Edward "Rock," 1950–73
Triplett, Ajax, 1973–79
Giles, James, 1979–83
Fields, Tony, 1983–84
Booker, Willie, 1984–Present

Baseball

Griffin, Peter, 1945–47
Moore, Oscar, 1947–59
Kittles, Costa "Pop," 1959–81
Gilliam, Melvin "Red," 1981–Present

Track and Field

Griffin, Peter, 1955–61
Hill, Richard, 1961–64
Gibson, Ken, 1964–66
Lang, Bobby, 1966–86

All Southern Intercollegiate Athletic Conference

Football

Varner, Alphonso, 1951
Woodard, Arthur, 1951
Saunders, Jasper, 1951
Moore, James, 1951
Kittles, Costa, 1951
Stephens, Bernard, 1951
Herout, Charles, 1951–52
Kenchion, William, 1951–52
Lee, Willie, 1951–53
Arnold, John, 1951–53
Irvin, Willie, 1952
Hepburn, Alkin, 1952
Moore, James, 1952
Gladden, Galvin, 1952–54
Marshall, Sam, 1953
Galimore, Willie, 1953, 1955–56
Barber, William, 1954
Boynton, Willie, 1954
Dean, Elvin, 1954
McCloung, William, 1954
Sullivan, Arnold, 1954
Anderson, Sam, 1955
Crowell, Carl, 1955–57
Frazier, Al, 1955–56
Morris, Riley, 1956
Lang, Robert, 1956
Hines, Charles, 1956–57
Wilder, Vernon, 1957
Gavin, Charles, 1957
Williams, James, 1957
Johnson, William, 1957
Wyche, William, 1957–58
Taylor, William, 1958
Hardee, Leroy, 1958
Latimer, David, 1958
Glover, John, 1958–59
Childs, Clarence, 1958–60
Clarrington, Willie, 1959
Sims, Willie, 1959
Miranda, Curtis, 1959–60
Miller, Jim, 1959–60
Carn, Bernie, 1960
Burns, Ralph, 1960

Paremore, Robert, 1960–62
Hayes, Robert, 1961–64
Denson, Al, 1961–63
Highsmith, Walter, 1961–64
Tullis, James, 1961–63
Wilson, William, 1961
Dixon, Hewritt, 1961–62
Rogers, Al, 1962
Brown, Robert, 1962
Robinson, Arthur, 1962–64
Perry, Cal, 1962
Miller, Fred, 1963
Daniels, David, 1963
Felts, Robert, 1963–64
Oates, Carlton, 1963–64
Sutton, Charles, 1963–64
Hart, Ernest, 1964
Williams, Archie, 1964

Basketball

Bostic, Charles, 1951
Pittman, Herman, 1951
Fears, Ernie, 1951
Washington, Earl, 1952
Hearns, Sam, 1952
Donald, Harold, 1953
Clayton, Mack, 1954
Beachum, Herb, 1954
Young, Roy, 1954–57
Cuyler, John, 1955
Stanley, James, 1955–60
Morgan, Leo, 1956–57
Gibson, Leroy, 1956–59
Collier, Leon, 1957–58
Forchion, James, 1960
Johnson, Melvin, 1960
Bellamy, Wate, 1960–62
Barnes, William, 1962
Kennedy, Walter, 1962
Allen, Ted, 1964
Collier, Willie, 1964–65
Walls, James, 1967
Jackson, Dennis, 1967
Lawson, Alfred, 1967–68

All Mid-Eastern Conference

Football

Ramsey, Gifford, 1980

Newton, Nathaniel, 1980
Coleman, Vincent, 1980–81
Wellons, Arthur, 1981
Alexander, Ray, 1981–83
Eason, R.C., 1981–83
Dawson, Rod, 1982
Hutchinson, Dorsey, 1982
Bronson, Sam, 1983

Basketball

Taylor, Walter, 1981
Spence, Darrell, 1981–82
Toomer, Michael, 1982–84
Broner, Larry, 1983

All-American (Black College)

Football

Powell, Nathaniel, 1947
Gary, Wilber, 1947
Montgomery, Theo, 1946
Mitchell, Bradley, 1947–48
Williams, Jim, 1948
Curtis, Ulysses, 1948
Kitles, Costa, 1950
Varner, Alphonso, 1951
Kenchon, William, 1951
Hepburn, Akin, 1952
Moore, James, 1952
Marshall, Samuel, 1953
Galimore, Willie, 1954–56
Gladden, Calvin, 1955
Frazier, Adolphus, 1955–56
Crowell, Carl, 1956–57
Wilder, Vernon, 1957
Whyche, Willie, 1958
Miranda, Curtis, 1959–61
Childs, Clarence, 1959–60
Paremore, Robert, 1961–62
Tullis, James, 1963
Denson, Alfred, 1963
Williams, Archie, 1964
Robinson, Arthur, 1964
Daniels, David, 1965
Hardee, Leroy, 1967
Eason, John, 1967
Lovett, Horace, 1969
McCaskill, Jimmy, 1969
Ginn, Hubert, 1969

Lawrence, Henry, 1972–73
Williams, Felix, 1974
Rackley, James, 1974
Poole, Frankie, 1974–75
Young, Charles, 1975
Burgess, Calvin, 1976
Grady, Jeffrey, 1977
Williams, Ike, 1977–78
McGriff, Tyrone, 1977–79
Lewis, Kiser, 1978–79
Oliver, Harrell, 1978–79
Ramsey, Gifford, 1980
Eason, R.C., 1982
Alexander, Ray, 1983

Florida A&M University's Hall of Fame

Thomas, Maxwell
Coleman, Abbie Carr
Jones, Thomas
Maloney, Charles
Lee, Willie
Tookes, Hansel E.
Wooten, Lonnie
Watts, Leon
Gentry, Howard
Gaither, A.S. "Jake"
Foote, Dr. L.H.E.
DaValt, Clarence
Bragg, J.B.
Beasley, Sylvester
Bostic, Charles
James, Alonzo "Babe"
Harris, John D.
Lawrence, Henry
Kirksey, Leander B.
Kidd, Arthur Leo
Moore, Dr. Oscar A.
Mitchell, Bradley
Perry, Dr. Benjamin L.
Poole, Thomas
Williams, Macon
Strachan, Stanley
Powell, Nathaniel
Rolle, Frankie S.
Small, James P.
Varner, Alphonso
Everett, James
Dawson, Andre

Calhoun, Soloman
Clark, Edward
Gibson, Leroy "Spike"
Gregory, Beulah
Griffin, Robert P.
Glover, John D.
Galimore, Willie
Gary, Wilbur
Denson, Alfred
Dixon, Hewritt
Childs, Clarence
Butler, Henry
Bell, William
Bragg, Eugene
Mayes, Jesse
McRae, Hal
Miranda, Curtis
Neely, Murray L.
Oglesby, Edward
Meek, Dr. Carrie P.
Paremore, Robert C.
Gibson, Althea
Pittman, Herman
Lee, J.R.E., Jr.
Curtis, Ulysses
Fears, Ernest D., Jr.
Hayes, Robert "Bob"
Jones, Reuben
Frazier, Adolphus
Lucas, William

Florida A&M Alumni in the National Football League

Felts, Robert, Baltimore Colts, (RB), 1965;
    Detroit Lions, (RB), 1965–67
Ginn, Hubert, Miami Dolphins, (RB), 1970–72, 1974–75;
    Baltimore Colts, (RB), 1973
    Oakland Raiders, (RB), 1976–78
Childs, Clarence, New York Giants, (DB), 1964–67;
    Chicago Bears, (DB), 1968
Galimore, Willie, Chicago Bears, (RB), 1957–63
Hazelton, Major, Chicago Bears, (DB), 1968–69
Lee, Herman, Chicago Bears, (T), 1958–66
Rogers, Mel, San Diego Chargers, (L), 1971–74;
    Los Angeles Rams, (L), 1976;
    Chicago Bears, (L), 1977
Riley, Ken, Cincinnati Bengals, (DB), 1969–83
Watts, Andre, Denver Broncos, (TE), 1967;
    Cincinnati Bengals, (TE), 1968;

San Diego Chargers, (TE), 1968

Coleman, Greg, Cleveland Browns, (P), 1977;
Minnesota Vikings, (P), 1978–85

McClung, Willie, Pittsburgh Steelers, (T), 1955–57;
Cleveland Browns, (T), 1958–59;
Detroit Lions, (T), 1960–61

Hayes, Robert, Dallas Cowboys, (WR), 1965–74;
San Francisco 49ers, (WR), 1975

Denson, Al, Denver Broncos, (WR), 1964–70;
Minnesota Vikings, (WR), 1971

Dixon, Hewritt, Denver Broncos, (RB), 1963–65;
Oakland Raiders, (RB), 1966–70

Frazier, Al, Denver Broncos, (RB), 1961–63

Highsmith, Walter, Denver Broncos, (C), 1968–69;
Houston Oilers, (C), 1972

Smith, Don, Denver Broncos, (G), 1967

Oats, Carlton, Oakland Raiders, (DT), 1965–72;
Green Bay Packers, (DT), 1973

James, Nathaniel, Cleveland Browns, (DB), 1968

Thomas, Eugene, Kansas City Chiefs, (RB), 1966–67

Holmes, John, Miami Dolphins, (DE), 1966

Woodson, Fred, Miami Dolphins, (G), 1967–69

Goodrum, Charles, Minnesota Vikings, 1972–78

Johnson, Preston, New England Patriots, (RB), 1971

Sykes, Alfred, New England Patriots, (WR), 1971

Hill, Ralph, New York Giants, (C), 1976–77

Finnie, Roger, New York Jets, (T), 1969–72;
St. Louis Cardinals, (DT), 1973–78

Daniels, David, Oakland Raiders, (DT), 1966

Eason, John, Oakland Raiders, (TE), 1978

Hawkins, Clarence, Oakland Raiders, (RB), 1979

Lawrence, Henry, Oakland/Los Angeles Raiders, (T), 1974–84

Morris, Riley, Oakland Raiders, (DE), 1960–62

White, Eugene, Oakland Raiders, (RB), 1962

Edwards, Glen, Pittsburgh Steelers, (DB), 1971–77;
San Diego Chargers, (DB), 1978–82

McGriff, Tyrone, Pittsburgh Steelers, (G), 1980–82

Paremore, Robert, St. Louis Cardinals, (RB), 1963–64

Kelly, John, Washington Redskins, (T), 1966–67

Middleton, Frank, Indianapolis Colts, (RB), 1984

Florida A&M Alumni in the National Basketball Association

Johnson, Clemon, Portland Trailblazers, (F), 1978–79;
Indiana Pacers, (F), 1979–82;
Philadelphia 76ers, (F), 1982–85;
Seattle Supersonics, 1986–Present

North Carolina
Agricultural and Technical State University
Greensboro, North Carolina 27411

Athletic Directors

Bell, Dr. William B.

Smith, Albert

Irvin, Cal

McKinley, Jim

Piggott, Dr. Bert

Moss, Orby

Coaches of Varsity Teams

Football

Bell, William, 1946–56

Piggott, Dr. Bert, 1957–67

Howell, Hornsby, 1968–76

McKinley, Jim, 1977–81

Forte, Mo, 1982–Present

Basketball

Irvin, Cal, 1954–72

Reynolds, Warren, 1972–77

Littles, Eugene, 1977–79

Corbett, Don,[1] 1979–Present

Baseball

Harris, Felix, 1949–55

Groomes, Mel, 1956–Present

All Central Intercollegiate Athletic Association

Football

Williams, Joseph, 1947

Jackson, Robert, 1947

Thompson, Sherwood, 1950

Jackson, Boyd, 1950

Boyers, William, 1950

Jackson, William, 1950–51

Funderburke, George, 1951

Farrar, Al, 1951

Washington, Leroy, 1951

Statum, Art, 1951–52

Hunter, Walter, 1951–52

Gibson, Jack, 1952

Smith, J.D., 1955

Oakley, Lloyd, 1958

Stanford, Lorenzo, 1960
Black, James, 1960
Ferguson, William, 1961
Gaines, Alexander, 1963
Gordon, Cornell, 1963
Francis, Ron, 1964
Bethea, Elvin, 1966–67
Pearson, Willie, 1967–68
Code, Merle, 1968–69
Holmes, Melvin, 1970
Westmoreland, Doug, 1970
Wright, Willie, 1970–71

All Mid-Eastern Athletic Conference

Football

Leonard, Lonnie, 1971
Middleton, Charles, 1971
Blacknall, Ben, 1971
Coleman, Ralph, 1971
Wideman, William, 1971–72
Hairston, John, 1972
Hicks, Osceola, 1972
Ross, Melvin, 1973
Collins, Carl, 1973
Holland, Al, 1973
Hampton, John, 1974
Bennett, Walter, 1974–75
Feaster, Dexter, 1974–76
Ragsdale, George, 1975
Turner, Ellsworth, 1975–77
Nibbs, Lucien, 1976
Holland, Jerald, 1976
Pride, Clayton, 1977
Holland, Glen, 1977
Warren, Thomas, 1977
Board, Dwaine, 1977–78
Brown, Wheeler, 1978
Jones, Nolan, 1978
Harris, Lon, 1978
Corrie, Tony, 1978
West, Michael, 1979
Johnson, Gerald, 1979
Westbrook, Eric, 1979
Britt, Clifton, 1980
Pitts, Wayman, 1980
Majors, Norton, 1980
Chesson, Frankie, 1980

Joyner, Michael, 1981
Robinson, Kevin, 1981
Jones, Michael, 1983
Harrison, Herbert, 1984
Williams, Tim, 1984
Riddick, Ernest, 1984–85
Hooker, Alan, 1985–86

Basketball

Austin, Elmer,[2] 1972
Harris, William, 1972–73
Outlaw, James, 1972, 1974
Spruill, Allen, 1975
Johnson, Ron, 1976
Sparrow, James,[3] 1976, 1978–79
Brawner, Joseph,[4] 1979–80
Anderson, James, 1981
Binion, Joe,[5] 1982–84
Brown, Jr., James, 1984–85
Boyd, Eric, 1984–85
Williams, Claude, 1986–87
Cale, George, 1986–87

All-American (Black College)

Football

Williams, Joseph, 1948
Boyers, William, 1950
Jackson, William, 1951
Hunter, Walter, 1951
Statum, Arthur, 1953
Phillips, Mel, 1959
Bethea, Elvin, 1966–67
Pearson, Willie, 1968
Code, Merle, 1969
Holmes, Mel, 1970
Coleman, Ralph, 1970
Wright, Willie, 1970
Blacknall, Ben, 1971
Leonard, Lonnie, 1971
Wideman, William, 1972
Holland, Al, 1974
Ragsdale, George, 1975
Turner, Ellsworth, 1975–76
Board, Dwaine, 1977–78
Jones, Michael, 1984

Basketball

Cotton, Joseph, 1958
Attles, Al, 1960
Harris, William, 1972–73
Sparrow, James, 1976
Binion, Joseph, 1983–84
Boyd, Eric, 1985
Brown, Jr., James, 1985

North Carolina Agricultural and Technical State University's Hall of Fame

Lane, James
DeBerry, Charles
Clark, Earl
Bruce, Sam
Neely, James
Smith, J.D.
Attles, Al
Raiford, C.L.
Alston, Thomas
Hamilton, Walter
Maye, Sr., John
Statum, Arthur
Jackson, Robert Stonewall
Thompson, Sherwood
Meadows, Helburn
Williams, Joseph
Gould, William
Earley, James
Armstrong, Nell J.
Kornegay, Robert
Douglass, Emanuel
Jewell, Harold
Bell, William
Hunter, Walter
Jackson, William
Martin, Julius
Conway, Thomas
Piggott, Bert C.
Martin, Ed
Wright, Roy
Blakely, William
Foster, Joseph O.
Wooden, Ralph
Gearring, Roy
Simmons, Hubert
Gibson, Jack

Bethea, Elvin
Day, Thomas
Phillips, Mel
Dillard, John
Cotton, Joseph
Griffin, C.C.
Lynch, Allen
Green, Harold
Code, Merl
Westmoreland, Richard
Harper, Estelle
Howell, Hornsby
Irvin, Cal
Graeber, Marvin
Canada, Ernest
Grier, Joseph
Shute, Matthew
Howell, C.O.
Gordon, Cornell
Evans, James
Grandy, Walter
Buggs, Ernest
Bradley, Chester
Wingate, Matthew
Rouse, Jr., Howard
Coefield, Aloon
Green, George
Hodges, Jr. Samuel
Jackson, Jesse
Knox, George
Watkins, Robert L.

North Carolina A&T Alumni in the National Football League

Smith, J.D., Chicago Bears, (RB), 1956;
    Dallas Cowboys, (RB), 1965–66
Taylor, Joe, Chicago Bears, (DB), 1967–74
Gordon, Cornell, New York Jets, (DB), 1965–69;
    Denver Broncos, (DB), 1970–72
Coleman, Ralph, Dallas Cowboys, (L), 1972
Bethea, Elvin, Houston Oilers, (DE), 1968–85
Pearson, Willie, Miami Dolphins, (DE), 1969
Westmoreland, Richard, San Diego Chargers, (DB), 1963–65;
    Miami Dolphins, (DB), 1966–69
Jackson, Robert, New York Giants, (RB), 1950–51
Small, George, New York Giants, (DT), 1980
Holmes, Mel, Pittsburgh Steelers, (T), 1971–73

Day, Thomas, St. Louis Cardinals, (G), 1960;
   San Diego Chargers, (G), 1967
Board, Dwaine, San Francisco 49ers, (DE), 1979–85

North Carolina A&T Alumni in the National Basketball Association

Attles, Alvin, San Francisco Warriors, (G), 1960–71

[1] Corbett, Don–1981–82; 1984–85 Mid-Eastern Athletic Conference Coach of the Year
[2] Austin, Elmer–1972 Mid-Eastern Conference Player of the Year
[3] Sparrow, James–1976 Mid-Eastern Athletic Conference Player of the Year
[4] Brawner, Joseph–1979 Mid-Eastern Athletic Conference Player of the Year
[5] Binion, Joe–1982–83 Mid-Eastern Athletic Conference Player of the Year

Howard University
Washington, D.C. 20059

Coaches of Varsity Teams

Football

Jackson, Edward, 1946–53
Johnson, Thomas, 1953–57
White, Robert, 1957–62
Sease, Tillman, 1962–69
Organ, John, 1969–70
Sease, Tillman, 1970–73
Wyche, Ed, 1973–74
Porter, Douglas, 1974–79
Keith, Floyd, 1979–83
Taylor, Joe, 1983–84
Jeffries, Willie, 1984–Present

Men's Basketball

Burr, Jr., John H., 1946–49
Jackson, Edward, 1949–51
Hart, Tom, 1951–58
Emery, Marshall, 1971–75
Williamson, A.B., 1975–Present

Tennis

Tyrance, Herman J., 1945–46
Jackson, M., 1948–49
Tyrance, Herman J., 1958–65
Simms, George, 1971–75
Johnson, Dr. Robert, 1976–83
Davis, Ed, 1984
Strickland, Larry, 1985

Track

Chambers, Ted, 1945–49
Moultrie, William, 1973–Present

Swimming

Johnson, Thomas, 1947–58
Pendeleton, Jr., Clarence M., 1970

Baseball

Hinton, Chuck, 1973–Present

All Central Intercollegiate Athletic Association

Football

Jordan, Otis, 1947
Marshall, Melvin, 1947
Carter, John, 1951
Neverson, Ed, 1951–52
Carroll, Bwano, 1952
Washington, Ken, 1957
Mabry, Ronald, 1970

Basketball

Harris, Thomas, 1956
Syphax, John, 1956–58
Hancock, Larry, 1961

All Central Intercollegiate Athletic Association Tournament Team

Basketball

Jett, George, 1948
Harris, Thomas, 1956
Taylor, Edward, 1966–67
Shingler, Aaron, 1967
Williams, Frank, 1967

All Mid-Eastern Athletic Conference

Football

Mabry, Ronald, 1971–72
Ridley, Frank, 1972
Richardson, Ed,[1] 1973
McGhee, Richard, 1973
Bethea, Clifton, 1973
Fuller, Norvell, 1973
Gamble, Julius, 1973–74
Banks, Michael[2], 1974
Napier, Keith, 1974, 1977

Harris, Benjamin, 1974, 1975
Tapp, Anthony, 1975
Rooney, General, 1975
Ambrose, Dan, 1975, 1977
Breakfield, James, 1976
Cunningham, Kevin, 1976
Wilson, Steven, 1978
Scott, Gregory, 1979
Fowler, Fitz, 1979
Facyson, Scott, 1979
Ward, Howard, 1980
Wilson, Ronald,[3] 1980
Bilberry, John, 1980
Singletary, Tracy,[4] 1980–82
Sellers, Robert, 1982
Nicholaison, John, 1983
Brown, Martin, 1983–84
Reed, Harvey, 1987

Basketball

Lewis, Robert, 1973
Hollins, Warren, 1973
Young, Arnold, 1973
Carroll, Achilles, 1974
Cotton, Vadnay, 1975–76
Glover, Gerald,[5] 1977–78
Dent, Dorian, 1978–79
Ratiff, James,[6] 1980–82
Spriggs, Larry,[7] 1980–81
Wright, Rodney, 1980, 1982
Perry, Bernard, 1983
Scott, Kevin, 1984
Wynn, David, 1984
Hill, Fred, 1985–86
McIlwaine, Robert, 1985–86

All-American (Black College)

Football

Harris, Benjamin, 1975
Reed, Harvery,[8] 1987

Basketball

Glover, Gerald, 1978
Ratiff, James, 1980
Spriggs, Larry, 1981

Men's Track

Corley, Hayward, MR, 1975
White, Gosnell, MR, 1975–77
Sojourner, Reginald, MR, 1,600MR, 1975, 1977–78
Massey, Richard, MR, 400M, 1,600MR, 1975–78
Jones, Zachary, MR, 1,600MR, 1977–78
Archie, Michael, MR, 1,600MR, 1977–78
Bridges, Olivser, MR, 400M, 1,600MR, 1981–83
Charleton, David, MR, 1,600MR, 1981–83
Oliver, Bernard, MR, 1981–82
Sims, Ed, MR, 1981–82
Wilson, Kenneth, 1,600MR, 1983
Louis, Richard, 1,600MR, 500M, 1983, 1985
Skerritt, Anton, 500M, 1985

Women's Track

Wilson, Dorothy, 1,600MR, 1982
Brooks, Kimberly, 1,600MR, 1982
Murphy, Debra, 1,600MR, 1982
Charles, Ruberta, 1,600MR, 1982, 1984
Pough, Michele, 1,600MR, 1984
Brooks, Kathy, 1,600MR, 1984
Allen, Teresa, LJ, 1985

Other Outstanding Athletes

Football

Jenkins, John
Redden, Herman
Thomas, Brian
Clarke, Thomas
Robinson, Theodore

Basketball

Council, Angelo
Hamilton, George
Wilson, Louis
Speight, Nate
Gaskins, Gerald

Baseball

Harris, Glen
Davis, Jerry

Howard University's Alumni in the National Football League

Williams, Howard, Green Bay Packers, (DB), 1962–63;
   San Francisco 49ers, (DB), 1963;
   Oakland Raiders, (DB), 1964–69
Mabra, Ron, Houston Oilers, (DB), 1973;
   Atlanta Falcons, (DB), 1975–76;
   New York Jets, (DB), 1977
Wilson, Steve, Dallas Cowboys, (DB), 1979–81;
   Denver Broncos, (DB), 1981–Present

Howard University's Alumni in the National Basketball Association

Spriggs, Larry, Houston Rockets, (F), 1982;
   Chicago Bulls, (F), 1982–83;
   Los Angeles Lakers, (F), 1983–86

[1] Richardson, Ed–1973 Mid-Eastern Athletic Conference Offensive Player of the Year
[2] Banks, Michael–1974 Mid-Eastern Athletic Conference Offensive Player of the Year
[3] Wilson, Ronald–1980 Mid-Eastern Athletic Conference Offensive Player of the Year
[4] Singletary, Tracy–1981–82 Mid-Eastern Athletic Conference Offensive Player of the Year
[5] Glover, Gerald–1978 Mid-Eastern Athletic Conference Player of the Year
[6] Ratiff, James–1980 Mid-Eastern Athletic Conference Player of the Year
[7] Spriggs, Larry–1981 Mid-Eastern Athletic Conference Player of the Year; 1979–81 Most Valuable Player at the Mid-Eastern Athletic Conference Tournament
[8] Reed, Harvey–Honorable Mention

Coppin State College
Baltimore, Maryland 21216

Athletic Directors

Byron, Dr. Cyril O.,[1] 1958–65
Jones, Joseph A., 1965–70
Harnett, Charles, 1970–74
Jones, Joseph A., 1974–79

Coaches of Varsity Teams

Basketball

Byron, Dr. Cyril O., 1958–65
Jones, Joseph A.,[2] 1965–69
Hardnett, Charles, 1969–74
Bates, John, 1974–Present

Baseball

Jones, Joseph A., 1968–69
Harnett, Charles, 1969–74
Linsey, James, 1974–79
Davis, Tommy, 1979–83
Smith, Reggie, 1983–Present

Men's and Women's Volleyball

Smith, Lewis, 1974–82

Men's and Women's Cross Country

Meyers, Dr. John, 1967–69
Jackson, Fletcher, 1969–74
Smith, Lewis, 1974–78
Merritt, Michael, 1983–84
Brown, Larry, 1984–Present

Tennis

Norton, Gregory, 1976–79

Women's Basketball

Alexander, Celestine, 1974–75
Bishop, Barbara, 1975–76
Koger, Anne, 1976–78
Travis, Ruth, 1978–80

All Mid-Eastern Intercollegiate Conference

Basketball

Edwards, Sidney, 1962
Briscoe, Thomas, 1963
Hayman, Warren, 1963
Bennett, James, 1964

All Potomac Intercollegiate Conference

Basketball

Martin, Hayzon, 1966
Green, Walter, 1966–68
Parker, Clyde, 1967
McNeil, Clayton, 1967
Hall, Larry, 1967
Carter, Colbert, 1968
Carter, Anthony, 1976–77
Heard, Warren, 1977

Baseball

Linsey, James, 1967
Logan, Marvin, 1967

Johnson, Randy, 1967
Hall, Larry, 1968

NAIA All-American

Basketball

Hayman, Warren, 1963
Briscoe, Thomas, 1963
Parker, Clyde, 1967
Hall, Larry, 1967
Green, Walter, 1967–68
Carter, Colbert, 1968
Pace, Joe, 1976–77
Heard, Warren, 1977
Carter, Anthony, 1977

Baseball

Linsey, James, 1967
Johnson, Randy, 1967

Coppin State College's Hall of Fame

Byron, Dr. Cyril O.[1]
Jones, Dr. Joseph A.[2]

Bates, John[3]
Edwards, Sidney
Briscoe, Thomas
Hayman, Warren
Bennett, James
Green, Walter
McNeill, Clayton
Hall, Larry
Carter, Colbert
Pace, Joe
Heard, Warren
Carter, Anthony
Johnson, Randy
Hall, Larry
Linsey, James

Coppin State Alumni in the National Basketball Association

Pace, Joe, Washington Bullets (C), 1976–78

[1] Byron, Dr. Cyril O.–first Athletic Director at Coppin State College
[2] Jones, Dr. Joseph A.–coached the first Coppin team that won an intercollegiate championship
[3] Bates, John–won the NAIA National Basketball Championship in 1976

SOUTHWESTERN ATHLETIC CONFERENCE

1. Alcorn State University
2. Grambling State University
3. Prairie View A&M University
4. Southern University

5. Jackson State University
6. Texas Southern University
7. Mississippi Valley State University

Alcorn State University
Lorman, Mississippi 39096

Athletic Directors

Casem, Marino H., 1964–85
Danzy, Sr., Theophilus, 1986

Coaches of Varsity Teams

Football

Casem, Marion H., 1963–85
Danzy, Sr., Theophilus, 1986–Present

Basketball

Whitney, Sr., David, 1968–Present

Women's Basketball

Walker, Shirley, 1978–Present

All Southwestern Athletic Conference

Football

Reed, Smith, 1963
Shivers, Samuel, 1964
Williams, J.C., 1966
Banks, Willie, 1967
Sowell, Rich, 1968
Carter, Fred, 1968
Ashford, Haywood, 1968–69
Young, Willie, 1968–69
Hadley, David, 1968–69

Jenkins, Rayford, 1968–69
Friday, James, 1970
Johnson, Cleo, 1970
Alexander, Willie, 1970
Gooden, Harry, 1970–71
Penchion, Robert, 1971
White, Louis, 1971
Thomas, Dennis, 1971, 1973
Price, Alexander, 1971–72
Pillars, Lawrence, 1972, 1974–75
Davis, Jimmy, 1973
Howard, Billy, 1973
Cameron, Larry, 1973
Brady, Barry, 1973–74
Wooley, William, 1973–74
Lee, Augusta, 1974, 1976
Pilate, Frank, 1974, 1976
Young, Ernest, 1974, 1976
Martin, Cecil, 1975
Holloway, Christopher, 1976
Cain, Percy, 1976
Sparks, Frederick, 1976
Warren, Larry, 1976
Thomas, John, 1976–77
Willis, Larry, 1978
Carson, James, 1978
Jackson, Will Arthur, 1978–79
Williams, Lee, 1979
Frazier, Leslie, 1979
Young, Roynell, 1979
Jones, Gregory, 1980
Rosales, Wilfredo, 1980
Joy, Darnell, 1982
Green, George, 1982
Knox, Tony, 1985
Reese, Michael, 1985
Barney, Milton, 1986
Mark, Milton, 1986

All Southwestern Athletic Conference

Basketball

Ned, Walter, 1966
Kelly, James, 1967–68
Norwood, Willie, 1967–69
Flowers, Robert, 1968
Keye, Julius, 1969
Wyatt, Levi, 1970, 1972

Sing, Sam, 1970
Bateman, Glen, 1971
Tatum, Andrew, 1973
Milton, Alfred, 1975
Robinson, Dellie, 1975–76
Monroe, Alfredo, 1977
Horton, James, 1978–79
Davis, Collie, 1979
Smith, Larry, 1979–80
Baker, Eddie, 1980
Wyatt, Clinton, 1980
Bell, E.J., 1980
Alexander, Dwight, 1981
Archie, Eddie, 1981
Irving, Albert, 1981–82
Collier, Thomas, 1983–84
Phelphs, Michael, 1983–84
Brandon, Aaron, 1985
Whitney, Jr., David, 1986
Palmer, David, 1986

Women's Basketball

Hooker, Teresa, 1986–87

All-American (Black College)

Football

Hadley, David, 1969
Carter, Fred, 1970
Gooden, Harry, 1971
Price, Alex, 1972
Fairley, Leonard, 1973
Dismuke, Jerry, 1974
Pillars, Lawrence, 1975
Lee, Augusta, 1976
Warren, Larry, 1976
Frazier, Leslie, 1979
Holt, Issac, 1984

Basketball

McGill, John, 1976

Alcorn State Alumni in the National Football League

Garror, Leon, Buffalo Bills, (S), 1972–73
Penchion, Robert, Buffalo Bills, (T), 1972–73;
   San Francisco 49ers, (T), 1974–75;
   Seattle Seahawks, (T), 1976

Washington, David, Denver Broncos, (L), 1971–72;
  Buffalo Bills, (L), 1972–74;
  San Francisco 49ers, (L), 1975–76;
  Detroit Lions, (L), 1978–79;
  New Orleans Saints, (L), 1980
Watkins, Larry, Detroit Lions, (RB), 1969;
  Buffalo Bills, (RB), 1973–74;
  New York Giants, (RB), 1975–77
Young, Willie, Buffalo Bills, (T), 1971;
  Miami Dolphins, (T), 1973
Frazier, Leslie, Chicago Bears, (DB), 1981
Bradley, Henry, Cleveland Browns, (DT), 1979–81
Brown, Boyd, Denver Broncos, (TE), 1974–76;
  New York Giants, (TE), 1977
Howard, William, Detroit Lions, (DT), 1974–76
McGee, Willie, San Diego Chargers, (WR), 1973;
  Los Angeles Rams, (WR), 1974–75;
  San Francisco 49ers, (WR), 1976;
  Detroit Lions, (WR), 1978
Purnell, Frank, Green Bay Packers, (RB), 1957
Springs, Jack, Pittsburgh Steelers, (G), 1952;
  Green Bay Packers, (G), 1955–56;
  New York Giants, (G), 1957
Alexander, Willie, Houston Oilers, (DB), 1974
Fairley, Leonard, Houston Oilers, (S), 1974
Giles, Jimmie, Houston Oilers, (TE), 1977;
  Tampa Bay Buccaneers, (TE), 1978–85
Owens, Joe, San Diego Chargers, (DE), 1970;
  New Orleans Saints, (DE), 1971–75;
  Houston Oilers, (DE), 1976
Rice, Floyd, Houston Oilers, (L), 1971–73;
  Oakland Raiders, (L), 1976–77;
  New Orleans Saints, (L), 1978
Sowell, Rich, New York Jets, (DB), 1971–76;
  Houston Oilers, (DB), 1977
Estes, Lawrence, Philadelphia Eagles, (DE), 1972;
  Kansas City Chiefs, (DE), 1975–76
Hadley, David, Kansas City Chiefs, (DB), 1970–72
Brown, Robert, St. Louis Cardinals, (TE), 1969–70;
  Minnesota Vikings, (TE), 1971;
  New Orleans Saints, (TE), 1972–73
Banks, Willie, Washington Redskins, (G), 1968–69;
  New York Giants, (G), 1970;
  New England Patriots, (G), 1973
Price, Elex, New Orleans Saints, (DT), 1973–80
Reed, Smith, New York Giants, (RB), 1965–66
Pillars, Lawrence, New York Jets, (DE), 1976–80;
  San Francisco 49ers, (DE), 1980–84
Wonsley, Otis, Washington Redskins, (RB), 1981–85

Alcorn State Alumni in the National Basketball Association

Smith, Larry, Golden State Warriors, (F), 1980–87

Grambling State University
Grambling, Louisiana 71245

Coaches of Varsity Teams

Football

Robinson, Ed,[1] 1946–Present

Basketball

Hobdy, Frederick, 1956–86
Hopkins, Robert, 1986–Present

Baseball

Jones, Ralph Waldo Emerson, 1946–77
Ellis, Wilbert, 1977–Present

All Southwestern Athletic Conference

Football

Caleb, Jamie, 1958
Richardson, Al, 1959
Powell, Preston, 1959–60
Taylor, Roosevelt, 1959–60
Ladd, Ernest, 1960
Robinson, Jerry, 1960–61
Simmons, Leon, 1960–61
Buchanon, Buck, 1960–62
Wilson, Nehimah, 1961
Boyette, Garland, 1961
Brown, Willie, 1961–62
Howell, Michael, 1961–62
Pryor, Wilbert, 1961–63
Howell, Lane, 1962
Garrett, J.D., 1962
Collins, Fred, 1963
Cullors, Arlen, 1963
Williams, Willie, 1963
Griffin, Jim, 1963
Dotson, Alphonso, 1964
Dyer, Henry, 1964–65
Cornish, Frank, 1964–65
Todd, James, 1964–66
Harris, James, 1965, 1968

Young, Willie, 1965
Davis, Norman, 1966–67
Atkins, Robert, 1966–67
Powell, Clarence, 1966–67
Joiner, Charles, 1967–68
Gasper, Cliff, 1967
Jones, Henry, 1968
Manning, Williams, 1968
Williams, Terry, 1968
Williams, Roger, 1968
Alexander, Glenn, 1968–69
Newsome, Billy, 1969
O'Neal, William, 1969
Breux, Walter, 1969
Lewis, Frank, 1969–70
Roundtree, Charles, 1969–70
McSwann, Artie, 1969–70
Armstrong, Willie, 1970
Holden, Sam, 1970
Robinson, Virgil, 1970
Freelon, Soloman, 1970
Harris, Richard, 1970
Turner, Eldridge, 1971
Mendenhall, John, 1971
Dennis, Steven, 1971–72
Baisy, Walter, 1971–72
Reed, Matthew, 1972
White, Sammie, 1972, 1975
Juread, Rodney, 1972
Dennis, Al, 1972
Smith, Charles, 1972
Bibbs, Ezil, 1972
Johnson, Gary, 1972, 1974
Scales, Dwight, 1973
Barber, Robert, 1974
Pennywell, Robert, 1974–75
Hunter, James, 1974–75
Singleton, Ronald, 1975
St. Claire, Michael, 1975
Harris, Michael, 1976
Williams, Douglas, 1977
Pennywell, Carlos, 1977
Woods, Robert, 1977
Price, Wayne, 1977
Moore, Michael, 1977
Hall, Russell, 1977
Bates, Calvin, 1977
Thompson, Tom, 1978
Hudson, Jeff, 1978

Parham, Robert, 1978–80
Allen, Aldrich, 1978–79
Butler, David, 1979
Ridge, Gerald, 1979
Gordon, Joe, 1979
Williams, Michael, 1979–80
Salter, Robert, 1979–80
Barker, Michael, 1980
Irving, Reginald, 1980
Walls, Everson, 1980
Johnson, Trumaine, 1980–81
Rosenburrow, Louis, 1981
Gorden, Jerry, 1981
Jackson, McKay, 1981
Johnson, Fred, 1981
King, Arthur, 1981
Elzy, Jerry, 1981
Robinson, Andre, 1981
Lewis, Al, 1981–82
Smith, Robert, 1981–82
Taylor, James, 1982
Moore, Levelle, 1984–85
Jackson, Kevin, 1984–85
Smith, Sean, 1985–86
Well, Arthur, 1986
Penn, Jerome, 1986
Anderson, Anthony, 1986

Basketball

Barr, Jerry, 1959
Hooper, James, 1959
Willis, Howard, 1959
Hardnett, Charles, 1959, 1962
Tippett, Rex, 1960–61
Reed, Willis, 1961, 1964
West, Hershell, 1963
Frazier, Wilbur, 1963–65
Comeaux, John, 1964–66
Jones, James, 1966–67
Davis, Howard, 1967
Hilton, Fred, 1969, 1971
Cannon, Emanuel, 1971
James, Aaron, 1972, 1974
Hart, Willie, 1972
Wright, Larry, 1975–76
Sykes, Terry, 1977
Lemelle, Martin, 1978–80
Tidwell, Gary, 1979
Williams, Robert, 1980–81

Simpson, Ken, 1981–82
Johnson, Napoleon, 1983–84
Lapoole, Willie, 1985

Other Outstanding Athletes

Baseball

Tommie Smith, Earl
Agee, Lee
Alexander, Matthew
Garr, Ralph
Jeter, John

All-American (Black College)

Football

Buchanan, Junious "Buck," 1962
Dotson, Alphonse, 1964
Young, Willie, 1965
Cornish, Frank, 1965
Manning, William, 1969
Harris, Richard, 1970
Roundtree, Charles, 1970
Freelon, Solomon, 1971
Mendenhall, John, 1972
Dennis, Steven, 1972
Johnson, Gary, 1972–74
Bryant, Willie, 1973
White, Sammie, 1975
Hunter, James, 1975
Williams, Doug, 1977
Gordon, Joe, 1979
Allen, Aldrich, 1979
Salters, Robert, 1979
Johnson, Trumaine, 1980, 1982
Barker, Michael, 1980
Robinson, Andre, 1981
Smith, Robert, 1983
Harris, James, 1985

Basketball

Hardnett, Charles, 1961–62
Reed, Willis, 1964
Comeaux, John, 1966
Wright, Larry, 1976

Grambling State Alumni in the National Football League

Davis, Norman, Baltimore Colts, (G), 1967;
    New Orleans Saints, (G), 1969;
    Philadelphia Eagles, (G), 1970
Fields, Gregory, Baltimore Colts, (DT), 1979–80
Newsome, Billy, Baltimore Colts, (DE), 1970–72;
    New Orleans Saints, (DE), 1973–74;
    New York Jets, (DE), 1975–76;
    Chicago Bears, (DE), 1977–78
Pennywell, Robert, Atlanta Falcons, (L), 1977–80
Smith, Michael, Atlanta Falcons, (WR), 1980
Crawford, Hilton, Buffalo Bills, (S), 1969
Harris, James, Buffalo Bills, (Q), 1969–71;
    Los Angeles Rams, (Q), 1973–76;
    San Diego Chargers, (Q), 1977–80
Lewis, Frank, Pittsburgh Steelers, (WR), 1971–77;
    Buffalo Bills, (WR), 1978–83
Cornish, Frank, Chicago Bears, (DT), 1966–70;
    Cincinnati Bengals, (DT), 1970;
    Miami Dolphins, (DT), 1970–71;
    Buffalo Bills, (DT), 1972
Harris, Richard, Philadelphia Eagles, (DE), 1971–73;
    Chicago Bears, (DT), 1974–75;
    Seattle Seahawks, (DT), 1976–77
Ladd, Ernest, San Diego Chargers, (DT), 1961–65;
    Houston Oilers, (DT), 1966–67;
    Kansas City Chiefs, (DT), 1967–68
Taylor, Roosevelt, Chicago Bears, (S), 1961–69;
    San Francisco 49ers, (S), 1969–71;
    Washington Redskins, (S), 1972
Wilson, Nemiah, Denver Broncos, (DB), 1965–67;
    Oakland Raiders, (DB), 1968–74;
    Chicago Bears, (DB), 1975
Griffin, James, San Diego Chargers, (DT), 1966–67;
    Cincinnati Bengals, (DT), 1968–69
Johnson, Essex, Cincinnati Bengals, (RB), 1968–75;
    Tampa Bay Buccaneers, (RB), 1976
Joiner, Charles, Houston Oilers, (WR), 1969–72;
    Cincinnati Bengals, (WR), 1972–75;
    San Diego Chargers, (WR), 1976–85
St. Clair, Richard Michael, Cleveland Browns, (DE), 1976–79;
    Cincinnati Bengals, (DE), 1980
Caleb, Jamie, Cleveland Browns, (RB), 1960–65;
    Minnesota Vikings, (RB), 1961
Davis, Henry, New York Giants, (L), 1968–69;
    Pittsburgh Steelers, (L), 1970–73

Howell, Michael, Cleveland Browns, (DB), 1965–72;
Miami Dolphins, (DB), 1972

McNeil, Clifton, Cleveland Browns, (WR), 1964–67;
San Francisco 49ers, (WR), 1968–69;
New York Giants, (WR), 1970–71;
Washington Redskins, (WR), 1971–72;
Houston Oilers, (WR), 1973

Powell, Preston, Cleveland Browns, (RB), 1961

Walls, Everson, Dallas Cowboys, (DB), 1981–86

Brown, Willie, Denver Broncos, (DB), 1963–66;
Oakland Raiders, (DB), 1967–78

Radford, Bruce, Denver Broncos, (DE), 1979;
Tampa Bay Buccaneers, (DE), 1980;
St. Louis Cardinals, (DE), 1981

Sellers, Goldie, Denver Broncos, (DB), 1966–67;
Kansas City Chiefs, (DB), 1968–69

Simmons, Leon, Denver Broncos, (L), 1963

Hunter, James, Detroit Lions, (DB), 1976–82

Mendenhall, John, New York Giants, (DT), 1972–79;
Green Bay Packers, (DT), 1980

Woods, Robert, Houston Oilers, (WR), 1978–79

Barber, Robert, Green Bay Packers, (DE), 1976–80

Davis, Willie, Cleveland Browns, (DE), 1958–59;
Green Bay Packers, (OT), 1980

Prather, Guy, Green Bay Packers, (L), 1981–85

Simon, Robert, Houston Oilers, (G), 1976

Atkins, Robert, St. Louis Cardinals, (DB), 1968–69;
Houston Oilers, (DB), 1970–76

Boyette, Garland, St. Louis Cardinals, (L), 1962–63;
Houston Oilers, (L), 1966–72

Watson, Ed, Houston Oilers, (L), 1969

Buchanan, Junious, Kansas City Chiefs, (DT), 1963–75

Dyer, Henry, Los Angeles Rams, (RB), 1966–68;
Washington Redskins, (RB), 1969–70

Scales, Dwight, Los Angeles Rams, (WR), 1976–78;
New York Giants, (WR), 1979;
San Diego Chargers, (WR), 1981

Williams, Roger, Los Angeles Rams, (DB), 1971–72

Younger, Paul, Los Angeles Rams, (RB), 1949–57;
Pittsburgh Steelers, (L), 1958

Dotson, Alphonse, Kansas City Chiefs, (DT), 1965;
Miami Dolphins, (DT), 1966;
Oakland Raiders, (DT), 1968–70

Roberson, Vern, Miami Dolphins, (S), 1977;
San Francisco 49ers, (S), 1978–79

White, Sammie, Minnesota Vikings, (WR), 1976–85

Garrett, J.D., Boston Patriots, (RB), 1964–67

Pennywell, Carlos, New England Patriots, (WR), 1978–81

Richardson, Virgil, New Orleans Saints, (RB), 1971–72

Bryant, William, New York Giants, (DB), 1976–78;
Philadelphia Eagles, (DB), 1978–79

Howell, Lane, New York Giants, (T), 1963–64;
Philadelphia Eagles, (T), 1965–69

Williams, Willie, New York Giants, (DB), 1965, 1967–73;
Oakland Raiders, (DB), 1966

Young, Willie, New York Giants, (T), 1966–75

Zeno, Coleman, New York Giants, (WR), 1971

Howell, Delles, New Orleans Saints, (DB), 1970–72;
New York Jets, (DB), 1973–75

Robinson, Jerry, San Diego Chargers, (WR), 1962–64;
New York Jets, (WR), 1965

Peeples, Woodrow, San Francisco 49ers, (G), 1968–77;
Philadelphia Eagles, (G), 1978–80

Johnson, Charles, San Francisco 49ers, (DB), 1979–80;
St. Louis Cardinals, (DB), 1981

Johnson, Gary, San Diego Chargers, (DT), 1975–81;
San Francisco 49ers, (DT), 1984

Grambling State Alumni in the National Basketball Association

Hopkins, Robert, Syracuse Nationals, (F), 1957–60

Reed, Willis, New York Knickerbockers, (C), 1964–74

Jones, James, Washington Bullets, (G), 1974–77

Hilton, Fred, Buffalo Braves, (G), 1971–73

Christian, Robert, Atlanta Hawks, (F), 1970–73;
Phoenix Suns, (F), 1973–74

James, Aaron, New Orleans Jazz, (F), 1974–79

Wright, Larry, Washington Bullets, (G), 1976–80;
Detroit Pistons, (G), 1980–81

[1] Robinson, Ed, has the most victories of any collegiate coach in history, W-336 L-113 T-15

Prairie View A&M University
Prairie View, Texas 77445

Athletic Directors

Jackson, Brutus N.

Coaches of Varsity Teams

Football

Nicks, William, 1951–67

McKinney, Jim, 1982–83

Haymon, Conway, 1984

Men's Basketball

Loore, Leroy, 1961–62
Duplantier, Jim, 1981–87

Women's Basketball

Atkins, Robert, 1983–Present

All Southwestern Athletic Conference

Football

Dillon, Ray, 1951
McGowan, Cotrell, 1951
Robinson, Leonard, 1951
Bellinger, Jack, 1951–53
Wright, Charles, 1951–54
Heard, Vance, 1952
Price, Jack, 1952
Bracklin, Charles, 1952, 1954
Childress, Elijah, 1952–54
Haywood, Charles, 1953
Payton, John, 1954–55
Jeffro, Algernon, 1955
Turner, Glover, 1955
Brooks, Leon, 1955
Tibbs, Heron, 1955–56
Stell, William, 1956
Daniels, Clem, 1956–57
Hunt, Jim, 1956, 1957
Hornsby, Gentras, 1957–59
Malone, Charles, 1957–58, 1960
Scott, Calvin, 1958
Granderson, Rufus, 1958–59
Harrington, John, 1958–59
McKee, Frank, 1959
Williams, Tom, 1960
Warner, Charles, 1962
Seals, Ezzell, 1963
Robinson, Carl, 1963
Taylor, Otis, 1963–64
Kearney, Jim, 1963–64
Dearborne, George, 1964
Chandler, Horace, 1965
Reed, Alvin, 1965
Williams, Clarence, 1968
Williams, Charles, 1969
Jernigan, John, 1969
Lee, Bivins, 1969–70
Fisher, Ed, 1970

Moore, John, 1971
Caple, Ellis, 1973
Riley, Eddie, 1974
Bohannon, David, 1975–76
Thompson, Ronald, 1976
Cowans, James, 1977–78
Thompson, Rodney, 1985
Thompson, Charles, 1986
Huffpower, Vincent, 1986

Basketball

Justice, Irving, 1953
Ludd, Clarence, 1954–56
Grimes, Harold, 1958
Beatty, Zelmo, 1959–60, 1962
Brackens, Harold, 1959
Lackey, Cornell, 1960
Jackson, Marvin, 1977
Hagan, Larry, 1979

All-American (Black College)

Football

Dillion, Ray Don, 1950–51
Wright, Charles, 1952–54
Brockins, Charles, 1953–54
Childress, Elijah, 1954
Payton, John, 1954
Tibbs, Nerron, 1955–56
Hornsby, Gentris, 1957–59
Granderson, Rufus, 1958–59
Scott, Calvin, 1959
Farrington, John, 1959
Webster, David, 1959
Malone, Charles, 1960
Seals, Archie, 1961
Taylor, Otis, 1963–64
Kearney, Jim, 1963–64
Cartwright, Seith, 1964
Dearborne, George, 1964
Seals, Ezell, 1964
Houston, Kenneth, 1967
Wallace, Alonzo, 1967
Williams, Clarence, 1968
Taylor, Finnis, 1968
Williams, Charles, 1969
Lee, Bivian, 1969–70
Moore, John, 1971

Sharpe, Talmadge, 1972
Caple, Ellis, 1973
Bohannon, David, 1975
Austin, Greg, 1975
Thompson, Ron, 1975–76
Bennett, Richard, 1975–76
Cowans, James, 1977
Knighton, Terry, 1977

Men's Basketball

Beatty, Zelmo-NAIA, 1960–62

Baseball

Andrews, Douglas, 1970–71

Other Outstanding Athletes

Baseball

Henderson, Steven
Hudson, Charles

Men's Basketball

Himes, Douglas
McQueen, Dewey
Lackey, Cornell
Manning, Guy
Gamble, James
Grimes, Harold
Stubblefield, Clarence
Redmond, Thomas

Prairie View A&M Alumni in the
National Football League

Mitchell, John, Atlanta Falcons, (TE), 1969–79
Neal, Louis, Atlanta Falcons, (WR), 1973–74
Teague, Matthew, Atlanta Falcons, (DB), 1981
Warner Charles, Kansas City Chiefs (DB), 1963–64;
    Buffalo Bills, (DB), 1964–66
Farrington, John, Chicago Bears, (WR), 1960–63
Aldridge, Allen, Green Bay Packers, (DE), 1971–72;
    Cleveland Browns, (DE), 1974
Kearney, Jim, Detroit Lions, (S), 1965–66;
    Kansas City Chiefs, (S), 1967–75;
    New England Patriots, (S), 1976
Brackins, Charles, Green Bay Packers, (RB), 1955
Williams, Clarence, Los Angeles Rams, (WR), 1970;
    Green Bay Packers, (WR), 1970–77
Harvey, Claude, Houston Oilers, (L), 1970–71

Houston, Ken, Houston Oilers, (S), 1967–72;
    Washington Redskins, (S), 1973–80
Anderson, Fred, Pittsburgh Steelers, (DE), 1978;
    Seattle Seahawks, (DE), 1980–82
Reed, Alvin, Houston Oilers, (TE), 1967–72;
    Washington Redskins, (TE), 1973–75
Whittington, C.L., Houston Oilers, (S), 1969
Woods, Glen, Houston Oilers, (DT), 1974–78
Austin, Hise, Kansas City Chiefs, (DB), 1975
Daniels, Clemon, Kansas City Chiefs, (RB), 1960;
    Oakland Raiders, (RB), 1961–67;
    San Francisco 49ers, (RB), 1968
Granderson, Rufus, Kansas City Chiefs, (T), 1960
Taylor, Otis, Kansas City Chiefs, (WR), 1965–75
Webster, David, Kansas City Chiefs, (DB), 1960–61
Wolf, James, Pittsburgh Steelers, (DT), 1974;
    Kansas City Chiefs, (DT), 1976
Adams, Sam, New England Patriots, (G), 1972–80;
    New Orleans Saints, (G), 1981
Hunt, Jim, New England Patriots, (DT), 1961–71
Lee, Bivian, New Orleans Saints, (DB), 1971–75
Brown, Otto, New York Giants, (DB), 1970–73

Prairie View A&M Alumni in the
National Basketball Association

Beatty, Zelmo, St. Louis Hawks, (C), 1962–68
    Atlanta Hawks, (C), 1968–69

Southern University
Baton Rouge, Louisiana 70813

Athletic Directors

Mumford, A.W., 1946–62
Lee, Robert, 1963–67
Jones, Ulyseus, 1967–79
Hines, Emory, 1980–81
Hill, Richard, 1981–Present

Coaches of Varsity Teams

Football

Mumford, A.W., 1946–61
Lee, Robert, 1962–65
Smith, Robert, 1965–78
Jackson, Cass, 1978–80
Washington, Otis, 1980–Present

Basketball

Stewart, Carl E., 1972–82
Stoglin, Andrew, 1982–85
Hopkins, Robert, 1985–86
Jobe, Ben, 1986–Present

All Southwestern Athletic Conference

Football

Moore, Curtis, 1951
Straughter, James, 1951
Holden, Robert, 1951
Posey, Odie, 1951
Greathouse, Lee, 1951
Wooten, Herman, 1951
Rutherford, Jack, 1951, 1953
Robinson, Sherman, 1952
Lowery, Ed, 1952
Bedford, Leon, 1952
Lomax, Willie, 1952–53
Moore, Leonard, 1953
Lemons, Charles, 1953–54
Dinkins, Robert, 1953–55
Spears, Elvin, 1953–54, 1956
Hardin, William, 1954
Meshack, Raoul, 1954–55
Simon, Emmitt, 1955
Pearson, Harold, 1955
Mitchell, John, 1955
Bates, Roman, 1956
Peterson, Philip, 1956
Culium, Art, 1956
Bruno, Clarence, 1957
Williams, Richard, 1957–58
McGee, George, 1958
Griffin, J.D., 1958
Thomas, John, 1958–59
Williams, Robert, 1958–60
Ross, Raymond, 1959–60
Gainor, Hubert, 1959
Lancaster, Cyrus, 1960
Evans, David, 1960–61
Simon, Junius, 1960–62
Davis, Donnie, 1961
Haymond, Alvin, 1962
Williams, Sid, 1962–63
McGee, Ben, 1963
Duncan, Leslie, 1963

Savage, Ken, 1964
Barnes, Peter, 1964–66
Clayton, John, 1965
Nixon, Rhome, 1966
Zenon, Joe, 1966
Holmes, Robert, 1967
Maples, Elmo, 1967
Beauchamp, Al, 1967
McClinton, Harold, 1967–68
Neal, Richard 1968
Lewis, Terry, 1969
Blount, Mel, 1969
Roche, Alden, 1969
Robertson, Isiah, 1970
Dunbar, Allen, 1971
Osbourne, James, 1971
Wright, James, 1971–72
Turk, Goodwin, 1971–73
Green, Henry, 1973
Holmes, Hulon, 1974
Robinson, John, 1974
Beckwirth, Carl, 1975
Henry, Lionel, 1975
Brooks, Perry, 1975
Briscoe, Greg, 1976
Stewart, Brainard, 1976
Labot, Gregory, 1977
Besaint, Nathaniel, 1977
Stewart, Charles, 1978–79
Times, Kenneth, 1979
Vaughn, Michael, 1980
Williams, Brian, 1980
Franklin, Jerrell, 1980
Robinson, Lloyd
Porter, Rufus, 1985
Swain, Connell, 1985

Basketball

Wyatt, Lawrence, 1952
Norwood, Sylvester, 1952
Johnson, James, 1952
Singleton, James, 1953
Cunningham, Clarence, 1953
Gray, Robert, 1953–56
Wise, Ellis, 1954
Hill, Roosevelt, 1957–58
Paul, Frank, 1958
Hayes, Ego, 1958

Thomas, Willie, 1960
Bond, Louis, 1960–62
Love, Robert, 1963–65
Boatwright, Homer, 1964
Hayes, Ron, 1964–65
Long, Ron, 1967
Wilson, Jasper, 1967–68
McTier, Larry, 1972
Frazier, Andrew, 1973
Keyes, Alexander, 1973
Barrow, Ron, 1974–76
Saunders, Frank, 1976–78
Green, Tom, 1977
Murphy, Tony, 1979–80
Garrett, Lionel, 1979
Jackson, Alvin, 1981
Broadway, Bryan, 1984
Lee, James, 1984
Gabriel, Byron, 1986

All-American (Black College)

Football

Robertson, Isiah, 1970
Wright, James, 1972
Turk, Godwin, 1973
Times, Ken, 1979

Southern University Alumni in the National Football League

Robertson, Isiah, Los Angeles Rams, (L), 1971–78;
  Buffalo Bills, (L), 1979–82
Osborne, Jim, Chicago Bears, (DT), 1972–84
Beauchamp, Al, Cincinnati Bengals, (L), 1969–75;
  St. Louis Cardinals, (L), 1976
Battle, Jim, Cleveland Browns, (G), 1966
Dunbar, Jubilee, Cleveland Browns, (WR), 1974
Ellis, Ken, Miami Dolphins, (DB), 1976;
  Cleveland Browns, (DB), 1977;
  Detroit Lions, (DB), 1979
  Los Angeles Rams, (DB), 1979
Jackson, Richard, Oakland Raiders, (L), 1966;
  Denver Broncos, (L), 1967–72;
  Cleveland Browns, (L), 1972
Pitts, Frank, Kansas City Chiefs, (WR), 1965–71;
  Cleveland Browns, (WR), 1971–73;
  Oakland Raiders, (WR), 1974

Williams, Sidney, Cleveland Browns, (L), 1964–66;
  Washington Redskins, (L), 1967
Davis, Donnie, Dallas Cowboys, (TE), 1962;
  Houston Oilers, (TE), 1970
Granger, Charles, Dallas Cowboys, (G-T), 1961;
  St. Louis Cardinals, (G-T), 1961
Roche, Alden, Denver Broncos, (DE), 1970;
  Green Bay Packers, (DE), 1971–76;
  Seattle Seahawks, (DE), 1977–78
Turk, Godwin, New York Jets, (L), 1974–75;
  Denver Broncos, (L), 1976–78
Green, Cleveland, Miami Dolphins, (T), 1979–85
Smith, Donnell, Green Bay Packers, (DE), 1971;
  New England Patriots, (DE), 1973–74
Barnes, Pete, Houston Oilers, (LB), 1967–68;
  San Diego Chargers, (L), 1970–72;
  St. Louis Cardinals, (L), 1973–75;
  New England Patriots, (L), 1976–77
Broadnax, Jerry, Houston Oilers, (TE), 1974
Davis, Marvin, Houston Oilers, (L), 1974
Haymond, Alvin, Philadelphia Eagles, (DB), 1968;
  Los Angeles Rams, (DB), 1969–71;
  Washington Redskins, (DB), 1972;
  Houston Oilers, (DB), 1973
Holmes, Robert, Kansas City Chiefs, (RB), 1968–71;
  Houston Oilers, (RB), 1971–72, 1975;
  San Diego Chargers, (RB), 1973
Rucker, Conrad, Houston Oilers, (G-T), 1978–79;
  Los Angeles Rams, (G-T), 1980
Hill, Mack Lee, Kansas City Chiefs, (RB), 1964–65
Porter, Lewis, Kansas City Chiefs, (WR), 1970
McGee, George, Boston Patriots, (T), 1960
Neal, Richard, New Orleans Saints, (DE), 1969–72, 1978;
  New York Jets, (DE), 1973–77
Brister, Willie, New York Jets, (TE), 1974–75
Carmichael, Harold, Philadelphia Eagles, (WR), 1971–84
Jackson, John, Philadelphia Eagles, (DE), 1977
Blount, Mel, Pittsburgh Steelers, (DB), 1970–83
Williams, Sid, Pittsburgh Steelers, (L), 1969
Times, Ken, St. Louis Cardinals, (DT), 1981
Williams, Herb, San Francisco 49ers, (DB), 1980;
  St. Louis Cardinals, (DB), 1981–82
Williams, Clyde, St. Louis Cardinals, (T), 1967–71
Mitchell, Ed, San Diego Chargers, (G), 1965–66
Brooks, Perry, Washington Redskins, (DT), 1978–84
McClinton, Harold, Washington Redskins, (L), 1969–78

***Southern University Alumni in the
National Basketball Association***

Love, Robert, Cincinnati Royals, (F), 1966–68;
    Milwaukee Bucks, (F), 1968–69;
    Chicago Bulls, (F), 1969–76;
    New Jersey Nets, (F), 1976–77
Green, Tom, Utah Jazz, (G), 1978–79
Saunders, Frank, Boston Celtics, (F), 1976–78;
    San Antonio Spurs, (F), 1978–79;
    Kansas City Kings, (F), 1981

Jackson State University
Jackson, Mississippi 39217

Athletic Directors

Ellis, T.B., 1946–77
Reed, Dr., Walter, 1977–Present

Coaches of Varsity Teams

Football

Ellis, T.B., 1946–53
Merritt, John, 1953–63
Clemons, John, 1963–64
Paige, Roderick, 1964–68
McPherson, W.S., 1968–70
Hill, Robert, 1971–76
Gordon, W.C., 1976–Present

Basketball

Ellis, T.B., 1949–51
Wilson, Harrison B., 1951–67
Covington, Paul, 1967–86
Prince, John, 1986–Present

Women's Basketball

Tucker, Peggy, 1948–52
Magee, Sadie, 1975–Present

Baseball

Smith, Allen, 1957–58
Gilliam, Joe, 1958–63
Andrews, Artis, 1963–65
Reed, Dr. Walter, 1965–66
Hill, Robert, 1966–70
Gordon, W.C., 1970–72
Braddy, Robert, 1972–Present

Track and Field

Norris, Edward P., 1946–50
Ellis, T.B., 1950–53
Merritt, John, 1953–54
Blackburn, Benjamin, 1954–64
Lattimore, Henry, 1964–69
Epps, Martin, 1968–Present

Women's Track and Field

Epps, Martin, 1969–Present

Tennis

Ellis, T.B., 1957–72
Shinall, John, 1972–84

Women's Tennis

Shinnall, John, 1982–84

Golf

Ellis, T.B., 1957–60
Smith, Allen, 1960–83
Marshall, James, 1983–Present

Volleyball

Jones, Kathy, 1975–76
Romain, Jean, 1976–78
Turner, James, 1978–Present

All Southwestern Athletic Conference

Football

Spencer, William, 1958
Dorsey, Frank, 1959
Richardson, Willie, 1959–62
Cooley, Archie, 1959
Rhoden, Israel, 1961
Curry, Roy, 1961–62
McGee, Ben, 1962–63
Biggs, Verlon, 1964
Richardson, Gloster, 1964
Hayes, James, 1964
Barney, Lem, 1964–66
Jackson, Harold, 1966
Hughes, Robert, 1966
Holifield, Jim, 1966
Funches, Tom, 1966–67
Outlaw, John, 1966–67
Jackson, Cephas, 1967
Griffin, Percey, 1968

Ellis, Charles, 1970
Collins, Sylvester, 1970–71
Keyes, Ray, 1970–72
Strickland, Otis, 1971
Barkum, Jerome, 1971
Marshall, James, 1971–73
Ellis, James, 1972
Gray, Leon, 1972
Richardson, Ernest, 1972
Payton, Walter, 1972–74
Slater, Jackie, 1972, 1974–75
Reese, Don, 1973
Tate, John, 1973
Philips, Rodney, 1974
Young, Rick, 1974
Collins, Willie, 1974
Brazile, Robert, 1974
Miley, Mac, 1975
Patton, Rick, 1975, 1977
Perry, Vernon, 1975
Sherrod, Leon, 1976
Reed, James, 1976
Tillman, Jeremiah, 1976
Sterling, Victor, 1976
Young, Anthony, 1976
Bullard, Louis, 1977
Williams, Charles, 1977
Griffin, Jessie, 1977
Barnet, Buster, 1978
Rice, Tom, 1978, 1980
Moore, Jeffrey, 1978
Hardy, Robert, 1978
Cloy, Clark, 1978
Young, Anthony, 1978
Perkins, Philip, 1978–79
Harrington, Perry, 1979
Walls, Lester, 1979
Hardy, Kevin, 1979
Werts, Larry, 1980
Straughters, Thomas, 1980–82
Roberts, Carl, 1981–82
Cowan, Larry, 1981
Lewis, Randall, 1981
Taylor, Keith, 1981
Fields, Michael, 1981
Rush, King David, 1981
Marshall, Al, 1981–82
Doss, Thomas, 1982

Simmons, Cleo, 1982
Sutton, Frank, 1982
Kirksey, Marlo, 1982
Johnson, Karl, 1982
Walker, Jackie, 1984–85
Hall, Victor, 1985
Tillman, Lewis, 1985
Woods, Darrell, 1985
Seals, Leon, 1985–86
Johnson, Carl, 1985–86
Harvey, James, 1986
Dent, Kevin, 1986

Basketball

Buckner, Cleveland, 1959–60
Barfield, James, 1960
Benton, James, 1964
Yarborough, Jerry, 1964–65
LeFlore, Lyvonne, 1964–65
Bingham, Charles, 1966
Manning, Ed, 1966–67
Warner, Cornell, 1969–71
Herdon, Lou, 1970
Shinall, John, 1970
Brown, Marvin, 1971
Kincaide, McKinley, 1971
Short, Eugene, 1973–74
Jones, Glendale, 1974–75
Ward, Henry, 1975
Short, Purvis, 1976–78
Norris, Sylvester, 1978
Walsh, Robert, 1979
Norris, Audie, 1979–82
Shavers, Doc, 1980–81
Williams, Henry, 1983
Walker, Jackie, 1984
Fonville, Lester, 1987
Hart, Jeff, 1985–87

Jackson State Alumni in the National Football League

Hilton, Roy, New York Giants, (DE), 1974;
    Atlanta Falcons, (DE), 1975
Hughes, Robert, Atlanta Falcons, (DE), 1967, 1969
Patton, Ricky, Atlanta Falcons, (RB), 1978;
    Green Bay Packers, (RB), 1979;
    San Francisco 49ers, (RB), 1980–82

Burnett, Buster, Buffalo Bills, (TE), 1981–84

Ward, Roscoe, New York Jets, (DB, KR), 1974–76;
New York Giants, (DB, KR), 1976;
Buffalo Bills, (DB, KR), 1976

Payton, Walter, Chicago Bears, (RB), 1975–86

Zanders, Emanuel, Chicago Bears, (G), 1981

Bacon, Coy, Los Angeles Rams, (DT), 1968–72;
San Diego Chargers, (DT), 1973–75;
Cincinnati Bengals, (DT), 1976–78;
Washington Redskins, (DT), 1978–81

Thomas, Lee, San Diego Chargers, (DE), 1971–72;
Cincinnati Bengals, (DE), 1973

Payton, Ed, Cleveland Browns, (KR), 1977;
Detroit Lions, (KR), 1977;
Kansas City Chiefs, (KR), 1978;
Minnesota Vikings, (KR), 1980–82

Richardson, Gloster, Kansas City Chiefs, (WR), 1967–70;
Dallas Cowboys, (WR), 1971;
Cleveland Browns, (WR), 1972–74

Houston, William, Dallas Cowboys, (WR), 1974

Barney, Lem, Detroit Lions, (DB), 1967–77

Greer, Albert, Detroit Lions, (E), 1963

Jackson, Ernest, Detroit Lions, (DB), 1979

Simmons, Cleo, Dallas Cowboys, (TE), 1983

Brazille, Robert, Houston Oilers, (L), 1975–76

Caster, Richard, New York Jets, (TE), 1970–77;
Houston Oilers, (TE), 1978–80;
New Orleans Saints, (TE), 1981;
Washington Redskins, (TE), 1981

Funchess, Thomas, Minnesota Vikings, (T), 1968–70;
Houston Oilers, (T), 1971–73;
Miami Dolphins, (T), 1974

Gray, Leon, New England Patriots, (T), 1973–78;
Houston Oilers, (T), 1979–86

Hayes, Jim, Houston Oilers, (DT), 1979

Perry, Vernon, Houston Oilers, (S), 1979

Thomas, Lee, Houston Oilers, (DE), 1975

Jackson, Harold, Los Angeles Rams, (WR), 1968, 1973–77;
Philadelphia Eagles, (WR), 1969–72;
New England Patriots, (WR), 1978–81

Molden, Frank, Los Angeles Rams, (DT), 1965;
Philadelphia Eagles, (DT), 1968

Phillips, Rod, Los Angeles Rams, (RB), 1975–78;
St. Louis Cardinals, (RB), 1979–80

Slater, Jackie, Los Angeles Rams, (G-T), 1976–86

Holifield, James, New York Giants, (DB), 1968–69

Reese, Don, Miami Dolphins, (DT), 1974–76;
New Orleans Saints, (DT), 1978–80;
San Diego Chargers, (DT), 1981

Richardson, Willie, Baltimore Colts, (WR), 1963–69, 1971;
Miami Dolphins, (WR), 1970

Young, Ricky, San Diego Chargers, (RB), 1975–77;
Minnesota Vikings, (RB), 1978–81

Cowan, Larry, New England Patriots, (RB), 1982

Outlaw, John, New England Patriots, (DB), 1969–72;
Philadelphia Eagles, (DB), 1973–78

Richardson, Tom, New England Patriots, (WR), 1969–70

Marshall, James, Nw Orleans Saints, (DB), 1980;

Zanders, Emanuel, New Orleans Saints, (G), 1974–80

Tate, John, New York Giants, (L), 1976

Barkum, Jerome, New York Jets, (WR, TE), 1972–83

Biggs, Verlon, New York Jets, (DE), 1965–70;
Washington Redskins, (DE), 1971, 1975

Harrington, Perry, Philadelphia Eagles, (RB), 1980–84;
St. Louis Cardinals, (RB), 1984

Harvey, Richard, Philadelphia Eagles, (DB), 1970

Curry, Roy, Pittsburgh Steelers, (RB), 1963

Duncan, Leslie, San Diego Chargers, (DB), 1964–70;
Washington Redskins, (DB), 1971–73

Hardy, Edgar, San Francisco 49ers, (G), 1973

Moore, Jeff, Seattle Seahawks, (RB), 1979–81;
San Francisco 49ers, (RB), 1982–83

Bullard, Louis, San Francisco 49ers, (T), 1978–80

Hardy, Robert, Seattle Seahawks, (DT), 1979–82

Jones, Michael, Seattle Seahawks, (L), 1977

Franklin, Larry, Tampa Bay Buccaneers, (WR), 1978

Jackson State University Alumni in the National Basketball Association

Buckner, Cleveland, New York Knickerbockers, (F), 1961–62

Manning, Ed, Baltimore Bullets, (F), 1967–69;
Chicago Bulls, (F), 1969–70;
Portland Trailblazers, (F), 1970–71

Short, Purvis, Golden State Warriors, (F), 1978–Present

Short, Eugene, New York Knickerbockers, (F), 1975–76;
Seattle Supersonics, (F), 1976–77

Norris, Audie, Portland Trailblazers, (F, C), 1982

Norris, Sylvester, San Antonio Spurs, (F), 1979–80

Jackson State University's Athletic Hall of Fame

Football

Alexander, A.A.
Banks, E.W.
Marshall, Luther
Sullivan, John L.
Stewart, Edgar

Greene, Percy
Jackson, Joseph H.
Ellis, T.B.
Westbrooks, C.D.
Brown, T.B.
Higgins, Commondore
Watson, Clarence
Higgins, Wallace
Biship, Edward J.
Wilson, Herbert
Wolfe, Robert
Hill, Thomas
Cooper, Robert
Grantham, John
Smith, Estus
Jones, Aaron
Witty, Jack
White, Wiley R.
Hill, Robert
Richardson, Willie
Chambliss, Jr., Alvin
Biggs, Verlon
Richardson, Gloster
Curry, Roy
Outlaw, John
Barney, Lem
Jackson, Hal
Duncan, Leslie
Magee, Jr., Ben
Payton, Walter
Gray, Leon
Brazile, Robert
Phillips, Rodney
Richardson, Allen
Lewis, James
Hardy, Edgar

Basketball

Ingram, Joel
Wood, Melvin
Buckner, Cleveland
Manning, Edward
Short, Eugene
Short, Purvis
Ward, Henry
Norris, Audie

Women's Basketball

Paige, Gloria
Hardy, Bertha
Bender, Evelyn
Robinson, Vanetta
Thomas, Lisa
Freeman, Gloria

Baseball

Moore, Kelvin
McDougal, Julius
Clark, David
Shinall, John, 1982–84

Texas Southern University
Houston, Texas 77004

Athletic Directors

Rettig, E.V.,[1] 1946–48
Durley, Alexander, 1949–64
McCleary, Dr. W.C., 1965–69
Rains, Dr. David D., 1969–71
Glosson, William H., 1981 (Jan. 1–June 31)
Redmond, Joseph (Acting), 1981 (June 1–Sept. 30)
Davis, Willie, 1981–82
White, Dr. Calvin, 1982–84
Robins, Dr. Thurman W., 1984–1985
Taylor, Lionel, 1985–Present

Coaches of Varsity Teams

Football

Retting, E.V., 1946–48
Durley, Alexander, 1949–64
Paul, Clifford, 1965–69
Benefield, Alfred, 1970
Pige, Dr. Roderick, 1971–75
Mosley, Wendell, 1976–78
Sorey, James, 1979–80
Redmond, James, 1981–83
Taylor, Lionel, 1984–Present

Basketball

Ewell, C.T.,[2] 1935–36
Patterson, Pat,[3] 1937–40
Redding, E.V., 1946–47
Lattimore, Oliver, 1948–49
Adams, Edward H., 1950–59

Morehead, I. Thomas, 1960–64
Whitney, David, 1964–69
Gordon, Lavalius, 1969–73
McCowan, Kenneth, 1973–75
Moreland, Robert E., 1975–Present

Track and Field

Retting, E.V., 1946–48
Wright, Stanley V., 1951–67
Paul, Clifford, 1968–69
Bethany, David, 1970–Present

Baseball

Adams, Edward H., 1950–57
Gaines, Vincent, 1958–65
Benefield, Alfred, 1966–70
Sistrunk, Allen, 1971–74
Hatty, Marshall, 1975–76
Perkins, Dwight, 1976–79
Moore, Leon, 1980–84
Hunter, Robert, 1985–Present

Tennis

Provost, Herbert, 1965–81
Wilkerson, John, 1981–82

Women's Basketball

Hooper, Steven T., 1973–76
Holden, Ricky, 1976–77
Gillespie, Nathaniel, 1977–82
Johnson, Brenda, 1982–84
Harris-Stewart, Lusia, 1984–86
Gatlin, Robert A., 1986–Present

Swimming

Means, Johnnie, 1965–75

Golf

Graves, Jackie, 1955–57
Mims, Alfred J., 1958–66
Glosson, William H., 1967
Powell, Lee, 1968–70
Glosson, William H., 1971

All Southwestern Athletic Conference

Football

Felder, Hollis, 1956
Williams, James, 1956

Durley, Alexander, 1956
Perkins, Willie, 1956–57, 1960
Sorey, James, 1956–59
Gardner, James, 1957
Glossen, William, 1958
Choice, Lloyd, 1960
Garcia, Lacy, 1961
Scoby, J.C., 1961
Jones, Homer, 1961–62
Hill, Winston, 1962
Rice, Andy, 1962
Driver, Herman, 1962, 1964
Wells, Warren, 1963
Woodard, Carl, 1963
Robey, Ed, 1964
Thompson, John, 1964–65
Hopkins, Roy, 1965–66
Ellison, Willie, 1966
Calloway, Ernest, 1966–67
Burrough, Ken, 1969
Blossom, Charles, 1969
Crowe, Larry, 1970
Adams, Julius, 1970
Allen, Nate, 1970
Holmes, Ernest, 1970
Hart, Harold, 1971
Thomas, David, 1971–73
Holmes, Michael, 1971–72
Holmes, Ron, 1972
Stafford, Charles, 1972–73
Baker, Melvin, 1973
Fergurson, Willie, 1973
Calloway, Kevin, 1973
Bolden, Don, 1975
Simmons, Alfonso, 1975
Colquitte, Donald, 1976–77
McMichael, Clarence, 1977
Johnson, Jacque, 1977
McNeal, Dwight, 1978
McIntosh, Jackie, 1978
Harris, Lee, 1979
Grisby, James, 1981
Sheppard, Dale, 1981

Basketball

Bolen, Ruben, 1955
Crawford, Clifford, 1955
Sauldsberry, Woody, 1955

Swain, Ben, 1955–58
Dunbar, Earl, 1956
Maura, Fred, 1956–57, 1959
Bobbitt, Robert, 1957–58
Taylor, Willie, 1957–59
Allen, James, 1967
Hart, Herbert, 1970
Aldridge, Ellis, 1971–72
Ford, Charles, 1972
Davis, Gaylord, 1976
Williams, Lawrence, 1977
Bradley, Alonzo, 1977
Blue, Fred, 1979
Kelly, Harry, 1980–83
Mitchell, Lattrell, 1983
Hilliard, Ed, 1984
Applewhite, Andre, 1984–85
Brooks, Lester, 1984–86
Gatlin, Robert, 1987

Baseball

Greene, Gerald, 1973
Brossard, Russell, 1975
Johnson, Ron, 1979
Long, Edeland, 1979
Cousinard, Prince, 1982
Charlot, Gary, 1983
Barlow, Tom, 1983
Lewis, Gerald, 1983
Carter, Glenn, 1983

Golf

Golden, Reginald, 1958–60
Evans, William, 1959
Henley, Sam, 1959–60
Ford, Raymond, 1960–61
Galley, Clyde, 1960–61
Tellison, Leonard, 1961
Gillespie, Lowie, 1961
Mitchell, Clyde, 1962
Dangerfield, Robert, 1973–75
Johnson, Bernard, 1974–75
Stewart, Henry, 1974–75
Maycock, Greg, 1976–78
Maycock, Philip, 1976–78

Texas Southern Alumni in the National Football League

Crowe, Larry, Atlanta Falcons, (DB), 1969–70;
  Philadelphia Eagles, (DB), 1972
Strahan, Art, Houston Oilers, (DE), 1965;
  Atlanta Falcons, (DE), 1968
Baker, Mel, Houston Oilers, (WR), 1972;
  Los Angeles Rams, (WR), 1974;
  San Diego Chargers, (WR), 1975;
  Buffalo Bills, (WR), 1977
Holmes, Michael, Buffalo Bills, (WR), 1976;
  Los Angeles Rams, (WR), 1976
Mays, David, Cleveland Browns, (Q), 1976–77
  Buffalo Bills, (Q), 1978
Sorey, Jim, Buffalo Bills, (DT), 1960–62
Dean, Fred, Chicago Bears, (G), 1977;
  Washington Redskins, (G), 1978–82
Rice, Andrew, Kansas City Chiefs, (DT), 1966;
  Cincinnati Bengals, (DT), 1968–69;
  San Diego Chargers, (DT), 1970–71;
  Chicago Bears, (DT), 1972–73
Jones, Homer, New York Giants, (WR), 1964–69;
  Cleveland Browns, (WR), 1970
Hill, Winston, New York Jets, (T), 1963–76
  Los Angeles Rams, (T), 1977
Mitchell, Leroy, Houston Oilers, (DB), 1969–70;
  Denver Broncos, (DB), 1971–73;
  New England Patriots, (DB), 1973–77
Allen, Nate, Kansas City Chiefs, (DB), 1971–74;
  San Francisco 49ers, (DB), 1975;
  Minnesota Vikings, (DB), 1976–78;
  Detroit Lions, (DB), 1979
Wells, Warren, Detroit Lions, (WR), 1964;
  Oakland Raiders, (WR), 1967–70
Askson, Bert, Pittsburgh Steelers, (DE), 1971;
  Green Bay Packers, (DE), 1975
Burrough, Ken, New Orleans Saints, (WR), 1970;
  Houston Oilers, (WR), 1971–83
Cheeks, B.W., Houston Oilers, (RB), 1965
Frazier, Charles, Houston Oilers, (WR), 1962–68;
  New England Patriots, (WR), 1969–70
Hicks, Wilmer Kenzie, Houston Oilers, (S, DB), 1964–69;
  New York Jets, (S, DB), 1970–72
Hopkins, Roy, Houston Oilers, (RB), 1967–71
Nicholson, Oliver, Houston Oilers, (L), 1975
Perkins, Willis, New England Patriots, (G), 1961;
  Houston Oilers, (G), 1961–63

White, John, Houston Oilers, (TE), 1960–61
Young, James, Houston Oilers, (DE), 1977–79
Ellison, Willie, Kansas City Chiefs, (RB), 1973–74
Hines, James, Miami Dolphins, (WR), 1969;
   Kansas City Chiefs, (WR), 1970
Mumphord, Lloyd, Miami Dolphins, (DB), 1969–74
Adams, Julius, New England Patriots, (DE), 1971–85
Holmes, Ernest, Pittsburgh Steelers, (NT, DT), 1972–77;
   New England Patriots, (NT, DT), 1978
Porter, Wilie, New England Patriots, (DB), 1968
Hart, Harold, Oakland Raiders, (RB), 1974–75;
   New York Giants, (RB), 1977
Pough, Ernest, Pittsburgh Steelers, (WR), 1976–77;
   New York Giants, (WR), 1978
Philyaw, Charles, Oakland Raiders, (DE), 1976–79
Calloway, Ernest, Philadelphia Eagles, (DT), 1969–72
Braxton, Eugene, Tampa Bay Buccaneers, (WR), 1983

Texas Southern Alumni in the National Basketball Association

Sauldesberry, Woodrow, Philadelphia Eagles, (F), 1957–60;
   Chicago Packers, (F), 1961–62
St. Louis Hawks, (F), 1962–63;
   Boston Celtics, (F), 1965–66
Swain, Ben, Boston Celtics, (F, C), 1958–59
Bradley, Alonzo, Houston Rockets, (F), 1977–80

[1] Rettig, E.V.–school was named the Texas State University for Negros
[2] Ewell, C.T.–school was named Houston Colored Junior College
[3] Patterson, Pat–school was named Houston College for Negros

Mississippi Valley State University
Itta Bena, Mississippi 38941

Athletic Directors

Prophet, Chuck, 1984–Present

Coaches of Varsity Teams

Football

Cooley, Archie, 1980–86
Pettiford, Ken, 1986–Present

Men's Basketball

Stribling, Lafayette, 1983–Present

Women's Basketball

Harris, Jesse L., 1974–Present

All Southwestern Athletic Conference

Football

McDaniels, David, 1967
Washington, Ted, 1971
Townsend, Arcellious, 1975
Dickinson, Parnell, 1975
Jackson, Charles, 1975
Stanfield, John, 1975–79
Battles, Derrick, 1976–77
Mullen, James, 1976
Whitlock, Tresvan, 1976
Williams, James, 1977
Kinnard, William, 1977–78
Williams, Melvin, 1978
Doaty, Donald, 1978
Stribblen, Earl, 1978
Harper, Larry, 1978
White, Carl, 1979
Taylor, Harold, 1979
Wright, Wally, 1980
Owens, Hubert, 1980
Hood, Dexter, 1980
Darns, Philip, 1980
Harmon, Larry, 1980
Culliver, Otis, 1980–82
Taylor, James, 1981
Bohannon, Fred, 1981
Jefferson, Clyde, 1982
Murry, Riley, 1982
Rew, Alvin, 1982
Mumphery, Lloyd, 1982
Rice, Jerry, 1982–83
Totten, Willie,[1] 1982–85
Totten, Willie, 1983–85
Clark, Lorenzo, 1985
Thomas, Joe, 1985
Byrum, Carl, 1985
Jones, Tyrone, 1985
Ware, Willie, 1985
Thompson, James, 1986
Jones, Paul, 1986
Brown, Vincent, 1986
Alexander, Clarence, 1986

Basketball

Robinson, Calvin, 1974
Williams, Ernest, 1979
Reed, Tony, 1980–81
Ellis, Henry, 1982–83
Phillips, Robert, 1984
Sanders, Robert, 1984–85

All-American

Football

White, Carl, 1979
Rice, Jerry, 1983–84
Totten, Willie,[1] 1984–85

[1] Totten, Willie–1984 Mississippi College Player of the Year; 1984 and 1985 Southwestern Athletic Conference Player of the Year; Division 1-AA All-time Career Yards per game leader, 13,007 yards in 40 games, 1982–1985

Mississippi Valley Alumni in the National Football League

Stanciel, Jeff, Atlanta Falcons, (RB), 1969
Gaddis, Robert, Buffalo Bills, (WR), 1976
Morgan, Melvin, Cincinnati Bengals, (DB), 1976–78; San Francisco 49ers, (DB), 1979–80
Feacher, Ricky, New England Patriots, (WR, KR), 1973; Cleveland Browns, (WR, KR), 1976–85
McDaniels, David, Dallas Cowboys, (WR), 1968
Washington, Ted, Houston Oilers, (L), 1973–86
Dorsey, Nate, New England Patriots, (DE), 1973
Bohannon, Fred, Pittsburgh Steelers, 1982
Washington, Sam, Pittsburgh Steelers, 1982
Rice, Jerry, San Francisco 49ers, (WR), 1985–Present
Darns, Phil, Tampa Bay Buccaneers, (DE), 1984
Dickinson, Parnell, Tampa Bay Buccaneers, (Q), 1976

BIG TEN CONFERENCE

1. Purdue University
2. University of Wisconsin
3. Northwestern University
4. Indiana University
5. Ohio State University

6. Iowa University
7. University of Illinois, at Urbana-Champaign
8. University of Minnesota
9. Michigan State University
10. University of Michigan

Purdue University
West Lafayette, Indiana 47097

Coaches of Varsity Teams

Women's Track

Grissom, Jo Ann, 1975–76

All Big Ten Conference

Football

Dillard, Mel, 1956
Wells, Harold, 1964
Singer, Karl, 1965
King, Charles, 1965
Olion, George, 1966–67
Keyes, Leroy,[1] 1967–68
Williams, Perry, 1967–68
Armstrong, Otis,[2] 1972
Burton, Larry, 1974
Smith, Blane, 1975–76

Arnold, Reginald, 1977
Turner, Keena, 1978–79
Young, David, 1979–80
Clark, Calvin, 1979–80
Looney, James, 1980
Bryant, Steven, 1981
Benson, Cliff, 1982
Griffin, Steven, 1984
Woodson, Rod, 1984, 1986

Basketball

Merriweather, Willie, 1959
Gilliam, Herman, 1969
Kendrick, Frank, 1974
Jordan, Walter, 1977–78
Carroll, Joe Barry, 1979–80
Edmonson, Keith, 1982
Cross, Russell, 1983
Mitchell, Todd, 1986–87
Lewis, Troy, 1986

Men's Track

Gay, Stan, 1968–69
Fulton, Mel, 1969
Laing, Derek, 1978
Cammack, Ken, 1978–80, 1980–82
McNair, Alvin, 1983–84

Women's Track

Payne, Peach, 1979
Perry, Sybil, 1982–85
Netterville, Yvonne, 1983–85

All-American

Football

Wells, Harold, 1964
Singer, Karl, 1965
Charles, John, 1966
Keyes, Leroy, 1967–68
Armstrong, Otis, 1972
Young, David, 1980
Carroll, Joe Barry, 1980
Woodson, Ron, 1987

Men's Track

Adams, Nate, 1963
Gay, Stan, 1968
Burton, Larry, 1974
Cammack, Ken, 1980
McNair, Alvin, 1983

Women's Track

Payne, Peach, 1979
Russell, Lorna, 1982
Perry, Sybil, 1982
Netterville, Yvonne, 1984

Other Outstanding Athletes

Basketball

McCants, Melvin

[1] Keyes, Leroy–1967 *Chicago Tribune Trophy recipient* (given to the Most Valuable Player in the Big-Ten Conference)
[2] Armstrong, Otis–1972 *Chicago Tribune* Trophy recipient (given to the Most Valuable Player in the Big-Ten Conference)

University of Wisconsin
Madison, Wisconsin 53711

Athletic Directors

Lee, John Robert E. (Assistant Athletic Director), 1976–84
Johnson, Dr. Diane (Assistant Athletic Director for Student Personnel Services), 1978–Present

Coaches of Varsity Teams

Football

Richardson, Les (Assistant), 1966–69
Martin, Jim (Assistant), 1970–73
Lee, John Robert E. (Assistant), 1974–75
Banks, Oree (Assistant), 1976
Jeter, Arnold (Assistant), 1977–Present
Knox, Clifford (Assistant), 1978–83
Jackson, Fred (Assistant), 1983–Present

Basketball

Cofield, William L. (Head), 1976–80
Weaver, Larry (Assistant), 1974–76
Reed, Larry (Assistant), 1976–80
McCallum, Ray (Assistant), 1984–Present

Women's Basketball

Qualls, Edwina (Head), 1976–Present
Richey-Walton, Kathy 1979–82

Women's Tennis

McKinney, Pam (Head), 1974–76

Men's Track

Dockery, Al (Assistant), 1974–Present

Women's Track

Henderson, Douglas (Assistant), 1983–Present

All Big-Ten Conference

Football

Holland, Louis, 1963
Gregory, William, 1970
Winfrey, Charles, 1970
Ferguson, Rufus, 1971–72
Snell, Ray, 1979
Sims, Darryl, 1981–82, 1984
Toon, Al, 1983–84
Johnson, Richard, 1984

Basketball

Franklin, Joe, 1968
Gaines, Arnold, 1978
Matthews, Westley, 1979
Gregory, Claude, 1981
Blackwell, Cory, 1983–84

Women's Basketball

Huff, Janet, 1984
Pruitt, Chris, 1984

Big-Ten Champions

Track

Nixon, Jesse, OD 440YD, 1963
Nixon, Jesse, ID 600YD, 1959
Pitts, Terry, ID 600YD, 1962
Higginbottom Elzie, ID OMR, 1962
Howard, Larry, ID 70YHH, 1962
Stalling, Reginald, ID OMR, 1966
Arrington, Ray, ID 880YR, 1967–69
Stalling, Reginald, ID OMR, 1966
Butler, Michael, ID 70YHH, 1967–69
Johnson, Greg, ID 70YLH, 1970
Johnson, Lawrence, ID 60YD, 1976
Higginbottom, Elzie, OD 440YD, 1963
Jackson, Aquine, OD 100YD, 1967
Arrington, Ray, OD MR, 1,500M, 880YR, 1967–69
Butler, Michael, OD 100YD, OD 120YHH, 1968–69
Bond, Michael, OD TJ, 1968–69
Hewlett, Dial, OD OMR, 1969
Floyd, Larry, OD OMR, 1969
Johnson, Greg, OD LJ, 1970
Johnson, Lawrence, OD 100MD, 200MD, OMR, 1976–77
Hands, Rich, OD 100MHH, 1977
Dixon, Leroy, OD 400MD, 1983
Toon, Al, ID TJ, 1984

All-American

Football

Withers, Ed, 1950
Johnson, Lawrence, 1978
Snell, Ray, 1979
Johnson, Richard, 1984

Track and Field

Nixon, Jesse, OD 400M, 1957
Higginbottom, Elzie, OD 400M, 1963
Poole, Rickey, ID 880YD, 1967
Butler, Michael, ID 60YDHH, 1967
Arrington, Ray, ID 1000YR, 1967–69
Arrington, Ray, OD 800M, 1968
Butler, Michael, OD 110HH, 1968
Johnson, Greg, ID LJ, 1970
Toon, Al, OD TJ, 1982–84
Toon, Al, ID TJ, 1984
Hackett, Robert, ID DMR, 1985

Wrestling

Kemp, Lee, 1975–78
Evans, David, 1979–80
Isom, Rudy, 1984

NCAA Champions

Boxing

Vernon, Cal—176 lbs., 1948
Pitts, Orville—178 lbs., 1956
McGhee, Brown—132 lbs., 1960

Madison, Wisconsin, Sports Hall of Fame (University of Wisconsin Hall of Fame)

Withers, Ed
Dockery, Al

Northwestern University
Evanston, Illinois 60201

Coaches of Varsity Teams

Football

Green, Dennis (Head), 1981–86
Peay, Francis (Head), 1986–Present

Women's Track and Cross Country

Todd, Dee, 1981–85

All Big-Ten Conference

Football

Burton, Ron, 1958–59
Kimbrough, Elbert, 1960
Echols, Fate, 1961
Lash, Jim, 1972
Craig, Steven, 1972–73
Shaw, Peter, 1975–76
Hinton, Chris, 1982
Cruise, Keith, 1984

Men's Basketball
McKinney, William, 1977

Women's Basketball
Browne, Anucha, 1983–85

All-American

Football

Burton, Ron, 1959
Hinton, Chris, 1982

Women's Basketball

Browne, Anucha, 1985

Northwestern University's Hall of Fame

Football
Burton, Ron

Track
Golliday, James

Indiana University
Bloomington, Indiana 47405

Coaches of Varsity Teams

Basketball
Wright, Joby (Assistant), 1985–Present

All Big-Ten Conference

Football

Taliaferro, George, 1948
Faison, Earl, 1960
Cunningham, Nate, 1968
Thomas, Donnie, 1975

Basketball

Garrett, William,[1] 1951
Bellamy, Walter, 1960–61
McGinnis, George, 1971
Wright, Joby, 1972
Downing, Steven,[2] 1973
Buckner, Quinn, 1974–75
May, Scott,[3] 1975–76
Woodson, Michael,[4] 1979
Thomas, Isiah, 1980–81
Tolbert, Ray,[5] 1981

All-American

Football
Taliaferro, George, 1948

Basketball

Garrett, William, 1951
Bellamy, Walter,[6] 1960–61
McGinnis, George, 1971
May, Scott, 1975–76
Thomas, Isiah,[7] 1981
Turner, Landon,[8] 1982

Track

Harris, Archie-Discus Throw

Indiana University's Hall of Fame

Basketball
Bellamy, Walter

Track

Bell, Greg[9]
Campbell, Milt[10]

Other Outstanding Athletes

Basketball

Wilkerson, Robert
Carter, Butch
Thomas, Jim
Thomas, Daryl
Smart, Keith
Garrett, Dean

[1] Garrett, William–the first black American to play basketball in the Big-Ten Conference
[2] Downing, Steven–1973 *Chicago Tribune* Trophy recipient (given to the Most Valuable Player in the Big-Ten Conference)
[3] May, Scott–1975 and 1976 *Chicago Tribune* Trophy recipient (given to the Most Valuable Player in the Big-Ten Conference); 1976 United Press International and Associated Press Player of the Year; member of the 1976 United States Olympic Basketball Team
[4] Woodson, Michael–1980 *Chicago Tribune* Trophy recipient (given to the Most Valuable Player in the Big-Ten Conference)
[5] Tolbert, Ray–1981 *Chicago Tribune* Trophy recipient (given to the Most Valuable Player in the Big-Ten Conference)
[6] Bellamy, Walter–member of the 1960 United States Olympic Basketball Team
[7] Thomas, Isiah–1981 Most Valuable Player in the Final Four Tournament; member of the 1980 United States Olympic Basketball Team
[8] Turner, Landon–(honorary)
[9] Bell, Greg–member of the 1956 United States Olympic Track and Field Team
[10] Campbell, Milt–member of the 1952 and 1956 United States Olympic Track and Field Team

Ohio State University
Columbus, Ohio 43210–1166

Athletic Directors

Delaney, Richard (Associate Director of Athletes), 1977–Present

Coaches of Varsity Teams

Women's Track and Field

Rallins, Mamie (Head), 1977–Present

Football

Hubbard, Rudy (Assistant), 1968–74

Men's Basketball

Cleamons, Jim (Assistant), 1980–86

All Big-Ten Conference

Football

Parker, Jim, 1955–56
Marshall, Jim, 1958
Warfield, Paul, 1962–63
Mayes, Rufus, 1968
Tatum, Jack, 1968–70
Brockington, John, 1970
Hicks, John, 1972–73
Colzie, Neal, 1973–74
Griffin, Archie,[1] 1973–75
Greene, Cornelius,[2] 1974–75
Johnson, Pete, 1975

Ward, Chris, 1975–77
Brown, Aaron, 1976–77
Gerald, Rod, 1977
Griffin, Ray, 1977
Murray, Calvin, 1980
Foster, Jerome, 1980–82
Spencer, Tim, 1981–82
Lane, Garcia, 1983
Byars, Keith,[3] 1983–84
Johnson, Thomas "Pepper," 1984
Carter, Chris, 1986

Men's Basketball

Cleamons, Jim, 1971
Ransey, Kelvin, 1978–80
Williams, Herb, 1980
Kellogg, Clark, 1982
Campbell, Tony, 1983–84
Stokes, Ron, 1985
Taylor, Troy, 1985
Sellers, Brad,[4] 1986
Hopson, Dennis, 1986–87

All-American

Football

Parker, Jim,[5] 1955–56
Marshall, Jim, 1958
Tatum, Jack, 1969–70
Brockington, John, 1970
Hicks, John,[6] 1972–73
Griffin, Archie,[7] 1974–75
Ward, Chris, 1976–77
Byars, Keith, 1984
Carter, Chris, 1986

Track

Whitfield, Mal,[8] 1948–49

Women's Track

Hightower, Stephanie,[9] 1978–80

Ohio State University's Hall of Fame

Football

Willis, Bill
Parker, Jim
Marshall, Jim
Warfield, Paul
Mayes, Rufus

Basketball

Cleamons, Jim

Track

Owens, Jesse
Albritton, David[9]
Whitfield, Malvin

Other Outstanding Athletes

Football

Workman, Vince

[1] Griffin, Archie–1973 and 1974 *Chicago Tribune* Trophy recipient (given to the Most Valuable Player in the Big-Ten Conference)
[2] Greene, Cornelius–1975 *Chicago Tribune* Trophy recipient (given to the Most Valuable Player in the Big-Ten Conference)
[3] Byars, Keith–1984 *Chicago Tribune* Trophy recipient (given to the Most Valuable Player in the Big-Ten Conference)
[4] Sellers, Brad–1986 Most Valuable Player in the National Invitational Tournament
[5] Parker, Jim–1956 Outland Trophy recipient
[6] Hicks, John–1973 Outland Trophy recipient; 1973 Vince Lombardi/Rotary Award recipient
[7] Griffin, Archie–1974 and 1975 Heisman Memorial Trophy recipient
[8] Whitfield, Mal–member of the 1948 United States Olympic Track and Field Team; 800 meters NCAA champion; 1948 and 1949, 1954 Sullivan Award recipient (given to the nation's top amateur athlete)
[9] Hightower, Stephanie–member of the 1980 United States Olympic Track and Field Team

Iowa University
Iowa City, Iowa 52242

Coaches of Varsity Teams

Men's Basketball

Raveling, George (Head), 1983–86

Women's Basketball

Stringer, Vivian (Head), 1983

Men's Track and Cross Country

Wheeler, Ted (Head), 1978

All Big-Ten Conference

Football

Jones, Calvin, 1953–55
Gilliam, Frank, 1956
Fleming, Willie, 1958
Jeter, Bob, 1959
Horris, Wilburn, 1960

Ferguson, Larry, 1960–62
Clemons, Craig, 1971
Rollins, Brian, 1973
Douthitt, Earl, 1974
Weiss, Leven, 1979
Mosley, Dennis, 1979
Tippett, Andre, 1981
Cole, Mel, 1981
Roby, Reggie, 1981–82
Station, Larry, 1983–84
Mitchell, Devon, 1984

Men's Basketball

Cain, Carl, 1956
Williams, Sam,[1] 1967–68
Johnson, John, 1970
Brown, Fred, 1971
Lester, Ron, 1978–79
Stokes, Greg, 1985
Marble, Roy, 1987

All-American

Football

Jones, Calvin,[2] 1954–55
Ferguson, Larry, 1960
Clemons, Craig, 1971
Roby, Reggie, 1981
Tippett, Andre, 1981
Station, Larry, 1984

Men's Basketball

Cain, Carl, 1956
Brown, Fred, 1971
Lester, Ron, 1979–80

Other Outstanding Athletes

Basketball

Payne, Michael
Horton, Ed

[1] Williams, Sam–1968 *Chicago Tribune* Trophy recipient (given to the Most Valuable Player in the Big-Ten Conference)
[2] Jones, Calvin–1955 Outland Trophy recipient

University of Illinois at Urbana-Champaign
Illinois 61820

Coaches of Varsity Teams

Men's Basketball

Yates, Tony (Assistant), 1974–83
Collins, James (Assistant), 1983–Present

Football

Solomon, Rich (Assistant), 1980–Present
Holton, Larry (Assistant), 1983

All Big-Ten Conference

Football

Owens, Ike, 1947
Caroline, J.C., 1953
Mitchell, Robert, 1955
Bennett, Tab, 1971
Beverly, Dwight, 1983
Williams, David, 1984
Hooks, Thomas, 1984
Swoope, Craig, 1983–84

Men's Basketball

Freeman, Don, 1966
Weatherspoon, Nick, 1973
Johnson, Eddie, 1981
Harper, Derek, 1983
Winters, Efrem, 1984–85
Douglas, Bruce, 1984–85
Welch, Anthony, 1985
Norman, Ken, 1986–87

Women's Basketball

Gantt, Kendra, 1982

Women's Track and Field

Washington, Bev, HJ, 1976–78
Conda, Roland, 400M, 1982–83
Grier, Gretchen, 800MR, 600YD, 1982–83
Dunlap, Kim, OD 400MR, 1983
Bass, Rachel, OD 400MR, 1983

All-American

Football

Caroline, J.C., 1953
Williams, David, 1984

Men's Basketball

Freeman, Don, 1966
Harper, Derek, 1983

Women's Track and Field

Ward, Cheryl, 3,200MR, 1982
Grier, Gretchen, 800MR, 3,200MR, 1982
Conda, Rolanda, 800MR, 1982

Other Outstanding Athletes

Football

Pearson, Preston
Perrin, Lonnie

Men's Basketball

Vaughn, Govoner[1]
Jackson, Mannie[2]
Montgomery, George
Matthews, Audie

[1] Vaughn, Govoner–one of the first black Americans to start for a University of Illinois basketball team
[2] Jackson, Mannie–one of the first black Americans to start for a University of Illinois basketball team

University of Minnesota
Minneapolis, Minnesota 55455

Coaches of Varsity Teams

Men's Basketball

Williams, James (Assistant, Interim Head Coach), 1985–86
Haskins, Clem (Head), 1986–Present

All Big-Ten Conference

Football

Zachary, Percy, 1952
Stephens, Sandy, 1961
Bell, Bob, 1961–62
Eller, Carl, 1963
Brown, Aaron, 1964–65
Williams, John, 1967
Boston, McKinley, 1967
Parsons, Ray, 1969
Simons, Keith, 1975
Barber, Marion, 1978–80
Brown, Keith, 1978
Bailey, Elmer, 1979
White, Gary, 1980
Thompson, Darryl, 1986

Men's Basketball

Hudson, Lou, 1965
Turner, Clyde, 1972
Behagan, Ron, 1973
Brewer, Jim,[1] 1973
Thompson, Mychal,[2] 1976–78
Mitchell, Darryl, 1982
Davis, Tom, 1985

University of Minnesota's Hall of Fame

Marshall, Bobby

All-American

Football

Stephens, Sandy, 1961
Bell, Robert,[3] 1961–62
Eller, Carl, 1963
Brown, Aaron, 1965

Men's Basketball

Hudson, Lou, 1965
Brewer, Jim, 1973
Behagan, Ron, 1973
Thompson, Mychal, 1978

Other Outstanding Athletes

Football

Upchurch, Rick
Dungy, Tony

Men's Basketball

Clark, Archie
Lockhart, Osborne
Williams, Ray
Tucker, Trent
Hall, Mark
Wilson, Mark

---

[1] Brewer, Jim–1972 *Chicago Tribune* Trophy recipient (given to the Most Valuable Player in the Big-Ten Conference)
[2] Thompson, Mychal–1978 *Chicago Tribune* Trophy recipient (given to the Most Valuable Player in the Big-Ten Conference)
[3] Bell, Robert–1962 Outland Trophy recipient

Michigan State University
East Lansing, Michigan 48824

Athletic Directors

Underwood, Jr., Dr. Clarence W. (Assistant Athletic Director), presently Assistant Commissioner of the Big-Ten Conference, 1971–81

Coaches of Varsity Teams

Women's Track and Field

Jackson, Nell (Head), 1973–77, 1979–81

Women's Track and Field, Cross Country

Dennis, Karen (Head), 1982

Football

Coleman, Don (Assistant), 1968
Lewis, Sherman (Assistant), 1969–75
Raye, James (Assistant), 1972–75
Greene, Ray (Assistant), 1976–77
Forte, Mo (Assistant), 1978–79
Willingham, Tyrone (Assistant), 1980–82
Baggett, Charles (Assistant), 1983–Present

Men's Basketball

Williams, Herb (Assistant), 1984
Perry, Derek (Assistant), 1985

All Big-Ten Conference

Football

Bolden, Leroy, 1953
Kelly, Ellison, 1957–58
Adderley, Herb, 1960
Lewis, Sherman, 1963
Rush, Jerry, 1964
Gordon, Richard, 1964
Washington, Eugene, 1965–66
Jones, Clinton, 1965–66
Smith, Charles "Bubba," 1965–66
Lucas, Harold, 1965
Webster, George, 1965–66
Thornhill, Charles, 1966
Phillips, Jesse, 1966
Bailey, Charles, 1968
Allen, Eric,[1] 1971
Dupree, Bill Joe, 1972

Clark, Gail, 1972
Jackson, Levi, 1974
Smith, Otto, 1974
Cobb, Michael, 1975–76
Hannon, Tom, 1975–76
Bethea, Larry,[2] 1977
Byrd, Eugene, 1978

All Big-Ten Conference

Football

Land, Melvin, 1978
Graves, Tom, 1978
Burroughs, James, 1981
Banks, Carl, 1981–83
White, Lorenzo, 1985
Ingram, Mark, 1986–87

Men's Basketball

McCoy, Julius, 1956
Green, John,[3] 1958–59
Walker, Horace, 1960
Washington, Stanley, 1966
Lafayette, Lee, 1969
Simpson, Ralph, 1970
Robinson, Michael, 1972–74
Hairston, Lindsay, 1974–75
Furlow, Terry, 1975–76
Johnson, Earvin,[4] 1978–79
Kelser, Gregory, 1979
Vincent, Jay, 1980–81
Smith, Kevin, 1982
Vincent, Sam, 1985
Johnson, Darryl, 1987

All-American

Football

Lewis, Sherman, 1963
Lucas, Harold, 1965
Smith, Charles "Bubba," 1965–66
Webster, George, 1965–66
Allen, Eric, 1971
Banks, Carl, 1983
White, Lorenzo, 1985

Men's Basketball

Green, John, 1959
Simpson, Ralph, 1970

Robinson, Michael, 1974
Johnson, Earvin, 1979

[1] Allen, Eric–1971 *Chicago Tribune* Trophy recipient (given to the Most Valuable Player in the Big-Ten Conference)
[2] Bethea, Larry–1977 *Chicago Tribune* Trophy recipient (given to the Most Valuable Player in the Big-Ten Conference)
[3] Green, John–1959 *Chicago Tribune* Trophy recipient (given to the Most Valuable Player in the Big-Ten Conference)
[4] Johnson, Earvin–1979 *Chicago Tribune* Trophy recipient (given to the Most Valuable Player in the Big-Ten Conference)

University of Michigan
Ann Arbor, Michigan 48109

All Big-Ten Conference

Football

Mann, Robert, 1947
Perry, Lowell, 1951
Johnson, Thomas, 1951
Walker, Art, 1952–54
Pace, James, 1957
McRae, Benjamin, 1961
Yearby, William, 1964–65
Ward, Carl, 1965
Johnson, Ron, 1967–68
Taylor, William, 1969–70
Hill, Henry, 1970
McKenzie, Reginald, 1970–71
Darden, Thomas, 1970–71
Taylor, Michael, 1971
Spearman, Clint, 1972
Logan, Randy, 1972
Brown, David, 1972–74
Franklin, Dennis, 1973
Bell, Gordon, 1975
Hicks, Dwight, 1977
Davis, Russell, 1978
Greer, Curtis, 1978–79
Woolfolk, Butch, 1979–81
Owens, Mel, 1980
Paris, Bubba, 1980–81
Carter, Anthony, 1980–82
Ricks, Lawrence, 1982–83
Humphries, Stefan, 1983
Morris, Jamie, 1985–86

Men's Basketball

Burton, Memie C., 1959
Buntin, William, 1963–65

Russell, Cazzie,[1] 1964–66
Wilmore, Henry, 1971–72
Russell, Campy,[2] 1974
Green, Rick, 1976–77
Hubbard, Phil, 1977
McGee, Michael, 1978–81
Turner, Eric, 1983
Tarpley, Roy,[3] 1985–86
Grant, Gary, 1985–87
Joubert, Antoine, 1986

Wrestling

Rawls, Jesse—167 Lbs. Champion, 1969

Baseball

Eaddy, Don, 1955

All-American

Football

Perry, Lowell, 1951
Walker, Art, 1954
Pace, James, 1957
Yearby, William, 1965
Johnson, Ron, 1968

Hill, Henry, 1970
McKenzie, Reginald, 1971
Taylor, Michael, 1971
Darden, Thomas, 1971
Logan, Randy, 1972
Brown, David, 1973–74
Carter, Anthony, 1980–82
Humphries, Stephan, 1983

Men's Basketball

Buntin, William, 1964–65
Russell, Cazzie, 1965–66
Wilmore, Henry, 1971–72
Russell, Campy, 1974
Green, Rick, 1977
Tarpley, Roy, 1985

Baseball

Eaddy, Don, 1955

[1] Russell, Cazzie–1965 and 1966 *Chicago Tribune* Trophy recipient (given to the Most Valuable Player in the Big-Ten Conference)
[2] Russell, Campy–1974 *Chicago Tribune* Trophy recipient (given to the Most Valuable Player in the Big-Ten Conference)
[3] Tarpley, Roy–1985 *Chicago Tribune* Trophy recipient (given to the Most Valuable Player in the Big-Ten Conference)

ATLANTIC COAST CONFERENCE

1. University of North Carolina, Chapel Hill
2. University of Virginia
3. Wake Forest University
4. University of Maryland, College Park
5. Georgia Institute of Technology
6. Duke University
7. Clemson University
8. North Carolina State University

University of North Carolina
Chapel Hill, North Carolina 27514

Coaches of Varsity Teams

Women's Basketball

Stroman, Debbie (Assistant), 1983

Football

Cale, Robert (Assistant), 1981–85
Gill, Ted (Assistant), 1984

All Atlantic Coast Conference

Football

Mattocks, Judge, 1969
Waddell, Charles, 1973
Betterson, James, 1974
Robinson, Ron, 1974
Powell, Delbert, 1976
Hardison, Dee, 1976–77
Broadway, Rod, 1977
Caldwell, Alan, 1977

Lawrence, Amos,[1] 1977–80
Barden, Ricky, 1978–80
Nicholson, Darrell,[2] 1980
Streater, Steve, 1980
Taylor, Lawrence,[3] 1980
Thompson, Donnell, 1980
Bryant, Kelvin, 1980–81
Fuller, William, 1981–83
Wilcher, Michael, 1982
Smith, Mark, 1983
Horton, Ethan, 1983–84

Basketball

Scott, Charles,[4] 1968–70
McAdoo, Robert,[5] 1972
Davis, Walter, 1976–77
Ford, Phil,[6] 1976–78
Wood, Al, 1979–81
Worthy, James,[7] 1981–82
Perkins, Sam,[8] 1982–84
Jordan, Michael,[9] 1983–84
Daugherty, Brad, 1985
Smith, Ken, 1985–87

Women's Basketball

Brown, Teresa, 1982–83

All-American

Football

Waddell, Charles, 1974
Hardison, Dee, 1977
Taylor, Lawrence, 1980
Fuller, William, 1982–83
Horton, Ethan, 1985

Basketball

Scott, Charles, 1969–70
Chamberlain, William, 1972
McAdoo, Robert, 1972
Ford, Phil 1976–78
Wood, Al,[10] 1980–81
Worthy, James, 1982
Perkins, Sam 1982–83
Jordan, Michael 1983–84

Smith, Ken,[11] 1985–86
Daugherty, Brad,[12] 1985

Women's Basketball

Brown, Teresa, 1984–85

Other Outstanding Athletes

Bradley, Dudley[13]

[1] Lawrence, Amos–1977 Atlantic Coast Conference Rookie of the Year
[2] Nicholson, Darrell–1978 Atlantic Coast Conference Rookie of the Year
[3] Taylor, Lawrence–1980 Atlantic Coast Conference Player of the Year
[4] Scott, Charles–1969 Everett Case Award recipient (given to the Most Valuable Player at the Atlantic Coast Conference Tournament)
[5] McAdoo, Robert–1972 Everett Case Award recipient (given to the Most Valuable Player at the Atlantic Coast Conference Tournament)
[6] Ford, Phil–1978 Atlantic Coast Conference Player of the Year, 1977 and 1978; Atlantic Coast Conference Athlete of the Year; member of the 1976 United States Olympic Basketball Team
[7] Worthy, James–1982 Everett Case Award recipient (most valuable player of the Atlantic Coast Conference Tournament)
[8] Perkins, Sam–1981 Atlantic Coast Conference Rookie of the Year; 1981 Everett Case Award recipient (Most Valuable Player of the Atlantic Coast Conference Tournament); member of the 1984 United States Olympic Basketball Team
[9] Jordan, Michael–1984 Atlantic Coast Conference Player of the Year; 1982 Atlantic Coast Conference Rookie of the Year; 1984 Atlantic Coast Conference Athlete of the Year; member of the 1984 United States Olympic Basketball Team
[10] Wood, Al–member of the 1980 United States Olympic Basketball Team
[11] Smith, Ken–Honorable Mention
[12] Daugherty, Brad–Honorable Mention
[13] Bradley, Dudley–1979 Everett Case Award recipient (Atlantic Coast Conference Tournament Most Valuable Player)

University of Virginia
Charlottesville, Virginia 22903

All Atlantic Coast Conference

Football

Davis, Harrison, 1973
Blount, Tony, 1979
Anderson, Stuart, 1980–81
Chester, Pat, 1982
Lyles, Lester, 1983
Word, Barry,[1] 1985–86

Basketball

Sampson, Ralph,[2] 1981–83
Wilson, Othell,[3] 1982–84

Baseball

Lantham, Tony, 1983

All-American

Basketball

Sampson, Ralph, 1981–83

Other Outstanding Athletes

Basketball

Drummond, Al[4]
Stroman, Debra[5]
Stokes, Ricky[6]

Football

Land, Stanley[7]
Davis, Harrison[8]
Merrit, Kent[9]
Rainey, John[10]

Men's Basketball

Edelin, Kenton

[1] Word, Barry–1985 Atlantic Coast Conference Player of the Year
[2] Sampson, Ralph–1981–83 Atlantic Coast Conference Player of the Year; 1981–83 United Press International Player of the Year; 1981–83 Associated Press Player of the Year; 1981–83 United States Basketball Writers Association Player of the Year; 1982–83 John Wooden Award recipient
[3] Wilson, Othell–Honorable Mention
[4] Drummond, Al–first black American to receive a scholarship to play basketball at the University of Virginia, 1970
[5] Stroman, Debra–first black Woman to receive a scholarship to play basketball at the University of Virginia, 1978
[6] Stokes, Ricky–received the 1984 Frances Pomeroy Naismaith Hall of Fame Award (given to the most outstanding senior male basketball player under six feet tall)
[7] Land, Stanley–one of the first black Americans to receive a scholarship to play football at the University of Virginia, 1970
[8] Davis, Harrison–one of the first black Americans to receive a scholarship to play football at the University of Virginia, 1970
[9] Merrit, Kent–one of the first black Americans to receive a scholarship to play football at the University of Virginia, 1970
[10] Rainey, John–one of the first black Americans to receive a scholarship to play football at the University of Virginia, 1970

Wake Forest University
Winston-Salem, North Carolina 27109

All Atlantic Coast Conference

Football

Hopkins, Larry, 1970–71
Gaines, Clark, 1975

McDougald, James, 1976–77, 1979
Tearry, Larry, 1977
Parker, James, 1979
Baumgardner, Wayne, 1979

Basketball

Davis, Charles,[1] 1969–71
Byers, Tony, 1973–74
Brown, Skip, 1975–77
Griffin, Rod,[2] 1976–78
Johnson, Frank, 1978–79, 1981
Teachey, Anthony, 1984
Green, Ken, 1984–85
Bogues, Tyrone "Muggsy," 1986–87

All-American

Basketball

Davis, Charles, 1971
Griffin, Rod, 1977–78
Johnson, Frank, 1981

Women's Basketball

Jackson, Keeva

Wake Forest University's Hall of Fame

Davis, Charles[3]

Other Outstanding Athletes

Basketball

Rudd, Delaney

[1] Davis, Charles–1971 Atlantic Coast Conference Player of the Year
[2] Griffin, Rod–1977 Atlantic Coast Conference Player of the Year
[3] Davis, Charles–First black American elected to the Wake Forest University Sports Hall of Fame

University of Maryland
College Park, Maryland 20740

Coaches of Varsity Teams

Football

Portee, Richard (Assistant), 1980–Present

Basketball

Dillard, Sherman (Assistant), 1980–85
Wade, Robert (Head), 1986–Present

All Atlantic Coast Conference

Football

Carter, Louis, 1973–74
Hughes, Leroy, 1975
Roy, Ken, 1976
Burress, Lloyd, 1978–80
Wysocki, Charles, 1979–80
Wilson, Eric, 1983

Basketball

Elmore, Len, 1972–74
Lucas, John, 1974–76
Brown, Owen, 1975
Howard, Maurice, 1975
Gibson, Larry, 1979
Williams, Charles "Buck," 1980–81
King, Albert,[1] 1980–81
Coleman, Ben, 1983
Branch, Adrian, 1983–85
Bias, Len,[2] 1985–86

Tennis

Lucas, John, 1974–75

All-American

Football

Carter, Louis, 1973–74
White, Walter, 1974
Hughes, LeRoy, 1975
Roy, Ken, 1976
Atkins, Steve, 1978
Burrus, Lloyd, 1978–80
Wysocki, Charles, 1979–80
Wilson, Eric, 1983

Basketball

Elmore, Len, 1974
Lucas, John, 1974–76
Gibson, Larry, 1980
King, Albert, 1980–81
Williams, Charles "Buck," 1980–81
Branch, Adrian, 1984–85
Bias, Len, 1985–86

Track

Nehemiah, Renaldo—110M, 1979–80

Other Outstanding Athletes

Football

Wilson, Tim
Hill, Greg
Covington, Keeta
Covington, Al
Kinard, Ben

Basketball

Brown, Darryl
Patton, Chris
Sheppard, Steve[3]
Graham, Ernest
Boston, Lawrence
Jones, Tom
Lewis, Derrick
Gatlin, Keith
Baxter, Jeff

[1] King, Albert–1980 Atlantic Coast Conference Player of the Year; 1980 Everett Case Award recipient (given to the Most Valuable Player at the Atlantic Coast Conference Tournament)
[2] Bias, Len–1985 Atlantic Coast Conference Player of the Year; 1986 Atlantic Coast Conference Player of the Year; 1984 Everett Case Award recipient (given to the Most Valuable Player at the Atlantic Coast Conference Tournament)
[3] Sheppard, Steve–member of the 1976 United States Olympic Basketball Team

Georgia Institute of Technology
Atlanta, Georgia 30332

Coaches of Varsity Teams

Strength Training

McCullough, William, 1975

Football

Charles, Russell (Assistant), 1975–76
Hunter, Willie (Assistant), 1977
Lavan, Al (Assistant), 1977–78
Crennel, Romeo (Assistant), 1980
Guy, John (Assistant), 1981–Present

Basketball

Jobe, Ben (Assistant), 1981–82
Clark, Perry (Assistant), 1983–Present

Women's Track and Cross Country

Todd, Dee (Head), 1985–Present

All Southeastern Independent

Football

Sims, David, 1974
Harris, Joe, 1974
Sanford, Lucius, 1975–77
Wilkes, Reggie, 1976
Ivery, Eddie Lee, 1978

All Metro Conference

Basketball

Brown, Tico, 1977
Drummer, Sam, 1978
Horton, Lenny, 1977–78

All Atlantic Coast Conference

Football

Lavette, Robert, 1984

Basketball

Salley, John, 1985
Dalrymple, Bruce,[1] 1985–86

Track

Horton, Bob, 1979
Larkin, Jeff, 1982
Stiles, Raymond, 1982
Armour, Michael, 1983–85
Bernard, Carlyle, 1983–85
Armour, Michael, 1983–85
Purvis, James, 1985
Morris, Dirk, 1985

All-American

Football

Sanford, Lucius, 1977
Bessillieu, Don, 1978

Track

Lowe, Larry, 1977–78
Hughes, Donald, 1978
Wade, Greg, 1978–79
Larkin, Jeff, 1979–80
Stiles, Raymond, 1982
Alexander, Phil, 1982
Bernard, Carlyle, 1983

Armour, Michael, 1983–84
McKay, Antonio, 1984–85
Morris, Dirk, 1985
Stanley, James, 1985

Georgia Institute of Technology's Hall of Fame

Football

Ivery, Eddie Lee

[1] Dalrymple, Bruce–1984 Atlantic Coast Conference Rookie of the Year

Duke University
Durham, North Carolina 27706

All Atlantic Coast Conference

Football

Jackson, Ernest,[1] 1971
Parker, Melvin, 1972
Clark, Ernest, 1973
Turner, Dennis, 1974
Slade, Tony, 1974–75
McGee, Carl, 1976
Tabron, Dennis, 1980–81
Jones, Cedric, 1981
Bowser, Charles, 1981
Grayson, Michael, 1983

Basketball

Banks, Eugene,[2] 1978–81
Taylor, Vince, 1982
Dawkins, John,[3] 1983–85
Amaker, Tom, 1987

Baseball

Doby, Larry, 1978–79

All-American

Football

Jackson, Ernest, 1971

Basketball

Banks, Eugene, 1981
Dawkins, John, 1985–86

Other Outstanding Athletes

Football

Dunn, Michael
Green, Jeff[4]
Benjamin, Anthony
Tilley, Emmett

Basketball

Hodge, Willie
Moses, George
Harrell, John
Henderson, David
King, Bill

Lacrosse

Henderson, Skip

Women's Basketball

Matthews, Kim

[1] Jackson, Ernest–1971 Atlantic Coast Conference Player of the Year
[2] Banks, Eugene–1978 Atlantic Coast Conference Rookie of the Year; Honorable Mention
[3] Dawkins, John–alternate member of the 1984 United States Olympic Basketball Team
[4] Green, Jeff–1976 Brian Piccolo Award recipient (given to the Atlantic Coast Conference Comeback Player of the Year)

Clemson University
Clemson, South Carolina 29631

Coaches of Varsity Teams

Football

Swinger, William (Assistant), 1973–75
Anderson, Willie (Assistant), 1975–81
McCorvey, Woodrow (Assistant), 1983–Present

Basketball

Bryant, Client (Assistant), 1977–84
Harris, Eugene (Assistant), 1984–Present
Washington, Rudy (Assistant), 1984–Present

All Atlantic Coast Conference

Football

Martin, Peanut, 1973
Anderson, Willie, 1974
Cunningham, Ben, 1975

Brooks, Jonathan, 1977
Butler, Jerry, 1977–78
Brown, Lester, 1978
Brown, Bubba, 1979
Durham, Steve, 1979
Jordan, Homer, 1981
Davis, Jeff, 1981
Tuttle, Perry, 1980–81
Bryant, Jeff, 1981
Kinard, Terry, 1981–82
Austin, Cliff, 1982
Headen, Andy, 1982
Rembert, John, 1982
Perry, William, 1982–84
Dunn, K.D., 1983
Pickett, Edgar, 1983
Robinson, James, 1983
Flager, Terrance, 1986

Basketball

Wise, Alan, 1975
Rollins, Wayne, 1975–77
Rome, Stan, 1977
Williams, Billy, 1980
Nance, Larry, 1981
Hamilton, Vincent, 1982
Grant, Horace, 1986–87

All-American

Football

Cunningham, Bennie, 1975
Butler, Jerry, 1978
Davis, Jeff, 1981
Tuttle, Perry, 1981
Bryant, Jeff, 1981
Rembert, John, 1982
Kinard, Terry, 1982
Robinson, James, 1983
Perry, William, 1984

Basketball

Rollins, Wayne, 1977

Wrestling

Loban, Noel
McGee, Herman[1]

Other Outstanding Athletes

Watson, Ron
Roulhac, Terrance
Reese, Steven
Magwood, Frank

[1] McGee, Herman–Assistant Trainer and Equipment Manager, 1948–57;
Honorary Associate of the Clemson Alumni Association; died in 1980 and was
recognized by South Carolina General Assembly with a Concurrent
Resolution

North Carolina State University
Raleigh, North Carolina 27650

Coaches of Varsity Teams

Basketball

Martin, Ray (Assistant), 1983–Present

All Atlantic Coast Conference

Football

Burden, Willie,[1] 1972–73
Brown, Ted, 1975–78
Stringer, Ralph, 1975–77
Carter, Richard, 1977
Gupton, Simon, 1978–79
Wilson, Woodrow, 1978–79
Green, Bubba, 1980
LeGrande, Donnie, 1981
McIntosh, Joe, 1981
Williams, Eric, 1982

Basketball

Heartly, Al,[2] 1971
Thompson, David,[3] 1973–75
Carr, Kenneth, 1976–77
Austin, Clyde, 1978

Whitney, Charles, 1978–80
Lowe, Sidney,[4] 1981–83
Whittenberg, Derek, 1982
Bailey, Thurl, 1983
Charles, Lorenzo, 1984–85
Washburn, Chris, 1986
Shackleford, Charles, 1987

All-American

Football

Brown, Ted, 1978

Basketball

Thompson, David, 1973–75
Carr, Kenneth, 1976
Whitney, Charles "Hawkeye,"[5] 1980
Charles, Lorenzo,[6] 1985

Other Outstanding Athletes

Football

Chesney, Clyde[7]

Basketball

McMillan, Nate
Myers, Ernest

[1] Burden, Willie–1973 Atlantic Coast Conference Player of the Year
[2] Heartly, Al–the first black American to play basketball at North Carolina
State University
[3] Thompson, David–1973, 1974, and 1975 Atlantic Coast Conference Player of
the Year; 1973 and 1975 Atlantic Coast Conference Athlete of the Year; 1974
and 1975 Associated Press Player of the Year; 1975 United Press
International Player of the Year; 1975 U.S. Basketball Writers Association
Player of the Year; Most Valuable Player in the 1974 NCAA Final Four
Tournament
[4] Lowe, Sidney–1983 Everett Case Award recipient (given to the Most Valuable
Player at the Atlantic Coast Conference Tournament)
[5] Whitney, Charles "Hawkeye"–Honorable Mention
[6] Charles, Lorenzo–Honorable Mention
[7] Chesney, Clyde–the first black American to be lettered in football at North
Carolina State University

PAC-TEN CONFERENCE

1. Stanford University
2. University of Washington
3. University of Southern California
4. University of California, Los Angeles
5. University of Arizona

6. Arizona State University
7. University of California, Berkeley
8. University of Oregon
9. Oregon State University
10. Washington State University

Stanford University
Stanford, California 94305

Athletic Directors

Johnson, Jim (Assistant to the Athletic Director)

Coaches of Varsity Teams

Track and Field

Johnson, Brooks (Head),[1] 1978–Present

Men's Basketball

Hunter, Robert (Assistant), 1982–84

All Pacific-Eight or Pacific-Ten Conference

Football

Washington, Eugene, 1967–68
Parish, Don, 1968–69
Hill, Tony, 1975
Lofton, James, 1977
Nelson, Darrin, 1977–81
Holloway, Brian, 1980
Williams, Vaughn, 1981–82
White, Vincent, 1982

Men's Basketball

Harris, Art, 1966
Belton, Kimberly, 1980
Jones, Keith, 1983

All-American

Men's Tennis

Bourne, Lloyd,[2] 1982

Women's Tennis

Morrison, Diane,[3] 1976–78

Men's Track and Field

Stoecker, Robert—Discus, 1965–66
Frische, Eric,[4] 1965

Rubin, Dale,[5] 1965
McIntyre, Robert,[6] 1965
Questad, Larry,[7] 1965

Women's Track

Jacoba, Regina—1500M, 1983–84

Other Outstanding Athletes

Football

Brown, Jackie
Barnes, Benny
Shockley, Hillary
Wilburn, Al
Tyler, Andre
Tolliver, Michael
Veris, Garin
Winsberry, John
Banks, Gordon
Harry, Emile

Men's Basketball

Tucker, Ed[8]
Griffin, Don
Perry, Wolfe

Baseball

Reynolds, Larry

Women's Basketball

Wilkes, Lucy
Smith, Louise[9]
Gore, Debbie

---

[1] Johnson, Brooks–Director of Track and Field; 1984 Head Coach of the United States Olympic Track and Field Team; first black Head Coach in Stanford University's history

[2] Bourne, Lloyd–1982 All-American Doubles Player (Partner; Peter Rennert)

[3] Morrison, Diane–1976, 1977, and 1978 All-American Doubles Player (Partner; Susie Henry); won the NCAA Doubles Championship, 1976 and 1977

[4] Frische, Eric–member of the 440-yard relay team

[5] Rubin, Dale–member of the 440-yard relay team

[6] McIntyre, Robert–member of the 440-yard relay team

[7] Questad, Larry–member of the 440-yard relay team

[8] Tucker, Ed–the first black American athlete at Stanford University, 1950–53

[9] Smith, Louise–first team, Northern California Conference, 1982

University of Washington
Seattle, Washington 98105

Administrators

Smith, Donald K. (Associate Athletic Director), 1972–Present

Coaches of Varsity Teams

Wrestling

Pleasant, Don (Head), 1974

Football

Jackson, Ray (Assistant), 1971–76

Basketball

Johnson, Robert (Assistant), 1975

All Coast

Football

Fleming, George,[1] 1960
Coffey, Junior, 1962–63
Greenlee, Tom, 1965–66
Brock, Lee, 1969
Jones, Calvin,[2] 1970–72
Jackson, Charles, 1976
Glasgow, Nesby, 1977–78
Jackson, Michael,[3] 1977–78
Lee, Mark,[4] 1979
Martin, Doug, 1978–79
Harrell, Bruce, 1979

Men's Basketball

Edwards, James, 1977

All Pacific-Eight or Pacific-Ten Conference

Men's Basketball

Edwards, James, 1977
Fortier, Paul, 1986

Track and Field

Gaines, Spider,[5] 1976

Wrestling

Pleasant, Don,[6] 1971
Renfro, Mel,[7] 1974

Gymnastics

Cooley, Melvin,[8] 1978

All-American

Football

Greenlee, Tom, 1966
Jones, Calvin, 1972

Men's Basketball

Edwards, James, 1976

Gymnastics

Cooley, Melvin, 1978

Other Outstanding Athletes

Football

Moon, Warren[9]

Basketball

Romar, Lorenzo[10]

Track

Gayton, Gary[11]
Franco, Pablo[12]

[1] Fleming, George–1960 Rose Bowl Co-Most Valuable Player
[2] Jones, Calvin–1972 University of Washington Player of the Year
[3] Jackson, Michael–1978 University of Washington Player of the Year
[4] Lee, Mark–1979 University of Washington Player of the Year
[5] Gaines, Spider–High Hurdles Champion, 1976
[6] Pleasant, Don–1971 150 Lbs. Champion
[7] Renfro, Mel–1974 177 Lbs. Champion
[8] Cooley, Melvin–1978 Horizontal Bars Champion
[9] Moon, Warren–1977 Pac-Eight Conference Co-Player of the Year; 1977 University of Washington Player of the Year; 1978 Rose Bowl Most Valuable Player
[10] Romar, Lorenzo–1980 Co-Captain
[11] Gayton, Gary–Two-Mile Run; 800 Meters
[12] Franco, Pablo–100-Meter and Mile Relay

University of Southern California
Los Angeles, California 90089–0602

Coaches of Varsity Teams

Men's Basketball

Raveling, George (Head), 1986–Present

Football and Baseball

Brown, Willie (Assistant)

Football

Jackson, John (Assistant)

Steele, Harold (Assistant)

Shaw, Nate (Assistant)

Basketball

Young, Draff (Assistant)

Washington, Rudy (Assistant)

Stewart, Stan (Assistant)

Women's Basketball

Williams, Fred (Assistant)

Football

Falks, Frank (Assistant)

Track

Davis, Leo

All Pacific-Eight or Pacific-Ten Conference

Football

Roberts, C.R., 1956

Buncom, Frank, 1961

Wilson, Ben, 1961

Brown, Willie, 1962–63

Garrett, Michael, 1963–65

Smith, Jeff, 1964–65

Walker, Jim, 1965

Shaw, Nate, 1965–66

May, Ray, 1966

McCullough, Earl, 1967

Simpson, O.J., 1967–68

Gunn, Jim, 1968–69

Cowlings, Al, 1969

Hudson, Tyrone, 1969

Davis, Clarence, 1969–70

Weaver, Charles, 1970

Hall, Willie, 1971

Young, Charles, 1972

Sims, James, 1972–73

Wood, Richard, 1972–74

Brown, Booker, 1973

Parker, Artimus, 1973

Swann, Lynn, 1973–74

Riley, Art, 1974

Powell, Ed, 1974

Phillips, Charles, 1974

Reece, Dan, 1974–75

Cobb, Marvin, 1974

Powell, Marvin, 1974–76

Jeter, Gary, 1974–76

Bell, Ricky,[1] 1975–76

Hickman, Donnie, 1976

Lewis, David, 1976

Martin, Rod, 1976

Thurman, Dennis, 1976–77

Underwood, Walter, 1977

White, Charles,[2] 1977–79

Williams, Kevin, 1978

Johnson, Dennis, 1978–79

Foster, Roy, 1979–81

Lott, Ron, 1979–80

Smith, Dennis, 1979–80

Allen, Marcus,[3] 1980

Edwards, Dennis, 1980–81

Banks, Chip, 1981–82

Slaton, Tony, 1981–82

Browner, Joey, 1982–83

Basketball

Hewitt, William, 1967–68

Calvin, Mack, 1969

Riley, Ron, 1972

Williams, Gus, 1975

Robinson, Cliff, 1978–79

Williams, Maurice, 1981–82

Anderson, Dwight, 1982

Hill, Jacque, 1983

All-American

Football

Garrett, Michael,[4] 1965

Shaw, Nate, 1966

Simpson, O.J.,[5] 1967–68

Gunn, Jim, 1969

Weaver, Charles, 1970

Young, Charles, 1972

Swann, Lynn, 1973

Brown, Booker, 1973

Parker, Artimus, 1973

Wood, Richard, 1973–74

Davis, Anthony, 1974

Bell, Ricky, 1975–76

Jeter, Gary, 1976

Thurman, Dennis, 1976–77

White, Charles,[6] 1978–79
Lott, Ron, 1980
Foster, Roy, 1981
Allen, Marcus, 1981
Banks, Chip, 1983

Basketball

Williams, Gus, 1975

Women's Basketball

McGee, Paula, 1982–83
Miller, Cheryl,[7] 1983–86
Lamb, Monica, 1987

NCAA Champions

Track and Field

McCullough, Earl—HH, 1967–68
Miller, Lennox—100MD, 1968
Edwards, Clancy—100MD, 1978
Mullins, William—400MD, 1978
Williams, Kevin—SR, 1978
Sanford, James, 1979

Other Outstanding Athletes

Baseball

Buford, Don
Wells, John
Edmonds, Stan
Fobbs, Larry

Women's Volleyball

Clark, Tracey

Women's Tennis
Allen, Leslie

Football

Jones, Jimmy

Track and Field

Cook, Darwin

[1] Bell, Ricky–1976 Pac-Eight Conference Player of the Year
[2] White, Charles–1978 and 1979 Pac-Ten Conference Player of the Year
[3] Allen, Marcus–1981 Pac-Ten Conference Player of the Year
[4] Garrett, Michael–1965 Heisman Memorial Trophy recipient
[5] Simpson, O.J.–1968 Heisman Memorial Trophy recipient; 1968 Walter Camp Award recipient
[6] White, Charles–1979 Heisman Memorial Trophy recipient; 1979 Walter Camp Award recipient

[7] Miller, Cheryl–1984 James Naismith Memorial Trophy recipient; member of the 1984 United States Olympic Basketball Team; 1985 and 1986 James Naismith Memorial Trophy recipient; 1984, 1985, and 1986 Broderick Award recipient; 1985 Wade Trophy recipient

University of California
Los Angeles, California 90024

Coaches of Varsity Teams

Basketball

Farmer, Larry (Head), 1981–84
Hazzard, Walt (Head), 1984–Present
MoCarter, Andre (Assistant)

Football

Williams, Ted (Assistant)
Jackson, Milt (Assistant)
Matthews, Billie (Assistant)
Durden, Earnel (Assistant)

All-Coast

Football

Jones, Ike, 1952

All-Pacific Coast Conference (Southern Division)

Basketball

Barksdale, Donald,[1] 1947
Minor, David, 1947–48
Moore, John, 1955
Naulls, Willie, 1955

All Pacific Coast and All Pacific-Ten Conference

Football

Loudd, Rommie, 1955
Cureton, Hardiman, 1955
Brown, Sam, 1955
Harris, Esker, 1956
Luster, Marv, 1960
Smith, Robert, 1961
Alexander, Kermit, 1962
Farr, Mel, 1965–66
Grant, Wes, 1969
Ballou, Michael, 1969

McAlister, James, 1972
Ellis, Allan, 1972
Johnson, Kermit, 1972–73
McNeill, Fred, 1973
Allen, Jimmy, 1973
Bright, James, 1973
Frazier, Cliff, 1975
Walker, Rick, 1976
Edwards, Oscar, 1976
Armstrong, Levi, 1976–77
Brown, Theotis, 1976–78
Robinson, Jerry, 1976–78
Easley, Ken, 1977–80
McNeil, Freeman, 1979–80
Eatman, Irv, 1980
Riley, Avon, 1980
Carney, Cormac, 1981–82
Morgan, Karl, 1982
Nelson, Kevin, 1983
Love, Duval, 1983
Rogers, Don, 1983
Green, Gaston, 1986

Basketball

Naulls, Willie, 1956
Taft, Morris, 1956
Torrence, Walter, 1959
Hazzard, Walter, 1963–64
Lynn, Michael, 1966
Allen, Lucius, 1967
Alcindor, Lewis,[2] 1967–69
Warren, Michael, 1968
Rowe, Curtis, 1969–71
Wicks, Sidney, 1970–71
Wilkes, Keith, 1973–74
Washington, Richard, 1976
Johnson, Marques,[3] 1976–77
Greenwood, David,[4] 1977–79
Hamilton, Roy, 1978–79
Sanders, Michael, 1981–82
Foster, Rod, 1981–83
Fields, Ken,[5] 1982–84
Jackson, Ralph, 1984
Miguel, Nigel, 1985
Miller, Reginald,[6] 1985–87
Richardson, Jerome, 1987

Baseball

Chambliss, Chris, 1969
Edwards, Michael, 1974

Track

Alexander, Kermit—TJ, 1962
Jackson, Norman—440 YRT, 1966
Copeland, Ron—HH, 1967
Smith, John—440YD, 1970
Collett, Wayne—440YD, 1971
Robinson, Reginald—440YRT, 1971
Echols, Reginald—440YRT, 1971
Edmonson, Warren—440YRT, 1971
Collett, Wayne—440YRT, 1971
Butts, James—TJ, 1972
Rich, Charles—HH, 1972
Gaddis, Ron—MR, 1972
Echols, Reginald—MR, 1972
Brown, Ben—MR, 1972
Tiff, Milan—TJ, 1973
Jackson, Clim—HH, 1975
Owens, James—HH, 1977
Thompson, Donn—MR, 1977
Myles, Bennie—MR, 1977
Banks, Willie—TJ, 1978
Brown, Eric—100M, 1981–82
Davis, Del—HJ, 1982

All-American

Football

Washington, Ken, 1939
Cureton, Hardiman, 1955
Loudd, Rommie, 1955
Alexander, Kermit, 1962
Farr, Mel, 1966
Ballou, Michael, 1969
Allen, James, 1973
Johnson, Kermit, 1973
McAlister, James, 1973
McNeil, Fred, 1973
Frazier, Cliff, 1975
Edwards, Oscar, 1976

Robinson, Jerry, 1976–78
Easley, Ken, 1978–80
McNeil, Freeman, 1980
Rogers, Don, 1983
Green, Gaston, 1986

Basketball

Naulls, Willie, 1956
Hazzard, Walter,[7] 1964
Alcindor, Lewis, 1967–69
Allen, Lucius, 1968
Rowe, Curtis, 1970
Wicks, Sidney,[8] 1970–71
Bibby, Henry, 1972
Wilkes, Keith, 1973–74
Washington, Richard, 1976
Johnson, Marques, 1977
Greenwood, David, 1978–79
Fields, Ken, 1984
Miller, Reginald, 1986–87

NCAA Champions

Track and Field

Luvalle, James,[9] 440YD, 1935
Lacefield, William, LJ, 1938
Robinson, Jackie, LJ, 1940
Brown, George,[10] LJ, 1951–52
Johnson, Jim, HH, 1960
Alexander, Kermit, TJ, 1962
Copeland, Ron, HH, 1966
Smith, John, MRT, 440YD, 1969–71
Collett, Wayne, MRT, 1969–71
Echols, Reginald, MRT, 1971–72
Edmonson, Warren, MRT, 100M, 1971–72
Butts, James, TJ, 1972
Gaddis, Ron, 1972–73
Peppers, Gordon, MRT, 1973
Tiff, Milan, TJ, 1973
Walters, Jerome, MRT, 1974
Herndon, Jerry, LJ, 1974
Owens, James, HH, 1977
Fosster, Greg, HH, 1978–80
Phillips, Andre, 1981
Davis, Del, HJ, 1982

National TAC Champions

Track and Field

Johnson, Rafer,[11] 1956–58, 1960
Smith, John, 440YD, 1970–71
Owens, James, HH, 1977
Tiff, Milan, TJ, 1977
Butts, James, TJ, 1978
Banks, Willie,[12] TJ, 1980–81, 1983
Foster, Greg,[13] HH, 1981–83

All-American

Tennis

Ashe, Arthur, Jr., 1963–65

Swimming

Silva, Chris, 1982

Women's Track

White, Sharon, 1975
Butler, Gayle, 1975
Roberson, Debra, 1976–77
Ashford, Evelyn,[14] 1976–78
Gourdine, Lisa, 1978
Warner, Cynthia, 1980
Ward, Andrea, 1980
Law, Kim, 1980
Fowler, Oralee, 1980
Cumbess, Cindy, 1980–81
Howard, Sherri, 1981
Emerson, Arlise, 1980–82
Jerald, Missy, 1981–82
Bolden, Jeannette,[15] 1981–83
Griffith, Florence,[16] 1982–83
Alston, Tonya, 1984
Joyner, Jackie,[17] 1984

All Western Collegiate Athletic Association

Women's Basketball

Thompson, Necie, 1980–83
Jones, Char, 1982–83
Joyner, Jackie, 1984

Women's Tennis

Blount, Rene, 1978

Other Outstanding Athletes

Basketball

Bunche, Dr. Ralph

Track

Bradley, Thomas

[1] Barksdale, Donald–first black American to be chosen for an Olympic team for basketball; member of the 1948 United States Olympic Basketball Team
[2] Alcindor, Lewis–aka Kareem Abdul-Jabbar; 1967 and 1969 United Press International Player of the Year; 1967 and 1969 Associated Press Player of the Year; 1967 and 1969 United States Basketball Writers Association Player of the Year
[3] Johnson, Marques–1977 Pacific-Eight Conference Player of the Year; 1977 United Press International Player of the Year; 1977 Associated Press Player of the Year; 1977 United States Basketball Writers Association Player of the Year; 1977 National Association of Basketball Coaches Player of the Year
[4] Greenwood, David–1978 Pacific-Eight Conference Player of the Year; 1979 Pacific-Ten Conference Player of the Year
[5] Fields, Ken–1983 Pacific-Ten Conference Player of the Year
[6] Miller, Reginald–1986 Pacific-Ten Conference Player of the Year
[7] Hazzard, Walter–1964 United States Basketball Writers Association Player of the Year
[8] Wicks, Sidney–1971 United States Basketball Writers Association Player of the Year
[9] Luvalle, James–member of the 1936 United States Olympic Track and Field Team
[10] Brown, George–member of the 1952 United States Olympic Track and Field Team
[11] Johnson, Rafer–Decathlon; member of the 1956 and 1960 United States Olympic Track and Field Teams
[12] Banks, Willie–member of the 1984 United States Olympic Track and Field Team
[13] Foster, Greg–member of the 1984 United States Olympic Track and Field Team
[14] Ashford, Evelyn–member of the 1984 United States Olympic Track and Field Team
[15] Bolden, Jeanette–member of the 1984 United States Olympic Track and Field Team
[16] Griffith, Florence–member of the 1984 United States Olympic Track and Field Team
[17] Joyner, Jackie–member of the 1984 United States Olympic Track and Field Team

University of Arizona
Tucson, Arizona 85721

Athletic Directors

Hopkins, Gayle (Assistant Director, Student-Athlete Services), 1983–Present

Coaches of Varsity Teams

Men's Basketball

Snowden, Fred[1] (Head), 1972–82
Byrdsong, Rick (Assistant), 1983–Present

Football

Keith, Floyd (Assistant), 1983–Present

Track and Field

Williams, Willie[2] (Head), 1970–82

All Border Conference

Football

Thompson, Bobby Lee, 1960

Men's Basketball

Johnson, Leo, 1950–51

All Western Athletic Conference

Football

Wallace, Jackie, 1971–72
Upchurch, Jim, 1974
Bell "T," 1974–75
Erby, Obra, 1975

Basketball

Norman, Coniel, 1973–74
Fleming, Al, 1974–76
Money, Eric, 1973–74
Elliott, Robert, 1975–77
Harris, Helman, 1977

All Pacific-Eight or Pacific-Ten Conference

Football

Crosby, Cleveland, 1978–79
Liggins, David, 1979–80
Hunley, Rick, 1981–82
Elliott, Sean, 1987

All-American

Football

Wallace, Jackie, 1972
Bell, "T," 1975
Oliver, Hubert, 1978–79
Crosby, Cleveland, 1979
Hunley, Rick, 1982

Men's Basketball

Elliott, Robert, 1976–77

[1] Snowden, Fred–first black head basketball coach at the University of Arizona; first black basketball coach at a major university
[2] Williams, Willie–1972 and 1973 NCAA District Seven Coach of the Year; first black head track coach at a major university

Arizona State University
Tempe, Arizona 85287

Athletic Directors

Frazier, Herman (Assistant Athletic Director), 1979–Present
Harris, Charles (Athletic Director), 1985–Present

Coaches of Varsity Teams

Wrestling

Douglas, Robert[1] (Head), 1974–Present

Football

Williams, Ivy (Assistant), 1982–Present
Shaw, Willie (Assistant), 1979–Present

All Border Conference

Football

Johnson, John Henry, 1952
Burton, Leon, 1957–58

All Western Athletic Conference

Football

Taylor, Charles, 1962–63
Lorick, Tony, 1962–63
Pitts, John, 1965
Hawkins, Ben, 1965
Culp, Curly, 1966–67
Hill, J.D., 1967–70
Malone, Art, 1968–69
Hall, Windlen, 1970
Holden, Steven, 1970–72
Green, Woody, 1971–73
McClanahan, Brent, 1972
Haynes, Michael, 1973–75
Gordon, Larry, 1975
Williams, Freddie, 1975
Jefferson, John, 1975–77
Harris, Al, 1977

Men's Basketball

Caldwell, Joe, 1963–64
Lewis, Fred, 1966
Hollins, Lionel, 1974–75
White, Rudy, 1975

All Pacific-Ten Conference

Football

Harris, Al, 1978
Riggs, Gerald, 1981
Maxwell, Vernon, 1981
Jeffcoat, Jim, 1982
Richardson, Michael, 1981–82
Clack, Darryl, 1982–83

Men's Basketball

Williams, Sam, 1981
Lister, Alton, 1981
Lever, Lafayette, 1981–82
Scott, Byron, 1983

All-American

Football

Hawkins, Ben, 1965
Culp, Curly, 1967
Malone, Art, 1969
Hill, J.D., 1970
Hall, Windlan, 1970–71
Green, Woody, 1972–73
Williams, Fred,[2] 1975
Gordon, Larry, 1975
Haynes, Michael, 1975
Jefferson, John, 1975–77
Harris, Al, 1977–78
Richardson, Michael,[3] 1980
Riggs, Gerald,[4] 1981
Maxwell, Vernon, 1982
Jeffcoat, Jim, 1982
Clack, Darryl, 1984

Men's Basketball

Williams, Sam,[5] 1981
Lister, Alton,[6] 1981
Scott, Byron, 1983

Baseball

Jackson, Reginald, 1966
McDowell, Oddibe,[7] 1984

[1] Douglas, Robert–first black head coach in the history of Arizona State University
[2] Williams, Fred–Honorable Mention
[3] Richardson, Michael–Honorable Mention
[4] Riggs, Gerald–Honorable Mention
[5] Williams, Sam–Honorable Mention
[6] Lister, Alton–Honorable Mention
[7] McDowell, Oddibe–1984 College Baseball Player of the Year; 1984 Pacific-Ten Conference Co-Player of the Year

University of California, Berkeley
Berkeley, California 97420

Coaches of Varsity Teams

Football

Johnson, John (Assistant), 1972–74
Jackson, Milton (Assistant), 1975–76
Malone, Fred (Assistant), 1977
Peay, Francis (Assistant), 1978–80
West, Charles (Assistant), 1972
Wright, Nathaniel (Assistant), 1982–83
Hardaway, Jerry (Assistant), 1984–85

Men's Basketball

Berry, William (Assistant), 1972–73
Bankhead, Robert (Assistant), 1976–77
Williams, Ronald (Assistant), 1983–85
Hodges, Morris (Assistant), 1984–85

Track

Craig, Charles (Assistant), 1970
Hunt, Ervin J. (Head), 1972–Present

All Pacific-Ten or Pacific-Eight Conference

Football

Williams, Samuel, 1954
Augustine, Irby, 1969
White, Sherman, 1970–71
Youngblood, Ray, 1970–71

Muncie, Harry Vance "Chuck," 1974–75
Deloach, Ralph, 1977
Dixon, Richard, 1980

Basketball

Schultz, Earl, 1960
Johnson, Charles, 1969
Chenier, Phil, 1971
Truitt, Ansley, 1972

Baseball

Booker, Rod, 1980

Men's Track and Field

White, Willie, 100Y, 1960
Strickland, Howard, 1974
Robinson, James, 800M, 1975
Cowling, Larry, 110MH, 1981
Bates, Paul, TJ, 1981
Robinson, Leonard, 400MH, 1983

Women's Basketball

Cook, Cynthia, 1983
Garrett, Mazetta, 1984

Women's Track

Culbaert, Connie, 1983
Arnold, Jean, 1984
Cole, Gina, 1984
Wite, Kim, 1984

Women's Tennis

Driver, Wendy, 1982

All-American

Football

White, Sherman, 1971
Muncie, Harry Vance "Chuck," 1975
Lewis, David, 1982

Baseball

Booker, Rod, 1980

Other Outstanding Athletes

Track

Williams, Archie[1]
Hart, Ed[2]

Basketball

Pressley, Robert

---

[1] Williams, Archie–member of the 1936 United States Olympic Track and Field Team
[2] Hart, Ed–member of the 1972 United States Olympic Track and Field Team

University of Oregon
Eugene, Oregon 97403

Coaches of Varsity Teams

Football

Couser, Ron (Assistant), 1971
Stratten, Ron (Assistant), 1968–72
Wade, Joe (Assistant), 1972–74
Blackburn, Carl (Assistant), 1976
Jackson, Milt (Assistant), 1977–78
Malone, Fred (Assistant), 1979–80
Skipper, Jim (Assistant), 1980–82
Owens, Robert (Assistant), 1983–84
Campbell, Gary (Assistant), 1983–84

Men's Basketball

Billingslea, Ron (Assistant), 1973–78
Kent, Ernest (Assistant), 1978–80
Jackson, Stuart (Assistant), 1983–84
Adams, Debbie (Assistant), 1983–84

All Pacific Coast, All Pacific-Eight, or All Pacific-Ten Conference

Football

Daniels, Chester, 1949
Barnes, Emery, 1952
West, Willie, 1958
Renfro, Mel, 1963
Smith, Jim "Yazoo," 1966–67
Moore, Bobby, aka Ahmad Rashad, 1969–71
Coleman, Lionel, 1970

Lewis, Reginald, 1973
Clark, Mario, 1975
Goldsmith, Vince, 1980
Brown, Steve, 1982
Barnes, Lew, 1983

Basketball

Franklin, Charles, 1957
Lee, Ron,[1] 1973–76
Ballard, Greg, 1977

Men's Track

Lewis, Woodley, NDC, BJ, 1948–50
Barnes, Emery, NDC, HJ, 1952
Davis, Otis, NDC, 220YD, 1958
Moore, Bouncey, LJ, 1970
Mack, David, 800M, 1980
Walcott, George, 200MC, 1983

Baseball

Reynolds, Donald, 1973

All-American

Football

Renfro, Mel, 1962
Moore, Bobby, 1971

Basketball

Lee, Ron, 1975
Ballard, Greg, 1977

Men's Track

Cook, Roscoe,[2] 1959
Davis, Otis,[3] 1960
Renfro, Mel, 1962
Buford, Vincent, S, 1970
Moore, Bouncy, LJ, 1970
Hearvy, Al, 1970–72
Vance, Weldon, 1971
Harris, Ivory, HH, 1971–72
Mack, Davis, 800M, 1980–81

Women's Track

Adams, Debbie,[4] 1979
Batiste, Melanie,[5] 1979–81

Massey, Rhonda,[6] 1979–80
Beasley, Queena,[7] 1983

Wrestling

Gibson, Greg, 1975

Other Outstanding Athletes

Football

Robinson, Robert[8]
Williams, Charles[9]
Lillard, Joe[10]
Glass, Leland

Basketball

Patterson, Charles[11]

Men's Basketball

Jones, Steven

[1] Lee, Ron–1976 Pacific-Eight Conference Player of the Year
[2] Cook, Roscoe–Collegiate Champion, 100-Yard Dash
[3] Davis, Otis–400 Meters; member of the 1960 United States Olympic Track and Field Team
[4] Adams, Debbie–AIAW All-American Mile Relay
[5] Batiste, Melanie–AIAW All-American Mile Relay
[6] Massey, Rhonda–AIAW All-American Mile Relay
[7] Beasley, Queena–NCAA All-American; Shot Put
[8] Robinson, Robert–competed in football, 1928–30
[9] Williams, Charles–competed in football, 1928–30
[10] Lillard, Joe–competed in football, 1931
[11] Patterson, Charles–the first black American to compete in basketball in the Pacific Coast Conference

Washington State University
Pullman, Washington 99164–1610

Coaches of Varsity Teams

Men's Basketball

Raveling, George (Head), 1973–83

Women's Basketball

Rhodes, Harold, 1982–Present

Women's Gymnastics

Sanders, Al, 1977–Present

Wrestling

Parker, Phil, 1979–Present

All Pacific-Eight or All Pacific-Ten Conference

Football

Williams, Clarence, 1964
Gaskins, Willie, 1965
Thomas, Lionel, 1969
Jackson, Bernard, 1971
Mims, Ron, 1971
Porter, Kerry, 1983
Mayes, Rueben, 1984

Basketball

Rhodes, Harold, 1977
Donaldson, James, 1978
Collins, Don,[1] 1978–80
Rison, Bryan, 1980
Harriel, Steven, 1983

Wrestling

James, Michael,[2] 1979
Ellis, Wendell,[3] 1984

All-American

Football

Mayes, Rueben, 1984

Wrestling

James, Michael, 1979
Ellis, Wendell, 1984

Basketball

Collins, Don, 1980

Washington State University's Hall of Fame

Foster, Wes
Reed, George

Other Outstanding Athletes

Football

Washington, Talmadge "Duke"
Reed, George
Jones, Andrew
Ransom, Eason
Grandberry, Ken
Harris, Tim
Williams, Mark

Basketball

Miller, Sam
Jeffries, Edgar
Davis, Ron
Hill, Angelo
House, Stuart

Baseball

Wilkins, Eric[4]

Track and Field

Foster, Wes
Richardson, Clint
Kimble, Ray
Brewster, James
Whitlock, Chris
Gordon, Lee

[1] Collins, Don–1980 Pacific-Ten Conference Player of the Year; Honorable Mention
[2] James, Michael–1979 Pacific-Ten Champion
[3] Ellis, Wendell–1984 Pacific-Ten Champion
[4] Wilkins, Eric–1977 Northern Division All-Star

Oregon State University
Corvallis, Oregon 97331

Coaches of Varsity Teams

Track

Simmons, Steven (Head), 1976–79

Football

Hilliard, Gene (Assistant), 1969–75
Shaw, Nate (Assistant), 1976–79
Ford, Robert (Assistant), 1980–81
Taylor, Lionel (Assistant), 1982–83
Brooks, Booker (Assistant), 1984

All Pacific Coast or Pacific-Ten Conference

Football

Durden, Earnel, 1956
Bates, Ted, 1958
Easley, Mel, 1969
Simmons, Victor, 1981
Ogelesby, Bryce, 1983
Bynum, Reginald, 1984

Basketball

White, Charles, 1966
Boyd, Fred, 1972
Shelton, Lonnie, 1975
Smith, Rocky, 1977
Lee, Ricky, 1978
Johnson, Steven,[1] 1979–80
Blume, Ray, 1980–81
Radford, Mark, 1981
Conner, Lester,[2] 1982
Green, A.C.,[3] 1983–84

All-American

Football

Bates, Ted, 1958

Basketball

White, Charles, 1966
Boyd, Fred, 1972
Blume, Ray, 1980
Johnson, Steven, 1980–81
Conner, Lester, 1982

Track

Turner, Willie—220 YD, 1970

[1] Johnson, Steven–1981 Pacific-Ten Conference Player of the Year
[2] Conner, Lester–1982 Pacific-Ten Conference Player of the Year
[3] Green, A.C.–1984 Pacific-Ten Conference Player of the Year

IVY LEAGUE CONFERENCE

1. Harvard University
2. Princeton University
3. Dartmouth College
4. Cornell University

5. Columbia University
6. Yale University
7. University of Pennsylvania
8. Brown University

Harvard University
Cambridge, Massachusetts 02138

Coaches of Varsity Teams

Men's Basketball

Sanders, Tom (Head), 1973–77
Roby, Peter P. (Head), 1985

All Ivy League

Men's Basketball

Lewis, Floyd, 1971

Harvard University's Hall of Fame

Cross Country

Wharton, Richard G.[1]

Other Outstanding Athletes

Men's Basketball

Brown, James[2]

[1] Wharton, Richard G.–earned varsity letters in cross country 1954–56
[2] Brown, James–played on the 1970–71 Harvard University teams

Princeton University
Princeton, New Jersey 08544

All Ivy League

Football

Isom, Robert, 1977

Basketball

Taylor, Brian,[1] 1971–72
Hill, Armond, 1975–76
Melville, Randy, 1981
Robinson, Craig,[2] 1982–83

Men's Track

Stevenson, Herman, 1970

Women's Track

Newsam, Mary Elizabeth

All-American

Basketball

Taylor, Brian, 1972

[1] Taylor, Brian–member of the Ivy League Silver Anniversary All-Star Team; Ivy League Silver Anniversary Player of the Era
[2] Robinson, Craig–1982 Ivy League Player of the Year (Co-Winner); 1983 Ivy League Player of the Year

Dartmouth College
Hanover, New Hampshire 03755

Coaches of Varsity Teams

Men's Basketball

Jackson, Marcus (Head), 1974–75
Minton, Reginald (Head), 1983–84

All Ivy League

Football

Holly, Edgar, 1965
Bogan, Willie,[1] 1970
Williams, Reginald,[2] 1973–75
Wilson, Harry, 1976
Press, Cody, 1979
Pierce, Jerry, 1980
Fernandes, Joe, 1981
Williams, Charles, 1981

Men's Basketball

Brown, James, 1973
Edmonds, Sterling, 1978
Lawrence, Larry,[3] 1979

Indoor Track

Norman, Ken, 600YDR, 1975–76
Nichols, Rich, 600YDR, 1976

Outdoor Track

Norman, Ken, 440YR, 400M, 1975–76
O'Neal, Shawn, 1,500M, 1982

All-American

Football

Williams, Reginald, 1975

Men's Basketball

Lawrence, Larry, 1979

Track

Norman, Ken, 1975–76
Nichols, Rich, 1975–76
Worrell, Carl, 1976
Coburn, Robert, 1978

Basketball

Raynor, Bill[4]
Cubas, Larry[5]

[1] Bogan, Willie–member of the Silver Anniversary All-Star Team (Second Team)
[2] Williams, Reginald–member of the Silver Anniversary All-Star Team (First Team); Ivy League Silver Anniversary Player of the Era
[3] Lawrence, Larry–1981 Ivy League Player of the Year
[4] Raynor, Bill–1972 Ivy League Rookie of the Year
[5] Cubas, Larry–1975 Ivy League Rookie of the Year

Cornell University
Ithaca, New York 14851

Coaches of Varsity Teams

Men's Basketball

Bluitt, Ben[1] (Head), 1974–81

Women's Track and Cross Country

Evans, Renee (Head), 1978–82

Women's Basketball

Anderson, Rhonda (Assistant), 1983–84

All Ivy League

Football

Jacobs, Theo, 1969
Starks, Bruce, 1974
Lee, Terry, 1977
Holland, Joe, 1978
Cotton, Virgil, 1978
Loyd, Phil, 1981
Harmon, Derrick,[2] 1982

Basketball

Morris, Gregory, 1967
Brown, Maynard, 1975
Vaughn, Bernard, 1977

All-American

Football

Harmon, Derrick, 1983

Women's Track

Roach, Palemetisa, 1975

Men's Track

Hall, Neal, 200M, 1977

Cornell University's Hall of Fame

Football

Pierce, Samuel
Talton, Ken

Basketball

Esdaile, Walter
Davis, Michael

Track

Leonard, Jim[3]

[1] Bluitt, Ben–first black head coach in Cornell University's history
[2] Harmon, Derrick–1983 Asa S. Bushnell Cup recipient
[3] Leonard, Jim–1972, 1974–75 Heptagonal Outdoor Triple Jump Champion

Columbia University—Barnard College
New York, New York 10027

Coaches of Varsity Teams

Women's Basketball

Samuel, Pat (Head, Barnard College), 1977–79

All Ivy League

Football

Parks, Jesse, 1970–71
Johnson, Charles, 1970
Evans, Michael, 1971
Gregory, Ted,[1] 1973
Jackson, Doug,[2] 1975

Basketball

McMillian, Jim,[3] 1968–70
Dotson, Heyward, 1969–70
Evans, Robert, 1973
Free, Ricky, 1977–78
Byrd, Alton,[4] 1977–79
Burnett, Darren, 1982–83

Wrestling

Thomas, Greg, 158 lbs., 1981

Fencing

Miller, Wayne, Sabre, 1978

All Eastern League

Baseball

Whilhite, Michael, 1977–78

All-American

Football

Gregory, Ted, 1973
Jackson, Doug, 1975

Men's Basketball

McMillian, Jim, 1968–70
Dotson, Heyward, 1968–70
Byrd, Alton,[6] 1978–79
Free, Ricky,[7] 1979
Burnett, Darren,[8] 1982–83

Track

Johnson, Ben, 1936
Allen, Charles, 1977

Other Outstanding Athletes

Football

Starke, George

Track

Armstrong, Paul

Fencing

Lottingham, Robert

[1] Gregory, Ted–member of the Ivy League Silver Anniversary All-Star Team (First Team)
[2] Jackson, Doug–1975 Asa S. Bushnell Cup recipient
[3] McMillian, Jim–member of the Ivy League Silver Anniversary All-Star Team (First Team); Ivy League Silver Anniversary Player of the ERA; member of the Ivy League Silver Anniversary All-Star Team (Second Team)
[4] Byrd, Alton–member of the Ivy League Silver Anniversary All-Star Team (Second Team)
[6] Byrd, Alton–Honorable Mention
[7] Free, Ricky–Honorable Mention
[8] Burnett, Darren–Honorable Mention

Yale University
New Haven, Connecticut 06250

Coaches of Varsity Teams

Men's Track and Cross Country

Calhoun, Lee (Head), 1975–80

Football

Martin, Don (Assistant), 1984–Present

All Ivy League

Football

Hill, Calvin,[1] 1967–68
Williams, Dick, 1968
Charity, Elvin,[2] 1973–74
Green, Rudy, 1974

Basketball

Graves, Earl (Butch), 1981–83

Wrestling

Traylor, Steve, 150 lbs., 1978–79
Washington, Allan, 158 lbs., 1979–80

Track

Jones, Paul, 1968
Hill, Calvin,[3] 1969
Martin, Don,[4] 1971
Osborne, Martin,[5] 1980
Profit, Eugene,[6] 1983
Miller, Larry,[7] 1984
Wiggins, Douglas,[8] 1985

Women's Track

Melton, Patricia,[9] 1981–82
Forbes, Moya,[10] 1982

All-American

Basketball

Graves, Earl "Butch,"[11] 1982–83

Women's Track

Melton, Patricia, 400MH, 1982

Other Outstanding Athletes

Basketball

Swift, Jay
Robinson, Ed

Football

Jackson, Levi[12]

Track

Motley, Wendell[13]

[1] Hill, Calvin–member of the Silver Anniversary All-Star Team (First Team); Ivy League Silver Anniversary Player of the Era
[2] Charity, Elvin–member of the Silver Anniversary Player of the Era
[3] Hill, Calvin–IC4A Long Jump Champion, Heptagonal Long and Triple Jump Champion
[4] Martin, Don–IC4A and Heptagonal Dash Champion
[5] Osborne, Martin–Steeplechase
[6] Profit, Eugene–Heptagonal Long Jump Champion
[7] Miller, Larry–Heptagonal Long Jump Champion
[8] Wiggins, Douglas–Heptagonal Long Jump Champion
[9] Melton, Patricia–400 Meter Hurdles
[10] Forbes, Moya–Indoor Heptagonal 200-Meter Champion
[11] Graves, Earl "Butch"–Honorable Mention
[12] Jackson, Levi–lettered four years; captain of the team his senior year, 1945–49
[13] Motley, Wendell–member of the 1964 United States Olympic Track and Field Team

University of Pennsylvania
Philadelphia, Pennsylvania 19104

Athletic Directors

Harris, Charles 1979–85

Coaches of Varsity Teams

Men's Basketball

Littlepage, Craig (Head), 1982–85

All Ivy League

Football

Smith, David, 1983

Men's Basketball

Calhoun, David "Corky,"[1] 1970–72
Hankinson, Phil,[2] 1972–73
Haigler, Ron,[3] 1973–75
McDonald, Keven,[4] 1976–78
Price, Anthony "Tony,"[5] 1979
Salters, James, 1980
Hall, Ken, 1981
Little, Paul,[6] 1982–83
Brown, Michael, 1983
Racine, Karl, 1984
Bromwell, Perry, 1987

All-American

Football

Bell, Edward B., 1952
Evans, Robert, 1953

Basketball

Calhoun, David, 1972

Other Outstanding Athletes

Men's Basketball

Littlepage, Craig[7]
Willis, Robert

Track and Cross Country

Cochran-Fikes, Denis Elton[8]

[1] Calhoun, David "Corky"–member of the Ivy League Silver Anniversary All-Star Team (First Team); Ivy League Silver Anniversary Player of the Era; 1972 Robert Geasey Memorial Trophy recipient (Big Five Most Valuable Player); Big-Five Hall of Fame; member of the 1970–80 Eastern College Athletic Conference All-Decade Team
[2] Hankinson, Phil–Big-Five Hall of Fame
[3] Haigler, Ron–1975 Ivy League Player of the Year; member of the Ivy League Silver Anniversary All-Star Team (First Team); Ivy League Silver Anniversary Player of the Era; Big-Five Hall of Fame
[4] McDonald, Keven–1978 Ivy League Player of the Year; member of the Ivy League Silver Anniversary All-Star Team (Second Team)
[5] Price, Anthony "Tony"–1979 Ivy League Player of the Year; member of the Ivy League Silver Anniversary All-Star Team (Second Team)
[6] Little, Paul–1982 Ivy League Co-Player of the Year
[7] Littlepage, Craig–Captain, 1973
[8] Cochran-Fikes, Denis Elton–captain of the team, 1974

Brown University
Providence, Rhode Island 02912

All Ivy League

Football

Taylor, William, 1974
Brown, Ron, 1978

Men's Basketball

Morris, Eddie, 1974

Brown, Phil, 1974–75
Saunders, Brian, 1976–77
Moss, Peter,[1] 1979–80

Other Outstanding Athletes

Basketball

Clarke, Vaughn
Armstead, Wayne

[1]Moss, Peter—1980 Ivy League Player of the Year

SOUTHWEST CONFERENCE

1. Texas Christian University
2. Rice University
3. Baylor University
4. Texas Tech University

5. Texas A&M University
6. Southern Methodist University
7. University of Texas, Austin
8. University of Houston, University Park

Texas Christian University
Fort Worth, Texas 76129

Coaches of Varsity Teams

Football

Frazier, Charles (Assistant)
Perry, Tom (Assistant)
Thomas, James (Assistant)

All Southwest Conference

Football

Davis, Charles, 1972
Washington, Stanley, 1980–81
Davis, Kenneth, 1984

Basketball

Kennedy, Eugene, 1971
Degrate, Simpson, 1972
Browder, Darrell, 1983
Lott, Carl, 1986

All-American

Football

Washington, Stanley, 1981
Davis, Kenneth, 1984

Track

Williams, Lee, 1974
Collins, William, 1974–75
Delaney, Phillip, 1974–75
McKinney, Andrew "Sam," 1975
Norris, Glen, 1975–76
Milton, Michael, 1976
Boone, Cleo, 1976
Thomas, Jerry, 1976
Epps, Phillip, 1982–83
Walker, David, 1983
Ingraham, Allen, 1983
Richard, James, 1983
Burnett, Keith, 1983–84
Cannon, Michael, 1984

Other Outstanding Athletes

Basketball

Cash, James[1]

[1] Cash, James–first black athlete to play basketball in the Southwest Conference, 1968

Rice University
Houston, Texas 77251

All Southwest Conference

Football

Vincent, Stahle, 1971
Barnes, Rodrigo, 1971
Walker, Cornelius, 1973

Basketball

Pierce, Ricky, 1980–82

All-American

Basketball

Pierce, Ricky, 1982

Baylor University
Waco, Texas 76706

Coaches of Varsity Teams

Basketball

Thomas, Roy (Assistant), 1976–80
Gentry, Alvin (Assistant), 1980–81
Procter, Joe (Assistant), 1981–Present

All Southwest Conference

Football

Dancer, Charles, 1973
Green, Gary, 1976
Singletary, Michael, 1978–80
Melontree, Andrew, 1979
Abercrombie, Walter, 1980
Gentry, Dennis, 1980
Benson, Charles, 1980–82
McNeil, Gerland, 1981–83
Anderson, Alfred, 1983
Everett, Thomas, 1986

Basketball

Bowman, Tommy, 1968–69
Chatmon, William, 1970–71
Johnson, Vinnie, 1978–79
Teagle, Terry, 1980–82

All-American

Football

Green, Gary, 1976
Singletary, Michael, 1978–80
Benson, Charles, 1982
McNeil, Gerald, 1983
Everett, Thomas, 1986

Basketball

Johnson, Vinnie, 1978

Women's Basketball

Polk, Debbie, 1981

Track and Field

Carter, Michael, 1975–76
Duncan, Davey, 1976
Reed, Scooter, 1976
Fisher, Michael, 1978
Clarke, Chris, 1978–80
Vaughn, Vance, 1980
Jefferson, Zeke, 1980–81
Davis, Bruce, 1981
McCullar, Arthur, 1981
Caldwell, Willie, 1982

Texas Tech University
Lubbock, Texas 79409

All Southwest Conference

Football

Tillman, Andre, 1973
Wallace, Kenneth, 1973
Burley, Ecomet, 1973–75
Williams, Lawrence, 1974
Issac, Larry, 1976
Howard, Thomas, 1976
Felton, Eric, 1977
Hadnot, James, 1978–79
Watts, Ted, 1980

Men's Basketball

Knolle, Gene, 1970–71
Lowery, Greg, 1972
Richardson, Ron, 1973
Bullock, Rick, 1974–76

Johnson, William, 1975
Russell, Michael, 1977–78

All-American

Football

Tillman, Andre, 1973
Howard, Thomas, 1976

Men's Track

Mays, James, 800M, 1981
Selmon, Thomas, 1981
Poyser, Delroy, 1983–84

Texas A&M University
College Station, Texas 77843–1228

Coaches of Varsity Teams

Football

Pugh, George (Assistant), 1982–Present

All Southwest Conference

Football

Gray, Tim, 1974
Bean, Bubba, 1974–75
Thomas, Pat, 1974–75
Woodard, George, 1976
Jackson, Robert, 1976
Hayes, Lester, 1976
Green, Jacob, 1978–79
Siler, Rich, 1983
Vick, Roger, 1986–87
Murray, Kevin, 1987

Men's Basketball

Davis, Barry, 1975
Parker, Sonny, 1975–76
Wright, Rynn, 1980

Baseball

Glenn, James, 1980
Metoyer, Tony, 1983

Track and Field

Harvey, Edgar, 1968
McElroy, Hugh, 1968

Mills, Curtis, 1970
Mills, Marvin, 1970
Blackmon, Willie, 1970–71
Taylor, Marvin, 1975–76
Jones, Scottie, 1975–76
Brooks, Ray, 1978
Figgs, Kent, 1978
Dickey, Curtis, 1978–80
Willis, Steven, 1979–80
Kerr, Leslie, 1979–81
Pittman, Vernon, 1979–82

Track

Jamerson, Reginald, 1980
Figgs, Karl, 1980
Washington, James, 1980–82
Gillespie, Michael, 1981–82
Austin, Darrell, 1982
Jones, Don, 1982
Tolson, Tony, 1982

All-American

Football

Thomas, Pat, 1974–75
Jackson, Robert, 1976
Green, Jacob, 1979

Track

Mills, Curtis, 1970
Dickey, Curtis, 1979–80
Henderson, Chapelle, 1983

Southern Methodist University
Dallas, Texas 75275

All Southwest Conference

Football

Levias, Jerry,[1] 1967–68
Maxson, Alvin, 1971–73
Harrison, Kenny, 1972
Roan, Oscar, 1974
Tolbert, Emanuel, 1977–78
Spivey, Lee, 1980
Armstrong, Harvey, 1980–81
Dickerson, Eric, 1981–82
Carter, Russell, 1981–83

Moten, Gary, 1981–82
Hopkins, Wes, 1982
Carter, Michael, 1983
Dupard, Reginald, 1983–84
King, Don, 1984
Beverly, Anthony, 1984

Men's Basketball

Triplett, Ruben, 1972
Hervey, Sam, 1973
Terrell, Ira, 1973–74, 1976
Wright, Carl, 1984

All-American

Football

Levias, Jerry, 1968
Tolbert, Emanuel, 1978
Armstrong, Harvey, 1981
Dickerson, Eric, 1982
Carter, Russell, 1983

Men's Track

Shaw, Rufus, 220M, 440YR, 1973–74
Pouncy, Joe, 220M, 440YR, 1973–74
Pouncy, Eugene, 100M, 440YR, 1973–74
Carter, Michael,[2] 1980

Tennis

Harmon, Rodney, 1982–83

Southern Methodist University's Hall of Fame

Levias, Jerry

[1] Levias, Jerry–the first black athlete to play football in the Southwest Conference
[2] Carter, Michael–shot put; member of the 1984 United States Olympic Track and Field Team

University of Texas at Austin
Austin, Texas 78713–7389

Coaches of Varsity Teams

Women's Basketball

Page, Rod (Head), 1973–76

All Southwest Conference

Football

Leakes, Roosevelt, 1973
Campbell, Earl, 1974–75, 1977
Clayborn, Raymond, 1975–76
Johnson, John, 1977–79
Jones, John "Lam,"[1] 1978–79
Hatchett, Derrick, 1979
Sims, Kenneth, 1980–81
Cade, Mossy, 1983
Gray, Jerry, 1983–84

Men's Basketball

Robinson, Larry, 1972–74
Baxter, Ron, 1978–80
Moore, John, 1979
Thompson, LaSalle, 1981–82

Women's Basketball

Mackey, Terri, 1983
Whaley, Esoleta, 1983
Smith, Annette,[2] 1983–84
Harris, Fran, 1984
Davis, Clarissa, 1986–87

Women's Track

Turner, Terry, MR, 440M, 1983–84
Walker, Florence, TMR, 1,600MR, 1983–84

All-American

Football

Leaks, Roosevelt, 1973
Campbell, Earl,[3] 1975–77
Johnson, John, 1978–79
Sims, Kenneth,[4] 1980–81
Cade, Mossy, 1983
Gray, Jerry, 1983–84

Women's Basketball

Mackey, Terri, 1982–83
Smith, Annette, 1983–84
Harris, Fran, 1984
Davis, Clarissa, 1986–87

Women's Track

Coleman, Robbin, 600YR, MR, 1982
Sherfield, Donna, MR, 400MR, 1982

Denny, Hollie, 400MR, 1982
Walker, Florence, MR, 1982
Turner, Terry, TJ, 1984
Johnson, Robyne, TJ, 1984

[1] Jones, John "Lam"—member of the 1976 United States Olympic Track and Field Team
[2] Smith, Annette—1983 and 1984 Southwest Conference Player of the Year
[3] Campbell, Earl—1977 Heisman Memorial Trophy recipient
[4] Sims, Kenneth—1981 Vince Lombardi Rotary Award recipient

University of Houston, University Park, Houston, Texas 77004

All Southwest Conference

Football

Whitley, Wilson, 1976
Francis, Anthony, 1976
Bass, Don, 1977
Davis, Danny, 1978
Taylor, Hosea, 1978–79
Hodge, David, 1979
Jones, Melvin, 1979
Clark, Terald, 1979
Mitchell, Leonard, 1980
Turner, Grady, 1981
Fifer, Maceo, 1981–82
Harris, Weedy, 1982
Turner, T.J., 1984

Basketball

Birdsong, Otis, 1976–77
Williams, Rob, 1980–82
Drexler, Clyde, 1983
Young, Michael, 1983–84
Franklin, Alvin, 1984–85
Winslow, Rick, 1987

All-American

Football

McVea, Warren, 1966–67
Wright, Elmo, 1970
Whitley, Wilson,[1] 1976
Jones, Melvin, 1979
Hodge, David, 1979
Mitchell, Leonard, 1980

Basketball

Hayes, Elvin, 1966–68
Taylor, Ollie, 1970
Chaney, Don, 1970
Davis, Dwight, 1972
Birdsong, Otis, 1977

Men's Track

Edwards, Rich, 1979
Lewis, Carl,[2] 1980–81
Clark, Cletus, 1981
Floyd, Stanley, 1982
Ketchum, Anthony, 1982
McNeil, Mark, 1982
Berry, Andre, 1982
Young, Charles, 1982
Baptiste, Kirk, 1983
Criddle, Byron, 1983

Women's Track

Clary, Rachel, 1981
Lavallias, Pat, 1982
Jefferson, Darlene, 1982
Lewis, Carol, 1982
Sutton, Valarie, 1982
Mastin, Tara, 1983

Other Outstanding Athletes

Basketball

Dunbar, Louis
Rose, Cecile
Winslow, Rick
Micheaux, Larry

Women's Volleyball

Crokett, Rita[3]
Hyman, Flo[4]
Magers, Rose[5]

[1] Whitley, Wilson—1976 Vince Lombardi/Rotary Award recipient
[2] Lewis, Carl—member of the 1984 United States Olympic Track and Field Team
[3] Crockett, Rita—member of the 1984 United States Olympic Volleyball Team
[4] Hyman, Flo—member of the 1984 United States Olympic Volleyball Team
[5] Magers, Rose—member of the 1984 United States Olympic Volleyball Team

ATLANTIC-TEN CONFERENCE

1. West Virginia University
2. St. Bonaventure University
3. Temple University
4. Duquesne University

5. Rutgers University
6. University of Massachusetts
7. University of Rhode Island
8. St. Joseph's University

West Virginia University
Morgantown, West Virginia 26507

Coaches of Varsity Teams

Football

Simmons, Robert (Assistant)
Ford, Garrett (Assistant)

Basketball

Robinson, Jackie Joe (Assistant)

All Southern Conference

Football

Ford, Garrett,[1] 1965–66
Crennell, Carl, 1967

Basketball

Williams, Ron,[2] 1966–68

All Atlantic-Ten Conference

Basketball

Robertson, Anthony, 1977
Robinson, Maurice, 1977–78
Moore, Lowes, 1978–80
Todd, Russell, 1981–83
Jones, Greg,[3] 1981–83
Rowe, Lester, 1984–85

All-American

Football

Talley, Darryl, 1982

Basketball

Williams, Ron, 1968
Jones, Greg,[3] 1983

West Virginia University's Hall of Fame

Williams, Ron
Jester, Robert

Other Outstanding Athletes

Football

Braxton, Jim
Buggs, Dan

Basketball

Robinson, Will
Prue, Darryl

Head Trainers

Ford, Bill (Graduate Assistant)
Davis, Jackie (Student Trainer)

[1] Ford, Garrett–1966 Southern Conference Co-Player of the Year
[2] Williams, Ron–1968 Southern Conference Athlete of the Year; 1968 Southern Conference Player of the Year
[3] Jones, Greg–1982 Atlantic-Ten Conference Player of the Year; 1983 Atlantic-Ten Conference Co-Player of the Year; Honorable Mention

St. Bonaventure University
St. Bonaventure, N.Y. 14778

All Atlantic-Ten Conference

Basketball

Belcher, Earl,[1] 1980–81
Jones, Mark, 1982–83

All-American

Basketball

Stith, Tom, 1961
Lanier, Robert, 1969–70
Sanders, Greg, 1978
Belcher, Earl, 1981

Other Outstanding Athletes

Basketball

Crawford, Fred[2]
Gantt, Matt
Stith, Tom
Hagan, Glenn[3]
Harrod, Delmar

Track

Major, Charles[4]

[1] Belcher, Earl–Honorable Mention
[2] Crawford, Fred–sixth all-time leading scorer in Saint Bonaventure University's history
[3] Hagan, Glenn–all-time assist leader in Saint Bonaventure Univesity's history
[4] Major, Charles–National Indoor High Jump Champion

Temple University
Philadelphia, Pennsylvania 19122

Coaches of Varsity Teams

Men's Basketball

Chaney, John,[1] (Head), 1983–Present

Track

Alexander, Charles (Head), 1977–Present

Women's Lacrosse

Green, Tina Sloan (Head), 1975–Present

Women's Gymnastics

Hurley, Evelyn (Head), 1976–80

Women's Fencing

Franke, Nikki (Head), 1972–Present

Women's Swimming

Cunningham, Malachi (Head), 1985

All Atlantic-Ten Conference

Men's Basketball

Stansbury, Terence,[2] 1983–84
Hall, Granger,[3] 1984–85
Rayne, Charles, 1985
Blackwell, Nate,[4] 1986–87

All-American

Men's Basketball

Lear, Hal, 1956
Rodgers, Guy,[5] 1957–58
Hall, Granger, 1982, 1984–85
Stansbury, Terence, 1984
Rayne, Charles,[6] 1985

Football

Singletary, William, 1972
Young, Anthony, 1984
Bowles, Todd, 1984
Palmer, Paul, 1986

Women's Basketball

Stephens, Marilyn, 1984

Gymnastics

Hill, Mel, 1972

Temple University's Hall of Fame

Football

Robinson, Tex
Cosby, William[7]
Council, Don[8]
Singletary, William

Basketball

Lear, Hal[9]
Rodgers, Guy
Williams, Jim[10]
Baum, John[11]
Broookins, Clarence
Johnson, Ollie[12]

[1] Chaney, John–1985 Atlantic-Ten Conference Coach of the Year
[2] Stansbury, Terence–1983 Robert Geasey Memorial Trophy recipient (Big-Five Most Valuable Player); 1984 Atlantic-Ten Conference Player of the Year
[3] Hall, Granger–1985 Atlantic-Ten Conference Player of the Year; Honorable Mention
[4] Blackwell, Nate–1987 Atlantic-Ten Conference Player of the Year
[5] Rodgers, Guy–1956-58 Robert Geasey Memorial Trophy recipient (Big-Five Most Valuable Player); Big-Five Hall of Fame
[6] Rayne, Charles–Honorable Mention
[7] Cosby, William–also competed in track and field
[8] Council, Don–aka Dhamiri Abayomi; also competed in track and field
[9] Lear, Hal–Big-Five Hall of Fame
[10] Williams, Jim–Big-Five Hall of Fame
[11] Baum, John–Big-Five Hall of Fame
[12] Johnson, Ollie–Big-Five Hall of Fame

Duquesne University
Pittsburgh, Pennsylvania 15282

All Atlantic-Ten Conference

Basketball

Nixon, Norm, 1977
Arnold, Doug, 1980
Flenory, B. B., 1980
Moore, John, 1981
Dixon, Ron, 1981
Atkins, Bruce,[1] 1981–82
Sellers, Emmett, 1984

All-American

Basketball

Cooper, Charles, 1950
Ricketts, Richard, 1955
Green, Sihugo, 1955–56

Duquesne University's Hall of Fame

Kemp, Ray
Jackson, Brue
Cooper, Charles
Ricketts, Richard
Green, Sihugo
Somerset, Willie
Nixon, Norm
Durham, Jarrett
Ricketts, Dave

Other Outstanding Athletes

Johnson, Fletcher[2]

[1]Atkins, Bruce—1979 Atlantic-Ten Conference Rookie of the Year
[2]Johnson, Fletcher—sixth man on the 1952–54 basketball team

Rutgers University
New Brunswick, New Jersey 08903

Coaches of Varsity Teams

Men's Basketball

Littlepage, Craig (Head), 1985–

Women's Track

Petway, Sandra (Head), 1973–80

Track

Williams, David (Head), 1984

Football

Brown, Sampson (Assistant), 1967–72
Cottrell, Ted (Assistant), 1973–80
Mosely, Earle (Assistant), 1980–83
Moses, Wayne (Assistant), 1984

Basketball

Baker, Joseph (Assistant), 1976–79
Perry, Art (Assistant), 1973–76, 1978–Present
Nance, Stanford (Assistant), 1978–79
Sellers, Phil (Assistant), 1980–Present

Track

Williams, Robert (Assistant), 1969–74
McBryde, Ken (Assistant), 1980–84
Freeman, Ron (Assistant), 1981–82

All Atlantic-Ten Conference

Jordan, Ed, 1977
Bailey, James[1], 1977–79
Troy, Kelvin, 1980–81
Hinson, Roy, 1982–83
Battle, John, 1984–85

All-American

Football

Jennings, James "J.J.," 1973
Toran, Nate, 1975–76
Steward, Ed, 1978

Basketball

Sellers, Phil, 1975–76
Dabney, Michael,[2] 1976
Copeland, Hollis,[3] 1977
Jordan, Ed,[4] 1977
Bailey, James, 1978
Hinson, Roy,[5] 1983
Battle, John,[6] 1984–85

Lacrosse

Ford, James,[7] 1978–80
Ray, Albert, 1981–83

Track

Grimes, Brian,[8] 1981
Belin, Ron,[9] 1981
Kirkland, Walter,[10] 1981

Women's Track

McCauley, Lori, 1984

Women's Basketball

Lawrence, Lorrie,[11] 1982

Other Outstanding Athletes

Basketball

Armstead, Eugene
Roundtree, Vinnie
Cason, Les
Anderson, Abdul
Black, Kevin
Tillman, Clarence

[1] Bailey, James–1978 and 1979 Atlantic-Ten Conference Player of the Year; member of the Eastern College Athletic Conference 1970–80 All Decade Basketball Team
[2] Dabney, Michael–Honorable Mention
[3] Copeland, Hollis–Honorable Mention
[4] Jordan, Ed–Honorable Mention
[5] Hinson, Roy–Honorable Mention
[6] Battle, John–Honorable Mention
[7] Ford, James–Honorable Mention
[8] Grimes, Brian–member of the 1981 Indoor 880 Relay National Championship Team
[9] Belin, Ron–member of the 1981 Indoor 880 Relay National Championship Team
[10] Kirkland, Walter–member of the 1981 Indoor 880 Relay National Championship Team
[11] Lawrence, Lorrie–Honorable Mention

University of Massachusetts
Amherst, Massachusetts 01003

Coaches of Varsity Teams

Basketball

Wilson, Ray (Assistant)

All Atlantic-Ten Conference

Basketball

Pyatt, Michael, 1978
Green, Edwin, 1984
Neysmith, Horace, 1985

All-American

Basketball

Erving, Julius,[1] 1970–71
Skinner, Al,[2] 1974

Football

Harris, Ron, 1976
Pearson, Gary,[3] 1982
Fuller, Grady, 1982

Other Outstanding Athletes

Basketball

Eldridge, Alexander
Claiborne, Derrick
Russell, Donald
Green, Edwin
Young, Ron
Smith, Carl

[1] Erving, Julius–member of the 1970–80 Eastern College Athletic Conference All Decade Basketball Team
[2] Skinner, Al–Honorable Mention
[3] Pearson, Gary–1982 Eastern College Athletic Conference Division 1-AA Player of the Year

University of Rhode Island
Kingston, Rhode Island 02881

Coaches of Varsity Teams

Basketball

English, Claude (Head), 1981–Present

Wrestling

Adams, Carl (Head), 1979–81

Basketball

Skinner, Al (Assistant), 1984–Present

Football

James, Ron (Graduate Assistant), 1976
Franklin, Gil (Graduate Assistant), 1982

All Yankee Conference

Football

Pina, Bernie, 1953
Gibbons, Charles, 1955

Adams, Jim, 1957
Thompson, John, 1966
Keene, Everett, 1968
McGee, Molly, 1971–73
Spann, Tom, 1976
Babbit, Charles, 1978
Benson, Estes, 1978
Shaw, Leroy, 1979
Whitfield, Cal, 1981
Roberson, Jim, 1982
Pelzer, Richard, 1983
Hill, Tony, 1983
Reilly, Dameon,[1] 1983–84

Basketball

Lee, Charles, 1962
Carey, Henry, 1966
Stephenson, Art, 1967–68
Johnson, Larry, 1967–68
English, Claude, 1969–70
Adger, Nate, 1971
Tolliver, Dwight, 1971
Hickson, Phil, 1972
Williams, Sylvester "Sly," 1978–79

All Atlantic-Ten Conference

Basketball

Wright, Jimmy, 1981
Owens, Horace "Pappy," 1981–83
Upshaw, Mark, 1982

Women's Basketball

Washington, Michelle, 1984

Baseball

Hill, Tony, 1984

All-American

Football

Gibbons, Charles,[2] 1955
Pelzer, Rich,[3] 1982

Basketball

Owens, Horace "Pappy,"[4] 1973
Williams, Sylvester "Sly," 1978–79

Men's Track

Brown, Herman "Butch," 1982–83

University of Rhode Island's Hall of Fame

Football

Gibbons, Charles
Brenner, Henry
McDaniel, Everett

Basketball, Football

Pina, Bernard

Basketball

Adams, James

[1] Reilly, Dameon–1983 Yankee Conference Rookie of the Year
[2] Gibbons, Charles–Little All-American
[3] Pelzer, Rich–Honorable Mention
[4] Owens, Horace "Pappy"–Honorable Mention

St. Joseph's University
Philadelphia, Pennsylvania 19131

All East Coast Conference

Basketball

Black, Norman, 1976–79
Williams, Marcellus "Boo," 1978–81
Griffin, Luke, 1980
Warrick, Bryan, 1981–82
Clark, Jeffrey A.,[1] 1982
Costner, Anthony, 1982

All Atlantic-Ten Conference

Basketball

Costner, Anthony, 1983–84
Martin, Maurice,[2] 1984–85
Blake, Rodney, 1987

All-American

Basketball

Anderson, Clifford T.,[3] 1967
Bantom, Michael,[4] 1973

Other Outstanding Athletes

Basketball

McFarlan, Alonzo
Benson, Edward L.
Grundy, Alfred L.
Mitchell, Dr., Eric I.

[1] Clark, Jeffrey A.–1982 All Big-Five; 1982 Robert Geasey Memorial Trophy winner (Big-Five Most Valuable Player)
[2] Martin, Maurice–1986 Atlantic-Ten Conference Player of the Year
[3] Anderson, Clifford T.–1965–67 All Big-Five; 1967 Robert Geasey Memorial Trophy winner (Big-Five Most Valuable Player)
[4] Bantom, Michael–member of the 1972 United States Olympic Basketball Team; 1972–73 All Big-Five

INDEPENDENTS

1. Case Western Reserve University
2. University of Miami
3. University of Notre Dame

4. De Paul University
5. Marquette University

Case Western Reserve University
Cleveland, Ohio 44106

All Mid-American Conference

Football

Delaney, Richard, 1954

All-American

Football

Delaney, Richard, 1954

University of Miami
Miami, Florida 33124

Coaches of Varsity Teams

Football

Reed, Lambert (Assistant), 1972–74
Morand, Elroy (Assistant), 1978
Alexander, Hubbard (Assistant), 1979–Present

Men's Basketball

Bryant, Clint (Assistant), 1985–Present

Women's Basketball

Rivers, Cherry (Assistant), 1984–Present

All South Independent

Football

Bellamy, Ray, 1968
Thompson, Woody, 1973

Anderson, Otis, 1977–78
Walker, Pat, 1980
Swain, John, 1980
Belk, Rocky, 1982
Bentley, Albert, 1983
Bellinger, Rodney, 1983
Ward, Alvin, 1983
Calhoun, Ken, 1984
Smith, Willie, 1984
Highsmith, Alonzo, 1984–86
Smith, Willie, 1985
Brown, Jerome, 1986
Blades, Bennie, 1986

All-American

Football

Foreman, Chuck, 1972
Owens, Burgess, 1972
Carter, Rubin, 1974
Edwards, Eddie, 1976
Latimer, Don, 1977
Marion, Fred, 1981
Williams, Lester, 1981
Brown, Eddie, 1984
Smith, Willie, 1985
Brown, Jerome, 1986
Blades, Bennie, 1986

Other Outstanding Athletes

Baseball

Brewer, Tony[i]
Jams, Calvin

Football

Shakespere, Stanley

University of Miami's Hall of Fame

Owens, Burgess

[1] Brewer, Tony–1978–79 College Baseball World Series All Tournament Team

University of Notre Dame
Notre Dame, Indiana 46556

Coaches of Varsity Teams

Men's Basketball

Brokaw, Gary (Assistant), 1981–86

All-American

Football

Arrington, Richard, 1965
Page, Alan, 1966
Gatewood, Tom, 1970
Ellis, Clarence, 1971
Townsend, Michael, 1973
Browner, Ross,[1] 1976–77
Bradley, Luther, 1977
Fry, Willie, 1977
Fergurson, Vegas, 1979
Hunter, Tony, 1982
Pinkett, Allen, 1983–84
Brown, Tim, 1986

Men's Basketball

Hawkins, Tom, 1958–59
Carr, Austin,[2] 1970–71
Jones, Collis, 1971
Shumate, John, 1973–74
Dantley, Adrian,[3] 1975–76
Woolridge, Orlando,[4] 1982
Rivers, David,[6] 1985–86

Track

Lewis, Aubrey, 1958
Gregory, Ron, 1961
Hurd, Willliam, 1969

Wrestling

Warrington, Richard, 1965

Other Outstanding Athletes

Football

Howard, Joe

Basketball

Catlett, Sid
Brokaw, Gary
Clay, Dwight
Martin, Ray

[1] Browner, Ross–1976 Outland Trophy recipient; 1977 Vince Lombardi/Rotary Award recipient
[2] Carr, Austin–1971 United Press International Player of the Year; 1971 Associated Press Player of the Year
[3] Dantley, Adrian–1976 United States Basketball Writers Association Player of the Year; member of the 1976 United States Olympic Basketball Team
[4] Woolridge, Orlando–Honorable Mention
[5] Rivers, David–Honorable Mention

De Paul University
Chicago, Illinois 60614

All-American

Men's Basketball

Aguirre, Mark,[1] 1980–81
Cummings, Terry, 1982

Other Outstanding Athletes

Men's Basketball

Robinzine, Sr., Bill[2]
Robinzine, Jr., Bill
Garland, Gary
Bradshaw, Clyde
Patterson, Ken
Corbin, Tyrone
Comegys, Dallas
Dillard, Skip
Watkins, Curtis

[1] Aguirre, Mark–1980 United Press International and Associated Press Player of the Year; 1980 United States Basketball Writers Association Player of the Year; member of the 1980 United States Olympic Basketball Team
[2] Robinzine, Sr., Bill—played guard for DePaul, 1955–56

Marquette University
Milwaukee, Wisconsin 53233

Coaches of Varsity Teams

Women's Tennis

Randolph, Sharon (Head), 1975–Present

Men's Basketball

Cobb, Ulrich (Assistant), 1979–86

All-American

Men's Basketball

Thompson, George, 1969
Meminger, Dean, 1970–71
Chones, Jim, 1972
Lackey, Robert, 1972
Lucas, Maurice, 1974
Ellis, Maurice, 175–77
Walton, Lloyd, 1975–76
Tatum, Earl, 1976
Lee, Alfred,[1] 1977–78
Whitehead, Jerome, 1978
Worthen, Sam, 1979–80
Rivers, Glen, 1982–83

Other Outstanding Athletes

Men's Basketball

Washington, Marcus
Toone, Bernard
Lee, Oliver

Wilson, Michael
Downing, Walter

[1] Lee, Alfred–1978 James Naismith Award recipient; 1978 Adolph Rupp Award recipient

Pennsylvania State University
University Park, Pennsylvania 16802

All-American

Football

Moore, Len, 1954–55
Robinson, David, 1962
Mitchell, Lydell, 1971
Harris, Pete, 1978
Clark, Bruce,[1] 1978–79
Robinson, Mark, 1982
Jackson, Ken, 1982–83
Dozier, D.J., 1985–86

Basketball

Arnelle, Jesse, 1954–55

Other Outstanding Athletes

Football

Hoggard, Dennis
Tripplett, Wallace
Pittman, Charles
Harris, Franco[2]

[1] Clark, Bruce–1978 Vince Lombardi/Rotary Award recipient; 1979 Downtown Athletic Club Defensive Lineman of the Year; 1979 Washington Pigskin Club NCAA Lineman of the Year
[2] Harris, Franco–gained 2002 yards in his career, 1969–71

EASTERN COLLEGES ATHLETIC CONFERENCE
(North Atlantic and South Divisions)

1. Northeastern University
2. University of Richmond

3. Boston University
4. James Madison University

Northeastern University
Boston, Massachusetts 02115

Coaches of Varsity Teams

Soccer

Smith, Winston (Head), 1984

All Eastern College Athletic Conference (North Atlantic)

Men's Basketball

Harris, Peter, 1980–81
Moss, Perry,[1] 1982
Halsel, Mark,[2] 1982–84
Lewis, Reginald,[3] 1984–87
Lafleur, Andre, 1986–87

All Greater Boston Conference

Track

Little, William,[4] 1960–62
Cater, William,[5] 1964
Allen, Arthur, 1985

Other Outstanding Athletes

Football

Mitchell, Clinton[6]
Willis, Keith[7]

Hockey

Turner, Wayne[8]

[1] Moss, Perry–1982 Eastern College Athletic Conference North Atlantic Player of the Year
[2] Halsel, Mark–1984 Eastern College Athletic Conference North Atlantic Player of the Year
[3] Lewis, Reginald–1984 Eastern College Athletic Conference North Atlantic Rookie of the Year; 1985 Eastern College Athletic Conference North Atlantic Player of the Year; 1986 Eastern College Athletic Conference North Atlantic Player of the Year
[4] Little, William–1960 Indoor 45-Yard High and Low Hurdles; 1961 Indoor 45-Yard High and Low Hurdles; 1962 Indoor 45-Yard Low Hurdles Champion
[5] Cater, William–1964 45-Yard Dash Champion; 1964 440-Yard Dash Champion
[6] Mitchell, Clinton–All New England Division 1–AA, 1981
[7] Willis, Keith–All New England
[8] Turner, Wayne–Co-Captain, 1980

University of Richmond
Richmond, Virginia 23173

Coaches of Varsity Teams

Football

Rucker, Ken (Assistant), 1982–83
Slade, Larry (Assistant), 1982–83

All Southern Conference

Men's Basketball

Stewart, Aron,[1] 1973–74

All Eastern College Athletic Conference (South)

Men's Basketball

Johnson, Kelvin, 1985
Newman, John, 1985

All Colonial Athletic Association

Men's Basketball

Newman, John, 1986

All-American

Football

Redden, Barry,[2] 1981

Men's Basketball

Stewart, Aron, 1973–74
Perry, Michael, 1980

Other Outstanding Athletes

Football

Seale, Mark
Jennings, Jarvis
Evans, Reginald

[1] Stewart, Aron–1973 Malcolm U. Pitt Award recipient (given to the Player of the Year in the Southern Conference); 1974 Most Valuable Player in the Southern Conference Tournament
[2] Redden, Barry–chosen by the Richmond Touchdown Club as the 1980 Virginia Division Defensive Player of the Year

Boston University
Boston, Massachusetts 02215

Coaches of Varsity Teams

Wrestling
Adams, Carl (Head), 1980–86

Men's Basketball
Jarvis, Michael (Head), 1985–Present

All New England

Men's Basketball
Cross, Randy, 1963–65

All Yankee Conference

Men's Basketball
Boyd, Ken, 1972–74

All Eastern College Athletic Conference (North Atlantic)

Men's Basketball
Plummer, Gary, 1984
Teague, Shawn, 1984–85
Irving, Dedrick, 1986–87

All-American

Football
Taylor, Bruce, 1969–70

Boston University's Hall of Fame

Football
Thomas, Charles
Taylor, Bruce
Rucker, Reggie
Byrd, George "Butch"

Men's Basketball
Cross, Randy
Boyd, Ken

Men's Track
Thomas, John[1]
Bruce, Dr., Bernard

Other Outstanding Athletes

Basketball
Brown, Arturo

Hockey
Wright, Eddie[2]

Basketball
Chesley, Walter

[1] Thomas, John–member of the 1960 and 1964 United States Olympic Track and Field Team
[2] Wright, Eddie–first black athlete to receive a hockey scholarship to an American university; first black hockey coach at any level in America (State University of New York at Buffalo)

James Madison University
Harrisonburg, Virginia 22807

Coaches of Varsity Teams

Football
Jackson, Charles (Graduate Assistant), 1981–83

Women's Basketball
Lacey, Trudy (Graduate Assistant), 1982–83

Track and Field
Harris, Gwen (Graduate Assistant), 1981–82
Love, Flossie, 1975–78

All Virginia College Athletic Association

Football
Slayton, Bernard, 1974
Stith, Ron, 1975

Basketball
Dillard, Sherman, 1974–75

All Eastern College Athletic Conference (South)

Football
Clark, Gary,[1] 1982

Basketball
Townes, Linton, 1981–82
Newman, John, 1985

Baseball

Bundy, Lorenzo, 1980–81

All-American

Football

Slayton, Bernard,[2] 1974
Thurman, Michael,[3] 1982
Clark, Gary,[4] 1982–83
Blackwell, John,[5] 1983

Basketball

Dillard, Sherman,[6] 1974–76
Townes, Linton,[7] 1981–82

Baseball

Sample, Billy,[8] 1976
Johnson, Katherine,[9] 1977

Other Outstanding Athletes

Volleyball

Chittams, Sheila

Women's Basketball

Johnson, Katherine

Men's Basketball

Mills, Wilbert
Baker, Leon

[1] Clark, Gary–Honorable Mention
[2] Slayton, Bernard–College Division; Honorable Mention
[3] Thurman, Michael–Division 1–AA
[4] Clark, Gary–Division 1–AA; Honorable Mention
[5] Blackwell, John–Division 1–AA
[6] Dillard, Sherman–College Division; Honorable Mention
[7] Townes, Linton–University Division
[8] Sample, Billy–NCAA Division II
[9] Johnson, Katherine–Honorable Mention

INDEPENDENTS (BLACK COLLEGES)

1. University of the District of Columbia
2. Lincoln University (Pennsylvania)
3. Kentucky State University
4. Cheyney University of Pennsylvania
5. Bishop College

University of the District of Columbia
Washington, D.C. 20008

Athletic Directors

Thompson, Oliver, 1977–78
Moss, Orby, 1978–82
Moore, Charles, 1982–83
Hall, Dr. Sydney O., 1983–Present

Coaches of Varsity Teams

Football

Payne, Carroll, 1977
Vactor, Ted, 1978–83
Moore, Charles, 1983
Frazier, Dr. Robert, 1984–Present

Men's Basketball

Waters, Emory, 1977
Barnes, Dempsey, 1978–79
Jones, Wil,[1] 1979–Present

Women's Basketball

Hall, Cynthia, 1977
Montgomery, Carolyn, 1978
Stockard, Bessie, 1979–81
McGriff, Windy, 1981–82
Stockard, Bessie, 1982–84
Cummings, Bertha, 1984–Present

Men's Track

Carr, Anthony, 1977
Stewart, James, 1978–82
Mullins, Stan, 1982–Present

Women's Track

Dixon, Adrian, 1977–79
Stanton, Harry, 1980–81
Mullins, Stan, 1982–Present

Cross Country

Dixon, Adrian, 1977–79

Men's and Women's Tennis

Hall, Dr. Sydney O., 1977–Present

Women's Volleyball

Best, Emma, 1977–78
Huff, Sandra, 1979–82
Newman, Sandra, 1984

Baseball

Wilkerson, Lefty, 1977–79
Frazier, Dr. Robert, 1985

Head Trainers

Wellington, Linwood, 1977–Present

All Eastern College Athletic Conference

Basketball

Jones, Earl, 1981–84
Britt, Michael, 1982–83

All-American

Football

Chisley, Charles, 1981

Basketball

Britt, Michael, 1981–82
Jones, Earl, 1982–83

Men's Track

Brown, Anthony, ID and OD, 1985

Women's Track

Young, Elizabeth, 1979
Young, Yolene, 1985
Bushrod, Diane, 1985
Gooding, Marcelle, ID and OD, 1985

Women's Basketball

Butler, Alice, 1981

University of the District of Columbia Alumni in the National Basketball Association

Jones, Earl, Los Angeles Lakers (C,F), 1984–85
 San Antonio Spurs (C,F), 1985–86

[1] Jones, Wil–won the 1982 NCAA Division II Men's Basketball Championship

Lincoln University
Lincoln University, Pennsylvania 19352

Athletic Directors

Rivero, Manuel, 1946–77
Jones, Melvin, 1977–85
Jones, Cyrus, 1986–Present

Coaches of Varsity Teams

Football

Stackhouse, Chester R., 1948
Gardner, R.N., 1952–60

Basketball

Rivero, Manuel, 1946–47
Stackhouse, Chester R., 1947–49
Rivero, Manuel, 1951–52
Hunter, W., 1952–56
Smith, Robert, 1957–66
Laisure, Floyd, 1967–68
Laisure, W.F., 1970–74
Randolph, D., 1974–77
Jones, Melvin, 1977–86

Baseball

Rivero, Manuel, 1949–70

Golf

Gardner, Robert N., 1955–59

Wrestling

Pearcy, Milton, 1947
Gardner, R.N., 1948–69
Cook, Allen B., 1970
Balent, Thomas J., 1971–72
Wolfe, William J., 1973
Kinder, Geoffrey C., 1974–76

Women's Basketball

Sloan, Clementine, 1971–75
Nolan, Joyce, 1975–76
Crittenden, Barbara J., 1976–86

Swimming

Jones, Sandrel, 1983–86

Tennis

Walker, Alfred, 1933–34
Hawkins, Dr. Theodore, 1945–46
Ross, Hubert B., 1958–59
O'Sheields, William, 1969–71
Rivero, Manuel, 1971–78
Randolph, Doug, 1979
Jones, Melvin, 1979–86

Bowling

Gardner, R.N., 1961–62, 1966–68
Thomas, James, 1980–86

Volleyball

White, Jean A., 1970–86

All Central Intercollegiate Athletic Association

Football

Bridgeforth, Sidney, 1946–47
Cowles, James, 1952

All Tournament Team

Basketball

Usry, James, 1946
Hall, William, 1946

All Delaware Valley Conference

Basketball

Hall, David, 1963
Hall, Ken, 1968
Moon, Lawrence, 1968

PAIAW All Conference

Women's Basketball

Cooper, Sonia, 1979–81
Williams, Tonya, 1981
Clayton, Bernadete, 1983
Clark, Trina, 1983–84
Anderson, Julia, 1984

All-American (Black College)

Basketball

Wright, Sterling "Tree,"[1] 1973
Gooden, George R.,[2] 1973

Track and Field

Parker, Alfonso, 1979
Wiliams, Robert, 1979
Hunt, Ron, 1979
Blanton, John, 1980
Bailey, Walter, 1980–81
Randolph, Michael, 1980–81
Hunt, William, 1981
Auston, Jeff, 1981–83
Youngblood, Van, 1981–83
Jones, Andre, 1982
Cunningham, Louis, 1982
Hammond, Robin, 1982
Fearon, Barry, 1983
Randolph, Cary, 1984

[1] Wright, Sterling "Tree"–Honorable Mention
[2] Gooden, George R.–Honorable Mention

**Kentucky State University
Frankfort, Kentucky 40601**

Athletic Directors

Willis, William
White, Robert, 1946–49
Exum, William, 1951–77
Burns, Ralph, 1977–79
Mitchell, Ron, 1979–83
Gibson, Kenneth, 1983–Present

Coaches of Varsity Teams

Football

White, Robert M., 1946
Taylor, Randolph, 1947–50
Edwards, George, 1951–56
Gilliam, Joseph, 1957–58
Taylor, Sam, 1958–62
Whedbee, Mel, 1962–66
Bates, Charles, 1966–69
Smith, Leroy, 1969–82
Mitchell, Ron, 1982
Kirksey, Larry, 1983
Williamson, William, 1984–Present

Men's Basketball

Kean, Henry Arthur
Fletcher, Joseph G., 1946–56

Brown, James B., 1957–64
McClendon, John, 1964–66
Williams, Robert D., 1966–67
Mitchell, Lucius, 1967–75
Oliver, James V., 1975–78
Thread, Floyd, 1978–80
McKinnie, Silas, 1980–81
Mitchell, Ron, 1981–82
Lykins, John, 1982–83
Skaggs, Richard, 1983–86
Peck, Paul, 1986–Present

Women's Basketball/Volleyball

Russell, Corneith, 1963–81
Mitchell, Ron, 1981

Track

Gibson, Kenneth, 1967–69
Taylor, C. Randolph
Exum, William
Taylor, C. Randolph

All Mid-Western Conference

Football

Corbin, Richard "Nick," 1946–48
Howard, Fred "Train," 1947
French, John, 1947
Sanders, Mack, 1947
Hanley, Alvin, 1947–48, 1950
Daniels, Harvey, 1948
Jackson, Pierre, 1948
Spurlin, James "Spike," 1948
Traylor, Eugene, 1950
Allen, Arthur, 1950
Fulgham, Joe, 1950
Singleton, Harvey, 1950–51
Cameron, Eugene, 1951
Jones, Joe, 1951
Jameson, Max, 1957
Harper, Samuel, 1962
Williamson, Thomas, 1962–63
Harts, Preston, 1962–63
Ricks, McCoy, 1963
Dennis, Cleotha, 1963
Jones, Clarence, 1963
White, Lee, 1963
Rhodes, Robert, 1964
Young, Larry, 1964

Jones, Melvin, 1964
White, William, 1964

Basketball

Gray, Grant, 1946
Robinson, Harold "Dribble," 1948
Dixon, Luther "Chest," 1947–49
Roberts, Richard, 1949
Stewart, Thomas L., 1958

All-American (Black College)

Football

Williamson, James, 1946
Jackson, Pierre "Red," 1948
Corbin, Richard "Chick," 1948
Hanley, Alvin, 1948
Daniels, Harry, 1948
Martin, D'Artagnan, 1970
Epps, Wiley, 1972
Oliver, Frank, 1974

All-American (NAIA)

Basketball

Grant, Travis, 1970–72
Smith, Elmore, 1970–72
Sibert, Sam, 1972
Carmichael, Harvey, 1974
Cunningham, Gerald, 1975–77
Linder, Lewis, 1975
Bates, Billy Ray, 1977–78

Track and Cross Country

Knox, Donald, 1964
Harris, Rudy, 1964
Ewing, Richard, 1964
Bradford, Mackey, 1965
Mullins, Stan, 1965
Kemp, James, 1967
Ray, Clarence, 1967
Wallace, Craig, 1968
Gary, Phillip, 1968
Penn, James, 1969
Jordan, Steven, 1970–72
Pinkston, Allen, 1970–71
Garrett, Dick, 1971
Murphy, Ronald, 1971
Stallworth, Charles, 1971

Colbert, Tom, 1972
Taylor, Charles, 1975
Williams, Randy, 1975–76
Abaernathy, Mel, 1975–76
Nichols, Willie, 1976
Anderson, Greg, 1976–77
Myree, Craig, 1976–77
Grimes, Hamil, 1976–78
Small, Trevor, 1977

Kentucky State University's Hall of Fame

Adams, Sam
Bailey, Melvin
Bumphas, Alphonso
Coleman, William
Corbin, Richard
Cyrus, Warren
Davidson, William
Edwards, George
Evans, James
Francis, Jewel
George, Warren
Glover, James
Hanley, Alvin
Hardin, Robert
Hunt, Leonard
Jackson, Pierre
Jones, Asbury
Kean, Henry Arthur
Kendall, Joseph
Livisay, Charles
Millere, Leon
Overstreet, Louis
Passmore, Norman
Phillips, Robert
Reed, William
Richardson, Robert
Rogers, Redford
Scaife, William
Stubblefield, Robert
Sykes, Harry
Thurman, Hoy
Toomer, Eugene
Trawick, Herbert
West, W.A.
Williamson, James
Page, Herbert

Thompson, Robert
Miller, Loraine
Dowery, Robert L.
Peoples, James
Roach, Sanford
Colins, Elmer C.
Chambers, James
Clairborne, Clifford
Hackett, J. Waymon
Singleton, Harvey
Golden
Wallace, Craig
Whitney, David
Frazier, James
Harts, Preston
Alexander, Ernest
Jones, Clarence
Merritt, John
Holloway, John
Barnes, Walter
Moses, Irving
Scott, George

Kentucky State Alumni in the National Football League

McKinney, Royce, Buffalo Bills, (DB), 1975
Oliver, Frank, Buffalo Bills, (DB), 1975;
    Tampa Bay Buccaneers, (DB), 1976
Rogers, Willie, Houston Oilers, 1972–75
Kenerson, John, Los Angeles Rams, (T), 1960
Martin, D'Artagnan, New Orleans Saints, (DB), 1971–72

Kentucky State Alumni in the National Basketball Association

Smith, Elmore, Buffalo Braves, (C), 1971–73;
    Milwaukee Bucks, (C), 1975–77;
    Cleveland Cavaliers, (C), 1977–81
Sibert, Sam, Kansas City Kings, (G), 1973
Grant, Travis, A.B.A., Indiana Pacers, (F), 1975–76
Theard, Floyd, A.B.A., Denver Nuggets (G), 1969–70
Bates, Billy Ray, Portland Trailblazers, (G), 1979–82;
    Washington Bullets, (G), 1982–83
A.B.A.-American Basketball Association

**University of Pennsylvania, at Cheyney
Cheyney, Pennsylvania 19319**

Athletic Directors

Wilson, Wade, 1951–56
O'Sheilds, William, 1956–65
Jones, Willard, 1965–67
Blitman, Harold, 1967–69
Lawrence, Edwin, 1967–69
Hinson, Andrew, 1969–Present

Women's Athletic Association Directors

Dudley, Mildred B., 1946–67
Terrell, Pheon, 1967–Present

Coaches of Varsity Teams

Men's All Sports

Johnson, Rufus C., 1946–47
O'Sheilds, William, 1947–56

Football

Stevenson, James, 1956–66
Hatcher, Cleophus C., 1966–68
Reed, Frederick, 1969–72
Williams, Joe, 1972–78

Men's Basketball

O'Shields, William, 1956–63
Blitman, Harold, 1964–68
Coma, Anthony S., 1969–71
Chaney, John, 1972–82

Men's Track

O'Shields, William, 1956–63
Davis, Ira, 1967–68
Scott, John, 1968–70
Thorpe, Noah H., 1971

Women's All Sports

Dudley, Mildred, 1946–63

Women's Basketball

Dudley, Mildred, 1965–66
Bembry, Joyce, 1967–68
Spencer, Deborah, 1969–70
Stringer, Vivian, 1971–82

Women's Volleyball

Dudley, Mildred, 1965–66
Barton, Margaret, 1967–70
Stringer, Vivian, 1971–82

Men's Cross Country

O'Shields, William, 1956–63

All Pennsylvania State College Conference

Football

Webster, Arnold,[1] 1955
Washington, James,[2] 1955
Davidson, Milton,[3] 1955
Frazier, Marvin, 1972
Scott, Harold, 1972
Purnell, Garnett, 1972
Clark, Robert, 1972
Zachary, Antonio,[4] 1972
Allen, Arthur, 1972
Anderson, Steven, 1972
Armstrong, William, 1973

Basketball

Washington, Tom, 1966
Booker, Harold, 1968
Fillmore, Greg,[5] 1968
Wilson, James, 1969
Eldridge, Leroy, 1971
Kirkland, Charles, 1972
Allen, William, 1973
Bell, Leon, 1973

Men's Track and Field

Williams, Jimmy,[6] 1965
Jones, Charles,[7] 1966
Kennard, David,[8] 1966
Allen, Glenn,[9] 1966–68

All-American (Small College)

Football

Covert, Alonzo, 1970
Frazier, Marvin, 1972
Henry, Arthur, 1973

Basketball

Kirkland, Charles, 1972
Fields, Andrew, 1979
Melton, George, 1981–82

Women's Basketball

Walker, Valerie, 1981–82
Laney, Yolanda, 1984

University of Pennsylvania at Cheyney Alumni in the National Basketball Association

Fillmore, Greg, New York Knicks (C), 1970–72

[1] Webster, Arnold–Honorable Mention
[2] Washington, James–Honorable Mention
[3] Davidson, Milton–Honorable Mention
[4] Zachary, Antonio–Honorable Mention
[5] Fillmore, Greg–New York Knicks, 1970–72
[6] Williams, Jimmy–1965 Pennsylvania State College Conference 100-Yard Dash Champion
[7] Jones, Charles–1966 Pennsylvania State College Conference Shot Put Champion
[8] Kennard, David–1966 Pennsylvania State College Conference Long Jump Champion
[9] Allen, Glenn–Cross Country Pennsylvania State College Conference Champion; 1966 One and Three-Mile Run

Bishop College
Dallas, Texas 75241

Coaches of Varsity Teams

Football

Little, Shannon D., 1946–51
Brinkley, Edward, 1951–52
James, Jesse, 1952–53
Gaines, Vincent, 1953–54
Jones, Nathan "Tricky," 1955–56
Fisher, Dwight "Red,"[1] 1957–73
Little, Shannon D., 1974–75
Peters, Edmond, 1975–76
Fisher, Dwight "Red," 1976–77
Johnson, Raymond, 1977–78
Jones, James, 1978–Present

Basketball

Jones, Emanuel, 1965–69
Alexander, Charles, 1969–72
Allen, Roy-Fisher Dwight, 1973
Lilly, Sylvester "Ben," 1974–Present

Women's Basketball

Robinson, Myrtle, 1978–82
Young, Abron, 1982–Present

Baseball

Garcia, Charles, 1968
Allen, Roy, 1970–74
Lane, Fred, 1975–76
Blackwell, James, 1977
Sheppard, Jerrell, 1978
Moten, Bobby, 1979–83
Young, Abron, 1983–Present

Softball

Johnson, James, 1982
Moten, Bobby, 1984

Men's and Women's Volleyball

Robinson, Myrtle, 1978–Present

All Southwestern Athletic Conference

Basketball

Fairfax, Ruben, 1952
Seabeery, Leland, 1953–55

All-District, All-Star (NAIA)

Football

Anderson, Lee G., 1966
Merchant, George, 1966
Vickers, Lester, 1966
McCoy, Arthur, 1969
McCoy, John, 1969
Jones, James L., 1969
O'Neil, Herbert, 1970
Ross, Jimmy, 1970
Thomas, Issac, 1971
Howard, Leroy, 1971
Sullivan, Grady, 1972
Bryant, Richard, 1973
Hinson, Robert, 1973
Dixon, George, 1978
Bush, John, 1978
Ina, Welby, 1978
Bolden, Willie, 1980
Harris, Edmond, 1980
Payne, Darryl, 1980
Nelson, Carlton, 1981

Basketball

Prince, Edgar, 1966
Smith, Paul, 1966
Lee, Raymond, 1966
Carter, Curtis, 1971
Collins, Willie, 1973

Baseball

Young, Abron, 1971
Seals, Teddie, 1973
Dennis, Ivan, 1974
Neisbet, Walter, 1983

All-American (NAIA)

Football

Holligan, Henry, 1964
Thomas, Emmit, 1965
West, Sam, 1965
Moten, Bobby, 1968
Johnson, Leonard, 1971
McGee, Anthony, 1971
Roberts, Robert, 1974
Brooks, Robert, 1975
Glanton, Derrick, 1977
Harris, Edmond, 1980
Nelson, Carlton, 1981
Devaugh, Dennis, 1981
Hill, Will, 1984
Parker, David, 1984
Jude, Charles, 1984
Phillips, Charles, 1984
Johnson, Kenneth, 1984

Basketball

Lilly, Sylvester, 1968
Perry, Leonard, 1968
Collins, Willie, 1973
Govan, Dwain, 1974
Lilly, Shannon, 1983
Wright, William, 1985

Women's Basketball

Shaw, Tina, 1984

Bishop College Alumni in the National Football League

Thomas, Ike, Dallas Cowboys, (DB), 1971;
  Green Bay Packers, (DB), 1972;
  Buffalo Bills, (DB), 1975
McGee, Tony, Chicago Bears, (DE), 1971–73;
  New England Patriots, (DE), 1974–81;
  Washington Redskins, (DE), 1982–84
Moten, Robert, Denver Broncos, (TE), 1968
Holigan, Henry, Houston Oilers, (RB), 1963
Thomas, Emmit, Kansas City Chiefs, (DB), 1966–78
Brooks, Robert, New York Giants, (DB), 1974–76

[1] Fisher, Dwight "Red"–NAIA Coach of the Year

West Virginia State College
Institute, West Virginia 25112

Coaches of Varsity Teams

Football

Cardwell, Mark, 1946–58
Burris, Chester A., 1959–62
Banks, Oree, 1977–83
Moore, Clifton, 1984–Present

Basketball

Cardwell, Mark, 1946–64
Enty, Frank, 1964–67
Gray, Grant, 1968–69
Burris, Chester A., 1969–72
Price, Curtis, 1973–76

Men's Track

Cardwell, Mark, 1947–60
Price, Roderick, 1960–63
Wilson, James, 1963–66
Harris, D., 1964–66
Smiley, Jr., Glover L., 1983–Present

Women's Track

Smiley, Jr., Grover L., 1979–85

Tennis

Hawkins, Charles C., 1947
Mills, Marvin, 1960–64

Golf

Hawkins, Dr., Charles, 1966
Burris, Chester, 1980–81

Baseball

Cardwell, Mark, 1945–54
Gray, Grant, 1954–66

Women's Basketball

Walker, Bettie J., 1954–58
Clark, Barbara, 1959–74
Randall, Edgar, 1981–85

Swimming

Eubanks, Audrey, 1947
Burris, Chester A., 1957, 1964
Wilson, James, 1960

Cross Country

Smiley, Jr., Grover L., 1984–85

Bowling

Oden, Barbara, 1971–73
Oden, Joe, 1975–79

All Central Intercollegiate Athletic Association

Football

Gamble, Samuel, 1946
Gilliam, Joseph, 1948
Fairfax, Charles, 1949
Dillard, Clyde, 1949
Wickcliffe, Edward, 1949
Clark, Clarence, 1949
Miller, Samuel, 1950
Hawkins, Robert, 1951, 1953
Curry, Rupert, 1951
Smith, Willie, 1951
Henderson, Herbert, 1952
Boone, James, 1953–54
Scruggs, O'Bryant, 1955

All Central Intercollegiate Athletic Association All Tournament

Basketball

Clark, Clarence,[1] 1948–49
Wilson, Robert, 1948–50
Lloyd, Earl, 1948–50
Perry, Ervell, 1951
Morris, James,[2] 1951

All-American (Black College or NAIA)

Football

Graves, Alfred, 1948–50
Ellis, Oliver, 1948–50
Curry, Rupert, 1948–50
Hightower, Walter, 1948–50
Miller, Samuel, 1948–50
Reed, Vincent, 1950
Newkirk, George, 1951–52
Brown, Roland, 1958
Carter, Robert, 1958
Ravenel, Harry, 1960
Dawson, Lummell, 1960
Spradley, Milton, 1960
Meadows, Floyd, 1960
Morgan, Chris, 1960
Gallion, Michael, 1960
Harris, Raymond, 1960

Baseball

Justice, Frank, 1959
Jackson, Al, 1959
Baldwin, Clyde, 1959
Goff, Wilbur, 1960–61
Hartney, Joe, 1962
Jeter, James, 1962

Basketball

Moore, Ron, 1987

All West Virginia Intercollegiate Athletic Conference

Track

Tucker, Sam
Harris, Michael
Pleasant, Ronald
Smiley, Jr., Glover L.
Early, Jerry
Taylor, Tyrone
Hairston, Kevin
Hairston, Mark
Curry, Sam
Tyson, Michael
Lester, Scott
Gilmer, Rodney
Davis, Ivory
Smith, Manuel

Savage, Bernard
Cunningham, Leon
Reid, Walter[3]
Lipscomb, William
Crummel, George[4]
Bethel, Antoine
Alcorn, James
Smith, Manuel

Football

Jones, Cornelius, 1962–64
Gilmore, John, 1963
Bailey, James, 1964
McClothen, Fred, 1964
Nicholson, William, 1967
Dawson, Joe, 1967
Simms, Jim, 1968
Ellis, Charles, 1969
Logan, Dick, 1969
Lee, Ed, 1970
Yalentine, John, 1973–74
Swann, Steve, 1974
Davidson, Ray, 1975
Anderson, Warren, 1975–76
Berger, Marshall, 1976
Atkinson, Terry, 1977–79
Weaver, Anthony, 1980
Hughes, Harold, 1980
Spradley, Milton, 1980–81
Harris, Clyde, 1982
Holman, Walter, 1982
Hankerson, Rufus, 1985

Boxing

Perry, Taylor, 1959

Women's Basketball

Gordon, Donna, 1985
Battle, Maria, 1985

West Virginia State Alumni in the National Basketball Association

Lloyd, Earl, Syracuse Nationals, 1952–58;
   Detroit Pistons, 1958–60

West Virginia State College Hall of Fame

Bailey, Dr., James A.
Bates, Dr., John M.
Clark, Clarence
Harvey, Dr., Harold N.
Meadows, Floyd
Robinson, Will
Burris, Chester A.
Hale, Vasco D.
Lloyd, Earl
Wickliffe, Edward V.
Moore, Dr., Oscar A.
Harvey, Dr., Harold N.
Greene, Oliver
Stewart, Jr., Colston R.
Wilson, Robert
Reed, Vincent E.
Clark, Dr., Benjamin
Burghardt, Dr., William F.
Middleton, Fred D.
Wilson, Robert
Jackson, Dr., William S.
Gamble, Samuel A.
Richardson, Marvin H.
Scott, James L.
Henderson, Herbert H.
Moore, William George
Cardwell, Mark H.
Burroughs, Knute W.
Hamblin, Adolph P.
Bates, Pervis

[1] Clark, Clarence–1948 Most Valuable Player of the CIAA Tournament
[2] Morris, James–1951 Most Valuable Player of the CIAA Tournament
[3] Ried, Walter–1975 WVIAC Track Man of the Year
[4] Crummel, George–1973 WVIAC Track Man of the Year

Langston University
Langston, Oklahoma 73050

All Southwestern Athletic Conference

Football

Sluby, Roscoe, 1951
Desmukes, Lamar, 1951–52
Clark, George, 1952
Roach, William, 1954
Brackeen, Curtis, 1955

Luster, Al, 1955
Clay, Curtis, 1955–56

Basketball

Johnson, Jack, 1952
Holmes, Clint, 1953
Dixon, Jay, 1955

Langston University Alumni in the National Football League

Bassett, Maurice, Cleveland Browns, (RB), 1954–56
Henderson, Thomas, Dallas Cowboys, (L), 1975–79;
   Houston Oilers, (L), 1980
   San Francisco 49ers, (L), 1980
Payne, Ken, Green Bay Packers, (WR), 1974–77
Howard, Eugene, Los Angeles Rams, (DB), 1971–72
Lawson, Odell, New England Patriots, (RB), 1970–71;
   New Orleans Saints, (RB), 1973–74
Williams, Gerald, Washington Redskins, (DB), 1976–78;
   San Francisco 49ers, (DB), 1979–80;
   St. Louis Cardinals, (DB), 1980
Williams, Ed, Tampa Bay Buccaneers, (RB), 1976–77

Tennessee State University
Nashville, Tennessee 37203

Athletic Directors

Kean, Henry Arthur, Sr., 1943–55
Gentry, Howard Cornelius, Sr., 1955–76
Adams, Sterling (Interim), 1983–

Coaches of Varsity Teams

Football

Kean, Henry A.—Member of the Helms Foundation College
Football Hall of Fame, 1946–54
Gentry, Howard, 1955–60
Simmons, Lawrence, 1961–62
Merritt, John, 1963–84
Thomas, William, 1984–Present

Basketball

Kean, Henry A., 1945–48
Matthews, Shelton, 1949
Kean, Henry A., 1950
Cash, Clarence, 1951–54

McLendon, John B., 1954–59
(McLendon, John B., 1959 NAIA Coach of the Year-first black
coach to serve on The United States Olympic Committee
1966.)
Hunter, Harold, 1959–68
Martin, Ed., 1972 NCAA College Division Coach of the Year,
1968–85
Meyers, Ed, 1985–86
Reid, Larry, 1986–Present

Swimming

Hughes, Thomas A., 1945–69

Baseball

Simmons, Lawrence E., 1954–56
Whitmon, Raymond, 1956
Robinson, Allen Steven, 1977–Present

Men's Track

Harris, Tom, 1945–55
Mack, Richard L., 1955–57
Kemp, Raymond, 1957–61
Stevens, Willie, 1961

Women's Track

Harris, Tom, 1946–50
Kincaide, C.J., 1950–53
Temple, Edward S., 1960 and 1964 United States Olympic
Women's Track and Field Coach, 1953
member of The United States Olympic Committee from
1960–80.

All Midwestern Conference

Football

Drummond, Robert, 1946
Smith, William, 1946
Washington, William, 1946
Taylor, Nathaniel, 1946–47
Herndon, Joe, 1948
Wynne, Raleigh, 1948
Gilchrist, George, 1948–49
Joseph, Jesse, 1949
Nails, Clarence, 1949
Carter, Carl, 1949–50
Lacy, Lafayette, 1950
Gillespie, Walter, 1950
Tanner, Willie, 1950

Turner, Harold, 1950–51
Stokes, Theodore, 1950–52
Gaines, Clarence, 1951
Claybourne, Edward, 1951
Anderson, Paul, 1951–52
Caldwell, James, 1951–52
Maiden, Matthew, 1952
Wood, Marshall, 1952
Kimble, Roy, 1953
Brownley, Clarence, 1953–54
Valentine, Fred, 1954
Champine, Daniel, 1954
Jamison, Leon, 1954–56
Howard, Clarence, 1955
Mitchell, Fay, 1955
Patton, Charles, 1955
Gavin, Charles, 1956
Suesbery, Wilbur, 1957
Wilburn, Jesse, 1957
Thomas, Woodrow, 1958
Sorrells, Calvin, 1958
Taylor, Don, 1958
Metcalfe, Fred, 1959
Arnold, Hank, 1959–61
Walker, Charles, 1959
Alexander, Hubbard, 1959–60
Balthazar, George, 1960
Ferguson, Charles, 1960

Basketball

Wilson, Clarence, 1946–47, 1949
Taylor, Nathaniel, 1946–49
Grider, Joshua, 1947–49
Lewis, Frank, 1949
Brown, Sage, 1950
Gibson, Tommy, 1950
Landry, John, 1951
Reed, Willie, 1951–53
Nesbit, Remus, 1954
Thomas, Willis, 1954
McNeal, Vernon, 1955
Kean, Henry A., Jr., 1955
Jackson, Ben, 1955–56
Barnett, Richard, 1956–59
Hamilton, Ronald, 1957–58
Barnhill, John, 1958–59
Werts, Gene, 1960

Meriwether, Porter, 1961
Johnson, Rossie, 1961
McIntyre, Larry, 1962

All-American (Black College)

Football

Washington, William, 1946
Whitmon, Raymond, 1946–47
Taylor, Nathaniel, 1946–47
Wynn, Releigh, 1947
Davis, Grannison, 1949
Gilchrist, George, 1949
Gillespie, Walter, 1950
Tanner, Willie, 1950
Turner, Harold, 1950–51
Caldwell, James, 1951–52
Maiden, Matthew, 1952
Kimble, Roy, 1953
Hairston, Perry, 1953
Patton, Charles, 1955
Buford, James, 1956
Mitchell, Fay, 1956
Gavin, Charles, 1956–57
Jamison, Leon, 1957
Walker, Charles, 1959
Balthazar, George, 1960
Reed, Robert, 1963–64
Carter, James, 1965
Dickey, Eldridge, 1965–66
Davis, Tom, 1966
Dixon, Harvey, 1966
Johnson, Leo, 1966
Humphrey, Claude, 1966–67
Marsalis, Jim, 1968
Drungo, Elbert, 1968
Brumfield, Claude, 1969
Holland, Vernon, 1969
Jones, Joe, 1969
Reese, Wayne, 1969
Davis, David, 1970
Gilliam, Jr., Joe, 1970–71
Brown, Nathaniel, 1971
Glover, Asberry, 1971
Thaxton, James, 1971
McTorry, Charles, 1971–72
Bryant, Waymon, 1971–73

Woods, Robert, 1972
Smith, Ollie P., 1972
Jones, Ed, 1972
Holland, John, 1972
Kindle, Gregory, 1973
Elam, Cleveland, 1974
Lyons, Granville, 1974
Haigler, Allen, 1974
Dorsey, Larry, 1974–75
Mitchell, Melvin, 1975
Davis, Oliver, 1976
Hicks, Sylvester, 1976–77
McRae, Jerrold, 1976–77
Johnson, Stanley George, 1977
Johnson, Dan, 1977
Wheeler, Dwight, 1977
Elias, Homer, 1977
Lawson, Sylvester, 1977
Adams, Joe, 1977, 1979–80
Smith, John Henry, 1979
Carter, Jimmy Paul, 1979
Fitzgerald, Maurice, 1979
Ford, Aaron, 1980
Taylor, James, 1980
Dent, Richard, 1980–82
Jones, Michael, 1981
Ransom, Brian, 1981
Moore, Steven, 1982
Taylor, Malcolm, 1982–83
Tate, Golden, 1982–83
Biggles, Kenneth, 1982
Tate, Walter, 1982–83
Robinson, Roger, 1982
Elam, Onzy, 1986

Men's Basketball

Jackson, Ben, NAIA, 1955
Satterwhite, James, NAIA, 1957
Barnhill, John, NAIA, 1957–59
Barnett, Richard, NAIA, NCAA Little All-American, Associated Press, 1957–59
Werts, Gene, NAIA, 1960
Johnson, Rossie, NAIA, 1960
Merriwether, Porter, NAIA, United Press International, 1960–61
McClain, Ted, Division II, 1971
Neal, Lloyd, Division II, 1972
Robinson, Leonard, Division II, 1974

Swimming

James, Clyde, NAIA, 1960–61

Men's Track

Boston, Ralph, AAU Broad Jump, 1960–61
(member of the 1964 and 1968 United States Olympic Track and Field Team)

All-American

Patterson, Audrey, AAU, 200M Champion, 1948
(member of the 1948 United States Olympic Track and Field Team)
Reed, Emma, AAU, High Jump, 1948
(member of the 1948 United States Olympic Track and Field Team)
Patton, Jean, AAU, 200M, 1951
Faggs, Starr Mae, AAU, 100 Yard Dash, 1954–56
(member of the 1952 and 1956 United States Olympic Track and Field Team)
Daniels, Isabelle, AAU, 400M Relay Team, 1956–59
(member of the 1952 United States Olympic Track and Field Team)
Slater Jones, Barbara, AAU, 1958–59
(member of the 1960 United States Olympic Track and Field Team)
Wilburn, Margaret Matthews, AAU, Broad Jump, Sprints, 1957–59
(member of the 1956 United States Olympic Track and Field Team)
White, Willye B., AAU, Long Jump 1960, 1964, 1968 and 1974, 1956–57
member of the 1956 United States Olympic Track and Field Team)
Rudolph, Wilma, AAU, 100M Dash, Relay Team, 1956–57, 1959, 1962
(member of the 1956 and 1960 United States Olympic Track and Field Team) 1960 Helms World Trophy recipient; 1961 James A. Sullivan Award recipient; 1960 Associated Press "Female Athlete of the Year" Award recipient
Grissom, Joe Ann, AAU, Hurdles, Broad Jump, 1959–61–63
member of the 1960 United States Olympic Track and Field Team)
Hudson, Martha, AAU, 100 Yard Dash, 1959
(member of the 1960 United States Olympic Track and Field Team)
Brown Reed, Vivian, AAU, 220 Yard Dash, 200 Meter Dash, 1961–62
(member of the 1964 United States Olympic Track and Field Team)

McGuire Duvall, Edith, AAU, 100 and 200 Meter Dash, 1961, 1963, 1966
  (member of the 1964 United States Olympic Track and Field Team)
Tyus Simberg, Wyomia, AAU, 100 Yard Dash, 100 Meter Dash, 1964
  (member of the 1964 and 1968 United States Olympic Track and Field Team)
Montgomery, Eleanor, AAU, High Jump, 1966–69
  (member of the 1968 United States Olympic Track and Field Team) 1969 Norman E. Seattle Award recipient
Manning Jackson, Madeline, AAU, 400 Meter Dash, 800 Meters, 1968–72
  (member of the 1968 United States Olympic Track and Field Team)
Watson, Martha, AAU, Long Jump, 1967–69
  (member of the 1964, 1968, 1972 United States Olympic Track and Field Team)
Render, Mattilene, AAU, 60 Yard Dash, 100 Yard Dash, 1969–71
Davis Hicks, Iris, AAU, 100 Meter Dash, 1969–73
Cheesebourough, Chandra, 1979 (member of the 1984 United States Olympic Track and Field Team)

Tennessee State University's Hall of Fame

Coaches

McClendon, John B.
Gentry, Howard Cornelius
Temple, Edward Stanley
Coleman, Alvin "Cat"
Gilliam, Sr., Joe W.
Little, Shannon
Kemp, Ray
Hughes, Tom
Merritt, John Ayers
Davis, Dr., Walter S.
Bell, Julian
Kean, Henry Arthur

Sports Information Director

Carmicheal, Luther, 1932–76

Football

Drummond, Robert
Strange, Forrest
Sumrall, Frederick
Bass, William
Gilchrist, George

Taylor, Nathaniel
Whitmon, Samuel
Jamison, Leon
Marsalis, James
Holland, Vernon
Gilliam, Jr., Joe
Tucker, William
Humphrey, Claude
Elam, Cleveland
Bryant, Waymon
Jones, Ed
Dickey, Eldridge

Men's Basketball

Grider, Joshua
Buie, Boyd
Wilson, Clarence
Barnhill, John
Barnett, Richard
McClain, Theodore
Neal, Lloyd
Merriweather, Porter

Baseball

Valentine, Fred
Altmon, George
Bowens, Sam
Robinson, Allen

Men's Track

Boston, Ralph
Stevens, Willie

Women's Track

Patton, Jean
Faggs, Mae
Williams, Lucinda
Daniels, Isabelle
White, Willye B.
Hudson, Martha
Jones, Barbara
Rudolph, Wilma
McGuire, Edith
Tyvs, Wyomia
Watson, Martha
Manning, Madeline

Boxing

Cox, William

Swimming

Stewart, Frank
Jackson, Donald
Gainor, Stanley
Jones, Leroy E.
James, Clyde

The 1958–59 Men's Basketball Team; National NAIA Champions

McClendon, John B. (Head Coach)
Mack, Richard (Assistant)
Hunter, Harold (Assistant)
Clark, Robert
Barnhill,John
Johnson, Rossie
Werts, Gene
Satterwhite, James
Davis, Melvin
Barnett, Richard
Merriweather, Porter
Warley, Ben
Brown, Hillary

Tennessee State University Alumni in the National Basketball Association

Barnett, Richard, Syracuse Nationals, 1959–61;
   Los Angeles Lakers, 1962–64;
   New York Knicks, 1965–74
Meriwether, Porter, Syracuse Nationals, 1962–63
Walker, Dwight, Atlanta Hawks, 1968–69;
   A.B.A. Denver Nuggets, 1969–72
Buckhalter, Joe, Cincinnati Royals, 1961–63
Warley, Ben, Syracuse Nationals, 1962–63;
   A.B.A. Denver Nuggets, 1969–70
Robinson, Leonard, Washington Bullets, 1974–77;
   Phoenix Suns, 1978–82;
   New York Knickerbockers, 1982–85
Barnhill, John, Washington Bullets, 1966–69;
   A.B.A. Indiana Pacers, 1969–72;
   San Diego Rockets, 1967–68
McClain, Ted, A.B.A. New York Nets, 1975–76;
   Philadelphia 76ers, 1977–78;
   Buffalo Braves, 1977–78
A.B.A., American Basketball Association
Daniel, 1954
Howard, Clarence, 1955
Mitchell, Fay, 1955

SOUTHERN INTERCOLLEGIATE ATHLETIC CONFERENCE

1. Savannah State College
2. Fort Valley State College
3. Bethune-Cookman College
4. Morris Brown College

5. Alabama A&M University
6. Clark College
7. Morehouse College
8. Fisk University

Savannah State College
Savannah, Georgia 31404

Athletic Directors

Wright, Theodore, 1947–63
Frazier, Albert, 1963–81
Ellington, Russell, 1982–Present

Coaches of Varsity Teams

Football

Martin, John, 1950–52
Frazier, Albert, 1953

Pearly, Ross, 1954–56
Washington, Richard, 1957–63
Richardson, Leo,[1] 1964–68
Myles, John, 1969–76
Ellis, Jr. Frank, 1977–Present

Men's Basketball

Myles, John,[2] 1946–47
Wright, Theodore,[3] 1947–62
Frazier, Albert, 1962–64
Richardson, Leo, 1964–71
Backus, Michael, 1971–76
Ellington, Russell, 1976–Present

Men's Track

Wright, Theodore, 1949–56
Washington, Richard, 1956–75, 1985

Women's Basketball

Webb, Ella, 1946–51
Fisher, Ella W., 1951–57
Westley, Jimmy, 1974–78
Trudell, Saralyn, 1978–84

Baseball

Myles, John, 1969–Present

All South Atlantic Athletic Conference

Football

Latimoer, Grady, 1946
Miller, Harrison, 1948

All Southeastern Athletic Conference

Football

Turner, Joseph, 1950
Slocum, Robert, 1950
Struchins, Albert, 1954
Weatherspoon, William, 1954
Collier, James, 1954
Butler, Robert, 1954
Batchelor, Willie, 1956
McGraw, Elijah, 1957–59
Brown, Leroy, 1958
Stanley, Ulysees, 1958
Dukes, Willie, 1958
Davis, Donald, 1958
King, Moses, 1958
Stephens, Jolly, 1958
Walker, Floyd, 1958
Strong, Johns, 1959–60
Bowens, James, 1960
Carter, Fred, 1960
Bell, Eddie, 1960
Saunders, Henry, 1961
Myers, Fred, 1961
Spann, Benjamin, 1961
Gold, Barry, 1965
Ellis, Frank, 1965
Bell, Frank, 1965–67
Brown, Judson, 1965–67

Leggett, Terry, 1966
Westmore, Carlos, 1966
Ford, Vaughn, 1966
Betts, Henry, 1966–67
Carter, Robert, 1966–67
Berry, Isiah, 1967
Trvell, David, 1967
Armstead, Willie, 1967
Dvon, Willie, 1967

All Southeastern Athletic Conference

Basketball

Jackson, Alfred, 1950–52
Brock, Otis, 1954–56
Lewis, Robert, 1954–56
Wright, Noel, 1954–56
Mathis, Johnny, 1963–64
Westley, Jimmy, 1967
Crump, Carl, 1967–68
Nichols, Alan, 1968
White, Vincent,[4] 1968–69

All Southeastern Intercollegiate Athletic Conference

Football

Garrett, Leonard, 1970
Daise, Rodney, 1970
Gibbs, Joseph, 1970
Alston, Andre, 1970
Harper, Frankie, 1970–72
Bennett, Lorenzo, 1970–72
Lawrence, Calvin, 1970–72
Jones, Dennis, 1971
Poythress, Elijah, 1971
Newberry, Rosby, 1971
Dupree, James, 1971
Giggs, Joe, 1971
Reynolds, Willie, 1971–72
Moffett, Carlton, 1971–72
Duncan, Nathaniel, 1972
Sears, Leon, 1972
Nunnally, Maurice, 1974
Singleton, Julius, 1974
Wilkins, Wofford, 1974
Stevens, Jerrold, 1974
Blitch, Lee, 1974–75

Jackson, Charles, 1974–75
Westberry, John, 1974–75
Best, Cleveland, 1975
Camp, Keith, 1975
Porter, John, 1975–77
Govan, Martin, 1975–77
Walker, Tim,[5] 1976–78
Rollins, Mitch, 1977
Slocum, Jr., Robert, 1977
Dickerson, John, 1977–78
Thurmond, Edwin, 1977–79
Winfield, Larry, 1979
Newton, Cecil, 1979–80
Dawson, Kenny, 1979–80
Walker, Tony, 1980
Wallace, Roland, 1980
Ellis, Stanley, 1980
Locke, Robert, 1980
Jordan, Tim, 1980–81
Miller, Ernest, 1982

Basketball

Jordan, Michael, 1971
White, Vincent, 1971
Ogden, Turner, 1975
Kenlaw, Sam, 1975
Grant, Sherman, 1977
Hubbard, Harold,[6] 1979–80
Riley, Ted[7]
Stocks, Michael, 1982

All Southeastern Athletic Conference

Women's Basketball

Girvin, Ida[8]
Gross, Eunice
Keith, Gwendolyn[9]
Moore, Rosa Lee
Bryant, Clara
Johnson, Luella
Bonner, Susie

All Georgia Association of Intercollegiate Athletics for Women

Williams, Delois, 1978

[1] Richardson, Leo–1967 Southeastern Athletic Conference Coach Of The Year
[2] Myles, John–he was a Student Player and Head Coach
[3] Wright, Theodore–1960 Southeastern Athletic Conference Coach Of The Year

[4] White, Vincent–1969 Most Valuable Player of the South Eastern Athletic Conference Tournament; 1970 Most Valuable Player of the Southern Intercollegiate Athletic Conference Tournament
[5] Walker, Tim–1980 Amateur Athlete of the Year in the State of Georgia
[6] Hubbard, Harold–1979 Southern Intercollegiate Athletic Conference Most Valuable Player
[7] Riley, Ted–1980 Southern Intercollegiate Athletic Conference Tournament Most Valuable Player
[8] Girvin, Ida–1948 South Eastern Athletic Conference Tournament Most Valuable Player
[9] Keith, Gwendolyn–1955 South Eastern Athletic Conference Tournament Most Valuable Player (Co Most Valuable Player of the League in 1956)

Clark College
Atlanta, Georgia 30314

All Southern Intercollegiate Athletic Conference

Football

Clark, Offie, 1952–53
Barnett, Algia, 1957
Dickerson, Lowell, 1962
Palmer, David, 1963
Nixon, Elmer, 1963
Mims, McDuffie, 1969
Mullins, Harold, 1969
Wilson, James, 1974
Wyche, Anthony, 1975
Pellman, John, 1978
Fowler, Edward, 1978
McPherson, Charles, 1978
Cheeks, Charles, 1978
Wilder, John, 1978
Mitchell, Melvin, 1980
Pollard, Walter, 1980
Brown, Rickey, 1982
Wilder, Leonard, 1982

Basketball

Turmon, Roman, 1951–52, 1954
Bunn, Junius, 1954
Hubbard, Harold, 1954
Threatt, Reginald, 1954
Jones, Edwin, 1958
Clark, Henry, 1961
Smith, Charles, 1961–63
Simpson, Walter, 1962–63
Dickerson, Lowell, 1963
Norton, Theodis, 1964
Brown, Sam, 1965
Jackson, Ron, 1965–66

Walls, James, 1966–67
Epps, III, L.S., 1967
Floyd, Anthony, 1967
Mincey, Elder, 1982–83
Carter, Steven, 1983
Hunter, Marvin, 1983
Duffy, Alvin, 1984
Lee, Ernest, 1984, 1986–87

All-American (Division II)

Basketball

Lee, Ernest, 1986–87

Clark Alumni in the National Football League

McCrary, Greg, Washington Redskins (TE), 1978–81
Nevett, Elijah, New Orleans Saints (DB), 1967–70

Fisk University
Nashville, Tennessee 37203

All Southern Intercollegiate Athletic Conference

Football

Fortson, Charles, 1951
Sharkey, Leo, 1952
Campbell, Al, 1952
Robinson, James, 1954
Anderson, Sam, 1955
Lester, Robert, 1955
Epps, Martin, 1955
Fair, John, 1956
Moore, Eugene, 1958–59
Hale, Robert, 1959
Lewis, John, 1959
James, Robert, 1968
Barber, Abraham, 1969
Bostic, Aaron, 1972
Jones, John, 1974
Johnson, Ray, 1975
Robinson, Dwayne, 1975
Pink, Willie, 1975
Thomas, Cloyd, 1975
Davis, Louis, 1975
Blackman, Lawrence, 1978

Basketball

Work, Fred, 1954–56
Drew, Weldon, 1955
Jobe, Ben, 1955–56
Gilliam, Robert, 1958–59
McAdoo, James, 1959
Washington, Alton, 1959–61
Glover, Renaldo, 1962–63, 1965
Lawson, Lamonte, 1963
Richardson, Lamar, 1965

Fisk Alumni in the National Football League

James, Robert, Buffalo Bills, (DB), 1969–74
Craig, Neal, Cleveland Browns, (S), 1975–76
Bolton, Andy, Seattle Seahawks, (RB), 1976;
    Detroit Lions, (RB) 1976–78
Jones, John, New York Jets, (QB), 1975

Fort Valley State College
Fort Valley, Georgia 31030

Athletic Directors

Craig, Richard, 1946–54
Gates, Osley S., 1954–56
Tabor, Alva, 1956–59
Hawkins, James E., 1962–80
Porter, Douglas T., 1980–Present

Coaches of Varsity Teams

Football

Craig, Richard, 1946–54
Gates, Osley S., 1954–56
Tabor, Alva, 1956–59
Varner, Alphonso, 1960–61
Hawkins, James E., 1962–63
Lomax, Leon J., 1963–77
Mangrum, LeLand, 1977–79
Porter, Douglas T., 1979–Present

Men's Basketball

Graig, Richard, 1946–54
Hawkins, James E., 1962–63
Lomax, Leon J., 1963–69
Clemons, William, 1972–75
White, Calvin, 1975–79

Mells, Ronald, 1980–82
Patrick, James, 1982–Present

Men's Track

Craig, Richard, 1946–54
Lomax, Leon J., 1963–66
Mangrum, Leland, 1974–77
Rhodes, John, 1977–80
Jackson, Thomas, 1980–82
Turner, Glen, 1983–86

Women's Track

Love, Flossie, 1960–73
Marshall, Doris Lee, 1974–Present

Women's Basketball

Love, Flossie, 1960–72
Brown, Jessie, 1972–83
Bartley, Lonnie, 1984–Present

Baseball

Hawkins, James E., 1962–70
Cole, James F., 1970–77
Marshall, Ulysses S., 1978–Present

All Southern Intercollegiate Athletic Conference

Football

Nelms, Lamar, 1947
Hollis, Webb, 1947
Bey, Ted, 1948
Wiggins, Julius, 1948
Fouch, John Rufus, 1951
Green, Levon, 1953
Peters, Willie, 1953–54
Peters, Edmond, 1957–58
Armster, Charles, 1958
Moore, Leroy, 1958
Brown, Ronald, 1958–59
Aycok, Issac, 1958–59
Atkins, John, 1958–59
Mangrum, Leland, 1959
Washington, Barney, 1960
Allen, James, 1960
Smith, Allen, 1964
Clark, Dennis, 1964
Bowden, David, 1965
Abrams, Eugene, 1966

Brown, Dean, 1966
Wright, Rayfield, 1966–67
Green, Willie, 1966
Ross, Sanford, 1966
Carey, Moses, 1966
Lewis, Arthur, 1966
Haynes, Randolph, 1966
Talton, David, 1966–68
Goff, George, 1967
Rittenberry, Walter, 1967
Street, Willie, 1967
Simon, Kenneth, 1967
Williams, Lewis, 1967
McCall, Hyrom, 1968
Redding, Frank, 1968
Young, Benjamin, 1968
Vickers, James, 1968
Bryant, Willie, 1968
Lowe, Ronnie, 1968–69
Dawsey, Kelley, 1969
Redding, Lovett, 1969
Reed, Arthur, 1969
Flowers, James, 1969

Basketball

Wright, Rayfield, 1967

All-American (Black College)

Football

Smith, Allen, 1966
Lowe, Ronald, 1969
White, Albert, 1972
Harris, Fred, 1974
Ingram, Lee, 1979
Canady, Willie, 1981
Taylor, Tugwan

Basketball

Gilmore, Walter, 1969

Fort Valley State College Hall of Fame

Lomax, Leon J.
Copeland, Alvin
Wright, Rayfield

Fort Valley Alumni in the National Football League

Moore, Leroy, Buffalo Bills, (DE), 1960, 1962–63
Smith, Allen, Buffalo, (RB), 1966–67
Brown, Dean, Cleveland Browns, (RB), 1969
Wright, Rayfield, Dallas Cowboys, (T), 1967–79

Bethune-Cookman College
Daytona Beach, Florida 32015

All Southern Intercollegiate Athletic Conference

Football

Thornton, Ray, 1951
McClairen, Jack, 1951–52
Hinton, Andy, 1952
Jefferson, Robert, 1952
Sanders, Clyde, 1953
Bethel, Matthew, 1953–54
Hill, Matthew, 1954
McArthur, Sylvester, 1955
Robinson, Eugene, 1956
Williams, Levon, 1956
Rainey, Henry, 1956
Graham, Doc, 1956
Sykes, Earl, 1956
Green, King, 1958
Burch, Curley, 1959
Dickerson, Robert, 1959–62
Crayton, Frank, 1960
Townsell, Robert, 1960–61
Frazier, Robert, 1961–62
Douglas, John, 1964
Little, Larry, 1964–66
Barber, Rudy, 1965
Knight, John, 1966
Washington, Richard, 1967
Frazier, Walter, 1967
Brown, Willie, 1967–68
Harrison, Wilbur, 1967–68
Wyatt, Alvin, 1967–69
Hardaway, Lamar, 1967–70
Grisby, Anthony, 1968
Richardson, Elijah, 1969
Mack, Winston, 1969
Moore, Maulty, 1969–70
Haywood, Al, 1970–71
Davis, Reginald, 1972

Walker, Randy, 1972–74
Allen, Wayne, 1972–74
Osborne, John, 1972
Straughn, Randy, 1972–73
Burton, Al, 1972–74
Clay, Clarence, 1973
Mackey, James, 1973–75
Dye, Michael, 1974
Smith, Victor, 1974
Jackson, Willie, 1974
Coleman, Bernard, 1975
Lee, Willie, 1975
Inman, Earl, 1975–76
Samuels, Andre, 1976
Burns, Robert, 1976
Shepherd, Tracey, 1976
White, Charles, 1976
Beverly, Reginald, 1976
Snell, Alcus, 1976
Cornelius, Charles, 1976
Claitt, Ricky, 1977
Thompson, Lynn, 1977
Willis, Gary, 1977
Mallory, Arthur, 1977
Young, Robert, 1977–79
Jones, David, 1979
Killings, Greg, 1979

Basketball

Hemsley, Hubert, 1953
Martin, Wycliff, 1953
Chaney, John, 1953–55
Humphrey, James, 1959
Fuller, Carl, 1965
Henderson, Mac, 1965
Allen, John, 1966, 1968–69
Fells, Otis, 1968

All Mid-Eastern Athletic Conference

Football

Sunkett, Gordon, 1980
Wright, Herb, 1980–81
Reese, Booker, 1980–81
Hammond, Steven, 1981
Bostic, John, 1981, 1983–84
Riggins, Charles, 1981
Bethune, Darryl, 1981
Patterson, Reno, 1982

Anderson, Troy, 1982
Washington, Alabaert, 1982
Morgan, Wilford, 1983
Daniels, Dennis, 1983
Williams, Lee, 1983
Hawk, Bernard, 1983–84
Gonzales, Leon, 1983–84
Young, Almon, 1984
Robinson, Charles, 1984
Goodman, Clenner, 1984
Simmons, Arthur, 1984
Green, King, 1984
Collier, Steven

Basketball

James, Ellis, 1981
Smith, Jarvis, 1982
Hill, Donald, 1985

All-American (Black College)

Football

Thornton, Raymond, 1951
McClairen, Jack "Cy," 1952
Hinson, Andy, 1952
Dickerson, Robert, 1961
Gipson, Elijah, 1965
Little, Larry, 1966
Wyatt, Alvin, 1969
Moore, Maulty, 1970
Ross, Nathaniel, 1971
Walker, Randy, 1972
Lee, Willie, 1975
Samuels, Tony, 1976
Cornelius, Charles, 1976
Inman, Earl, 1977
Reese, Booker, 1979
Williams, Lee, 1983

Bethune-Cookman Alumni in the National Football League

Simmons, Jerry, Pittsburgh Steelers, (WR), 1965–66;
    New Orleans Saints, (WR), 1967; *
    Atlanta Falcons, (WR), 1967–69;
    Chicago Bears, (WR), 1969;
    Denver Broncos, (WR), 1971–74
Wyatt, Alvin, Oakland Raiders, (DB), 1970;
    Buffalo Bills, (DB), 1971–73;
    Houston Oilers, (DB), 1973

Clark, Boobie, Cincinnati Bengals, (RB), 1973–78;
    Houston Oilers, (RB), 1979–80
Moore, Maulty, Miami Dolphins, (DT), 1972–74;
    Cincinnati Bengals, (DT), 1975;
    Tampa Bay Buccaneers, (DT), 1976
Haywood, Al, Denver Broncos, (RB), 1975
Anderson, Terry, Miami Dolphins, (WR), 1977–78;
    Washington Redskins, (WR), 1978;
    San Francisco 49ers, (WR), 1980
Samuels, Tony, Kansas City Chiefs, (TE), 1977–80;
    Tampa Bay Buccaneers, (TE) 1980
Barber, Rudy, Miami Dolphins, (LB), 1968
Cornelius, Charles, Miami Dolphins, (DB), 1977–78
Little, Larry, San Diego Chargers, (G), 1967–68;
    Miami Dolphins, (G), 1969–80
Washington, Richard, Miami Dolphins, (DB), 1968
White, Charles, New York Jets, (RB), 1977;
    Tampa Bay Buccaneers, (RB), 1978
Inmon, Earl, Tampa Bay Buccaneers, (LB), 1978
Reese, Booker, Tampa Bay Buccaneers, (DE), 1982–84
Claitt, Rickey, Washington Redskins, (RB), 1980–81
Lee, Willie, Kansas City Chiefs, (DT), 1976–77
McClairen, Jack, Pittsburgh Steelers, (E), 1955–60
Burton, Al, Houston Oilers, (DE), 1976;
    New York Jets, (DE), 1977

Morris Brown College
Atlanta, Georgia 30314

All Southern Intercollegiate Athletic Conference

Football

Harvell, Reginald, 1951
Benson, Ted, 1951
Williams, John, 1951
Moseley, Henry, 1951–52
Neeson, Alvin, 1951–53
Parham, Donald, 1952
Southern, Brandon, 1952–54
Glover, Frank, 1953
Reynolds, John, 1954–55
Williams, George, 1955
Cooper, Willie, 1955
Glover, Howard, 1955–56
Reed, Lambert, 1956–58
Bolden, Charles, 1957–59
Bivins, Charles, 1957–59

Bing, Louis, 1959
Robertson, Eugene, 1961
Thomas, Calvin, 1961
Croft, David, 1961
Hubbard, Simon, 1961–62
Dean, Eddie, 1961–64
Benson, Charles, 1962
Moore, George, 1963–64
Atkinson, George, 1965–67
Hart, Thomas, 1967
Coster, William, 1969
Barker, Charles, 1969
Myles, George, 1969
Henderson, Larry, 1969
Denson, Ron, 1970
Townsend, James, 1970
Jenkins, Alfred, 1972
Thompson, Gregory, 1972
Payne, Donald, 1975–76
Rankin, Alexander, 1976
Ingram, Willie, 1976
Blackwell, Willie, 1976
Williams, Veotis, 1979
Williams, Cecil, 1979
Dedrick, Thomas, 1979
Lamar, B.J., 1979
Lee, Gerald, 1979
Powers, Larry, 1980
Stewart, Anthony, 1980
Parker, Ozie, 1980
Knight, Arthur, 1980
Hill, Derek, 1980
Walker, Randy, 1982
Harris, Ananais, 1982
Cambridge, Neil, 1982–83
Flagg, Michael, 1983
Winfrey, Leon, 1983–84
Liverpool, James, 1983–84

Basketball

Benson, Ted, 1951
Andrews, James, 1951
Hannol, G.B., 1951
Glover, Frank, 1951–52
Williams, George, 1957
Glover, Howard, 1957
Bell, Curtis, 1957–59
Ross, Erwin, 1959–60
Scott, James, 1960

Morris Brown Alumni in the National Football League

Jenkins, Alfred, Atlanta Falcons, (WR), 1975–83
Bivins, Charles, Chicago Bears, (RB), 1960–66;
  Buffalo Bills, (RB), 1967;
  Pittsburgh Steelers, (RB), 1967
Hart, Tom, San Francisco 49ers, (DE), 1968—76;
  Chicago Bears, (DE), 1978–79
Mosely, Henry, Chicago Bears, (RB), 1955
Atkinson, George, Oakland Raiders, (DB), 1968–77;
  Denver Broncos, (DB), 1979
Johnson, Ezra, Green Bay Packers, (DE), 1977–85
Brannon, Soloman, Kansas City Chiefs, (DB), 1965–66;
  New York Jets, (DB), 1967
Christopher, Herb, Kansas City Chiefs, (S), 1979–82
Davis, Jerry, New York Jets, (DB), 1975

Alabama A&M University
Normal, Alabama 35762

All Southern Intercollegiate Athletic Conference

Football

Hinton, Willie, 1952
Turner, Eldridge, 1953
Clark, Robert, 1955
Ashley, David, 1955
Jones, Cleon, 1961
LeGrlande, Bernard, 1965
Thomas, Hardin, 1965
Jackson, Onree, 1966–68
Kindricks, William, 1967
Harris, Curtis, 1969
Shephard, Charles, 1971
Jackson, Nathaniel, 1972
Stallworth, John, 1972–73
Hinton, Robert, 1972–74
Weathers, Larry, 1972–74
Smith, Jack, 1973
McDonald, Curtis, 1975
Horton, Donald M., 1975
Lyons, Wayne, 1977
Watson, Cleveland, 1977
Rice, Charles, 1977–79
Dean, Roy, 1977–79
Holman, Roderick, 1977–79
Newsome, Thomas, 1977–79

French, Ernest, 1977–80
Holt, Kennedy, 1979
Ligon, Malcolm, 1980
Shackleford, William, 1980
Fox, Michael, 1980
McCord, Prince, 1980
Tate, Jerome, 1980
Harris, Ananias, 1980–82
McGraw, Reginald, 1982
Gibson, Reginald, 1982
Addison, Larry, 1984
Johnson, Maurice, 1984
Whaley, Kevin, 1984
Malone, Joey, 1984

Basketball

Phillips, Ed, 1968
Goston, John, 1975
Williams, Joe, 1975
Davis, Homer, 1975–77
Edwards, Jackie, 1975–77
Hill, Cornelius, 1979
Randle, Terry, 1980
Dixon, Dan, 1982–83
Hunter, Marvin, 1983
Thomas, Leafus, 1984
Reedus, Don, 1984

SOUTHLAND CONFERENCE

1. Louisiana Tech University
2. Lamar University
3. McNeese State University

4. Northeast Louisiana University
5. North Texas State University
6. University of Southwestern Louisiana

Louisiana Tech University
Ruston, Louisiana 71272

Coaches of Varsity Teams

Football

Baldwin, Jerry (Assistant), 1983–Present

All Southland Conference

Football

Dean, Fred, 1972–74
Wilborn, Wenford, 1973–74
McDaniel, Charles, 1974
Eddings, Gerald, 1975–77
White, John Henry, 1976–77
Anderson, Larry, 1976–77
Foppe, Rob, 1977
Paggett, Ron, 1977
Blackshire, James, 1977–78
McCann, Ardis, 1978
Yates, George, 1978
Robinson, John, 1978–80
Young, Andre, 1979
Dejean, Haywood, 1981
Landry, Doug, 1983–84

Washington, Donald, 1984
Johnson, Walter, 1984
Adams, Doyle, 1984

Basketball

Knowles, Andy, 1972
Green, Michael,[1] 1972–73
Wells, Lanky, 1975–77
Alexander, Randy, 1978
King, Victor, 1978–79
Ivory, Joe, 1980
Simmons, David, 1981
Malone, Karl, 1983–85
Simmons, Willie, 1985

Track

Holman, Victor, ID HH 1981
Webb, Darrell, ID HJ 1981

All Southland Conference

Track

Thornton, George, OD HJ 1973
Smith, Wesley, OD LJ 1974–75
Ford, Monroe, OD LJ 1976
Woods, Wendell, LJ 1978

Webb, Darrell, HJ 1980
Garrett, Cornell,[1] 00M 1981

All-American

Football

Dean, Fred, 1974
Johnson, Walter, 1984
Landry, Doug, 1984

Men's Basketball

Green, Michael, 1973
Malone, Karl, 1985

Women's Basketball

Kelly, Pam,[2] 1980–82
Turner, Angela,[3] 1982
Lawrence, Janis,[4] 1983–84

[1] Green, Michael—All Gulf States Conference, 1971
[2] Kelly, Pam—1982 Wade Trophy recipient; 1982 Broderick Award recipient
[3] Turner, Angela—1981 Most Valuable Player at the AIAW National Tournament
[4] Lawrence, Janis—member of the 1984 United States Olympic Women's Basketball Team; 1984 Wade Trophy recipient; Most Valuable Player at the 1984 NCAA Final Four Tournament

Lamar University
Beaumont, Texas 77710

Coaches of Varsity Teams

Football

Payton, John (Assistant), 1970–82
Pope, Kenneth (Assistant), 1979–80
Bell, James (Assistant), 1983–84
Chandler, Otis (Assistant), 1983–84

All Southland Conference

Football

Gillory, Anthony, 1964
Wynn, Spergon, 1966–67
Smiley, Tom, 1967
Gibbs, Patrick, 1971
Matthews, Doug, 1972
Bowser, Joe, 1972–73
Colbert, Randy, 1972–74
Babineaux, Leon, 1973–74
Hill, Donald, 1974
Black, Ronald, 1974

Bell, Kevin, 1974
Davis, Donnie, 1974–76
Enard, Victor, 1977–79
Mask, Alfred, 1979
Robinson, Howard, 1979
Phoenix, Kurt, 1980
Choice, Sam, 1980
Harris, Herbert, 1981
Seale, Eugene, 1983

Basketball

Dow, Earl, 1968–69
Adams, Luke, 1970–71
Nickson, Alfred, 1974
Jones, Henry, 1976
Davis, B.B., 1978–79, 1981
Oliver, Michael, 1979–81
Kea, Clarence, 1980
Sewel, Thomas, 1983–84
Robinson, Lamont, 1984

Baseball

Mack, Anthony, 1981–82
Clark, Jerald, 1984–85

All-American

Football

Wynn, Spergon,[1] 1967
Seale, Eugene,[2] 1983

Basketball

Dow, Earl, 1969

Track and Field

LeBlac, Joe, 1964
Gipson, Efren "De De," 1973–74
Harris, Jackie, MR
Nichols, Jerry, MR 1984
Amboree, Troy, MR 1984

Lamar University's Hall of Fame

Wynn, Spergon
Smiley, Tom
Dow, Earl
Thomas, Waverly
Gipson, Efren (De De)

[1] Wynn, Spergon—Little All-American
[2] Seale, Eugene—Division 1–AA

McNeese State University
Lake Charles, Louisiana 70609

Coaches of Varsity Teams

Men's Basketball

Brown, William (Assistant), 1982–Present

All Southland Conference

Football

Allen, Nathaniel, 1972
Kimble, Barry, 1976
Wilson, Robert, 1976
Jefferson, Charles, 1976–78
Price, Harry, 1979
Shankle, Artie, 1979
McClendon, Theron, 1980
Starring, Stephen, 1980–81
Smith, Leonard, 1981
Jordan, Buford, 1981–83

Men's Basketball

Ray, Henry, 1974–75
Lawrence, Edmund, 1975–76
McClaurin, Chirley, 1977
Lawrence, David, 1979–80
Chaffould, Fred, 1982
Dumars, Joe, 1982–84

Men's Track

Collins, Davis, QM 1974
Dunn, Donald, 100M, 200M 1974
Deveaux, Steven, TJ 1974
Smith, Ray, SP 1974
Lloyd, Edward, HJ 1980
Starring, Stephen, HH 1981–83
Young, Verril, HJ 1983
Andrus, Craig, J 1983–84

Women's Basketball

Jean, Pat, 1981–83

All-American

Football

Moore, James, 1972
Smith, Leonard, 1982

Men's Basketball

Lawrence, David, 1980

Track

Starring, Stephen, HH 1983

Northeast Louisiana University
Monroe, Louisiana 7209

Coaches of Varsity Teams

Football

Thomas, Dennis (Assistant), 1974–75
Coleman, Fred (Assistant), 1984–Present
Burnette, Jesse (Assistant), 1984–Present

All Southland Conference

Football

Christophe, Arthur, 1982
Outley, David, 1983
Jones, Ben, 1983
Evans, Joey, 1983–84

Men's Basketball

Hayes, Arthur, 1985

All-American

Football

Profit, Joe,[1] 1970
Edwards, James,[2] 1972
Fleming, Glenn,[3] 1973–74

Basketball

Natt, Calvin, 1978–79

Track

Shanklin, Warren, HJ[4] 1975

Other Outstanding Athletes

Basketball

Harris, Andrew

[1] Profit, Joe—(NAIA) 1971 Gulf States Conference Athlete of the Year; the first black athlete to play football at a predominantly white college in Louisiana
[2] Edwards, James—(NAIA) All-American
[3] Fleming, Glenn—(NAIA) All-American
[4] Shanklin, Warren—1975 NCAA Division I National Champion

North Texas State University
Denton, Texas 76203

Administrators

Greene, Charles Edward "Joe," 1982–85

Coaches of Varsity Teams

Football

Barnes, Nelson (Assistant)
Shanklin, Ron (Assistant)
Jackson, Carl (Assistant)
Williams, Vic (Assistant)

Basketball

Gales, James (Assistant)

Track

Brown, Abe

All Missouri Valley Conference

Football

Haynes, Abner, 1958–59
Perkins, Arthur, 1960
Christle, William, 1961
Love, John, 1965
Harkless, Burkley, 1965
Woods, William, 1966
Greene, Joe, 1966–68
Beatty, Charles, 1967
Shanklin, Ron, 1967–69
Taylor, Leo, 1968
Holloway, Glen, 1968–69
Hardman, Cedric, 1969
Edwards, Dralves, 1970
Dunlap, Leonard, 1970
Scales, Hurles, 1972

Basketball

Savage, John, 1962–64
Russell, Rubin, 1966–67
Hamilton, Joe, 1969–70
Iverson, Robert, 1974–75

All Southland Conference

Football

Hickman, Ron, 1983
Cooks, Rayford, 1983
Harper, Lester, 1983

Men's Basketball

Lyons, Kenneth, 1983

University of Southwestern Louisiana
Lafayette, Louisiana 70501

Coaches of Varsity Teams

Football

Culley, David (Assistant), 1985

Men's Basketball

Donaldson, Dennis (Assistant), 1984

All Southland Conference

Men's Basketball

Lamar, Dwight, 1972–73
Ebron, Roy, 1972–73
Toney, Andrew, 1978–80
Figaro, Kevin, 1981

All-American

Men's Basketball

Winkler, Marvin, 1970
Lamar, Dwight, 1972–73
Toney, Andrew, 1980

Other Outstanding Athletes

Football

Jackson, Thomas
Perkins, Pierre

Men's Basketball

Ivory, Elvin
Warner, Graylin
Allen, Alonzo

METRO CONFERENCE

1. University of Louisville
2. St. Louis University
3. University of Cincinnati
4. University of South Carolina

5. University of Southern Mississippi
6. Virginia Polytechnic Institute
7. Tulane University
8. Memphis State University

University of Louisville
Louisville, Kentucky 40292

Athletic Directors

Hill, Richard (Assistant Athletic Director)

Coaches of Varsity Teams

Football

Coe, Charles (Assistant)
Lavan, All (Assistant)
Mann, Richard (Assistant)
Walters, Trent (Assistant)
Dickerson, Ron (Assistant)

Basketball

Houston, Wade, (Assistant)

All Missouri Valley Conference

Football

Bouggess, Lee, 1968–69
Jones, Horrace, 1970
Jackson, Tom,[1] 1970–72
Stevens, Howard,[2] 1971–72

Basketball

Unseld, Westley, 1966–68
Beard, Alfred "Butch," 1967–69
Price, Jim, 1971–72
Murphy, Allen, 1973–75
Bridgeman, Ulysses "Junior,"[3] 1973–75

All Metro Conference

Basketball

Cox, Westley, 1977
Williams, Larry, 1977–79
Wilson, Rick,[4] 1978
Griffith, Darrell,[5] 1978–80

Turner, Robert, 1979
Smith, Derek,[6] 1981
McCray, Rodney,[7] 1981–83
Eaves, Jerry, 1982
Gordon, Lancaster, 1983–84
Wagner, Milt, 1983–84, 1986
Jones, Charles 1984

All-American

Basketball

Unseld, Westley, 1967–68
Murphy, Allen,[8] 1975
Bridgeman, Ulysses "Junior," 1975
Griffith, Darrell, 1980

Other Outstanding Athletes

Football

Lyles, Lenny
Green, Ernie
Johnson, Charles
Patrick, Wayne
Walker, Cleo
Bishop, Richard
Poole, Nathan
Miller, Kevin
Smith, Marty
Johnson, Ed
Woodruff, Dwayne
Wilson, Otis
Craft, Don
Clayton, Mark
Minnifield, Frank
Givins, Ernest

Basketball

Bacon, Henry
Bond, Philip
Thomas, Ron
Branch, Tony

Gallon, Rick
Thompson, Billy
McCray, Scooter
Forrest, Manuel
Ellison, Pervis[9]
Kimbro, Tony

[1] Jackson, Tom—1972 Missouri Valley Conference Defensive Player of the Year
[2] Stevens, Howard—1971 and 1972 Missouri Valley Conference Offensive Player of the Year
[3] Bridgeman, Ulysses "Junior"—1974 and 1975 Missouri Valley Conference Player of the Year; Honorable Mention
[4] Wilson Rick—1978 Metro Conference Co-Player of the Year
[5] Griffith, Darrell—1980 Metro Conference Player of the Year
[6] Smith, Derek—1981 Metro Conference Co-Player of the Year
[7] McCray, Rodney—1983 Metro Conference Player of the Year; member of the 1980 United States Olympic Basketball Team
[8] Murphy, Allen—Honorable Mention
[9] Ellison, Pervis—1986 NCAA Final Four Tournament Most Valuable Player; 1986 Metro Conference Freshman of the Year

St. Louis University
St. Louis, Missouri 63108

Coaches of Varsity Teams

Men's Basketball

Coleman, Ron, 1977–78

All Missouri Valley Conference

Men's Basketball

Parks, Richard, 1966
Moore, Eugene, 1966
Wiley, Joe, 1970
Irving, Jim, 1971
Rogers, Harry, 1972–73
Leonard, Jesse, 1973

All Metro Conference

Men's Basketball

Johnson, Carol, 1977
Henderson, Kelvin, 1979
Burns, David, 1980–81

All Mid-Western Collegiate Conference

Men's Basketball

Burden, Luther, 1983–85

University of Cincinnati
Cincinnati, Ohio 45221–0021

Athletic Directors

Yates, Tony[1] (Associate Athletic Director), 1984–Present
Purnell, Garnett[2] (Assistant Athletic Director, Academic Counseling and Development), 1985

Coaches of Varsity Teams

Football

Godette, Cary (Assistant), 1983–Present
Ivory, Bruce (Assistant), 1984

Basketball

Yates, Tony (Head), 1984–Present
Turner, Ken (Assistant), 1984–Present

All Missouri Valley Conference

Football

Owens, Brig, 1963–64
Nelson, Al

Basketball

Robertson, Oscar, 1959–60
Hogue, Paul, 1960–62
Thacker, Tom, 1961–63
Yates, Tony, 1963
Wilson, George, 1963–64
Roberson, Rick, 1967–68
Ard, Jim,[2] 1968–70

All Metro Conference

Football

Bell, Farley, 1979
Bettis, James, 1981
Gibson, Antonio, 1981–82
Harvin, Allen, 1982
Jamison, George, 1983
Taylor, Reginald, 1984
Foster, Deno, 1984
Gordon, Alex, 1986

Men's Basketball

Miller, Robert, 1977–78
Lee, Eddie, 1979–80

Jones, Dwight, 1982–83
McMillan, Derrick, 1985
McClendon, Roger, 1986–87

All-American

Football

Nelson, Al, 1965
Bell, Robert, 1970
Jenkins, Keith, 1975
Sanders, Clarence, 1975
Woods, Michael, 1977
Bettis, James, 1981
Gibson, Antonio, 1981–82
Barrett, Danny, 1982
Harvin, Allen, 1982
Jamison, George, 1983
Taylor, Reginald, 1984
Foster, Deno, 1984
Gordon, Alex, 1987

Men's Basketball

Robertson, Oscar,[3] 1958–60
Hogue, Paul,[4] 1962
Thacker, Tom, 1963
Yates, Tony, 1963
Wilson, Goerge,[5] 1963
Batts, Lloyd, 1973
Miller, Robert, 1978
McClendon, Roger, 1987

Other Outstanding Athletes

Football

Bonds, Jay

[1] Yates, Tony—1985 Metro Conference Coach of the Year
[2] Ard, Jim—1970 Missouri Valley Conference Player of the Year
[3] Robertson, Oscar—1958–60 United Press International College Player of the Year; 1959 and 1960 United States Basketball Writers' Associate College Player of the Year; member of the 1960 United States Olympic Basketball Team
[4] Hogue, Paul—1962 Helms Foundation Player of the Year
[5] Wilson, George—member of the 1964 United States Olympic Basketball Team

University of South Carolina
Columbia, South Carolina 29208

Athletic Directors

White, Harold (Academic Counselor, formerly Assistant Football Coach), 1972–Present
Dickerson, Ron (Assistant Athletic Director, Non Revenue Sports), 1981–82

Coaches of Varsity Teams

Football

Banks, Oree (Assistant), 1973–74
Goodwin, Sam (Assistant), 1982
Black, William (Assistant), 1984–Present
Diggs, Richard (Assistant), 1984–Present

Basketball

Jobe, Ben (Assistant), 1973–78

All Metro Conference

Track

Rhodes, Vernon, 200 and 400M 1984
Johnsson, Earl, Decathlon 1984
Taylor, Ollie, 100M 1984
Smith, Wayne, LJ 1984

All-American

Football

Rogers, George,[1] 1979–80
Scott, Willie, 1981

Basketball

Boswell, Thomas, 1975
English, Alexander, 1976
Frederick, Zam, 1981

Women's Basketball

Foster, Sheila, 1982

Baseball

Wilson, William Hayward, 1977

Track and Field

Thomas, George, 1977
Adams, Rolando, 1979

Rambo, Tony, 1980
Kirkland, Gus, 1981

Other Outstanding Athletes

Basketball

Hodges, Cedrick
Dozier, Terry

[1] Rogers, George—1980 Heisman Trophy recipient

University of Southern Mississippi
Hattiesburg, Mississippi 39406–3161

Coaches of Varsity Teams

Cross Country/Track

Bell, Marshall (Head), 1978–84

Women's Basketball

Jones, Shirley (Assistant), 1983–84

Football

Cheatham, Ronald (Assistant), 1976–83
Horton, Freeman (Assistant), 1984

Basketball

Moore, Ralph (Assistant), 1984

All South Independent

Football

Cook, Fred, 1972–73
Cheatham, Ronald, 1974
Thomas, Norris, 1975
Garry, Ben, 1976–77
Parker, Anthony, 1977–78
Taylor, Ronald, 1978–79
Dixon, Hanford, 1979–80
Harvey, Marvin, 1979–80
Winder, Sammy, 1980–81
Collier, Reggie, 1981–82
Baylis, Jerald, 1981–83
Dejarnette, Sam, 1982
Lipps, Louis, 1983

Basketball

Prince, John, 1977
Dawson, Joe, 1980–82

All Metro Conference

Basketball

Green, Curtis, 1982
Siler, Ken, 1986–87

All-American

Football

Cook, Fred, 1973
Collier, Reggie, 1981

Basketball

Prince, John, 1977
Dawson, Joe, 1981–82

Other Outstanding Athletes

Women's Basketball

Jones, Shirley
Lyons, Diane
Smith, Rose
Backstrom, Diane
Smith, Wilhelmina
Winston, Bridget

Volleyball

Sims, Sheila

Cross Country

Young, Donnie

Baseball

Burnett, Ivie

Virginia Polytechnic Institute
Blacksburg, Virginia 24061

Coaches of Varsity Teams

Men's Basketball

Allen, Frank (Assistant), 1975–Present

All Metro Conference

Men's Basketball

Robinson, Wayne, 1979–80
Solomon, Dale,[1] 1979–82

Curry, Dell,[2] 1984–86
Young, Perry, 1985

All-American

Football
Smith, Bruce,[3] 1983–84

Basketball
Curry, Dell, 1986

Other Outstanding Athletes

Men's Basketball
Pierre, Russell
Davis, Russell
Thorpe, Duke
Ashfold, Marshall
Hanson, Les
Lancaster, Wally

Track
Gaines, Jerry[4]

[1] Solomon, Dale—1979 Metro Conference Freshman of the Year
[2] Curry, Dell—1986 Metro Conference Player of the Year
[3] Smith, Bruce—1984 Outland Trophy recipient; 1984 Washington, D.C., Touchdown Club Lineman of the Year
[4] Gaines, Jerry—the first black athlete to attend Virginia Tech Institute, 1967

Tulane University
New Orleans, Louisiana 70118

Coaches of Varsity Teams

Basketball
Lewis, James (Assistant), 1976–81
Saulny, Kirk (Assistant), 1981–Present

All South Independent

Football
Hall, Charles, 1972–74
Mitchell, Martin, 1976
Alexis, Alton, 1979
Hall, Nickie, 1980
Cole, Kevin, 1980
Simon, Wilfred, 1980
Griffin, Robert, 1980–82
Holeman, Rodney, 1981

Douglas, Brian, 1981
Smith, Wayne, 1983
Dent, Burnell, 1986

All Metro Conference

Basketball
Thompson, Paul, 1980–81, 1983
Williams, John,[1] 1982–84

Trainers
Henry, John

Tulane University's Hall of Fame

Hall, Charles

[1] Williams, John—1984 Metro Conference Player of the Year

Memphis State University
Memphis, Tennessee 38152

Coaches of Varsity Teams

Men's Basketball
Finch, Larry (Head), 1986–Present

Football
Fox, James (Assistant)
Manuel, Fred (Assistant)

Women's Basketball
Booker, Betty (Assistant)

All Missouri Valley Conference

Basketball
Finch, Larry,[1] 1971–73
Robinson, Ron, 1971–73
Kenon, Larry,[2] 1973

All South Independent

Football
Harris, Eric, 1973–74, 1976
Thompson, James, 1974
Moon, Ronald, 1974
Ward, Robert, 1974
Jones, Earl, 1974–75

Dandridge, Jerry, 1974–75
Middleton, Terdell, 1975
Patterson, Lloyd, 1976–77
Gray, Ernest, 1977–78
Walker, Johnny, 1982
Harris, Tim, 1983
Fairs, Eric, 1983

All Metro Conference

Football

Knowlton, Jerry, 1980
Adams, Stanley, 1980
Thomas, Michael, 1980
Chatman, Marvin, 1981
Montgomery, Greg, 1981–82
Walker, Johnny, 1982
Harris, Tim, 1983
Fairs, Eric, 1983
Nabors, Percy, 1983
Crawford, Derrick, 1983
Burroughs, Derrick, 1984
Williams, Punkin, 1984

Basketball

Reed, Dexter, 1977
Wright, Alvin, 1978
Bradley, James, 1978–79
Lee, Keith,[3] 1982–84
Parks, Bobby, 1983
Haynes, Phillip, 1984
Bedford, William, 1986

All-American

Football

Dandridge, Jerry,[4] 1975
Harris, Eric,[5] 1976

Patterson, Lloyd,[6] 1976
Gray, Earnest,[7] 1977
Simpson, Keith, 1978
Harris, Tim,[8] 1983

Basketball

Finch, Larry, 1972–73
Kenon, Larry, 1972–73
Lee, Keith, 1982–84

Other Outstanding Athletes

Basketball

Jones, Rich
Douglas, James
Hillard, Marion
Jackson, Otis
Gunn, John[9]
Phillips, Derrick
Turner, Andre
Lee, Rodney
Boyd, Dwight
Askew, Vincent

Women's Basketball

Street, Regina

[1] Finch, Larry—1972 Missouri Valley Conference Player of the Year
[2] Kenon, Larry—1973 Missouri Valley Conference Player of the Year
[3] Lee, Keith—1982 Metro Conference Player of the Year; 1982 Metro Conference Freshman of the Year; 1982 John Gunn Outstanding Player Award recipient (Metro Conference Tournament Most Valuable Player)
[4] Dandridge, Jerry—Honorable Mention
[5] Harris, Eric—Honorable Mention
[6] Patterson, Lloyd—Honorable Mention
[7] Gray, Earnest—Honorable Mention
[8] Harris, Tim—Honorable Mention
[9] Gunn, John—died in 1976 of complications from Stevens-Johnson Syndrome. An award is given in his honor at the Metro Conference Tournament (John Gunn Outstanding Player Award)

METRO ATLANTIC CONFERENCE

1. Fordham University
2. La Salle University
3. St. Peter's College

4. College of the Holy Cross
5. Iona College

Fordham University
Bronx, New York 10458

Coaches of Varsity Teams

Football

Tutein, O'Neal (Head), 1981–Present

Baseball

Blair, Paul (Head), 1983

All Metro Atlantic Athletic Conference

Basketball

Tongal, Dud, 1982
Bona, Ed, 1982
Maxwell, David, 1982–83
Roberson, David, 1984
Samuels, Steven, 1984–85
McIntosh, Tony, 1984–85

All-American

Basketball

Yelverton, Charles, 1971
Charles, Ken,[1] 1973
Maxwell, David,[2] 1983

Fordham University's Hall of Fame

Basketball

Melvin, Robert
Yelverton, Charles
Charles, Kenny

Track

Perry, Sam

[1] Charles, Ken—Honorable Mention
[2] Maxwell, David—Honorable Mention

La Salle University
Philadelphia, Pennsylvania 19141

Coaches of Varsity Teams

Men's Basketball

Rines, Sam (Assistant, Part-Time), 1979

All East Coast Conference

Men's Basketball

Taylor, Bill,[1] 1975
Bryant, Joe,[2] 1975
Wise, Charles,[3] 1975–76
Brooks, Michael,[4] 1977–80
Lewis, Ralph,[5] 1983

All-American

Men's Basketball

Durrett, Ken,[6] 1970–71
Brooks, Michael, 1979–80

Other Outstanding Athletes

Men's Basketball

Lewis, Alonzo[7]
Marshall, Hubie[8]
Williams, Bernie[9]
Moore, Jackie[10]

[1] Taylor, Bill—Big-Five Hall of Fame
[2] Bryant, Joe—Big-Five Hall of Fame
[3] Wise, Charles—1976 Robert Geasey Memorial Trophy recipient (given to the Big-Five Most Valuable Player); Big-Five Hall of Fame
[4] Brooks, Michael—1978–80 East Coast Conference Player of the Year; 1978–80 Robert Geasey Memorial Trophy recipient (given to the Big-Five Most Valuable Player); member of the 1980 United States Olympic Basketball Team; 1980 United States Basketball Writers Association Player of the Year; Member of the 1970–80 Eastern College Athletic Conference All-Decade Team
[5] Lewis, Ralph—1984 Robert Geasey Memorial Trophy recipient (given to the Big-Five Most Valuable Player)
[6] Durrett, Ken—1969–70 Robert Geasey Memorial Trophy co-recipient (given to the Big-Five Most Valuable Player); 1971 Robert Geasey Memorial Trophy recipient; Big-Five Hall of Fame
[7] Lewis, Alonzo—Big-Five Hall of Fame
[8] Marshall, Hubie—1966–67 All Big-Five; Big-Five Hall of Fame
[9] Williams, Bernie—1969 All Big-Five; Big-Five Hall of Fame
[10] Moore, Jackie—played on the 1952 National Invitational Tournament Championship Team

St. Peter's College
Jersey City, New Jersey 07306

Athletic Directors

Spriggs, Ed (Assistant Director of Athletics—Recreation), 1983

Coaches of Varsity Teams

Football
Wright, Robert (Head), 1969–72

Women's Volleyball
Minter, Sheryl (Head), 1984

Football
Morgan, Robert (Head), 1984

All Metro Atlantic Athletic Conference

Basketball
Brown, Wiliam,[1] 1982
Gibbs, Shelton, 1982–84
Jamison, Phil, 1983
Best, Tom, 1983–84
Hayes, Leonard, 1985

Women's Basketball
Berry, Amanda, 1983–84

All-American

Basketball
Webster, Elnardo,[3] 1969

St. Peter's College Hall of Fame

Basketball
Lurie, Harry
Webster, Elnardo
Slappy, Ken

Other Outstanding Athletes

Football
Bethea, Keith
Lamb, Greg

Basketball
Anderson, Cliff
Richard, Steven
Brandon, Jim

[1] Brown, William—1982 Metro Atlantic Athletic Conference Player of the Year
[2] Berry, Amanda—1984 Metro Atlantic Athletic Conference Tournament Most Valuable Player
[3] Webster, Elnardo—Helms Foundation

College of the Holy Cross
Worcester, Massachusetts 01610

Coaches of Varsity Teams

Football
Gentry, Curtis (Assistant), 1971–74

Basketball
Baker, Rodney J. (Assistant), 1978–80

All Metro Atlantic Athletic Conference

Basketball
Floyd, Ernie,[1] 1984

College of the Holy Cross Hall of Fame

Football
Wilson, Joseph[2]

Other Outstanding Athletes

Basketball
Grayson, Stanley E.

Head Trainers

Scott, Charles[3]

[1] Floyd, Ernie—1980 Eastern College Athletic Conference Co-Rookie of the Year
[2] Wilson, Joseph—College of the Holy Cross All-Time Leading Rusher
[3] Scott, Charles—Head Trainer for Football, Baseball, Track during the 1920s and 1930s

Iona College
New Rochelle, New York 10801

Coaches of Varsity Teams

Men's Basketball
Brokaw, Gary (Head), 1986–Present

All Metro Atlantic Athletic Conference

Men's Basketball

Burtt, Steven,[1] 1982–84
Springer, Gary, 1982–84
Hargraves, Tony, 1984
Grimes, Rory, 1985

All-American

Men's Basketball

Burtt, Steven, 1983–84

Other Outstanding Athletes

Men's Basketball

Simmons, Rich

[1] Burtt, Steven—1983 and 1984 Metro Atlantic Athletic Conference Player of the Year; Honorable Mention

BIG SKY CONFERENCE

1. Idaho State University

2. Northern Arizona University

Idaho State University
Pocatello, Idaho 83209

Coaches of Varsity Teams

Football

Lewis, Marvin (Assistant), 1981–Present

All Rocky Mountain Conference

Football

Douglas, George, 1965
Thomas, Otis, 1967
Harris, Leroy, 1967–68
Bell, Ed, 1968–69
Chandler, Larry, 1969
Price, Phil, 1971
Garnett, Rene, 1972
Johnson, Michael, 1979
Childs, Rod, 1980–81
Qualls, Carl, 1983

Basketball

Crump, Art, 1964
Frazier, Len "Buddy," 1966
Boone, Ron, 1967–68
Parks, Charles, 1967–68
Wilson, Ed, 1968
Simmons, O'Neal, 1969–70
Humes, Willie, 1970–71

Hicks, Edison, 1972–73
Griffin, Greg, 1976–77
Thompson, Ed, 1977
Butler, Lawrence, 1978–79
Fleury, Jackie, 1983
Williams, Michael, 1984

Track and Field

Malstrom, William, TJ 1964
Frazier, Len "Buddy," 220Y 1965
Bell, Ed, 220Y 1969
Lawson, Carl, 100Y, 220Y 1971–74
Bolden, Anthony, HH 1975–77
Tullock, Richard, LJ 1976–78
Wilson, Paul, LJ 1977

Wrestling

Harris, Leroy—167 lbs., 177 lbs. 1968–69
Shade, Tim—152 lbs., 150 lbs. 1969–70
Allen, Jim—175 lbs. 1975
Bagley, Arnie—Heavyweight 1981–84

Other Outstanding Athletes

Boxing

Webb, Ellsworth "Spider"[1]
McCullom, Robert "Bobby"[2]
Sanders, Hayes Edward[3]
Espy, Hal[4]

Football

Larue, Bernard "Jake"[5]

Idaho State University's Hall of Fame

Beckham, Samuel B.
Bell, Ed
Boone, Ron
Larue, Bernard "Jake"
Crump, Arthur M.
Sanders, Hayes Edward
Watkins, Homer
Webb, Ellsworth
McCullom, Robert

[1] Webb, Ellsworth "Spider"—1952 NCAA Boxing Champion
[2] McCullom, Robert "Bobby"—1955 NCAA Boxing Champion
[3] Sanders, Hayes Edward—member of the 1952 United States Olympic Boxing Team
[4] Espy, Hal—1958 and 1959 NCAA Heavyweight Champion
[5] Larue, Bernard "Jake"—also competed in basketball (1947–49)

Northern Arizona University
Flagstaff, Arizona 86011

Coaches of Varsity Teams

Football

Cockerham, William (Assistant), 1982–84
Jackson, Moody (Assistant), 1984–Present

All Big Sky Conference

Football

Mullen, Rufus, 1972

Smith, Jim, 1973
Golden, Carl, 1976–77
Smith, Harold, 1976–78
Judie, Ed, 1979
Mandley, Peter, 1980, 1982–83
Gee, James, 1983–84

Basketball

Mannon, Walter, 1971–72
Payne, Nate, 1974–75
Allen, David, 1984

Baseball

Galloway, Clint, 1973–74

All-American

Judie, Ed, 1979
Mandley, Peter, 1982–83
Gee, James, 1983

Basketball

Nash, Willie, 1966
Mannon, Walt,[1] 1972

Cross Country

Chumley, Larry, 1984

Northern Arizona University's Hall of Fame

Football

Harris, Cleveland "Chick"
Lee, Charles
Randolph, Earl
Maddox, Hosie

[1] Mannon, Walt—Honorable Mention

OHIO VALLEY CONFERENCE

1. Eastern Kentucky University
2. Tennessee Technological University
3. Austin Peay State University

4. Middle Tennessee State University
5. Youngstown State University

Eastern Kentucky University
Richmond, Kentucky 40475

Coaches of Varsity Teams

Rifle Coach

Beard, Sgt. Nelson (Head), 1979–82

Football

Taylor, Teddy (Assistant), 1979–Present

Basketball

Washington, Robert (Assistant), 1980–82

All Ohio Valley Conference

Football

Marsh, Aaron, 1966–67
Taylor, Ted, 1967–69
Brooks, James, 1969–71
Wilson, James, 1971
Porter, James, 1971
Chambers, Wallace, 1972
Croudep, James, 1972
Thompson, Alfred, 1973
Hardin, Junior, 1974
Hatley, Robyn, 1974–75
Talbert, Everett,[1] 1974–76
Boyd, Elmo, 1975
Kelly, Roosevelt, 1976
Miller, Anthony, 1977
Patton, Dale, 1978–79
Richard, Joe, 1978–79
Lawson, Darryl, 1980
Shelton, James, 1980
Floyd, George,[2] 1980
Thompson, Terrence, 1981
Parrish, Jerry, 1981
Armstrong, Tron, 1982
Hill, David, 1983
Jones, Anthony, 1983

Basketball

Washington, Robert, 1967–69

Smith, Garfield, 1968
Woods, Willie, 1970
Mitchell, Charles, 1972–73
Brown, Carl, 1974–76
Joiner, Lovell, 1978
Elliott, Ken, 1979
Tillman, James,[3] 1979–80
Jones, Bruce, 1979–80
Baker, Tom, 1981

All-American

Football

Chambers, Wally, 1967
Marsh, Aaron, 1967
Taylor, Ted, 1969
Talbert, Everett, 1974
Hardin, Junior, 1975
Kelly, Roosevelt, 1976
Floyd, George, 1980–81

Basketball

Tillman, James, 1979

[1] Talbert, Everett—1974 Ohio Valley Conference Offensive Player of the Year; 1976 Ohio Valley Conference Offensive Co-Player of the Year
[2] Floyd, George—1980–81 Ohio Valley Conference Defensive Player of the Year
[3] Tillman, James—1980 Ohio Valley Conference Player of the Year

Tennessee Technological University
Cookeville, Tennessee 38505

Coaches of Varsity Teams

Basketball

Taylor, Steven (Assistant)

Soccer

Smith, Steven (Head)

All Ohio Valley Conference

Football

Axel, Jeff, 1971–72

Byrd, Allen, 1972
Grooms, Elois, 1974
Fore, Cecil, 1977–78
Rockymore, Fred, 1979

Basketball

Jordan, Henry, 1966
Pack, Wayne, 1971–73
Lewis, Al, 1972
Stone, Rich, 1972
Jones, Frank, 1974–76
Porter, Robert, 1978
Troupe, Brian, 1979
Taylor, Steven, 1983

All-American

Football

Grooms, Elois, 1974

Other Outstanding Athletes

Track and Field

Moore, Rodney

Austin Peay State University
Clarksville, Tennessee 37040

Coaches of Varsity Teams

Men's Basketball

Jackson, Howard (Head), 1984–86

All Ohio Valley Conference

Men's Basketball

Jackson, Howard, 1972–73
Williams, James,[1] 1973–74
Odums, Dan, 1974
Howard, Percy, 1975
Howard, Otis, 1976–78
Sanders, Roosevelt, 1980

All-American

Men's Basketball

Williams, James, 1974

[1] Williams, James—1974 Ohio Valley Conference Player of the Year

Middle Tennessee State University
Murfreesboro, Tennessee 37132

Coaches of Varsity Teams

Football

Martin, Leo (Assistant), 1978
West, Lou (Assistant), 1981–82
Culley, David (Assistant), 1982

Basketball

Crawford, Coleman (Assistant), 1982–84
Radford, Ralph (Assistant), 1984–Present

All Ohio Valley Conference

Football

Porter, Nate, 1973
Moore, Michael,[1] 1975–77
Bell, Reginald, 1977
Bell, Mo, 1977
Wright, Stan, 1978
Griffin, James, 1981–82
Toles, Emanuel, 1982
Hall, Vincent, 1983
Griffin, Don, 1983

Basketball

Brown, Willie, 1968–69
Riley, Ken, 1970–71
Sykes, Herman, 1972
Powell, James, 1973–74
Peeler, Steven, 1975
Sorrell, George,[2] 1975
Joyner, Gregory, 1977–79
Taylor, Claude, 1978
Coleman, Leroy, 1980
Beck, Jerry,[3] 1980–82

All-American

Football

Moore, Michael, 1976

Track

McClure, Barry, TJ 1972–73
Haynes, Tom, TJ and LJ[4] 1975
Dupree, Rayfield, TJ[5] 1977
Artis, Greg, LJ[6] 1980–82

Lloyd, Eddie, TJ 1982
Meeks, Orestes, 1982
Johnson, Dwight, LJ 1984

[1] Moore, Michael—1975 Ohio Valley Conference Offensive Player of the Year
[2] Sorrell, George—1975 Ohio Valley Conference Player of the Year
[3] Beck, Jerry—1981–82 Ohio Valley Conference Player of the Year
[4] Haynes, Tom—member of the 1976 United States Olympic Track and Field Team
[5] Dupree, Rayfield—member of the 1976 United States Olympic Track and Field Team
[6] Artis, Greg—1981 Ohio Valley Conference Athlete of the Year

Youngstown State University
Youngstown, Ohio 44555

All Mid-Continent Conference

Football

Brumfield, Marscheil 1977–78

All Ohio Valley Conference

Football

Wicks, Paris 1981–82
Goode, John 1983

All-American

Football

Wicks, Paris 1981–82
Goode, John, 1983

Men's Basketball

Covington, Jeff 1977–78

BOXING

AFRICAN-AMERICAN WORLD BOXING CHAMPIONS

Weight Class	Name	Year
heavyweight	Louis, Joe	1937–49
light-heavyweight	Lewis, John Henry	1935–38
middleweight	Flowers, Tiger	1926
middleweight	Jones, Gorilla	1931–32
welterweight	Thompson, Cecil (aka Young Jack)	1930–31
welterweight	Armstrong, Henry	1938–40
lightweight	Armstrong, Henry	1938–39
lightweight	Walker, Sidney (aka Beau Jack)	1942–43, 1943–44 (New York)
lightweight	Montgomery, Bob	1943, 1944–47 (New York)
featherweight	Armstrong, Henry	1937–38
featherweight	Wilson, Jackie	1941–43 (NBA)

JOE LOUIS

(Joseph Louis Barrow)

(The Brown Bomber)

Born, May 13, 1914, Lafayette, Alabama. Weight, 188-218 lbs. Height, 6 ft. 1¾ in. Managed by Julian Black and John Roxborough; later by Marshall Miles.

1934 National AAU Light Heavyweight Champion

1934

July	4–Jack Kracken, Chicago	KO	1
July	12–Willie Davies, Chicago	KO	3
July	30–Larry Udell, Chicago	KO	2
Aug.	13–Jack Kranz, Chicago	W	8
Aug.	27–Buck Everett, Chicago	KO	2
Sept.	11–Alex Borchuk, Detroit	KO	4
Sept.	26–Adolph Wiater, Chicago	W	10
Oct.	24–Art Sykes, Chicago	KO	8
Oct.	31–Jack O'Dowd, Detroit	KO	2
Nov.	14–Stanley Poreda, Chicago	KO	1
Nov.	30–Charley Massera, Chicago	KO	3
Dec.	14–Lee Ramage, Chicago	KO	8

1935

Jan.	4–Patsy Perroni, Detroit	W	10
Jan.	11–Hans Birkie, Pittsburgh	KO	10
Feb.	21–Lee Ramage, Los Angeles	KO	2
Mar.	8–Donald (Reds) Barry, San Francisco	KO	3
Mar.	29–Natie Brown, Detroit	W	10
Apr.	12–Roy Lazer, Chicago	KO	3
Apr.	22–Biff Bennett, Dayton	Exh. KO	1
Apr.	25–Roscoe Toles, Flint	Exh. KO	6
May	3–Willie Davis, Peoria	Exh. KO	2
May	7–Gene Stanton, Kalamazoo	Exh. KO	3
June	25–Primo Carnera, New York	KO	6
Aug.	7–King Levinsky, Chicago	KO	1
Sept.	24–Max Baer, New York	KO	4
Dec.	14–Paulino Uzcudun, New York	KO	4

1936

Jan.	17–Charley Retzlaff, Chicago	KO	1
June	19–Max Schmeling, New York	KO by	12
Aug.	18–Jack Sharkey, New York	KO	3
Sept.	22–Al Ettore, Philadelphia	KO	5
Oct.	9–Jorge Brescia, New York	KO	3
Oct.	14–Willie Davies, South Bend	Exh. KO	3
Oct.	14–K.O. Brown, South Bend	Exh. KO	3
Nov.	20–Paul Williams, New Orleans	Exh. KO	2
Nov.	20–Tom Jones, New Orleans	Exh. KO	3
Dec.	14–Eddie Simms, Cleveland	KO	1

1937

Jan.	11–Stanley Ketchell, Buffalo	Exh. KO	2
Jan.	29–Bob Pastor, New York	W	10
Feb.	17–Natie Brown, Kansas City	KO	4
June	22–James J. Braddock, Chicago	KO	8
	(Won World Heavyweight Title)		
Aug.	30–Tommy Farr, New York	W	15
	(Retained World Heavyweight Title)		

1938

Feb.	23–Nathan Mann, New York	KO	3
	(Retained World Heavyweight Title)		
Apr.	1–Harry Thomas, Chicago	KO	5
	(Retained World Heavyweight Title)		
June	22–Max Schmeling, New York	KO	1
	(Retained World Heavyweight Title)		

1939

Jan.	25–John Henry Lewis, New York	KO	1
	(Retained World Heavyweight Title)		
Apr.	17–Jack Roper, Los Angeles	KO	1
	Retained World Heavyweight Title)		
June	28–Tony Galento, New York	KO	4
	(Retained World Heavyweight Title)		
Sept.	20–Bob Pastor, Detroit	KO	11
	(Retained World Heavyweight Title)		

1940

Feb.	9–Arturo Godoy, New York	W	15
	(Retained World Heavyweight Title)		
Mar.	29–Johnny Paychek, New York	KO	2
	(Retained World Heavyweight Title)		
June	20–Arturo Godoy, New York	KO	8
	(Retained World Heavyweight Title)		
Dec.	16–Al McCoy, Boston	KO	6
	(Retained World Heavyweight Title)		

1941

Jan.	31–Red Burman, New York	KO	5
	(Retained World Heavyweight Title)		
Feb.	17–Gus Dorazio, Philadelphia	KO	2
	(Retained World Heavyweight Title)		
Mar.	21–Abe Simon, Detroit	KO	13
	(Retained World Heavyweight Title)		
Apr.	8–Tony Musto, St. Louis	KO	9
	(Retained World Heavyweight Title)		
May	23–Buddy Baer, Washington, D.C.	W disq.	7
	(Retained World Heavyweight Title)		

June 18–Billy Conn, New York . . . . KO 13
    (Retained World Heavyweight Title)
July 11–Jim Robinson, Minneapolis . . . . Exh. KO 1
Sept. 29–Lou Nova, New York . . . . KO 6
    (Retained World Heavyweight Title)
Nov. 25–George Giambastiani, Los Angeles . . . . . . Exh. 4

1942

Jan. 9–Buddy Baer, New York . . . . KO 1
    (Retained World Heavyweight Title)
Mar. 27–Abe Simon, New York . . . . KO 6
    (Retained World Heavyweight Title)
June 5–George Nicholson, Fort Hamilton . . . . Exh. 3

1943
(Inactive)

1944

Nov. 3–Johnny Demson, Detroit . . . . Exh. KO 2
Nov. 6–Charley Crump, Baltimore . . . . Exh. 3
Nov. 9–Dee Amos, Hartford. . . . . Exh. 3
Nov. 13–Jimmy Bell, Washington, D.C.. . . . . Exh. 3
Nov. 14–Johnny Davis, Buffalo . . . . Exh. KO 1
Nov. 15–Dee Amos, Elizabeth . . . . Exh. 3
Nov. 17–Dee Amos, Camden . . . . Exh. 3
Nov. 24–Dan Merritt, Chicago . . . . Exh. 3

1945

Nov. 15–Sugar Lip Anderson, San
    Francisco . . . . Exh. 2
Nov. 15–Big Boy Brown, San Francisco. . . . . Exh. 2
Nov. 29–Big Boy Brown, Sacramento . . . . Exh. 2
Nov. 29–Bobby Lee, Sacramento . . . . Exh. 2
Dec. 10–Bob Frazier, Victoria . . . . Exh. 3
Dec. 11–Big Boy Brown, Portland. . . . . Exh. 2
Dec. 11–Dave Johnson, Portland . . . . Exh. 2
Dec. 12–Big Boy Brown, Eugene . . . . Exh. 3
Dec. 13–Big Boy Brown, Vancouver . . . . Exh. 3

1946

June 19–Billy Conn, New York . . . . KO 8
    (Retained World Heavyweight Title)
Sept. 18–Tami Mauriello, New York. . . . . KO 1
    (Retained World Heavyweight Title)
Nov. 11–Cleo Everett, Honolulu. . . . . Exh. 4
Nov. 11–Wayne Powell, Honolulu . . . . Exh. 2
Nov. 25–Perk Daniels, Mexicali . . . . Exh. 4

1947

Feb. 7–Arturo Godoy, Mexico City . . . . Exh. 10
Dec. 5–Jersey Joe Walcott, New York . . . . W 15
    (Retained World Heavyweight Title)

1948

June 25–Jersey Joe Walcott, New York . . . . KO 11
    (Retained World Heavyweight Title)

1949

Mar. 1–Announced retirement.

1950

Sept. 27–Ezzard Charles, New York . . . . L 15
    (For World Heavyweight Title)
Nov. 29–Cesar Brion, New York. . . . . W 10

1951

Jan. 3–Freddie Beshore, Detroit . . . . KO 4
Feb. 7–Omelio Agramonte, Miami . . . . W 10
Feb. 23–Andy Walker, San Francisco. . . . . KO 10
May 2–Omelio Agramonte, Detroit. . . . . W 10
June 15–Lee Savold, New York . . . . KO 6
Aug. 1–Cesar Brion, San Francisco . . . . W 10
Aug. 15–Jimmy Bivins, Baltimore . . . . W 10
Oct. 26–Rocky Marciano, New York . . . . KO by 8

TB	KO	WD	WF	D	LD	LF	KOBO	ND	NC
66	49	13	1	0	1	0	2	0	0

Elected to Boxing Hall of Fame, 1954.
Died, April 12, 1981, Las Veas, Nevada.

JOHN HENRY LEWIS

Born, May 1, 1914, Los Angeles, Calif. Weight, 174 lbs. Height, 5 ft. 11 in. Managed by Ernie Lira, Larry White, Frank Schuler, Gus Greenlee.

1930

  –Roy Gunn. . . . . KO 3
  –Kid Val Don . . . . KO 3
  –Sammy Bass . . . . KO 1
  –Ray Imm . . . . KO 4
  –Jake Henderson . . . . KO 4
  –Young Tiger Flowers . . . . KO 6

1931

Jan. 30–Palmleaf Wright, Phoenix . . . . KO 2
Feb. 6–Bob Richardson, Phoenix . . . . KO 2

Mar. 11 –Sam Terrain, Prescott................ KO 4

May 15 –Tony Cadena, Phoenix................. KO 1

May 29 –Evans Fortune, Phoenix .... KO 3

July 1 –Lloyd Phelps, Mesa .... W 8

Sept. 14 –Joe Arcienega, Phoenix.............. KO 5

Nov. 27 –The School Boy, Phoenix.............. KO 3

1932

Career totals to March, 1932: 20 bouts, 18 kayoes, two wins on points.

Apr. 22 –Yale Okun, San Francisco .... W 10

July 13 –Peitro Georgi, San Francisco........... KO 1

July 29 –Jimmy Hanna, San Francisco.......... KO 6

Sept. 21 –James J. Braddock, San Francisco........ W 10

Oct. 5 –Fred Lenhart, San Francisco........... KO 4

Oct. 26 –Lou Scozza, San Francisco .... W 10

Nov. 16 –Maxie Rosenbloom, San Francisco........ L 10

Dec. 9 –Tuffy Dial, Phoenix.................. KO 4

1933

Feb. 7 –Terris Hill, San Francisco .... KO 4

Apr. 7 –Emmett Rocco, San Francisco.......... KO 7

May 15 –Tom Patrick, San Francisco............ W 10

June 10 –Fred Lenhart, San Francisco .... D 10

July 10 –Maxie Rosenbloom, San Francisco .... W 10

July 31 –Maxie Rosenbloom, San Francisco .... W 10

Oct. 31 –Frank Rowsey, Los Angeles............ W 10

1934

Feb. 9 –Bobby Brown, Tucson .... KO 1

June 6 –Sandy Casanova, Ft. Hauchuca......... KO 3

July 12 –Bobby Brown, Tucson .... KO 3

Sept. 3 –Tony Poloni, Reno................... KO 1

Sept. 12 –Norman Conrad, Oakland .... W 10

Sept. 20 –Young Firpo, Portland .... D 10

Oct. 3 –Red Barry, San Francisco .... D 10

Oct. 17 –Pietro Georgi, Oakland .... KO 2

Oct. 31 –Earl Wise, Oakland .... KO 3

Nov. 16 –James J. Braddock, New York .... L 10

Nov. 23 –Yale Okun, New York .... KO 3

Dec. 14 –Tony Shucco, New York .... W 10

1935

Jan. 29 –Don Petrin, Pittsburgh .... KO 7

Feb. 25 –Frank Wojack, Syracuse .... KO 3

Mar. 4 –Terry Mitchell, Syracuse .... KO 6

Mar. 13 –Emilio Martinez, Denver.............. W 10

Apr. 12 –Bob Olin, San Francisco............... W 10

May 10 –Frank Rowsey, San Francisco........... W 10

June 3 –Tommy Patrick, Pittsburgh .... KO 1

June 24 –Izzy Singer, Paterson .... KO 1

July 8 –Lou Poster, Cleveland................. KO 5

July 17 –Maxie Rosenbloom, Oakland .... L 10

July 24 –Abe Feldman, New York .... L 10

Oct. 31 –Bob Olin, St. Louis .... W 15

(Won World Light Heavyweight Title)

Nov. 29 –Maxie Rosenbloom, San Francisco........ L 10

Dec. 11 –Georgie Simpson, Oakland .... KO 2

Dec. 19 –Coleman Johns, Phoenix.............. KO 2

Dec. 20 –Dutch Weimer, Tucson .... W 10

1936

Jan. 10 –Tiger Jack Fox, Spokane .... KO 3

Jan. 17 –Al Stillman, St. Louis .... KO 4

Jan. 29 –Emilio Martinez, Denver............... L 10

Jan. 31 –Cyclone Lynch, Walsenburg............. KO 1

Mar. 6 –Eddie Simms, St. Louis .... W 10

Mar. 13 –Jock McAvoy, New York................ W 15

(Retained World Light Heavyweight Title)

Apr. 7 –George Nichols, Buffalo .... D 10

Apr. 22 –Izzy Singer, Chicago .... W 10

May 27 –Charlie Massera, Pittsburgh .... W 10

May 29 –Bob Godwin, New York............... KO 1

June 8 –John Anderson, New York............. W 10

June 12 –Dutch Weimer, York .... KO 5

June 17 –Tony Shucco, St. Louis .... KO 8

June 22 –Jimmy Merriott, Peoria................ KO 3

July 10 –Max Marek, Chicago................. W 10

July 30 –Al Gainer, Pittsburgh .... W 12

Aug. 12 –George Nichols, St. Louis .... W 10

Sept. 17 –Tiger Hairston, Charleston .... KO 1

Oct. 2 –Red Burman, Chicago................ KO 2

Nov. 9 –Len Harvey, London.................. W 15

(Retained World Light Heavyweight Title)

1937

Jan. 4 –Al Ettore, Philadelphia .... D 10

Jan. 11 –Art Sykes, Pittsburgh .... KO 6

Jan. 28 –Chester Palutis, Scranton .... KO 7

Feb. 8 –Al Ettore, Philadelphia .... W 15

Mar. 15 –Hans Birkie, Philadelphia .... W 10

Apr. 2 –Donald (Reds) Barry, St. Louis .... KO 5

Apr. 9 –Babe Davis, Indianapolis .... KO 3

Apr. 13 –Harold Murphy, Omaha............... KO 4

Apr. 19 –Pret Farrar, Des Moines .... KO 6

May 4 –Emilio Martinez, St. Louis .... W 10

May   14–Patsy Perroni, New York . . . . W 10
May   21–Jack Kranz, Kansas City . . . . KO   3
June   3–Bob Olin, St. Louis . . . . KO   8
       (Retained World Light Heavyweight Title)
June   15–Al Ettore, Philadelphia . . . . W 10
June   28–Willie Reddish, Washington. . . . . W 10
Aug.   19–Italo Colonello, Pittsburgh . . . . W 12
Oct.   15–Isadore Gastanga, Detroit . . . . L 10
Nov.   26–Salvadore Ruggierello, Minneapolis . . . . KO   4
Dec.   12–Isadore Gastanaga, St. Louis. . . . . KO   9
Dec.   17–Johnny Risko, Cleveland . . . . W 10

1938

Jan.   10–Leonard Neblitt, Nashville . . . . KO   8
Jan.   18–Marty Gallagher, St. Louis . . . . KO   3
Jan.   31–Emil Scholz, Pittsburgh . . . . W 10
Feb.   11–Fred Lenhart, St. Louis . . . . KO   3
Mar.   25–Bud Mignault, St. Paul . . . . W 10
Apr.   4–Bob Tow, Philadelphia . . . . W 10
Apr.   25–Emilio Martinez, Minneapolis . . . . KO   4
       (Retained World Light Heavyweight Title)
May   5–Domenic Ceccarelli, Baltimore . . . . W 10
May   19–Elmer Ray, Atlanta . . . . KO 12
Aug.   25–Domenic Ceccarelli, Nutley. . . . . KO   3
Sept. 15–Jimmy Adamick, Philadelphia . . . . W 10
Oct.   28–Al Gainer, New Haven. . . . . W 15
       (Retained World Light Heavyweight Title)

1939

Jan.   25–Joe Louis, New York . . . . KO by 1
       (For World Heavyweight Title)
June   –
Announced retirement.

TB	KO	WD	WF	D	LD	LF	KOBO	ND	NC
116	64	39	0	5	7	0	1	0	0

Died, April 18, 1974, Berkeley, Calif.

THEODORE (TIGER) FLOWERS

(The Georgia Deacon)
Born, August 5, 1895, Camille, Georgia. Weight, 160 lbs.
Height, 5ft. 10 in. Southpaw. Managed by Walk Miller.

1918

Knockouts: Billy Hooper, 11; Kid Fox, 2; Batt Hazel, 8. Won: Batt Henry Williams, 20; Rufus Cameron, 10; Batt Mims, 15.

1919

Knockout: Rough House Baker, 3. Won: Batt Mims, 10; Bill Hooper, 20.

1920

Knockouts: Tiger Moore, 2; Kid Palmer, 3. Won: Sailor Darden, 15; Batt Mims, 10.

1921

Knockouts: Kid Brown, 8; Batt Troupe, 3; Kid Brown, 2; Whitey Black, 1; Kid Williams, 3; Gorilla Jones, 4; Jim Barry, 5; Mexican Kid Brown, 1. Won: Billy Hooper, 10; Batt Mims, 10; Batt Mims, 10; Batt Gahee, 10; Batt Gahee, 8; Whitey Black, 8; Jim Barry, 15. Knockout by: Panama Joe Gans, 5.

1922

Knockouts: Jack Ray, 2; Kid Brown, 2; Kid Paddy, 1; Kid Davis, 1; Eddie Palmer, 10. Won: Billy Britton, 15; Battling Gahee, 8; Frankie Murphy, 15; Andy Kid Palmer, 15; Frankie Carbone, 10; (foul) Eddie Palmer, 8. Knocked out by: Kid Norfolk, 3; Sam Langford, 2; Lee Anderson, 7; Jamaica Kid, 2. Draw: Battling Norfolk, 8.

1923

Feb.   21–Bob Lawson, Nashville . . . . W   8
Feb.   28–Batt Mims, Nashville . . . . W   8
Mar.   10–Evansville Jack Ray, Nashville . . . . KO   3
Apr.   20–Jamaica Kid, Toledo . . . . ND 12
May   8–Kid Norfolk, Springfield . . . . KO by   1
May   15–Tom King, Juarez, Mexico. . . . . W 15
May   25–Panama Joe Gans, Toledo . . . . ND 12
July   3–Tut Jackson, Atlanta . . . . W 12
July   30–Whitey Black, Detroit . . . . ND 10
Sept.   3–Jamaica Kid, Atlanta . . . . W 12
Sept. 16–Jim Flynn, Mexico City . . . . W   5
Nov.   7–George Robinson, Atlanta . . . . D 12
Dec.   6–Rufus Cameron, Albany. . . . . KO   4

1924

Jan.   23–Herbert Moore, Nashville . . . . KO   1
Jan.   30–Sam Goodrich, San Antonio . . . . W 12
Feb.   18–Bob Lawson, Toledo . . . . KO 10
Feb.   25–Battling Gahee, Barberton . . . . W 12
Mar.   3–Jamaica Kid, Fremont. . . . . ND 10
Mar.   19–Bob Lawson, Nashville . . . . KO   5
Mar.   29–Lee Anderson, N.Y.C. . . . . W 12
Apr.   9–Dave Thorton, Nashville . . . . KO   2
Apr.   19–Jimmy Darcy, N.Y.C.. . . . . W 10
Apr.   29–Geo. Robinson, Atlanta. . . . . W 10
May   3–Ted Jamieson, N.Y.C. . . . . W 12

May   14–Willie Walker, N.Y.C. . . . . KO   7
June   14–Joe Lohman, N.Y.C. . . . . W   12
June   20–Batt. Gahee, Fremont . . . . ND   10
June   27–Jamaica Kid, Grand Rapids . . . . WF   3
July   3–Lee Anderson, Atlanta . . . . WF   6
July   22–Jamaica Kid, Covington. . . . . WF   3
Aug.   2–Jack Townsend, N.Y.C. . . . . KO   11
Aug.   12–Oscar Mortimer, San Antonio . . . . KO   3
Aug.   21–Harry Greb. Fremont . . . . ND   10
Sept.   1–Tut Jackson, Martins Ferry . . . . ND   10
Sept.   15–Jamaica Kid, Columbus . . . . W   12
Sept.   22–Lee Anderson, Columbus . . . . W   12
Sept.   28–Battling Gahee, Zanesville. . . . . KO   4
Sept.   29–Tut Jackson, Canton . . . . KO   1
Oct.   11–Jamaica Kid, N.Y.C. . . . . KO   7
Oct.   21–Cleve Hawkins, Atlanta . . . . KO   3
Oct.   23–Joe Lohman, Hamilton . . . . WF   4
Nov.   1–George Robinson, N.Y.C. . . . . W   12
Nov.   10–*Jerry Hayes, Philadelphia . . . . KO   2
Nov.   10–*Hughie Clemons, Philadelphia . . . . KO   2
Nov.   27–Clem Johnson, Canton . . . . ND   12
Dec.   1–Battling Gahee, Columbus. . . . . KO   2
Dec.   9–Johnny Wilson, N.Y.C. . . . . KO   3
Dec.   15–Jack Townsend, Philadelphia . . . . KO   5
Dec.   26–Frankie Schoell, Buffalo . . . . D   6

*Both in same night.

1925

Jan.   1–Joe Lohman, Brooklyn . . . . KO   3
Jan.   5–Billy Britton, Boston. . . . . KO   4
Jan.   7–Dan Dowd, Providence . . . . KO   6
Jan.   16–Jack Delaney, N.Y.C. . . . . KO by   2
Jan.   28–Tommy Robson, Boston . . . . KO   8
Feb.   2–Ted Moore, Newark . . . . ND   12
Feb.   5–Jamaica Kid, Dayton . . . . KO   10
Feb.   14–Jackie Clarke, N.Y.C. . . . . KO   5
Feb.   16–Lou Bogash, Boston . . . . LF   3
Mar.   4–Jack Delaney, N.Y.C. . . . . KO by   4
Mar.   16–Sailor Darden, Toledo . . . . W   12
Mar.   20–Lou Bogash, Boston. . . . . W   10
Apr.   29–Sailor Darden, Savannah . . . . KO   5
May   18–Pal Reed, Boston . . . . W   10
May   26–Lou Bogash, Bridgeport . . . . W   12
June   4–Jock Malone, E. Chicago. . . . . ND   10
June   8–Lee Anderson, Phildalephia . . . . W   10
July   24–Lou Bogash, Aurora . . . . ND   10
July   20–Pat McCarthy, Boston. . . . . W   10
Aug.   28–Jock Malone, Boston . . . . W   10
Sept.   7–*Ted Moore, Cleveland . . . . NC   6

Oct.   23–Jock Malone, St. Paul. . . . . ND   10
Oct.   28–Chuck Wiggins, E. Chicago . . . . ND   10
Dec.   10–Frank Moody, Boston . . . . W   10
Dec.   23–Mike McTigue, N.Y.C. L   10
                    *Referee stopped fight.

1926

Feb.   26–Harry Greb, N.Y.C. . . . . W   15
                (Won World Middleweight Title)
Apr.   16–Panama Joe Gans, Wilkes-Barre . . . . W   10
June   18–Young Bob Fitzsimmons, Jersey City . . . . . . ND   10
June   28–Ray Neuman, Boston . . . . W   10
July   11–Lee Anderson, Juarez, Mexico . . . . KO   2
July   24–Eddie Huffman, Los Angeles. . . . . W   10
Aug.   10–Batt. McCreary, Atlanta . . . . WF   2
Aug.   19–*Harry Greb, N.Y.C. . . . . W   15
Sept.   16–Happy Hunter, Memphis . . . . KO   3
Oct.   15–Maxie Rosenbloom, Boston . . . . LF   9
Nov.   22–Eddie Huffman, Chicago. . . . . W   10
Dec.   3–Mickey Walker, Chicago L   10
                (Lost World Middleweight Title)

*Title bout.

1927

Jan.   7–Tut Jackson, Grand Rapids . . . . KO   2
Jan.   22–Leo Lomski, Los Angeles L   10
Feb.   18–Lou Bogash, Boston. . . . . W   10
Mar.   29–Soldier Geo. Jones, Atlanta. . . . . KO   1
Apr.   29–Chuck Wiggins, Buffalo. . . . . W   10
May   13–Chuck Wiggins, Grand Rapids . . . . W   10
May   27–Eddie Huffman, Boston . . . . W   10
June   16–Bob Sage, Detroit . . . . W   10
July   3–Maxie Rosenbloom, Chicago . . . . D   10
July   28–Bing Conley, Norwalk. . . . . W   10
Aug.   3–Chuck Wiggins, Cleveland . . . . D   10
Aug.   11–Harry Dillon, Portland . . . . W   10
Aug.   16–Jock Malone, Seattle . . . . W   6
Sept.   1–Joe Anderson, N.Y.C. . . . . W   10
Sept.   30–Pete Latzo, Wilkes-Barre . . . . W   10
Oct.   17–Joe Lohman, Canton . . . . W   10
Nov.   9–Maxie Rosenbloom, Detroit. . . . . D   10
Nov.   12–Leo Gates, N.Y.C. . . . . KO   4

TB	KO	WD	WF	D	LD	LF	KOBO	ND	NC
149	49	61	5	6	3	2	8	14	1

Died, November 16, 1927, New York City, N.Y.,
following an operation.
Elected to Boxing Hall of Fame, 1971.

WILLIAM (GORILLA) JONES

Born, May 4, 1910, Memphis, Tenn. Weight, 147-160 lbs. Height, 5 ft. 6 in. Managed by Suey Welch.

1928

Jan. 27–George Moore, Akron	KO 5
Feb. 23–Black Fitz, Barberton	KO 3
Mar. 1–Sailor Maxwell, Canton	KO 4
Mar. 29–K.O. Kelly, Akron	W 10
Apr. 10–Joe Feldman, Cleveland	KO 1
Apr. 27–Ben Spively, Marietta	KO 4
May 4–Alvin Spence, Cleveland	KO 1
May 17–Young Saylor, Marietta	ND 10
May 29–Allan Beatty, McKeesport	KO 10
June 1–Bobby Brown, Cleveland	L 10
June 18–Mickey Fedor, Akron	KO 5
July 18–Jim Williams, Akron	KO 3
July 25–Bobby Brown, Cleveland	KO 3
Aug. 14–Billy Algers, Akron	W 10
Aug. 29–Sammy Baker, Cleveland	ND 10
Sept. 13–Tommy Freeman, Cleveland	ND 10
Sept. 18–Bobby LaSalle, Cleveland	W 10
Oct. 2–Billy Leonard, Akron	KO 1
Oct. 11–Heavy Andrews, Erie	W 10
Oct. 19–Bucky Lawless, Erie	ND 10
Oct. 25–Bucky Lawless, Erie	W 10
Nov. 2–Jimmy Finley, Akron	W 10
Nov. 16–Pal Silvers, New York	W 8
Dec. 28–Tony Vaccarelli, New York	D 10

1929

Jan. 8–Arturo Shackels, Cleveland	KO 1
Jan. 14–Arturo Shackels, Buffalo	W 10
Feb. 15–Jack Murphy, Erie	KO 4
Feb. 18–Bucky Lawless, Buffalo	L 10
Feb. 25–Nick Testo, Holyoke	LF 5
Mar. 11–Joe Zelinsky, Springfield	KO 1
Apr. 2–George Fifield, Akron	KO 1
Apr. 9–Tommy Freeman, Cleveland	D 12
May 3–Al Mello, New York	W 10
May 17–Izzy Grove, New York	KO 6
June 3–Al Mello, Boston	KO 6
June 14–Jack Palmer, Chicago	KO 5
June 25–Jack McVey, Boston	W 10
July 16–Bucky Lawless, Cleveland	L 12
Aug. 1–Battling Groves, Memphis	KO 3
Aug. 12–Pete Meyers, San Francisco	KO 5

Aug. 20–Fred Mahan, Los Angeles	KO 6
Oct. 9–Jack Horner, Akron	KO 2
Oct. 21–Jackie Fields, San Francisco	L 10
Nov. 8–Jack Sparr, San Diego	KO 4
Dec. 4–Nick Testo, Akron	KO 6
Dec. 13–Jackie Fields, Boston	NC 7

1930

Jan. 1–Billy Angelo, Philadelphia	W 10
Jan. 17–Floyd Hybert, Holyoke	KO 3
Jan. 27–Izzy Grove, New York	KO 6
Feb. 7–Eddie Roberts, San Francisco	D 10
Feb. 14–Wesley Ketchell, San Francisco	W 10
Mar. 14–Meyer Grace, Akron	KO 4
Mar. 17–Jock Malone, St. Paul	ND 10
Apr. 14–Gene Cardi, Wheeling	KO 7
Apr. 22–Roy (Tiger) Williams, Dayton	L 12
May 12–Bucky Lawless, Holyoke	L 10
May 26–Vincent Forgione, Pittsburgh	W 10
June 2–Henry Goldberg, W. Springfield	W 10
June 25–Vincent Forgione, Cleveland	W 10
July 18–Bucky Lawless, San Francisco	KO 9
Aug. 8–Manuel Quintero, San Francisco	D 10
Aug. 15–Ham Jenkins, Denver	W 10
Sept. 4–Harry Smith, Long Island City	NC 9
Sept. 15–Cowboy Jack Willis, Canton	W 10
Oct. 23–Harry Smith, New York	L 10
Nov. 10–Abe Lichtenstein, Rochester	W 10
Nov. 28–Jackie Brady, Erie	L 10
Dec. 26–Clyde Chastain, Akron	KO 4

1931

Jan. 13–Johnny Burns, Oakland	KO 7
Jan. 28–Chick Devlin, San Francisco	D 10
Jan. 30–Mike Hector, Stockton	W 10
Feb. 6–Frank Rowsey, San Francisco	KO 8
Feb. 17–Herman Ratzleff, Portland	W 10
Mar. 11–Bud Gorman, Oakland	W 10
Apr. 14–Paul Pirrone, Cleveland	W 10
Apr. 28–Ham Jenkins, Kansas City	W 10
May 25–Bucky Lawless, Chicago	L 10
Aug. 25–Tiger Thomas, Milwaukee	W 10
Sept. 17–Clyde Chastain, Milwaukee	KO 6
Oct. 21–Johnny Roberts, Akron	KO 3
Nov. 3–George Nichols, Milwaukee	W 10
Nov. 19–Frankie O'Brien, Milwaukee	W 10
Dec. 11–Henry Firpo, Milwaukee	W 10

1932

Jan. 25–Oddone Piazza, Milwaukee . . . . KO 6
(Won Vacant World Middleweight Title)
Mar. 14–Frankie O'Brien, Holyoke . . . . L disq. 8
Mar. 31–Chuck Burns, Akron . . . . KO 3
Apr. 7–Bud Saltis, Green Bay . . . . W 10
Apr. 26–Young Terry, Trenton . . . . W 12
(Retained World Middleweight Title)
June 11–Marcel Thil, Paris. . . . . L disq. 11
(Lost World Middleweight Title)
Aug. 9–Jack December, Cleveland . . . . KO 2
Aug. 29–Kid Leonard, Davenport . . . . W 10
Oct. 3–Johnny Peppe, Atlantic City. . . . . W 8
Nov. 24–Jackie Purvis, Akron . . . . KO 3
Dec. 1–Willie Oster, Davenport . . . . W 10
Dec. 5–Manny Davis, Manche . . . . WF 6
Dec. 26–Tommy Freeman, Pittsburgh . . . . D 10

1933

Jan. 13–Young Stuhley, Clinton . . . . KO 4
Jan. 30–Sammy Slaughter, Cleveland . . . . KO 7
(Won Vacant NBA American Middleweight Title)
Feb. 21–Kid Baker, Indianapolis. . . . . W 10
Feb. 28–Willie Oster, Toledo . . . . KO 3
Apr. 19–Ben Jeby, Cleveland . . . . NC 6
June 30–Babe Marino, San Francisco . . . . KO 10
July 18–Wesley Ketchell, Los Angeles . . . . W 10
July 28–Vearl Whitehead, Los Angeles. . . . . L disq. 10
Aug. 8–Vearl Whitehead, Lost Angeles . . . . D 10
Aug. 25–Harold Hoxwood, Salt Lake City . . . . D 10
Sept. 3–Manuel Victoria, Tijuana . . . . KO 7
Sept. 15–Johnny Romero, San Diego . . . . KO 3
Sept. 21–Billy Papke, Pasadena . . . . KO 8
Oct. 6–Mike Payan, San Diego . . . . W 10
Oct. 12–Lou Bertman, Phoenix . . . . KO 2
Oct. 27–Ed Murdock, San Diego . . . . KO 10
Dec. 5–Frank Remus, Seattle . . . . KO 6

1934

Jan. 16–Tony Poloni, Los Angeles . . . . W 10
Feb. 9–Max Maxwell, San Diego. . . . . D 10
Feb. 23–Dutch Weimer, San Diego . . . . L 10
May 22–Freddie Steele, Seattle. . . . . D 10
June 19–Emilio Martinez, Denver . . . . L 10
Aug. 21–Oscar Rankin, Los Angeles . . . . L 10

1935

Sept. 17–Freddie Steele, Seattle . . . . L 10

1936

Jan. 1–Tait Littman, Milwaukee . . . . KO 1
Jan. 27–Tait Littman, Milwaukee . . . . KO 10
Aug. 5–Art Taylor, Phoenix . . . . D 10
Dec. 4–Mickey Bottone, Milwaukee. . . . . KO 1

1937

Jan. 1–Freddie Steele, Milwaukee . . . . L 10
(For NBA-New York World Middleweight Title)
Jan. 29–Frankie Battaglia, Milwaukee. . . . . D 10
Apr. 13–Battling Nelson, Omaha . . . . KO 4
July –Frankie Misko, Sioux City . . . . KO 5
Aug. 9–Tommy Freeman, Council Bluffs . . . . W 10
Oct. 27–Andy Miller, Sioux City. . . . . W 8
Nov. 23–Alabama Kid, Springfield. . . . . L 10
Dec. 15–Bob Turner, Akron . . . . W 10

1938

Jan. 12–Frankie Hughes, Akron . . . . W 10
Jan. 19–Tiger Carsonia, Louisville . . . . KO 2
Feb. 16–Johnny Davis, Akron . . . . KO 8
Feb. 23–Jack Moran, Akron . . . . W 10
Apr. 4–King Wyatt, Fort Wayne. . . . . D 10
May 10–Babe Risko, Akron . . . . L 10

1939

Jan. 24–Angelo Puglisi, Seattle . . . . W 10

1940

May 29–Vern Earling, Kellogg . . . . L 10

TB	KO	WD	WF	D	LD	LF	KOBO	ND	NC
140	55	42	1	13	17	4	0	5	3

Died, January 4, 1982, Los Angeles Calif.

HENRY ARMSTRONG

(Henry Jackson)
(Homicide Hank)
Born, December 12, 1912, Columbus, Miss. Weight, 124-146
lbs. Height, 5 ft. 5½ in. Managed by Wirt Ross, Eddie Mead.

1931

July 27–Al Iovino, North Braddock. . . . . KO by 3
Aug. –Sammy Burns, Millville. . . . . W 6

1932

Aug. 30–Eddie Trujillo, Los Angeles . . . . L 4

Sept. 27–Al Greenfield, Los Angeles L   4
       –Max Tarley . . . . W   4
       –Young Bud Taylor . . . . KO   2
       –Vince Trujillo . . . . KO   2
Dec.   13–Gene Espinosa, Los Angeles. . . . . W   4

1933

       –Mickey Ryan . . . . W   6
       –Georgie Dundee . . . . W   6
       –Steve Harky . . . . W   6
Mar.   21–Paul Wangley, Los Angeles . . . . KO   4
       –Young Corpus . . . . W   6
       –Johnny Granone . . . . KO   5
May   31–Max Tarley, Los Angeles . . . . KO   3
July   11–Baby Manuel, Los Angeles. L   6
Aug.   8–Bobby Calmes, Los Angeles . . . . KO   5
Aug.   30–Hoyt Jones, Los Angeles. . . . . D   4
Sept. 5–Perfecto Lopez, Los Angeles. . . . . D   4
Oct.   11–Perfecto Lopez, Los Angeles . . . . D   4
Nov.   3–Kid Moro, Pismo Beach . . . . W 10
Nov.   23–Kid Moro, Stockton . . . . D 10
Dec.   14–Gene Espinosa, Sacramento . . . . KO   7
Dec.   –Kid Moro, Watsonville. . . . . D 10

1934

Jan.   26–Baby Manuel, Sacramento. . . . . W 10
Feb.   13–Benny Pelz, Los Angeles. . . . . W   6
Mar.   17–Young Danny, Los Angeles . . . . KO   1
May   22–Johnny DeFoe, Los Angeles . . . . KO   6
June   5–Vincente Torres, Los Angeles . . . . W   4
June   14–Davy Abad, Sacramento . . . . W 10
July   17–Perfecto Lopez, Los Angeles . . . . W   6
Aug.   28–Perfecto Lopez, Los Angeles. . . . . KO   5
       –Mark Diaz . . . . W   8
       –Tully Corvo . . . . KO   7
Nov.   3–Baby Arizmendi, Mexico City . . . . L 10
Dec.   2–Joe Gonde, Mexico City . . . . KO   7
Dec.   15–Ventura Arana, Mexico City. . . . . KO   5

1935

Jan.   2–Baby Arizmendi, Mexico City . . . . L 12
       (For Vacant Calif.-Mexican World Featherweight Title)
Mar.   19–Sal Hernandez, Los Angeles . . . . KO   2
Mar.   31–Davy Abad, Mexico City . . . . L 10
Apr.   16–Frankie Covelli, Los Angeles. . . . . W   8
May   28–Davy Abad, LosAngeles. . . . . W 10
June   25–Varias Milling, Los Angeles. . . . . W 10
Sept. 18–Perfecto Lopez, San Francisco . . . . D   8

Oct.   21–Lester Marston, Oakland . . . . KO   7
Nov.   12–Leo Lomelli, Oakland . . . . KO   6
Nov.   27–Midget Wolgast, Oakland . . . . W 10
Dec.   6–Alton Black, Reno. . . . . KO   8

1936

Jan.   1–Joe Conde, Mexico City. . . . . L 10
Feb.   26–Ritchie Fontaine, Oakland . . . . L 10
Mar.   31–Ritchie Fontaine, Los Angeles. . . . . W 10
Apr.   17–Alton Black, Reno. . . . . KO   8
May   19–Pancho Leyvas, Los Angeles . . . . KO   4
June   22–Johnny DeFoe, Butte . . . . W 10
Aug.   4–Baby Arizmendi, Los Angeles . . . . W 10
       (Won Calif.-Mexican World Featherweight Title)
Aug.   28–Juan Zurita, Los Angeles . . . . KO   4
Sept. 3–Buzz Brown, Portland. . . . . W 10
Sept. 8–Dommy Ganzon, Sacramento . . . . KO   1
Oct.   27–Mike Belloise, Los Angeles . . . . W 10
Nov.   2–Gene Espinosa, Los Angeles . . . . KO   1
Nov.   17–Joey Alcanter, St. Louis . . . . KO   6
Dec.   3–Tony Chavez, St. Louis . . . . LF   8

1937

Jan.   1–Baby Casanova, Mexico City . . . . KO   3
Jan.   19–Tony Chavez, Los Angeles . . . . KO 10
Feb.   2–Moon Mullins, Los Angeles. . . . . KO   2
Feb.   19–Varias Milling, San Diego . . . . KO   4
Mar.   2–Joe Rivers, Los Angeles . . . . KO   4
Mar.   12–Mike Belloise, New York. . . . . KO   4
Mar.   19–Aldo Spoldi, New York . . . . W 10
Apr.   6–Pete De Grasse, Los Angeles . . . . KO 10
May   4–Frankie Klick, Los Angeles . . . . KO   4
May   28–Wally Hally, Los Angeles . . . . KO   4
June   9–Mark Diaz, Pasadena . . . . KO   4
June   15–Jackie Carter, Los Angeles . . . . KO   4
July   8–Alf Blatch, New York. . . . . KO   3
July   19–Lew Massey, Brooklyn . . . . KO   4
July   27–Benny Bass, Philadelphia . . . . KO   4
Aug.   13–Eddie Brink, New York . . . . KO   3
Aug.   16–Johnny Cabello, Washington, D.C. . . . . KO   2
Aug.   31–Orville Drouillard, Detroit. . . . . KO   5
Sept. 9–Charley Burns, Pittsburgh. . . . . KO   4
Sept. 16–Johnny DeFoe, New York . . . . KO   4
Sept. 21–Bobby Dean, Youngston . . . . KO   1
Oct.   18–Joe Marcienti, Philadelphia. . . . . KO   3
Oct.   29–Petey Sarron, New York . . . . KO   6
       (Won World Featherweight Title)
Nov.   19–Billy Beauhuld, New York . . . . KO   5

Nov. 23–Joey Brown, Buffalo . . . . KO 2
Dec. 6–Tony Chavez, Cleveland. . . . . KO 1
Dec. 12–Johnny Jones, New Orleans . . . . KO 2

1938

Jan. 12–Enrico Venturi, New York . . . . KO 6
Jan. 21–Frankie Castillo, Phoenix . . . . KO 3
Jan. 22–Tommy Brown, Tucson . . . . KO 2
Feb. 1–Chalky Wright, Los Angeles. . . . . KO 3
Feb. 9–Al Citrino, San Francisco . . . . KO 4
Feb. 25–Everett Rightmire, Chicago . . . . KO 4
Feb. 28–Charley Burns, Minneapolis . . . . KO 2
Mar. 15–Baby Arizmendi, Los Angeles . . . . W 10
Mar. 25–Eddie Zivic, Detroit . . . . KO 4
Mar. 30–Lew Feldman, New York . . . . KO 5
May 31–Barney Ross, Long Island City. . . . . W 15
(Won World Welterweight Title)
Aug. 17–Lou Ambers, New York. . . . . W 15
(Won World Lightweight Title)
–Relinquished world featherweight title.
Nov. 25–Ceferino Garcia, New York . . . . W 15
(Retained World Welterweight Title)
Dec. 5–Al Manfredo, Cleveland. . . . . KO 3

1939

Jan. 10–Baby Arizmendi, Los Angeles . . . . W 10
(Retained World Welterweight Title)
Mar. 4–Bobby Pacho, Havana, Cuba . . . . KO 4
(Retained World Welterweight Title)
Mar. 16–Lew Feldman, St. Louis . . . . KO 1
(Retained World Welterweight Title)
Mar. 31–Davey Day, New York . . . . KO 12
(Retained World Welterweight Title)
May 25–Ernie Roderick, London . . . . W 15
(Retained World Welterweight Title)
Aug. 22–Lou Ambers, New York . . . . L 15
(Lost World Lightweight Title)
Oct. 9–Al Manfredo, Des Moines . . . . KO 4
(Retained World Welterweight Title)
Oct. 13–Howard Scott, Minneapolis . . . . KO 2
(Retained World Welterweight Title)
Oct. 20–Ritchie Fointaine, Seattle . . . . KO 3
(Retained World Welterweight Title)
Oct. 24–Jimmy Garrison, Los Angeles . . . . W 10
(Retained World Welterweight Title)
Oct. 30–Bobby Pacho, Denver . . . . KO 4
(Retained World Welterweight Title)
Dec. 11–Jimmy Garrison, Cleveland . . . . KO 7
(Retained World Welterweight Title)

1940

Jan. 4–Joe Ghnouly, St. Louis . . . . KO 5
(Retained World Welterweight Title)
Jan. 24–Pedro Montanez, New York . . . . KO 9
(Retained World Welterweight Title)
Mar. 1–Ceferino Garcia, Los Angeles . . . . D 10
(For World Middleweight Title)
Apr. 26–Paul Junior, Boston . . . . KO 7
(Retained World Welterweight Title)
May 24–Ralph Zanelli, Boston . . . . KO 5
(Retained World Welterweight Title)
June 21–Paul Junior, Portland . . . . KO 3
(Retained World Welterweight Title)
July 17–Lew Jenkins, New York. . . . . KO 6
Sept. 23–Phil Furr, Washington, D.C. . . . . KO 4
(Retained World Welterweight Title)
Oct. 4–Fritzie Zivic, New York . . . . L 15
(Lost World Welterweight Title)

1941

Jan. 17–Fritzie Zivic, New York . . . . KO by 12
(For World Welterweight Title)
Oct. 1–Knocked out two opponents in two rounds each
in exhibition bouts in Oklahoma City.
Oct. 12–Knocked out two opponents in two rounds each
in exhibition bouts.

1942

June 1–Johnny Taylor, San Jose . . . . KO 4
June 24–Sheik Rangel, Oakland . . . . W 10
July 3–Reuben Shank, Denver . . . . L 10
July 20–Joe Ybarra, Sacramento . . . . KO 3
Aug. 3–Aldo Spoldi, San Francisco . . . . KO 7
Aug. 13–Jackie Burke, Ogden, ... W 10
Aug. 26–Rudolfo Ramirez, Oakland. . . . . KO 8
Sept. 4–Leo Rodak, San Francisco. . . . . KO 8
Sept. 7–Johnny Taylor, Pittman . . . . KO 3
Sept. 30–Earl Turner, Oakland . . . . KO 4
Oct. 13–Juan Zurita, Los Angeles . . . . KO 2
Oct. 26–Fritzie Zivic, San Francisco. . . . . W 10
Dec. 4–Lew Jenkins, Portland. . . . . KO
Dec. 14–Saverio Turiello, San Francisco . . . . KO

1943

Jan. 5–Jimmy McDaniels, Los Angeles . . . . W
Mar. 2–Willie Joyce, Los Angeles L
Mar. 8–Tippy Larkin, San Francisco . . . . KO
Mar. 22–Al Tribuani, Philadelphia. . . . . W

Apr.	2–Beau Jack, New York..................	L
Apr.	30–Saverio Turiello, Washington, D.C.	KO
May	7–Tommy Jessup, Boston	KO
May	24–Maxie Shapiro, Philadelphia	KO
June	11–Sammy Angott, New York	W
July	24–Willie Joyce, Hollywood	W
Aug.	6–Jimmy Garrison, Portland.	W
Aug.	14–Joey Silva, Spokane, Wash.	W
Aug.	27–Ray Robinson, New York	L

1944

Jan.	14–Aldo Spoldi, Portland.	KO
Jan.	26–Saverio Turiello, Kansas City............	KO
Feb.	7–Lew Hanbury, Washington, D.C.	KO
Feb.	23–Jimmy Garrison, Kansas City...........	KO
Feb.	29–Jackie Byrd, Des Moines..............	KO
Mar.	14–Johnny Jones, Miami	KO
Mar.	20–Frankie Wills, Washington, D.C.	W
Mar.	24–Ralph Zanelli, Boston................	W
Apr.	25–John Thomas, Los Angeles	W
May	16–Ralph Zanelli, Boston................	W
May	22–Aaron Perry, Washington, D.C.	KO
June	2–Willie Joyce, Chicago	L
June	15–Al (Bummy) Davis, New York	KO
June	21–Nick Latsios, Washington, D.C...........	W
July	4–John Thomas, Los Angeles	L
July	14–Slugger White, Hollywood..............	D
Aug.	21–Willie Joyce, San Francisco.............	W
Sept.	15–Aldo Spoldi, St. Louis................	KO
Nov.	4–Mike Belloise, Portland..............	KO

1945

Jan.	17–Chester Slider, Oakland	D
Feb.	6–Genaro Rojo, Los Angeles	W
Feb.	14–Chester Slider, Oakland	L

TB	KO	WD	WF	D	LD	LF	KOBO	ND	NC
174	98	47	0	9	17	1	2	0	0

Elected to Boxing Hall of Fame, 1954.

YOUNG JACK THOMPSON
(Cecil Lewis Thompson)

Born, 1904, Los Angeles, Calif. Weight, 145 lbs. Height, 5 ft. 8 in. Managed by Clyde Hudkins, Ray Alvis.

1922

Nov.	20–Bud Kelly, San Francisco..............	KO	2

1923

Feb.	13–Billy Springfield, San Francisco........	KO by	2
Dec.	6–Joe Powell, San Jose.	KO	2
Dec.	20–Manny (Kid) Robinson, San Jose.........	W	4

1924

Jan.	4–Kid Martin, San Francisco..............	KO	2
Apr.	24–Leo Spencer, San Meteo	L	4
May	15–Joe Powell, San Jose.................	L	5
May	29–Pete Francis, San Jose	D	4
June	24–Angelo Papas, San Meteo	D	4
Aug.	7–Henry Faligano, San Jose	D	4
Aug.	19–Min Minnick, San Jose	L	4
Sept.	22–Min Minnick, San Jose	D	4

1925

Jan.	21–Eddie Cortez, Los Angeles	KO	1
Feb.	4–Joe Martinez, Los Angeles	KO	6
Feb.	18–Eddie Sylvester, Los Angeles............	KO	3
Mar.	11–Charley Burns, Los Angeles	W	10
Mar.	13–Joe Carter, San Diego................	KO	1
Mar.	20–Kid Bello, San Diego	D	6
Apr.	3–Battling Ward, San Diego	W	6
Apr.	13–Battling Ward, Los Angeles	KO	4
May	1–Charley Feraci, San Dlego..............	L	10
July	24–Young Harry Wills, San Dlego	D	10
	7–Harry Scott, Oakland	L	6

1926

Jan.	14–Tarzan Lopez, Pasadena	KO	3
Jan.	22–Baby Pete, San Diego	W	6
Feb.	10–Bobby Ertle, Oakland	KO	1
Mar.	9–Joe Layman, Vernon	D	6
Mar.	31–Young Sam Langford, Los Angeles	L	
	–Billy Sprinfield......................	D	6
May	18–Young Corbett III, Fresno	L	6
May	21–Ad Ruiz, San Diego	W	6
May	28–Buddy Bairie, San Diego...............	W	
June	18–Billy McCann, San Diego	KO	8
July	24–Harry Whybrow, Los Angeles...........	KO	2
Sept.	28–Jack Silver, Los Angeles	KO	8
Oct.	15–Billy Adams, San Francisco	KO	5
Nov.	5–Billy Alger, San Francisco	W	10
Nov.	14–Ted Makagon, San Francisco	D	10
Nov.	23–Russ Whalen, Los Angeles	L	10

1927

Feb.	11–Tommy Cello, San Francisco	D	10

Feb.	18–Harry (Kid) Brown, San Francisco	KO	5
Mar.	4–King Tut, San Francisco	W	10
Mar.	11–Harry (Kid) Brown, San Francisco	W	10
Apr.	8–Irineo Flores, San Francisco	KO	2
June	24–Young Corbett III, San Freancisco	D	10
July	22–Charley Feraci, San Francisco	KO	5
	–Frankie Turner	KO	8
	–Charley Pitts	KO	4

1928

Jan.	17–Johnny Adams, Los Angeles	KO	4
Jan.	27–Don Fraser, San Francisco	KO	3
Feb.	13–Young Corbett III, San Francisco	L	10
Mar.	16–Johnny O'Donnell, San Francisco	KO	8
Apr.	11–Jimmy Duffy, Oakland	LF	9
June	8–Billy Light, Chicago	W	8
July	11–Russie LeRoy, Chicago	KO	5
Aug.	10–Eddie Dempsey, Chicago	KO	4
Aug.	22–Gene Cardi, Cleveland	KO	6
Aug.	30–Joe Dundee, Chicago	KO	2
Oct.	1–Jackie Fields, San Francisco	L	10
Oct.	31–Danny Gordon, Chicago	KO	2
Dec.	7–Red Bragan, Buffalo	KO	4
	–Sam Bruce, Buffalo	KO	10

1929

Jan.	25–Red Herring, Buffalo	KO	7
Jan.	30–Harry Dudley, Kansas City	KO	5
Feb.	18–Ham Jenkins, Kansas City	W	10
Mar.	8–Heavy Andrews, Buffalo	W	10
Mar.	25–Jackie Fields, Chicago	L	10
	(For NBA Welterweight Title)		
June	24–Jimmy Evans, San Francisco	KO	9
Aug.	7–Jimmy Duffy, Oakland	W	10
Oct.	2–Jimmy Duffy, Oakland	KO	10
Oct.	9–Freddie Fitzgerald, Oakland	L	10
Nov.	18–Billy White, Pittsburgh	KO	8
Dec.	10–Billy Wells, Minneapolis	W	10

1930

Jan.	10–Tommy Freeman, Detroit	L	10
Feb.	3–Bucky Lawless, Rochester	L	10
Mar.	2–Freddie Fltzgerald, Chicago	W	10
Mar.	28–Jimmy McLarnin, New York	L	10
May	9–Jackie Fields, Detroit	W	15
	(Won World Welterweight Title)		
June	6–Billy Wells, Omaha	KO	2
June	9–Jerry Dolan, Portland, Ore.	KO	3

June	17–Joe Cordoza, Los Angeles	KO	3
July	4–Young Corbett III, San Francisco	L	10
Sept.	5–Tommy Freeman, Cleveland	L	15
	(Lost World Welterweight Title)		

1931

Mar.	4–Babe Anderson, Oakland	KO	9
Mar.	19–Larry (Kid) Kaufman, Moline, Ill.	KO	3
Apr.	14–Tommy Freeman, Cleveland	KO	12
	(Regained World Welterweight Title)		
May	8–Bucky Lawless, Chicago	L	10
May	27–Pete August, Newark	W	10
June	19–Speedball Turner, Little Rock	KO	3
July	23–Lou Brouillard, Boston	L	10
Sept.	6–Tommy Jones, Flint, Mich.	KO	3
Oct.	23–Lou Brouillard, Boston	L	15
	(Lost World Welterweight Title)		

1932

Jan.	27–Jimmy Evans, Oakland	L	10
Mar.	4–Billy Wells, Stockton	KO	6
Mar.	11–Al Trulmans, San Diego	W	10
Mar.	25–Charlie Cobb, San Diego	L	10
May	25–Leonard Bennet, Seattle	W	6

TB	KO	WD	WF	D	LD	LF	KOBO	ND	NC
97	43	18	0	11	23	1	1	0	0

Died April 9 1946 Los Angeles Calif.

JACKIE WILSON

(Jack Benjamin Wilson)
Born, 1911, Arkansas. Weight, 115-131 lbs. Height, 5 ft. 5 in.
Managed by Billy Daly, Jack Laken, Pete Reilly, Harry Burnkrant.

1929

Dec.	6–Jimmy Thomas, Pittsburgh	W	6
Dec.	20–Young Ketchell, Pittsburgh	W	6

1930

Mar.	18–Lefty Foster, Johnstown, Pa.	W	4
Apr.	17–Ross Fields, McKeesport, Pa.	D	4
Apr.	24–Jack Benton, McKeesport	W	6
May	5–Mose Butch, Pittsburgh	D	6
July	14–Jackie Ward, North Braddock, Pa.	L	6
Aug.	14–Mose Butch, Millvale, Pa.	L	6
Sept.	11–Mose Butch, Millvale, Pa.	L	6
Nov.	28–Bid Maloney, Pittsburgh	KO	4

1931

	–Tony Marino, Pittsburgh	W	6
	–Babe Peleco, Pittsburgh	W	6
	–Tony Marino, Pittsburgh	D	6
	–Marty Gold, Pittsburgh	W	6
Sept. 24	–Johnny Datto, Pittsburgh	KO by	3
Dec.	–Steve Senich, Pittsburgh	W	6

1932

Jan. 1	–Ross Fields, Pittsburgh	W	6
Feb. 26	–Willie Davies, Pittsburgh	W	10
Mar.	–Mose Butch, Pittsburgh	W	10
Mar. 21	–Baby Face Mathison, Pittsburgh	W	8
May 16	–Steve Senich, Pittsburgh	W	8
June	–Johnny Cataline, Pittsburgh	W	8
June 23	–Chico Cisneros, Pittsburgh	L	10
Sept.	–Joey Bozak, Pittsburgh	W	8
Dec.	–Ross Fields, Pittsburgh	KO by	10

1933

Jan.	–Billy Landers	D	8
Feb. 3	–Midget Wolgast, Pittsburgh	D	10
Mar. 3	–Ross Fields, Pittsburgh	W	10
Mar. 17	–Johnny Mitchell, Pittsburgh	W	10
Apr. 3	–Tommy Paul, Pittsburgh	W	10
Apr. 13	–Johnny Pena, Chicago	W	10
May 8	–Eddie Shea, Pittsburgh	W	10
June 5	–Tommy Paul, Pittsburgh	KO	8
July 20	–Benny Britt, Fort Hamilton	W	10
Aig. 18	–Ernie Ratner, Long Branch	W	10
Nov. 22	–Johnny Fitzpatrick, Chicago	W	8
Dec. 4	–Dario Moreno, Chicago	KO	6
Dec. 20	–Everett Rightmire, Sioux City	D	8

1934

Jan. 8	–Johnny Mitchell, Chicago	KO	6
	–Jimmy Gilligan, Toronto	W	6
	–Bud Dempsey	KO	1
July 19	–Mose Butch, Pittsburgh	W	10
Oct.	–Joe Conde, Mexico City	L	10
Dec. 23	–Mose Butch, Pittsburgh	W	10

1935

May 27	–Al Farrone, Pittsburgh	W	6
June 10	–Frankie Wolfram, Pittsburgh	W	8
July 4	–Sammy Crocetti, Dubois	W	
July 22	–Sammy Angott, Pittsburgh	W	6
Oct. 10	–Billy Gannon, Liverpool	W	10
Oct. 24	–Spike Robinson, Belfast	W	12

Nov. 7	–Cuthbert Taylor, Liverpool	W	10
Dec. 12	–Gilbert Johnston, Liverpool	KO	5

1936

Jan. 12	–Ronnie James, London	L	10
Jan. 27	–Jane Linehan, Cork	W	10
Feb. 21	–Stan, Jehu, Manchester	W	10
Mar. 6	–Douglas Kestress, Manchester	W	10
Mar. 31	–Johnny McGrory, Glasgow	KO	10
May 8	–Jack Middleton, Plymouth	KO	2
May 22	–George Gee, Plymouth	KO	7
June 16	–Tommy Rogers, Wolverhampton	KO	4
Oct. 12	–Bobby Dean, Pittsburgh	KO	2
Dec. 3	–Lee Sheppard, Pittsburgh	W	10

1937

Feb. 9	–Freddie Miller, Pittsburgh	W	10
Feb. 22	–Mike Belloise, Pittsburgh	W	10
Mar. 22	–Charley Burns, Lancaster	W	8
Apr. 12	–Armando Sicilia, Springfield	D	8
Apr. 26	–Freddie Miller, Cincinnati	W	10
May 10	–Joey Brown, Lancaster	KO	4
June 15	–Pete DeGrasse, Los Angeles	W	10
July 6	–Speedy Dado, Stockton	W	10
July 26	–Ritchie Fontaine, Los Angeles	L	10
Aug. 6	–Al Manriquez, Sioux City	W	10
Aug. 19	–Leo Rodak, St. Louis	D	10
Sept. 17	–Leo Rodak, St. Louis	D	15
Oct. 12	–Everett Rightmire, St. Louis	L	10

1938

Jan. 10	–Leo Rodak, Chicago	D	10
Jan. 21	–Varias Millig, Chicago	W	10
Mar. 22	–Sammy Angott, Milwaukee	L	10
May 9	–Norment Quarles, Baltimore	W	10
June 17	–Leo Rodak, Baltimore	L	15
	(For Vacant Maryland World Featherweight Title)		
Nov. 4	–Jiggs McKnight, Clarksburg	KO	8

1939

Feb. 4	–Mickey Miller, Melbourne	KO	4
Feb. 13	–Joe Hall, Sydney	W	12
Feb. 25	–Joe Hall, Melbourne	W	12
Mar. 3	–Sammy Garcia, Brisbane	L	12
Mar. 11	–Claude Varner, Melbourne	W	12
Mar. 31	–Henry Moreno, Brisbane	W	12
Apr. 11	–Koe Velasco, Sydney	WF	8
Apr. 26	–Joe Hall, Melbourne	WF	10
May 31	–Mickey Miller, Melbourne	W	12

June 28–Henry Moreno, Melbourne . . . . W 12
July 6–Kui Kong, Sydney . . . . WF 8
Aug. 3–Kui Kong Young, Sydney . . . . W 12
Nov. 8–Armando Sicilia, Pittsburgh . . . . W 10
Nov. 20–Emil Joseph, Pittsburgh . . . . W 10

1940

Feb. 12–Frank Covelli, Chicago . . . . W 10
Mar. 31–Harris Blake, New Orleans . . . . L 10
Apr. 25–Bobby Green, Lancaster . . . . W 10
June 3–Leo Rodak, Chicago . . . . L 10
Aug. 20–Harry Jeffra, Youngstown . . . . L 10
Dec. 12–Frank Terranova, Baltimore . . . . W 8

1941

Jan. 23–Maxie Shapiro, Baltimore . . . . W 10
Feb. 11–Joe Marinelli, Youngstown . . . . W 10
Mar. 31–Matt Perfecti, Baltimore . . . . W 10
Apr. 21–Leo Rodak, Cincinnati . . . . L 10
May 19–Baby Arizmendi, Los Angeles . . . . KO 8
July 17–Chalky Wright, Baltimore . . . . L 10
Oct. 27–Leo Rodak, Toledo, Ohio . . . . L 10
Nov. 18–Richie Lemos, Los Angeles . . . . W 12
(Won NBA Featherweight Title)
Dec. 16–Richie Lemos, Los Angeles . . . . W 12
(Retained NBA Featherweight Title)

1942

Feb. 20–Abe Denner, Boston . . . . L 10
Mar. 2–Terry Young, New York . . . . L 8

1943

Jan. 18–Jackie Callura, Providence . . . . L 15
(Lost NBA Featherweight Title)
Mar. 18–Jackie Callura, Boston . . . . L 15
(For NBA Featherweight Title)
Apr. 26–Willie Pep. Pittsburgh . . . . L 12
May 17–Danny Petro, Washington, D.C. . . . . KO 10
June 7–Jimmy Phillips, Washington, D.C. . . . . W 10
June 28–Lew Hanbury, Washington, D.C. . . . . KO 7
July 26–Tony Costa, Providence . . . . W 10

Aug. 30–Lulu Costantino, Washington . . . . W 10
Oct. 4–Larry Bolvin, Providence . . . . L 10
Oct. 22–Freddie Pope, Cleveland . . . . L 10
Dec. 6–Tony Costa, Providence . . . . LF 6

1944

Sept. 19–Cleo Shans, Washington, D.C. . . . . W 10
Oct. 17–Pedro Hernandez, Washington . . . . L 10

1945

Jan. 8–Harry Jeffs, Baltimore . . . . W 10
Jan. 22–Pedro Hernandez, Washington . . . . W 10
Mar. 12–Cleo Shans, Baltimore . . . . W 10
Apr. 9–Chalky Wright, Baltimore . . . . NC 7
June 25–Freddie Russo, Baltimore . . . . L 10

1946

Mar. 11–Willie Joyce, Washington . . . . KO by 5
Mar. 26–Willie Pep, Kansas City . . . . L 10
May 3–Jackie Graves, Minneapolis . . . . L 8
June 18–Enrique Bolanos, Los Angeles . . . . KO by 7
Sept. 11–Star Misamis, Oakland . . . . L 10
Sept. 25–Star Misamis, Oakland . . . . L 10
Oct. 22–Luis Castillo, San Jose . . . . W 10
Nov. 18–Luis Castillo, San Jose . . . . L 10
Dec. 17–Mario Trigo, San Jose . . . . L 10

1947

Jan. 8–Speedy Cabanella, Sacramento . . . . L 10
Jan. 20–Buddy Jacklich, San Francisco . . . . L 10
Apr. 7–Freddie Steele, Vancouver . . . . KO 7
Apr. 25–Manny Ortega, El Paso . . . . KO by 10
May 12–Jackie Turner, Vancouver . . . . L 10
May 30–Jackie Turner, Vancouver . . . . L 10
Sept. 1–Joey Dolan, Spokane, Wash . . . . L 10
Sept. 22–Simon Vegara, Ocean Park . . . . KO by 9

TB	KO	WD	WF	D	LD	LF	KOBO	ND	NC
147	18	72	3	10	36	1	6	0	1

Died, December 2, 1966, Torrance, Pa.

BASEBALL

AFRICAN-AMERICAN BASEBALL PLAYERS AT WHITE COLLEGES

Name	Position	Years	College
John Prim	Left Field	1920	U. of Washington
F. M. Sheffield	Second Base	1921	Oberlin
Sam Taylor	na	1922–23	Northwestern U.
George Gossen	Shortstop	1922–24	Boston U.
Joe Washington	Left Field	1923	New York U.
Earl Brown	Pitcher	1924	Harvard
G. Lewis Chandler	na	1925	Middleburg
Ralph Bunche	na	1925–27	UCLA
Leslie Sims	na	1926	Northeastern U.
Booker T. Spencer	na	1926	Western Reserve U.
Kenny Washington	Shortstop	1938	UCLA
Jackie Robinson	Infielder	1938	UCLA
Ray Bartlett	Outfielder	1938	UCLA

na = position not available

BLACK COLLEGE CONFERENCE WINNERS

	CIAA	SWAC	SIAC	EIAC	SCAC	MWAC
1916			Morris Brown & Morehouse			
1917			Morris Brown & Morehouse			
1918			Talladega			
1919			Morehouse			
1920			Atlanta U.			
1921			Morehouse			
1922			Morehouse			
1923			Morehouse			
1924	Va. Normal		Atlanta U.			
1925	Va. Union		Morehouse			
1926	Va. Normal		Morehouse & Alabama State			
1927	Va. State		Alabama State		Alcorn A&M	
1928	Va. State		Atlanta U.		Alcorn A&M	
1929	Va. State		Alabama State		Alcorn A&M	
1930	Lincoln (Pa.)					
1931	Va. State				Alcorn A&M	
1932	Va. State					
1933	Va. State					
1934	Va. State & Hampton					
1935						
1936					Okolona	
1937					Piney Woods	
1938					Okolona	
1939						
1940						
1941	Va. Union					
1942	N. Car. College					
1943						
1944						
1945	Morgan					

ALL-TIME REGISTER OF PLAYERS, MANAGERS, UMPIRES, AND OFFICIALS

Career	Last Name	First Name	Teams	Positions
1920	Barber	–	Hilldale	Secondbase
	Becker	–	Dayton Marcos	Firstbase
	Blukoi	Frank	Kansas City Monarchs	Secondbase
	Carter	–	Detroit Stars	Catcher
	Clark	Albert	Dayton Marcos	Ball Player
	Davis	James	Chicago Giants	Pitcher
	Forest	Charles	St. Louis Giants	Ball Player
	Goliath	Fred	Chicago Giants	Outfielder
	Grant	Art	Baltimore Black Sox	Ball Player
	Grey	William	Dayton Marcos	Pitcher
	Harper	–	Norfolk Stars	Shortstop
			Hilldale	
	Houston	–	Indianapolis ABC's	Pitcher
	Johnson	M.	Lincoln Giants	Outfielder
	Leary	–	Dayton Marcos	Third base
	Lewis	Cary B.	Negro National League	Secretary*
			Constitution of Negro National League	Co-Designer*
	Longware	–	Detroit Stars	Secondbase
	Ridgely	–	Lincoln Giants	Shortstop
	Washington	Blue	Kansas City Monarchs	Firstbase
	Wingfield	–	Dayton Marcos	Secondbase
1920–1921	Busby	Maurice	All Cubans	Pitcher
			Bacharach Giants	
	McLain	–	Columbus Buckeyes	Secondbase
			Indianapolis ABC's	Thirdbase
	Raglan	–	Columbus Buckeyes	Pitcher
			Kansas City Monarchs	
			Indianapolis ABC's	
1920–1922	Archer	–	Baltimore Black Sox	Pitcher
			Lincoln Giants	
	Dudley	C.A.	St. Louis Stars	Outfielder
			St. Louis Giants	
	Taylor	Big	Kansas City Monarchs	Pitcher
			Chicago Giants	
1920–1923	Hill	Fred	Milwaukee Bears	Thirdbase
			St. Louis Giants	Outfielder
			Detroit Stars	Secondbase
	White	Butler	Chicago Giants	Firstbase
	Wilson	Carter	Peter's Union Giants	Outfielder
			Gilkerson's Union Giants	
	York	Jim	Bacharach Giants	Catcher
			Norfolk Stars	
			Hilldale	

Career	Last Name	First Name	Teams	Positions
1920–1924	Holtz	Eddie	Chicago American Giants St. Louis Stars St. Louis Giants	Secondbase
	Moore	N.	Detroit Stars	Outfielder
	Pullen	C. Neil	Baltimore Black Sox Brooklyn Royal Giants Kansas City Monarchs	Catcher
1920–1925	Ewing	–	Indianapolis ABC's Chicago American Giants Columbus Buckeyes	Catcher
	Green	Curtis	Brooklyn Cuban Giants Birmingham Black Barons	Outfielder Firstbase
	Long	–	Indianapolis ABC's Detroit Stars	Outfielder
	Luther	–	Lincoln Giants Chicago American Giants Hilldale Chicago Giants	Pitcher
	Owens	Aubrey	New Orleans Caulfield Ads Indianapolis ABC's Chicago Giants Chicago American Giants	Pitcher
	Taylor	John	Lincoln Giants Chicago Giants	Pitcher
	Thompson	James	Birmingham Black Barons Milwaukee Bears Dayton Marcos	Catcher Outfielder
1920–1926	Fiall	George	Harrisburg Giants Lincoln Giants Baltimore Black Sox	Thirdbase Shortstop
	Jefferson	Ralph	Bacharach Giants Washington Potomacs Indianapolis ABC's Philadelphia Royal Stars Philadelphia Giants	Outfielder
	Norman	–	Cleveland Elites Lincoln Giants	Shortstop
1920–1929	Kenyon	Harry C.	Lincoln Giants Memphis Red Sox Hilldale Kansas City Monarchs Detroit Stars Brooklyn Royal Giants Indianapolis ABC's Chicago American Giants	Outfielder Secondbase Manager* Pitcher

Career	Last Name	First Name	Teams	Positions
	Marshall	Jack	Kansas City Monarchs	Pitcher
			Chicago American Giants	
			Detroit Stars	
	Means	Lewis	Bacharach Giants	Firstbase
				Secondbase
1920–1930	Murray	Mitchell	St. Louis Stars	Catcher
			Cleveland Tate Stars	
			Indianapolis ABC's	
			Toledo Tigers	
			Chicago American Giants	
			Dayton Marcos	
	Reavis	–	Pennsylvania Red Caps of New York	Pitcher
			Lincoln Giants	
1920–1932	Day	Wilson C.		
		(Connie)	Baltimore Black Sox	Thirdbase
			Bacharach Giants	Shortstop
			Indianapolis ABC's	Secondbase
			Harrisburg Giants	
1920–1933	Riggins	Orville	New York Black Yankees	Thirdbase
			Cleveland Hornets	Secondbase
			Detroit Stars	Shortstop
			Lincoln Giants	Manager*
			Brooklyn Royal Giants	
			Homestead Grays	
	Rile	Edward (Ed)	Cole's American Giants	Firstbase
			Indianapolis ABC's	Pitcher
			Columbus Buckeyes	
			Chicago American Giants	
			Brooklyn Royal Giants	
			Lincoln Giants	
1920–1934	Cobb	L.S.N.	Negro Southern League	Secretary*
			Birmingham Black Barons	Officer*
			St. Louis Giants	Officer*
	Mothel	Carrol (Dirk)	Kansas City Monarchs	Shortstop
			Cleveland Stars	Outfielder
			All Nations	Catcher
				Second base
1920–1935	Streeter	Samuel (Sam)	Lincoln Giants	Pitcher
			Pittsburgh Crawfords	
			Homestead Grays	
			Atlanta Black Crackers	
			Montgomery Gray Sox	
			Birmingham Giants	
			Chicago American Giants	
			Cleveland Cubs	

*Managerial position

Career	Last Name	First Name	Teams	Positions
1920–1936	Bennette	George (Jew Baby)	Chicago Union Giants Memphis Red Sox Indianapolis ABC's Columbus Buckeyes Detroit Stars Chicago Giants	Outfielder
1920–1940	Jenkins	Clarence (Fats)	New York Black Yankees Brooklyn Royal Giants Harrisburg Giants Philadelphia Stars Brooklyn Eagles Bacharach Giants Lincoln Giants	Outfielder Manager*
1920–1941	Cooper	Andy (Lefty)	Kansas City Monarchs Detroit Stars St. Louis Stars Chicago American Giants	Pitcher Manager* Pitcher
	Ellis	–	Nashville Elite Giants Dayton Marcos	Firstbase
	Green	(Fat)	Nashville Elite Giants	Catcher
	Greyer	–	Baltimore Black Sox	Firstbase
	Griffin	(Horse)	Nashville Elite Giants	Secondbase
	Hall	–	St. Louis Stars	Pitcher
	Hamilton	–	Kansas City Monarchs	Pitcher
	Hancock	–	St. Louis Giants	Catcher
	King	–	Kansas City Monarchs	Outfielder
	Knight	–	Detroit Stars	Outfielder
	Latimer	–	Indianapolis ABC's	Pitcher
	McAllister	–	Kansas City Monarchs	Outfielder
	McCarthy	C.H.	Southeastern Negro League	President*
	Moore	Ralph	Cleveland Tate Stars	Pitcher
	Moore	Roy	Cleveland Tate Stars	Firstbase
	Noel	–	Nashville Elite Giants	Pitcher
	Otis	Amos	Nashville Elite Giants	Outfielder
	Potter	–	Kansas City Monarchs	Catcher
	Rutledge	–	Dayton Marcos	Pitcher
	Smith	Lefty	Kansas City Monarchs	Pitcher
	Southy	–	Lincoln Giants	Shortstop
	Staples	John	Montgomery Grey Sox	Manager*
	Ware	–	Nashville Elite Giants	Outfielder
1920–1942	Britt	George (Chippy)	Brooklyn Royal Giants Newark Dodgers Dayton Marcos	Infielder Pitcher Catcher

*Managerial position

Career	Last Name	First Name	Teams	Positions
			Baltimore Black Sox	
			Homestead Grays	
			Columbus Elite Giants	
			Washington Black Senators	
			Jacksonville Red Caps	
			Columbus Buckeyes	
			Hilldale	
1920–1943	Lee	Holsey S. (Scrip)	Negro National League	Umpire,* Firstbase
			Bacharach Giants	Pitcher
			Richmond Giants	Outfielder
			Baltimore Black Sox	
			Norfolk Stars	
			Norfolk Giants	
			Philadelphia Stars	
1920–1948	Jeffries	Harry	Chicago Columbia Giants	Firstbase
			Knoxville Giants	Catcher
			Chicago American Giants	Shortstop
			Cleveland Tigers	Thirdbase
			Detroit Stars	Manager*
1921	Allison	–	Nashville Elite Giants	Catcher
	Arnet	–	Bacharach Giants	Pitcher
	Barr	–	Kansas City Monarchs	Shortstop
				Thirdbase
	Billings	William	Nashville Elite Giants	Pitcher
	Bix	–	St. Louis Giants	Pitcher
	Blanchard	–	Kansas City Monarchs	Outfielder
				Firstbase
	Brady	Lefty	Cleveland Tate Stars	Pitcher
	Brown	–	Columbus Buckeyes	Outfielder
	Carey	–	Dayton Marcos	Thirdbase
	Coleman	–	Dayton Marcos	Firstbase
			Columbus Buckeyes	Outfielder
	Cooper	E.	Cleveland Tate Stars	Firstbase
	Dickerson	Lou	Hilldale	Pitcher
	Dobbins	–	Hilldale	Shortstop
	Ford	–	Baltimore Black Sox	Secondbase
			Harrisburg Giants	
	Harris	–	Hilldale	Pitcher
			Harrisburg Giants	
			Brooklyn Royal Giants	
	Logan	–	Baltimore Black Sox	Pitcher
	Phillips	–	Detroit Stars	Secondbase
			Nashville Elite Giants	Shortstop
	Raggs	Harry	Baltimore Black Sox	Outfielder
			Norfolk Giants	
			Harrisburg Giants	
	Thomas	D.	St. Louis Stars	Secondbase
			Indianapolis ABC's	

*Managerial position

Career	Last Name	First Name	Teams	Positions
1921–1922	Dickey	(Steel Arm)	St. Louis Stars Montgomery Grey Sox	Pitcher
	Haynes	Willie	Hilldale Dallas Giants	Pitcher
	Howard	–	Harrisburg Giants Norfolk Giants	Shortstop
	Howard	–	Indianapolis ABC's Detroit Stars	Ball Player
	Oldham	Jimmy	St. Louis Stars St. Louis Giants	Pitcher
	O'Neill	Charles	Bacharach Giants Columbus Buckeyes	Catcher
	Ricks	–	Cleveland Tate Stars Dayton Marcos	Pitcher Outfielder
	Thomas	–	Baltimore Black Sox	Catcher
	Wilson	Charles	Detroit Stars Columbus Buckeyes	Pitcher
1921–1923	Fagan	Bob	St. Louis Stars Kansas City Monarchs	Secondbase
	Holland	Bill	Brooklyn Royal Giants New York Black Yankees Detroit Stars Philadelphia Stars Lincoln Giants Chicago American Giants	Manager* Pitcher
1921–1924	George	John	Harrisburg Giants New York Black Yankees Chicago American Giants	Outfielder
	Hutt	–	St. Louis Giants Dayton Marcos Toledo Tigers	Firstbase
	Ray	–	Cleveland Tate Stars Kansas City Monarchs Cleveland Browns St. Louis Stars Chicago Giants	Catcher Pitcher
	Smith	William	Baltimore Black Sox	Outfielder
	Smith	Wyman	Baltimore Black Sox	Outfielder
1921–1925	Brown	Maywood	Indianapolis ABC's	Pitcher
	Forrest	–	Lincoln Giants	Outfielder
	Kemp	John	Lincoln Giants Baltimore Black Sox Memphis Red Sox Norfolk Giants Philadelphia Royal Stars	Outfielder
	Perry	–	Lincoln Giants Cleveland Browns Washington Potomacs	Shortstop Thirdbase Secondbase

*Managerial position

Career	Last Name	First Name	Teams	Positions
	Roth	Herman (Bobby)	Detroit Stars Bacharach Giants Milwaukee Bears Birmingham Black Barons New Orleans Crescent Stars Chicago American Giants Detroit Stars	Catcher
	Williams	Gerard	Homestead Grays Indianapolis ABC's	Shortstop
	Wilson	E.	Detroit Stars Dayton Marcos	Thirdbase Secondbase
1921–1926	Keaton	–	Cleveland Tate Stars Dayton Marcos	Pitcher
	McClain	Edward (Boots)	Toledo Tigers Dayton Marcos Detroit Stars Cleveland Tate Stars Cleveland Browns	Shortstop Pitcher
	Moore	Walter (Dobie)	Kansas City Monarchs	Outfielder Shortstop
1921–1927	Hampton	Lewis	Bacharach Giants Indianapolis ABC's Washington Potomacs Columbus Buckeyes Detroit Stars Lincoln Giants	Pitcher
	Sweatt	George	Kansas City Monarchs Chicago Giants Chicago American Giants	Secondbase Thirdbase Outfielder
	Wagner	Bill	Brooklyn Royal Giants Lincoln Giants	Secondbase Shortstop Manager
	Weley	Connie	Indianapolis ABC's Columbus Buckeyes Memphis Red Sox Pittsburgh Keystones	Outfielder
1921–1928	Carpenter	Wayne	Indianapolis ABC's St. Louis Giants Lincoln Giants Baltimore Black Sox Wilmington Potomacs Bacharach Giants Brooklyn Royal Giants Newark Stars Washington Potomacs	Pitcher

*Managerial position

Career	Last Name	First Name	Teams	Positions
1921–1929	Force	William	Baltimore Black Sox	Pitcher
			Detroit Stars	
1921–1930	Almon	Harry	Homestead Grays	Pitcher
			Birmingham Black Barons	
	McClure	Robert (Rob)	Baltimore Black Sox	Pitcher
			Indianapolis ABC's	
			Brooklyn Royal Giants	
			Cleveland Tate Stars	
			Bacharach Giants	
	Washington	Namon	Brooklyn Royal Giants	Shortstop
			Indianapolis ABC's	Outfielder
			Brooklyn Cuban Giants	
			Philadelphia Tigers	
			Lincoln Giants	
1921–1931	Bell	Clifford (Cliff)	Cleveland Cubs	Pitcher
			Detroit Stars	
			Kansas City Monarchs	
			Memphis Red Sox	
	Jackson	Richard	Hilldale	Thirdbase
			Harrisburg Giants	Secondbase
			Baltimore Black Sox	Shortstop
			Bacharach Giants	
	Lowe	William	Memphis Red Sox	Shortstop
			Chattanooga Black Lockouts	Outfielder
			Detroit Stars	Secondbase
			Indianapolis ABC's	Manager*
	Smith	Clarence	Birmingham Black Barons	Outfielder
			Columbus Buckeyes	Manager*
			Baltimore Black Sox	
			Cleveland Cubs	
			Detroit Stars	
1921–1932	Foreman	F. (Hooks)	Indianapolis ABC's	Catcher
			Washington Pilots	
			Kansas City Monarchs	
	Hudspeth	Robert (Highpockets)	Hilldale	Firstbase
			Columbus Buckeyes	
			New York Black Yankees	
			Indianapolis ABC's	
			Bacharach Giants	
			Lincoln Giants	
			Brooklyn Royal Giants	
1921–1933	Stratton	Leroy	Milwaukee Bears	Thirdbase
			Nashville Elite Giants	Shortstop
			Birmingham Black Barons	Secondbase
				Manager*

*Managerial position

Career	Last Name	First Name	Teams	Positions
	Williams	Poindexter	Birmingham Black Barons	Catcher
			Detroit Stars	Manager*
			Homestead Grays	
			Chicago American Giants	
			Louisville White Sox	
			Homestead Grays	
			Kansas City Monarchs	
1921–1934	Holloway	Crush	Hilldale	Outfielder
			Bacharach Giants	
			Indianapolis ABC's	
			Detroit Stars	
			Baltimore Black Sox	
1921–1935	Daniels	Leon (Pepper)	Brooklyn Eagles	Firstbase
			Harrisburgh Giants	Catcher
			Cuban Stars	
			Detroit Stars	
	Gisentaner	Willie (Lefty)	Pittsburgh Crawfords	Pitcher
			Newark Stars	
			Washington Potomacs	
			Kansas City Monarchs	
			Nashville Elite Giants	
			Cuban Stars (East)	
			Jarrosbirg Giants	
			Louisville Red Caps	
			Homestead Grays	
			Louisville White Sox	
	White	Chaney	Homestead Grays	Outfielder
			Wilmington Potomacs	
			Hilldale	
			Philadelphia Stars	
			Quaker Giants	
			Darby Daisies	
1921–1937	Stephens	Paul (Jake)	Pittsburgh Crawfords	Shortstop
			Hilldale	
			New York Black Yankees	
			Homestead Grays	
			Philadelphia Stars	
			Philadelphia Giants	
1921–1938	Crump	James	Philadelphia Stars	Secondbase
			Norfolk Giants	
			Hilldale	
			Negro National League	Umpire*
	Johnson	William J. (Judy)	Darby Daisies	Shortstop
			Pittsburgh Crawfords	Thirdbase
			Homestead Grays	Manager*
			Hilldale	

*Managerial position

Career	Last Name	First Name	Teams	Positions
1921–1940	Cooper	Daltie	Nashville Elite Giants	Pitcher
			Harrisburg Giants	
			Hilldale	
			Newark Eagles	
			Homestead Grays	
			Lincoln Giants	
			Bacharach Giants	
			Indianapolis ABC's	
1921–1942	Stearns	Norman (Turkey)	Philadelphia Stars	Outfielder
			Detroit Stars	
			Montgomery Grey Sox	
			Detroit Black Sox	
			Cole's American Giants	
			Kansas City Monarchs	
			Lincoln Giants	
			Chicago American Giants	
1921–1944	Rector	Cornelius (Connie)	New York Black Yankees	Pitcher
			Hilldale	
			New York Cubans	
			Brooklyn Royal Giants	
			Lincoln Giants	
1921–1945	Cannady	Walter (Rey)	New York Black Yankees	Pitcher
			New York Cubans	Secondbase
			Dayton Marcos	Outfielder
			Cleveland Tate Stars	Firstbase
			Cincinnati Indianapolis Clowns	Thirdbase
			Chicago American Giants	Manager*
			Columbus Buckeyes	
			Brooklyn Royal Giants	
			Darby Daisies	
			Homestead Grays	
			Harrisburg Giants	
			Lincoln Giants	
			Hilldale and Pittsburgh Crawfords	
1922	Bennett	–	Pittsburgh Keystones	Catcher
	Boyd	Fred	Cleveland Tate Stars	Outfielder
	Campbell	–	Pittsburgh Keystones	Outfielder
	Devoe	J.R.	Cleveland Tate Stars	Business Manager*
	Friely	–	Bacharach Giants	Secondbase
	Gray	G.E.	Pittsburgh Keystones	Outfielder
	Harper	(Chick)	Detroit Stars	Pitcher
	Howard	–	Baltimore Black Sox	Pitcher
	Jeffries	E.	Chicago Giants	Catcher
	Johnson	S.	Philadelphia Royal Stars	Thirdbase
	Knight	–	Baltimore Black Sox	Outfielder

*Managerial position

Career	Last Name	First Name	Teams	Positions
	Kyle	–	Baltimore Black Sox	Outfielder
	Lewis	Ira F.	Pittsburgh Keystones	Secretary*
	Lindner	–	Kansas City Monarchs	Pitcher
	McClelland	J.W.	St. Louis Stars	Club Officer*
	McDevitt	John J.	Baltimore Black Sox	Club Officer*
	Pace	–	Pittsburgh Keystones	Catcher
	Page	–	Pittsburgh Keystones	Catcher
	Richardson	Dewey	Hilldale	Catcher
	Spencer	–	Pittsburgh Keystones	Outfielder
	Stitler	–	Bacharach Giants	Pitcher
	Weeks	William	Bacharach Giants	Club Officer*
	White	–	Pittsburgh Keystones	Secondbase
	Williams	A.N.	Pittsburgh Keystones	Club Officer*
	Williams	Matt	Pittsburgh Keystones	Thirdbase Shortstop
1922–1923	Davis		Bacharach Giants	Thirdbase
	Fisher	George	Harrisburg Giants Richmond Giants	Outfielder
	Gooden	Ernest (Pud)	Toledo Tigers Pittsburgh Keystones Chicago American Giants	Thirdbase Second base
	Henderson	–	Cleveland Tate Stars	Thirdbase Outfielder
	Holt	Johnny	Toledo Tigers Pittsburgh Keystones	Outfielder
	Risley	–	Washington Potomacs Baltimore Black Sox	Thirdbase
	Smith	L.	Baltimore Black Sox	Outfielder
	Spedden	Charles P.	Baltimore Black Sox	Club Officer
	Strong	–	Milwaukee Bears New Orleans Crecent Stars	Pitcher
	Strong	F.	Chicago American Giants Cleveland Tate Stars	Pitcher
1922–1924	Blackman	Henry	Baltimore Black Sox Indianapolis ABC's	Thirdbase
	Johnson	Nat	Cleveland Browns Bacharach Giants	Pitcher
	Taylor	Mrs. Charles I.	Indianapolis ABC's	Club Officer*
	Wilson	J.	Baltimore Black Sox	Secondbase Firstbase
1922–1925	Albritton	Alexander (Alex)	Hilldale Baltimore Black Sox Washington Potomacs	Pitcher
	Anderson	Theodore (Bubbles)	Washington Potomacs Indianapolis ABC's	Secondbase

*Managerial Position

Career	Last Name	First Name	Teams	Positions
			Kansas City Monarchs	
			Birmingham Black Barons	
	Brown	Elias	Wilmington Potomacs	Outfielder
			New York Bacharach Giants	Thirdbase
			Washington Potomacs	Secondbase
	Combs	A. (Jack)	Detroit Stars	Pitcher
	Jordan	H. (Hen)	Harrisburg Giants	Outfielder
				Catcher
	Ross	H.	Washington Potomacs	Pitcher
			Indianapolis ABC's	
			Chicago American Giant	
1922–1926	Bell	Fred (Lefty)	St. Louis Stars	Pitcher
	Bonner	Robert	Toledo Stars	Catcher
			Cleveland Elites	Secondbase
			Cleveland Tate Stars	Firstbase
			St. Louis Stars	
	Johnson	C.	Harrisburg Giants	Shortstop
			Cleveland Tate Stars	Secondbase
			Baltimore Black Sox	
	Johnson	J.	Cleveland Elites	Pitcher
			Cleveland Tate Stars	
	McCall	William (Bill)	Kansas City Monarchs	Pitcher
			Indianapolis ABC's	
			Pittsburgh Keystones	
			Birmingham Black Barons	
			Chicago American Giants	
1922–1927	Branahan	J.	Cleveland Tate Stars	Pitcher
			Detroit Stars	
			Harrisburg Giants	
			Cleveland Elites	
			Cleveland Hornets	
	Duncan	Warren	Bacharach Giants	Outfielder
				Catcher
	Ward	Ira	Chicago Giants	Firstbase
				Shortstop
	Wilson	Andrew	Milwaukee Bears	Outfielder
			New Orleans Crescent Stars	
			Chicago Giants	
1922–1928	Corbett	Charles	Harrisburg Giants	Pitcher
			Pittsburgh Keystones	
			Indianapolis ABC's	
	Poles	E. (Possum)	Harrisburg Giants	Thirdbase
			Baltimore Black Sox	Shortstop

*Managerial Position

Career	Last Name	First Name	Teams	Positions
	Young	Berdell	Lincoln Giants	Outfielder
			Bacharach Giants	
1922–1929	Jones	John	Detroit Stars	Firstbase
				Outfielder
	Mason	Charles	Bacharach Giants	Pitcher
			Homestead Grays	Outfielder
			Richmond Giants	
			Newark Stars	
			Lincoln Giants	
	Moody	Willis	Homestead Grays	Outfielder
	Williams	Henry	St. Louis Stars	Catcher
			Kansas City Monarchs	
1922–1930	Barnes	Fat	Cleveland Tigers	Catcher
			Memphis Red Sox	
			Cleveland Tate Stars	
			Cleveland Hornets	
			St. Louis Stars	
			Detroit Stars	
			Cleveland Browns	
	Bray	James	Chicago American Giants	Outfielder
			Chicago Giants	Catcher
	Thompson	Lloyd P.	Hilldale	Club Officer*
1922–1931	Kent	Richard	St. Louis Stars	Club Officer*
	Lindsay	Clarence	Wilmington Potomacs	Shortstop
			Richmond Giants	
			Pennsylvania Red Caps of New York	
			Bacharach Giants	
			Richmond Giants	
	Watson	J.	Brooklyn Royal Giants	Outfielder
			Bacharach Giants	
			Detroit Stars	
1922–1932	Keyes	George	Negro National League	Club Officer*
			St. Louis Stars	Club Officer*
	Reed	Ambrose	Atlanta Black Crackers	Firstbase
			Bacharach Giants	Outfielder
			Hilldale	Thirdbase
			Pittsburgh Crawfords	Secondbase
	Rossiter	George	Baltimore Black Sox	Club Officer*
	Russell	Branch	Cleveland Stars	Outfielder
			Kansas City Monarchs	Thirdbase
			Cleveland Cubs	
			St. Louis Stars	
1922–1933	Collins	George	Milwaukee Bears	Secondbase
			New Orleans Crescent Stars	Outfielder
	Johnson	Oscar (Heavy)	Harrisburg Giants	Secondbase
			Cleveland Tigers	Outfielder

*Managerial Position

Career	Last Name	First Name	Teams	Positions
			Baltimore Black Sox	Catcher
			Memphis Red Sox	
			Kansas City Monarchs	
	Johnston	Wade	Baltimore Black Sox	Outfielder
			Cleveland Tate Stars	
			Detroit Stars	
			Kansas City Monarchs	
	Wilson	Percy	Milwaukee Bears	Firstbase
			New Orleans Crescent Stars	
1922–1934	Muse	B.	Monroe Monarchs	Pitcher
			Hilldale	
1922–1937	Dixon	Herbert (Rap)	Darby Daisies	Outfielder
			Brooklyn Eagles	
			Pittsburgh Crawfords	
			Harrisburg Giants	
			Baltimore Black Sox	
			Homestead Grays	
			Philadelphia Stars	
	Gilmore	Quincy J.	Texas-Oklahoma-Louisiana League	President*
			Negro National League	Secretary*
			Kansas City Monarchs	Business Manager*
	Washington	Jap	Pittsburgh Crawfords	Outfielder
			Homestead Grays	Thirdbase
			Pittsburgh Keystones	Firstbase
			Negro National League	Umpire*
1922–1938	Richardson	Henry	Pittsburgh Crawfords	Outfielder
			Washington Pilots	Pitcher
			Baltimore Black Sox	
			Bacharach Giants	
			Washington Black Senators	
1922–1939	Joseph	Newton (Newt)	Birmingham Black Barons	Thirdbase
			Satchell Paige's All-Stars	Secondbase
			Kansas City Monarchs	Manager*
1922–1942	Henry	Charles (Charlie)	Bacharach Giants	Manager*
			Hilldale	Pitcher
			Detroit Black Sox	
			Harrisburg Giants	
			Detroit Stars	
1922–1944	Allen	Newton (Newt)	St. Louis Stars	Outfielder
			All Nations	Secondbase
			Kansas City Monarchs	Shortstop
				Manager*
1922–1945	Burnett	Fred	Brooklyn Eagles	Coach
			Pittsburgh Crawfords	Outfielder
			Pittsburgh Keystones	Manager*
			Brooklyn Royal Giants	Firstbase

*Managerial Position

Career	Last Name	First Name	Teams	Positions
			Indianapolis ABC's	Catcher
			Harrisburgh Giants	
			Baltimore Black Sox	
			Homestead Grays	
			Lincoln Giants	
1922–1946	Bell	James (Cool Papa)	Memphis Red Sox	Pitcher
			St. Louis Stars	Outfielder
			Homestead Grays	
			Detroit Wolves	
			Chicago American Giants	
			Pittsburgh Crawfords	
			Kansas City Monarchs	
1922–1948	Clarke	Robert	Baltimore Elite Giants	Manager*
			Richmond Giants	Catcher
			Philadelphia Stars	
			Baltimore Black Sox	
			New York Black Yankees	
1922–1950	Porter	Andrew (Andy)	Indianapolis Clowns	Pitcher
			Washington Elite Giants	
			Nashville Elite Giants	
			Cleveland Cubs	
			Baltimore Elite Giants	
1923	Atkins	–	Toledo Tigers	Shortstop
	Augustine	Leon	Negro National League	Umpire*
	Calhoun	–	Toledo Tigers	Secondbase
	Chase	–	Toledo Tigers	Outfielder
	Clark	–	Brooklyn Royal Giants	Pitcher
	Cole	–	Toledo Tigers	Pitcher
	Collins	–	Toledo Tigers	Pitcher
	Curtis	–	Harrisburg Giants	Pitcher
	Embry	William	Negro National League	Umpire*
	Gibbons	–	Harrisburg Giants	Thirdbase
	Graves	Lawrence	Harrisburg Giants	Pitcher
	Gray	–	Cleveland Tate Stars	Firstbase
	Holcomb	–	Detroit Stars	Pitcher
	Johnson	Ray	St. Louis Stars	Outfielder
	Johnston	Tom	Negro National League	Umpire*
	Matthews	–	Toledo Tigers	Thirdbase
	McMillan	Earl	Toledo Tigers	Outfielder
	Reel	–	Toledo Tigers	Outfielder
	Roberts	Harry	Baltimore Black Sox	Outfielder
	Spike	–	Washington Potomacs	Pitcher
	Stevens	L.	Toledo Tigers	Firstbase
				Pitcher
	Thompson	–	Harrisburg Giants	Pitcher
	Turner	–	Toledo Tigers	Outfielder

*Managerial Position

Career	Last Name	First Name	Teams	Positions
	Walker	–	Milwaukee Bears	Pitcher
	White	–	Toledo Tigers	Thirdbase
	Williams	Bert	Philadelphia Giants	Club Officer*
	Williams	Lem	Negro National League	Umpire*
	Wingfield	–	Toledo Tigers	Pitcher
	Wisher	–	Harrisburg Giants	Outfielder
1923–1924	Clark	–	Washington Potomacs	Pitcher
				Firstbase
	Gordon	Herman	Birmingham Black Barons	Outfielder
			Toledo Tigers	Pitcher
	Hammond	–	Cleveland Browns	Shortstop
			Cleveland Tate Stars	Thirdbase
	Newsome	Omer	Washington Potomacs	Pitcher
			Indianapolis ABC's	
	Wolfolk	Lewis	Chicago American Giants	Pitcher
1923–1925	Wiley	F.	Pennsylvania Red Caps of New York	Pitcher
			Lincoln Giants	Outfielder
				Secondbase
	Wilson	Benjamin	Pennsylvania Red Caps of New York	Outfielder
		(Benny)	Lincoln Giants	
1923–1926	Alexander	Grover Cleveland	Indianapolis ABC's	Pitcher
		(Buck)	Chicago Giants	
			Cleveland Elites	
			Detroit Stars	
	Brown	Earl	Lincoln Giants	Pitcher
	Goodrich	Joe	Philadelphia Giants	Shortstop
			Washington Potomacs	Secondbase
				Thirdbase
	Harper	John	Lincoln Giants	Pitcher
			Bacharach Giants	
	Manese	E.	Kansas City Monarchs	Secondbase
			Indianapolis ABC's	
			Detroit Stars	
	Rush	Joe	Negro National League	Secretary*
			Negro Southern League	President*
			Birmingham Black Barons	Club Officer*
1923–1927	Hill	–	Brooklyn Royal Giants	Thirdbase
	Miles	W.	Cleveland Elites	Firstbase
			Toledo Tigers	Outfielder
			Cleveland Hornets	Thirdbase
			Cleveland Browns	
			Cleveland Tate Stars	
1923–1928	Lewis	R.S. (Bubbles)	Negro National League	Vice-President*
			Memphis Red Sox	Club Officer*
	Lockhart	Hubert	Bacharach Giants	Pitcher

*Managerial Position

Career	Last Name	First Name	Teams	Positions
	Mitchell	Hooks	Bacharach Giants	Pitcher
			Baltimore Black Sox	
			Harrisburg Giants	
	Smith	Cleveland (Cleo)	Philadelphia Tigers	Shortstop
			Baltimore Black Sox	Thirdbase
			Homestead Grays	Secondbase
			Lincoln Giants	
	Wheeler	Joe	Brooklyn Cuban Giants	Pitcher
			Baltimore Black Sox	
	Willett	–	Cleveland Tigers	Outfielder
			Cleveland Browns	Shortstop
			Lincoln Giants	
1923–1929	Campbell	William (Zip)	Hilldale	Pitcher
			Washington Potomacs	
			Lincoln Giants	
			Philadelphia Giants	
	Gee	Richard (Rich)	Lincoln Giants	Outfielder
				Catcher
	Summers	S.	Cleveland Tigers	Outfielder
			Cleveland Elites	
			Chicago American Giants	
			Toledo Tigers	
			Cleveland Browns	
			Cleveland Hornets	
1923–1930	Harney	George	Chicago American Giants	Pitcher
1923–1931	Gray	Willie (Dolly)	Lincoln Giants	Outfielder
			Homestead Grays	
			Pennsylvania Red Caps of New York	
			Cleveland Tate Stars	
	Leonard	Bobo	Homestead Grays	Outfielder
			Chicago American Giants	
			Pennsylvania Red Caps of New York	
			Baltimore Black Sox	
			Bacharach Giants	
			Lincoln Giants	
	Levis	Oscar (Oscal)	Darby Daisies	Pitcher
			Hilldale	
			Baltimore Black Sox	
			Cuban Stars (East)	
1923–1932	Gurley	James	Chicago American Giants	Pitcher
			St. Louis Stars	Outfielder
			Memphis Red Sox	Firstbase
			Montgomery Grey Sox	
	Huff	Eddie	Dayton Marcos	Catcher
			Bacharach Giants	Manager*
				Outfielder

*Managerial Position

Career	Last Name	First Name	Teams	Positions
	Jamison	Caesar	Negro National League	Umpire*
			East-West League	
1923–1933	Miller	Percy	St. Louis Giants	Pitcher
			Nashville Elite Giants	
			St. Louis Stars	
	Owens	Willie	Chicago American Giants	Pitcher
			Detroit Stars	Secondbase
			Memphis Red Sox	Shortstop
			Washington Potomacs	
			Dayton Marcos	
			Birmingham Black Barons	
			Indianapolis ABC's	
	Pryor	Anderson	Memphis Red Sox	Shortstop
			Detroit Stars	Secondbase
			Milwaukee Bears	
1923–1934	Bobo	Willie	Nashville Elite Giants	Firstbase
			Kansas City Monarchs	
			All Nations	
			St. Louis Stars	
	Boggs	G.	Detroit Stars	Outfielder
			Milwaukee Bears	Pitcher
	Carter	Clifford	Philadelphia Stars	Pitcher
			Baltimore Black Sox	
			Harrisburg Giants	
			Hilldale	
			Philadelphia Tigers	
			Bacharach Giants	
	Davis	Walter	Chicago Columbia Giants	Firstbase
		(Steel Arm)	Cole's American Giants	Pitcher
			Chicago American Giants	Outfielder
			Nashville Elite Giants	
			Detroit Stars	
1923–1935	Washington	Peter (Pete)	Philadelphia Stars	Outfielder
			Washington Potomacs	
			Baltimore Black Sox	
			Wilmington Potomacs	
1923–1936	Yancey	William J.	Brooklyn Eagles	Shortstop
		(Bill, Yank)	Hilldale	
			Philadelphia Giants	
			Darby Daisies	
			Philadelphia Stars	
			New York Black Yankees	
			Lincoln Giants	
			Philadelphia Tigers	
1923–1937	Donaldson	W.W. (Billy)	Negro National League	Umpire*

*Managerial Position

Career	Last Name	First Name	Teams	Positions
	Foster	Willie H. (Bill)	Homestead Grays	Pitcher
			Memphis Red Sox	Manager
			Chicago American Giants	
			Cole's American Giants	
			Kansas City Monarchs	
1923–1939	Hensley	(Slap)	Detroit Stars	Pitcher
			Indianapolis ABC's	
			St. Louis Stars	
			Chicago American Giants	
			Toledo Tigers	
			Cleveland Giants	
1923–1943	Gholston	Bert E.	Negro National League	Umpire*
			East-West League	Umpire*
1923–1946	Thomas	David (Showboat)	New York Black Yankees	Outfielder
			Montgomery Grey Sox	Firstbase
			Baltimore Black Sox	Manager*
			New York Cubans	
			Washington Black Senators	
			Brooklyn Royal Giants	
			Birmingham Black Barons	
1923–1948	Bell	William	Newark Dodgers	Pitcher
			Kansas City Monarchs	Manager*
			Pittsburgh Crawfords	
			Newark Eagles	
			Homestead Grays	
			Detroit Wolves	
1923–1950	Harris	Victor (Vic)	Chicago American Giants	Outfielder
			Baltimore Elite Giants	Coach*
			Birmingham Black Barons	Manager*
			Pittsburgh Crawfords	
			Cleveland Tate Stars	
			Homestead Grays	
			Cleveland Browns	
1924	Bostick	–	St. Louis Giants	Outfielder
	Brown	Hap	Cleveland Browns	Pitcher
	Evans	W.P.	Chicago American Giants	Outfielder
	Hamilton	George	Memphis Red Sox	Catcher
	Hunter	–	Memphis Red Sox	Pitcher
	Means	–	Birmingham Black Barons	Catcher
	Mitchell	Robert	St. Louis Stars	Utility Player
	Rich	–	St. Louis Giants	Thirdbase
	Robinson	George	Washington Potomacs	Club Officer*
	Rose	–	St. Louis Stars	Pitcher
	Smith	–	Washington Potomacs	Pitcher
	Smith	W.	Hilldale	Shortstop
	Stovall	–	Cleveland Browns	Pitcher

*Managerial Position

Career	Last Name	First Name	Teams	Positions
	Walters	–	Cleveland Browns	Pitcher
	Williams	F.	Washington Potomacs	Ball Player
	Young	–	St. Louis Stars	Pitcher
1924–1925	Salmon	Harry	Homestead Grays	Pitcher
			Birmingham Black Barons	
	Terrell	–	Detroit Stars	Pitcher
1924–1926	Cunningham	Marion (Daddy)	Montgomery Grey Sox	Manager*
			Memphis Red Sox	Firstbase
	Daniels	Hammond	Bacharach Giants	Club Officer*
	Ducey	–	Dayton Marcos	Outfielder
			St. Louis Giants	Infielder
	Lindsey	Bill	Dayton Marcos	Pitcher
			Washington Potomacs	
			Lincoln Giants	
	Meyers	George	Dayton Marcos	Pitcher
			St. Louis Stars	
	Watts	Eddie	Cleveland Hornets	Firstbase
			St. Louis Stars	Secondbase
			Cleveland Elites	
1924–1927	Hamilton	J.H.	Birmingham Black Barons	Thirdbase
			Washington Potomacs	
	Spearman	William	Cleveland Elites	Pitcher
			Memphis Red Sox	
	Strothers	C.W.	Harrisburg Giants	Club Officer*
1924–1928	Miller	Bob	Memphis Red Sox	Thirdbase
				Secondbase
	Moore	Squire (Square)	Cleveland Hornets	Pitcher
			Memphis Red Sox	
			Cleveland Tigers	
			Kansas City Monarchs	
1924–1929	Jackson	Tom	Cleveland Tigers	Pitcher
			Nashville Elite Giants	
			St. Louis Stars	
	Macklin	–	Chicago Giants	Outfielder
				Thirdbase
	Poindexter	Robert	Memphis Red Sox	Firstbase
			Birmingham Black Barons	Pitcher
			Chicago American Giants	
	Wesley	Charles	Birmingham Black Barons	Secondbase
				Manager*
1924–1930	Smith	Charles (Chino)	Brooklyn Royal Giants	Secondbase
			Lincoln Giants	Outfielder
			Philadelphia Giants	
1924–1931	Jackson	Stanford	Chicago American Giants	Shortstop
			Memphis Red Sox	Outfielder
				Secondbase
				Thirdbase

*Managerial Position

Career	Last Name	First Name	Teams	Positions
	Williams	Charles (Arthur)	Memphis Red Sox Chicago Columbia Giants Indianapolis ABC's Lincoln Giants	Secondbase Shortstop
1924–1932	Morris	Harold (Yellowhorse)	Detroit Stars Monroe Monarchs Chicago American Giants Kansas City Monarchs	Pitcher
1924–1933	Russell	John Henry	Indianapolis ABC's Memphis Red Sox Detroit Wolves St. Louis Stars	Thirdbase Secondbase
1924–1934	McAllister	George	Memphis Red Sox Birmingham Black Barons Chicago American Giants Indianapolis ABC's Cleveland Red Sox Homestead Grays	Firstbase
1924–1936	Beverly	Charles	Cleveland Stars New Orleans Crescent Stars Birmingham Black Barons Pittsburgh Crawfords Newark Eagles Kansas City Monarchs	Pitcher
	Glass	Carl	Cincinnati Tigers Memphis Red Sox	Pitcher Manager*
1924–1940	Creary	A.D. (Dewey)	Detroit Wolves Washington Pilots Brooklyn Royal Giants St. Louis Stars Kansas City Monarchs Philadelphia Stars Columbus Blue Birds Cleveland Giants	Thirdbase
	Redus	Wilson	Cleveland Red Sox St. Louis Stars Chicago American Giants Cleveland Giants Kansas City Monarchs Columbus Blue Birds Cleveland Stars	Outfielder Manager*
1924–1945	Davis	Roosevelt	Cincinnati Clowns Cincinnati-Indianapolis Clowns Memphis Red Sox Brooklyn Royal Giants Philadelphia Stars	Pitcher

*Managerial Position

Career	Last Name	First Name	Teams	Positions
			St. Louis Stars	
			Columbus Blue Birds	
			Pittsburgh Crawfords	
			New York Black Yankees	
			Chicago Brown Bombers	
			Baltimore Elite Giants	
	Wilson	Judson	Homestead Grays	Firstbase
		(Jud, Bojung)	Philadelphia Stars	Thirdbase
			Baltimore Black Sox	Manager*
1924–1950	Meredith	Buford	Nashville Elite Giants	Secondbase
		(Geetchie)	Birmingham Black Barons	Shortstop
1925	Allison	–	Indianapolis ABC's	Secondbase
	Bebley	–	Birmingham Black Barons	Pitcher
	Bragg	Eugene	Chicago American Giants	Catcher
	Collins	–	Indianapolis ABC's	Shortstop
	Davis	(Red)	Indianapolis ABC's	Outfielder
	Ellis	–	Cleveland Browns	Thirdbase
	Evans	William	Lincoln Giants	Pitcher
	Hartley	(Hop)	Kansas City Monarchs	Pitcher
	Henderson	–	Birmingham Black Barons	Catcher
	Hodges	–	Lincoln Giants	Pitcher
	Jeffries	M.	Baltimore Black Sox	Thirdbase
	Johnson	Monk	Lincoln Giants	Ball Player
	Johnson	W.	Wilmington Potomacs	Ball Player
	Lair	–	Pennsylvania Red Caps of New York	Outfielder
	Lillie	–	Birmingham Black Barons	Utility Player
	Morrison	W.	Cleveland Browns	Firstbase
	Overton	John	Indianapolis ABC's	Club Officer*
	Page	R.	Indianapolis ABC's	Club Officer*
	Pryor	Edward	Lincoln Giants	Secondbase
	Richardson	George	Detroit Stars	Club Officer*
	Richardson	John	Birmingham Black Barons	Ball Player
	Robinson	–	Birmingham Black Barons	Pitcher
	Saunders	–	Pennsylvania Red Caps of New York	Catcher
	Savage	–	Bacharach Giants	Pitcher
	Smith	–	St. Louis Stars	Catcher
	Street	Albert	Chicago American Giants	Infielder
	Taylor	C.	Lincoln Giants	Outfielder
	Williams	A.D.	Indianapolis ABC's	Club Officer*
1925–1926	Baldwin	–	Cleveland Elites	Secondbase
			Indianapolis ABC's	Shortstop
	Gee	Tom	Lincoln Giants	Catcher
	Martin	(Stack)	Indianapolis ABC's	Outfielder
	Mungin	–	Baltimore Black Sox	Pitcher
	Nuttall	H.	Lincoln Giants	Pitcher
	Offert	–	Indianapolis ABC's	Pitcher

*Managerial Position

Career	Last Name	First Name	Teams	Positions
	Pierce	Herbert	Homestead Grays	Catcher
	Stevens	Frank	Indianapolis ABC's	Pitcher
			Chicago American Giants	
	Tyler	Roy	Chicago American Giants	Outfielder
				Pitcher
1925–1927	Broiles	–	St. Louis Stars	Pitcher
	Chambers	Rube	Lincoln Giants	Pitcher
	Robinson	Newt	Lincoln Giants	Shortstop
			Hilldale	
	Smith	J.	Brooklyn Royal Giants	Shortstop
				Secondbase
	Stamps	Hulan (Lefty)	Memphis Red Sox	Pitcher
1925–1928	Grier	Claude (Red)	Bacharach Giants	Pitcher
			Wilmington Potomacs	
	Johnson	John B.	Brooklyn Cuban Giants	President*
				Manager*
	Lewis	Milton	Bacharach Giants	Firstbase
			Wilmington Potomacs	Secondbase
	Pierce	Steve	Detroit Stars	Club Officer*
	Strong	J.T.	Baltimore Black Sox	Pitcher
1925–1929	Miller	Eddie (Buck)	Indianapolis ABC's	Pitcher
			Chicago American Giants	
1925–1930	Dean		Pennsylvania Red Caps of New York	Thirdbase
			Lincoln Giants	Secondbase
	Graham	Dennis	Homestead Grays	Outfielder
	Roesirk	John	Detroit Stars	Club Officer*
	Ross	William	Cleveland Hornets	Pitcher
			St. Louis Stars	
			Homestead Grays	
1925–1931	Davis	Saul	Memphis Red Sox	Secondbase
			Birmingham Black Barons	Thirdbase
			Detroit Stars	Shortstop
			Chicago American Giants	
			Cleveland Tigers	
	Orange	Grady	Kansas City Monarchs	Thirdbase
			Detroit Stars	Shortstop
			Birmingham Black Barons	Secondbase
1925–1932	Baker	Henry	Indianapolis ABC's	Outfielder
	Dean	Nelson	Detroit Stars	Pitcher
			Cleveland Hornets	
			Cleveland Tigers	
			Kansas City Monarchs	
			Cleveland Stars	
	Duff	E.	Indianapolis ABC's	Outfielder
			Cuban Stars	
			Cleveland Hornets	
			Cleveland Tigers	

*Managerial Position

Career	Last Name	First Name	Teams	Positions
	Tyler	William (Steel Arm)	Cole's American Giants Memphis Red Sox Kansas City Monarchs Detroit Stars	Pitcher
1925–1933	Dallard	William (Eggie)	Bacharach Giants Quaker Giants Philadelphia Stars Baltimore Black Sox Wilmington Potomacs Darby Daisies	Outfielder Catcher Secondbase Firstbase
	Finley	Thomas (Tom)	Brooklyn Royal Giants Baltimore Black Sox New York Black Yankees Philadelphia Stars Lincoln Giants Pennsylvania Red Caps of New York Bacharach Giants	Catcher Thirdbase
1925–1934	Robinson	William	Cleveland Stars Cleveland Red Sox Indianapolis ABC's Memphis Red Sox Detroit Stars Cleveland Elites	Shortstop Thirdbase
	Ward	C.	Louisville Black Caps Memphis Red Sox Cincinnati Tigers Chicago Columbia Giants	Outfielder
1925–1936	Taylor	Leroy R.	Homestead Grays Chicago American Giants Indianapolis ABC's Cleveland Red Sox Detroit Wolves	Outfielder
1925–1937	Dwight	Eddie	Kansas City Monarchs Indianapolis ABC's	Outfielder
1925–1939	Moorhead	Albert	Chicago Giants	Catcher
1925–1942	Jacksman	Bill	Brooklyn Eagles Lincoln Giants Boston Royal Giants Quaker Giants	Pitcher
1925–1948	Brewer	Chet	Washington Pilots Cleveland Buckeyes Kansas City Monarchs Chicago American Giants New York Cubans Philadelphia Stars	Pitcher

Career	Last Name	First Name	Teams	Positions
1925–1949	Mitchell	George	Mounds City Illinois Blues	Pitcher
			Indianapolis ABC's	Business Manager*
			New York Black Yankees	Manager*
			Chicago American Giants	
			Montgomery Grey Sox	
			Cleveland Cubs	
			New Orleans-St. Louis Stars	
			Houston Eagles	
			Harrisburgh-St. Louis Stars	
	Wells	Willie	Newark Eagles	Thirdbase
			St. Louis Stars	Shortstop
			Cole's American Giants	Manager*
			Memphis Red Sox	
			Baltimore Elite Giants	
			Kansas City Monarchs	
			Chicago American Giants	
			Detroit Wolves	
			Indianapolis Clowns	
			New York Black Yankees	
1926	Ash	–	Hilldale	Pitcher
	Bowers	–	Baltimore Black Sox	Pitcher
	Brooks	–	Dayton Marcos	Outfielder
				Thirdbase
	Carpenter	Clay	Baltimore Black Sox	Pitcher
	Caulfield	Fred	New Orleans Ads	Manager*
	Coleman	–	Lincoln Giants	Pitcher
	Gantz	–	Harrisburg Giants	Catcher
	Hanson	Harry	Negro Southern League	Vice-President
	Heywood	Dobie	Lincoln Giants	Pitcher
	Jackson	(Lefty)	Philadelphia Giants	Pitcher
	Jenkins	Clarence	Philadelphia Giants	Catcher
	Johnson	P.	Baltimore Black Sox	Pitcher
	Kirksey	–	Dayton Marcos	Catcher
	Lewis	Charles	Lincoln Giants	Shortstop
	Montgomery	A.G.	Negro Southern League	Secretary*
	Nestor	S.	Lincoln Giants	Outfielder
	Roddy	B.M.	Negro Southern League	President*
	Russell	E.	Harrisburg Giants	Thirdbase
	Saunders	Bob	Kansas City Monarchs	Pitcher
	Ware	William	Chicago American Giants	Firstbase
	Whitlock	–	Dayton Marcos	Firstbase
	Willburn	–	Baltimore Black Sox	Pitcher
	Brown	G.	St. Louis Stars	Pitcher
1926–1927	Brown	L.A.	St. Louis Stars	Agent*
	Evans	–	Cleveland Hornets	Outfielder
			Dayton Marcos	

*Managerial Position

Career	Last Name	First Name	Teams	Positions
1926–1928	Craig	Charles	Lincoln Giants	Pitcher
			Brooklyn Cuban Giants	
	Dudley	Edward	Lincoln Giants	Pitcher
			Brooklyn Royal Giants	
	Gilmore	–	Lincoln Giants	Pitcher
	Roberts	Rags	Homestead Grays	Catcher
1926–1929	Russ	Pythias	Chicago American Giants	Shortstop
				Catcher
1926–1930	Pitchett	Wilbur	Brooklyn Cuban Giants	Pitcher
			Hilldale	
			Baltimore Black Sox	
			Harrisburg Giants	
1926–1931	Cephus	Goldie	Bacharach Giants	Outfielder
			Philadelphia Giants	
	Harding	Hallie	Chicago Columbia Giants	Secondbase
			Detroit Stars	Shortstop
			Indianapolis ABC's	Thirdbase
			Bacharach Giants	
			Kansas City Monarchs	
	Zomphier	Charles	Memphis Red Sox	Thirdbase
			Cleveland Hornets	Shortstop
			Cleveland Cubs	Secondbase
			Cleveland Elites	
			Cleveland Tigers	
1926–1932	Thompson	Sandy	Chicago Columbia Giants	Outfielder
			Birmingham Black Barons	
			Cole's American Giants	
			Chicago American Giants	
1926–1933	Blanchard	Chester	Dayton Marcos	Utility Player
1926–1934	Ewell	–	Cincinnati Tigers	Catcher
			Indianapolis ABC's	
	Farrell	Luther	New York Black Yankees	Pitcher
			New York Cubans	
			Bacharach Giants	
1926–1937	Page	Theodore (Ted)	Philadelphia Stars	Outfielder
			Homestead Grays	
			Baltimore Black Sox	
			Newark Eagles	
			Pittsburgh Crawfords	
			Newark Eagles	
			Brooklyn Royal Giants	
			New York Black Yankees	
	Young	T.J. (Tom)	Detroit Wolves	Catcher
			Kansas City Monarchs	
			Pittsburgh Crawfords	

Career	Last Name	First Name	Teams	Positions
			St. Louis Stars	
			New York Cubans	
1926–1938	Yokeley	Loymon	Philadelphia Stars	Pitcher
			Baltimore Black Sox	
			Washington Black Senators	
			Bacharach Giants	
1926–1944	Marshall	William	Gilkerson's Union Giants	Thirdbase
		(Jack, Bolsy)	Philadelphia Stars	Firstbase
			Cole's American Giants	Secondbase
			Dayton Marcos	
			Cincinnati-Indianapolis Clowns	
			Chicago Columbia Giants	
1926–1949	Welch	Winfield (Scott)	Monroe Monarchs	Ball Player
			Chicago American Giants	Manager*
			Birmingham Black Barons	
			Shreveport Giants	
			New Orleans Black Pelicans	
			Cincinnati Buckeyes	
			Cincinnati Crescents	
			New York Cubans	
1926–1950	Paige	Leroy (Satchel)	Pittsburgh Crawfords	Pitcher
			Cleveland Cubs	
			Satchel Paige's All-Stars	
			Birmingham Black Barons	
			Kansas City Monarchs	
			Chattanooga Black Lockouts	
	Parnell	Roy (Red)	Philadelphia Stars	Manager*
			Houston Eagles	Firstbase
			Columbus Elite Giants	Outfielder
			Birmingham Black Barons	
			New Orleans Crescent Stars	
			Indianapolis ABC's	
			Monroe Monarchs	
			Memphis Red Sox	
	Pollack	Syd	Indianapolis Clowns	Club Officer*
			Ethiopian Clowns	Club Officer*
			Havana Red Sox	Club Officer*
			Cuban House of David	Club Officer*
			Cincinnati Clowns	Club Officer*
			Cuban Stars	Club Officer*
1927	Arnold	–	Brooklyn Royal Giants	Outfielder
	Bobo	J.	Cleveland Hornets	Outfielder
	Everett	–	Kansas City Monarchs	Shortstop
	Harness	Robert	Chicago Giants	Pitcher
	Harris	–	Lincoln Giants	Firstbase
	Martin	–	Detroit Stars	Firstbase

*Managerial Position

Career	Last Name	First Name	Teams	Positions
	Miller	A.	Memphis Red Sox	Outfielder
	Monroe	Bill	Baltimore Black Sox	Thirdbase
	Payne	–	Brooklyn Royal Giants	Secondbase
	Sockard	–	Cleveland Hornets	Thirdbase
	Stephens	–	Cleveland Hornets	Firstbase
				Outfielder
	Young	M.	Kansas City Monarchs	Pitcher
1927–1928	Goldie	–	Cleveland Tigers	Firstbase
			Indianapolis ABC's	
	Nutter	Issac	Eastern League	President*
			Bacharach Giants	Club Officer*
	Pryor	Bill	Memphis Red Sox	Pitcher
1927–1929	Guy	Wesley	Chicago Giants	Pitcher
	McHaskell	J.C.	Memphis Red Sox	Firstbase
	Ziegler	William	Chicago Giants	Outfielder
1927–1930	Byrd	James F.	Hilldale	Agent*
	Freeman	Charlie	Hilldale	Club Officer*
	Johnson	G.	Birmingham Black Barons	Secondbase
			Detroit Stars	Thirdbase
1927–1931	Hicks	Wesley	Memphis Red Sox	Outfielder
			Kansas City Monarchs	
			Chicago American Giants	
	Hueston	William C.	Negro National League	President*
	Johnson	William (Bill)	Philadelphia Tigers	Outfielder
			Pennsylvania Red Caps of New York	Catcher
			Hilldale	Manager*
1927–1932	Burdine	J.	Birmingham Black Barons	Outfielder
				Pitcher
	McDonald	Luther (Vet)	Chicago American Giants	Pitcher
			St. Louis Stars	
			Cole's American Giants	
			Chicago Columbia Giants	
	Trimble	William E.	Chicago American Giants	Club Officer*
1927–1933	Britt	Charles (Charlie)	Homestead Grays	Thirdbase
1927–1934	Bailey	Percy (Bill)	New York Black Yankees	Pitcher
			Detroit Stars	
			Baltimore Black Sox	
			Cole's American Giants	
			Nashville Elite Giants	
1927–1935	Charleston	Porter	Philadelphia Stars	Pitcher
			Hilldale	
			Darby Daisies	
1927–1936	Dials	Odem	Memphis Red Sox	Outfielder
			Cleveland Giants	
			Chicago American Giants	

*Managerial Position

Career	Last Name	First Name	Teams	Positions
1927–1937	Hampton	Eppie	Washington Pilots New Orleans Crescent Stars Memphis Red Sox	Pitcher Catcher
1927–1938	Giles	George	St. Louis Stars Kansas City Monarchs New York Black Yankees Philadelphia Stars	Firstbase
1927–1939	Trent	Theodore (Ted)	Detroit Wolves Chicago American Giants St. Louis Stars Cole's American Giants Homestead Grays	Pitcher
1927–1945	Miller	Dempsey (Dimp)	Detroit Stars Cleveland Tigers Cleveland Hornets Detroit Giants Nashville Elite Giants	Pitcher Manager*
	Powell	Willie (Wee Willie)	Detroit Stars Chicago American Giants Cole's American Giants Cleveland Red Sox	Pitcher
	Rogers	Nat	Cole's American Giants Memphis Red Sox Chicago American Giants Chicago Columbia Giants	Outfielder
1927–1946	Palm	Clarence (Spoony)	Brooklyn Eagles Philadelphia Stars Birmingham Black Barons Detroit Stars Cleveland Giants Homestead Grays New York Black Yankees	Catcher
	Radcliffe	Alex	Cincinnati-Indianapolis Clowns Cole's American Giants New York Cubans Memphis Red Sox Chicago Giants Chicago American Giants Kansas City Monarchs	Thirdbase Shortstop
1927–1947	Hall	Perry	Chicago Giants Cleveland Tigers Indianapolis Athletics Memphis Red Sox	Outfielder Thirdbase

*Managerial Position

Career	Last Name	First Name	Teams	Positions
1928	Barkins	W.C.	Cleveland Stars	Club Officer*
	Black	Howard	Brooklyn Cuban Giants	Infielder
	Boone	Robert	Negro National League	Umpire*
	Bryant	–	Harrisburg Giants	Ball Player
	Clark	Eggie	Memphis Red Sox	Outfielder
	Coleman	Gilbert	Brooklyn Cuban Giants	Infielder
	Collier	–	Bacharach Giants	Catcher
	Collins	–	Baltimore Black Sox	Pitcher
	Cooper	Alex	Harrisburg Giants	Outfielder
			Philadelphia Tigers	Outfielder
	Cooper	(Chief)	Negro National League	Umpire*
	Edwards	Chancellor (Jack)	Cleveland Tigers	Catcher
	Flournoy	Fred	Brooklyn Cuban Giants	Catcher
	Goodman	–	Harrisburg Giants	Outfielder
	Greene	–	Bacharach Giants	Firstbase
	Greene	Walter	Brooklyn Cuban Giants	Outfielder
	Haley	(Red)	Chicago American Giants	Secondbase
	Harps	Fred	Brooklyn Cuban Giants	Infielder
	Holtz	Joseph	Brooklyn Cuban Giants	Outfielder
	Hopwood	–	Kansas City Monarchs	Outfielder
	Jackson	–	Bacharach Giants	Outfielder
	Jackson	Carlton	Harrisburg Giants	Club Officer
	Jenkins	Tom	Hilldale	Secretary*
	Johnson	C. (Sess)	Philadelphia Tigers	Firstbase
	Johnson	Robert	Brooklyn Cuban Giants	Infielder
	Johnson	W.	Detroit Stars	Outfielder
	Jones	Alvin	Harrisburg Giants	Club Officer*
	Jones	Alvin	Harrisburg Giants	Club Officer*
	Lucas	(Scotty)	Philadelphia Tigers	Club Officer*
	Mayers	George	Hilldale	Club Officer*
	Mayo	George	Hilldale	Club Officer*
	Stevenson	–	Cleveland Tigers	Pitcher
	Stockard	T.	Cleveland Tigers	Shortstop
	Terrell	S.M.	Cleveland Stars	Club Officer*
	Turner	–	St. Louis Stars	Pitcher
	Tyler	Edward	Brooklyn Cuban Giants	Pitcher
	Washington	Issac	Bacharach Giants	Club Officer*
	Williams	Craig (Stringbean)	Brooklyn Cuban Giants	Pitcher
1928–1929	Melton	Elbert	Lincoln Giants	Outfielder
			Brooklyn Cuban Giants	
1928–1930	Rogers	William	Memphis Red Sox	Outfielder
			Chicago American Giants	
1928–1931	Jackson	R.T.	Negro Southern League	President*
			Birmingham Black Barons	Club Officer*

*Managerial Position

Career	Last Name	First Name	Teams	Positions
	Walker	Moses L.	Detroit Stars	Club Officer*
1928–1932	Alexander	Chuffy	Monroe Monarchs	Firstbase
			Birmingham Black Barons	Thirdbase
	Cooper	Alfred (Army)	Cleveland Stars	Ball Player
			Knasas City Monarchs	
	Livingston	L.D. (Goo Goo)	New York Black Yankees	Outfielder
			Pittsburgh Crawfords	
			Kansas City Monarchs	
	O'Den	J.	Knoxville Giants	Outfielder
			Louisville Black Caps	Shortstop
			Birmingham Black Barons	
1928–1933	Mosley	William	Detroit Stars	Club Officer*
	Womack	–	Columbus Turfs	Firstbase
			Indianapolis ABC's	
			Cleveland Tigers	
			Baltimore Black Sox	
			Cuban Stars	
1928–1934	Cannon	Richard (Speedball)	Louisville Red Caps	Pitcher
			St. Louis Stars	
			Birmingham Black Barons	
			Nashville Elite Giants	
	Dixon	John	Cleveland Giants	Shortstop
			Cleveland Red Sox	Pitcher
			Cleveland Tigers	
			Cuban Stars	
			Detroit Stars	
	Williams	J.	Detroit Stars	Pitcher
			St. Louis Stars	Outfielder
			Homestead Grays	
			Indianapolis ABC's	
1928–1935	Strong	Joseph C. (Joe)	Homestead Grays	Pitcher
			Hilldale	
			St. Louis Stars	
1928–1937	Davis	Albert	Baltimore Black Sox	Pitcher
			Detroit Stars	
1928–1939	Willis	Jim	Columbus Elite Giants	Pitcher
			Birmingham Black Barons	
			Washington Elite Giants	
			Cleveland Cubs	
			Nashville Elite Giants	
			Baltimore Elite Giants	
1928–1940	Burton	–	Birmingham Black Barons	Infielder
				Pitcher
				Outfielder
1928–1945	Dukes	Tommy	Memphis Red Sox	Thirdbase
			Columbus Elite Giants	Catcher

*Managerial Position

Career	Last Name	First Name	Teams	Positions
			Indianapolis Crawfords	
			Toledo Crawfords	
			Chicago American Giants	
			Homestead	
1928–1947	Perkins	W.G. (Bill)	Cleveland Cubs	Outfielder
			New York Black Yankees	Catcher
			Philadelphia Stars	Manager*
			Birmingham Black Barons	
			Baltimore Elite Giants	
1928–1948	Stanley	John (Neck)	Baltimore Black Sox	Pitcher
			Bacharach Giants	
			Brooklyn Royal Giants	
			Philadelphia Stars	
			Quaker Giants	
			Lincoln Giants	
			New York Cubans	
			New York Black Yankees	
1928–1950	Radcliffe	Theodore (Double Duty)	Memphis Red Sox	Pitcher
			Birmingham Black Barons	Catcher
			St. Louis Stars	Manager*
			Detroit Stars	
			Homestead Grays	
			Brooklyn Eagles	
			Columbus Blue Birds	
			Cincinnati Tigers	
			Pittsburgh Crawfords	
			Louisville Buckeyes	
			Chicago American Giants	
1929	Bell	Julian	Birmingham Black Barons	Pitcher
	Broadnax	Willie	Memphis Red Sox	Outfielder
				Pitcher
	Cade	–	Bacharach Giants	Pitcher
	Dandridge	Troy	Chicago Giants	Thirdbase
	Diamond	(Black)	Birmingham Black Barons	Pitcher
	Everett	Dean	Lincoln Giants	Pitcher
	Gay	H.	Chicago American Giants	Outfielder
				Pitcher
	Gransberry	Bill	Chicago Giants	Firstbase
			Chicago American Giants	Outfielder
	Harland	Bill	Lincoln Giants	Pitcher
	Jackson	C.	Homestead Grays	Thirdbase
	Lindsey	Ben	Bacharach Giants	Shortstop
	Nesbit	Dr. E.E.	Memphis Red Sox	Club Officer*
	Pennington	–	Nashville Elite Giants	Pitcher
	Robeson	Bobbie	Detroit Stars	Shortstop
	Robsell	–	Birmingham Black Barons	Outfielder
	Ronsell	–	Birmingham Black Barons	Outfielder

*Managerial Position

Career	Last Name	First Name	Teams	Positions
	Stevens	–	Bacharach Giants	Pitcher
	Thomas	Boy	Lincoln Giants	Pitcher
	Washington	–	Nashville Elite Giants	Catcher
	White	Red	Nashville Elite Giants	Pitcher
	Wilson	Chubby	Bacharach Giants	Outfielder
	Wyatt	–	Detroit Stars	Catcher
1929–1930	Edward	Jesse	Nashville Elite Giants	Outfielder
				Secondbase
	Ewing	(Buck)	Homestead Grays	Catcher
	Green	Julius	Detroit Stars	Outfielder
			Memphis Red Sox	
	Johnson	Claude (Hooks)	Memphis Red Sox	Pitcher
			Detroit Stars	Thirdbase
	Thomas	L.	Birmingham Black Barons	Outfielder
				Firstbase
				Catcher
1929–1931	Harps	Walter	Chicago American Giants	Catcher
				Firstbase
	Miller	Buck	Chicago Columbia Giants	Thirdbase
			Homestead Grays	Shortstop
			Chicago American Giants	
	Russell	–	Memphis Red Sox	Outfielder
			Nashville Elite Giants	
	Thrilkill	–	Nashville Elite Giants	Outfielder
				Shortstop
1929–1932	Charleston	Red	Nashville Elite Giants	Catcher
	Dallas	(Big Boy)	Monroe Monarchs	Thirdbase
			Birmingham Black Barons	
	Holsey	(Frog)	Cleveland Cubs	Pitcher
			Chicago American Giants	
			Nashville Elite Giants	
			Columbia Giants	
	Williams	Jim (Bullet)	Cleveland Cubs	Pitcher
			Nashville Elite Giants	
			Detroit Wolves	
	Winston	–	Chicago Columbia Giants	Outfielder
			Chicago Giants	Pitcher
			Atlanta Black Crackers	
1929–1933	Lattimore	–	Columbus Blue Birds	Catcher
			Baltimore Black Sox	
			Brooklyn Royal Giants	
	Warmack	Sam	Bacharach Giants	Outfielder
			Hilldale	
	Williams	H.	New Orleans Crescent Stars	Pitcher
			Monroe Monarchs	
			Homestead Grays	

*Managerial Position

Career	Last Name	First Name	Teams	Positions
	Williams	W.	Brooklyn Royal Giants	Secondbase
			Bacharach Giants	Shortstop
1929–1934	Buford	(Black Bottom)	Detroit Stars	Secondbase
			Louisville Red Cars	Thirdbase
			Nashville Elite Giants	Shortstop
			Cleveland Cubs	
	Cooper	Anthony	Cleveland Stars	Shortstop
			Baltimore Black Sox	
			Birmingham Black Barons	
			Cleveland Red Sox	
	Harris	Henry	Louisville Black Caps	Shortstop
			Memphis Red Sox	
			Baltimore Black Sox	
	Lane	Alto	Cincinnati Tigers	Pitcher
			Indianapolis ABC's	
			Memphis Red Sox	
	Mitchell	Bud	Bacharach Giants	Pitcher
			Hilldale	Outfielder
			Darby Daisies	Catcher
	Ridley	Jack	Cleveland Cubs	Outfielder
			Nashville Elite Giants	
			Louisville Red Caps	
	Wilson	W. Rollo	Negro National League	Commissioner*
			American Negro League	Secretary*
	Wright	Henry	Cleveland Cubs	Pitcher
			Nashville Elite Giants	
1929–1935	Laurent	Milton	Nashville Elite Giants	Outfielder
			Cleveland Cubs	Catcher
			New Orleans Crescent Stars	Firstbase
			Memphis Red Sox	Secondbase
			Birmingham Black Barons	
1929–1936	Carter	Paul	New York Black Yankees	Pitcher
			Hilldale	
			Philadelphia Stars	
			Darby Daisies	
1929–1937	Turner	E.C. (Pop)	Cleveland Cubs	Shortstop
			Homestead Grays	Thirdbase
			Cole's American Giants	
			Birmingham Black Barons	Umpire*
			Negro National League	
1929–1938	Pipkin	Robert (Lefty)	New Orleans Crescent Stars	Pitcher
			Cleveland Cubs	
			Birmingham Black Barons	
	Williams	Nish	Washington Elite Giants	Thirdbase
			Nashville Elite Giants	Firstbase
			Birmingham Black Barons	Catcher

*Managerial Position

Career	Last Name	First Name	Teams	Positions
			Cleveland Cubs	Outfielder
			Columbus Elite Giants	
1929–1942	Matlock	Leroy	Detroit Wolves	Pitcher
			New York Cubans	
			St. Louis Stars	
			Washington Pilots	
			Homestead Grays	
			Pittsburgh Crawfords	
1929–1943	Forbes	Frank	New York Cubans	Business Manager, Umpire*
			Negro National League	Promoter*
1929–1945	Brooks	Ameal	Columbus Blue Birds	Catcher
			New York Cubans	
			Chicago American Giants	
			Cole's American Giants	
			New York Black Yankees	
			Cuban Stars	
			Cleveland Cubs	
1929–1946	Cornelius	Willie	Nashville Elite Giants	Pitcher
			Cole's American Giants	
			Memphis Red Sox	
			Chicago American Giants	
	Parker	Thomas (Big Train)	Boston Blues	Outfielder
			New Orleans-St. Louis Stars	Pitcher
			Memphis Red Sox	Manager*
			Monroe Monarchs	
			Indianapolis ABC's	
			Harrisburg-St. Louis Stars	
			New York Cubans	
			Homestead Grays	
1929–1950	Martin	Dr. J.B.	Negro Southern League	President*
			Negro American League	President*
			Negro Dixie League	President*
			Chicago American Giants	Club Officer*
			Memphis Red Sox	
	Martin	Dr. W.S.	Negro American League	Club Officer*
			Negro Southern League	President*
			Memphis Red Sox	Club Officer*
	Walker	Jesse (Hoss)	Cincinnati-Indianapolis Clowns	Thirdbase
			Nashville Elite Giants	Shortstop
			Washington Elite Giants	Manager*
			Cleveland Cubs	Club Officer*
			Nashville Cubs	
			Baltimore Elite Giants	
			Bacharach Giants	
			Birmingham Black Barons	
			New York Black Yankees	
			Cincinnati Clowns	

*Managerial Position

Career	Last Name	First Name	Teams	Positions
1930	Anderson	–	Nashville Elite Giants	Outfielder
	Austin	–	Nashville Elite Giants	Pitcher
	Banks	–	Hilldale	Secondbase
	Bauzz	–	Cuban Stars	Shortstop
	Berry	E.	Detroit Stars	Secondbase
			Memphis Red Sox	Shortstop
	Charleston	Benny	Homestead Grays	Outfielder
	Creek	Willie	Brooklyn Royal Giants	Catcher
	Davis	Dwight	Detroit Stars	Pitcher
	Johnson	(Lefty)	Memphis Red Sox	Pitcher
	McCauley	–	Nashville Elite Giants	Pitcher
	Mitchell	Otto	Birmingham Black Barons	Secondbase
	Morrison	Jimmy	Memphis Red Sox	Utility Player
	Page	–	Brooklyn Royal Giants	Outfielder
			Quaker Giants	Firstbase
	Stratton	–	Hilldale	Catcher
	Trammel	–	Birmingham Black Barons	Firstbase
	Turner	–	Kansas City Monarchs	Firstbase
	West	C.	Memphis Red Sox	Secondbase
			Birmingham Black Barons	
	Weston	–	Hilldale	Pitcher
1930–1931	Love	William	Detroit Stars	Outfielder
				Catcher
	Williams	Zeke	Cleveland Cubs	Catcher
			Birmingham Black Barons	
1930–1932	Fields	Benny	Cleveland Cubs	Secondbase
			Memphis Red Sox	Outfielder
	Gillespie	Murray (Lefty)	Nashville Elite Giants	Pitcher
			Memphis Red Sox	
	Harris	Bill	Indianapolis ABC's	Catcher
			Memphis Red Sox	
			Monroe Monarchs	
1930–1933	Anderson	–	Baltimore Black Sox	Catcher
			Chicago American	
	Hayes	(Bun)	Washington Pilots	Pitcher
			Baltimore Black Sox	
1930–1934	Burnham	Willie	Monroe Monarchs	Pitcher
	Evans	Bill (Happy)	Detroit Wolves	Shortstop
			Homestead Grays	Outfielder
			Brooklyn Royal Giants	
			Washington Pilots	
	Huber	–	Nashville Elite Giants	Outfielder
			Memphis Red Sox	Catcher
	Lackey	Obie	Pittsburgh Crawfords	Pitcher
			Hilldale	Secondbase
			Bacharach Giants	Shortstop

*Managerial Position

Career	Last Name	First Name	Teams	Positions
	Vance	Columbus	Detroit Wolves	Pitcher
			Birmingham Black Barons	
			Detroit Stars	
			Homestead Grays	
	Walker	Charlie	Homestead Grays	Club Officer*
1930–1935	Stovall	Fred	Monroe Monarchs	Club Officer
1930–1936	Binder	James (Jimmy)	Detroit Stars	Secondbase
			Washington Elite Giants	Thirdbase
			Memphis Red Sox	
			Homestead Grays	
			Indianapolis ABC's	
	Tye	Dan	Cincinnati Tigers	Shortstop
			Memphis Red Sox	Pitcher
				Thirdbase
1930–1937	Cunningham	Harry (Baby)	Memphis Red Sox	Pitcher
1930–1939	Houston	Jess	Cincinnati Tigers	Infielder
			Chicago American Giants	Pitcher
			Memphis Red Sox	
1930–1940	Burbage	Benjamin (Buddy)	Washington Black Senators	Outfielder
			Newark Dodgers	
			Hilldale	
			Pittsburgh Crawfords	
			Bacharach Giants	
			Homestead Giants	
			Brooklyn Royal Giants	
1930–1941	Dunn	Jake	Nashville Elite Giants	Outfielder
			Washington Pilots	Shortstop
			Baltimore Black Sox	Secondbase
			Detroit Stars	Manager*
			Philadelphia Stars	
1930–1942	Andrews	Herman (Jabo)	Washington Black Senators	Pitcher
			Detroit Wolves	Outfielder
			Pittsburgh Crawfords	Manager*
			Birmingham Black Barons	
			Indianapolis ABC's	
			Pittsburgh Crawfords	
			Homestead Grays	
			Chicago American Giants	
			Jacksonville Red Caps	
			Columbus Blue Birds	
1930–1943	Williams	Chester	Philadelphia Stars	Secondbase
			Pittsburgh Crawfords	Shortstop
			Memphis Red Sox	
			Homestead Grays	

*Managerial Position

Career	Last Name	First Name	Teams	Positions
1930–1944	Smith	Robert (Bob)	Memphis Red Sox	Thirdbase
			Chicago American Giants	Catcher
			Birmingham Black Barons	
			Pittsburgh Crawfords	
			St. Louis Stars	
			New Orleans-St. Louis Stars	
1930–1945	Crutchfield	John W. (Jimmie)	Pittsburgh Crawfords	Outfielder
			Indianapolis ABC's	
			Indianapolis Crawfords	
			Toledo Crawfords	
			Birmingham Black Barons	
			Cleveland Buckeyes	
			Newark Eagles	
			Chicago American Giants	
	Markham	John	Monroe Monarchs	Pitcher
			Birmingham Black Barons	
			Kansas City Monarchs	
	McDuffie	Terris	Newark Eagles	
			Birmingham Black Barons	
			Homestead Grays	
			New York Black Yankees	
			Philadelphia Stars	
			Baltimore Black Sox	
1930–1946	Gibson	Joshua (Josh)	Pittsburgh Crawfords	Outfielder
			Homestead Grays	Catcher
1930–1947	West	James (Jim)	Washington Elite Giants	Firstbase
			Birmingham Black Barons	
			Philadelphia Stars	
			Cleveland Cubs	
			New York Black Yankees	
			Nashville Elite Giants	
			Columbus Elite Giants	
			Baltimore Elite Giants	
1930–1948	Brown	Raymond	Detroit Wolves	Pitcher
			Homestead Grays	
			Dayton Marcos	
			Indianapolis ABC's	
1930–1949	Trouppe	Quincy Thomas	Indianapolis ABC's	Pitcher
			Detroit Wolves	Outfielder
			New York Cubans	Catcher
			Kansas City Monarchs	Manager*
			Cleveland Buckeyes	
			Homestead Grays	
			Chicago American Giants	

*Managerial Position

Career	Last Name	First Name	Teams	Positions
1930–1950	Bankhead	Samuel (Sam)	Homestead Grays	Pitcher
			Birmingham Black Barons	Secondbase
			Pittsburgh Crawfords	Outfielder
			Nashville Elite Giants	Shortstop
				Manager*
	Brown	T.J. (Tom)	Cleveland Buckeyes	Thirdbase
			Memphis Red Sox	Shortstop
	Curry	Homer (Goose)	New York Black Yankees	Pitcher
			Philadelphia Stars	Outfielder
			Newark Eagles	Manager*
			Memphis Red Sox	
			Washington Elite Giants	
			Baltimore Elite Giants	
	McHenry	Henry	Philadelphia Stars	Pitcher
			Indianapolis Clowns	
			Kansas City Monarchs	
			New York Black Yankees	
1931	Adkins	Clarence	Nashville Elite Giants	Outfielder
	Capers	Lefty	Louisville White Sox	Pitcher
	Carter	Bo	Chattanooga Black Lookouts	President*
	Chapman	–	Chicago Columbia Giants	Pitcher
	Clark	–	Kansas City Monarchs	Pitcher
	Cooley	–	Birmingham Black Barons	Catcher
	Cox	Hannibal	Nashville Elite Giants	Outfielder
	Dials	Alonzo	Detroit Stars	Firstbase
	Forkins	Marty	New York Black Yankees	Club Officer*
	Hughes	Robert	Louisville White Sox	Pitcher
	Lindsey	–	Indianapolis ABC's	Pitcher
	Moody	–	Memphis Red Sox	Shortstop
	Mott	–	Birmingham Black Barons	Thirdbase
	Owens	–	Nashville Elite Giants	Pitcher
	Peak	Rufus	Detroit Stars	Club Officer*
	Poinsette	Robert	New York Black Yankees	Outfielder
	Powell	–	Memphis Red Sox	Secondbase
	Powell	J.J.	Little Rock Black Travelers	Club Officer*
	Roberts	–	Chicago Columbia Giants	Catcher
	Robinson	Bill (Bojangles)	New York Yankees	Club Officer*
			New York Stars	Club Officer*
	Smith	C.	Chicago Columbia Giants	Firstbase
	Spencer	Zack	Chicago Columbia Giants	Pitcher
	Thomas	Henry	New York Black Yankees	Outfielder
	Thornton	H.	Memphis Red Sox	Outfielder
	Van Buren	–	Memphis Red Sox	Outfielder
	Vaughn	Joe	Negro Southern League	Secretary*
	Veal	–	Birmingham Black Barons	Outfielder
				Pitcher

*Managerial Position

Career	Last Name	First Name	Teams	Positions
	Wallace	–	Cleveland Cubs	Thirdbase
	Watson	Everett	Detroit Stars	Club Officer*
	Williams	L.R.	Cleveland Stars	Club Officer*
	Winfield	–	Memphis Red Sox	Shortstop
1931–1932	Brown	William M.	Montgomery Grey Sox	Officer*
	Drew	John M.	Hilldale	Club Officer*
			Darby Daisies	
	Johnson	J.	Memphis Red Sox	Firstbase
	Ousley	Guy	Cleveland Cubs	Secondbase
			Columbia Giants	Thirdbase
			Memphis Red Sox	Shortstop
	Petway	–	Birmingham Black Barons	Secondbase
			Nashville Elite Giants	Shortstop
	Pope	–	Montgomery Grey Sox	Pitcher
			Louisville White Sox	
	Williams	B.	Indianapolis ABC's	Outfielder
			Montgomery Grey Sox	
1931–1933	Howard	W.	Birmingham Black Barons	Thirdbase
				Firstbase
	McNeil	–	Nashville Elite Giants	Outfielder
			Louisville White Sox	
			Louisville Black Caps	
	Nelson	–	Montgomery Grey Sox	Pitcher
1931–1934	Cates	Joe	Louisville Red Caps	Shortstop
			Louisville White Sox	
	English	–	Louisville Red Caps	Outfielder
			Louisville Black Caps	Catcher
			Louisville White Sox	
	Henry	Otis	Monroe Monarchs	Thirdbase
			Memphis Red Sox	Secondbase
	Holmes	Frank	Philadelphia Stars	Pitcher
			Bacharach Giants	
	Terry	–	Homestead Grays	Thirdbase
			Indianapolis ABC's	Secondbase
			Cincinnati Tigers	
	Wiggins	Joe	Bacharach Giants	Thirdbase
			Nashville Elite Giants	
	Williams	Elbert	Monroe Monarchs	Pitcher
			Louisville White Sox	
1931–1935	Gilcrest	Dennis	Columbus Blue Birds	Secondbase
			Indianapolis ABC's	Catcher
			Brooklyn Eagles	
			Cleveland Red Sox	
	Hunter	Bertrum	Pittsburgh Crawfords	Pitcher
			St. Louis Stars	
			Detroit Wolves	

*Managerial Position

Career	Last Name	First Name	Teams	Positions
1931–1936	Harris	(Popsickle)	Cleveland Stars	Firstbase
			Kansas City Monarchs	
	Peterson	Harvey	Cincinnati Tigers	Pitcher
			Birmingham Black Barons	Outfielder
			Montgomery Grey Sox	
			Memphis Red Sox	
	Saunders	–	Monroe Monarchs	Shortstop
			Detroit Stars	Secondbase
			Louisville Red Caps	
			Bacharach Giants	
1931–1937	Griffin	Robert	St. Louis Stars	Pitcher
			Chicago Columbia Giant	
	Lewis	Clarence (Foots)	Memphis Red Sox	Shortstop
	Lyons	Granville	Louisville Red Caps	Pitcher
			Nashville Elite Giants	Firstbase
			Memphis Red Sox	
			Detroit Stars	
			Philadelphia Stars	
1931–1939	Williams	P.	Toledo Crawfords	Secondbase
			Baltimore Black Sox	
1931–1940	McBride	Fred	Chicago American Giants	Outfielder
			Indianapolis ABC's	Firstbase
	Wright	Zollie	Washington Elite Giants	Outfielder
			New Orleans Crescent Stars	
			Memphis Red Sox	
			New York Black Yankees	
			Monroe Monarchs	
			Washington Black Senators	
			Columbus Elite Giants	
1931–1941	Byas	Richard T.	Memphis Red Sox	Outfielder
		(Scubby)	Kansas City Monarchs	Catcher
			Newark Dodgers	Firstbase
1931–1942	Thompson	Samuel	Philadelphia Stars	Pitcher
		(Sad Sam)	Kansas City Monarchs	
			Chicago American Giants	
			Columbus Elite Giants	
			Indianapolis ABC's	
			Detroit Stars	
1931–1943	Casey	William (Mickey)	Philadelphia Stars	Catcher
			Baltimore Black Sox	Manager*
			Baltimore Grays	
			Bacharach Giants	
			Washington Black Senators	
			New York Cubans	
			Cuban Stars	
			New York Black Yankees	

*Managerial Position

Career	Last Name	First Name	Teams	Positions
	Everett	Jimmy	Cincinnati Clowns	Outfielder
			Pennsylvania Red Caps of New York	Pitcher
	Hardy	Paul	Chicago American Giants	Catcher
			Memphis Red Sox	
			Detroit Stars	
			Columbus Elite Giants	
			Birmingham Black Barons	
			Baltimore Elite Giants	
			Montogomery Grey Sox	
			Kansas City Monarchs	
1931–1944	Burch	Walter	Cleveland Buckeyes	Shortstop
			Bacharach Giants	Catcher
			Pittsburgh Cranfords	Secondbase
			Hilldale	Manager
			New Orleans-St. Louis Stars	
			Cleveland Bears	
			St. Louis Stars	
	Taylor	Raymond	Cleveland Buckeyes	Catcher
			Kansas City Monarchs	
			Memphis Red Sox	
			Cincinnati Buckeyes	
1931–1945	Ford	James (Jimmy)	New Orleans-St. Louis Stars	Secondbase
			Cincinnati Clowns	Thirdbase
			Memphis Red Sox	
			St. Louis Stars	
			Philadelphia Stars	
	Greenlee	W.A. (Gus)	United States Baseball League	Founder*
			Pittsburgh Crawfords	Club Officer*
			Second Negro National League	Founder, President*
	Stone	Ed	Newark Leagues	Outfielder
			Philadelphia Stars	
			Bacharach Giants	
			Brooklyn Eagles	
1931–1946	Calhoun	Walter (Lefty)	Harrisburg-St. Louis Stars	Pitcher
			New Orleans-St. Louis Stars	
			Birmingham Black Barons	
			Washington Black Senators	
			Pittsburgh Crawfords	
			Montogomery Grey Sox	
			New York Black Yankees	
			Cleveland Buckeyes	
			St. Louis Stars	
			Indianapolis ABC's	
	Carlisle	Matthew	Homestead Grays	Shortstop
			Birmingham Black Barons	Secondbase
			Memphis Red Sox	

*Managerial Position

Career	Last Name	First Name	Teams	Positions
			Montogomery Grey Sox	
	Hughes	Sammy T.	Washington Elite Giants	Secondbase
			Homestead Grays	
			Baltimore Elite Giants	
			Columbus Elite Giants	
			Louisville White Sox	
			Nashville Elite Giants	
1931–1947	Show	Felton	Baltimore Elite Giants	Secondbase
			Nashville Cubs	Thirdbase
			Louisville Black Caps	Manager*
			Washington Elite Giants	
			Louisville White Sox	
			Columbus Elite Giants	
			Nashville Elite Giants	
	Williams	Harry	Harrisburg-St. Louis Stars	Shortstop
			Baltimore Black Sox	Secondbase
			Pittsburgh Crawfords	Thirdbase
			Brooklyn Eagles	Manager*
			Baltimore Elite Giants	
			New Orleans Creoles	
			New York Cubans	
			Newark Eagles	
			Homestead Grays	
			New York Black Yankees	
1931–1950	Boone	Alonzo	Cleveland Buckeyes	Manager*
			Cleveland Cubs	Pitcher
			Cincinnati Buckeyes	
			Louisville Buckeyes	
			Chicago American Giants	
			Birmingham Black Barons	
	Jackson	R.B.	Negro Southern Leagues	President, Vice-President*
			Nashville Black Vols	Club Officer*
1932	Anderson	–	Indianapolis ABC's	Outfielder
	Barnes	O.	New York Black Yankees	Club Officer*
	Bashum		Indianapolis ABC's	Catcher
	Bridgefort	R.	Cleveland Cubs	Club Officer*
	Briggery	–	Atlanta Black Crackers	Shortstop
	Brown	Oliver	Newark Browns	Business Manager*
	Campbell	Buddy	Cole's American Giants	Catcher
	Carter	–	Birmingham Black Barons	Catcher
	Claxton	James E.	Cuban Stars	Pitcher
	Clay	–	Kansas City Monarchs	Pitcher
	Cross	Norman	Cole's American Giants	Ball Player
	Cummings	–	Louisville Black Caps	Catcher
	Curtis	–	Louisville Black Caps	Catcher
	Davis	(Big Boy)	Indianapolis ABC's	Pitcher

*Managerial Position

Career	Last Name	First Name	Teams	Positions
	Drake	Andrew	Birmingham Black Barons	Catcher
	Dubisson	D.J.	Little Rock Greys	Club Officer*
	Durant	–	Washington Pilots	Pitcher
	Dykes	John	Washington Pilots	Club Officer*
	English	H.D.	Monroe Monarchs	Club Officer*
	Fisher	–	Columbus Turfs	Pitcher
	Floyd	J.J.	Little Rock Greys	Club Officer*
	Gadsden	Gus	Hilldale	Outfielder
	Gladney	–	Indianapolis ABC's	Shortstop
	Goins	–	Montgomery Grey Sox	Pitcher
	Goodson	M.E.	New York Black Yankees	Club Officer*
	Hackett	–	Washington Pilots	Pitcher
	Harris	Dixon	Homestead Grays	Ballplayer
	Harris	G.	Louisville Black Caps	Secondbase
	Hawley	–	Memphis Red Sox	Catcher
	Henderson	H. (Long)	Nashville Elite Giants	Firstbase
	Herman	–	Memphis Red Sox	Outfielder
	Jasper	–	Birmingham Black Barons	Pitcher
	Johnson	R.	Washington Pilots	Outfielder
	Kinard	–	Washington Pilots	Thirdbase
	Lewis	F.	Montgomery Grey Sox	Outfielder
	Lightner	–	Cole's American Giants	Pitcher
	Lyles	–	Indianapolis Clowns	Catcher
	Martin	Alexander	Cleveland Cubs	Club Officer
	McCoy	Roy	Washington Pilots	Club Officer*
	Mimms	–	Columbia Turfs	Pitcher
	Peeks	A.J.	Atlanta Black Crackers	Club Officer*
	Rhodes	Dusty	Louisville Black Caps	Pitcher
	Savage	Artie	Cleveland Stars	Club Officer*
	Thurman	–	Louisville Black Caps	Outfielder Pitcher
	Walker	H.	Monroe Monarchs	Catcher
	Walker	W.	Monroe Monarchs	Outfielder
	Ware	–	Cleveland Stars	Outfielder
1932–1933	Cooke	James	Bacharach Giants Baltimore Black Sox	Pitcher
	Henderson	L.	Birmingham Black Barons Montgomery Grey Sox Nashville Elite Giants	Shortstop Thirdbase
	Johnson	Jim	Bacharach Giants Hilldale	Shortstop
	Neeley	–	Cuban Stars Louisville Black Caps	Pitcher
	Smith	B.	Birmingham Black Barons	Firstbase Pitcher
	Waddy	Lefty	Detroit Stars Indianapolis ABC's	Pitcher

*Managerial Position

Career	Last Name	First Name	Teams	Positions
1932–1934	Harris	(Moocha)	Kansas City Monarchs	Outfielder
			Detroit Wolves	
			New Orleans Crescent Stars	
	Jackson	A.	Birmingham Black Barons	Shortstop
			Montgomery Grey Sox	Thirdbase
	Jones	J.	Memphis Red Sox	Outfielder
	Mason	Jim	Memphis Red Sox	Outfielder
			Washington Pilots	Firstbase
	Oliver	–	Birmingham Black Barons	Outfielder
				Catcher
1932–1935	Blake	Big Red	New York Black Yankees	Pitcher
			New York Cubans	
			Baltimore Black Sox	
	Cole	Robert A.	Negro National League	Treasurer*
			Chicago American Giants	Club Officer*
			Negro Southern League	Vice-President*
	Sampson	–	Brooklyn Royal Giants	Shortstop
			Atlanta Black Crackers	
1932–1936	Bennett	–	Cleveland Cubs	Secondbase
			Memphis Red Sox	
1932–1937	Graves	Bob	Indianapolis Athletics	Pitcher
			Indianapolis ABC's	
	Lillard	Joe	Cincinnati Tigers	Catcher
			Cole's American Giants	Pitcher
				Outfielder
	Tate	Roosevelt		
		(Speed)	Memphis Red Sox	Outfielder
			Birmingham Black Barons	
			Cincinnati Tigers	
			Nashville Elite Giants	
	Thornton	Jack	Atlanta Black Crackers	Firstbase
				Pitcher
				Secondbase
1932–1938	Allen	Clifford Crooks	Memphis Red Sox	Pitcher
			Hilldale	
			Homestead Grays	
			Baltimore Black Sox	
	Else	Harry	Kansas City Monarchs	Catcher
			Monroe Monarchs	
	Kincannon	Harry	New York Black Yankees	Pitcher
			Washington Black Senators	
			Pittsburgh Crawfords	
			Philadelphia Stars	
1932–1940	Frazier	O.	Cleveland Bears	Thirdbase
			Montgomery Grey Sox	Secondbase
			Jacksonville Red Caps	

*Managerial Position

Career	Last Name	First Name	Teams	Positions
	Long	Bang	Indianapolis Athletics Atlanta Black Crackers Philadelphia Stars Chicago American Giants	Thirdbase
1932–1941	Williams	Roy	Brooklyn Eagles Columbus Blue Birds Pittsburgh Crawfords Baltimore Elite Giants Baltimore Black Sox Philadelphia Stars Brooklyn Royal Giants New York Black Yankees	Pitcher
1932–1943	Green	James	Kansas City Monarchs Atlanta Black Crackers	Firstbase Catcher
	Powell	Melvin (Put)	Chicago American Giants Chicago Brown Bombers Cole's American Giants	Outfielder Pitcher
1932–1944	Morney	Leroy	Birmingham Black Barons Monroe Monarchs Washington Elite Giants Cincinnati Clowns New York Black Yankees Cleveland Giants Columbus Elite Giants Monroe Monarchs Columbus Blue Birds	Thirdbase Shortstop Secondbase
1932–1945	Adams	Emery (Ace)	New York Black Yankees Baltimore Black Sox Memphis Red Sox	Pitcher
	Harvey	William (Bill)	Pittsburgh Crawfords Baltimore Elite Giants Memphis Red Sox	Pitcher
	Ray	John	Kansas City Monarchs Montgomery Grey Sox Cleveland Bears Cincinnati-Indianapolis Clowns Birmingham Black Barons Jacksonville Red Caps	Outfielder
	Welmaker	Roy	Homestead Grays Atlanta Black Crackers Philadelphia Stars	Pitcher
	Wright	Burnis (Bill)	Washington Elite Giants Nashville Elite Giants Philadelphia Stars Baltimore Elite Giants Columbus Elite Giants	Outfielder

*Managerial Position

Career	Last Name	First Name	Teams	Positions
1932–1946	Clark	John L.	Homestead Grays	Secretary, Publicity Man*
			Negro National League	Business Manager*
			Pittsburgh Crawfords	
	Howard	Herman (Red)	Washington Elite Giants	Pitcher
			Atlanta Black Crackers	
			Birmingham Black Barons	
			Jacksonville Red Caps	
			Indianapolis ABC's	
			Memphis Red Sox	
			Indianapolis Athletics	
			Chicago American Giants	
	Sprearman	Clyde (Splo)	Newark Eagels	Outfielder
			Birmingham Black Barons	
			Pittsburgh Crawfords	
			New York Cubans	
			Philadelphia Stars	
			Chicago American Giants	
			New York Black Yankees	
1932–1947	Morris	Barney	New York Cubans	Pitcher
			Monroe Monarchs	
			Cuban Stars	
			Pittsburgh Crawfords	
1932–1948	Benjamin	Jerry	Toledo Crawfords	Outfielder
			New York Cubans	
			Memphis Red Sox	
			Homestead Grays	
			Detroit Stars	
			Birmingham Black Barons	
	Bremer	Eugene (Gene)	Memphis Red Sox	Pitcher
			Cleveland Buckeyes	
			New Orleans Crescent Stars	
			Kansas City Monarchs	
			Cincinnati Buckeyes	
			Cincinnati Tigers	
1932–1949	Brown	Barney	Philadelphia Stars	Pitcher
			New York Black Yankees	
			Cuban Stars (East-West)	
	Byrd	William (Bill)	Baltimore Elite Giants	Outfielder
			Columbus Blue Birds	Pitcher
			Washington Elite Giants	
			Columbus Turfs	
	Carter	Ernest (Spoon)	Birmingham Black Barons	Pitcher
			Cleveland Red Sox	
			Toledo Crawfords	
			Indianapolis Crawfords	
			Pittsburgh Crawfords	

*Managerial Position

Career	Last Name	First Name	Teams	Positions
			Memphis Red Sox	
			Newark Eagles	
			Philadelphia Stars	
1933	Armour	–	Detroit Stars	Pitcher
	Borden	–	Birmingham Black Barons	Shortstop
	Boyd	–	Kansas City Monarchs	Outfielder
	Busby	–	Detroit Stars	Outfielder
	Caldwell	–	Birmingham Black Barons	Outfielder
	Cambria	Joe	Baltimore Black Sox	Club Officer*
	Carter	Dr. A.B.	Negro Southern League	Vice President*
	Dial	Kermit	Columbus Blue Birds	Secondbase
	Freeman	Bill	Cuban Stars	Pitcher
	Jordan	–	Chicago American Giants	Pitcher
	Kerner	–	Columbus Blue Birds	Outfielder
	McClain	Bill	Columbus Blue Birds	Pitcher
	Norwood	Walter	Detroit Stars	Club Officer
	Payne	–	Homestead Grays	Outfielder
	Peacock	–	Homestead Grays	Thirdbase
	Peebles	A.J.	Columbus Blue Birds	Club Officer*
	Pierson	–	Homestead Grays	Thirdbase
	Russell	–	Brooklyn Royal Giants	Pitcher
	Snowden	–	Detroit Stars	Pitcher
	Stevens	Jim	Philadelphia Stars	Secondbase
	Thompson	–	Cuban Stars	Pitcher
	Tindle	Levy	Detroit Stars	Club Officer*
1933–1934	Bention	–	Brooklyn Royal Giants	Outfielder
			Bacharach Giants	
	Johnson	H.	Birmingham Black Barons	Outfielder
	Nash	William	Birmingham Black Barons	Outfielder
				Pitcher
	Roberts	R.	Cleveland Red Sox	Pitcher
			Cleveland Giants	
1933–1935	Griffin	C.B.	Brooklyn Eagles	Outfielder
			Columbus Blue Birds	
			Cleveland Red Sox	
1933–1937	Brown	(Lefty)	Memphis Red Sox	Pitcher
	Gill	–	Indianapolis Athletics	Thirdbase
			Detroit Stars	Firstbase
			Louisville Red Caps	Outfielder
	Webster	Jim	Detroit Stars	Catcher
1933–1938	Jones	Stuart (Slim)	Philadelphia Stars	Pitcher
			Baltimore Black Sox	
	Pelham	William	Atlanta Black Crackers	Shortstop
			Bacharach Giants	
	Smith	C.	Birmingham Black Barons	Catcher
1933–1939	Williams	Ray	New York Black Yankees	Pitcher

*Managerial Position

Career	Last Name	First Name	Teams	Positions
1933–1940	Bell	James (Steel Arm)	Indianapolis Crawfords Montgomery Grey Sox	Catcher
	Spencer	Pee Wee	Toledo Crawfords Indianapolis Crawfords Chicago American Giants	Thirdbase Catcher
1933–1942	Hall	Horace G.	Negro American League Chicago American Giants	Vice-President* Club Officer*
1933–1944	Bibbs	Rainey	Kansas City Monarchs Cleveland Buckeyes Chicago American Giants Detroit Stars Indianapolis Crawfords Cincinnati Tigers	Thirdbase Shortstop Secondbase
1933–1945	Smith	Hilton	Kansas City Monarchs Monroe Monarchs	Pitcher
1933–1948	Gaston	Robert (Rab Roy)	Homestead Grays	Catcher
	Greene	James (Joe)	Atlanta Black Crackers Cleveland Buckeyes Homestead Grays Kansas City Monarchs	Catcher
1933–1949	Dandridge	Raymond (Hooks)	Newark Dodgers New York Cubans Detroit Stars Newark Eagles	Secondbase Thirdbase Shortstop
	Woods	Parnell	Jacksonville Red Caps Cleveland Buckeyes Birmingham Black Barons Louisville Buckeyes Cleveland Bears	Manager* Thirdbase
1933–1950	Leonard	Walter (Buck)	Homestead Grays Brooklyn Royal Giants	Outfielder Firstbase
	Martin	Dr. B.B.	Negro Southern League Memphis Red Sox	Club Officer* Club Officer*
	Washington	John	Baltimore Elite Giants Montgomery Grey Sox Houston Eagles New York Black Yankees Birmingham Black Barons Pittsburgh Crawfords	Firstbase
1934	Blakely	–	Cincinnati Tigers	Catcher
	Brown	Jim	Monroe Monarchs	Shortstop
	Byrd	Prentice	Cleveland Red Sox	Club Officer*
	Charter	William	Louisville Red Caps	Outfielder
	Cheatham	–	Homestead Grays Pittsburgh Crawfords	Pitcher

*Managerial Position

Career	Last Name	First Name	Teams	Positions
	Crawford	Willie W.	Birmingham Black Barons	Outfielder
	Cunningham	–	Baltimore Black Sox	Outfielder
	Davis	Hy	Newark Dodgers	Firstbase
			Hilldale	
	Dixon	P.	Baltimore Black Sox	Outfielder
	Dixon	T.	Baltimore Black Sox	Catcher
	Evans	–	Cincinnati Tigers	Shortstop
				Outfielder
				Thirdbase
	Foster	Leland	Monroe Monarchs	Pitcher
	Hairston	(Rap)	Newark Dodgers	Ball Player
	Hamilton	Theron B.	Homestead Grays	Vice-President*
	Hendrix	–	Nashville Elite Giants	Pitcher
	Hughes	C.	Cleveland Red Sox	Secondbase
	Johnson	Bill	New York Black Yankees	Catcher
	Jones	A.	Birmingham Black Barons	Pitcher
	Jones	B.	Cleveland Red Sox	Outfielder
	Jones	W.	Birmingham Black Barons	Outfielder
	Jones	W.	Memphis Red Sox	Shortstop
			Chicago Unions	
	Key	Ludie	Birmingham Black Barons	President*
	Lemon	–	Indianapolis ABC's	Secondbase
	Liggons	James	Memphis Red Sox	Outfielder
			Monroe Monarchs	Pitcher
	Lisby	–	Bacharach Giants	Pitcher
			Newark Dodgers	
	Meadows	–	Cincinnati Tigers	Outfielder
	Miller	–	Cincinnati Tigers	Secondbase
	Milton	C.	Cleveland Red Sox	Infielder
	Nunley	–	Memphis Red Sox	Firstbase
	Passon	Harry	Bacharach Giants	Club Officer*
	Postell	–	Cincinnati Tigers	Secondbase
	Rice	–	Cincinnati Tigers	Outfielder
	Rogers	–	Cincinnati Tigers	Pitcher
	Starks	Leslie	Newark Dodgers	Outfielder
	Vaughn	–	Newark Dodgers	Pitcher
	Vincent	Irving (Lefty)	Pittsburgh Crawfords	Pitcher
	White	Arthur	Newark Dodgers	Pitcher
	White	Zarlie	Monroe Monarchs	Ball Player
1934–1935	Arnold	Paul	Newark Dodgers	Outfielder
	Clark	Roy	Newark Dodgers	Pitcher
	Johnson	Bert	Newark Dodgers	Outfielder
	Merritt	Schute	Newark Dodgers	Utility Player
	Reese	James	Brooklyn Eagles	Pitcher
			Cleveland Red Sox	
	Tyler	Charles H.	Newark Dodgers	Club Officer*

*Managerial Position

Career	Last Name	First Name	Teams	Positions
1934–1937	Brooks	Jesse	Kansas City Monarchs	Outfielder
			Cleveland Red Sox	Thirdbase
	Dula	Louis	Homestead Grays	Pitcher
	Johnson	Frank	Memphis Red Sox	Manager*
			Monroe Monarchs	
	Williams	Jim	Philadelphia Stars	Firstbase
			Newark Dodgers	Outfielder
			New York Black Yankees	
1934–1938	Maxwell	Zearle (Jiggs)	Memphis Red Sox	Secondbase
			Monroe Monarchs	Thirdbase
1934–1940	Gillard	Luther	Chicago American Giants	Firstbase
			Memphis Red Sox	Outfielder
			Indianapolis Crawfords	
	Harris	Curtis	Philadelphia Stars	Shortstop
			Pittsburgh Crawfords	Firstbase
				Secondbase
				Catcher
	Patterson	Pat	Philadelphia Stars	Outfielder
			Houston Eagles	Thirdbase
			Newark Eagles	Secondbase
			Cleveland Red Sox	
			Pittsburgh Crawfords	
			Kansas City Monarchs	
	Smith	Ernest	Chicago American Giants	Catcher
			Monroe Monarchs	
1934–1941	Griffin	Robert (Rob)	Columbus Elite Giants	Pitcher
			New York Black Yankees	
			Baltimore Elite Giants	
			Nashville Elite Giants	
	Milton	Henry	Brooklyn Royal Giants	Outfielder
			Indianapolis ABC's	
			Kansas City Monarchs	
			Chicago Giants	
1934–1942	Ellis	(Rocky)	Jacksonville Red Caps	Pitcher
			Homestead Grays	
			Hilldale	
			Philadelphia Stars	
			Baltimore Grays	
	Reed	John	Chicago American Giants	Pitcher
			Cole's American Giants	
			Chicago Brown Bombers	
			Indianapolis ABC's	
1934–1943	Evans	Robert (Bob)	New York Black Yankees	Pitcher
			Newark Eagles	
			Newark Dodgers	
			Jacksonville Red Caps	

*Managerial Position

Career	Last Name	First Name	Teams	Positions
	Lyles	John	Chicago American Giants	Shortstop
			Indianapolis ABC's	Outfielder
			Cleveland Bears	
			Cincinnati Buckeyes	
			Homestead Grays	
			Cleveland Buckeyes	
	McCoy	Chink	Harrisburg-St. Louis Stars	Catcher
			Newark Dodgers	
1934–1944	Clayton	Zack	Chicago American Giants	Firstbase
			New York Black Yankees	
			Coles American Giants	
			Bacharach Giants	
	Moss	Porter	Memphis Red Sox	Pitcher
			Cincinnati Tigers	
1934–1945	Glover	Thomas (Lefty)	New Orleans Black Pelicans	Pitcher
			Washington Elite Giants	
			Memphis Red Sox	
			Cleveland Red Sox	
			Birmingham Black Barons	
			Baltimore Elite Giants	
	Jackson	Norman (Jelly)	Homestead Grays	Secondbase
			Cleveland Red Sox	Shortstop
1934–1946	Mayweather	Eldridge	Kansas City Monarchs	Firstbase
			New Orleans-St. Louis Stars	
			Boston Blues	
			Monroe Monarchs	
			St. Louis Stars	
	Taylor	Olan (Jelly)	Memphis Red Sox	Catcher
			Birmingham Black Barons	Firstbase
			Cincinnati Tigers	Manager*
1934–1947	Bissant	John	Birmingham Black Barons	Pitcher
			Cole's American Giants	Outfielder
			Chicago Brown Bombers	
			Chicago American Giants	
1934–1948	Benson	Gene	Bacharach Giants	Outfielder
			Newark Eagles	
			Philadelphia Stars	
			Pittsburgh Crawfords	
1934–1949	Davenport	Lloyd	Philadelphia Stars	Outfielder
		(Bear Man)	Chicago American Giants	Manager*
			Pittsburgh Crawfords	
			Louisville Buckeyes	
			Cleveland Buckeyes	
			Monroe Monarchs	
			Cincinnati Tigers	
			Memphis Red Sox	

*Managerial Position

Career	Last Name	First Name	Teams	Positions
	Jackson	Rufus (Sonnyman)	Homestead Grays	President* Treasurer*
	Longley	Wyman Red	Memphis Red Sox	Catcher Shortstop Firstbase Secondbase Outfielder Thirdbase
1934–1950	Bassett	Lloyd (Pepper)	Pittsburgh Crawfords New Orleans Crescent Stars Birmingham Black Barons Cincinnati-Indianapolis Clowns Philadelphia Stars Chicago American Giants	Catcher
	Cowan	John	Memphis Red Sox Birmingham Black Barons Cleveland Buckeyes	Secondbase Thirdbase
	Day	Leon	Newark Eagles Brooklyn Eagles Baltimore Elite Giants Bacharach Giants	Pitcher
	Hayes	John	Boston Blues New York Yankees Newark Eagles Baltimore Elite Giants Newark Dodgers	Catcher
	Partlon	Roy	Philadelphia Stars Cincinnati Tigers Homestead Grays Memphis Red Sox	Pitcher
1935	Gayin	–	Brooklyn Eagles	Pitcher
	Jones	(Country)	Brooklyn Royal Giants	Secondbase
	Moles	Lefty	Philadelphia Stars	Pitcher
	Raynolds	Joe	Philadelphia Stars	Pitcher
	White	Eugene	Brooklyn Eagles	Thirdbase
1935–1939	Brown	Ossie	St. Louis Stars Indianapolis Athletics Cole's American Giants Indianapolis ABC's	Outfielder Pitcher
1935–1940	Bond	Timothy	Newark Dodgers Pittsburgh Crawfords Chicago American Giants	Thirdbase Shortstop
	Duncan	Charlie	St. Louis Stars Atlanta Black Crackers Indianapolis ABC's	Pitcher

*Managerial Position

Career	Last Name	First Name	Teams	Positions
	Miller	Leroy (Flash)	New York Black Yankees Newark Dodgers	Secondbase Shortstop
1935–1945	Taylor	John	Cuban Stars New York Cubans	Pitcher
1935–1946	Craig	John	Negro National League	Umpire*
	Manley	Abraham	Negro National League	Vice President*, Treasurer*
			Newark Eagles Brooklyn Eagles	Club Officer*
1935–1948	Manley	Effa (Mrs. Abraham)	Brooklyn Eagles	
1935–1950	Napier	Euthumn (Eddie)	Pittsburgh Crawfords Homestead Grays	Catcher
1936	Blavis	Fox	Homestead Grays	Thirdbase
	Cleage	Pete	Negro National League St. Louis Stars	Umpire* Outfielder
	Lebeaux	–	Chicago American Giants	Shortstop
	Nicholas	–	Newark Eagles	Pitcher
1936–1937	Harris	V.	Cincinnati Tigers	Outfielder Pitcher Secondbase
	Thomas	D.	Cincinnati Tigers	Pitcher
	Waite	Arnold	Homestead Grays	Pitcher
1936–1938	Madison	–	Memphis Red Sox Kansas City Monarchs	Outfielder Thirdbase Pitcher
1936–1939	Johnson	Josh	Homestead Grays New York Black Yankees Cincinnati Tigers	Pitcher Catcher
1936–1940	Wilson	Lefty	Memphis Red Sox Kansas City Monarchs	Pitcher
1936–1941	Henderson	Curtis (Curt)	Washington Black Senators Philadelphia Stars New York Black Yankees Chicago American Giants Indianapolis Crawfords	Thirdbase Shortstop
	Kranson	Floyd	Memphis Red Sox Kansas City Monarchs	Pitcher
1936–1945	Christopher	Thaddeus (Taad)	Cleveland Buckeyes Newark Eagles Cincinnati Clowns New York Black Yankees Pittsburgh Crawfords Cincinnati Clowns	Firstbase Outfielder

*Managerial Position

Career	Last Name	First Name	Teams	Positions
1936–1946	Spearman	Henry (Splo)	Baltimore Elite Giants Pittsburgh Crawfords Philadelphia Stars Homestead Grays Washington Black Senators	Firstbase Thirdbase
1936–1947	Armour	Alfred (Buddy)	Harrisburg-St. Louis Stars St. Louis Stars Chicago American Giants New Orleans-St. Louis Stars Cleveland Buckeyes	Shortstop Outfielder
1936–1948	Barker	Marvin	Philadelphia Stars New York Black Yankees	Thirdbase Secondbase Outfielder Manager*
1936–1949	Easterling	Howard	Chicago American Giants New York Cubans Cincinnati Tigers Homestead Grays	Shortstop Secondbase Thirdbase
	Smith	Theolic (Fireball)	New Orleans-St. Louis Stars St. Louis Stars Kansas City Monarchs Pittsburgh Crawfords Cleveland Buckeyes	Pitcher
1936–1950	Brown	Willand	Kansas City Monarchs	Shortstop Outfielder
	Robinson	Neil	Memphis Red Sox Homestead Grays Cincinnati Tigers	Shortstop Outfielder
	Ruffin	Leon	Philadelphia Stars Newark Eagles Houston Eagles Pittsburgh Crawfords	Catcher Manager*
1937	Baker	Norman	Newark Eagles	Pitcher
	Bames	–	Birmingham Black Barons	Catcher
	Bleach	–	Detroit Stars	Secondbase
	Bledsoe	–	St. Louis Stars	Ball Player
	Bryant	R.B.	Memphis Red Sox	Shortstop
	Burke	–	Indianapolis Athletics	Shortstop
	Clark	Milton, J. Jr.	Chicago American Giants	Secretary
	Coleman	–	Birmingham Black Barons	Shortstop
	Cook	–	Indianapolis Athletics	Pitcher
	David	William	St. Louis Stars	Outfielder Thirdbase
	Davis	William	St. Louis Stars	Outfielder Thirdbase

*Managerial Position

Career	Last Name	First Name	Teams	Positions
	Dunbar	Vet	Indianapolis Athletics	Catcher
				Infielder
	Edwards	–	St. Louis Stars	Secondbase
				Catcher
	Farrell	–	Birmingham Black Barons	Pitcher
	Fellows	–	Birmingham Black Barons	Catcher
				Pitcher
	Floyd	–	Indianapolis Athletics	Pitcher
	Good	Cleveland	Newark Eagles	Pitcher
	Hale	–	Detroit Start	Shortstop
	Hannibal	–	Indianapolis Athletics	Pitcher
	Harvey	–	Philadelphia jStars	Shortstop
	Haslett	Claude	Indianapolis Athletics	Pitcher
			Memphis Red Sox	
	Henry	–	Indianapolis Athletics	Outfielder
	Hill	–	Atlanta Black Crackers	Outfielder
	Humes	John	Newark Eagles	Pitcher
	Humphries	–	Atlanta Black Crackers	Outfielder
	Jackson	S.	Memphis Red Sox	Catcher
	Johnson	Joseph	Indianapolis Athletics	Club Officer*
	Justice	Charley	Detroit Stars	Pitcher
	Mays	–	St. Louis Stars	Pitcher
	Mays	Dave	Kansas City Monarchs	Outfielder
	McIntosh–	–	Detroit Stars	Utility Player
	Miller	–	Indianapolis Athletics	Firstbase
	Monroe	Al	Negro American League	Secretary*
	Morgan	J.L.	Indianapolis Athletics	Outfielder
			Memphis Red Sox	
	Petway	Shirley	Detroit Stars	Catcher
	Pfiffer	–	St. Louis Stars	Thirdbase
	Pierson	–	St. Louis Stars	Outfielder
	Reed	–	St. Louis Stars	Outfielder
	Salters	Edward	Detroit STars	Outfielder
	Thornton	Jesse	Indianapolis Athletics	Alub Officer*
	Titus	James	Detroit Stars	Club Officer*
	Underwood	Ely	Detroit Stars	Outfielder
	Walker	–	Indianapolis Athletics	Catcher
	Walker	A.M.	Birmingham Black Barons	Manager*
	Watkins	G.C.	Indianapolis Athletics	Club Officer*
	Wilson	Felton	Detroit Stars	Catcher
1937–1938	Baker	W.B.	Atlanta Black Crackers	Business
				Manager*
	Barnes	Ed	Kansas City Monarchs	Pitcher
	Blackman	–	Birmingham Black Barons	Pitcher
			Chicago American Giants	

*Managerial Position

Career	Last Name	First Name	Teams	Positions
	Eaton	–	Birmingham Black Barons	Pitcher
	Glenn	–	Atlanta Black Crackers	Thirdbase
	Hadley	–	Atlanta Blacvk Crackers	Outfielder
				Catcher
	McCall	Butch	Birmingham Black Barons	Firstbase
			Chicago American Giants	
	Miles	John (Mule)	Chicago American Giants	Outfielder
	Moore	Henry L.	Birmingham Black Barons	Club Officer*
			St. Louis Stars	
	Powell	Eddie	New York Black Yankees	Catcher
1937–1939	Direaux	Jimmy	Baltimore Elite Glants	Pitcher
			Washington Elite Giants	
	Dunlap	Herman	Chicago American Giants	Outfielder
	Kemp	James	Indianapolis ABC's	Secondbase
			Atlanta Black Crackers	
			Jacksonville Red Caps	
	Owens	–	Indianapolis ABC's	Outfielder
			Birmingham Black Barons	
1937–1940	Hall	(Bad News)	Indianapolis Crawfords	Thirdbase
			Indianapolis Athletics	
	Moore	James	Atlanta Blacck Crackers	Firstbase
		(Red)	Baltimore Elite Giants	
			Newark Eagles	
	Sparks	Joe	Chicago American Giants	Secondbase
			St. Louis Stars	
1937–1941	Reeves	Donald	Chicago American Giants	Outfielder
			Atlanta Blacck Crackers	Firstbase
			Indianapolis ABC's	
1937–1942	Brown	Ulysses	Jacksonville Red Caps	Outfielder
		(Buster)	Cincinnati Buckeyes	Catcher
			Newark Eagles	
	Gilyard	Luther	St. Louis Stars	Firstbase
			Birmingham Black Barons	
			Chicago American Giants	
	Lamar	Clarence	Cleveland Bears	Shortstop
			St. Louis Stars	
			Jacksonville Red Caps	
	Royall	John	Jacksonville Red Caps	Pitcher
			New York Black Yankees	
			Indianapolis Athletics	
1937–1943	Bowen	Chuck	Chicago Brown Bombers	Outfielder
			Indianapolis Athletics	
	Bradley	Frank	Kansas City Monarchs	Pitcher
			Cincinnati Tigers	
	Cox	Roosevelt	Cuban Stars	Thirdbase
			Detroit Stars	Secondbase

*Managerial Position

Career	Last Name	First Name	Teams	Positions
			Kansas City Monarchs	Shortstop
			New York Cubans	
	Dunn	Alphonse (Blue)	Birmingham Black Barons	Outfielder
			Detroit Stars	Firstbase
			New York Cubans	
1937–1945	Campanella	Roy	Baltimore Elite Giants	Catcher
	Canada	James	Jacksonville Red Caps	Firstbase
			Baltimore Elite Giants	
			Birmingham Black Barons	
			Memphis Red Sox	
	Childs	Andy	Memphis Red Sox	Pitcher
			Indianapolis Athletics	Secondbase
	McQueen	Pete	New York Black Yankees	Outfielder
			Memphis Red Sox	
	Thomas	Walter	Kansas City Monarchs	Outfielder
			Detroit Stars	Pitcher
1937–1946	Hoskins	William (Bill)	Baltimore Elite Giants	Outfielder
			Detroit Stars	
			New York Black Yankees	
			Memphis Red Sox	
	Whatley	David (Speed)	Homestead Grays	Outfielder
			Pittsburgh Crawfords	
			Chicago American Giants	
	Wilson	Emmett	Boston Blues	Outfielder
			Cincinnati Clowns	
			Cincinnati Buckeyes	
			Pittsburgh Crawfords	
1937–1947	Wilson	Dan	Harrisburg-St. Louis Stars	Shortstop
			Pittsburgh Crawfords	Outfielder
			Philadelphia Stars	Thirdbase
			New York Black Yankees	Secondbase
			St. Louis Stars	
			Homestead Grays	
			New Orleans-St. Louis Stars	
1937–1948	Barbee	Bud	Cincinnati Clowns	Pitcher
			Baltimore Elite Giants	Firstbase
			Philadelphia Stars	Manager*
			New York Black Yankees	
			Raleigh Times	
			Cincinnati-Indianapolis Clowns	
	Carter	Marlin (Mel)	Memphis Red Sox	Secondbase
			Cincinnati Tigers	Thirdbase
			Chicago American Giants	
			Atlanta Black Crackers	
	Strong	T.R. (Ted)	Kansas City Monarchs	Infielder
			Indianapolis Athletics	Outfielder

*Managerial Position

Career	Last Name	First Name	Teams	Positions
			Indianapolis Clowns	Manager*
			Indianapolis ABC's	
	Williams	James (Jim)	Birmingham Black Barons	Outfielder
			Homestead Grays	Manager*
			Durham Eagles	
			Toledo Crawfords	
			New York Cubans	
			Cleveland Bears	
			New York Gorhams	
			New York Black Yankees	
	Wright	John Richard	Pittsburgh Crawfords	Pitcher
			Indianapolis Crawfords	
1937–1949	Blueitt	Virgil	Negro American League	Umpire*
	Evans	Felix (Chin)	Birmingham Black Barons	Outfielder
			Atlanta BLack Crackers	Pitcher
			Indianapolis ABC's	
			Memphis Red Sox	
	Hyde	Cowan (Bubber)	Memphis Red Sox	Outfielder
			Cincinnati Tigers	
1937–1950	Clarkson	James (Bus)	Baltimore Elite Giants	Secondbase
			Newark Eagles	Outfielder
			Pittsburgh Crawfords	Shortstop
			Indianapolis Crawfords	
			Toledo Crawfords	
			Philadelphia Stars	
	Douglas	Jesse	Kansas City Monarchs	Outfielder
			Memphis Red Sox	Infielder
			Birmingham Black Barons	
			Chicago American Giants	
	Gaines	Jonas	Baltimore Elite Giants	Pitcher
			Philadelphia Stars	
			Newark Eagles	
	Jefferson	Willie	Memphis Red Sox	Pitcher
			Cleveland Buckeyes	
			Cincinnati Tigers	
			Cincinnati Buckeyes	
	Kimbro	Henry	Baltimore Elite Giants	Manager*
			New York Black Yankees	Outfielder
			Washington Elite Giants	
	Little	William	Chicago American Giants	Club Officer*
	Pearson	Leonard (Lennie)	Baltimore Elite Giants	Shortstop
			Newark Eagles	Outfielder
				Firstbase
				Thirdbase
				Manager*
	Walker	George (Little)	Kansas City Monarchs	Pitcher
			Homestead Grays	

*Managerial Position

Career	Last Name	First Name	Teams	Positions
1938	Barnes	Tubby	Birmingham Black Barons	Catcher
	Betts	–	Kansas City Monarchs	Pitcher
	Bubbles	–	Atlanta Black Crackers	Pitcher
	Cephas	–	Birmingham Black Barons	Shortstop
	Clarke	–	Washington Black Senators	Secondbase
	Crumbley	Alex	New York Black Yankees	Outfielder
	Holiday	–	Atlanta Black Crackers	Outfielder
	McDonald	Earl	Washington Black Senators	Club Officer
	Osley	–	Birmingham Black Barons	Pitcher
	Parker	Jack	Pittsburgh Crawfords	Infielder
	Pope	–	Atlanta Black Crackers	Outfielder
	Roberts	Charley	Washington Black Senators	Pitcher
	Smith	Charlie	Washington Black Senators	Infielder
	Smith	Clyde	Pittsburgh Crawfords	Thirdbase
	Sparrow	Roy	Washington Black Senators	Club Officer
	Thurston	–	Birmingham Black Barons	Pitcher
	Tyson	–	Birmingham Black Barons	Catcher
	Walton	Fuzzy	Pittsburgh Crawfords	Outfielder
1938–1939	Carter	Jimmy	Philadelphia Stars	Pitcher
	Davis	S.	Indianapolis ABC's	Thirdbase
			Atlanta Black Crackers	Outfielder
	Dixon	Ed	Baltimore Elite Giants	Pitcher
			Atlanta Black Crackers	
			Indianapolis ABC's	
	Johnson	Byron	Kansas City Monarchs	Shortstop
	Johnson	Jack	Toledo Crawfords	Thirdbase
			Homestead Grays	
	Robinson	J.	St. Louis Stars	Thirdbase
			Indianapolis ABC's	
1938–1940	Armstead	–	St. Louis Stars	Pitcher
			Indianapolis ABC's	
	Brooks	Alex	Brooklyn Royal Giants	Outfielder
			New York Black Yankees	
	Hairston	Napoleon	Indianapolis Crawfords	Outfielder
			Pittsburgh Crawfords	
	Jackson	(Big Train)	Memphis Red Sox	Pitcher
			Kansas City Monarchs	
	Moses	–	Kansas City Monarchs	Pitcher
	Thomas	Dan	Birmingham Black Barons	Outfielder
			Jacksonville Red Caps	
			Chicago American Giants	
1938–1941	Bruton	Jack	New Orleans-St. Louis Stars	Outfielder
			Philadelphia Stars	Pitcher
			Cleveland Bears	
	Campbell	David (Dave)	Philadelphia Stars	Secondbase
			New York Black Yankees	

Career	Last Name	First Name	Teams	Positions
	Jones	–	Cleveland Bears	Firstbase
			Jacksonville Red Caps	
	Missouri	Jim	Philadelphia Stars	Pitcher
	Mitchell	Alonzo	Cleveland Bears	Pitcher
			Jacksonville Red Caps	Firstbase
				Manager*
1938–1942	Bradford	William (Bill)	Birmingham Black Barons	Outfielder
			Indianapolis ABC's	
			Memphis Red Sox	
			St. Louis Stars	
	Cooper	W. (Bill)	Philadelphia Stars	Catcher
			Atlanta Black Crackers	
	Taylor	Robert	New Orleans-St. Louis Stars	Catcher
			Indianapolis ABC's	
			New York Black Yankees	
			St. Louis Stars	
	Turner	Flash	Cleveland Bears	Firstbase
			Jacksonville Red Caps	Catcher
				Outfielder
				Secondbase
1938–1943	Cleveland	Howard (Duke)	Cleveland Buckeyes	Outfielder
			Jacksonville Red Caps	
			Cleveland Bears	
	Riddie	Marshall	New Orleans-St. Louis Stars	Secondbase
			Indianapolis ABC's	
			Cleveland Bears	
			St. Louis Stars	
1938–1945	Barnhill	Herbert (Herb)	Kansas City Monarchs	Catcher
			Jacksonville Red Caps	
			Chicago American Giants	
	Holmes	Leroy (Phillie)	Atlanta Black Crackers	Shortstop
			Jacksonville Red Caps	
			New York Black Yankees	
			Cleveland Bears	
			Cincinnati-Indianapolis Clowns	
	Wilson	Fred	Cincinnati Clowns	Pitcher
			New York Black Yankees	Outfielder
			Cincinnati-Indianapolis Clowns	Manager*
			Newark Eagles	
1938–1946	Bryant	(Lefty)	Memphis Red Sox	Pitcher
			Kansas City Monarchs	
			All Nations	
	Horne	William (Billy)	Chicago American Giants	Secondbase
			Cleveland Buckeyes	Shortstop
			Cincinnati Buckeyes	
			Monroe Monarchs	

*Managerial Position

Career	Last Name	First Name	Teams	Positions
	McAllister	Frank (Chip)	Harrisburg-St. Louis Stars Indianapolis ABC's New York Black Yankees St. Louis Stars Brooklyn Brown Dodgers New Orleans-St. Louis Stars	Pitcher
	Starks	James	Harrisburg-St. Louis Stars New York Black Yankees	Firstbase
1938–1947	Henry	Leo (Preacher)	Cleveland Bears Jacksonville Red Caps Indianapolis Clowns Cincinnati Clowns	Pitcher
	Young	Edward (Pep)	Kansas City Monarchs Chicago American Giants Homestead Grays	Thirdbase Catcher Firstbase
1938–1948	Irvin	Monford Merrill (Monte)	Newark Eagles	Thirdbase Shortstop Outfielder
1938–1949	Cain	Marlon (Sugar)	Brooklyn Royal Giants Indianapolis Clowns Pittsburgh Crawfords	Pitcher
	McCreary	Fred	Negro National League	Umpire*
	Summers	Lonnie	Chicago American Giants Baltimore Elite Giants	Catcher Outfielder
1938–1950	Baird	Thomas	Kansas City Monarchs Negro American League	Club Officer* Agent*
	Butts	Thomas (Tommy, Peewee)	Baltimore Elite Giants Atlanta Black Crackers Indianapolis ABC's	Shortstop
	O'Neil	John (Buck)	Kansas City Monarchs	Manager* Firstbase
1939	Andrews	–	Cleveland Bears	Pitcher
	Beverle	–	Baltimore Elite Giants	Thirdbase
	Brown	Oscar	Baltimore Elite Giants Indianapolis ABC's	Catcher
	Davis	W.	Indianapolis ABC's	Outfielder
	Johnson	(Pee Wee)	Newark Eagles	Secondbase
	Johnson	Robert	New York Black Yankees	Outfielder
	Mitchell	Arthur	New York Black Yankees	Infielder
	Phillips	John	Baltimore Elite Giants	Pitcher
	Reveria	Charlie	Baltimore Elite Giants	Thirdbase
	Reverle	–	Baltimore Elite Giants	Thirdbase
	Richardson	Jim	New York Black Yankees	Pitcher
	Robinson	Charles	Chicago American Giants	Outfielder
	Robinson	Joshua	New York Black Yankees	Outfielder
	Rogers	–	Chicago American Giants	Pitcher

*Managerial Position

Career	Last Name	First Name	Teams	Positions
	Smith	P.	St. Louis Stars	Pitcher
	Taylor	Shine	Toledo Crawfords	Outfielder
	Treadway	–	Kansas City Monarchs	Pitcher
	Williams	–	Indianapolis ABC's	Catcher
	Wilson	Alec	New York Black Yankees	Outfielder
1939–1940	Bowe	Randolph (Bob, Lefty)	Chicago American Giants Kansas City Monarchs	Pitcher
	Burris	Samuel	Birmingham Black Barons Memphis Red Sox	Pitcher
	Davidson	Charles	Brooklyn Royal Giants New York Black Yankees	Pitcher
	Dean	Bob	St. Louis Stars	Pitcher
	Decuir	Lionel	Kansas City Monarchs	Catcher
	Harvey	Willie	Indianapolis Crawfords Pittsburgh Crawfords	Pitcher
	Johnson	Jimmy (Slim)	Indianapolis Crawfords Toledo Crawfords	Pitcher
	Williams	Clarence	Baltimore Elite Giants	Outfielder Pitcher
1939–1941	Biot	Charlie	Baltimore Elite Giants New York Black Yankees Newark Eagles	Outfielder
	Brown	Jesse	Baltimore Elite Giants New York Black Yankees Newark Eagles	Pitcher
	Dukes	–	Jacksonville Red Caps Cleveland Bears	Outfielder
	Greer	J.B.	Knoxville Red Caps Cleveland Bears Jacksonville Red Caps	Club Officer*
	Hubert	Willie (Bubber)	Cincinnati Buckeyes Brooklyn Brown Dodgers Pittsburgh Crawfords Newark Eagles Baltimore Grays Baltimore Elite Giants Homestead Grays	Pitcher
1939–1942	Boone	Oscar	Chicago American Giants Indianapolis ABC's	Firstbase Catcher
	Green	Leslie (Chin)	New York Black Yankees St. Louis Stars	Outfielder
	Jackson	Robert R.	Negro American League	Commissioner
	Owens	Raymond (Smoky)	Jacksonville Red Caps Cleveland Bears Cincinnati Clowns New Orleans-St. Louis Stars	Outfielder Pitcher

Career	Last Name	First Name	Teams	Positions
1939–1943	Cole	Ralph (Punjab)	Cleveland Bears	Outfielder
			Jacksonville Red Caps	
			Cincinnati Clowns	
	Cozart	Harry	Newark Eagles	Pitcher
1939–1945	Hill	Jimmy (Lefty)	Newark Eagles	Pitcher
	Rigney	H.G. (Hank)	Toledo Rays	Club Officer*
			Toledo Crawfords	Club Officer*
			Indianapolis Crawfords	
1939–1946	Roberts	Speck	Newark Eagles	Pitcher
			Homestead Grays	
			New York Black Yankees	
1939–1947	Parks	John	Newark Eagles	Outfielder
			New York Black Yankees	Catcher
1939–1948	Harden	John	Indianapolis ABC's	Club Officer*
			Atlanta Black Crackers	
			New York Black Yankees	
			Negro Southern League	Treasurer*
	Young	Frank A. (Fay)	Negro American League	Secretary*
1939–1949	Forrest	Percy	Indianapolis Clowns	Pitcher
			Newark Eagles	
			Chicago American Giants	
			New York Black Yankees	
	Hutchinson	Willie (Ace)	Memphis Red Sox	Pitcher
			Kansas City Monarchs	
	Manning	Maxwell (Max)	Houston Eagles	Pitcher
			Newark Eagles	
1939–1950	Hayes	Thomas H.	Negro American League	Vice-President, President*
			Birmingham Black Barons	Club Officer*
	Lockett	Lester	Baltimore Elite Giants	Thirdbase
			Birmingham Black Barons	Secondbase
			Memphis Red Sox	
			Cincinnati-Indianapolis Clowns	
			Chicago American Giants	
	Robinson	Norman	Birmingham Black Barons	Shortstop
			Baltimore Elite Giants	Outfielder
1940	Bass	Red	Homestead Grays	Catcher
	Bea	Bill	Philadelphia Stars	Utility Player
			New York Black Yankees	
	Boone	Steve (Lefty)	Memphis Red Sox	Pitcher
	Bordes	Ed	Cleveland Bears	Utility Player
	Byatt	–	Philadelphia Stars	Firstbase
	Craig	Dick	Indianapolis Crawfords	Firstbase
	Dalton	Rossie	Chicago American Giants	Utility Player
	Debran	Roy	New York Black Yankees	Outfielder
	Fulcur	Robert	Chicago American Giants	Pitcher

Career	Last Name	First Name	Teams	Positions
	Gibson	Ted	Columbus Buckeyes	Infielder
	Gregory	–	Birmingham Black Barons	Pitcher
	Harding	Tom	Indianapolis Crawfords	Outfielder
	Harris	Samuel	Chicago American Giants	Pitcher
	Hayes	–	St. Louis Stars	Secondbase
			Philadelphia Stars	Shortstop
	Hicks	Eugene	Homestead Grays	Pitcher
	Jeffries	Jeff	Brooklyn Royal Giants	Pitcher
	Lawson	–	Philadelphia Stars	Pitcher
	Mickey	James	Birmingham Black Barons	Thirdbase
			Chicago American Giants	Shortstop
	Moody	–	Birmingham Black Barons	Pitcher
	Nears	Red	Memphis Red Sox	Outfielder
				Catcher
	Newman	–	Memphis Red Sox	Pitcher
	Newson	–	Newark Eagles	Outfielder
	Payne	Rusty	Indianapolis Crawfords	Outfielder
	Reynolds	Jimmy	Indianapolis Crawfords	Thirdbase
	Robinson	Bobby	St. Louis Stars	Utility Player
	Russell	–	Cuban Stars	Outfielder
	Samuels	–	Philadelphia Stars	Pitcher
	Saunders	Leo	Birmingham Black Barons	Shortstop
			Chicago American Giants	Pitcher
	Savage	Junior	Memphis Red Sox	Pitcher
	Summerall	Big	Memphis Red Sox	Pitcher
	Vines	Eddie	Birmingham Black Barons	Thirdbase
			Chicago American Giants	Pitcher
	White	Lefty	Cleveland Bears	Pitcher
	Wilson	James	Indianapolis Crawfords	Secondbase
				Outfielder
	Wise	Russell	Indianapolis Crawfords	Firstbase
1940–1941	Awkward	Russell	Newark Eagles	Outfielder
			Cuban Stars	
	Dumas	Jim	Memphis Red Sox	Pitcher
	Nixon	–	Birmingham Black Barons	Outfielder
	Redd	Ulysses A.	Birmingham Black Barons	Shortstop
			Chicago American Giants	
	Sampson	Sam	Jacksonville Red Caps	Secondbase
			Cleveland Bears	
	Washington	Fay	New Orleans-St. Louis Stars	Pitcher
			St. Louis Stars	
1940–1942	Dawson	Johnny	Kansas City Monarchs	Catcher
			Memphis Red Sox	
	Hamilton	J.C. (Ed)	Homestead Grays	Pitcher
	Hudson	William	Chicago American Giants	Pitcher
	Jordan	–	New York Black Yankees	Shortstop
			Philadelphia Stars	

Career	Last Name	First Name	Teams	Positions
	Robinson	Walter (Skindown)	Jacksonville Red Caps	Secondbase
			Cleveland Bears	
	Sarvis	Andrew (Smoky)	Jacksonville Red Caps	Pitcher
			Cleveland Bears	
	Sheed	Eddie (Lefty)	Birmingham Black Barons	Pitcher
	Turner	Little Lefty	Baltimore Elite Giants	Firstbase
			Indianapolis Crawfords	
1940–1943	Cyrus	Herb	Kansas City Monarchs	Thirdbase
	Ferrell	Willie (Red)	Chicago American Giants	Pitcher
			Homestead Grays	
			Cincinnati Clowns	
	Smith	Lefty	Chicago American Giants	Pitcher
1940–1945	Gray	–	Harrisburg-St. Louis Stars	Catcher
			St. Louis Stars	
			New York Black Yankees	
			Kansas City Monarchs	
	Matchett	Jack	Kansas City Monarchs	Pitcher
	Matthews	Francis	Boston Royal Giants	Firstbase
			Newark Eagles	
	Moreland	Nate	Kansas City Monarchs	Pitcher
			Baltimore Elite Giants	
1940–1946	Bennett	Bradford	St. Louis Stars	Outfielder
			New York Black Yankees	
			Boston Blues	
			New Orleans-St. Louis Stars	
1940–1947	Anderson	William (Bill)	New York Cubans	Pitcher
			Brooklyn Royal Giants	
			Cuban Stars	
	Bankhead	Daniel Robert (Dan)	Birmingham Black Barons	
			Memphis Red Sox	Pitcher
	Israel	Clarence	Homestead Grays	Secondbase
			Newark Eagles	Thirdbase
	Morton	Cy	Chicago American Giants	Secondbase
			Philadelphia Stars	Shortstop
			Pittsburgh Crawfords	
	Warren	Jesse	Birmingham Black Barons	Thirdbase
			Memphis Red Sox	Secondbase
			Chicago American Giants	Pitcher
			New Orleans-St. Louis Stars	
1940–1948	Duckett	Mahlon	Philadelphia Stars	Shortstop
				Secondbase
				Thirdbase
	Hooker	Len	Newark Eagles	Pitcher

Career	Last Name	First Name	Teams	Positions
	Miller	Henry	Philadelphia Stars	Pitcher
	Sampson	Thomas (Tommy)	Birmingham Black Barons	Firstbase
			Chicago American Giants	Secondbase
			New York Cubans	Manager*
	Smith	John	Chicago American Giants	Pitcher
			Indianapolis Crawfords	Outfielder
			New York Yankees	
1940–1949	Alexander	Ted	Kansas City Monarchs	Pitcher
			Newark Eagles	
			Birmingham Black Barons	
			Chicago American Giants	
			Cleveland Bears	
	Bostock	Lyman	Chicago American Giants	Outfielder
			Birmingham Black Barons	Firstbase
			New York Cubans	
	Jessup	Gentry	Birmingham Black Barons	Pitcher
			Chicago American Giants	
	Mathis	Verdel	Memphis Red Sox	Outfielder
				Firstbase
	McDaniels	Booker	Memphis Red Sox	Outfielder
			Kansas City Monarchs	Pitcher
	Smith	Eugene (Gene)	Cleveland Buckeyes	Pitcher
			New Orleans-St. Louis Stars	
			Louisville Buckeyes	
			New York Black Yankees	
			St. Louis Stars	
	Williams	Jesse	Indianapolis Clowns	Thirdbase
			Kansas City Monarchs	Shortstop
1940–1950	Britton	John (Jack)	Indianapolis Clowns	Thirdbase
			St. Louis Stars	
			Cincinnati Clowns	
			Birmingham Black Barons	
	Haywood	Albert (Buster)	Indianapolis Clowns	Manager*
			Chicago American Giants	Catcher
			New York Cubans	
			Birmingham Black Barons	
			Cincinnati-Indianapolis Clowns	
	Johnson	Clifford (Cliff)	Kansas City Monarchs	Pitcher
			Indianapolis Crawfords	
	Merchant	Henry	Indianapolis Clowns	Outfielder
			Cincinnati-Indianapolis Clowns	Pitcher
			Chicago American Giants	
	Pennington	Arthur (Art)	Pittsburgh Crawfords	Secondbase
			Chicago American Giants	Outfielder
				Firstbase

*Managerial Position

Career	Last Name	First Name	Teams	Positions
	Perry	Alonzo	Birmingham Black Barons	Firstbase
			Homestead Grays	Pitcher
	Ware	Archie V.	Louisville Buckeyes	Firstbase
			Chicago American Giants	
			Indianapolis Clowns	
			Kansas City Monarchs	
			Cleveland Buckeyes	
1941	Berkley	–	New Orleans-St. Louis Stars	Pitcher
	Cooper	A.	New York Black Yankees	Secondbase
				Outfielder
				Shortstop
	Harris	(Lefty)	Cuban Stars	Pitcher
	Heat	–	Cuban Stars	Pitcher
	Johnson	Lee	Birmingham Black Barons	Catcher
	Kelly	–	Jacksonville Red Caps	Pitcher
	Listach	–	Birmingham Black Barons	Outfielder
	Marsellas	David	New York Black Yankees	Catcher
	Patterson	–	New York Black Yankees	Outfielder
	Riddick	Vernon	Newark Eagles	Shortstop
	Sampson	Eddie	Birmingham Black Barons	Outfielder
	Smith	G.	Kansas City Monarchs	Pitcher
	Spencer	Willie	Birmingham Black Barons	Outfielder
1941–1942	Barnes	Jimmy	Baltimore Elite Giants	Pitcher
	Broom	–	Jacksonville Red Caps	Pitcher
	Buchanan	Chester (Buck)	Philadelphia Stars	Pitcher
	Flowers	Jake	New York Black Yankees	Infielder
	Houston	Bill	Homestead Grays	Pitcher
	Tatum	Reece (Goose)	Cincinnati Clowns	Firstbase
			Birmingham Black Barons	Outfielder
			Indianapolis Clowns	
			Minneapolis-St. Paul Gophers	
			Cincinnati-Indianapolis Clowns	
	Walls	Greenie		Umpire*
	Watts	Herman (Lefty)	Cleveland Buckeyes	Pitcher
			Jacksonville Red Caps	
1941–1943	Ferrell	Truchart	Chicago American Giants	Outfielder
				Pitcher
	Hobgood	Freddie (Lefty)	Newark Eagles	Pitcher
1941–1945	Boone	Charles (Lefty)	Pittsburgh Crawfords	Pitcher
			Harrisburg-St. Louis Stars	
			New Orleans-St. Louis Stars	
	Greenege	Victor (Slicker)	New York Cubans	Pitcher
			Cuban Stars	
	Sutton	Leroy	Chicago American Giants	Pitcher
			New Orleans-St. Louis Stars	
			Cincinnati-Indianapolis Clowns	

*Managerial Position

Career	Last Name	First Name	Teams	Positions
1941–1946	Fillmore	Joe	Baltimore Grays	Pitcher
			Philadelphia Stars	
	Shead	Sylvester	Cincinnati Clowns	Secondbase
			Kansas City Monarchs	Outfielder
			New York Black Yankees	
1941–1947	Robinson	Ray	Philadelphia Stars	Pitcher
			Newark Eagles	
			Cincinnati Buckeyes	
1941–1948	Brown	James (Jim)	Newark Eagles	Outfielder
				Pitcher
	Davis	Spencer (Babe)	Winston-Salem Giants	Shortstop
			New York Black Yankees	Manager*
	Keyes	Steve (Youngie)	Philadelphia Stars	Pitcher
			Memphis Red Sox	
1941-1949	Barnhill	David (Dave)	New York Cubans	Pitcher
			New Orleans-St. Louis Stars	
	Fields	Wilmer (Red)	Homestead Grays	Outfielder
				Pitcher
				Thirdbase
	Gipson	Alvin (Bubber)	Houston Eagles	Pitcher
			Birmingham Black Barons	
			Chicago American Giants	
	McKinnis	Gread (Lefty)	Pittsburgh Crawfords	Pitcher
			Birmingham Black Barons	
			Chicago American Giants	
	Wright	Ernest (Ernie)	Negro American League	Vice-President*
			Cincinnati Buckeyes	Club Officer*
			Cleveland White Sox	Club Officer*
			Cleveland Buckeyes	Club Officer*
1941–1950	Steele	Edward (Ed)	Birmingham Black Barons	Outfielder
1942	Brooks	–	Memphis Red Sox	Pitcher
	Brown	G.	Cincinnati Buckeyes	Outfielder
	Burgess	–	Chicago American Giants	Pitcher
	Campbell	Hunter	Cincinnati Clowns	Officer*
	Charleston	–	Cincinnati Buckeyes	Catcher
	Corcoran	Tom	Homestead Grays	Pitcher
	Cowans	Russ	Negro Baseball League of America	Secretary*
	Dunn	–	Jacksonville Red Caps	Pitcher
	Harris	Sonny	Cincinnati Buckeyes	Outfielder
	Hubbard	Dehart	Cleveland-Cincinnati Buckeyes	Secretary*
	Ingram	–	Jacksonville Red Caps	Pitcher
	James	Tice	Cincinnati Clowns	Ball Player
	James	(Winky)	Cincinnati Buckeyes	Shortstop
	Longest	Jimmy	Chicago Brown Bombers	Firstbase
	Lugo	Leo	Cincinnati-Indianapolis Clowns	Ball Player
	McKellam	–	Cincinnati Buckeyes	Pitcher

*Managerial Position

Career	Last Name	First Name	Teams	Positions
	Montgomery	Lou	Cincinnati Clowns	Outfielder
				Pitcher
	Pipkin	Black Diamond	Birmingham Black Barons	Pitcher
	Sampson	John	New York Cubans	Outfielder
	Smith	E.	Cincinnati Buckeyes	Thirdbase
			Jacksonville Red Caps	
	Sykes	Joe	Cincinnati Clowns	Ball Player
	Thompson	Copperknee	Minneapolis-St. Paul Gophers	Infielder
			Cincinnati Clowns	
	Walker	Larry	Newark Eagles	Thirdbase
	Wilbert	Art	Minneapolis-St. Paul Gophers	Outfielder
			Cincinnati Clowns	
1942–1943	Fagan	–	Jacksonville Red Caps	Infielder
			Philadelphia Stars	
			Memphis Red Sox	
	Lindsay	Leonard	Birmingham Black Barons	Pitcher
			Cincinnati Clowns	Firstbase
	Phillips	Norris	Kansas City Monarchs	Pitcher
1942–1945	Johnson	John (Johnny)	New York Black Yankees	Pitcher
			Birmingham Black Barons	
			Homestead Grays	
	Smith	Henry	Cincinnati Clowns	Shortstop
			Chicago American Giants	Secondbase
			Jacksonville Red Caps	
			Cincinnati-Indianapolis Clowns	
	Young	Roy	Negro American League	Umpire*
1942–1946	Johnson	Allen	Harrisburg-St. Louis Stars	Club Officer*
			St. Louis Stars	
			Boston Blues	
			New York Black Yankees	
	Spencer	Joseph B.	Homestead Grays	Shortstop
			Birmingham Black Barons	Secondbase
			New York Cubans	
			Pittsburgh Crawfords	
	West	Ollie	Birmingham Black Barons	Pitcher
			Pittsburgh Crawfords	
			Chicago American Giants	
	Williams	Frank	Homestead Grays	Outfielder
	Wyatt	Ralph	Homestead Grays	Shortstop
			Chicago American Giants	
1942–1947	Allen	(Buster)	Cincinnati-Indianapolis Clowns	Pitcher
			Memphis Red Sox	
			Cincinnati Clowns	
			Jacksonville Red Caps	
	Crue	Martin (Matty)	New York Cubans	Pitcher

*Managerial Position

Career	Last Name	First Name	Teams	Positions
	Farmer	Greene	New York Cubans	Outfielder
			Cincinnati Clowns	
			New York Black Yankees	
	Longest	Bernell	Chicago American Giants	Secondbase
			Chicago Brown Bombers	
1942–1948	Green	Vernon	Baltimore Elite Giants	Club Officer*
	Jethroe	Samuel (Sam)	Cleveland Buckeyes	Outfielder
			Cincinnati Buckeyes	
	Marcell	Everett	Newark Eagles	Catcher
			Chicago American Giants	
1942–1949	Brown	John W.	Houston Eagles	Pitcher
			St. Louis Giants	
			Cleveland Buckeyes	
	Hoskins	David (Dave)	Homestead Grays	Pitcher
			Cincinnati Clowns	Outfielder
			Louisville Buckeyes	
			Chicago American Giants	
	McLaurin	Felix	New York Black Yankees	Outfielder
			Jacksonville Red Caps	
			Chicago American Giants	
			Birmingham Black Barons	
	Williams	Marvin	Philadelphia Stars	Secondbase
1942–1950	Davis	Edward A. (Eddie-Peanuts)	Cincinnati Clowns	
			Indianapolis Clowns	
			Cincinnati-Indianapolis Clowns	
	Grace	Willie	Cleveland Buckeyes	Outfielder
			Houston Eagles	
			Louisville Buckeyes	
			Cincinnati Buckeyes	
	Hayes	Wilbur	Negro American League	Sergeant-at-Arms*
			Cleveland Buckeyes	Club Officer*
			Cincinnati Buckeyes	
	Humes	John	Memphis Red Sox	Catcher
			Chicago American Giants	Pitcher
			Cincinnati Clowns	
			Birmingham Black Barons	
	Jefferson	George Leo	Cleveland Buckeyes	Pitcher
			Jacksonville Red Caps	
	Louden	Louis	Cuban Stars	Catcher
			New York Cubans	
	Neil	Ray	Indianapolis Clowns	Secondbase
			Cincinnati Clowns	
	Rhodes	Harry	Chicago American Giants	Firstbase
				Pitcher
	Robinson	Frazier	Baltimore Elite Giants	Catcher
			Baltimore Grays	

*Managerial Position

Career	Last Name	First Name	Teams	Positions
1943	Buster	Herbert	Chicago American Giants	Infielder
	Carter	–	Harrisburg-St. Louis Stars	Thirdbase
	Clayton	Leroy	Chicago Brown Bombers	Catcher
	Cox	–	Memphis Red Sox	Pitcher
	Crawford	John	Negro National League	Umpire*
	Daniels	(School)	Birmingham Black Barons	Pitcher
	Evans	(Cowboy)	Cincinnati Clowns	Pitcher
	Evans	Ulysses	Chicago Brown Bombers	Pitcher
			Cincinnati Clowns	
	Garrett	William	New York Black Yankees	Club Officer*
	Gibson	Jerry	Cincinnati Tigers	Ball Player
	Grimes	–	Cleveland Buckeyes	Outfielder
	Harris	Charlie	Chicago Brown Bombers	Infielder
			Cincinnati Clowns	
	Higdon	Barney	Cincinnati Clowns	Pitcher
	Hurdley	Johnny Lee	Cleveland Buckeyes	Outfielder
				Catcher
	King	Brendan	Cincinnati Clowns	Pitcher
	Lett	Roger	Cincinnati Clowns	Ball Player
	Lewis	Henry N.	Atlanta Black Crackers	Manager*
	Lewis	Jim	Chicago Brown Bombers	Pitcher
	Moore	Charles	Negro National League	Umpire*
	Morehead	Albert	Chicago Brown Bombers	Catcher
			Birmingham Black Barons	
	Parker	–	Kansas City Monarchs	Pitcher
	Ray	Richard	Chicago Brown Bombers	Outfielder
	Richardson	–	Newark Eagles	Shortstop
	Smith	Douglas	Baltimore Elite Giants	Club Officer*
	Stevenson	Willie	Homestead Grays	Pitcher
	Thomas	William	Chicago Brown Bombers	Outfielder
	Turner	Oliver	Chicago Brown Bombers	Pitcher
	Tyler	Eugene	Chicago Brown Bombers	Catcher
	Waller	George	Chicago Brown Bombers	Infielder
	Williams	E.	Harrisburg-St. Louis Stars	Outfielder
1943–1944	Britton	George	Cleveland Buckeyes	Catcher
	Burns	Willie	Cincinnati-Indianapolis Clowns	Pitcher
			Memphis Red Sox	
1943–1945	Harden	Lovell	Cleveland Buckeyes	Pitcher
	Haynes	Sam	Kansas City Monarchs	Catcher
	Locke	Eddie	Kansas City Monarchs	Pitcher
			Cincinnati Clowns	
	McDaniels	Fred	Memphis Red Sox	Outfielder
	Rowe	Schoolboy	Pittsburgh Crawfords	Pitcher
			Chicago Brown Bombers	
	Smith	Quincy	Birmingham Black Barons	Outfielder
			Cleveland Buckeyes	

*Managerial Position

Career	Last Name	First Name	Teams	Positions
	Washington	Lafayette	Cincinnati-Indianapolis Clowns	Pitcher
			Kansas City Monarchs	
			Chicago American Giants	
			Birmingham Black Barons	
1943–1946	Charter	W.M. (Bill)	Chicago American Giants	Catcher
1943–1947	Doby	Lawrence Eugene		
		(Larry)	Newark Eagles	Secondbase
1943–1948	Thompson	Henry Curtis	Kansas City Monarchs	Secondbase
				Outfielder
				Shortstop
	Williams	Johnny	Indianapolis Clowns	Pitcher
			Chicago Brown Bombers	
			Cincinnati-Indianapolis Clowns	
1943–1949	Nelson	Clyde	Chicago American Giants	Firstbase
			Indianapolis Clowns	Secondbase
			Chicago Brown Bombers	
			Cleveland Buckeyes	
	Russell	Frank (Junior)	Baltimore Elite Giants	Outfielder
				Secondbase
1943–1950	Black	Joseph (Joe)	Baltimore Elite Giants	Pitcher
	Cash	William (Bill,		
		Ready)	Philadelphia Stars	Thirdbase
				Catcher
				Outfielder
	Davis	John	Houston Eagles	Outfielder
			Newark Eagles	
	Davis	Lorenzo (Piper)	Birmingham Black Barons	Shortstop
				Secondbase
				Firstbase
				Manager
	Newberry	James (Jimmy)	Birmingham Black Barons	Pitcher
	Tut	Richard (King)	Indianapolis Clowns	Firstbase
			Cincinnati Clowns	
1944	Harriston	Clyde	Cincinnati-Indianapolis Clowns	Ball Player
			Birmingham Black Barons	
	Jackson	Samuel	Chicago American Giants	Ball Player
	Johnson	Robert	Kansas City Monarchs	Infielder
	Jones	Collis	Birmingham Black Barons	Utility Player
	Mahoney	Ulysses	Philadelphia Stars	Pitcher
	Smith	Mance	Kansas City Monarchs	Ball Player
	Waldon	Allie	Chicago American Giants	Ball Player
	White	Edward	Homestead Grays	Pitcher
	Wingo	Doc	Kansas City Monarchs	Ball Player
1944–1945	Battle	Ray	Homestead Grays	Thirdbase
	Chatman	Edgar	Memphis Red Sox	Pitcher
	Felder	Kendall	Chicago American Giants	Ball Player

Career	Last Name	First Name	Teams	Positions
			Memphis Red Sox	
			Birmingham Black Barons	
	Harper	David (Dave)	Kansas City Monarchs	Ball Player
	Jones	Alonzo	Memphis Red Sox	Pitcher
			Chicago American Giants	
	Keyes	Robert	Memphis Red Sox	Pitcher
	King	Wilbur	Chicago American Giants	Shortstop
			Cleveland Buckeyes	
			Memphis Red Sox	
	Ligon	Rufus	Memphis Red Sox	Pitcher
	Moody	Lee	Kansas City Monarchs	Firstbase
	Newcombe	Donald (Don)	Newark Eagles	Pitcher
	Troy	Donald	Baltimore Elite Giants	Pitcher
	Williams	Jesse	Cleveland Buckeyes	Ball Player
	Young	Leandy	Birmingham Black Barons	Outfielder
1944–1946	Carswell	Frank	Cleveland Buckeyes	Pitcher
1944–1947	Baker	Rufus	New York Black Yankees	Outfielder
	Braitwaite	Archie	Philadelphia Stars	Outfielder
			Newark Eagles	
	McFarland	John	New York Black Yankees	Pitcher
	Wylie	Ensloe	Memphis Red Sox	Pitcher
			Kansas City Monarchs	
1944–1948	Austin	Frank	Philadelphia Stars	Shortstop
	Bumpus	Earl	Chicago American Giants	Outfielder
			Kansas City Monarchs	Pitcher
			Birmingham Black Barons	
	Dennis	Wesley	Philadelphia Stars	Outfielder
			Baltimore Elite Giants	Firstbase
	Leak	Curtis A.	Negro National League	Club Officer*
			New York Black Yankees	
	Watkins	Murray	Philadelphia Stars	Thirdbase
			Newark Eagles	
	Wilson	Arthur Lee (Artie)	Birmingham Black Barons	Shortstop
1944–1949	Makell	Frank	Baltimore Elite Giants	Catcher
			Newark Eagles	
	Minor	George	Louisville Buckeyes	Outfielder
			Chicago American Giants	
			Cleveland Buckeyes	
1944–1950	Glenn	Stanley	Philadelphia Stars	Catcher
	Harvey	Robert (Rob)	Houston Eagles	Outfielder
			Newark Eagles	
	Jones	Clinton (Casey)	Memphis Red Sox	Catcher
	Ricks	William (Bill)	Philadelphia Stars	Pitcher
	Sovell	Herbert (Herb)	Kansas City Monarchs	Infielder
	Wynn	Willie	New York Cubans	Catcher
			Newark Eagles	

*Managerial Position

Career	Last Name	First Name	Teams	Positions
1945	Baker	Edgar	Memphis Red Sox	Pitcher
	Bennett	Jim	Cincinnati-Indianapolis Clowns	Pitcher
	Cotton	James	Chattanooga Choo Choos	Catcher
				Pitcher
				Club Officer*
	Cromartie	Leroy	Cincinnati Indianapolis Clowns	Ball Player
	Davis	Lee	Kansas City Monarchs	Pitcher
	Davis	Willie	Mobile Black Shippers	Club Officer*
	Duncan	Frank, Jr.	Baltimore Elite Giants	Pitcher
	Foster	Jim	Chicago Brown Bombers	Club Officer*
	Gulley	Napoleon	Cleveland Buckeyes	Pitcher
	Hall	Joseph W.	Hilldale Club of Philadelphia	Club Officer*
	Hinton	Archie	Baltimore Elite Giants	Infielder
				Pitcher
	Humber	–	Newark Eagles	Secondbase
	Johnson	W.	Memphis Red Sox	Pitcher
	Jackson	B.	Homestead Grays	Thirdbase
	Johnson	Leaman	Memphis Red Sox	Shortstop
	Kelly	–	New York Black Yankees	Ball Player
	Leftwich	John	Homestead Grays	Pitcher
	Lewis	Henry N.	Knoxville Black Smokies	Club Officer*
	Linton	Benjamin	Detroit Giants	Club Officer
	Mack	–	New York Black Yankees	Pitcher
	Matthews	Clifford	New Orleans Black Pelicans	Club Officer*
	Mazaar	Robert	Hilldale Club of Philadelphia	Club Officer*
	McCall	Henry	Chicago American Giants	Utility Player
	McMeans	Willie	Chicago American Giants	Pitcher
	Noble	Sam	New York Cubans	Catcher
	Parks	Sam	Memphis Grey Sox	Club Officer*
	Robinson	Jackie	Kansas City Monarchs	Secondbase
	Smith	Ollie	Cincinnati-Indianapolis Clowns	Pitcher
	Spencer	J.C.	Birmingham Black Barons	Secondbase
	Surkett	–	Philadelphia Stars	Pitcher
	Thompson	Jimmy	Negro American League	Umpire*
	Williams	Eddie	Kansas City Monarchs	Outfielder
	Williams	S.	Newark Eagles	Pitcher
	Young	Wilbur	Birmingham Black Barons	Pitcher
1945–1946	Blair	Garnet	Homestead Grays	Pitcher
	Kimbrough	Larry	Philadelphia Stars	Pitcher
	Oliver	John	Cleveland Buckeyes	Shortstop
			Memphis Red Sox	
	Poole	Claude	New York Black Yankees	Pitcher
1945–1947	Barrow	Wesley	Baltimore Elite Giants	Manager*
			Nashville Cubs	
			New Orleans Black Pelicans	
	Watson	Amos	Baltimore Elite Giants	Pitcher
			Cincinnati-Indianapolis Clowns	

*Managerial Position

Career	Last Name	First Name	Teams	Positions
1945–1948	Ashby	Earl	Newark Eagles Cleveland Buckeyes Homestead Grays Birmingham Black Barons	Catcher
	Looke	Clarence	Chicago American Giants	Firstbase Pitcher
	Moore	C.L.	Negro American Association Asheville Blues	President* Club Officer*
	Peace	Warren	Newark Eagles	Pitcher
1945–1949	Bell	Herman	Birmingham Black Barons	Catcher
	Gerrard	Alphonso	Indianapolis Clowns New York Black Yankees Chicago American Giants	Outfielder
	Glenn	Hubert (Country)	Brooklyn Brown Dodgers Indianapolis Clowns New York Black Yankees	Pitcher
	McCoy	Walter	Chicago American Giants	Pitcher
	McMullin	Clarence	Houston Eagles Kansas City Monarchs	Outfielder
	Pearson	Frank	Memphis Red Sox	Pitcher
	Walker	Robert T.	Homestead Grays	Pitcher
1945–1950	Clark	Cleveland	New York Cubans	Outfielder
	Drake	Yerdes	Indianapolis Clowns Cincinnati-Indianapolis Clowns	Outfielder
	Gilliam	James (Junior)	Baltimore Elite Giants Nashville Black Vols	Secondbase
	Hairston	Samuel (Sam)	Indianapolis Clowns Cincinnati-Indianapolis Clowns	Thirdbase Catcher
	Hardy	Walter	New York Cubans New York Black Yankees	Secondbase Shortstop

*Managerial Position

BASKETBALL

SOUTHWESTERN ATHLETIC CONFERENCE CHAMPIONS (MEN, 1956–1984)

Year	School	Coach
1956	Texas Southern	Ed Adams
1957	Texas Southern	Ed Adams
1958	Texas Southern	Ed Adams
1959	Grambling	Fred Hobdy
1960	Grambling	Fred Hobdy
1961	Prairie View	Leroy Moore
1962	Prairie View	Leroy Moore
1963	Grambling	Fred Hobdy
1964	Grambling	Fred Hobdy
1965	Jackson State	Paul Covington
1965	Southern	Richard Mack
1966	Alcorn State	E.E. Simmons
1966	Grambling	Fred Hobdy
1967	Alcorn State	Bob Hopkins
1967	Arkansas AM&N	Coach Clemmons
1969	Alcorn State	Davey Whitney
1970	Jackson State	Paul Covington
1971	Grambling	Fred Hobdy
1972	Grambling	Fred Hobdy
1973	Alcorn State	Davey Whitney
1974	Jackson State	Paul Covington
1975	Jackson State	Paul Covington
1976	Alcorn State	Davey Whitney
1977	Texas Southern	Bob Moreland
1978	Southern	Carl Stewart
1979	Alcorn State	Davey Whitney
1980	Alcorn State	Davey Whitney
1981	Alcorn State	Davey Whitney
1982	Alcorn State	Davey Whitney
1983	Alcorn State	Davey Whitney
1984	Southern	Bob Hopkins

SIAC TOURNAMENT CHAMPIONS (1950–1984) DIVISION II

Year	School	Coach
1950	Morris Brown	H.B. Thompson
1951	Morris Brown	H.B. Thompson
1952	Florida A&M	Ed Oglesby
1953	Bethune-Cookman	Rudolph Matthews
1954	Clark	Leonidis Epps
1955	Florida A&M	Ed Oglesby
1956	Knoxville	Julian Bell
1957	Florida A&M	Ed Oglesby
1958	Knoxville	Julian Bell
1959	Florida A&M	Ed Oglesby
1960	Florida A&M	Ed Oglesby
1961	Benedict	John Brown
1962	Florida A&M	Ed Oglesby
1963	Fisk	H.B. Thompson
1964	South Carolina State	Ed Martin
1965	Clark	Leonidis Epps
1966	South Carolina State	Ed Martin
1967	Florida A&M	Ed Oglesby
1968	Bethune-Cookman	Jack McClairen
1969	Fort Valley State	Leon Lomax
1970	Savannah State	Leo Richardson
1971	Alabama State	Bernard Boozer

Year	School	Coach
1972	Alabama State	Bernard Boozer
1973	Albany State	Oliver Jones
1974	Fisk	Ron Lawson
1975	Alabama A&M	Clarence Blackmon
1976	Alabama A&M	Clarence Blackmon
1977	Florida A&M	Ajax Triplett
1978	Florida A&M	Ajax Triplett
1979	Tuskegee	Charles Thompson
1980	Bethune-Cookman	Jack McClairen
1981	Morehouse	Arthur McAfee
1982	Morris Brown	Billy Wade
1983	Albany State	Oliver Jones
1984	Albany State	Oliver Jones

SIAC
TOURNAMENT CHAMPIONS (1950–1984)
DIVISION III

Year	School	Coach
1979	Savannah State	Russ Ellington
1980	Savannah State	Russ Ellington
1981	Savannah State	Russ Ellington
1982	Miles	McKinley Young
1983	LeMoyne-Owen	Jerry Johnson
1984	LeMoyne-Owen	Jerry Johnson

MEAC CHAMPIONS
(1972–1984)

Year	School	Coach
1972	North Carolina A&T	Cal Irvin
1973	Maryland Eastern Shore	John Bates
1974	Morgan State	Nat Frazier
	Maryland Eastern Shore	John Bates
1975	North Carolina A&T	Warren Reynolds
1976	North Carolina A&T	Warren Reynolds
	Morgan State	Nat Frazier
1977	South Carolina State	Tim Autry
1978	North Carolina A&T	Gene Littles
1979	North Carolina A&T	Gene Littles
1980	Howard University	A.B. Williamson
1981	North Carolina A&T	Don Corbett

Year	School	Coach
1982	North Carolina A&T	Don Corbett
1983	North Carolina A&T	Don Corbett
1984	North Carolina A&T	Don Corbett

CIAA CHAMPIONS
(1950–1984)

Year	School	Coach
1950	North Carolina College	John McLendon
1951	Virginia Union	Tom Harris
1952	Virginia Union	Tom Harris
1953	Winston-Salem	Big House Gaines
1954	Virginia Union	Tom Harris
1955	Virginia Union	Tom Harris
1956	Maryland State	Nat Taylor
1957	Winston-Salem	Big House Gaines
1958	North Carolina A&T	Cal Irvin
1959	North Carolina A&T	Cal Irvin
1960	Winston-Salem	Big House Gaines
1961	Winston-Salem	Big House Gaines
1962	North Carolina A&T	Cal Irvin
1963	Winston-Salem	Big House Gaines
1964	North Carolina A&T	Cal Irvin
1965	Norfolk State	Ernie Fears
1966	Winston-Salem	Big House Gaines
1967	North Carolina A&T	Cal Irvin
1968	Norfolk State	Ernie Fears
1969	Elizabeth City	Bobby Vaughan
1970	Winston-Salem	Big House Gaines
1971	Norfolk State	Robert Smith
1972	Norfolk State	Robert Smith
1973	Fayetteville State	Thomas Reeves
1974	Norfolk State	Charles Christian
1975	Norfolk State	Charles Christian
1976	Norfolk State	Charles Christian
1977	Winston-Salem	Big House Gaines
1978	Norfolk State	Charles Christian
1979	Virginia Union	Dave Robbins
1980	Virginia Union	Dave Robbins
1981	Elizabeth City	Bobby Vaughan
1982	Hampton Institute	Hank Ford
1983	Hampton Institute	Hank Ford
1984	Norfolk State	Charles Christian

BLACK COLLEGE CONFERENCE WINNERS

	CIAA	SWAC	SIAC	EIAC	SCAC	MWAC
1916			Morehouse			
1917			Morehouse			
1918			Morehouse			
1919			Morehouse			
1920			Morehouse			
1921			Morehouse			
1922			Morehouse			
1923			Morehouse			
1924	Hampton		Morehouse			
1925	Hampton		Morehouse			
1926	Hampton		Morehouse			
1927	Hampton		Clark			
1928	Va. Seminary		Clark			
1929	Va. Seminary		M'house-Clark			
1930	Lincoln (Pa.)		Knoxville			
1931		Morgan State		Morris Brown		
1932	Morgan State		Morris Brown			
1933	Morgan State		Tuskegee			
1934	Howard		Tuskegee		Alcorn A & M	Wilberforce
1935	Howard		Alabama State		Alcorn A & M	Wilberforce
1936	Hampton		Alabama State		Alcorn A & M	Wilberforce
1937	N. Car. A & T		Morehouse		Alcorn A & M	Lincoln (Pa.)
1938	Va. State		Xavier		Alcorn A & M	W. Va. State
1939	Va. Union	Wiley	Clark		Alcorn A & M	W. Va. State
1940	*Va. Union	Bishop	Clark	Miner T.C.	Alcorn A & M	Kentucky State
1941		Bishop	Xavier	Fayetteville	Tougaloo	
1942		Langston	Fla. A & M		Tougaloo	
1943		Southern	S. Car. State		M.I. College	
1944		Langston	Tuskegee		M.I. College	
1945		Langston	Fla. A & M		S. Christian	

[1]The asterisk refers to a contested title. Va. Union says it won the CIAA title, but the CIAA refused to award it to them because they played against a professional team.

BLACK PLAYERS AT WHITE COLLEGES
(1920–1946)

Name	Year	College
Maynard Garner	1920–21	Hamilton
John H. Johnson	1920–21	Columbia U.
Ralph Bunche	1921–22	UCLA
Ross Owens	1923	South Dakota St.
Charles Drew	1923–25	Amherst
Ernie Page	1924–26	Western Illinois
George Gregory	1927–31	Columbia
James Barnes	1928–30	Oberlin
Sam Barnes	1928–30	Oberlin
DL:*Horace Johnson	1936–38	Dakota College
Bobby Yancey	1937	Boston U.
Ben Franklin	1937	Boston U.
Lawrence Bleach	1937	Detroit U.
William "Dolly" King	1937–39	Long Island U.
Frank "Doc" Kelker	1938–40	Western Reserve
Jim Coward	1938–41	Brooklyn College
Jackie Robinson	1939–41	UCLA
William Sidat-Singh	1939–41	Syracuse
Sonny Jameson	1941–45	CCNY
Ed Younger	1942–44	Long Island U.
Dick Wilkins	1942–44	Oregon
Clifton Mobley	1942–43	Wayne State
Jay Swift	1943–45	Yale
Arthur Wilson	1944–46	Princeton

ALL-CENTRAL INTERCOLLEGIATE ATHLETIC ASSOCIATION BASKETBALL TEAMS (1954–1984)

Year	Name	School
1954	Jones, Samuel	North Carolina College
	Bacote, Ralph	St. Paul's College
	Harrison, Charles	North Carolina College
	Garrett, Ernest	Morgan State
	Burks, Clarence	St. Augustine's College
1955	Burks, Clarence	St. Augustine's College
	Sanders, Claude	Johnson C. Smith
	Gwinn, Stephen	Virginia Union
	Defares, Jack	Winston-Salem State
	Garrett, Ernest	Morgan State
1956	Syphax, John	Howard University
	Amos, Edwin	Hampton Institute
	Lloyd, Theophalius	Maryland State
	Defares, Jack	Winston-Salem State
	Smith, William	North Carolina A&T
	Harris, Thomas	Howard University
1957	Jones, Samuel	North Carolina Central
	Evans, Ronald	Fayetteville State
	Amos, Edwin	Hampton Institute
	Syphax, John	Howard University
	Defares, Jack	Winston-Salem State
1958	Garner, Ronald	Morgan State
	Sligh, James	North Carolina College
	Brightful, Charles	Morgan State
	John, Wilfred	Winston-Salem State
	Syphax, John	Howard University
	Howell, Joseph	North Carolina A&T
1959	Crenshaw, Joseph	Johnson C. Smith
	Trader, Nathaniel	Hampton Institute
	Bell, Carlton	North Carolina College

Year	Name	School	Year	Name	School
	Hill, Cleo	Winston-Salem State		Mitchell, Ira	Shaw University
	Howell, Joseph	North Carolina A&T		Cunningham, Tom	Winston-Salem State
1960	Spraggins, Warren	Virginia Union		Manning, Theodore	North Carolina College
	Attles, Alvin	North Carolina A&T		Ridgill, Howard	Winston-Salem State
	Simmons, Samuel	Virginia State		Stubbins, Gary	Elizabeth City State
	Johnson, Harold	Morgan State		Pitts, Richard	Norfolk State
	Hill, Cleo	Winston-Salem	1967	Monroe, Earl	Winston-Salem State
1961	Jackson, Jackie	Virginia Union		Davis, Lee	North Carolina College
	Ward, Walter	Hampton Institute		Lewis, Frederick	Elizabeth City State
	Hancock, Larry	Howard University		Reid, James	Winston-Salem State
	Hill, Cleo	Winston-Salem State		Randolph, Reginald	Johnson C. Smith
	Spraggins, Warren	Virginia Union		Horton, Ronald	Delaware State
1962	Trotman, Marvin	Elizabeth City State		Campbell, Ted	North Carolina A&T
	Foree, George	Winston-Salem State		Stubbins, Gary	Elizabeth City State
	Johnson, Harold	Morgan State		Davis, Michael	Virginia Union
	Williams, Jesse	Maryland State		Grant, James	Norfolk State
	Hester, James	Johnson C. Smith	1968	Looney, Rodney	Virginia State
1963	Neal, Fred	Johnson C. Smith		Dandridge, Robert	Norfolk State
	Stephens, Frank	Virginia Union		Smith, Oscar	Elizabeth City State
	Blount, Theodore	Winston-Salem State		Horton, Ronald	Delaware State
	Brock, Ernest	Virginia State		English, William	Winston-Salem State
	Glover, Richard	Winston-Salem State		Kirkland, Richard	Norfolk State
1964	Parker, Joseph	North Carolina College		Smiley, Eugene	Winston-Salem State
	Blount, Theodore	Winston-Salem State		Davis, Lee	North Carolina Central
	Bibby, Fred	Fayetteville State		Lewis, Frederick	Elizabeth City State
	Williams, Edward	Maryland State		Davis, Michael	Virginia Union
	McHartley, Maurice	North Carolina A&T	1969	Monroe, William	Fayetteville State
	Curry, Willie	Winston-Salem State		Bonaparte, Charles	Norfolk State
	Brock, Ernest	Virginia State		Walker, Vernon	North Carolina A&T
	Jackson, James	North Carolina A&T		Cherry, Daryl	North Carolina A&T
	Williams, Edward	Maryland State		Ford, Jake	Maryland State
	Davis, Warren	North Carolina A&T		Dandridge, Robert	Norfolk State
1965	Mulcare, Irving	North Carolina A&T		Pridgen, Joseph	North Carolina College
	Blount, Theodore	Winston-Salem State		Oliver, Israel	Elizabeth City State
	Morris, John	Norfolk State		English, William	Winston-Salem State
	Manning, Theodore	North Carolina College		Davis, Michael	Virginia Union
	Monroe, Earl	Winston-Salem State	1970	Utley, Kelly	Shaw University
	Turk, James	Morgan State		Butts, Robert	Johnson C. Smith
	Todd, Richard	Elizabeth City State		Gale, Michael	Elizabeth City State
	Mulcare, Irving	North Carolina A&T		Ford, Jake	Maryland State
	Turner, Charles	Johnson C. Smith		McCrimmon, Ron	North Carolina Central
	Pitts, Richard	Norfolk State		Green, Michael	St. Paul's College
1966	Monroe, Earl	Winston-Salem State		Williams, Donald	Winston-Salem State
	Rue, Al	Delaware State		Oliver, Israel	Elizabeth City State
	Grant, James	Norfolk State		Morgan, James	Maryland State
	Todd, Richard	Elizabeth City State		McKinney, Johnny	Norfolk State

Year	Name	School	Year	Name	School
1971	Sneed, Michael	Fayetteville State		Carrington, Gregory	Virginia Union
	Prichett, Curtis	St. Augustine's College		Burns, Melvin	Norfolk State
	Smith, Sandy	Winston-Salem State		Cunningham, Eugene	Norfolk State
	Austin, Elmer	North Carolina A&T		Cooper, George	Johnson C. Smith
	Butts, Robert	Johnson C. Smith		Roberts, Donnie	St. Paul's College
	Harris, William	North Carolina A&T		Paulin, Thomas	Winston-Salem State
	Jones, Leroy	Norfolk State		Carr, Charles	Elizabeth City State
	Utley, Kelly	Shaw University		Hamilton, Jerry	Livingstone College
	Peele, Rudolph	Norfolk State	1976	Cozart, William	St. Paul's College
	Haskins, Raymond	Shaw University		Helton, Donald	Winston-Salem State
	Leggett, Redden	North Carolina Central		Lewis, Robert	Johnson C. Smith
	Gale, Michael	Elizabeth City State		Paulin, Thomas	Winston-Salem State
1972	Williams, Earl	Winston, Salem State		Cunningham, Eugene	Norfolk State
	Peele, Rudolph	Norfolk State		Epps, Raymond	Norfolk State
	Wilson, Ronald	Norfolk State		Bell, Jerome	Virginia State
	Sneed, Michael	Fayetteville State		Tisdol, Doward	Virginia State
	Carmichael, Len	Elizabeth City State		Roberts, Donnie	St. Paul's College
	Haskins, Raymond	Shaw University		Terry, Carlos	Winston-Salem State
	Pritchett, Curtis	St. Augustine's College	1977	Tisdol, Doward	Virginia State
	Johnson, Linwood	Virginia State		Barrows, John	Fayetteville State
	Jones, Leroy	Norfolk State		Entzminger, Herbert	Johnson C. Smith
	Smith, Sandy	Winston-Salem State		Payne, Marvin	Hampton Institute
1973	Youngblood, Willie	Hampton Institute		Blue, Thomas	Elizabeth City State
	Agee, Daniel	Shaw University		Epps, Raymond	Norfolk State
	Cogdill, Alton	Fayetteville State		Best, Tyrone	Hampton Institute
	Hunter, Ralph	Virginia Union		Lewis, Curvan	Virginia Union
	Johnson, Linwood	Virginia State		Terry, Carlos	Winston-Salem State
	Jones, Leroy	Norfolk State		Wilkerson, Jesse	Norfolk State
	Chavious, Arthur	Winston-Salem State		Powell, Sean	St. Augustine's College
	Williams, Earl	Winston-Salem State		Cozart, William	St. Paul's College
	Windley, Glen	Elizabeth City State	1978	Mayhorn, Rick	Hampton Institute
	Wilson, Ronald	Norfolk State		Threatt, Tony	Hampton Institute
	Hazley, Andrew	Virginia Union		Evans, Kenny	Norfolk State
1974	Cunningham, Eugene	Norfolk State		Entzminger, Herbert	Johnson C. Smith
	Britt, Wayne	Hampton Institute		Gaines, Reginald	Winston-Salem State
	Cooper, George	Johnson C. Smith		Proctor, Francis	Johnson C. Smith
	Hamilton, Jerry	Livingstone College		Robinson, Michael	Winston-Salem State
	Mitchell, Roosevelt	Norfolk State		Isabelle, Robert	Norfolk State
	Richardson, Andrew	Shaw University		Terry, Carlos	Winston-Salem State
	Williams, Earl	Winston-Salem State		Tolliver, Keith	Hampton Institute
	Kitt, Harold	Winston-Salem State	1979	Gaskins, Arthur	Elizabeth City State
	Johnson, Linwood	Virginia State		Evans, Kenneth	Norfolk State
	Windley, Glen	Elizabeth City State		Jefferson, Edward	Fayetteville State
1975	Blue, Thomas	Elizabeth City State		Valentine, Keith	Virginia Union
	Tisdol, Doward	Virginia State		Hart, Jon	Livingstone College
	Moye, Joseph	Shaw University		Ware, Daniel	Virginia State

Year	Name	School
	Tibbs, William	Johnson C. Smith
	Harold, David	Winston-Salem State
	Procter, Francis	Johnson C. Smith
	Gaines, Reginald	Winston-Salem State
	Payne, Marvin	Hampton Institute
	Mahorn, Rick	Hampton Institute
1980	Holmes, Larry	Virginia Union
	Robinson, Michael	Winston-Salem State
	Evans, Kenneth	Norfolk State
	Gaskins, Arthur	Elizabeth City State
	Oliver, Larcell	Johnson C. Smith
	Procter, Francis	Johnson C. Smith
	Cooper, William	St. Augustine's College
	Lily, Derwin	Virginia Union
	Jackson, Gregory	St. Paul's College
	Mahorn, Rick	Hampton Institute
	Gaines, Reginald	Winston-Salem State
	Tibbs, Terry	Norfolk State
	Bishop, John	North Carolina Central
	Warwick, Daryl	Hampton Institute
	Stith, Darrell	Virginia State
	Pope, David	Norfolk State
1981	Mims, Steve	Fayetteville State
	Norman, Julius	Virginia State
	Oliver, Larcell	Johnson C. Smith
	Lewis, Bernard	St. Paul's College
	Jackson, Gregory	St. Paul's College
	Boggan, Anthony	St. Augustine's College
	Flores, Phil	Johnson C. Smith
1982	Washington, Anthony	Hampton Institute
	Davis, Antonio	Livingstone's College
	McNeil, Bonny	Fayetteville State
	Stuckey, Sammy	Shaw University
	Greene, Therman	Winston-Salem State
	Bland, Pierce	Elizabeth City State
	Carroll, Donald	St. Augustine's College
	Oakley, Charles	Virginia Union
	Pope, David	Norfolk State
	Norman, Julius	Virginia State
	Oliver, Larcell	Johnson C. Smith
	Tibbs, William	Johnson C. Smith
1983	Pope, David	Norfolk State
	Washington, Anthony	Hampton Institute
	Hines, Gregory	Hampton Institute
	Binlon, David	North Carolina Central
	Oakley, Charles	Virginia Union

Year	Name	School
1984	McGrudder, Roosevelt	Johnson C. Smith
	Pope, David	Norfolk State
	Tally, Ralph	Norfolk State
	Russell, Troy	Winston-Salem State
	Francis, Randy	St. Augustine's College
	Lacy, David	Shaw University
	Bell, Charles	St. Paul's College
	Rogers, Anthony	St. Augustine's College
	Person, William	Fayetteville State
	Miller, Cedric	Hampton Institute
	Murphy, Charles	North Carolina Central
	Oakley, Charles	Virginia Union

ALL-SOUTHWESTERN ATHLETIC CONFERENCE BASKETBALL TEAMS (1958–1981)

Year	Name	School
1958	***First Team***	
	Taylor, Willie	Texas Southern
	Bobbitt, Robert	Texas Southern
	Hill, Roosevelt	Southern University
	Grimes, Harold	Prairie View A&M
	Swain, Ben	Texas Southern
	Second Team	
	Groce, Luther	Texas College
	Paul, Frank	Southern University
	Chatam, E.C.	Arkansas AM&N
	Hudson, Odell	Texas College
	Hayes, Ego	Southern Unviersity
1959	***First Team***	
	Beatty, Zelmo	Prairie View A&M
	Buckner, Cleveland	Jackson State
	Barr, Jerry	Grambling State
	Hooper, James	Grambling State
	Taylor, Willie	Texas Southern
	Second Team	
	Brackens, Harold	Prairie View A&M
	Willis, Howard	Grambling State
	Harper, Charles	Wiley College
	Grimes, Harold	Prairie View A&M
	Maura, Fred	Texas Southern
	Hardnett, Charles	Grambling State
1960	***First Team***	
	Tippett, Rex	Grambling State

Year	Name	School
	Buckner, Cleveland	Jackson State
	Mack Allen, James	Arkansas AM&N
	Bond, Louis	Southern University
	Beatty, Zelmo	Prairie View AM&N
	Second Team	
	Barfield, James	Jackson State
	Hardnett, Charles	Grambling State
	Thomas, Willie	Southern University
	Lackey, Cornell	Prairie View A&M
	Hayes, Ego	Southern University
1961	**First Team**	
	Hardnett, Charles	Grambling State
	Reed, Willis	Grambling State
	Tippett, Rex	Grambling State
	Bond, Louis	Southern, University
	Mack Allen, James	Arkansas AM&N
1962	**First Team**	
	Reed, Willis	Grambling State
	Hardnett, Charles	Grambling State
	Love, Robert	Southern University
	Beatty, Zelmo	Prairie View A&M
	Bond, Louis	Southern, University
	Mack Allen, James	Arkansas AM&N
1963	**First Team**	
	Frazier, Wilbur	Grambling State
	Reed, Willis	Grambling State
	Love, Robert	Southern University
	West, Hershell	Grambling State
	Mack Allen, James	Arkansas, AM&N
1964	**First Team**	
	Love, Robert	Southern University
	Frazier, Wilbur	Grambling State
	Yarborough, Jerry	Jackson State
	Mack Allen, James	Arkansas AM&N
	Reed, Willis	Grambling State
	Second Team	
	Boatwright, Homer	Southern University
	Leflore, Lyvonne	Jackson State
	Comeaux, John	Grambling State
	Bevins, Harold	Arkansas AM&N
	Hayes, Ron	Southern University
	Benton, James	Jackson State
1965	**First Team**	
	Frazier, Wilbur	Grambling State
	Love, Robert	Southern University

Year	Name	School
	Yarborough, Jerry	Jackson State
	Comeaux, John	Grambling State
	Richardson, Don	Arkansas AM&N
	Second Team	
	Leflore, Lyvonne	Jackson State
	Richardson, Sam	Wiley College
	Bevins, Harold	Arkansas AM&N
	Hayes, Ron	Southern University
	Allen, Robert	Arkansas AM&N
1966	**First Team**	
	Comeaux, John	Grambling State
	Manning, Ed	Jackson State
	Ned, Walter	Alcorn State
1966	**Second Team**	
	Jones, James	Grambling State
	Bingham, Charles	Jackson State
1967	**First Team**	
	Allen, Robert	Arkansas AM&N
	Manning, Ed	Jackson State
	Jones, James	Grambling State
	Davis, Howard	Grambling State
	Wilson, Jasper	Southern University
	Second Team	
	Norwood, Willie	Alcorn State
	Kelly, James	Alcorn State
	Flowers, Robert	Alcorn State
	Long, Ron	Southern University
	Allen, James	Texas Southern
1968	**First Team**	
	Norwood, Willie	Alcorn State
	Flowers, Robert	Alcorn State
	Kelly, James	Alcorn State
	Wilson, James	Arkansas AM&N
	Wilson, Jasper	Southern University
1969	**First Team**	
	Norwood, Willie	Alcorn State
	Warner, Cornell	Jackson State
	Hilton, Fred	Grambling State
	Keye, Julius	Alcorn State
	Hart, Herb	Texas Southern
1970	**First Team**	
	Wyatt, Levi	Alcorn State
	Herdon, Lou	Jackson State
	Hart, Herb	Texas Southern

Year	Name	School	Year	Name	School
	Shinall, John	Jackson State	1976	*First Team*	
	Warner, Cornell	Jackson State		Robinson, Dellie	Alcorn State
	Sing, Sam	Alcorn State		Short, Purvis	Jackson State
1971	*First Team*			Davis, Gaylord	Texas Southern
	Wyatt, Levi	Alcorn State		Saunders, Frankie	Southern University
	Brown, Marvin	Jackson State		Barrow, Ron	Southern University
	Hilton, Fred	Grambling State		Wright, Larry	Grambling State
	Aldridge, Ellis	Texas Southern	1977	*First Team*	
	Warner, Cornell	Jackson State		Sykes, Terry	Grambling State
	Second Team			Short, Purvis	Jackson State
	Bateman, Glen	Alcorn State		Jackson, Marvin	Prairie View A&M
	Kincaid, McKincey	Jakcson State		Williams, Lawrence	Texas Southern
	Mason, Floyd	Alcorn State		Bradley, Alonzo	Texas Southern
	Cannon, Emanuel	Grambling State		Green, Tom	Southern University
	Golden, Russell	Jackson State		Monroe, Alfredo	Alcorn State
1972	*First Team*		1978	*First Team*	
	James, Aaron	Grambling State		Saunders, Frank	Southern University
	Wyatt, Levi	Alcorn State		Short, Purvis	Jackson State
	McTier, Larry	Southern University		Horton, James	Alcorn State
	Ford, Charles	Texas Southern		Norris, Sylvester	Jackson State
	Aldridge, Ellis	Texas Southern		Lemelle, Martin	Grambling State
	Hart, Willie	Grambling State	1979	*First Team*	
1973	*First Team*			Murphy, Tony	Southern University
	James, Aaron	Grambling State		Garrett, Lionel	Southern Unviersity
	Keyes, Alex	Southern University		Norris, Audie	Jackson State
	Frazier, Andrew	Southern University		Davis, Collie	Alcorn State
	Short, Eugene	Jackson State		Lemelle, Martin	Grambling State
	Tatum, Andrew	Alcorn State		Smith, Larry	Alcorn State
1974	*First Team*			*Second Team*	
	Jones, Glendale	Jackson State		Walsh, Robert	Jackson State
	Short, Eugene	Jackson State		Hagan, Larry	Prairie View A&M
	Robinson, Calvin	Mississippi Valley State		Tidwell, Gary	Grambling State
	Barrow, Ron	Southern University		Williams, Ernest	Mississippi Valley State
	James, Aaron	Grambling State		Blue, Fred	Texas Southern
1975	*First Team*			Horton, James	Alcorn State
	Barrow, Ron	Southern University	1980	*First Team*	
	Milton, Alfred	Alcorn State		Smith, Larry	Alcorn State
	Ward, Henry	Jackson State		Norris, Audie	Jackson State
	Wright, Larry	Grambling State		Murphy, Tony	Southern University
	Robinson, Dellie	Alcorn State		Lemelle, Martin	Grambling State
	Jones, Glendale	Jackson State		Kelly, Harry	Texas Southern

Year	Name	School
	Second Team	
	Shavers, Doc	Jackson State
	Reed, Tony	Mississippi Valley State
	Williams, Robert	Grambling State
	Baker, Eddie	Alcorn State
	Bell, E.J.	Alcorn State
	Wyatt, Clinton	Alcorn State
1981	**First Team**	
	Jackson, Alvin	Southern University
	Kelly, Harry	Texas Southern

Year	Name	School
	Williams, Robert	Grambling State
	Reed, Tony	Mississippi Valley State
	Irving, Albert	Alcorn State
	Loder, Kevin	Alabama State
	Second Team	
	Alexander, Dwight	Alcorn State
	Shavers, Doc	Jackson State
	Norris, Audie	Jackson State
	Simpson, Ken	Grambling State
	Baker, Eddie	Alcorn State

TENNIS

AMERICAN TENNIS ASSOCIATION CHAMPIONSHIP ROLL

Men's Singles

Year	Place Played	Names
1917	Baltimore	Tally Holmes
1918	New York	Tally Holmes
1919	New York	Sylvester Smith
1920	New York	B. M. Clark
1921	Washington	Tally Holmes
1922	Philadelphia	Edgar G. Brown
1923	Chicago	Edgar G. Brown
1924	Baltimore	Tally Holmes
1925	Bordentown	Theodore Thompson
1926	St. Louis	Eyre Saitch
1927	Hampton	Theodore Thompson
1928	Bordentown	Edgar G. Brown

Year	Place Played	Names
1929	Bordentown	Edgar G. Brown
1930	Indianapolis	Douglas Turner
1931	Tuskegee	Reginald Weir
1932	Shady Rest	Reginald Weir
1933	Hampton	Reginald Weir
1934	Lincoln	Nathaniel Jackson
1935	Institute	Franklin Jackson
1936	Wilberforce	Lloyd Scott
1937	Tuskegee	Reginald Weir
1938	Lincoln	Franklin Jackson
1939	Hampton	Jimmie McDaniel
1940	Wilberforce	Jimmie McDaniel
1941	Tuskegee	Jimmie McDaniel
1942	Lincoln	Reginald Weir
1944	New York	Lloyd Scott
1945	New York	Lloyd Scott

Note: Only in rare instances were tournaments held in 1943. Thus, most of the following statistics do not include entries for that year.

Year	Place Played	Names
1946	Wilberforce	Jimmie McDaniel
1947	Tuskegee	George Stewart
1948	Orangeburg	George Stewart
1949	Wilberforce	Unfinished*
1950	Wilberforce	Oscar Johnson
1951	Wilberforce	George Stewart
1952	Wilberforce	George Stewart
1953	Daytona Beach	George Stewart
1954	Daytona Beach	Earthna Jacquet
1955	Wilberforce	Robert Ryland
1956	Wilberforce	Robert Ryland
1957	Wilberforce	George Stewart
1958	Wilberforce	Wilbert Davis
1959	Wilberforce	Wilbert Davis
1960	Hampton	Arthur Ashe, Jr.
1961	Hampton	Arthur Ashe, Jr.
1962	Wilberforce	Arthur Ashe, Jr.
1963	Wilberforce	Wilbert Davis
1964	Wilberforce	George Stewart
1965	Wilberforce	Luis Glass
1966	Wilberforce	Wilbert Davis
1967	Wilberforce	Wilbert Davis
1968	Wilberforce	Robert Binns
1969	St. Louis	Marty Gool
1970	St. Louis	Gene Fluri
1971	St. Louis	John Wilkerson
1972	Boston	Horace Reid
1973	Boston	Arthur Carrington
1974	Washington, DC	R. D. Guedes
1975	San Diego	Benny Sims
1976	New Orleans	Terrance Jackson
1977	New Orleans	Terrance Jackson
1978	Princeton	Rodney Harmon
1979	Atlanta	Warick Jones
1980	Atlanta	Kelvin Belcher
1981	Detroit	Kelvin Belcher
1982	San Diego	Warrick Jones
1983	Boston	Adrian Clark
1984	Atlanta	Young Kwon
1985	Washington, DC	Phillip Williamson

Men's (35) Junior Veterans Singles

Year	Place Played	Names
1970	St. Louis	Ronald Charity
1971	St. Louis	Clyde C. Freeman
1972	Boston	Norman Fitz

Year	Place Played	Names
1973	Boston	Walter Gundlach
1974	Washington, DC	Norman Fitz
1975	San Diego	John Wilkerson
1976	New Orleans	John Wilkerson
1977	New Orleans	Thomas Jefferson
1978	Princeton	John Wilkerson
1979	Atlanta	Willis Thomas, Jr.
1980	Atlanta	Willis Thomas, Jr.
1981	Detroit	John Wilkerson
1982	San Diego	Bill Scott
1983	Boston	Lee Townsel
1984	Atlanta	Ollen A. Dupree
1985	Washington, DC	John Quick

Men's 45 Senior Singles

Year	Place Played	Names
1933	Hampton	J. P. Wilkinson
1934	Lincoln	Fred Johnson
1935	Institute	C. W. Furlonge
1936	Wilberforce	C. W. Furlonge
1937	Tuskegee	Fred Johnson
1938	Lincoln	Fred Johnson
1939	Hampton	John B. Garrett
1940	Wilberforce	John B. Garrett
1941	Tuskegee	John B. Garrett
1942	Lincoln	John B. Garrett
1944	New York	John B. Garrett
1945	New York	John B. Garrett
1946	Wilberforce	John B. Garrett
1947	Tuskegee	John B. Garrett
1948	Orangeburg	John B. Garrett
1949	Wilberforce	John B. Garrett
1950	Wilberforce	Henry Graham
1951	Wilberforce	Walter R. Thomas
1952	Wilberforce	Wilber A. Clarke
1953	Daytona Beach	Maceo Hill
1954	Daytona Beach	Maceo Hill
1955	Wilberforce	Walter Onque
1956	Wilberforce	Ronald Fieulleteau
1957	Wilberforce	Edgar Lee
1958	Wilberforce	Edgar Lee
1959	Wilberforce	Edgar Lee
1960	Hampton	Edgar Lee
1961	Hampton	Edgar Lee
1962	Wilberforce	Edgar Lee
1963	Wilberforce	Edward Van Beverhoudt

Year	Placed Played	Names
1964	Wilberforce	Edgar Lee
1965	Wilberforce	Edgar Lee
1966	Wilberforce	Col. William Campbell
1967	Wilberforce	Louis Graves
1968	Wilberforce	Robert Miller
1969	St. Louis	Edgar Lee
1970	St. Louis	Ralph Legall
1971	St. Louis	Ronald Fieulleteau
1972	Boston	Robert Miller
1973	Boston	Robert Miller
1974	Washington, DC	Ralph Legall
1975	San Diego	Melvin Lewis
1976	New Orleans	Ronald Charity
1977	New Orleans	Chris Scott
1978	Princeton	Billy Davis
1979	Atlanta	Orlando Cummings
1980	Atlanta	Orlando Cummings
1981	Detroit	Norman Fitz
1982	San Diego	George Herring
1983	Boston	George Herring
1984	Atlanta	Alberto Loney
1985	Washington, DC	Daniel Hoskins

Men's 50 Senior Singles

Year	Place Played	Names
1978	Princeton	Joseph Buckhalter
1979	Atlanta	Willie Young
1980	Atlanta	Willie Young
1981	Detroit	Jack Novick
1982	San Diego	Milvin Lewis
1983	Boston	Ronald Charity
1984	Atlanta	Ronald Charity
1985	Washington, DC	Bernard Cross

Men's 55 Senior Singles

Year	Place Played	Names
1972	Boston	Edgar Lee
1973	—	—
1974	Washington, DC	Rex Matthews
1975	San Diego	Ronald Fieulleteau
1976	New Orleans	Ronald Fieulleteau
1977	New Orleans	Ronald Fieulleteau

Year	Place Played	Names
1978	Princeton	Robert Ryland
1979	Atlanta	Ronald Fieulleteau
1980	Atlanta	Ronald Fieulleteau
1981	Detroit	William Ray
1982	San Diego	Stan Potts
1983	Boston	Robert Miller
1984	Atlanta	Jack Novick
1985	Washington, DC	Riddick Van

Men's 60 and Over Senior Singles

Year	Place Played	Names
1978	Princeton	Marion Rice
1979	Atlanta	Nehemiah Atkinson
1980	Atlanta	Nehemiah Atkinson
1981	Detroit	Ernest Greene
1982	San Diego	Ernest Greene
1983	Boston	Ernest Greene
1984	Atlanta	George Simkins
1985	Washington, DC	George Simkins

Men's 65 Senior Singles—New Event

Year	Place Played	Names
1984	Atlanta	Nehemiah Atkinson
1985	Washington, DC	Marion Rice

Women's Singles

Year	Place Played	Names
1917	Baltimore	Lucy Slowe
1918	New York	M. Rae
1919	New York	M. Rae
1920	New York	M. Rae
1921	Washington, DC	Lucy Slowe
1922	Philadelphia	Isadore Channels
1923	Chicago	Isadore Channels
1924	Baltimore	Isadore Channels
1925	Bordentown	Lulu Ballard
1926	St. Louis	Isadore Channels
1927	Hampton	Lulu Ballard
1928	Bordentown	Lulu Ballard
1929	Bordentown	Ora Washington
1930	Indianapolis	Ora Washington

Year	Place Played	Names
1931	Tuskegee	Ora Washington
1932	Shady Rest	Ora Washington
1933	Hampton	Ora Washington
1934	Lincoln	Ora Washington
1935	Institute	Ora Washington
1936	Wilberforce	Lulu Ballard
1937	Tuskegee	Ora Washington
1938	Lincoln	Flora Lomax
1939	Hampton	Flora Lomax
1940	Wilberforce	Agnes Lawson
1941	Tuskegee	Flora Lomax
1942	Lincoln	FLora Lomax
1944	New York	Roumania Peters
1945	New York	Kathryn Irvis
1946	Wilberforce	Roumania Peters
1947	Tuskegee	Althea Gibson
1948	Orangeburg	Althea Gibson
1949	Wilberforce	Althea Gibson
1950	Wilberforce	Althea Gibson
1951	Wilberforce	Althea Gibson
1953	Daytona Beach	Althea Gibson
1954	Daytona Beach	Althea Gibson
1955	Wilberforce	Althea Gibson
1956	Wilberforce	Althea Gibson
1957	Wilberforce	Gwendolyn McEvans
1958	Wilberforce	Mary E. Fine
1959	Wilberforce	Gwendolyn McEvans
1960	Hampton	Mimi Kanarek
1961	Hampton	Carolyn Williams
1962	Wilberforce	Carolyn Liguori
1963	Wilberforce	Ginger Pfiefer
1964	Wilberforce	Bonnie Logan
1965	Wilberforce	Bonnie Logan
1966	Wilberforce	Bonnie Logan
1967	Wilberforce	Bonnie Logan
1968	Wilberforce	Bonnie Logan
1969	St. Louis	Bonnie Logan
1970	St. Louis	Bonnie Logan
1971	St. Louis	Bessie Stockard
1972	Boston	Lorraine Bryant
1973	Boston	Mimi Kanarek
1974	Washington, DC	Jean Burnett
1975	San Diego	Diane Morrison
1976	New Orleans	Kim Sands

Year	Place Played	Names
1977	New Orleans	Leslie Allen
1978	Princeton	Joann Jacobs
1979	Atlanta	Zina Garrison
1980	Atlanta	Zina Garrison
1981	Detroit	Lori McNeil
1982	San Diego	Lucy Bacerra
1983	Boston	Lisa DeAngeles
1984	Atlanta	Shandra Livingston
1985	Washington, DC	Kyle Copeland

Women's 35 Junior Veterans Singles

Year	Place Played	Names
1974	Washington, DC	Jerri Traylor
1975	San Diego	Angela Grant
1976	New Orleans	Angela Grant
1977	—	—
1978	Princeton	Pat Stewart
1979	Atlanta	Angela Grant
1980	Atlanta	Angela Grant
1981	Detroit	Jean Burnett
1982	San Diego	Ann Ross Eaton
1983	Boston	Ann Ross Eaton
1984	Atlanta	Sallie Middleton
1985	Washington, DC	Ann Ross Eaton

Women's 45 Senior Singles—New Event

Year	Place Played	Names
1984	Atlanta	Angela Grant
1985	Washington, DC	Queen Patterson

Women's 50 Senior Singles

Year	Place Played	Names
1947	Tuskegee	Blanche Winston
1948	Orangeburg	Eleese Thornton
1949	Wilberforce	Eleese Thornton
1950	Wilberforce	Jane Hudlin
1951	Wilberforce	Eleese Thornton
1952	Wilberforce	Jane Hudlin
1953	Daytona Beach	Jane Hudlin
1954	Daytona Beach	Olga Bethel
1955	Wilberforce	Eleese Thornton
1956	Wilberforce	Eleese Thornton
1957	Wilberforce	Eleese Thornton
1958	Wilberforce	Flora Bray
1959	Wilberforce	Flora Bray

Year	Place Played	Names
1960	Hampton	Flora Bray
1961	Hampton	Helen Watanable
1962	Wilberforce	Helen Watanable
1963	Wilberforce	Helen Watanable
1964	Wilberforce	HElen Watanable
1965	Wilberforce	Helen Watanable
1966	Wilberforce	Doris Harrison
1967	Wilberforce	Doris Harrison
1968	Wilberforce	Dorothy Kornegay
1969	St. Louis	Dorothy Kornegay
1970	St. Louis	Dorothy Kornegay
1971	St. Louis	Alphoniza Edwards
1972	Boston	Kay Evans
1973	Boston	Alphonzia Edwards
1974	—	—
1975	San Diego	Alphonzia Edwards
1976	New Orleans	Jean Richardson
1977	New Orleans	Jean Richardson
1978	Princeton	Jean Richardson
1979	Atlanta	Jean Richardson
1980	Atlanta	Pat Stewart
1981	Detroit	Jean Richardson
1982	San Diego	Pat Stewart
1983	Boston	Virginia Glass
1984	Atlanta	Ann Givins
1985	Washington, DC	Bessie Stockard

Men's Doubles

Year	Place Played	Names
1917	Baltimore	Tally Holmes & Sylvester Smith
1918	New York	D. Monroe & Percy Richardson
1919	New York	Tally Holmes & Sylvester Smith
1920	New York	E. K. Jones & B. M. Clark
1921	Washington, DC	Tally Holmes & Sylvester Smith
1922	Philadelphia	Tally Holmes & Sylvester Smith
1923	Chicago	John L. McGriff, Sr. & Ellwood D. Downing
1924	Baltimore	Tally Holmes & Theodore Thompson

Year	Place Played	Names
1925	Bordentown	Tally Holmes & Theodore Thompson
1926	St. Louis	Eyre Saitch & Theodore Thompson
1927	Hampton	Tally Holmes & Theodore Thompson
1928	Bordentown	Eyre Saitch & Sylvester Smith
1929	Bordentown	Eyre Saitch & Sylvester Smith
1930	Indianapolis	John L. McGriff, Sr. & Ellwood D. Downing
1931	Tuskegee	Nathaniel Jackson & Franklin Jackson
1932	Shady Rest	Richard Hudlin & Douglas Turner
1933	Hampton	Nathaniel Jackson & Franklin Jackson
1934	Lincoln	Nathaniel Jackson & Franklin Jackson
1935	Institute	Nathaniel Jackson & Franklin Jackson
1936	Wilberforce	Nathaniel Jackson & Franklin Jackson
1937	Tuskegee	James Stocks & Thomas Walker
1938	Lincoln	Nathaniel Jackson & Franklin Jackson
1939	Hampton	Jimmie McDaniel & Richard Cohen
1940	Wilberforce	Clifford Russell & Howard Minnis
1941	Tuskegee	Jimmie McDaniel & Richard Cohen
1942	Lincoln	Clifford Russell & Howard Minnis
1944	New York	Ronald Fieulleteau & Howard Minnis
1945	New York	Lloyd Scott & Louis Graves
1946	Wilberforce	Jimmie McDaniel & James L. Stocks
1947	Tuskegee	John Chandler & Harold Mitchell
1948	Orangeburg	George Stewart & Hubert Eaton

Year	Place Played	Names	Year	Place Played	Names
1949	Wilberforce	George Stewart & Hubert Eaton	1974	Washington, DC	Bruce Foxworth & Roger Guedes
1950	Wilberforce	James Stocks & Oscar Johnson	1975	San Diego	M. Andrews & Lawrence King
1951	Wilberforce	George Stewart & Hubert Eaton	1976	New Orleans	Terrence Scott & T. Jackson
1952	Wilberforce	Jimmie McDaniel & Earthna Jacquet	1977	New Orleans	Marrell Harmon & Weldon Rogers
1953	Daytona Beach	Unfinished	1978	Princeton	Rodney Harmon & Marrell Harmon
1954	Daytona Beach	Earthna Jacquet & Wilbert Davis	1979	Atlanta	Melvin McCurley & O. Ongunrinde
1955	Wilberforce	Clyde Freeman & Harold Freeman	1980	Atlanta	Michael Delane & Greg Williams
1956	Wilberforce	George Stewart & Hubert Eaton	1981	Detroit	Kelvin Belcher & F. Otabar
1957	Wilberforce	George Stewart & John Chandler	1982	San Diego	Troy Collins & Angel Lopez
1958	Wilberforce	Wilbur Jenkins & Thomas Calhoun	1983	Boston	Godwin Emeh & M. Menezes
1959	Wilberforce	Jow Pierce & Shaw Emmons	1984	Atlanta	Kyle Anderson & Alex Diaz
1960	Hampton	Wilbur Jenkins & Thomas Calhoun	1985	Washington, DC	Franklin Hatchett & Mark Riley

Men's 35 Junior Veterans Doubles

Year	Place Played	Names	Year	Place Played	Names
1961	Hampton	Arthur Ashe & Ronald Charity	1972	Boston	Norman Fitz & Thomas Calhoun
1962	Wilberforce	Wilbert Davis & Robert Davis	1973	Boston	Norman Fitz & Vernon Morgan
1963	Wilberforce	Howard Minnie & William Monroe	1974	Washington, DC	Thomas Jefferson & C. Johnson
1964	Wilberforce	Luis Glass & Lenward Simpson	1975	San Diego	R. Bacon & J. Movido
1965	Wilberforce	Luis Glass & Lenward Simpson	1976	New Orleans	P. Gates & D. Hutson,ql
1966	Wilberforce	Arthur Carrington & John Mudd	1977	New Orleans	Thomas Jefferson & Al Hagan
1967	Wilberforce	Arthur Carrington & John Mudd	1978	Princeton	Willis Thomas, Jr. & Phillip Lucas
1968	Wilberforce	Marty Gool & Gregory Morton	1979	Atlanta	Phillip Lucas & Willie Thomas, Jr.
1969	St. Louis	Marty Gool & Gregory Morton	1980	Atlanta	Thomas Jefferson & Donald Bennett
1970	St. Louis	Gene Fluri & Tom Fluri	1981	Detroit	James Bland 7 Ollen Dupree
1971	St. Louis	William Heinbecker & Jerry Johnson	1982	San Diego	Jack Rathburn & Jim Kelly
1972	Boston	Unfinished	1983	Boston	James Bland & Ollen Dupree
1973	Boston	Shri Anadon & Luis Glass	1984	Atlanta	John quick & Melvin Pinn
			1985	Washington, DC	Eddie Davis & Fred Drilling

Men's 45 Senior Doubles

Year	Place Played	Names
1955	Wilberforce	C. Albert Dixon & Walter Thomas
1956	Wilberforce	Dudley Woodard & Maceo Hill
1957	Wilberforce	Edgar Lee & George Watson
1958	Wilberforce	Edgar Lee & George Watson
1959	Wilberforce	Dan Kean & John Chandler
1960	Hampton	Edgar Lee & John F. D Manns
1961	Hampton	Edgar Lee & John F. D. Manns
1962	Wilberforce	Edgar Lee & John F. D Manns
1963	Wilberforce	Edgar Lee & John F. D. Manns
1964	Wilberforce	Edgar Lee & John F. D. Manns
1965	Wilberforce	Edgar Lee & John F. D. Manns
1966	Wilberforce	Walter Onque & Ronald Fieulleteau
1967	Wilberforce	Edgar Lee & John F. D. Manns
1968	Wilberforce	Edgar Lee & John F. D. Manns
1969	St. Louis	Robert Ryland & Edward Van Beverhoudt
1970	St. Louis	Ralph Legall & Royal Madison
1971	St. Louis	Ralph Legall & Royal Madison
1972	Boston	Royal Madison & Nehemiah Atkinson
1973	Boston	Edgar Lee & John F. D. Manns
1974	Washington, DC	Edgar Lee & John F. D. Manns
1975	San Diego	R. Bowles & F. Simmons
1976	New Orleans	Edgar Lee & Ronald Charity
1977	New Orleans	Ralph Legall & Chris Scott
1978	Princeton	J. Buckhalter & C. Walker

Year	Place Played	Names
1979	Atlanta	Harold Freeman & Clyde Freeman
1980	Atlanta	Orlando Cummings & John Sample
1981	Detroit	Orlando Cummings & John Sample
1982	San Diego	Melvin Lewis & Frank Simmons
1983	Boston	Howard Bolling & Frank Simmons
1984	Atlanta	Dan Hoskins & Paul Gates
1985	Washington, DC	Lee Townsel & Paul Gates

Men's 55 Senior Doubles

Year	Place Played	Names
1980	Atlanta	NEhemiah Atkinson & Royal Madison
1981	Detroit	Nehemiah Atkinson & Royal Madison
1982	San Diego	Norman Appel & Stan Potts
1983	Boston	Robert Miller & Edgar Lee
1984	Atlanta	George Simkins & Frank Herberer
1985	Washington, DC	George Simkins & Frank Herberer

Women's Doubles

Year	Place Played	Names
1924	Baltimore	Isadore Channels & Emma Leonard
1925	Bordentown	Ora Washington & Lulu Ballard
1926	St. Louis	Ora Washington & Lulu Ballard
1927	Hampton	Ora Washington & Lulu Ballard
1928	Bordentown	Ora Washington & Lulu Ballard
1929	Bordentown	Ora Washington & Lulu Ballard
1930	Indianapolis	Ora Washington & Blanche Winston
1931	Tuskegee	Ora Washington & Blanche Winston
1932	Shady Rest	Ora Washington & Lulu Ballard
1933	Hampton	Ora Washington & Anita Grant

Year	Place Played	Names
1934	Lincoln	Ora Washington & Lulu Ballard
1935	Institute	Ora Washington & Lulu Ballard
1936	Wilberforce	Ora Washington & Lulu Ballard
1937	Tuskegee	Bertha Iassacs & Lilyan Spencer
1938	Lincoln	Margaret Peters & Roumania Peters
1939	Hampton	Margaret Peters & Roumania Peters
1940	Wilberforce	Margaret Peters & Roumania Peters
1941	Tuskegee	Margaret Peters & Roumania Peters
1942	Lincoln	Lillian Van Buren & Flora Lomax
1944	New York	Margaret Peters & Roumania Peters
1945	New York	Margaret Peters & Roumania Peters
1946	Wilberforce	Margaret Peters & Roumania Peters
1947	Tuskegee	Margaret Peters & Roumania Peters
1948	Orangeburg	Margaret Peters & Roumania Peters
1949	Wilberforce	Margaret Peters & Roumania Peters
1950	Wilberforce	Margaret Peters & Roumania Peters
1951	Wilberforce	Margaret Peters & Roumania Peters
1952	Wilberforce	Margaret Peters & Roumania Peters
1953	Daytona Beach	Margaret Peters & Roumania Peters
1954	Daytona Beach	Evelyn George & Ivy C. Ransey
1955	Wilberforce	Eva F. Bracy & Mary E. Fine
1956	Wilberforce	Angela Imala & Lorraine Williams
1957	Wilberforce	Eva. F. Bracy & Mary E. Fine

Year	Place Played	Names
1958	Wilberforce	Eva. F. Bracy & Mary E. Fine
1959	Wilberforce	Marlene Everson & Darnella Everson
1960	Hampton	Bessie A. Stockard & Carolyn Williams
1961	Hampton	Carolyn Williams & Marreline Faggett
1962	Wilberforce	Mimi Kanarek & Carolyn Liquori
1963	Wilberforce	Maimee Frye & Ginger Pfiefer
1964	Wilberforce	Sylvia Hooks & Bonnie Logan
1965	Wilberforce	Jean Richardson & Helen Watanable
1966	Wilberforce	Bonnie Logan & Bessie Stockard
1967	Wilberforce	Bessie Stockard & Sylvia Hooks
1968	Wilberforce	Bessie Stockard & Anne Koger
1969	St. Louis	Reuter & Beauchamp
1970	St. Louis	Reuter & Beauchamp
1971	St. Louis	Pamela Steinmetz & Bunny Wall
1972	Boston	Elaine Busch & Brenda Johnson
1973	Boston	Jean Burnett & Arvelia Meyers
1974	Washington, DC	Bessie Stockard & Barbara Faulkner
1975	San Diego	S. Dancy & Lisa Rapfogel
1976	New Orleans	Margo Tiff & Brenda Richards
1977	New Orleans	Karen Harden & Brenda Richards
1978	Princeton	Jean Burnett & Brenda Richards
1979	Atlanta	Carol Watson & Jean Burnett
1980	Atlanta	Zina Garrison & Lori McNeil
1981	Detroit	Zina Garrison & Lori McNeil

Year	Place Played	Names
1982	San Diego	Kathy Foxworth & Lori McNeil
1983	Boston	Joan Jackson & Renee Ralph
1984	Atlanta	Patricia Collins & Michelle Wreen
1985	Washington, DC	Ronita Elder & Helyn Edwards

Women's 35 Junior Veterans Doubles

Year	Place Played	Names
1977	New Orleans	Ruth Dupree & Bessie Stockard
1978	Princeton	Virginia Glass & Patricia Stewart
1979	Atlanta	Virginia Glass & Patricia Stewart
1980	Atlanta	Virginia Glass & Patricia Stewart
1981	Detroit	Angela Grant & Helen Watson
1982	San Diego	Chris Machado & Corrinne Fagerburg
1983	Boston	Ann Eaton & Sallie Middleton
1984	Atlanta	Ann Eaton & Sallie Middleton
1985	Washington, DC	Ann Eaton & Sallie Middleton

Women's 45 Senior Doubles

Year	Place Played	Names
1964	Wilberforce	Thelma Wells & Mary Radcliffe
1965	Wilberforce	Lena Walden & Anita Harris
1966	Wilberforce	Doris Harrison & Helen Watanable
1967	Wilberforce	Anita Harris & Doris Harrison
1968	Wilberforce	Anita Harris & Dorothy Kornegay
1969	St. Louis	Pratt & Zancy
1970	St. Louis	Zancy & Kolar
1971	St. Louis	Flora Bray & Alphonsia Edwards

Year	Place Played	Names
1972	Boston	Anita Harris & Dorothy Kornegay
1973	Boston	Flora Bray & Alphonsia Edwards
1974	Washington, DC	Alphonsia Edwards & Flora Bray
1975	San Diego	Alphonsia Edwards & Virginia Glass
1976	New Orleans	Virginia Glass & Alphonsia Edwards
1977	New Orleans	Jean Richardson & Eleese Thornton
1978	Princeton	Elaine Busch & Ella Simpson
1979	Atlanta	Elaine Busch & Ella Simpson
1980	Atlanta	Ann Givens & Helen Watson
1981	Detroit	Elaine Busch & Ruth Dupree
1982	San Diego	Virginia Glass & Patricia Stewart
1983	Boston	Elaine Busch & Ella Simpson
1984	Atlanta	Angela Grant & Helen Watson
1985	Washington, DC	Elaine Busch & Queen Patterson

Mixed Doubles

Year	Place Played	Names
1924	Baltimore	Nellie Nicholson & B. M. Rhetta
1925	Bordentown	C. O. Seames & L. C. Downing
1926	St. Louis	E. Robinson & E. Cole
1927	Hampton	Blanche Winston & Louis Jones
1928	Bordentown	Blanche Winston & W. A. Kean
1929	Bordentown	Anita Grant & O. B. Williams
1930	Indianapolis	Anita Grant & O. B. Williams
1931	Tuskegee	Anne Roberts & Theodore Thompson

Year	Place Played	Names	Year	Place Played	Names
1932	Shady Rest	Martha Davis & Henry Williams	1958	Wilberforce	Gwen McEvans & Clyde Freeman
1933	Hampton	Emma Leonard & C. O. Hilton	1959	Wilberforce	Gwen McEvans & Clyde Freeman
1934	Lincoln	Emma Leonard & C. O. Hilton	1960	Hampton	Elaine Busch & George Stewart
1935	—	—	1961	Hampton	Mimi Kanarek & Ernest Ingram
1936	—	—			
1937	Tuskegee	Flora Lomax & William H. Hall	1962	Wilberforce	Mimi Kanarek & Ernest Ingram
1938	Lincoln, PA	Lulu Ballard & Gerald Norman, Jr.	1963	Wilberforce	Lucy McEvans & Charles Berry
1939	Hampton	Ora Washington & Sylvester Smith	1964	Wilberforce	Bessie Stockard & Charles Berry
1940	Wilberforce	Flora Lomax & William H. Hall	1965	Wilberforce	Sylvia Hooks & William Morton, Jr.
1941	Tuskegee	Eoline Thornton & Harold Mitchell	1966	Wilberforce	Sylvia Hooks & William Morton, Jr.
1942	Lincoln, PA	Kathryn Jones & William E. Jones	1967	Wilberforce	Bonnie Logan & Lenward Simpson
1944	New York	Lillian Van Buren & Delbert Russell	1968	Wilberforce	Bonnie Logan & Lenward Simpson
1945	New York	Lillian Van Buren & Delbert Russell	1969	St. Louis	Bonnie Logan & Lenward Simpson
1946	Wilberforce	Ora Washington & George Stewart	1970	St. Louis	Bonnie Logan & Lenward Simpson
1947	Tuskegee	Ora Washington & George Stewart	1971	St. Louis	Beverly Hussell & Alberto Loney
1948	Orangeburg	Althea Gibson & R. Walter Johnson	1972	Boston	Lee Stavins & Chris Scott
1949	Wilberforce	Althea Gibson & R. Walter Johnson	1973	Boston	Ann Koger & Tyrone Mapp
			1974	Washington, DC	Ann Koger & Tyrone Mapp
1950	Wilberforce	Althea Gibson & R. Walter Johnson	1975	San Diego	R. Harris & D. Stewart
1951	Wilberforce	Mary Atta Fine & Leo Fine	1976	New Orleans	Marilyn Supeville & Jessie Holt
1952	Wilberforce	Althea Gibson & R. Walter Johnson	1977	New Orleans	Leslie Allen & Maurice Hunter
1953	Daytona Beach	Althea Gibson & R. Walter Johnson	1978	Princeton	Sallie Elam & Jessie Holt
1954	Daytona Beach	Althea Gibson & R. Walter Johnson	1979	Atlanta	Sallie Elam & Jessie Holt
			1980	Atlanta	Sallie Middleton & Jessie Holt, Jr.
1955	Wilberforce	Althea Gibson & R. Walter Johnson	1981	—	—
1956	Wilberforce	G. McEvans & W. A. Campbell	1982	San Diego	Katherine Willette & Angel Lopez
1957	Wilberforce	Doris Harrison & Ernie Ingram	1983	Boston	Lisa Foxworth & H. Sanco
			1984	Atlanta	Kathy Foxworth & Sidney Cooper
			1985	Washington, DC	Kathy Foxworth & Paul Geiger

Senior Mixed Doubles

Year	Place Played	Names
1980	Atlanta	Virginia Glass & Charles Massey
1981	Detroit	Jean Richardson & Frank Simmons
1982	San Diego	Jean Richardson & Frank Simmons
1983	Boston	Virginia Glass & Frank Simmons
1984	Atlanta	Virginia Glass & Frank Simmons
1985	Washington, DC	Eva Rice & Henry Philmon

Boys' 18 and Under Singles

Year	Place Played	Names
1924	Baltimore	Russell Smith
1925	Bordentown	Lenoir Cook
1926	St. Louis	Maceo Hill
1927	Hampton	Douglas Turner
1928	Bordentown	Reginal Weir
1929	Bordentown	Nathaniel Jackson
1930	Indianapolis	Nathaniel Jackson
1931	Tuskegee	Franklin Jackson
1932	Shady Rest	Franklin Jackson
1933	Hampton	Hubert Eaton
1934	Lincoln	Theodore Cousins
1935	Institute	Ernest McCampbell
1936	Wilberforce	Johnson Wells
1937	Tuskegee	Johnson Wells
1938	Lincoln	Johnson Wells
1939	Hampton	Robert Ryland
1940	Wilberforce	Joseph King
1941	Tuskegee	Raymond Jackson
1942	Lincoln	Richard Cunningham
1944	New York	Carl Williams
1945	New York	Franklin Bailey
1946	Wilberforce	Clyde Freeman
1947	Tuskegee	Clyde Freeman
1948	Orangeburg	Wilbert Davis
1949	Wilberforce	Robert Dibble
1950	Wilberforce	James Thompkins
1951	Wilberforce	Larry Green
1952	Wilberforce	William Winn
1953	Daytona Beach	William Winn
1954	Daytona Beach	Donald Archer
1955	Wilberforce	Willis Fennell
1956	Wilberforce	William Neilson

Year	Place Played	Names
1957	Wilberforce	Horace Cunningham
1958	Wilberforce	Joe Williams
1959	Wilberforce	Charles Brown
1960	Hampton	Arthur Ashe, Jr.
1961	Hampton	Robert Davis
1962	Wilberforce	William Morton
1963	—	—
1964	—	—
1965	—	—
1966	Wilberforce	Donald Ringgold
1967	—	—
1968	—	—
1969	St. Louis	David Williams
1970	St. Louis	Steve Gilliam
1971	—	—
1972	Boston	Bruce Foxworth
1973	Boston	Robert Johnson
1974	—	—
1975	San Diego	Tony Brock
1976	New Orleans	Rodney Harmon
1977	New Orleans	Rodney Harmon
1978	Princeton	Larry Thomas
1979	Atlanta	Todd Nelson
1980	Atlanta	Mark Stephens
1981	Detroit	Patrick Lindsay
1982	San Diego	Philip Williamson
1983	Boston	Datus Murray
1984	Atlanta	Ulyses Currie
1985	Washington, DC	Patrick Perry

Boys' 16 and Under Singles

Year	Place Played	Names
1937	Tuskegee	Marshall Arnold
1938	Lincoln	Weldon Collins
1939	Hampton	Robert Issacs
1940	Wilberforce	Charles Lewis, Jr.
1941	Tuskegee	John D. Rhodes
1942	Lincoln	Matthew Branche
1944	New York	Clyde Freeman
1945	New York	Wilbert Davis
1946	Wilberforce	Thomas Freeman
1947	Tuskegee	James Thompkins
1948	Orangeburg	Harold Freeman
1949	Wilberforce	Donald Archer
1950	Wilberforce	William Winn
1951	Wilberforce	James Green
1952	Wilberforce	Robert Colburn

Year	Place Played	Names
1953	Daytona Beach	Rudy Hernando
1954	Daytona Beach	Willis Fennell
1955	Wilberforce	Willis Fennell
1956	Wilberforce	Joseph Wiliams
1957	Wilberforce	Arthur Ashe, Jr.
1958	Wilberforce	Arthur Ashe, Jr.
1959	Wilberforce	Charles Berry
1960	Hampton	James Malone, Jr.
1961	Hampton	Sidney Glass
1962	Wilberforce	Lenward Simpson
1963	—	—
1964	—	—
1965	—	—
1966	Wilberforce	John Lucas
1967	—	—
1968	—	—
1969	St. Louis	Paul Farrow
1970	St. Louis	Paul Farrow
1971	—	—
1972	Boston	Juan Farrow
1973	Boston	Maurice Hunter
1974	—	—
1975	San Diego	Marell Harmon
1976	New Orleans	Rodney Harmon
1977	New Orleans	Glenn Merritt
1978	Princeton	Mark Stephens
1979	Atlanta	Young Kwon
1980	Atlanta	Mark Stephens
1981	Detroit	George Kennard
1982	San Diego	Otis Allmon
1983	Boston	Patrick Perry
1984	Atlanta	John Moses
1985	Washington, DC	Christopher Thompson

Year	Place Played	Names
1972	Boston	Walter Robinson
1973	Boston	Miles Gray
1974	Washington, DC	Marcel Freeman
1975	San Diego	Sy Fountain
1976	New Orleans	Jerome Jones
1977	New Orleans	Mark Stephens
1978	Princeton	Young Kwon
1979	Atlanta	Young Kwon
1980	Atlanta	Bryon Shelton
1981	Detroit	Brian Flowers
1982	San Diego	Raunn Ross
1983	Boston	No Champion
1984	Atlanta	Akada Mashaka
1985	Washington, DC	Bill Potoczny

Boys' 12 and Under Singles

Year	Place Played	Names
1955	Wilberforce	Arthur Ashe, Jr.
1956	Wilberforce	James Ford
1957	—	—
1958	—	—
1959	Wilberforce	Sydney Glass
1960	Hampton	Luis Glass
1961	Hampton	Elmer Reid
1962	Wilberforce	Lenward Simpson
1963	—	—
1964	—	—
1965	—	—
1966	Wilberforce	John Lucas
1967	—	—
1968	Wilberforce	Juan Farrow
1969	—	—
1970	St. Louis	Juan Farrow
1971	—	—
1972	Boston	Alex Crosby
1973	Boston	Gary Brown
1974	Washington, DC	Lange Johnson
1975	San Diego	Barry Fields
1976	New Orleans	Barry Fields
1977	New Orleans	Anthony Minnis
1978	Princeton	Barry Fields
1979	Atlanta	Brian Flowers
1980	Atlanta	Raunn Ross
1981	Detroit	Raunn Ross
1982	San Diego	Mark Ellison
1983	Boston	Steve Perry
1984	Atlanta	Akada Mashaka
1985	Washington, DC	Mark Young

Boys' 10 and Under Singles

Year	Place Played	Names
1973	Boston	Frank Wilson
1974	Washington, DC	J. Johnson
1975	San Diego	Daryl Lindsey
1976	New Orleans	Brent Fields
1977	—	—
1978	Princeton	Raunn Ross
1979	Atlanta	Raunn Ross
1980	Atlanta	Charles Stafford
1981	Detroit	Steve Perry
1982	San Diego	Malcolm Greene
1983	Boston	Michael Holmes

Year	Place Played	Names
1984	Atlanta	Michael Holmes
1985	Washington, DC	Matthew Halfpenny

Girls' 18 and Under Singles

Year	Place Played	Names
1935	Institute	Mae Hamlin
1936	Wilberforce	Angelina Spencer
1937	Tuskegee	Mae Hamlin
1938	Lincoln	Mayme Stanley
1939	Hampton	Vivian Murphy
1940	Wilberforce	Helen Mutchinson
1941	Tuskegee	Thelma McDaniels
1942	Lincoln	Nana Davis
1944	New York	Althea Gibson
1945	New York	Althea Gibson
1946	Wilberforce	Gwendolyn Whittington
1947	Tuskegee	Wilma McGhee
1948	Orangeburg	Helen Mundy
1949	Wilberforce	Helen Mundy
1950	Wilberforce	Florence Gibson
1951	Wilberforce	Lorraine Williams
1952	Wilberforce	Barbara Pratt
1953	Daytona Beach	Barbara Pratt
1954	Daytona Beach	Blacnher Bailey
1955	Wilberforce	Emily Wilson
1956	Wilberforce	Clara Henry
1957	Wilberforce	Gwendolyn McEvans
1958	Wilberforce	Darnella Everson
1959	Wilberforce	Marlene Everson
1960	Hampton	Carolyn Williams
1961	Hampton	Carolyn Williams
1962	Wilberforce	Carolyn Williams
1963	—	—
1964	—	—
1965	—	—
1966	Wilberforce	Tam O'Shaughnessy
1967	—	—
1968	—	—
1969	St. Louis	Jackie Holloway
1970	St. Louis	Jolynn Johnson
1971	—	—
1972	Boston	Deborah Hunter
1973	Boston	Linda Jones
1974	Washington, DC	Lisa Hopewell
1975	San Diego	Lisa Rapfogel

Year	Place Played	Names
1976	New Orleans	Tina McCall
1977	New Orleans	Natalie Morales
1978	Princeton	Zina Garrison
1979	Atlanta	Lori McNeil
1980	Atlanta	Veronica Gholston
1981	Detroit	Katrina Adams
1982	San Diego	Julie Banks
1983	Boston	Valerie Rhodes
1984	Atlanta	Kelley N. Wilson
1985	Washington, DC	Stacey Martin

Girls' 16 and Under Singles

Year	Place Played	Names
1955	Wilberforce	Alice Faggett
1956	Wilberforce	Mary Henry
1957	—	—
1958	Wilberforce	Lucy E. McEvans
1959	Wilberforce	Lucy E. McEvans
1960	Hampton	Sylvia Hooks
1961	Hampton	Sylvia Hooks
1962	Wilberforce	Sylvia Hooks
1963	—	—
1964	—	—
1965	—	—
1966	Wilberforce	Tam O'Shaughnessy
1967	—	—
1968	—	—
1969	St. Louis	Jackie Holloway
1970	St. Louis	Sheryl Moser
1971	—	—
1972	Boston	M. Dickerson
1973	Boston	Lisa Foxworth
1974	Washington, DC	Shelly Solomon
1975	San Diego	Margaret Dudash
1976	New Orleans	Kyle Copeland
1977	New Orleans	Penny Watkins
1978	Princeton	Lori McNeil
1979	Atlanta	Kathy Foxworth
1980	Atlanta	Raku Robinson
1981	Detroit	Stacey Knowles
1982	San Diego	Sophia Ray
1983	Boston	Rachelle Mack
1984	Atlanta	Shelley Mack
1985	Washington, DC	Jeri Ingram

Girls' 14 and Under Singles

Year	Place Played	Names
1959	Wilberforce	Bonnie Logan
1960	Hampton	Bonnie Logan
1961	Hampton	Bonnie Logan
1962	Wilberforce	Bonnie Logan
1970	St. Louis	Sherri Wynn
1971	—	—
1972	Boston	Janet Leonard
1973	Boston	Lisa Foxworth
1974	Washington, DC	Karen Royal
1975	San Diego	Wendy Driver
1976	New Orleans	Mattie Middleton
1977	New Orleans	Zina Garrison
1978	Princeton	Lori McNeil
1979	Atlanta	Julia Banks
1980	Atlanta	Katrina Adams
1981	Detroit	Katrina Adams
1982	San Diego	Rachelle Mack
1983	Boston	Rachelle Mack
1984	Atlanta	Renika Shaw
1985	Washington, DC	Francine McLeod

Girls' 12 and Under Singles

Year	Place Played	Names
1972	Boston	Lisa Banks
1973	Boston	Penny Watkins
1974	Washington, DC	Kathy Foxworth
1975	San Diego	Lynn Lewis
1976	New Orleans	Kathy Foxworth
1977	New Orleans	Kathy Foxworth
1978	Princeton	Karen Locklear
1979	Atlanta	Katrina Adams
1980	Atlanta	Katrina Adams
1981	Detroit	Rachelle Mack
1982	San Diego	Rachelle Mack
1983	Boston	Erica Lewis
1984	Atlanta	Chervon Stafford
1985	Washington, DC	Valerie Poulos

Girls' 10 and Under Singles

Year	Place Played	Names
1974	Washington, DC	Kathy Foxworth
1975	San Diego	Cari Hagey
1976	New Orleans	Karen Locklear
1977	—	—
1978	Princeton	Katrina Adams

Year	Place Played	Names
1979	Atlanta	Rachelle Mack
1980	Atlanta	Rachelle Mack
1981	Detroit	Elena Hunt
1982	—	—
1983	Boston	Christine Walker
1984	Atlanta	Thanh Thai
1985	Washington, DC	Joi Mitchell

Boys' 18 and Under Doubles

Year	Place Played	Names
1973	Boston	William Feliciano & Rod Young
1974	Washington, DC	Tom Jones & J. Mitchell
1975	San Diego	Morris Strode & Nick White
1976	New Orleans	L. Barnett & C. Richardson
1977	New Orleans	Sidney Cooper & Larry Thomas
1978	Princeton	S. Cooper & E. McNeil
1979	Atlanta	Jerome Lawrence & Darryl Whitley
1980	Atlanta	Leonard Booker & William Lindsey
1981	Detroit	W. Marshall & M. Mitchell
1982	San Diego	Edward Baylor & Rozelle Lightfoot
1983	Boston	Chris Carrig & Leslie Smith
1984	Atlanta	Paul Manning & James Lundy
1985	Washington, DC	Rajat Dhanda & Patrick Perry

Boys' 16 and Under Doubles

Year	Place Played	Names
1955	Wilberforce	Joseph Williams & Christopher Hand
1956	Wilberforce	Arthur Ashe, Jr. & Willis Thomas
1957	—	—
1958	Wilberforce	Arthur Ashe, Jr. & Willis Thomas
1959	Wilberforce	Paul Kelly & Gilbert DeLorne
1960	Hampton	Luis Glass & Sidney Glass
1961	Hampton	Luis Glass & Sidney Glass
1962	Wilberforce	E. Allen & G. Morton
1963-1968	—	—

Year	Place Played	Names
1969	St. Louis	Paul Farrow & D. Nottingham
1970	St. Louis	R. Cunningham & Y. Garrett
1971	—	—
1972	Boston	J. Walton & E. Cruzat
1973	Boston	Maurice Hunter & Walter Robinson
1974	Washington, DC	Peter Lamb & Juan Farrow
1975	San Diego	Garrison Brown & Morrell Harmon
1976	New Orleans	Ricky Crowe & Glennys Merritt
1977	New Orleans	Kelvin Belcher & Eric McNeil
1978	Princeton	Darryl Whitney & Jerome Lawrence
1979	Atlanta	Jerome Smith & Craig Dawson
1980	Atlanta	Joey Gordon & Eric Smith
1981	Detroit	Otis Allmon & Chris Henderson
1982	San Diego	Otis Allmon & Chris Henderson
1983	Boston	Rajat Dhanda & Radek Kocek
1984	Atlanta	Charles Middleton & Jeffrey Gordon
1985	Washington, DC	Bryant Owens & Charles Ashe

Boys' 14 and Under Doubles

Year	Place Played	Names
1972	Boston	Blackburn & Knight
1973	Boston	Eddie Walls & Miles Gray
1974	Washington, DC	Rodney Harmon & Victor Bryant
1975	San Diego	Rodney Harmon & Glennys Merritt
1976	New Orleans	Barry Fields & T. Owens
1977	New Orleans	Darryl Whitley & Lorenzo Hollifield
1978	Princeton	Brent Fields & Barry Fields
1979	Atlanta	Brent Fields & Kenny Fields

Year	Place Played	Names
1980	Atlanta	Brent Fields & Kenny Fields
1981	Detroit	Marlon Henderson & Staton Norris
1982	San Diego	Vincent Mackey & Steven Joyner
1983	Boston	Mark Anderson & Ronnie Holmes
1984	Atlanta	Steve Perry & Karl Headen
1985	Washington, DC	Jerry O'Sullivan & Karl Headen

Boys' 12 and Under Doubles

Year	Place Played	Names
1955	Wilberforce	Arthur Ashe, Jr. & John Thomas
1956	Wilberforce	Gilbert DeLorne & John Merritt
1957	—	—
1958	—	—
1959	Wilberforce	Sidney Glass & Luis Glass
1960	Hampton	William Jones & J. S. Lewis
1961	Hampton	William Reid & John Ashe
1962	Wilberforce	Jeffrey Thomas & Donald Ringgold
1963-1965		
	—	—
1966	Wilberforce	W. Filician & T. Yen
1967	—	—
1968	—	—
1969	St. Louis	C. Hooper & Rovti Johnson
1970	St. Louis	Juan Farrow & Junie Chatman
1971	—	—
1972	Boston	Alex Crosby & Charles Francis
1973	Boston	Gary Brown & Goodie Feliciano
1974	Washington, DC	Glennis Burton & Tony Burton
1975	San Diego	Barry Fields & Thomas Owens
1976	New Orleans	Brent Fields & Barry Fields
1977	—	
1978	Princeton	Brent Fields & Barry Fields

Year	Place Played	Names
1979	Atlanta	Averil Chestnut & Brian Flowers
1980	Atlanta	Marlowe Henderson & Brett Hood
1981	Detroit	Andrew LeBlanc & Carl Headen
1982	San Diego	Mark Ellison & Roger Ray
1983	Boston	Steve Perry & Torre Neblett
1984	Atlanta	Spencer Belcher & Tyron Horton
1985	Washington, DC	Billy Burns & Mike Dean

Boys' 10 and Under Doubles

Year	Place Played	Names
1978	Princeton	Jeffrey Gordon & Raunn Ross
1979	Atlanta	Raunn Ross & Ronald Thomas
1980	Atlanta	Troy Cephas & Scott Devine
1981	Detroit	Malcolm Greene & Steven Perry
1982	San Diego	Patrick Jefferson & Robert Wheeler
1983	—	—
1984	—	—
1985	—	—

Girls' 18 and Under Doubles

Year	Place Played	Names
1955	Wilberforce	Eula M. Brown & Clara I. Henry
1956	Wilberforce	Cora Organ & Clara I. Henry
1957	—	—
1958	Wilberforce	Darnella Everson & Marlen Everson
1959	Wilbergorce	Lucy E. McEvans & Marlene Everson
1960	Hampton	Carolyn Williams & carolyn Archie
1961	Hampton	Sylvia Hooks & Lucy McEvans
1962	Wilberforce	Sylvia Hooks & Lucy McEvans

Year	Place Played	Names
1963-1968	—	—
1969	St. Louis	V. Green & S. Boone
1970	St. Louis	S. Pettus & P. McKinney
1971	—	—
1972	Boston	B. Cook & D. Bolen
1973	Boston	Darlene Tellis & Deborah Hunter
1974	Washington, DC	Darlene Tellis & Deborah Hunter
1975	San Diego	Deborah Hunter & Karen Royal
1976	New Orleans	M. Peatros & L. Foxworth
1977	New Orleans	Lawanda Briley & Marilyn Ruiz
1978	Princeton	Tina Hoskins & V. Griffin
1979	Atlanta	Babette Flennoy & Veronica Gholston
1980	Atlanta	Pamela Henderson & Lashaun Thomas
1981	Detroit	Pamela Henderson & Lashaun Thomas
1982	San Diego	Monica Raspberry & Ella Neely
1983	Boston	Patricia Collins & Pamela Willis
1984	—	—
1985	Washington, DC	Stacey Martin & Jeri Ingram

Girls' 16 and Under Doubles

Year	Place Played	Names
1955	Wilberforce	Alice M. Faggett & Mary Brown
1956	Wilberforce	Mary Henry & Alice Faggett
1957	—	—
1958	—	—
1959	Wilberforce	Imogene Williams & Judith Prince
1960	Hampton	Imogene Williams & Judith Prince
1961	Hampton	Ianisceta DeJesus & Beryl Sansom
1962	Wilberforce	B. Sanson & G. Adcock
1963-1969	—	—
1970	St. Louis	S. Boone & V. Green
1971	—	—

Year	Place Played	Names
1972	Boston	A. Hunter & D. Tellis
1973	Boston	Robin Tellis & Deborah Hunter
1974	Washington, DC	D. Hunter & K. Royal
1975	San Diego	Letitia King & Teri Williams
1976	New Orleans	M. Middleton & N. Mowles
1977	New Orleans	Natalie Morales & Mattie Middleton
1978	Princeton	N. Horowitz & J. Alexander
1979	Atlanta	D. Douglas & L. Pilot
1980	Atlanta	Dimitre Fulton & Diana White
1981	—	—
1982	San Diego	Nikki Gross & Crystal Polee
1983	Boston	Shanet Hutchinson & Kim Hutchinson
1984	Atlanta	No Champions
1985	Washington, DC	Jeanine septh & Dawnine Septh

Girls' 14 and Under Doubles

1973	Boston	Penny Watkins & Lori Tellis
1974	Washington, DC	Penny Watkins & Lori Tellis
1975	San Diego	Carol Hamilton & Lisa Hamilton
1976	New Orleans	Liza Cruzat & Kathy Foxworth
1977	New Orleans	Zina Garrison & Lori McNeil
1978	Princeton	Zina Garrison & Lori McNeil
1979	Atlanta	Katrina Adams & Stacey Knowles
1980	—	—
1981	Detroit	Gina Toole & Ginger Wilson
1982	San Diego	Lisa Knazze & Wendy Mitchell
1983	Boston	Courtney Tarpley & Kyla Upshaw
1984	Atlanta	Courtney Tarpley & Kyla Upshaw
1985	Washington, DC	Karen O'Sullivan & Tanis Robinson

Girls' 12 and Under Doubles

Year	Place Played	Names
1959	Wilberforce	Beryl Sanson & Bonnie Logan
1960	Hampton	Janice Cobbins & Patricia Brown
1961	Hampton	Bonnie Logan & Anne Koger
1962-1965	—	—
1966	Wilberforce	S. Pettus & P. McKinney
1967	—	
1968	—	
1969	St. Louis	S. Boone & V. Greene
1970	St. Louis	S. Boone & V. Greene
1971	—	
1972	Boston	B. Leonard & H. Jackson
1973	Boston	Kathy Foxworth & Kellie Sloane
1974	Washington, DC	Kathy Foxworth & Liza Cruzat
1975	—	
1976	New Orleans	Zina Garrison & Lori McNeil
1977	New Orleans	Kim Wynn & Sharon Holland
1978	Princeton	E. Cheng & M. Cheng
1979	Atlanta	A. Johnson & C. Anderson
1980	Atlanta	Candi Cephas & Lisa Matthews
1981	Detroit	Kathy Wilson & Lisa Knazze
1982	—	—
1983	—	—
1984	—	—
1985	—	—

Girls' 10 and Under Doubles

1978	Princeton	Katrina Adams & Paula Minnis
1979-1985	—	

Boys' Junior Doubles

1937	Tuskegee	Eugene Harrington & George Cox
1938	—	—

Year	Place Played	Names
1939	Hampton	Joseph King & Marshall Arnold
1940	Wilberforce	Robert Asford & Ronald McDaniel
1941	Tuskegee	Jack Points & Richard Cunningham
1942	Lincoln	Jefferson Craig & Dewitt Willis
1944	New York	Franklin Bailey & Carl Williams
1945	New York	Fred Wilson & Wilbert Davis
1946	Wilberforce	Clyde Freeman & Thomas Freeman
1947	Tuskegee	Clyde Freeman & Thomas Freeman
1948	Orangeburg	Maynard Driver & James Thompkins
1949	Wilberforce	Maynard Driver & James Thompkins
1950	Wilberforce	James Thompkins & Harold Freeman
1951	Wilberforce	Robert Ford & Harold Freeman
1952	Wilberforce	George Fryman & Thomas Shulman
1953	Daytona Beach	Rudy Hernando & Neil Flattery
1954	Daytona Beach	Willis Fennell & Frank Johnson
1955	Wilberforce	Samuel Bacote & Donald Archer
1956	Wilberforce	Irwin Holmes & Joe Williams
1957	Wilberforce	Horace Cunningham & Albert Brooks

Year	Place Played	Names
1958	Wilberforce	Horace Cunningham & William Neilson
1959	Wilberforce	Michael Bibb & John McGill
1960	Hampton	Henry Bowers & Denton Johnson, Jr.
1961	Hampton	Charles Barry & Phillip Lucas
1962	Wilberforce	William Morton & James Malone
1963-1967	—	—
1968	Wilberforce	J. Blair & R. Reynolds
1969	St. Louis	S. Gilliam & B. Clark
1970	—	—
1971	—	—
1972	Boston	Bruce Foxworth & Kevin Bolar

Junior Mixed Doubles

Year	Place Played	Names
1955	Wilberforce	Clara Henry & Joseph W. Clift
1956	Wilberforce	Clara Henry & Henry Lives
1957	—	—
1958	—	—
1959	Wilberforce	Beverly Leverson & John McGill
1960	Hampton	Lucy Evans & Denton Johnson, Jr.
1961	Hampton	Carolyn Williams & LaMar Williams
1962	Wilberforce	Bonnie Logan & Lenward Simpson
1963-1969	—	—
1970	St. Louis	Sheryl Moser & Robert Goode
1971-1985	—	—

BLACK COLLEGE CONFERENCE WINNERS

	CIAA	SWAC	SIAC	EIAC	SCAC	MWAC
1924	Howard					
1925	Va. Normal & Shaw					
1926	Va. Seminary & Shaw					
1927	Hampton & Va. Seminary		Tuskegee			
1928	Va. Seminary & Shaw		Tuskegee			
1929	Hampton & Shaw		Tuskegee			
1930	Hampton & Va. Union		Tuskegee			
1931	Howard & Va. State		Tuskegee			
1932	Howard & Hampton		Tuskegee			
1933						
1934	J.C. Smith		Tuskegee			
1935	J.C. Smith		Tuskegee			
1936	J.C. Smith		Tuskegee			
1937	Morgan		Tuskegee		Wilberforce	
1938	St. Augustine		Tuskegee			West Va. State
1939	St. Augustine				Tuskegee	West Va. State
1940			Tuskegee	Tougaloo	West Va. State	
1941	J.C. Smith	Southern	Tuskegee	Tougaloo		
1942	J.C. Smith	Southern	Tuskegee	Tougaloo		
1943		Southern	Tuskegee			
1944			Tuskegee	Okolona		
1945			Tuskegee			

GOLF

UNITED GOLFER'S ASSOCIATION TOURNAMENT WINNERS

1926–Harry Jackson, pro	Stowe, MA	
1927–Robert "Pat" Ball, pro	Stowe, MA	
1928–Frank Gaskins, amateur	Stowe, MA	
Porter Washington, pro		
1929–Frank Gaskins, amateur	Shady Rest, NJ	
Pat Ball, pro		
1930–George Roddy, amateur	Casa Loma, WI	
Marie Thompson, woman		
Edison Marshall, pro		
1931–James McKoy, amateur	Kankakee, IL	
Marie Thompson, woman		
Edison Marshall, pro		
1932–Frank Gaskins, amateur	Indianapolis, IN	
Lucy Williams		
John Dendy		
1933–Isaac Ellis, amateur	Kankakee, IL	
Julia Siler		
Howard Wheeler		
1934–Percy Jones, amateur	Detroit, MI	
Ella Able		
Robert "Pat" Ball		
1935–Frank Radcliffe, amateur	Yorktown Heights, NY	
Ella Able		
Solomon Hughes		
1936–Clifford Taylor, amateur	Philadelphia, PA	
Lucy Williams		
John Dendy		
1937–George Roddy, amateur	Cleveland, OH	
Lucy Williams		
John Dendy		
1938–Dr. Remus Robinson, amateur	Kankakee, IL	
Melanie Moye		
Howard Wheeler		
1939–Gus Price, amateur	Los Angeles, CA	
Geneva Wilson		
Cliff Strickland		
1940–Dr. Remus Robinson, amateur	Chicago, IL	
Melanie Moye		
Hugh Smith		
1941–Cliff Taylor, amateur	Boston, MA	
Cleo Ball (wife of "Pat")		
Robert "Pat" Ball		
*1942–1945 No Tournament		

TRACK & FIELD

WOMAN'S AFRICAN-AMERICAN AAU WINNERS THROUGH 1945

100 Meters

1938 Lula Hymes	Tuskegee	12.4
1940 Jean Lane	Wilberforce	12.0
1941 Jean Lane	Wilberforce	12.4
1942 Alice Coachman	Tuskegee	12.1
1945 Alice Coachman	Tuskegee	12.0

200 Meters

1928 Florence Wright	(Headlight AC)	27.4 (200 yards)
1937 Gertrude Johnson	(Mercury AC)	26.0
1941 Jean Lane	Wilberforce	25.2

100 Meters Hurdles

1937 Cora Gaines	Tuskegee	12.8
1941 Lelia Perry	Tuskegee	13.2
1942 Lillie Purifoy	Tuskegee	12.6
1944 Lillie Purifoy	Tuskegee	12.8
1945 Lillie Purifoy	Tuskegee	12.5

High Jump

1939 Alice Coachman	Tuskegee	5'-2"
1940 Alice Coachman	Tuskegee	4'-11"
1941 Alice Coachman	Tuskegee	5'-2 3/4"
1942 Alice Coachman	Tuskegee	4'-8"
1943 Alice Coachman	Tuskegee	5'-0"
1944 Alice Coachman	Tuskegee	5'-1 5/8"
1945 Alice Coachman	Tuskegee	5'-0"

Long Jump

1935 Etta Tate	(Unattached)	16'-6"
1936 Mable Smith	Tuskegee	18'-0"
1937 Lula Hymes	Tuskegee	17'-8 1/2"
1938 Lula Hymes	Tuskegee	17'-2"

Shot Put

1942 Ramona Harris	(Unattached)	37'-10 1/2"

Discus Throw

1944 Hattie Turner	Tuskegee	101'-7 3/4"

AMERICAN RECORDS HELD BY AFRICAN-AMERICANS AT THE END OF 1945
(MEN'S RECORDS)

60 yards

Ralph Metcalfe	6.1	March 11, 1933
Jesse Owens		March 9, 1935
Herbert Thompson		February 4, 1939
Bill Carter		March 15, 1941
Barney Ewell		February 7, 1942
Herbert Thompson		March 14, 1942
Herbert Thompson		March 27, 1943
Edward Conwell		February 26, 1944
Edward Conwell		March 9, 1946

100 yards

Jesse Owens	9.4	May 25, 1935

220 yards

Jesse Owens	20.3	May 25, 1935

880 yards

John Woodruff	1:47.7	March 14, 1940

1,000 yards

John Borican	2:08.8	March 11, 1939

Metric Distances

60 Meters

Jesse Owens	6.6	February 23, 1935
Herbert Thompson	6.6	February 25, 1939

100 Meters

Jesse Owens	10.2	June 20, 1936

400 Meters

James Herbert	48.4	March 14, 1940

800 Meters

John Woodruff	1:48.6	June 7, 1940

1600 Meter Relay

Stanford Braun, Harold Bogrow, James McPoland, JAMES HERBERT*	3:15.0	March 14, 1940

4 Mile Relay

M. Truitt, JAMES SMITH,* T. Deckard, D. Lash	17:16.1	April 23, 1937

220 Yard Hurdles

Harrison Dillard	22.5	June 8, 1946

Running High Jump

Ed Burke	6'9 1/4"	February 27, 1937
Mel Walker	6'9 3/4"	March 20, 1937

Running Broad Jump

Jesse Owens	26'8 1/4"	May 25, 1935

Women's Records

50 yard run

Elizabeth Robinson	5.8	July 27, 1929

50 Meter Run

Alice Coachman	6.4	July 14, 1944

100 yard dash

Jean Lane	10.9	May 29, 1940

220 yard run

Elizabeth Robinson	25.1	June 20, 1931

Running Broad Jump

Lula Mae Hymes	18'1 1/2"	September 3, 1939

400 Meter Relay

Tuskegee Institute (Lucy Newell, Jessie Abbott, Rowena Harris, Lula Mae Hymes)	49.3	July 13, 1940

*In relays, names in capitals are black runners; other relay runners are white.

WORLD RECORDS HELD BY AFRICAN-AMERICANS AT THE END OF 1945

100 Meters

Jesse Owens	10.2	June 20, 1936

200 Meters

Jesse Owens	20.7	August 5, 1936

4 × 100 Meter Relay

Jesse Owens Ralph Metcalfe Frank Draper (white) Frank Wykoff (white)	39.8	August 9, 1936

Long Jump

Jesse Owens	8.13 m (26' 81/4")	May 25, 1935

MEN'S AFRICAN-AMERICAN NCAA WINNERS THROUGH 1945

100 Meters

1925	William DeHart Hubbard	(Michigan)	9.8	100 yards
1932	Ralph Metcalfe	(Marquette)	10.2	
1933	Ralph Metcalfe	(Marquette)	9.4	100 yards
1934	Ralph Metcalfe	(Marquette)	9.7	100 yards
1935	Jesse Owens	(Ohio State)	9.8	100 yards
1936	Jesse Owens	(Ohio State)	10.2	
1938	Mozelle Ellerbe	(Tuskegee)	9.7	100 yards
1939	Mozelle Ellerbe	(Tuskegee)	9.8	100 yards
1940	Barney Ewell	(Penn State)	9.6	100 yards
1941	Barney Ewell	(Penn State)	9.6	100 yards
1944	Buddy Young	(Illinois)	9.7	100 yards

200 Meters

1931	Eddie Tolan	(Michigan)	21.5	200 yards
1932	Ralph Metcalfe	(Marquette)	20.3	
1933	Ralph Metcalfe	(Marquette)	20.4	200 yards
1934	Ralph Metcalfe	(Marquette)	20.9	200 yards
1935	Jesse Owens	(Ohio State)	21.5	200 yards
1936	Jesse Owens	(Ohio State)	21.3	
1937	Ben Johnson	(Columbia)	21.3	200 yards
1938	Mark Robinson	(Oregon)	21.3	200 yards
1940	Barney Ewell	(Penn State)	21.1	200 yards
1941	Barney Ewell	(Penn State)	21.1	200 yards
1944	Buddy Young	(Illinois)	21.6	200 yards

400 Meters

1935	James Luvalle	(UCLA)	47.7	440 yards
1936	Archie Williams	(California)	47.0	440 yards
1944	Elmore Harris	(Morgan State)	47.9	440 yards

800 Meters

1937	John Woodruff	(Pittsburgh)	1:50.3	880 yards
1938	John Woodruff	(Pittsburgh)	1:52.3	880 yards
1939	John Woodruff	(Pittsburgh)	1:51.3	880 yards

110 Meter High Hurdles

1940	Ed Dugger	(Tufts)	13.9	120 yards

High Jump

1936	Mel Walker	(Ohio State)	6'-6 ⅛"
	Dave Albritton	(Ohio State)	
1937	Gil Cruter	(Colorado)	6'-6 ¼"
	Dave Albritton	(Ohio State)	
1938	Gil Cruter	(Colorado)	6'-8 ¾"
	Dave Albritton	(Ohio State)	
1942	Adam Berry	(Southern U.)	6'-7 ¾"

Long Jump

1923	DeHart Hubbard	(Michigan)	25' 2"
1925	DeHart Hubbard	(Michigan)	25' 10⅞"
1929	Ed Gordon	(Iowa)	24' 8½"
1930	Ed Gordon	(Iowa)	25' 0"
1931	Ed Gordon	(Iowa)	24' 11⅜"
1933	John Brooks	(Chicago)	24' 4¾"
1935	Jesse Owens	(Ohio State)	26' 1⅜"
1936	Jesse Owens	(Ohio State)	25' 10⅞"
1937	Kermit King	(Pittsburgh)	25' 3¼"
1938	William Lacefield	(UCLA)	25' 1⅛"
1940	Jackie Robinson	(UCLA)	24' 10¼"

Discus Throw

1940	Archie Harris	(Indiana)	162'-4¼"
1941	Archie Harris	(Indiana)	174'-8¾"

Javelin Throw

1932	George Williams	Hampton	215'-0"

AFRICAN-AMERICAN OLYMPIANS

Year	Name	Medal	Event	Mark	City
1924	William DeHart Hubbard	Gold	Long Jump	24'5"	Paris
1924	Edward Gourdin	Silver	Long Jump	23'10"	Paris
1924	Earl Johnson	Bronze	10,000 Meters	—	Paris
1932	Eddie Tolan	Gold	100 Meters	10.3	Los Angeles
1932	Eddie Tolan	Gold	200 Meters	21.2	Los Angeles
1932	Ralph Metcalfe	Silver	100 Meters	10.3	Los Angeles
1932	Ralph Metcalfe	Bronze	200 Meters	21.5	Los Angeles
1932	Edward Gordon	Gold	Long Jump	25'0 ¾"	Los Angeles
1936	Cornelius Johnson	Gold	High Jump	6'8"	Berlin
1936	David Albritton	Silver	High Jump	6'6 ¾"	Berlin
1936	Jesse Owens	Gold	100 Meters	10.3	Berlin
1936	Jesse Owens	Gold	200 Meters	20.7	Berlin
1936	Jesse Owens	Gold	Long Jump	25'5 ½"	Berlin
1936	Jesse Owens**	Gold	400M- Relay	39.8	Berlin
1936	Archie Williams	Gold	400 Meters	46.5	Berlin
1936	James Luvalle	Bronze	400 Meters	46.8	Berlin
1936	John Woodruff	Gold	800 Meters	1:52.9	Berlin
1936	Mack Robinson	Silver	200 Meters	21.1	Berlin
1936	Ralph Metcalfe**	Gold	400M- Relay	39.8	Berlin
1936	Ralph Metcalfe	Silver	100 Meters	10.4	Berlin
1936	Fritz Pollard, Jr.	Bronze	110M- Hurdles	14.4	Berlin

**White teammates on Gold Medal 400 Meter Relay team were Frank Wykoff, Foy Draper.

MEN'S AFRICAN-AMERICAN AAU WINNERS
THROUGH 1945

100 Meters

1912 Howard Drew (Springfield HS)	10.0	100 yards
1913 Howard Drew (Springfield HS)	10.0	100 yards
1916 Andy Ward (Chicago AA)	10.0	100 yards
1917 Andy Ward (Chicago AA)	10.2	100 yards
1929 Eddie Tolan (Michigan)	10.0	100 yards
1930 Eddie Tolan (Michigan)	9.7	100 yards
1932 Ralph Metcalfe (Marquette)	10.6	
1933 Ralph Metcalfe (Marquette)	10.5	
1934 Ralph Metcalfe (Marquette)	10.4	
1935 Eulace Peacock (Shore AC)	10.2	
1936 Jesse Owens (Ohio State)	10.4	
1938 Ben Johnson (NY Curb Exchange)	10.7	
1941 Barney Ewell (US Army)	10.3	
1944 Buddy Young (Illinois)	10.5	
1945 Barney Ewell (US Army)	10.3	

200 Meters

1913 Howard Drew (Springfield HS)	22.8	220 yards
1916 Andy Ward (Chicago AA)	21.6	220 yards
1917 Andy Ward (Chicago AA)	22.2	220 yards
1929 Eddie Tolan (Michigan)	21.9	220 yards
1931 Eddie Tolan (Unattached)	21.0	220 yards
1932 Ralph Metcalfe (Marquette)	21.5	
1933 Ralph Metcalfe (Marquette)	21.1	
1934 Ralph Metcalfe (Marquette)	21.3	
1935 Ralph Metcalfe (Marquette U. Club)	21.0	
1936 Ralph Metcalfe (Marquette U. Club)	21.2	
1938 Mack Robinson (Oregon)	21.3	
1939 Barney Ewell (Penn State)	21.0	
1945 Elmore Harris (Shore AC)	21.9	

400 Meters

1914 Ted Meredith (Meadow Club)	50.2	440 yards
1915 Ted Meredith (Meadow Club)	47.0	440 yards
1925 Cecil Cooke (Salem Crescent AC)	49.2	440 yards
1944 Elmore Harris (Shore AC)	48.0	

800 Meters

1934 Ben Eastman (SF Olympic Club)	1:50.4
1937 John Woodruff (Pittsburgh)	1:50.0
1942 John Borican (Asbury Park AC)	1:51.2
1944 Robert Kelly (Illinois)	1:51.8
1945 Robert Kelly (Illinois)	1:54.1

10,000 Meters

1921 Earl Johnson	(Thomson Steel)	25:53.4
1922 Earl Johnson	(Thomson Steel)	25:33.0
1923 Earl Johnson	(Thomson Steel)	26:52.0

110 Meter Hurdles

1918 Earl Thomson	(Canada)	15.2	110 yards
1921 Earl Thomson	(Boston AA/Can.)	15.0	110 yards
1922 Earl Thomson	(Unattached/Can.)	15.3	110 yards

High Jump

1932 Cornelius Johnson	(Calif. HS)	6'6 ⅝"
1933 Cornelius Johnson	(Calif. HS)	6'7"
1934 Cornelius Johnson	(Compton JC)	6'8 ⅝"
1935 Cornelius Johnson	(Compton JC)	6'7"
1936 Cornelius Johnson	(Compton JC)	6'8"
Mel Walker	(Ohio State)	6'8"
Dave Albritton	(Ohio State)	6'8"
1937 Dave Albritton	(Ohio State)	6'8 ⅝"
1938 Dave Albritton	(Ohio State)	6'7"
Mel Walker	(Unattached)	6'7"
1942 Adam Berry	(Southern U)	6'7"
1945 Dave Albritton	(Unattached)	6'5 ¾"
Josh Williamson	(US Army)	6'5 ¾"

Long Jump

1920 Sol Butler	(Dubuque Col.)	24'-8"
1921 Ned Gourdin	(Harvard)	23'-7 ¾"
1922 William DeHart Hubbard	(Unattached)	24'-5 ⅛"
1923 William DeHart Hubbard	(Michigan)	24'-7 ¾"
1924 William DeHart Hubbard	(Michigan)	24'-0"
1925 William DeHart Hubbard	(Unattached)	25'-4 ⅜"
1926 William DeHart Hubbard	(Century AC)	25'-2 ½"
1927 William DeHart Hubbard	(Unattached)	25'-8 ¾"
1929 Ed Gordon, Jr.	(U. of Iowa)	24'-4 ¼"
1933 Jesse Owens	(Ohio H.S.)	24'-6 ⅜"
1934 Jesse Owens	(Ohio State)	25'-0 ⅞"
1935 Eulace Peacock	(Shore AC)	26'-3"
1936 Jesse Owens	(Ohio State)	26'-3"
1937 Kermit King	(Pittsburgh)	25'-1 ½"
1938 William Lacefield	(UCLA)	25'-0 ³⁄₁₀"
1939 William Lacefield	(Unattached)	25'-5 ½"
1945 Herb Douglas	(Unattached)	24'-0 ⅛"

Triple Jump

1922 William DeHart Hubbard	(Unattached)	48'-1 ½"
1923 William DeHart Hubbard	(Michigan)	47'-0 ½"
1944 Don Barksdale	(US Army)	47'-2 ⅞"

Shot Put

1939 Lilburn Williams   (Xavier)   53'-7"

Discus Throw

1941 Archie Harris   (Unattached)   167'-9 ½"

Decathlon

1940 William Watson   (Unattached)   7523
                                                                               points
1941 John Borican   (Asbury Park AC)   5666
1943 William Watson   (Detroit Police)   5994

BLACK COLLEGE CONFERENCE WINNERS

	CIAA	SWAC	SIAC	EIAC	SCAC	MWAC
1924	Hampton					
1925	Hampton					
1926	Hampton					
1927	Hampton					
1928	Lincoln					
1929	Hampton					
1930	Morgan					
1931	Hampton					
1932	St. Paul					
1933	Morgan					Wilberforce
1934	Va. Union					Wilberforce
1935	Hampton					Wilberforce
1936	Va. State & Morgan					Wilberforce
1937	Hampton					No Meet
1938	Va. State	Bishop	Xavier			Wilberforce
1939	Va. State	Bishop	Xavier			Lincoln U. (Mo.)
1940		Prairie View			Alcorn A & M	Lincoln U. (Mo.)
1941	Hampton	Southern			Dillard	
1942		Southern			Alcorn A & M	
1943		Southern				
1944		Prairie View			Tougaloo	
1945	Morgan	Wiley			Okolona	

FOOTBALL

ALL-CENTRAL INTERCOLLEGIATE ATHLETIC ASSOCIATION TEAMS

Year	Name	School
1923	Parker, Wallace	St. Paul's College
	Lancaster, J.W.L.	Lincoln University
	Byrd, Franz	Lincoln University
	Butler, Adee	Hampton Institute
	Miller, R.E.	Virginia Union
	Jones, James	Hampton Institute
	Johnson, R.W.	Lincoln University
	Coston, W.R.C.	Lincoln University
	Morgan, Chris	Lincoln University
	Coleman, Theodore	Hampton Institute
	Doneby, Charles	Howard University
1924	Galloway	Lincoln University
	Goodman, G.W.	Lincoln University
	Shields, James	Virginia Union
	Whedbee, Melvin	Virginia Seminary and College
	Crudup, B.D.	Lincoln University
	Lee, William	Hampton Institute
	Gill, H.H.	Shaw University
	Alexander, James	Hampton Institute
	Lancaster, J.W.L.	Lincoln University
	Morgan, Chris	Lincoln University
	Byrd, Franz	Lincoln University

Year	Name	School
1925	Polk, Samuel	Virginia Seminary and College
	Hoyle, Herbert	Virginia Seminary
	Lee, William	Hampton Institute
	Davis, George	Hampton Institute
	Coleman, Herman	North Carolina A&T
	Martin, J.J.	Shaw University
	Slaughter, Tanner	Virginia State
	Pindle, O.A.	Hampton Institute
	Alexander, James	Hampton Institute
	Wheedbee, Melvin	Virginia Seminary
	Brown, Governor	Virginia Seminary
1926	Brown, Governor	Virginia Seminary
	Hester, Clarence	North Carolina A&T
	Anderson, Roger	Virginia Union
	Breaux, Inman	Virginia Union
	Miller, Jessie	North Carolina A&T
	Polk, Samuel	Virginia Seminary
	Davis, George	Hampton Institute
	Williams, William	Hampton Institute
	Munday, Reuben	Hampton Institute
	Lee, William	Hampton Institute
	Coleman, Herman	North Carolina A&T
1927	Robinson, Theodore	Hampton Institute
	Fowler, Milton	Virginia Seminary and College

Year	Name	School	Year	Name	School
	Lane, J.F.	North Carolina A&T		Unthank, James	Hampton Institute
	Slaughter, Tanner	Virginia State		Johnson, L.M.	Virginia State
	Breaux, Inman	Virginia Union		Dabney, Red	Virginia State
	Washington, Herm	Virginia Union		Lewis, Roscoe	Virginia State
	Miller, J.	North Carolina A&T		Kane	Lincoln University
	Patterson, M.E.	North Carolina A&T		Williams, John	Virginia Union
	Streeter, J.A.	North Carolina A&T		Gaines, Samuel	Hampton Institute
	Coleman, Herman	North Carolina A&T		Conrad, Thomas	Morgan State
	Lee, William	Hampton Institute	1932	Poole, Everett	Virginia Union
1928	Dabney, Red	Virginia State		Boyd, Theodore	Virginia State
	Fowler, Milton	Virginia Seminary		Malone, William	North Carolina College
	Davis, Edward	Virginia Seminary		Bounds, Earl	Virginia State
	Gates, Harold	Hampton Institute		Williams, Lloyd	Virginia Union
	Hill, Carl	Hampton Institute		Jenkins, Samuel	Virginia Union
	Gaines, Samuel	Hampton Institute		Williams, James	Morgan State
	Pegram, Richard	Virginia State		Rivers, George	Hampton Institute
	Jones, Oscar	Hampton Institute		Unthank, James	Morgan State
	Shelton, James	Virginia State		Lewis, Roscoe	Virginia State
	Perkins, Sylvester	Hampton Institute		Conrad, Thomas	Morgan State
	Lane, J.F.	North Carolina A&T	1933	Richmond, Ivory	Hampton Institute
1929	Royall, Samuel	Virginia State		Wilson, Howard	Morgan State
	Gaines, Samuel	Hampton Institute		Ware, Joseph	Howard University
	Burton, Thomas	Virginia Union		Cole, Joseph	Howard University
	Syndor, J.	Lincoln University		Conrad, Thomas	Morgan State
	Thompson, B.H.	Virginia Union		Holmes, Irvin	North Carolina College
	Oliver, Basil	Virginia State		Williams, James	Morgan State
	Lee, Albert	Virginia State		Carmichael, Ellis	Bluefield State
	Bounds, Earl	Virginia State		Crawford, Hubert	Morgan State
	Johnson, L.M.	Virginia State		Bergen, C.W.	Lincoln University
	Smith, Bernard	Virginia Union		Unthank, James	Hampton Institute
	McGowan, Charles	Hampton Institute	1934	Gaither, Booker	Howard University
1930	Marshall, John	Howard University		Poole, Everett	Virginia Union
	Oliver, Basil	Virginia State		Drake, Carl	Morgan State
	Robinson, Theodore	Virginia Union		Jenkins, Samuel	Virginia Union
	Robinson, Maxie	Virginia Union		Troupe, Otis	Morgan State
	Gaines, Samuel	Hampton Institute	1935	Thompson, Herbert	Bluefield State
	Bogle, John	Johnson C. Smith		Norman, McHenry	North Carolina A&T
	Thomas, Maxwell	Hampton Institute		Alston, Edward	North Carolina College
	Lewis, Roscoe	Virginia State		Banks, Franklin	Bluefield State
	Williams, John	Virginia Union		Crawford, Hubert	Morgan State
	Bonds, Earl	Virginia State		Hursey, Julius	North Carolina College
	Conrad, Thomas	Morgan State	1936	Johnson, Matthew	Bluefield State
1931	Rivers, George	Hampton Institute		Link, Algie	Bluefield State
	Scott, Cabell	Virginia State		Owens, Larney	Hampton Institute
	Edwards	Hampton Institute		Craddock, Claiborne	Virginia State

Year	Name	School	Year	Name	School
	Briscoe, Henry	Virginia State		Toliver, Howard	Johnson C. Smith
	Flippen, John	Bluefield State		Cooper, Fred	Virginia Union
	Sowell, Richard	Morgan State		Powell, Kenneth	Johnson C. Smith
	Hopson, Raymond	Hampton Institute		Harris, Donald	Virginia State
	Mosby, Walter	Morgan State		Stuart, James	Hampton Institute
	Dixon, Richard	Virginia State	1941	Hall, William	North Carolina College
	Simpson, William	Morgan State		Worthy, Fred	Shaw University
1937	Briscoe, Henry	Virginia State		Fauntleroy, Arthur	Morgan State
	Meadows, Milton	Johnson C. Smith		Gaines, William	North Carolina College
	Craddock, Claiborne	Virginia State		Givens, Oscar	Morgan State
	Mosby, Walter	Morgan State		Brayboy, Jack	Johnson C. Smith
	Campbell, Francis	Virginia Union		Carter, Oscar	Virginia State
	Lampkin, William	Morgan State		Grice, William	Hampton Institute
	Brewer, James	Virginia State		Moseby, Wallace	Morgan State
	White, Robert	Howard University		Mack, George	North Carolina College
	Brown, Wendell	Lincoln University		Clarke, George	North Carolina A&T
	Sowell, Richard	Morgan State	1942	Malone, Gerald	Johnson C. Smith
1938	Frazier, Ivan	Virginia Union		Lynch, Wesley	West Virginia State
	Govan, Claude	Shaw University		Whittingham, Mitch	Morgan State
	Lamb, George	Virginia State		Ware, David	Hampton Institute
	Ryans, Mason	Morgan State		Grimsley, Preston	Morgan State
	Brewer, John	Virginia State		Brayboy, Jack	Johnson C. Smith
	Lynch, Allen	North Carolina A&T		Gaines, William	North Carolina College
	Gordon, Frank	Morgan State		Hurley, Walter	Virginia State
	Briscoe, Henry	Virginia State		Thomas, Henry	Bluefield State
	Brewer, James	Virginia State		Williams, Charles	Virginia State
	Nelson, James	Virginia State		Givens, Oscar	Morgan State
	Meadows, Milton	Johnson C. Smith	1943	Irvin, Calvin	Morgan State
1939	Cooper, Fred	Virginia Union		King, Bob	Hampton Institute
	Bruee, Samuel	North Carolina A&T		Mann, Robert	Hampton Institute
	Johnson, William	Bluefield State		Gaines, Clarence	Morgan State
	Perry, Leroy	Bluefield State		Battle, David	Virginia State
	Moseby, Wallace	Morgan State		Gearing, Roy	North Carolina A&T
	Griffin, James	Hampton Institute		Couch, Flan	Morgan State
	Holly, Waymond	Morgan State		Burgess, Fred	Morgan State
	Brewer, James	Virginia State		Ferebee, Melvin	Virginia State
	Stuart, James	Hampton Institute		Fletcher, Elbie	Johnson C. Smith
	Bartee, Lawrence	Virginia State	1944	Perry, General	Virginia State
	Meadows, Milton	Johnson C. Smith		Frazier, Charles	Morgan State
1940	Moseby, Wallace	Morgan State		Fisher, James	Johnson C. Smith
	Kee, Horace	Morgan State		Weaver, Charles	North Carolina A&T
	Brayboy, Jack	Johnson C. Smith		Day, Terry	Morgan State
	Peekman, William	North Carolina College		Porter, Leroy	Virginia State
	Reeves, Milton	Bluefield State		Taylor, Morris	Virginia State
	Cain, William	Morgan State		Whaley, Benjamin	Virginia State

Year	Name	School
	Burgess, Fred	Morgan State
	Gaines, Clarence	Morgan State
1945	Green, Linwood	West Virginia State
	Jones, John	Virginia State
	Galbreath, Carl	North Carolina College
	Price, Charles	Virginia State
	Jolly, Francis	Virginia State
	Robinson, James	West Virginia State
	Rahming, E.	Morgan State
	Turner, Ed	Johnson C. Smith
	Rawls, Wilbert	West Virginia State
	Childs, Leroy	North Carolina A&T
	Battle, David	Virginia State
1946	Casey, Tom	Hampton Institute
	Gamble, Samuel	West Virginia State
	Galbreath, Carl	North Carolina College
	Hurley, Walter	Virginia State
	Brown, John	North Carolina College
	Weaver, Charles	North Carolina A&T
	Fauntleroy, Arthur	Morgan State
	Bridgeforth, Sidney	Lincoln University
	Witcher, Alfred	Bluefield State
	Givens, Oscar	Morgan State
	Whaley, Benjamin	Virginia State
1947	Bellamy, Twillie	Shaw University
	Jordan, Otis	Howard University
	Hurley, Walter	Virginia State
	Casey, Tom	Hampton Institute
	Marshall, Melvin	Howard University
	Whaley, Benjamin	Virginia State
	Williams, Joseph	North Carolina A&T
	Fauntleroy, Arthur	Morgan State
	Bridgeforth, Sidney	Lincoln University
	Brown, John	North Carolina College
	Jones, John	Virginia State
1948	Gilliam, Joseph	West Virginia State
	Whaley, Benjamin	Virginia State
	Lewis, W.C.	Hampton Institute
	Clark, Clarence	West Virginia State
	Rooks, George	Morgan State
	Bailey, James	West Virginia State
	Goodall, Luther	Hampton Institute
	Cragway, Roy	Morgan State
	Bellamy, Twillie	Shaw University
	Scheneck, Edward	Delaware State

Year	Name	School
1949	Fairfax, Charles	West Virginia State
	Nelson, Athelstan	Morgan State
	Rooks, George	Morgan State
	Hunter, Timothy	Morgan State
	Dillard, Clyde	West Virginia State
	Roper, Edward	Shaw University
	Bellamy, Twille	Shaw University
	Way, Leroy	Shaw University
	Whaley, Marvin	Morgan State
	Wickcliffe, Edward	West Virginia State
	Clark, Clarence	West Virginia State
1950	Miles, Roland	St. Augustine's
	Taylor, Butch	North Carolina College
	Clements, Jesse	St. Augustine's
	Miller, Samuel	West Virginia State
	Warlick, Ernest	North Carolina College
	Jackson, Boyd	North Carolina A&T
	Thompson, Sherwood	North Carolina A&T
	Rooks, George	Morgan State
	Robinson, Charles	Morgan State
	Jackson, William	North Carolina A&T
	Boyers, William	North Carolina A&T
1951	**Offense**	
	Hawkins, Robert	West Virginia State
	Jackson, William	North Carolina A&T
	Keene, Floyd	Virginia State
	Smith, Ergie	Bluefield State
	Ayers, Robert	Hampton Institute
	Brown, Roosevelt	Morgan State
	Curry, Rupert	West Virginia State
	Funderburke, George	North Carolina A&T
	Rodez, Andrew	Virginia Union
	Smith, Willie	West Virginia State
	Crawley, William	North Carolina College
	Defense	
	Washington, Leroy	North Carolina College
	Miles, Leo	Virginia State
	Neverson, Ed	Howard University
	Spencer, Mel	North Carolina College
	Statum, Arthur	North Carolina A&T
	Hunter, Walter	North Carolina A&T
	Wallace, Cleo	Winston-Salem State
	Warlick, Ernest	North Carolina College
	Swann, David	Bluefield State
	Farrer, Al	North Carolina A&T
	Carter, John	Howard University

Year	Name	School	Year	Name	School
1952	**Offense**		1955	Sample, John	Maryland State
	Miles, Leo	Virginia State		Porter, Charles	Morgan State
	Petty, Howard	Johnson C. Smith		Harris, Thomas	Bluefield State
	Keene, Floyd	Virginia State		Rozier, Jack	Morgan State
	Brown, Roosevelt	Morgan State		Scruggs, O'Bryant	West Virginia State
	Cowles, James	Lincoln University		Nash, John	Virginia State
	Thompson, Charles	Virginia State		Plunkett, Sherman	Maryland State
	Neverson, Ed	Howard University		Douglas, Arthur	Maryland State
	Henderson, Herbert	West Virginia State		Boone, Matthew	North Carolina College
	Callahan, Robert	Virginia State		Smith, J.D.	North Carolina A&T
	Miller, Vandy	West Virginia State		Prather, Gilbert	Morgan State
	Hunter, Walter	North Carolina A&T	1956	Sample, John	Maryland State
	Defense			Vaughn, Vernon	Maryland State
	Vaughn, Leroy	Virginia Union		Hoover, John	Bluefield State
	Ellerbe, Steve	Virginia State		Nicholson, Joseph	St. Augustine's
	Carter, Sidney	Virginia State		Richards, Earl	St. Augustine's
	Wilson, Wilbur	Virginia State		Evans, Raleigh	Maryland State
	Gibson, Jack	North Carolina A&T		Brown, George	Hampton Institute
	Carroll, Bwano	Howard University		Montgomery, Al	North Carolina College
	Bundy, John	Delaware State		Baker, John	North Carolina College
	Curry, Rupert	West Virginia State		McArthur, Jerome	Morgan State
	McAllister, William	St. Augustine's		Rozier, Jack	Morgan State
	Floyd, Charles	North Carolina College	1957	Hammonds, Eugene	Shaw University
1953	Buford, William	Morgan State		Mouton, Alpha	Maryland State
	Hawkins, Robert	West Virginia State		Baker, John	North Carolina College
	Eason, Harry	Hampton Institute		Dupree, Benjamin	Winston-Salem State
	Person, Joseph	North Carolina College		Pinkston, Frank	Virginia Union
	Day, Norman	Virginia State		Vaughn, Vernon	Maryland State
	Gaines, Al	Morgan State		Washington, Ken	Howard University
	Bundy, John	Delaware State		Rowe, Robert	Winston-Salem State
	Thornton, Amos	North Carolina College		Coley, James	Maryland State
	Freeman, Clinton	Virginia State		Evans, Raleigh	Maryland State
	Boone, James	West Virginia State		Sample, John	Maryland State
	Williams, Charles	Virginia State	1958	Moody, George	Virginia State
1954	Parks, Frank	Bluefield State		Oakly, Lloyd	North Carolina A&T
	Harvey, Otto	North Carolina College		Gatling, Isaac	North Carolina College
	Plunkett, Sherman	Maryland State		Knight, Glenfield	Shaw University
	Day, Norman	Virginia State		Forbes, James	North Carolina College
	Jeter, Emmett	Delaware State		Wallace, George	North Carolina College
	Thornton, Amos	North Carolina College		Brown, Roger	Maryland State
	Sample, John	Maryland State		Jiles, Alfred	Maryland State
	Evans, Jerome	North Carolina College		Jackson, Clifton	North Carolina College
	Boone, James	West Virinia State		McClain, Albert	Shaw University
	Nash, John	Virginia State		Brewington, Jim	North Carolina College
	Freeman, Clinton	Virginia State			

Year	Name	School	Year	Name	School
1960	Stanford, Lorenzo	North Carolina A&T	1966	*Offense*	
	Braxton, Hezekiah	Virginia Union		Nock, George	Morgan State
	Guthrie, Nelson	Winston-Salem State		Sharper, Harry	Virginia State
	Holmes, Charles	Maryland State		Shell, Art	Maryland State
	Bey, Charles	Hampton Institute		Mayo, Earl	Morgan State
	Knight, Glenfield	Shaw University		Tyler, Alfred	Livingstone College
	Hobbs, John	Maryland State		Sutton, Sylvester	Livingstone College
	Black, James	North Carolina A&T		Palmore, Harvey	Morgan State
	Gray, Harold	Maryland State		Moore, Horace	Virginia Union
	Jeter, DeWayne	Virginia State		Bowers, Sandy	Hampton Institute
	Taylor, Robert	Maryland State		Phillips, James	Morgan State
1961	Clark, Otis	Shaw University		Jones, Edwin	North Carolina College
	Holmes, Charles	Maryland State		*Defense*	
	Wilkins, Richard	North Carolina College		Duncan, James	Maryland State
	Ferguson, Willie	North Carolina A&T		Bethea, Elvin	North Carolina A&T
	Norman, Pettis	Johnson C. Smith		Dabney, Carlton	Morgan State
	Hinton, Charles	North Carolina College		Chavis, Jesse	Virginia Union
	Guthrie, Nelson	Winston-Salem State		Chrenshaw, Chauncey	Shaw University
	Tinkler, William	Morgan State		Beard, Eugene	Virginia Union
	Young, Robert	Morgan State		Johnson, Wade	Morgan State
	McNeil, Robert	Virginia State		Smith, Raymond	Norfolk State
	Taylor, Robert	Maryland State		Lanier, Willie	Morgan State
1963	Dobbins, Oliver	Morgan State		Bell, Louis	North Carolina College
	Pugh, Jethro	Elizabeth City State		Queen, Jeffrey	Morgan State
	Baker, John	Norfolk State	1967	*Offense*	
	Gordon, Cornell	North Carolina A&T		Pearson, Willie	North Carolina A&T
	Watkins, Joseph	Virginia State		Robinson, Bertram	Hampton Institute
	Gaines, Alex	North Carolina A&T		Shell, Arthur	Maryland State
	Currington, Robert	North Carolina College		Nock, George	Morgan State
	Hayes, William	North Carolina College		Johnson, Daryl	Morgan State
	Davis, Jones	Virginia Union		Dean, Thomas	Morgan State
	Sheppard, Leroy	Morgan State		Martin, Julian	North Carolina College
	Anderson, Roger	Virginia Union		Helms, Dewey	Virginia State
1964	Boozer, Emerson	Maryland State		Bethea, Elvin	North Carolina A&T
	Beard, Monroe	Virginia Union		Kirksey, Roy	Maryland State
	Pugh, Jethroe	Maryland State		Boyd, Gerald	Morgan State
	Francis, Ronald	North Carolina A&T		*Defense*	
	Little, Thurlis	Elizabeth City State		Chavis, Jesse	Virginia Union
	Souels, Richard	Winston-Salem State		Queen, Jeffrey	Morgan State
	Golder, Edward	Virginia State		Hayes, Edward	Morgan State
	Hamilton, Henry	Virginia Union		Farmer, Edward	Johnson C. Smith
	Williams, Joseph	Maryland State		Mitchell, James	Virginia State
	Kelly, William	Virginia Union		Wilkerson, Doug	North Carolina College
	Phillips, James	Morgan State		Belk, William	Maryland State
				Thompson, William	Maryland State

Year	Name	School	Year	Name	School
	Dabney, Carlton	Morgan State		Washington, Mark	Morgan State
	Duncan, James	Maryland State		Quinn, Peter	North Carolina College
	Patterson, Donald	Virginia Union		Lewis, Alvin	Elizabeth City State
1968	*Offense*			Singletary, Sam	North Carolina College
	Denson, Moses	Maryland State		Baylor, Robert	Maryland State
	Walton, John	Elizabeth City State	1970	*Offense*	
	Pearson, Willie	North Carolina A&T		Wynecoff, Rodderick	Shaw University
	Grady, Daniel	Winston-Salem State		Duncan, Elroy	Johnson C. Smith
	Smith, Robert	Morgan State		Davis, Steve	Delaware State
	Wiliams, Ervin	Maryland State		Bell, Harold	Morgan State
	Jarvis, Raymond	Norfolk State		Wright, Willie	North Carolina A&T
	Ferguson, Eugene	Norfolk State		Williams, Torain	Elizabeth City State
	Smith, Gregory	Livingstone College		Holmes, Melvin	North Carolina A&T
	Wilkerson, Doug	North Carolina College		Caraway, Bruce	Morgan State
	Chester, Raymond	Morgan State		Jarvis, Raymond	Norfolk State
				Clanton, Larry	North Carolina College
	Defense			Branton, Robert	Livingstone College
	Thompson, William	Maryland State			
	Code, Merle	North Carolina A&T		*Defense*	
	Robinson, Bertram	Hampton Institute		Westmoreland, Douglas	North Carolina A&T
	Paige, Lonnie	North Carolina College		Leigh, Ronald	Elizabeth City State
	Baylor, Robert	Maryland State		Fairley, John	Johnson C. Smith
	Irons, Gerald	Maryland State		Germany, Willie	Morgan State
	Farmer, Edgar	Johnson C. Smith		Holloway, Robert	North Carolina College
	Klutz, Paul	Livingstone College		Jones, Larry	Johnson C. Smith
	Hayes, Edward	Morgan State		Brooks, Larry	Virginia State
	Mitchell, James	Virginia State		Cox, Ronald	Fayetteville State
				Mabry, Ronald	Howard University
1969	*Offense*			Quinn, Peter	North Carolina College
	Dusenberry, William	Johnson C. Smith		Jones, Glen	Delaware State
	Matthews, Herm	North Carolina College	1971	*Offense*	
	Jarvis, Raymond	Norfolk State		Duke, Bruce	Johnson C. Smith
	Carson, Ollis	North Carolina College		Mayes, Myron	Virginia State
	McManus, Allen	Winston-Salem State		Price, Perry	Livingstone College
	Gantt, Jerome	North Carolina College		Belton, Andy	Elizabeth City State
	Wilkerson, Doug	North Carolina College		Chambers, William	Virginia State
	Smith, Robert	Morgan State		Sawyer, Frank	Livingstone College
	Bell, Ernest	Elizabeth City State		Reynolds, Oliver	Elizabeth City State
	Russell, Anthony	Elizabeth City State		Winslow, Joe	Virginia State
	Martin, Julian	North Carolina College		Johnson, Robert	Hampton Institute
				Corbett, Billy	Johnson C. Smith
	Defense			Bullock, Ronald	Virginia State
	Moore, Donnell	Elizabeth City State			
	Robinson, Bertram	Hampton Institute		*Defense*	
	Code, Merle	North Carolina A&T		Jenkins, Oscar	Virginia Union
	Klutz, Paul	Livingstone College		Jackson, Roddrick	Virginia State
	Reid, Paul	Johnson C. Smith		Harper, William	Virginia State
	Mitchell, James	Virginia State			

Year	Name	School	Year	Name	School
	Allen, John	Virginia State		**Defense**	
	Gunn, William	Johnson C. Smith		Carmichael, Bruce	Elizabeth City State
	Brooks, Larry	Virginia State		McCray, Frank	Virginia Union
	Overton, Thomas	Virginia State		Stukes, David	Elizabeth City State
	Dreher, Damon	Virginia Union		Reed, Larry	Virginia Union
	Jones, Leroy	Norfolk State		Pearson, Joseph	Virginia State
	Brooks, David	Livingstone College		Macon, Richard	Virginia Union
	Davis, Ronald	Virginia State		Leonard, Anthony	Virginia Union
1972	**Offense**			Eley, Vincent	Virginia Union
	Phiffer, Curtis	Winston-Salem State		Barbour, Bennie	Winston-Salem State
	Nelson, Frederick	Winston-Salem State		Wright, Michael	Fayetteville State
	Chavis, Robert	Virginia State		Ballard, Horace	Livingstone College
	Walker, Larry	Fayetteville State	1974	**Offense**	
	Caul, Robert	Virginia State		Newsome, Jerome	Elizabeth City State
	Garner, Robert	Winston-Salem State		Roberts, Larry	Virginia Union
	Chambers, William	Virginia State		Woodson, James	St. Paul's College
	Lide, William	Johnson C. Smith		White, Clarence	Virginia Union
	Morrison, Marvin	Winston-Salem State		Tate, Donald	Virginia Union
	Carter, Luther	Johnson C. Smith		Graeff, Steve	Norfolk State
	Williams, Lofell	Virginia Union		Godwin, James	Fayetteville State
				Ritter, Sylvester	Livingstone College
	Defense			Hill, George	Johnson C. Smith
	Strickland, Irving	Virginia Union		Scott, Herbert	Virginia Union
	Harris, Ronald	Virginia State		Brooks, John	Elizabeth City State
	Gregg, Edward	Winston-Salem State		**Defense**	
	Barbour, Bennie	Winston-Salem State		Pearson, Joseph	Virginia State
	Hathaway, Harold	Virginia State		Leonard, Anthony	Virginia Union
	Farrar, John	Livingstone College		Bailey, Willie	Johnson C. Smith
	Green, Van	Shaw University		Richardson, Curtis	Winston-Salem State
	Jones, Bob	Virginia Union		Young, John	Fayetteville State
	Johnson, Larry	Elizabeth City State		Trotter, Moses	Norfolk State
	Hayes, Michael	Virginia State		Jones, Michael	Virginia Union
	Jones, Leroy	Norfolk State		Artis, William	Shaw University
1973	**Offense**			Miller, John	Livingstone College
	Pointer, Clarence	Fayetteville State		Barbour, Bennie	Winston-Salem State
	Davis, James	Winston-Salem State		Cooney, Andrew	Livingstone College
	Sawyer, Frank	Livingstone College	1975	**Offense**	
	Carter, Luther	Johnson C. Smith		Newsome, Jerome	Elizabeth City State
	Shepherd, Larry	Virginia Union		Godwin, James	Fayetteville State
	Scott, Herbert	Virginia Union		Rodgers, Johnny	Winston-Salem State
	Brooks, John	Elizabeth City State		Morrison, Marvin	Winston-Salem State
	Roberts, Larry	Virginia Union		Holmes, Alfred	Elizabeth City State
	Santiful, Adolph	Norfolk State		Cosby, Samuel	St. Paul's College
	Dunn, Walter	Virginia State		Woodson, James	St. Paul's College
	Thomas, Robert	Livingstone College		Bascomb, Carl	Hampton Institute

Year	Name	School	Year	Name	School
	Spindle, Linwood	Johnson C. Smith		Midgett, Reginald	Hampton Institute
	Simmons, Jackie	Fayetteville State		Weeks, Robert	Winston-Salem State
	Curry, Dexter	Norfolk State		Woodson, James	St. Paul's College
	Defense			Hargove, Fred	Elizabeth City State
	McCray, Frank	Virginia Union		Lyman, Curtis	Virginia Union
	Robinson, Linwood	Virginia State		Youngs, Ernesto	Virginia Union
	Lee, Larry	Livingstone College		**Defense**	
	Miller, Johnny	Livingstone College		Stoutamire, John	Livingstone College
	Franks, Maurice	Fayetteville State		Washington Cornelius	Winston-Salem State
	Seward, Larry	Virginia Union		Dark, Frank	Virginia Union
	Corley, Ronald	Johnson C. Smith		Doss, Reggie	Hampton Institute
	Williford, Larry	Virginia Union		Winbush, James	Winston-Salem State
	Nance, Roger	Norfolk State		Ellis, Michael	Norfolk State
	Leonard, Anthony	Virginia Union		Young, Calvin	Virginia Union
	Bey, Ronald Allen	Hampton Institute		Farrington, Lester	Elizabeth City State
				Cuthrell, Herman	Livingstone College
1976	**Offense**			Moore, Chris	Virginia State
	Thomas, Judge	Virginia Union		Crawley, Michael	Virginia Union
	Travis, Burnis	Fayetteville State	1978	**Offense**	
	Hines, Herbert	Virginia State		Thomas, Judge	Virginia Union
	Grimsley, Chet	Johnson C. Smith		Stroman, Charles	Johnson C. Smith
	Curry, Dexter	Norfolk State		Sweatt, Dwight	Norfolk State
	Hill, Darryl	Virginia Union		Diggs, William	Winston-Salem State
	Rodgers, Johnny	Winston-Salem State		Blount, Kermit	Winston-Salem State
	Powell, Robert	Norfolk State		Newsome, Tim	WInston-Salem State
	Woodson, James	St. Paul's College		Travis, Burnis	Fayetteville State
	Crawley, Michael	Virginia Union		Lyman, Curtis	Virginia Union
	Cosby, Samuel	St. Paul's College		Youngs, Ernesto	Virginia Union
				Jones, Leroy	Norfolk State
	Defense				
	Franks, Maurice	Fayetteville State		**Defense**	
	Cuthrell, Herman	Livingstone College		Adams, Leroy	Virginia Union
	Moore, Chris	Virginia State		Belle, Joe	Norfolk State
	McNeil, Dale	Virginia Union		Rose, Don	Hampton Institute
	Johnson, Bernard	Virginia Union		Moses, Waddell	Elizabeth City State
	Dossy, Reginald	Hampton Institute		Thompson, Tony	Elizabeth City State
	Corley, Ronald	Johnson C. Smith		Crawley, Michael	Virginia Union
	Flowers, Jim	Norfolk State		Harrington, Baxter	Winston-Salem State
	Williams, Curtis	Shaw University		Grimes, Willie	St. Paul's College
	Cooney, Andrew	Livingstone College		Pugh, James	Elizabeth City State
	Pleasants, Curtis	Virginia State		Jordan, Willie	Winston-Salem State
				Bullock, Plummer	Virginia Union
1977	**Offense**				
	Crawford, Rufus	Virginia State	1979	**Offense**	
	Hines, Herbert	Virginia State		Gray, Willie	Fayetteville State
	Blount, Kermit	Winston-Salem State		Hill, Michael	Elizabeth City State
	Newsome, Tim	Winston-Salem State		South, Victor	Hampton Institute
	Harrington, LaRue	Norfolk State		Robinson, James	Norfolk State

Year	Name	School	Year	Name	School
	Barnett, Oswald	Virginia Union		Collier, Robert	Virginia Union
	Barnwell, Malcolm	Virginia Union		White, Joseph	Livingstone College
	Newsome, Tim	Winston-Salem State		Lewis, John	Winston-Salem State
	Harrington, LaRue	Norfolk State		**Defense**	
	Long, Jesse	Livingstone College		Riddick, Andrew	North Carolina Central
	Lyman, Curtis	Virginia Union		Bryson, Dan	Winston-Salem State
	Tyson, James	Winston-Salem State		Drew, Dwayne	Virginia Union
	Guions, Ronald	Fayetteville State		Hamilton, James	Elizabeth City State
	Whaff, Wilbert	Virginia Union		Stokes, Harrison	Winston-Salem State
	Burnette, Carter	Virginia Union		Johnson, Brad	Virginia State
	Defense			Ingram, Lorenzo	North Carolina Central
	Adams, Leroy	Virginia Union		Dillon, William	Virginia Union
	Hall, Ike	Fayetteville State		Tongue, Margo	Bowie State
	Wring, Alfred	Johnson C. Smith		McKinstry, Chris	North Carolina Central
	Jacobs, Daniel	Winston-Salem State		Mayo, Gary	Virginia Union
	Wilson, Fred	Elizabeth City State		Futrell, Robert	Elizabeth City State
	Mack, Winfred	Winston-Salem State	1982	**Offense**	
	Sturdifen, Melvin	Norfolk State		McDowell, Nate	Johnson C. Smith
	White, Ernest	Hampton Institute		Thomas, John	Johnson C. Smith
	Ellis, Michael	Norfolk State		Tate, Benjamin	North Carolina Central
	Banks, Layard	Virginia State		Cathion, Keith	Virginia Union
	Bullock, Plummer	Virginia Union		Washington, Sam	North Carolina Central
	Wadford, Bertie	Fayetteville State		Barringer, Larry	Virginia Union
1980	**Offense**			White, Joseph	Livingstone College
	Smith, Anthony	Hampton Institute		Jordan, Roy	Virginia Union
	Jones, Arrington	Winston-Salem State		Nimmons, Jonathan	Winston-Salem State
	High, John	Norfolk State		Hunter, Victor	North Carolina Central
	Gunn, Jeffrey	Norfolk State		Moore, Danny	Winston-Salem State
	Barnett, Oswald	Virginia Union		**Defense**	
	Parson, Keith	Winston-Salem State		Dillon, William	Virginia Union
	Bell, Willie	St. Paul's College		Scott, Joseph	Norfolk State
	Mahan, Dennis	Hampton Institute		Pierce, Allen	North Carolina Central
	Johnson, Michael	Hampton Institute		Jackson, Reginald	Hampton University
	Whitehurst, Stanley	Elizabeth City State		Bingham, Michael	Virginia Union
	Lesane, Lydell	St. Paul's College		Beauford, Daniel	Johnson C. Smith
	Smith, Gary	North Carolina Central		Ingram, Lorenzo	North Carolina Central
1981	**Offense**			Martn, Kevin	Fayetteville State
	Fraylon, Gerald	North Carolina Central		Drew, Dwayne	Virginia Union
	Nimmons, Jonathan	Winston-Salem State		Evans, Brian	Norfolk State
	Wall, William	Virginia Union		Stokes, Harrison	Winston-Salem State
	James, Elvin	Elizabeth City State		Futrell, Robert	Elizabeth City State
	McDowell, Nate	Johnson C. Smith	1983	**Offense**	
	Gunn, Jeffrey	Norfolk State		Nimmons, Jonathan	Winston-Salem State
	Whitfield, Dwayne	Elizabeth City State		Clark, Robert	North Carolina Central
	Barringer, Larry	Virginia Union		Moore, Dan	Winston-Salem State

Year	Name	School	Year	Name	School
	Kelly, Tyrone	Fayetteville State		Ward, Quenton	Norfolk State
	Campbell, Kelvin	Virginia Union		Ward, James	Virginia State
	Powell, Alvin	Winston-Salem State		Smith, Leon	Norfolk State
	Barringer, Larry	Virginia Union		Jones, Glen	Norfolk State
	Goodhope, Orlando	Norfolk State		Wallace, Melvin	Norfolk State
	Ford, Paul	Livingstone College		Banks, Reginald	Elizabeth City State
	Kersey, Clifton	North Carolina Central		Grooms, Samuel	Virginia Union
				Green, John	Virginia State
	Defense			Brown, Arnold	North Carolina Central
	Robinson, Mark	Virginia State		Austin, Juan	Fayetteville State
	Frizzell, William	North Carolina Central		Lewis, Aaron	Fayetteville State
	Simms, Kendrick	Fayetteville State	1985	*Offense*	
	Cameron, Jack	Winston-Salem State		Turner, Barry	Winston-Salem State
	Curtis, Larry	Virginia Union		Clark, Robert	North Carolina Central
	Drew, Dwayne	Virginia Union		Green, Robert	North Carolina Central
	Smith, Leon	Norfolk State		Horn, Leonardo	Winston-Salem State
	Readon, Issacs	Hampton Institute		Painter, Carl	Hampton University
	Grooms, Samuel	Virginia Union		Patton, Gerald	North Carolina Central
	Ward, James	Virginia State		Browder, Dale	Norfolk State
	Wicker, Anthony	Johnson C. Smith		Cunningham, Kevin	Livingstone College
	Futrell, Robert	Elizabeth City State		Holland, Keith	Winston-Salem State
	Sauls, Eddie	Winston-Salem State		Skinner, Darryl	Hampton University
1984	*Offense*			McNeill, Terrence	North Carolina Central
	Mosley, Rufus	Livingston, College		Harvey, Earl	North Carolina Central
	Patton, Gerald	North Carolina Central		*Defense*	
	Hines, Ernest	Norfolk State		Blaylock, Anthony	Winston-Salem State
	James, Jeffrey	Winston-Salem State		Beasley Derrick	Winston-Salem State
	Green, Robert	Livingston College		Jeffries, Franklin	Saint Paul's College
	Clark, Robert	North Carolina Central		Wallace, Melvin	North Carolina Central
	Johnson, Anthony	Norfolk State		Harris, Charles	Fayetteville State
	Moore, Danny	Winston-Salem State		Asbury, Jerry	Livingstone College
	White, Joseph	Livingston College		Readon, Ike	Hampton University
	Smith, Tyrone	Winston-Salem State		Coles, John	Winston Salem State
	Langhorne, Reginald	Elizabeth City State		Cofield, Tim	Elizabeth City State
	Bailey, Clarence	Hampton University		Warren, Craig	Johnson C. Smith
	Defense			Lewis, Aaron	Fayetteville State
	Readon, Issac	Hampton University			

BLACK COLLEGE CONFERENCE WINNERS

	CIAA	SWAC	SIAC	EIAC	SCAC	MWAC
1916			Morehouse			
1917			Tuskegee			
1918			Talledega			
1919			Fisk			
1920			Morehouse			
1921		Wiley	Morehouse			
1922		Paul Quinn	Morehouse			
1923	Hampton	Wiley	Morehouse & Fisk			
1924	Va. Union	Paul Quinn	Tuskegee			
1925	Lincoln	Bishop	Tuskegee			
1926	Hampton	Sam Houston	Tuskegee			
1927	Hampton	Wiley	Tuskegee			
1928	N.Car. A&T	Wiley	Tuskegee			
1929	Hampton	Wiley	Talladega			
1930	Va. State	Wiley	Tuskegee		Tougaloo	
1931	Morgan	Prairie View	Tuskegee			
1932	Hampton	Wiley	Tuskegee		Alcorn A & M	
1933	Morgan	Langston & Prairie View	Tuskegee		Alcorn A & M	Wilberforce
1934	Morgan	Texas College	Morris Brown		Alcorn A & M	Wilberforce
1935	Morgan	Texas College	Alabama State		Tougaloo	Kentucky State
1936	Morgan	Langston & Texas College	Tuskegee		Tougaloo	Kentucky State
1937	Va. State	Texas College	Fla. A&M		Alcorn A & M	West Va. State
1938	Morgan	Langston & Southern	Fla. A&M		Alcorn A & M	Kentucky State
1939	Va. State	Langston	Alabama State		Leland	Kentucky State
1940		Langston & Southern	Fla. A&M	Fayetteville	Alcorn A &M	
1941	Morgan	Prairie View		Winston Salem	Leland	
1942		Texas College		Norfolk State	Leland	
1943						
1944		Langston & Texas & Wiley	Tuskegee			
1945	Va. State	Wiley				

AFRICAN-AMERICAN PROFESSIONAL FOOTBALL PLAYERS

1920	Akron Pros	Frederick Pollard, Paul Robeson
	Cleveland	Robert Marshall
	Hammond Pros	Paul Robeson
	Rock Island (Illinois)	Robert Marshall
1921	Akron Pros	Frederick Pollard, Paul Robeson
	Rock Island	Robert Marshall
	Canton Bulldogs (Ohio)	Jaye "Inky" Williams
	Hammond Pros	Jaye "Inky" Williams
1922	Milwaukee Badgers	Frederick Pollard, Paul Robeson, Fred Slater
	Hammond Pros	Jaye "Inky" Williams, John Shelbourne
	Rock Island	Fred Slater
1923	Hammond Pros	Frederick Pollard, Jaye "Inky" Williams
	Rock Island	Fred Slater, Edward Butler
	Milwaukee	James Turner
	Minneapolis	Dick Hudson
1924	Hammond Pros	Frederick Pollard, Jaye "Inky" Williams, Ed Butler
	Rock Island	Fred Slater
	Akron Pros	Edward Butler, Charles West
	Dayton	Jaye "Inky" Williams
1925	Akrons Pros	Frederick Pollard
	Hammond Pros	Frederick Pollard, Jaye "Inky" Williams, Dick Hudson
	Providence (Rhode Island)	Frederick Pollard
	Cleveland	Jaye "Inky" Williams
	Rock Island	Fred Slater
1926	Akron	Frederick Pollard
	Hammond Pros	Jaye "Inky" Williams, Ed Butler, Dick Hudson
	Rock Island	Fred Slater
	Canton Bulldogs	Edward Butler
	Chicago Cardinals	Fred Slater
1927	Chicago Cardinals	Fred Slater
1928	Chicago Cardinals	Fred Slater, Harold Bradley
1929	Chicago Cardinals	Fred Slater
1930	Chicago Cardinals	Fred Slater
1931	Chicago Cardinals	Fred Slater
1932	Chicago Cardinals	Joe Lillard
1933	Chicago Cardinals	Joe Lillard
	Pittsburgh Steelers	Raymond Kemp

1934–1945 All black players were banned from the National Football League

BLACK FOOTBALL PLAYERS AT WHITE COLLEGES

Name	Position	Years	School
John Shelburne	FB	1919–1921	Dartmouth
Edward Niles	HB	1919–1921	Colby
Bill West		1919–1921	Colby
Duke Slater	T	1919–1921	Iowa
Harry Graves	HB	1919–1922	Michigan State
Harry Jefferson	G	1919–1922	Ohio U.
Charles Howard	FB	1919–1922	Drake
George Calloway	G	1920–1921	Columbia
Joseph Collins	HB	1920–1921	Coe College
Charles West	HB	1920–1923	Washington & Jefferson
Hamilton Greene	HB	1921	U. of Washington
Sam Taylor	HB	1922	Northwestern
Ernie Page	E	1923	Western Illinois
John Southern	T	1923	Butler
Victor Crawford		1923–1924	Vermont
Charles Drew	HB	1923–1925	Amherst
Benjamin Goode	HB	1924	Michigan State
Ledrue Galloway		1924	Iowa
Harry Payne		1924	Vermont
Charles Ray		1924–1926	Bates
Dave Ray	HB	1924–1926	Bates
T.D. Hansbury	G	1925–1926	Oberlin
C.R. Taylor		1925–1926	Tufts
Ray Vaughn	FB	1926–1928	Colgate
E.S. Jamison	G	1927	Oberlin
Tom Verdell	HB	1927–1928	Northwestern
David Myers	T-E-QB-HB	1927–1930	New York U.
Chester Jackson	E	1928	Syracuse
Alonzo Watford	FB-LB	1928	Butler
Leslie J. Hart	HB	1928	Colgate
Brice Taylor	HB	1929	California
William O'Shields	E	1929	New York U.
William Bell	T	1929–1931	Ohio State
Ray Kemp	QB	1929–1931	Duquesne
Joe Lillard	HB	1930–1931	Oregon
Edward Atkinson	HB	1931	Loyola, California
Ellsworth Harpole	G	1931–1933	Minnesota
Carlos Berry	G	1931–1935	Oberlin
Ozzie Simmons	FB	1933–1934	Iowa
All Duvalle	T	1933–1935	Loyola, California
Jesse Chase	T	1934	Boston U.
Moreland Forte	E	1935–1936	Boston U.
Clarence Hinton	HB	1935–1937	Northwestern

Name	Position	Years	School
Dwight Reed	E	1935–1937	Minnesota
Robert Brooks		1936	Western Reserve
Horace Johnson	HB	1936–1937	North Dakota
Horace Bell	G	1936–1938	Ohio State
Edward Williams	E	1936–1938	New York U.
Walter McCowen	E-T	1936–1938	Loyola, California
Kenny Washington	FB	1936–1939	UCLA
William "Dolly" King	FB	1937	Long Island U.
Wilmeth Sidat-Singh	QB	1937	Syracuse
Thomas Harding	FB	1937	Butler
Charles Russell	HB	1937	U. of Washington
John Ore	T-E	1937–1938	Washington & Jefferson
Homer Harris	T	1937--1938	Iowa
Woodrow Strode	FB	1937–1939	UCLA
Bernard Jefferson	HB	1937–1939	Northwestern
Fritz Pollard, Jr.	HB	1937–1940	North Dakota
Roland Bernard		1938	Boston U.
Horace Bell		1938	Minnesota
Archie Harris	E	1938	Indiana
Frank "Doc" Kelker	E	1938–1940	Western Reserve
Lou Montgomery	HB	1939	Boston College
Jerome "Brud" Holland	E-T	1939	Cornell
Willis Ward	RB	1939	Michigan
Jim Smith		1939–1940	Northwestern
Ray Bartlett	HB	1939–1940	UCLA
Jackie Robinson	QB-HB	1939–1940	UCLA
Julius Franks	G	1939–1941	Michigan
Willard Cushingberry	E	1940	Drake
Sam Pierce	HB	1940	Cornell
Charles Anderson	E	1940	Ohio State
Leonard Bates	HB	1940–1941	New York U.
Perry Harris	HB	1940–1941	Drake
Bert Piggott	HB	1940–1946	Illinois
Ernie Parks	HB	1943–1944	Ohio State
Buddy Young	FB	1944	Illinois

MILTON ROBERTS' ALL-TIME BLACK COLLEGE SQUAD
(1920–1930)

Name	Position	School
C. Felton "Zip" Gayles	E	Morehouse
Napolean Rivers	E	Talladega University
Milledge Hall	E	Alabama State
Murray Jeffries	E	Bluefield Institute
Porter James	E	Talladega University
Ralph Garner	E	Talladega, Alabama S.
Owen Duncan	E	Tuskegee University
Milton Fowler	E	Va. Seminary, Wilberforce
Jimmy Lunceford	E	Fisk University
John Williams	E	Langston University
Byrd Crudup	E	Lincoln University
Henry "Hank" Carrothers	E	Virginia Union
Samuel "Hank" Archer	E	Morehouse College
Leander Rogers	E	Lincoln U. (Missouri)
George Calloway	T	Lincoln University
Ted Gallion	T	Bluefield Institute
Earl Cunningham	T	Bluefield Institute
Alexander L. Irving	T	Morehouse College
William "Wild Man" Lee	T	Hampton University
Ernie Hughes	T	Clark, Prairie View A & M
Booker T. Pierce	T	St. Paul's, Fisk
		Atlanta University
T. Jeff Lamar	T	Atlanta U., Va. Union
Jack Nurse	T	Howard University
Wayman Coston	T	Lincoln University
Theodore T. Coleman	T	Hampton University
Dan "Butch" Brown	T	W. Va. Institute
Raymond Doakes	T	Howard University
Walter Cromwell	T	Knoxville College
William Jennings	T	Tuskegee, Paul Quinn
Earl J. "Ox" Clemons	T	Paul Quinn, Morris Brown
Robert "Bobo" Miller	G	Va. Union, Howard U.
Marion "Bull" Bates	G	Prairie View A & M
Jesse Miller	G	North Carolina A & T
James L. "Liver" Scott	G	W. Virginia State
Moses B. Slaughter	G	Paul Quinn, Atlanta U.,
		Fisk University
Dudley Redd	G	Wiley College
Tom "Crow" Hawkins	G	Howard University
William H. Sweet	G	Fla. A & M, Wilberforce
Oscar "Bull" Tadlock	C	Tuskegee University
Aubrey Tobin	C	Tuskegee, Va. Union
Chris Morgan	C	W. Va., Lincoln U.

Name	Position	School
William Buchanan	C	Wilberforce University
Charles B. Clark	QB	Morehouse College
Mel Whedbee	QB	Va. Sem., Atlanta U.
		Fisk University
Loranzo "Cute" Carter	QB	Howard University
Eugene Bragg	QB	Talladega, Fla. A & M
Paul Smith	QB	Tuskegee University
Claire "Halley" Harding	QB	Wilberforce, Wiley C.
Leigh Gordon	QB	Talladega University
Inman Breaux	QB	Virginia Union U.
Ed Ritchie	QB	Wilberforce University
Herb Cain	QB	Bluefield Institute
William Mobley	QB	Tuskegee University
Booker T. Robinson	QB	Langston University
Jack Coles	QB	Va. State, Howard U.
John Joyner	QB	Tuskegee University
Allen C. Jackson	QB	Virginia Union U.
Lawrence "Zip" Johnson	QB	Virginia State U.
Arthur Turner	QB	New Orleans U.
Cecil Williams	QB	Benedict College
William Golden	QB	Rust College
George H. Mitchell	QB	Shaw University
Pat Nesbit	QB	Tennessee State
Leo Grant	HB	Jarvis College
Pythias Russ	HB	Walden, Sam Houston
Mark Cardwell	HB	W. Va. State
Benjamin Stevenson	HB	Tuskegee University
David L. Gunn	HB	Hampton University
Franz A. "Jazz" Byrd	HB	Lincoln University
Albert V. Parker	HB	Straight College
R.W. "Whirlwind" Johnson	HB	Lincoln University
Fleming "Sleepy" Edwards	HB	Talladega, Morris Brown
Henderson "Tubby" Johnson	HB	Fisk University
Joe Wiggins	HB	Va. State, Atlanta U.
		Fisk University
Elmer Baker	HB	Hampton, Clark College
Henry "Bus" Coleman	HB	North Carolina A&T
Harry "Wu Fang" Ward	HB	Wilberforce University
Ray Sheppard	HB	Paul Quinn, Atlanta U.
Harold Chambers	HB	Va. State, Clark C.
Nat Pendleton	HB	Bishop College
A. Joe Lockhart	HB	Morris Brown
John Nance	HB	Knoxville, Tenn. State
Clarence "Snaky" Beck	HB	Clark College
Howard "Ned" Love	HB	Prairie View A&M
Julie Martin	HB	Va. Union, Shaw, Lincoln

Name	Position	School
Eric "Ric" Roberts	HB	Clark College
Horatius "Cy" Cotton	HB	Morris Brown, S. Carolina S.
James "Horse" Lane	FB	North Carolina A & T
Aaron Lane	FB	Howard University
Charles Doneghy	FB	Howard University
Elmer "Bull" Moore	FB	Wilberforce University
Ernest Bailey	FB	Tuskegee University
Artis Graves	FB	Morristown, Bluefield I.
Nelson Miles	FB	Alcorn State
Earl "Tubby" Bounds	FB	Virginia State University
Eugene Triplett	FB	Lane College
Ben Cavil	FB	Wiley College

1930–1940

Name	Position	School
James Brewer	E	Virginia State University
Leross Baker	E	Morris Brown
Donald Reeves	E	Clark College
William Reed	E	Kentucky State
Lorry "Broadriver" Dawkins	E	South Carolina State
Leroy "Roughhouse" Haynes	E	Morehouse College
Charles Spearman	E	Lemoyne College
Robert Hardin	E	Kentucky State College
Major Powell	T	Morris Brown
William "Wild Man" Coleman	T	Kentucky State College
Ben McKenny	T	Tuskegee University
Murray Neely	T	Florida A & M
Sam "Thunderbolt" Gaines	T	Hampton University
Richard "Dynamite" Kane	T	Lincoln University
William Coger	G	Alabama State
Frank Bogle	G	Johnson C. Smith
Reedy Spignor	G	Bishop, Southern U.
Eolus Von Rettig	G	Bishop, Wilberforce U.
John Hurse	G	Xavier University
James Ware	G	W. Virginia State
Roy Gant	G	Florida A&M
Cliff Brown	G	Morris Brown
Ralph "Hogmaw" Robinson	C	Atlanta U., Fisk, Clark
Vernon Smith	C	Morehouse College
Forrest Strange	C	Tennessee State
Pat McPherson	C	Lincoln, Wilberforce U.
Lloyd "Sodi" White	C	Talladega University
Pete Griffen	C	Florida A & M
Roscoe "Turk" Lewis	C	Virginia State U.

Name	Position	School
Henry "Hank" Butler	QB	Florida A & M
Joe "Tarzan" Kendall	QB	W. Kentucky, Ken. State
John Cox	QB	Tenn. State, Morristown
Eddie Robinson	QB	Leland College
Geo. "Big Bertha" Edwards	HB	Kentucky State College
James "Blue Dean" Everett	HB	Edward Waters, Fla. A & M
Otis Troupe	HB	Morgan State
Henry Briscoe	HB	Virginia State University
Raymond "Pelican" Hill	HB	Southern University
Tom "Tank" Conrad	HB	Morgan State
Floyd Meadows	HB	W. Virginia State
Andrew "Pat" Patterson	HB	Wiley College
Shelton Mason	HB	Prairie View A & M
Tim Crisp	HB	Langston University
Stanley Strachan	HB	Florida A & M
William "Shag" Jones	HB	Morris Brown
William Porter	HB	S. Carolina State
Ivory "Ike" Richmond	HB	Arkansas St., Hampton U.
Charles "Cat" Guthrie	HB	Southern University
Eugene Bailey	FB	Virginia State University
Claude Willis	FB	Claflin College
Jeru J. Marks	FB	Prairie View A & M
Elza "Tip" Odell	FB	Wiley College
Alonzo Adams	FB	Florida A & M
Fred "Cannonball" Cooper	FB	Virginia Union U.

1940–1942

Name	Position	School
Jack Brayboy	E	Johnson C. Smith
William Wysinger	T	Morris Brown
Haywood Settles	T	Morris Brown
William "Gus" Gaines	T	North Carolina State
Herbert "Lord" Trawick	G	Kentucky State
Ulysses Jones	G	Southern University
Alva Tabor	QB	Ft. Valley St., Tuskegee U.
William Bass	HB	Kentucky State, Tenn. State
Leonard "Senrab" Barnes	HB	Southern University
John "Big Train" Moody	FB	Morris Brown

Orange Blossom Classic

Year	Winner	Score	Opponent	Score	Site
1933	Florida A & M	9	Howard U.	6	Jacksonville, Fla.
1934	Florida A & M	13	Virginia St.	12	Jacksonville, Fla.
1935	Kentucky St.	19	Florida A & M	10	Jacksonville, Fla.
1936	Prairie View	25	Florida A & M	0	Jacksonville, Fla.
1937	Florida A & M	25	Hampton Inst.	20	Orlando, Fla.
1938	Florida A & M	9	Kentucky State	7	Orlando, Fla.
1939	Florida A & M	42	Wiley (Texas)	0	Orlando, Fla.
1940	Florida A & M	0	Wilberforce	0	Orlando, Fla.
1941	Florida A & M	15	Tuskegee	7	Orlando, Fla.
1942	Florida A & M	12	Texas College	6	Jacksonville, Fla.
1943	Hampton Inst.	39	Florida A & M	0	Jacksonville, Fla.
1944	Virginia State	19	Florida A & M	6	Tampa, Fla.
1945	Wiley (Texas)	32	Florida A & M	6	Tampa, Fla.

Sources

BOOKS

Aaron, Henry. *Aaron.* New York: Thomas Y. Crowell Publishers, 1974.

Abdul-Jabbar, Kareem, and Knobler, Peter. *Giant Steps.* New York: Bantam Books, 1983.

Achebe, Chinua. *Things Fall Apart.* New York: McDowell Obolensky, 1959.

Adelman, Bob, and Hall, Susan. *Out of Left Field: Willie Stargell and the Pittsburgh Pirates.* Boston: Little, Brown and Company 1974.

Adelman, Melvin L. *A Sporting Time: New York City and the Rise of Modern Athletics 1820–70.* Urbana, Illinois: University of Illinois Press, 1986.

Adu Boahen, Clark; Desmond, Clarke; John H., Curtin, Philip; Davidson, Basil; Samkange, Stanlake; Schaar, Stuart; Shepperson, George; Shinnie, Margaret; Vansina, Jan; Wallerstein, Immanuel; Willis, John R. *The Horizon History of Africa.* New York: American Heritage Publishing Company, 1971.

Alexander, Charles C. *Ty Cobb.* New York: Oxford University Press, 1984.

Ali, Muhammad. *The Greatest: My Own Story.* New York: Random House, 1975.

Allen, Maury. *Mr. October: The Reggie Jackson Story.* New York: New American Library, 1982.

Anderson, Dave. *Sports of Our Times.* New York: Random House, 1979.

Aptheker, Herbert. *A Documentary History of the Negro People in the United States: 1910–1932.* Secaucus, New Jersey: Citadel Press, 1973.

Ashe, Arthur. *Off the Court.* New York: New American Library, 1981.

——————*Portrait in Motion.* Boston, Massachusetts: Houghton Mifflin Company, 1975.

Astor, Gerald. *And a Credit to His Race: The Hard Life and Times of Joseph Louis Barrow.* New York: Saturday Review Press, 1974.

Baker, William J. *Jesse Owens: An American Life.* New York: The Free Press, 1986.

Barber, Red. *1947: When All Hell Broke Loose in Baseball.* Garden Clty, New York: Doubleday and Company, 1982.

Beart, Charles. *"Jeux et Jouets de L'Ouest Africain"* (a monograph). Tome 1. Number 42.

Behee, John. *Hail to the Victors!* Ann Arbor, Michigan: Ulrich's Books, 1974.

Bell, Marty. *The Legend of Dr. J.* New York: New American Library, 1975.

Bennett, Lerone, Jr. *Wade in the Water: Great Moments in Black History.* Chicago: Johnson Publishing Company, 1979.

Berkow, Ira. *Oscar Robertson: The Golden Year 1964.* Englewood Cliffs, New Jersey: Prentice Hall, 1971.

——————. *The DuSable Panthers.* New York: Atheneum Publishers, 1978.

Blassingame, John W. *Black New Orleans: 1860–1880.* Chicago: University of Chicago Press, 1973.

——————. *Slave Testimony: Two Centuries of Letters, Speeches, Interviews and Autobiographies.* Baton Rouge, Louisiana: Louisiana State University Press, 1977.

Boss, David. *The Pro-Football Experience.* New York: Harry N. Abrams, Inc., 1973.

Broderick, Francis L., and Meier, August. *Negro Protest Thought in the Twentieth Century.* Indianapolis: Bobbs-Merrill Company, 1965.

Brondfield, Jerry. *Kareem Abdul-Jabbar, Magic Johnson and the Los Angeles Lakers.* New York: Scholastic Book Services, 1981.

Brown, Gene. *The Complete Book of Basketball.* New York: Arno Press, 1980.

Brown, Jimmy. *Off My Chest.* New York: Doubleday and Company, 1964.

Brown, Larry. *I'll Always Get Up.* New York: Simon and Schuster, 1973.

477

Brown, Paul. *PB: The Paul Brown Story.* New York: Atheneum Publishers, 1979.

Butler, Hal. *The Willie Horton Story.* New York: Julian Messner Company, 1970.

Campanella, Roy. *It's Good to Be Alive.* Boston: Little, Brown and Company, 1959.

Carter, Rubin "Hurricane." *The Sixteenth Round.* New York: Viking Press, 1974.

Cashmore, Ernest. *Black Sportsmen.* London: Routledge and Kegan Paul, 1982.

Chalk, Ocania. *Black College Sport.* New York: Dodd, Mead and Company, 1976.

——————. *Pioneers of Black Sport.* New York: Dodd, Mead and Company, 1975.

Chamberlain, Wilt, and Shaw, David. *Wilt: Just Like Any Other 7-Foot Black Millionaire Who Lives Next Door.* New York: Macmillan Publishing Company, 1973.

Chambers, Lucille Arcola. *America's Tenth Men.* New York: Twayne Publishers, 1957.

Chambers, Ted. *The History of Athletics and Physical Education at Howard University.* Washington, D.C.: Vantage Press, 1986.

Chew, Peter. *The Kentucky Derby: The First 100 Years.* Boston: Houghton Mifflin and Company, 1974.

Chisholm, J. Francis. *Brewery Gulch: Frontier Days of Old Arizona, Last Outpost of the Great Southwest.* San Antonio: Naylor Company, 1949.

Cohen, Joel H. *Hammerin' Hank of the Braves.* New York: Scholastic Book Services, 1971.

Considine, Tim. *The Language of Sport.* New York: World Almanac Publications, 1982.

Corbett, J. James. *The Roar of the Crowd: The True Tale of the Rise and Fall of a Champion.* Garden City, New York: Garden City Publishing Company, 1926.

Cottrell, John. *Man of Destiny: The Story of Muhammed Ali.* London: Frederick Muller Press, 1967.

Cummings, John. *Negro Population in the United States, 1790–1915.* New York: Arno Press, 1968.

Cunard, Nancy. *Negro Anthology 1913–1933.* London: Wishart and Company, 1934.

Davies, Marianna W. *Contributions of Black Women to America.* Columbia, South Carolina: Kenday Press, Inc., 1982.

Davis, Edwin Adams, and Hogan, William Ranson. *The Barber of Natchez.* Baton Rouge, Louisiana: Louisiana State University Press, 1973.

Diamond, Wilfred. *How Great Was Joe Louis?* New York: Paebar Company, 1950.

Dolan, Edward F., Jr., and Lyttle, Richard B. *Jimmy Young: Heavyweight Challenge.* Garden City; New York: Doubleday and Company, 1979.

Donaldson, Thomas. *Idaho of Yesterday.* Westport, Connecticut: Greenwood Press, 1970.

Douglass, Frederick. *The Life and Times of Frederick Douglass.* New York: Bonanza Books, 1962.

Drake, St. Clair, and Cayton, Horace R. *Black Metropolis: A Study of Negro Life in a Northern City.* New York: Harcourt, Brace and Company, 1945.

Du Bois, W. E. Burghardt. *The Souls of Black Folk.* New York: Washington Square Press, 1970.

Duncan, Otis Dudley, and Duncan, Beverly. *The Negro Population of Chicago.* Chicago: University of Chicago Press, 1957.

Durant, John, and Bettman, Otto. *Pictorial History of American Sports from Colonial Times to the Present.* Cranberry, New Jersey: A.S. Barnes and Company, 1973.

Durham, Philip, and Jones, Everette L. *The Negro Cowboys.* New York: Dodd, Mead and Company, 1965.

Eaton, Hubert A. *Every Man Should Try.* Wilmington, North Carolina: Bonaparte Press, 1984.

Edwards, Audrey, and Wohl, Gary. *Muhammad Ali: The People's Champ.* Boston: 1977.

Edwards, Harry. *Sociology of Sport.* Homewood, Illinois: The Dorsey Press, 1973.

——————. *The Revolt of the Black Athlete.* New York: The Free Press, 1970.

——————. *The Struggle That Must Be: An Autobiography.* New York: Macmillan Publishing, 1980.

Egan, Pierce. *Boxiana.* London: G. Smeeton Publishers, 1812.

Ehre, Edward, and *The Sporting News. Best Sport Stories 1982.* New York: E. P. Dutton, 1982.

Einstein, Charles. *Willie Mays: Born to Play Ball.* New York: G. P. Putnam's Sons, 1955.

Eisenstadt, Murray. *The Negro in American Life.* New York: Oxford Book Company, 1968.

Farr, Finis. *Black Champion: The Life and Times of Jack Johnson.* London: Macmillan and Company, 1964.

——————. *Black Champions: The Life and Times of Jack Johnson.* New York: Charles Scribner's Sons, 1964.

Figler, Stephen, and Figler, Howard. *The Athlete's Game Plan for College and Career*. Princeton, New Jersey: Peterson's Guide, 1984.

Fisher, Galen M. *John R. Mott: Architect of Cooperation and Unity*. New York: Associated Press, 1962.

——————. *Public Affairs and the YMCA: 1844–1944*. New York: Association Press, 1948.

Fitzgerald, Ray. *Champions Remembered*. Brattleboro, Vermont: The Stephen Greene Press, 1982.

Fleischer, Nat. *All-Time Ring Record Book*. Norwalk, Connecticut: O'Brian Suburban Press, 1944.

——————. *Black Dynamite: The Story of the Negro in the Prize Ring from 1782 to 1938*. New York: *Ring* magazine, 1947.

——————. *All-Time Ring Record Book*. Norwalk, Connecticut: O'Brian Suburban Press, 1947.

Fletcher, Marvin E. *The Black Soldier Athlete in the United States Army 1890–1916*. Athens, Ohio: 1973.

Flood, Kurt. *The Way It Is*. New York: Trident Press, 1971.

Foner, Philip S. *Paul Robeson Speaks: Writings, Speeches and Interviews*. London: Quartette Books, 1978.

Foreman, Thomas Elton. *"Discrimination Against the Negro in American Athletics* (a monograph). Fresno, California: Fresno State College, 1957.

Fox, Larry. *Willis Reed: Take Charge Man of the Knicks*. New York: Grosset and Dunlap, 1970.

Franklin, John Hope. *The Free Negro in North Carolina 1790–1860*. New York: W. W. Norton and Company, 1969.

Frazier, Walt, and Berkow, Ira. *Rockin' Steady*. Englewood Cliffs, New Jersey: Prentice Hall Inc., 1974.

Frazier, Walt, and Jares, Joe. *The Walt Frazier Story: Clyde*. New York: Grosset and Dunlap, 1970.

Frommer, Harvey. *Rickey and Robinson: The Men Who Broke Baseball's Color Barrier*. New York: Macmillan Publishing Company, 1982.

The Fulani of Northern Nigeria. Lagos, Nigeria: Government Printing Office, 1945.

Gallagher, Robert C. *Ernie Davis: The Elmira Express*. Silver Spring, Maryland: Bartleby Press, 1983.

Gary, Lawrence E. *Black Men*. Beverly Hills, California: Sage Publications, 1981.

Gayle, Addison, Jr. *The Black Aesthetic*. Garden City, New York: Anchor Books, 1972.

Genovese, Eugene D. *Roll Jordan Roll: The World the Slaves Made*. New York: Random House, 1974.

Gewecke, Cliff. *Advantage Ashe*. New York: Coward McCann, 1965.

Gibson, Althea. *I Always Wanted to Be Somebody*. New York: Harper and Brothers, 1958.

Gibson, Bob. *From Ghetto to Glory: The Story of Bob Gibson*. Englewood, New Jersey: Prentice Hall Inc., 1968.

Goldstein, Allan. *A Fistful of Sugar*. New York: Coward, McCann and Geoghegan, 1981.

Graffis, Herb. *PGA: Official History of the PGA of America*. New York: Thomas Y. Crowell Publishers, 1975.

Griffin, Archie. *Archie: The Archie Griffin Story*. Garden City, New York: Doubleday and Company, 1977.

Grun, Bernard. *The Timetables of History*. New York: Simon and Schuster, 1979.

Halberstam, David. *The Breaks of the Game*. New York: Alfred A. Knopf, 1981.

Hamilton, Virginia. *Paul Robeson: The Life and Times of a Free Black Man*. New York: Harper and Row, 1974.

Harris, Merv. *On Court with the Superstars of the NBA*. New York: The Viking Press, 1973.

Haskins, James. *Sugar Ray Leonard*. New York: Lothrop, Lee and Shepard, 1982.

Hayes, Elvin, and Gilbert, Bill. *They Call Me "The Big E."* Englewood Cliffs, New Jersey: Prentice Hall, 1978.

Heller, Peter. *In This Corner: Forty World Champions Tell Their Stories*. New York: Simon and Schuster, 1973.

Henderson, Edwin B. *The Negro in Sports*. Washington, D.C.: Associated Publishers Inc., 1949.

Henderson, Edwin B., and *Sport* magazine. *The Black Athlete: Emergence and Arrival*. Cornwell Heights, Pennsylvania: Pennsylvania Publishers Company Inc., 1968.

Henderson, James H. M., and Henderson, Betty F. *Molder of Men: Portrait of a "Grand Old Man"— Edwin Bancroft Henderson*. New York: Vantage Press, 1985.

Hirschberg, Al. *Henry Aaron: Quiet Superstar*. New York: G. P. Putnam's Sons, 1974.

Hollander, Zander. *Great American Athletes of the Twentieth Century.* New York: Random House, 1966.

Holmes, Dwight Oliver Wendell. *The Evolution of the Negro College.* New York: Arno Press, 1969.

Holway, John B. *"Bullet Joe and the Monarchs"* (a monograph). Washington, D.C.: Capitol Press, 1984.

Isaac, Stan. *Jim Brown: The Golden Year 1964.* Englewood Cliffs, New Jersey: Prentice Hall Inc., 1970.

Isaacs, Neil D. *All the Moves: A History of College Basketball.* New York: Harper and Row, 1984.

Jackson, Reggie. *Reggie.* New York: Ballantine Books, 1984.

——————. *Reggie: A Season with a Superstar.* Chicago: Playboy Press Books, 1975.

James, C. L. R. *Beyond a Boundary.* New York: Pantheon Books, 1983.

Jares, Joe. *Basketball: The American Game.* Chicago: Follett Publishing Company, 1971.

"The Jesse Owens Dossier." Obtained from the Federal Bureau of Investigation Under the Freedom of Information Act.

Johnson, Arthur T., and Frey, James H. *Government and Sport: The Public Policy Issues.* Totowa, New Jersey: Rowman and Allanheld, 1985.

Johnson, Charles S. *Patterns of Negro Segregation.* New York: Harper and Brothers, 1943.

Johnson, Earvin "Magic," and Levin, Richard. *Magic.* New York: The Viking Press, 1983.

Johnson, Jack. *Jack Johnson Is a Dandy: An Autobiography.* New York: New American Library, 1969.

——————. *Jack Johnson: In the Ring and Out.* Chicago: National Sports Publishing Company, 1927.

Johnson, James Weldon. *Black Manhattan.* New York: Atheneum Press, 1977.

Jones, Cleon. *Cleon.* New York: Coward-McCann, Inc., 1970.

Jones, Wally, and Washington, Jim. *Black Champions Challenge American Sports.* New York: David McKay Company, Inc., 1972.

Jones, William H. *Recreation and Amusement Among Negros in Washington.* Westport, Connecticut: Negro Universities Press, 1970.

Jordan, Pat. *Black Coach.* New York: Dodd, Mead and Company, 1971.

Kaletsky, Richard. *Ali and Me: Through the Ropes.* Bethany, Connecticut: Andrienne Publications, 1982.

Katz, William Loren. *The Black West.* Garden City, New York: Anchor Books, 1973.

Keeneland Association Library. *Thoroughbred Record.* Lexington, Kentucky: Keeneland Association Library.

Kountze, Mabe "Doc." *Fifty Sport Years Along Memory Lane.* Medford, Massachusetts: Mystic Valley Press, 1979.

Kowet, Don. *Vida Blue: Coming Up Again.* New York: G. P. Putnam's Sons, 1974.

Lapchick, Richard Edward. *The Politics of Race and International Sport: The Case of South Africa.* Westport, Connecticut: Greenwood Press, 1975.

Leach, George B. *Kentucky Derby Diamond Jubilee.* New York: Gibbs Inman Publishers, 1949.

LeFlore, Ron. *Break Out: From Prison to the Big Leagues.* New York: New York. Harper and Row, 1978.

Lewis, David Levering. *When Harlem Was in Vogue.* New York: Alfred A. Knopf, 1981.

Lewis, Dwight, and Thomas, Susan. *A Will to Win.* Mount Juliet, Tennessee: Cumberland Press, 1983.

Lewis, William H. *"How to Play Football"* (a monograph). Boston: 1903.

Libby, Bill, and Haywood, Spencer. *Stand Up for Something: The Spencer Haywood Story.* New York: Grosset and Dunlap, 1972.

Libby, Bill *Goliath: The Wilt Chamberlain Story.* New York: Dodd, Mead and Company, 1977.

Lipman, David, and Wilks, Ed. *Bob Gibson: Pitching Ace.* New York: G. P. Putnam's Sons, 1975.

Lipsyte, Robert. *Free to Be Muhammad Ali.* New York: Harper and Row, 1978.

——————. *Sports World: An American Dreamland.* New York: Quadrangle Books, 1975.

Louis, Joe. *Joe Louis: My Life.* New York: Harcourt Brace Jovanovich, 1978.

Louis, Joe. *My Life Story.* New York: Duell, Sloan and Pearce, 1947.

Lyle, Sparky, and Golenbock, Peter. *The Bronx Zoo.* New York: Crown Publishers Inc., 1979.

Mackler, Bernard. *Black Superstars: Getting Ahead in Today's America.* New York: *Conch* magazine Limited Publishers, 1977.

Mailer, Norman. *The Fight.* Boston: Little, Brown and Company, 1975.

Major, Gerri. *Black Society*. Chicago: Johnson Publishing Company, Inc., 1976.

Matthews, Vincent. *My Race Be Won*. New York: Charter House Publishers, 1974.

Mays, Willie, and Einstein, Charles. *Willie Mays: My Life in and Out of Baseball*. New York: E. P. Dutton and Company, 1966.

McAdoo, Harriett Pipes, and McAdoo, John Lewis. *Black Children: Social, Educational, and Parental Environments*. Beverly Hills, California: Sage Publications, 1985.

McCallum, John D. *The World Heavyweight Boxing Championship: A History*. Radnor, Pennsylvania: Chilton Book Company, 1974.

McPhee, John. *A Sense of Where You Are: A Profile of William Warren Bradley*. New York City: New York. Farrar, Straus and Giroux, 1965.

McPhee, John. *Levels of the Game*. New York: Farrar, Straus and Giroux, 1969.

Michelson, Herb. *Almost a Famous Person*. New York: Harcourt Brace Jovanovich, 1980.

Michener, James A. *Sports in America*. New York: Fawcett Crest, 1976.

Miller, Margery. *Joe Louis: American*. New York: Hill and Wang, 1945.

Moore, Archie, and Pearl, Leonard B. *Any Boy Can: The Archie Moore Story*. Englewood Cliffs, New Jersey: Prentice Hall, Inc., 1971.

Morris, Willie. *The Courting of Marcus Dupree*. Garden City, New York: Doubleday and Company, 1983.

Movius, Geoffrey H. *The Second Book of Harvard Athletics, 1923–1963*. Cambridge, Massachusetts: The Harvard Varsity Club, 1964.

Murray, Florence. *The Negro Handbook, 1944*. New York: Current Reference Publications, 1944.

Nazel, Joseph. *Jackie Robinson: A Biography*. Los Angeles: Holloway House Publishing Company, 1982.

Neft, David S., Cohen, Richard M., and Deutsch, Jordan A. *The Sports Encyclopedia: Pro Football the Modern Era, 1960 to Present*. New York: Simon and Schuster, 1982.

Neft, David S., Cohen, Richard M., and Deutsch, Jordan A. *Pro-Football: The Early Years, 1895–1959*. Ridgefield, Connecticut: Sports Products, Inc., 1978.

Negro Population in the United States, 1790–1915. New York: Arno Press, 1968.

Newcombe, Jack. *Floyd Patterson: Heavyweight King*. New York: Bartholomew House Inc., 1961.

Noll, Roger G. *Government and the Sports Business*. Washington, D.C.: The Brookings Institution, 1974.

Norback, Craig, and Norback, Peter. *The New American Guide to Athletics, Sports, and Recreation*. New York: The New American Library, 1979.

Norman, Gardner L. *Athletics of the Ancient World*. Chicago: Associated Publishers, 1930.

O'Connor, Dick. *Reggie Jackson: Yankee Superstar*. New York: Scholastic Book Services, 1978.

The Official 1985 National Football League Record and Fact Book. New York: National Football League, 1986.

Olsen, Jack. *Black Is Best: The Riddle of Cassius Clay*. New York: G. P. Putnam's Sons, 1967.

Orr, Jack. *The Black Athlete: His Story in American History*. New York: Lion Books Publishing, 1969.

Owens, Jesse. *Blackthink: My Life as Black Man and White Man*. New York: William Morrow and Company, 1970.

——————. *I Have Changed*. New York: William Morrow and Company, 1972.

——————. *Jesse: The Man Who Outran Hitler*. New York: Fawcett Gold Medal Books, 1978.

Pachter, Mark. *Champions of American Sport*. New York: National Portrait Gallery, Smithsonian Institute, 1981.

Parker, Inez Moore, and Callison, Helen Vassy. *The Biddle Johnson C. Smith University Story*. Charlotte, North Carolina: Charlotte Publishing Company, 1975.

Palmer, Charles B. *For Gold and Glory: The Story of Thoroughbred Racing in America*. New York: Karrick and Evans Inc., 1939.

Patterson, Floyd, and Gross, Milton. *Victory Over Myself*. New York: Bernard Geis Associates and Random House, 1962.

Paul Robeson Archives. *Paul Robeson Tribute and Selected Writings*. New York: Paul Robeson Archives, 1976.

Payton, Walter. *Sweetness*. Chicago: Contemporary Books, Inc., 1978.

Pepe, Phil. *Stand Tall: The Lew Alcindor Story*. New York: Grosset and Dunlap, 1970.

Peterson, James A. *Slater of Iowa*. Chicago: Hinkley and Schmitt, 1958.

Peterson, Robert. *Only the Ball Was White.* Englewood Cliffs, New Jersey: Prentice Hall Inc., 1970.

Phillips, Ulrich Bonnell. *American Negro Slavery.* Baton Rouge, Louisiana: Louisiana State University Press, 1966.

Picott, J. Rupert. *"Selected Black Sports Immortals"* (a monograph). Washington, D.C.: Association for the Study of Afro-American Life and History, Inc., 1981.

Plimpton, George. *Sports!* New York: Abbeville Press/Harry N. Abrams, 1978.

Plosky, Harry A., and Brown, Roscoe C., Jr. *The Negro Almanac.* New York: Bellwhether Publishing Company, 1967.

Puckett, Newbell N. *The Magic and Folk Beliefs of the Southern Negro.* New York: Dover Publications, 1969.

Rader, Benjamin G. *American Sports.* Englewood Cliffs, New Jersey: Prentice Hall, 1983.

Randolph, Jack. *"Tom Molineux: America's 'Almost' Champion"* (a monograph).

Randolph, Wilma. *Wilma.* New York: New American Library, 1977.

Reed, Willis. *A View from the Rim: Willis Reed on Basketball.* Philadelphia: J. B. Lippincott, 1971.

Reichler, Joseph L. *The Baseball Encyclopedia.* New York: Macmillan Publishing Company, Inc., 1985.

Reidenbaugh, Lowell. *The Sporting News First Hundred Years, 1886–1986.* St. Louis: Sporting News Publishing Company, 1985.

Reuter, Edward Byron. *The Mulatto in the United States.* New York: Negro Universities Press, 1969.

Ritter, Lawrence, and Honig, Donald. *The 100 Greatest Baseball Players of All Time.* New York: Crown Publishers, 1981.

Roberts, Randy. *Papa Jack: Jack Johnson and the Era of White Hopes.* New York: The Free Press, 1983.

Robertson, Lawson. *College Athletics.* New York: American Sports Publishing Company, 1923.

Robeson, Susan. *The Whole World in His Hands: A Pictorial Biography of Paul Robeson.* Secaucus, New Jersey: Citadel Press, 1981.

Robinson, Frank. *Frank: The First Year.* New York: Holt, Rinehart and Winston, 1976.

Robinson, Frank. *My Life in Baseball.* Garden City, New York: Doubleday and Company, 1968.

Robinson, Jackie. *I Never Had It Made.* Greenwich, Connecticut: Fawcett Publications, 1972.

——————. *Jackie Robinson: My Own Story.* New York: Greenberg Publishers, 1948.

Robinson, Louie, Jr. *Arthur Ashe: Tennis Champion.* Garden City, New York: Doubleday and Company Inc., 1967.

Rogosin, Don. *Invisible Men: Life in Baseball's Negro Leagues.* New York: Atheneum Publishers, 1983.

Ross, Frank Alexander, and Kennedy, Louise Benable. *A Bibliography of Negro Migration.* New York: Columbia University Press, 1934.

Ruck, Ron. *Sandlot Seasons: Sport in Black Pittsburgh.* Urbana, Illinois: University of Illinois Press, 1987.

Russell, Bill, and Branch, Taylor. *Second Win: The Memoirs of an Opinionated Man.* New York: Random House, 1979.

Russell, Cazzie L., Jr. *Me, Cazzie Russell.* Westwood, New Jersey: Fleming H. Revell, 1967.

Russell, John A. *The Free Negro in Virginia: 1619–1865.* New York: Negro Universities Press, 1969.

Rust, Art, Jr. *"Get That Nigger Off the Field!"* New York: Delacorte Press, 1976.

Rust, Art, Jr., and Rust, Edna. *Recollections of a Baseball Junkie.* New York: William Morrow and Company, 1985.

Rust, Edna, and Rust, Art, Jr. *Art Rust's Illustrated History of the Black Athlete.* Garden City, New York. Doubleday and Company Inc., 1985.

Sample, Johnny. *Confessions of a Dirty Ball Player.* New York: The Dial Press, 1970.

Savin, Francine. *Women Who Win.* New York: Dell Publishing Company, 1975.

Saxon, Walt. *Darryl Strawberry.* New York: Dell Books, 1985.

Schapp, Dick. *The Perfect Jump.* New York: New American Library, 1976.

——————. *Sport.* New York: Arbor House, 1975.

Schneider, Russell, Jr. *Frank Robinson: The Making of a Manager.* New York: Coward, McCann and Geoghegan, 1976.

Schoolcraft, M. H. "Letters on the Condition of the African Race in the United States by a Southern Lady" (a monograph). Philadelphia: T. K. and P. G. Collins, 1852.

Schoor, Gene. *Dave Winfield: The 23 Million Dollar Man.* Briarcliff Manor, New York: Stein and Day Publishers, 1982.

——————. *Willie Mays: Modest Champion.* New York: G. P. Putnam's Sons, 1960.

Schubert, Frank N. "*The Black Regular Army Regiments in Wyoming, 1885–1912*" (a thesis). Laramie, Wyoming: University of Wyoming, 1970.

Scott, Jack. *The Athletic Revolution.* New York: The Free Press, 1971.

Silvermen, Al. *Best from Sport: An Anthology of Fifteen Years of Sport Magazine.* New York: Bartholomew House, Inc., 1961.

——————. *I Am Third: Gale Sayers.* New York: Viking Press, 1970.

Simpson, O. J. *O.J. : The Education of a Rich Rookie.* New York: The Macmillan Company, 1970.

Sims, Mary S. *The Natural History of a Social Institution—YMCA.* New York: Association Press, 1929.

Smith, Harry Worcester. *Life and Sport in Aiken.* Aiken, South Carolina: Derrydale Press, 1935.

"Softball Hall of Famers" (a monograph). Oklahoma City: Amateur Softball Association.

Sowell, Thomas. *Ethnic America: A History.* New York: Basic Books Inc., 1981.

Spalding's Athletic Library. *Interscholastic Athletic Association Guide Book for 1910, 1911, and 1913.* New York: American Sports Publishing Company.

Spink, J. G. Taylor. *Judge Landis and Twenty-Five Years of Baseball.* New York: Thomas Y. Crowell Publishers, 1947.

Spradling, Mary Mace. *In Black and White.* Detroit: Gale Research Company, 1980.

Stagg, Amos Alonzo, and Williams, H. C. "A Scientific and Practical Treatise on American Football for Schools and Colleges" (a monograph). Chicago: University of Chicago, 1893.

Staples, Robert. *Black Masculinity: The Black Male's Role in American Society.* San Francisco: The Black Scholar Press, 1982.

Stargell, Willie, and Bird, Tom. *Willie Stargell: An Autobiography.* New York: Harper and Row Publishers, 1984.

Stern, Robert. *They Were Number One: A History of the NCAA Basketball Tournament.* New York: Leisure Press, 1983.

Stingley, Darryl. *Darryl Stingley: Happy to be Alive.* New York: Beaufort Books Inc., 1983.

Sugar, Bert Randolph, and *Ring* magazine. *The Great Fights.* New York: Rutledge Press, 1981.

Super, Paul. *Formative Ideas in the YMCA.* New York: Association Press, 1929.

Tatum, Jack. *They Call Me Assassin.* New York: Everest House Publishers, 1979.

Taylor, Marshall W. "Major." *The Fastest Bicycle Rider in the World.* Worcester, Massachusetts: Wormley Publishing Company, 1928.

The Annals of America. Chicago: Encyclopedia Britannica Inc., 1976.

The Horizon History of Africa. New York: American Heritage Publishing Company, 1971.

The International Amateur Athletic Association Federation Statistics Handbook. Los Angeles: International Amateur Athletic Federation, 1984.

The Official Results of the 1984 Olympic Games. Los Angeles: Los Angeles Olympic Committee, 1984.

The Ring Record Book and Boxing Encyclopedia. New York: Atheneum Publishers, 1987.

The *Sporting Life's* Official Baseball Guide: 1890.

The Sporting News Official NBA Guide: 1984–1985. St. Louis: The Sporting News, 1985.

Trengove, Allan. *The Story of the Davis Cup.* London: Stanley Paul Publishers, 1985.

Truehart, William Elton. "The Consequences of Federal and State Resource Allocation and Development Policies for Traditionally Black Land-Grant Institutions: 1862–1954" (a thesis). Cambridge, Massachusetts: Doctoral Thesis for Graduate School of Education, Harvard University, 1979.

Tygiel, Jules. *Baseball's Great Experiment: Jackie Robinson and His Legacy.* New York: Oxford University Press, 1983.

United States Tennis Association. *The Official USTA Year Book and Tennis Guide.* Lynn, Massachusetts: H. O. Zimman Inc., 1986.

Wallechinsky, David. *The Complete Book of the Olympics.* New York: Penguin Books, 1984.

White, Solomon. *Sol White's Official Baseball Guide.* Philadelphia: Camden House, Inc., 1984.

Who's Who Among Black Americans. *Who's Who Among Black Americans, 1975-76.* Northbrook, Illinois: 1976.

Wills, Maury, and Gardner, Steve. *It Pays to Steal.* Englewood Cliffs, New Jersey: Prentice Hall Inc., 1963.

Winters, Manque. *Professional Sports: The Community College Connection*. Inglewood, California: Winnor Press, 1982.

Woodward, Bob, and Armstrong, Scott. *The Brethren: Inside the Supreme Court*. New York: Simon and Schuster, 1979.

Works Projects Administration. *Houston, Texas: A History and Guide*. Houston: Anson Jones Press, 1945.

Yannakis, Andrew; McIntrye, Thomas D.; Melnick, Merrill J.; and Hart, Dale P. *Sport Sociology: Contemporary Themes*. Dubuque, Iowa: Kendall/Hunt Publishing Company, 1976.

Young, A. S. "Doc." *Great Negro Baseball Stars*. New York: Barnes and Company, 1953.

—————. *Negro Firsts in Sports*. Chicago: Johnson Publishing Company, 1963.

Zinkoff, Dave. *Go, Man, Go!: Around the World with the Harlem Globetrotters*. New York: Pyramid Books, 1958.

NEWSPAPERS

The Aftro-American Newspaper (New York, New York)
The Atlanta Constitution (Atlanta, Georgia)
The Atlanta Independent (Atlanta, Georgia)
The Atlanta Daily World (Atlanta, Georgia)
The Birmingham Reporter (Birmingham, Alabama)
The Boston Chronicle (Boston, Massachusetts)
The Boston Globe (Boston, Massachusetts)
The Boston Guardian (Boston, Massachusetts)
The Brooklyn Daily Union (Brooklyn, New York)
The Brooklyn Times (Brooklyn, New York)
The California Eagle (Los Angeles, California)
The Cape May Star and Wave (Cape May, New Jersey)
The Cedar Rapids Republican (Cedar Rapids, Iowa)
The Chicago Bee (Chicago, Illinois)
The Chicago Defender (Chicago, Illinois)
The Chicago Tribune (Chicago, Illinois)
The City Sun (Brooklyn, New York)
The Cleveland Advocate (Cleveland, Ohio)
The Cleveland Call & Post (Cleveland, Ohio)
The Cleveland Gazette (Cleveland, Ohio)
The Daily Houston Telegraph (Houston, Texas)
The Daily Worker (New York, New York)

The Dallas Times Herald (Dallas, Texas)
The Detroit Free Press (Detroit, Michigan)
The Detroit Plain Dealer (Detroit, Michigan)
The East Tennessee News (Johnson City, Tennessee)
The Galesburg Register (Galesburg, Illinois)
The Harvard Crimson (Harvard University)
The Indianapolis Freeman (Indianapolis, Indiana)
The Interstate Tattler (New York, New York)
The Irish Times (Dublin, Ireland)
The Jamestown Evening Journal (Jamestown, New York)
The London Times (London, England)
The Los Angeles Sentinel (Los Angeles, California)
The Los Angeles Times (Los Angeles, California)
The Louisville Courier Journal (Louisville, Kentucky)
The Macon Telegram (Macon, Georgia)
The Miami Herald (Miami, Florida)
The Minnesota Journal (Mahtomedi, Minnesota)
The Montgomery Advertiser (Montgomery, Alabama)
The Morning Telegraph (New York, New York)
The Morning Transcript (Lexington, Kentucky)
The Nashville Tennessee Banner (Nashville, Tennessee)
The Newark Call (Newark, New Jersey)
The Newark Evening News (Newark, New Jersey)
The New Orleans Daily-Picayune (New Orleans, Louisiana)
The New Orleans Pelican (New Orleans, Louisiana)
The New Orleans Times (New Orleans, Louisiana)
The New Orleans Times-Democrat (New Orleans, Louisiana)
The New Orleans Weekly Louisianian (New Orleans, Louisiana)
The New York Age (New York, New York)
The New York American (New York, New York)
The New York Amsterdam News (New York, New York)
The New York City Illustrated News (New York, New York)
The New York Herald (New York, New York)
The New York Herald-Tribune (New York, New York)
The New York News (New York, New York)
The New York Post (New York, New York)
The New York Sun (New York, New York)
The New York World (New York, New York)
The Norfolk Journal and Guide (Norfolk, Virginia)

The Philadelphia Public Ledger (Philadelphia, Pennsylvania)

The Philadelphia Tribune (Philadelphia, Pennsylvania)

The Pittsburgh American (Pittsburgh, Pennsylvania)

The Pittsburgh Courier (Pittsburgh, Pennsylvania)

The Police Gazette (New York, New York)

The Record and Sun (Pennsylvania)

The Richmond News Leader (Richmond, Virginia)

The Richmond Planet (Richmond, Virginia)

The Richmond Times-Dispatch (Richmond, Virginia)

The Rochester Democrat and Chronicle (Rochester, New York)

The Rocky Mount Telegram (Rocky Mount, North Carolina)

The Rocky Mountain News (Denver, Colorado)

The Rome Tribune-Herald (Rome, Georgia)

The South Side Signal (Long Island, New York)

The Spirit of the Times

The Sporting Life (Philadelphia, Pennsylvania)

The St. Louis Argus (St. Louis, Missouri)

The St. Louis Post-Dispatch (St. Louis, Missouri)

The St. Louis Star (St. Louis, Missouri)

The Syracuse Standard (Syracuse, New York)

The Times Plain Dealer

The Washington Post (Washington, D.C.)

Tombstone Epitaph (Tombstone, Arizona)

MAGAZINES AND MAGAZINE ARTICLES

Abbotts Monthly

Backstretch

Black Enterprise (New York)

Black Sports (New York)

Black Tennis (Houston, Texas)

Boxing Scene (Palisades, New York)

Lowe, Albert S. "Camp Life of The Tenth U.S. Cavalry." *The Colored American* (Boston, Massachusetts), Volume 7, Number 3, 1904.

Collier's

Commonwealth (Charlottesville, Virginia)

Crisis

Ebony

Edwards, Harry. "Black Athletes and Sports in America." *The Western Journal of Black Studies*, Volume 6, Number 3, Fall 1982.

Esquire

Garvey, Edward R. "From Chattel to Employee: The Athlete's Quest for Freedom And Dignity." *Annals of the American Academy of Political and Social Science*. Vol. 445, September 1979.

Harper's Weekly

Hewetson, W. T. "The Social Life of the Southern Negro." *Chautauquan Magazine*, Volume 26, page 295, October 1897–March 1898.

Inside Sports

Lapchick, Richard E. "South Africa: Sport and Apartheid Politics." *Annals of the American Academy of Political and Social Science*, September 1979.

Lowe, Albert S. "Camp Life of The Tenth U.S. Cavalry." *The Colored American* (Boston, Massachusetts), Volume 7, Number 3, 1904.

New Directions: The Howard University Magazine (Washington, D.C.)

New York Times Sunday Magazine

Newsweek

Opportunity

Racquet Quarterly (New York)

Reach's Official Baseball Guide

Roberts, Milton. "50 Years of the Best in Black College Football." *Black Sports*, June 1976.

———————. "First Black Pro Gridder." *Black Sports*, November 1975.

Spivey, Donald, "The Black Athlete in Big-Time Intercollegiate Sports, 1941–1968." *Phylon*, Volume 44, pages 116–25, June 1983.

Sport

Sports Illustrated

Stumpf, Florence, and Cozens, Fred. "Some Aspects of the Role of Games, Sports and Recreational Activites in the Culture of Modern Primitive Peoples." *Research Quarterly*, 1949.

Tennis (Trumbull; Connecticut)

The Black Scholar (San Francisco)

The Negro History Bulletin

Time

Wiggins, David K. "The Play of Slave Children in the Plantation Communities of the Old South,

1820–1860. *"Journal of Sport History,* Volume 7, Number 2.

——————. "Sport and Popular Pastimes: Shadow of the Slave Quarter." *Canadian Journal of History of Sport and Physical Education,* Vol. 11, May 1980.

ORGANIZATIONS, FOUNDATIONS, AND INSTITUTIONS

The Carter G. Woodson Institute for Afro-American and African Studies, University of Virginia, Charlottesville, Virginia

The Jackie Robinson Foundation
The Jesse Owens Foundation
Moorland Spingarn Research Library, Howard University
Norfolk, Virginia, Public Library
Northern University: Center for the Study of Sport in Society
Schomburg Library for Research in Black Culture
Tuskegee University Archives

Index